Fodor's 2003

Ireland

The Guide
for All Budgets

Completely
Updated

Where to Stay, Eat,
and Explore

On and Off
the Beaten Path

When to Go,
What to Pack

Maps, Travel Tips,
and Web Sites

Fodor's Travel Publications • New York, Toronto, London, Sydney, Auckland
www.fodors.com

Fodor's Ireland 2003

EDITOR: Diane Mehta

Editorial Contributors: John Babb, Muriel Bolger, Graham Bolger, Geoff Hill, Alannah Hopkin, Anto Howard, Elizabeth Whisler

Editorial Production: Ira-Neil Dittersdorf

Maps: David Lindroth, *cartographer*; Rebecca Baer and Bob Blake, *map editors*

Design: Fabrizio La Rocca, *creative director*; Guido Caroti, *art director*; Jolie Novak, *senior picture editor*; Melanie Marin, *photo editor*

Cover Design: Pentagram

Production/Manufacturing: Yexenia (Jessie) Markland

Cover Photo (Dingle Peninsula): Nik Wheeler

Copyright

Important Tip

Although all prices, opening times, and other details in this book are based on information supplied to us at press time, changes occur all the time in the travel world, and Fodor's cannot accept responsibility for facts that become outdated or for inadvertent errors or omissions. So **always confirm information when it matters,** especially if you're making a detour to visit a specific place.

Special Sales

Fodor's Travel Publications are available at special discounts for bulk purchases for sales promotions or premiums. Special editions, including personalized covers, excerpts of existing guides, and corporate imprints, can be created in large quantities for special needs. For more information, contact your local bookseller or write to Special Markets, Fodor's Travel Publications, 1745 Broadway, New York, NY 10019. Inquiries from Canada should be directed to your local Canadian bookseller or sent to Random House of Canada, Ltd., Marketing Department, 2775 Matheson Boulevard East, Mississauga, Ontario L4W 4P7. Inquiries from the United Kingdom should be sent to Fodor's Travel Publications, 20 Vauxhall Bridge Road, London SW1V 2SA, England.

PRINTED IN THE UNITED STATES OF AMERICA

10 9 8 7 6 5 4 3 2 1

CONTENTS

On the Road with Fodor's *v*
Smart Travel Tips A to Z *vii*

1   Destination: Ireland   1

Eire Apparent *2*
What's Where *3*
Pleasures and Pastimes *5*

Fodor's Choice *9*
Great Itineraries *11*

2   Dublin   14

Exploring Dublin *19*
CLOSE-UP: *The Age of Elegance: Dublin's Georgian Style 32*
CLOSE-UP: *Ancestor-Hunting 33*
CLOSE-UP: *Rejoice! A Walk Through James Joyce's Dublin and Ulysses 53*

Dining *58*
Lodging *69*
Nightlife and the Arts *80*
Outdoor Activities and Sports *90*
Shopping *94*
Side Trips *101*
Dublin A to Z *111*

3   Dublin Environs   118

North of Dublin in the Boyne Valley *122*
County Wicklow's Coast and Mountains *133*

County Kildare and West Wicklow *141*
Dublin Environs A to Z *147*

4   The Midlands   150

The Eastern Midlands *155*
The Northern Midlands *159*

North Tipperary and the West Midlands *164*
The Midlands A to Z *172*

5   The Southeast   175

On the Road to Kilkenny City and Wexford Town *182*
Along the Coast to Waterford *195*

The Nire Valley, the Blackwater Valley, and County Tipperary *205*
The Southeast A to Z *211*

6   The Southwest   214

Cork City *222*
East Cork and the Blackwater Valley *235*
Kinsale to Glengariff via Bantry Bay *240*
CLOSE-UP: *Back of the Beyond 247*
The Ring of Kerry *250*

In and Around Killarney *256*
The Dingle Peninsula *263*
North Kerry and Shannonside *270*
CLOSE-UP: *Risen from the Ashes: Frank McCourt's Limerick 275*
The Southwest A to Z *279*

7   The West   285

The Burren and Beyond—   CLOSE-UP: *Pub Etiquette 314*
West Clare to South Galway   The Aran Islands *316*
292   Through Connemara and
Galway City *304*   County Mayo *319*
CLOSE-UP: *A Year-Round*   The North Mayo Coast *332*
Fleadh 312   The West A to Z *333*

8   The Northwest   338

Yeats Country—Sligo Town   Northern Donegal *363*
and Environs *345*   The Northwest A to Z *373*
Around Donegal Bay *355*

9   Northern Ireland   378

Belfast *386*   CLOSE-UP: *A Political ABC*
CLOSE-UP: *Belfast's Wall*   *416*
Murals 389   Around Counties Tyrone,
CLOSE-UP: *Churches Around*   Fermanagh, Armagh, and
the City 395   Down *419*
Around Counties Antrim and   Northern Ireland A to Z *428*
Derry *405*

10   Irish Greens   435

11   Background and Essentials   444

Portraits of Ireland *445*   Chronology *452*
Books and Movies *448*   Irish Family Names *456*

Index   460

Maps

Dublin City Center *24–25*   The Southwest *220-221*
Dublin West *41*   Cork City *226*
Dublin Dining *60–61*   Killarney and Environs *259*
Dublin Lodging *76–77*   The West *291*
Dublin Pubs *87*   Galway City *307*
Dublin Shopping *95*   Yeats Country and Around
County Dublin: Southside *103*   Donegal Bay *344*
County Dublin: Northside *107*   Sligo Town *347*
Dublin Environs *123*   The Northern Peninsulas *364*
The Midlands *154*   Northern Ireland *384–385*
The Southeast *180–181*   Belfast *392*
Kilkenny City *186*   Derry *414*
Wexford Town *192*   Ireland *458–459*
Waterford City *199*

ON THE ROAD WITH FODOR'S

A TRIP TAKES YOU OUT OF YOURSELF. Concerns of life at home completely disappear, driven away by more immediate thoughts—about, say, what marvels will beguile the next day, or where you'll have dinner. That's where Fodor's comes in. We make sure that you know all your options, so that you don't miss something that's around the next bend just because you didn't know it was there. Mindful that the best memories of your trip might have nothing to do with what you came to Ireland to see, we guide you to sights large and small all over the country. You might set out to explore Georgian Dublin and sample the fine restaurants there, but back at home you find yourself unable to forget the wild, rugged coastline, the languid days of golfing and fly-fishing, or the out-of-the-way pubs you discovered. With Fodor's at your side, serendipitous discoveries are never far away.

About Our Writers

Our success in showing you every corner of Ireland is a credit to our extraordinary writers. Although there's no substitute for travel advice from a good friend who knows your style, our contributors are the next best thing—the kind of people you would poll for travel advice if you knew them.

John Babb honed his journalistic skills at the Canadian Broadcasting Corporation in Toronto before he moved to Warsaw, Poland, where he spent two years working as a business journalist. He has been laying low in Dublin for the last two years, studying Irish culture.

Graham Bolger is a freelance writer who contributes to a wide variety of titles in Ireland, specializing in travel, music, and technical writing. He is currently working on a series of self-help books. A consummate fan of all things edible, he updated the Dublin dining section and the Southeast and Irish Greens chapters.

Freelance editor and journalist **Muriel Bolger** is a travel writer and regular contributor to several magazines and newspapers in Ireland, including Food & Wine Magazine. She updated the Southeast and Irish Greens chapters. Her interests are eclectic and only exclude deep-sea diving and space exploration. She edits Irish Interiors and Irish Exteriors magazines, too.

Geoff Hill is the travel editor of the News Letter, Northern Ireland's main morning newspaper. In a previous life, he was Ireland's most capped (experienced) volleyball player and a much younger man. In the past six years he's won a UK travel writer of the year award twice and been shortlisted four times. He's also the current Irish travel writer of the year and the Mexican Government European travel writer of the year, although he's still trying to work out exactly what that means. He's also a novelist and writes about travel regularly for the London Daily Telegraph and the Sunday edition of the Independent. He lives in Belfast with his fiancée, a cat, and a hammock.

A full-time freelance writer who lives near the sea in County Cork, **Alannah Hopkin,** our veteran contributor, has worked on the guide since 1985. This year she covered the Midlands and Southwest. Alannah has published a book on the cult of St. Patrick, a book-length guide to County Cork, two novels, and several short stories. She writes on travel and the arts for the London Sunday Times and contributes regularly to the Irish Examiner and the Irish Times.

Anto Howard, who worked on the Dublin and Dublin Environs chapters, is a Northside Dublin native who studied at Trinity College before acquiring his U.S. green card. He lived in New York, where he worked as a travel writer, editor, and playwright, before returning to Ireland. Anto (short for Anthony) is also the author of Fodor's Escape to Ireland.

Elizabeth A. Whisler, who updated the West and Background and Essentials chapters, is a New England native who lived in Northern Ireland for the past five years. She received a master's degree in Irish Literature from the University of Ulster and worked as the Director of the U.S. State Department's Irish Peace Process Cultural and Training Program. She has traveled through all 32 counties of Ireland.

You can rest assured that you're in good hands—and that no property mentioned in the book has paid to be included. Each has been selected strictly on its merits, as the best of its type in its price range.

How to Use This Book

Up front is Smart Travel Tips A to Z, arranged alphabetically by topic and loaded with tips, Web sites, and contact information. Destination: Ireland helps get you in the mood for your trip. Subsequent chapters in *Ireland* are arranged regionally. All city chapters begin with exploring information, with a section for each neighborhood (each recommending a good tour and listing sights alphabetically). All regional chapters are divided geographically; within each area, towns are covered in logical geographical order, and attractive stretches of road between them are indicated by the designation En Route. To help you decide what you'll have time to visit, all chapters begin with our writers' favorite itineraries. (Mix itineraries from several chapters, and you can put together a really exceptional trip.) The A to Z section that ends every chapter lists additional resources. The chapters that follow Exploring are arranged alphabetically. At the end of the book you'll find Background and Essentials, including Portraits, essays about Ireland's turbulent history—from its agrarian beginnings through the Great Famine and up to the Irish diaspora—and a timeline charting everything from Stone Age settlers to current-day political developments. The Books and Movies section suggests enriching reading and viewing.

Icons and Symbols
★　Our special recommendations
✕　Restaurant
🏠　Lodging establishment
✕🏠　Lodging establishment whose restaurant warrants a special trip
🐤　Good for kids (rubber duck)
☞　Sends you to another section of the guide for more information

✉　Address
☎　Telephone number
🕐　Opening and closing times
💵　Admission prices

Numbers in white and black circles ③ ❸ that appear on the maps, in the margins, and within the tours correspond to one another.

For hotels, you can assume that all rooms have private baths, phones, TVs, and air-conditioning unless otherwise noted and that all hotels operate on the European Plan (with no meals) if we don't specify another meal plan. We always list a property's facilities but not whether you'll be charged extra to use them, so when pricing accommodations, do ask what's included. For restaurants, it's always a good idea to book ahead; we mention reservations only when they're essential or are not accepted. All restaurants we list are open daily for lunch and dinner unless stated otherwise; dress is mentioned only when men are required to wear a jacket or a jacket and tie. Look for an overview of local dining-out habits in Smart Travel Tips A to Z and in the Pleasures and Pastimes section that follows each chapter introduction.

Don't Forget to Write

Your experiences—positive and negative—matter to us. If we have missed or misstated something, we want to hear about it. We follow up on all suggestions. Contact the Ireland editor at editors@ fodors.com or c/o Fodor's at 1745 Broadway, New York, New York 10019. And have a fabulous trip!

Karen Cure
Karen Cure
Editorial Director

ESSENTIAL INFORMATION

ADDRESSES

We have tried to provide full addresses for hotels, restaurants, and sights, though many of Ireland's villages and towns are so tiny they barely have street names, much less house numbers. If in doubt, ask for directions.

AIR TRAVEL

From North America and the United Kingdom, Aer Lingus is the main carrier to Ireland. Indirect flights from the United States and Canada fly via London and then switch to Aer Lingus or British Midlands for the final leg to Dublin. There are no direct flights from Australia or New Zealand. Regular service is available from most major airports in Ireland to most major cities in England and Scotland, including Leeds, Manchester, and Glasgow. In general, flying into Ireland tends to be a relatively hassle-free experience, although an increase in traffic in the last decade has caused a slight increase in flight delays and waiting for baggage to clear customs.

BOOKING

When you book **look for nonstop flights** and **remember that "direct" flights stop at least once.** Try to avoid connecting flights, which require a change of plane. For more booking tips and to check prices and make on-line flight reservations, log on to www.fodors.com.

CARRIERS

When flying internationally, you must usually choose between a domestic carrier, the national flag carrier of the country you are visiting, and a foreign carrier from a third country. National flag carriers have the greatest number of nonstops. Domestic carriers may have better connections to your home town and serve a greater number of gateway cities.

Third-party carriers may have a price advantage.

Aer Lingus is the national flag carrier of Ireland, with regularly scheduled flights to Shannon and Dublin from New York's JFK, Boston's Logan, Chicago's O'Hare, and LAX. Delta has a daily departure from Atlanta that flies first to Shannon and on to Dublin. Continental flies daily direct to Dublin and Shannon, departing from Newark Airport in New Jersey. With the exception of special offers, the prices of the four airlines tend to be similar. British Midlands offers regularly scheduled flights to Belfast from London Heathrow Airport.

London to Dublin is now one of the busiest international air routes in the world, and four main carriers, as well as numerous smaller airlines, provide daily service on this route. With such healthy competition, there are plenty of bargains to be found. Ryanair, a relatively new Irish airline, is famous for its cheap, no-frills service.

Aer Lingus provides service around Ireland to Dublin, Cork, Galway, Kerry, and Shannon. Aer Arann Express, which used to run only an island-hopping service, has recently expanded into the domestic market, flying from Dublin to Cork, Derry, Donegal, Galway, Knock, and Sligo. British Airways also offers daily flights from Dublin to Derry.

➤ MAJOR AIRLINES: **Aer Lingus** (☎ 800/474–74247 in the U.S. and Canada; 0845/973–7747 or 020/8899–4747 in the U.K.; 02/9244–2123 in Australia; 09/308–3351 in New Zealand, WEB www.aerlingus.com). **British Airways** (☎ 0845/773–3377 in the U.K., WEB www.britishairways.com). **British Midlands** (☎ 0870/607–0555 in the U.K., WEB www.britishmidland.co.uk). **Continental** (☎ 800/231–0856 in the U.S., WEB www.continental.com). **Delta**

(☎ 800/241–4141 in the U.S. and Canada, WEB www.delta.com). **Ryanair** (☎ 08701/569–569 in the U.K., WEB www.ryanair.com).

➤ AROUND IRELAND: **Aer Arann Express** (☎ 1890/462–726 in the Republic of Ireland, 0800/587–2324 in the U.K., 3531/814–1058 in the U.S., Canada, Australia, and New Zealand, WEB www.aerarannexpress. com). **Aer Lingus** (☎ 800/474–74247 in the U.S. and Canada; 0845/973–7747 or 020/8899–4747 in the U.K.; 02/9244–2123 in Australia; 09/308–3351 in New Zealand, WEB www. aerlingus.com). **British Airways** (☎ 800/147–9297 in the U.S. and Canada; 0845/773–3377 in the U.K; 02/8904–8800 in Australia; 0800/274–8477 in New Zealand, WEB www. britishairways.com).

CHECK-IN AND BOARDING

Checking in and boarding an outbound plane in Ireland tends to be fairly hassle-free. Security is professional but not overbearing, and airport staff are usually helpful and patient. During the busy summer season lines can get longer, and you should play it safe and arrive the suggested two hours before your flight. You'll need to show your passport before checking in.

Assuming that not everyone with a ticket will show up, airlines routinely overbook planes. When everyone does, airlines ask for volunteers to give up their seats. In return, these volunteers usually get a certificate for a free flight and are rebooked on the next flight out. If there are not enough volunteers, the airline must choose who will be denied boarding. The first to get bumped are passengers who checked in late and those flying on discounted tickets, so **get to the gate and check in as early as possible,** especially during peak periods.

CUTTING COSTS

The least expensive airfares to Ireland must usually be purchased in advance and are nonrefundable. It's smart to **call a number of airlines, and when you are quoted a good price, book it on the spot**—the same fare may not be available the next day. Always **check different routings** and look into

using different airports. Travel agents, especially low-fare specialists (☞ Discounts and Deals), are helpful.

Consolidators are another good source. They buy tickets for scheduled international flights at reduced rates from the airlines, then sell them at prices that beat the best fare available directly from the airlines, usually without restrictions. Sometimes you can even get your money back if you need to return the ticket. Carefully read the fine print detailing penalties for changes and cancellations, and **confirm your consolidator reservation with the airline.**

When you **fly as a courier,** you trade your checked-luggage space for a ticket deeply subsidized by a courier service. There are restrictions on when you can book and how long you can stay.

Charter carriers, such as Sceptre Charters, offer flights to Dublin and Shannon from various U.S. cities. Air Canada Vacations and Regent Holidays fly from Canada. Note that in certain seasons, usually fall and winter, their charter deals include mandatory hotel and car-rental packages.

To save money on flights from the United Kingdom and back, **look into an APEX or Super-PEX ticket.** APEX tickets must be booked in advance and have certain restrictions. Super-PEX tickets can be purchased at the airport on the day of departure—subject to availability.

➤ CHARTERS: **Sceptre Charters** (☎ 800/221–0924, WEB www. sceptreireland.com). **Air Canada Vacations** (☎ 888/247–2262, WEB www.aircanadavacations.com).**Regent Holidays** (☎ 800/387–4860 in Canada).

➤ CONSOLIDATORS: **Air Canada Vacations** (☎ 888/247–2262, WEB www. aircanadavacations.com). **Cheap Tickets** (☎ 800/377–1000). **Discount Airline Ticket Service** (☎ 800/576–1600). **Regent Holidays** (☎ 800/387–4860). **Sceptre Ireland** (☎ 800/221–0924, WEB www.sceptreireland.com). **Unitravel** (☎ 800/325–2222). **Up & Away Travel** (☎ 212/889–2345, WEB www.upandaway.com). **World Travel Network** (☎ 800/409–6753).

➤ COURIERS: **Now Voyager** (☏ 212/431–1616).

ENJOYING THE FLIGHT

State your seat preference when purchasing your ticket, and then repeat it when you confirm and when you check in. For more legroom, you can request one of the few emergency-aisle seats at check-in, if you are capable of lifting at least 50 pounds—a Federal Aviation Administration requirement of passengers in these seats. Seats behind a bulkhead also offer more legroom, but they don't have under-seat storage. Don't sit in the row in front of the emergency aisle or in front of a bulkhead, where seats may not recline.

Ask the airline whether a snack or meal is served on the flight. If you have dietary concerns, **request special meals when booking.** These can be vegetarian, low-cholesterol, or kosher, for example. It's a good idea to pack some healthy snacks and a small (plastic) bottle of water in your carry-on bag. On long flights, try to maintain a normal routine, to help fight jet lag. At night, **get some sleep.** By day, **eat light meals, drink water** (not alcohol), and **move around the cabin** to stretch your legs. For additional jet-lag tips consult *Fodor's FYI: Travel Fit & Healthy* (available at bookstores everywhere).

Smoking policies vary from carrier to carrier. Many airlines prohibit smoking on all of their international flights; others allow smoking only on certain routes or certain departures. Ask your carrier about its policy.

FLYING TIMES

Flying time to Ireland is 6½ hours from New York, 7½ hours from Chicago, 10 hours from Los Angeles, 1 hour from London, and 27 hours from Sydney.

HOW TO COMPLAIN

If your baggage goes astray or your flight goes awry, complain right away. Most carriers require that you **file a claim immediately.**

➤ AIRLINE COMPLAINTS: U.S. Department of Transportation **Aviation Consumer Protection Division** (✉ C-75, Room 4107, Washington, DC 20590, ☏ 202/366–2220, WEB www.dot.gov/airconsumer). **Federal Aviation Administration Consumer Hotline** (☏ 800/322–7873).

RECONFIRMING

Even if an airline says there's no need to reconfirm, it's best to do so anyway 12–14 hours before your flight to ensure that your seat is held; you can also check to see if the flight schedule has changed.

AIRPORTS

The major gateways to Ireland are Dublin Airport (DUB), 10 km (6 mi) north of the city center, and Shannon Airport (SNN) on the west coast, 25½ km (16 mi) west of Limerick. Two airports serve Belfast: Belfast International Airport (BFS) at Aldergrove, 24 km (15 mi) from the city, handles local and U.K. flights, as well as all other international traffic; Belfast City Airport (BHD), 6½ km (4 mi) from the city, handles local and United Kingdom flights only. In addition, the City of Derry Airport (LDY) receives flights from Dublin, Manchester, Birmingham, and Glasgow in the United Kingdom and Scotland.

➤ AIRPORT INFORMATION: **Belfast City Airport** (☏ 028/9045–7745, WEB www.belfastcityairport.com). **Belfast International Airport at Aldergrove** (☏ 028/9448–4848, WEB www.bial.co.uk). **City of Derry Airport** (☏ 028/7181–0784, WEB www.derry.net/airport). **Dublin Airport** (☏ 01/814–1111, WEB www.aer-rianta.ie). **Shannon Airport** (☏ 061/712–000, WEB www.shannonairport.com).

DUTY-FREE SHOPPING

Duty-free shopping for people traveling between European Union (EU) countries ended July 1, 1999. You can, however, purchase duty-free goods when traveling between any EU country and a non-EU country. For duty-free allowances when entering Ireland from a non-EU country, *see* Customs & Duties.

BIKE TRAVEL

Ireland is a cyclist's paradise. The scenery is phenomenal, the roads are flat and uncrowded, and the distance from one village to the next is rarely more than 16 km (10 mi). The massive influx of EU money into the roads over the last decade has banished many of the dreaded pothole-covered byways to the distant past. On the downside, though, foul weather and rough roads in remote areas are all too common, so rain gear and spare parts are a must.

There are plenty of bike rental shops in the country. Most offer 18- to 24-gear mountain bikes with index gears and rear carriers for about €12.70 per day or €63.50 per week. A refundable deposit of €63.50 is often required. For a fee of €15.25 or so, you can rent a bike at one location and drop it off at another. Raleigh Ireland has dealers all over the country who do repairs and rentals.

➤ BIKE MAPS: **Discovery Series** (✉ Ordnance Survey, Phoenix Park, Dublin 8, ☎ 01/820–6439 or 01/820–6443).

➤ BIKE RENTALS: **Raleigh Ireland** (✉ Raleigh House, Kylemore Rd., Dublin 10, ☎ 01/626–1333).

BIKES IN FLIGHT

Most airlines accommodate bikes as luggage, provided they are dismantled and boxed. Airlines sell bike boxes, which are often free at bike shops, for about $5 (it's at least $100 for bike bags). International travelers can sometimes substitute a bike for a piece of checked luggage at no charge; otherwise, the cost is about $100. Domestic and Canadian airlines charge $25–$50.

Most ferries will transport your bicycle for free. If there's room, Irish buses and Irish Rail will transport bikes for a small fee.

BOAT AND FERRY TRAVEL

There are two principal ferry routes to the Irish Republic: to Dublin from Holyhead on the Isle of Anglesea, and to Rosslare from Fishguard or Pembroke in Wales. Two main companies sail the Dublin route: Irish Ferries from Dublin port and Stena Sealink, whose ferries go both to Dublin port and Dun Laoghaire, 4 km (2½ mi) south of the city center. SeaCat Ferries also has a service to Dublin from Liverpool between March and November. Trains leave London (Euston) for Liverpool throughout the day. The trip takes about four hours. Prices and departure times vary according to season, so call to confirm. In summer, reservations are strongly recommended. Dozens of taxis wait to take you into town from both Dublin port and Dun Laoghaire, or you can take DART (Dublin Area Rapid Transit) or a bus to the city center.

Irish Ferries operates the Pembroke–Rosslare route; Stena Sealink operates the Fishguard–Rosslare route. To connect with the Fishguard sailings, take one of the many direct trains from London (Paddington). A connecting train at Rosslare will get you to Waterford by about 8:30 PM, to Cork by about midnight. For the Pembroke sailings, you have to change trains at Swansea. Sailing time for both routes is four hours.

Swansea Cork Ferries operate a service between Swansea and Cork from mid-March to early November. The crossing takes 12 hours, but easy access by road to both ports make this longer sea route a good choice for motorists heading for the Southwest.

The cost of your trip can vary substantially, so **spend time with a travel agent and compare prices carefully;** flying is sometimes cheaper, and fares to Dublin are cheapest. For example, the fare for a family (car and driver plus four adults) on the Fishguard-to-Rosslare route ranges from €144.75 to €328.85. **Book well in advance at peak periods.** Students and others under 26 should take advantage of the cheap fares offered by Eurotrain.

Car ferries run to Northern Ireland from the Scottish ports of Stranraer and Troon. Trains leave London (Euston) for Stranraer Harbor several times a day. Sealink Ferries crosses the water to the Port of Belfast. The whole trip is around 13 hours. Sea-Cat, a huge car-ferry catamaran, crosses from Troon into Belfast in 2½ hours.

If you're traveling from County Kerry to County Clare and the West of Ireland, you can take the ferry from Tarbert (in County Kerry), leaving every hour on the half hour. Going the other way, ferries leave from Killimer (in County Clare) every hour on the hour. The 30-minute journey across the Shannon Estuary costs €8.90 per car, €2.55 for foot passengers.

A 10-minute car ferry crosses the River Suir between Ballyhack in County Wexford and Passage East in County Waterford, which will introduce you to two pretty fishing villages, Ballyhack and Arthurstown. The ferry operates continuously during daylight hours and costs €4.45 per car, €1 for foot passengers.

The Cork Harbor crossing is a scenic route that allows those traveling from West Cork or Kinsale to Cobh and the east coast to bypass the city center. The five-minute car ferry runs from Glenbrook (near Ringaskiddy) in the west to Carrigaloe (near Cobh) in the east and operates continuously from 7:15 AM to 12:45 AM daily. It costs €3.80 per car, €.75 for foot passengers.

You can reach many, but not all, of Ireland's islands by ferry. There are regular services to the Aran Islands from Galway City, Rossaveal in County Galway, and Doolin in County Clare. Ferries also sail to Inishbofin off the Galway coast and Arranmore off the Donegal coast, and to Bere, Sherkin, and Cape Clear islands off the coast of County Cork. The islands are all small enough to explore on foot, so the ferries are for foot passengers and bicycles only. Other islands—the Blaskets and the Skelligs in Kerry, Rathlin, and Tory off the Donegal coast—can be reached by private arrangements with local boatmen. Full details on ferries to the islands are available in a publication from the Irish Tourist Board (ITB).

FARES AND SCHEDULES

You can get schedules and purchase tickets, with a credit card if you like, from the offices listed below. You can also pick them up at Dublin Tourism offices and from any major travel agent in Ireland or the United Kingdom. Payment must be made in the currency of the country of the port of departure.

➤ BOAT AND FERRY INFORMATION: **Cork Swansea Ferries** (✉ 52 S. Mall St., Cork, ☎ 021/271166, WEB www. commerce.ie/cs/scf). **Irish Ferries** (✉ Merrion Row, Dublin, ☎ 01/638–3333, WEB www.irishferries.ie). **SeaCat** (✉ Donegal Quay, Belfast, ☎ 028/9031–2301, WEB www.seacat.co.uk). **Stena Sealink** (✉ Ferryport, Dun Laoghaire, ☎ 01/204–7777 or 01/204–7700, WEB www.stenaline.co.uk).

BUS TRAVEL

IN THE REPUBLIC OF IRELAND

Buses are a cheap, flexible way to explore the countryside. Expressway bus services, with the most modern buses, cover the country's major routes. Outside the peak season, services are limited, and some routes (e.g., Killarney–Dingle) disappear altogether. There is often only one service a day on the express routes— and one a week to some of the more remote villages.

Long-distance bus services are operated by Bus Éireann, which also provides local services in Cork, Galway, Limerick, and Waterford. To ensure that your proposed bus journey is feasible, **buy a copy of Bus Éireann's timetable**—€1.30 from any bus terminal.

Many of the destination indicators on bus routes are in Irish, so **make sure you get on the right bus.** Asking someone to translate is often the best way to avoid a mishap.

IN NORTHERN IRELAND

In Northern Ireland, all buses are operated by the state-owned Ulsterbus. Service is generally good, with particularly useful links to those towns not served by train. Ulsterbus also offers tours.

FROM THE U.K.

Buses to Belfast run from London and from Birmingham, making the Stranraer–Port of Belfast crossing. Contact National Express. The numbers listed are in London, so be sure to add the 44 country code and drop the 0 from the area code when dialing from abroad.

Numerous bus services run between Britain and the Irish Republic, but

be ready for long hours on the road and possible delays. All buses to the Republic use either the Holyhead–Dublin or Fishguard/Pembroke–Rosslare ferry routes. National Express, a consortium of bus companies, has Supabus (as its buses are known) services from all major British cities to more than 90 Irish destinations. Slattery's, an Irish company, has services from London, Manchester, Liverpool, Oxford, Birmingham, Leeds, and North Wales to more than 100 Irish destinations.

FARES AND SCHEDULES

Pick up a timetable at any bus station or call the numbers below for a schedule. It's best to avoid Friday-evening and Sunday-morning travel, as this is when throngs of workers from the country return to and depart from Dublin on the weekends.

➤ BUS INFORMATION: **Bus Éireann** (☎ 01/836–6111 in the Republic of Ireland, WEB www.buseireann.ie). **National Express** (☎ 08705/808–080 in the U.K., WEB www.nationalexpress. co.uk). **Slattery's** (☎ 020/7482–1604 in the U.K.). **Ulsterbus** (☎ 028/9033–3000 in Northern Ireland, WEB www. ulsterbus.co.uk).

PAYING AND CUTTING COSTS

You can buy tickets at the main tourist offices, at the bus station, or on the bus (cash only for the latter option). Buses have only one class, and prices are similar for all seats.

Several opportunities are available to save money, however, by buying multiday passes—some can be combined with the rail service for added flexibility. There are also some cost-cutting passes that will give access to travel in both Northern Ireland and the Republic of Ireland. All of these passes offer a terrific value. A Freedom of Northern Ireland ticket costs U.K.£38 for seven days' unlimited travel. A one-day ticket costs U.K.£10. Several passes offer discounts on both the bus and rail system in the Irish Republic, including the **Irish Explorer Rail and Bus Pass,** the **Irish Rambler Card,** the **Irish Rover Card,** and the **Emerald Card.** Contact Bus Éireann or Ulsterbus for details on passes.

RESERVATIONS

Check the bus office to see if reservations are accepted for your route; if not, show up early to get a seat. Note: prepaid tickets don't apply to a particular bus time, just a route, so if one vehicle is full you can try another.

BUSINESS HOURS

Business hours are generally 9–5, sometimes later in the larger towns. In smaller towns, stores often close from 1 to 2 for lunch. If a holiday falls on a weekend, most businesses are closed on Monday as well.

BANKS AND OFFICES

Banks are open 10–4, Monday–Friday. In small towns they may close from 12:30 to 1:30. They remain open until 5 one afternoon per week; the day of week varies, although it's usually Thursday. Post offices are open weekdays 9–5 and Saturdays 9–1; some of the smaller country offices close for lunch.

In Northern Ireland bank hours are weekdays 9:30–4:30. Post offices are open weekdays 9–5:30, Saturday 9–1. Some close for an hour at lunch.

GAS STATIONS

There are some 24-hour gas stations along the highways; otherwise, hours vary from morning rush hour to late evenings.

MUSEUMS AND SIGHTS

Museums and sights are generally open Tuesday–Saturday 10–5 and Sunday 2–5.

PHARMACIES

Most pharmacies are open Monday–Saturday 9–5:30 or 6. Larger towns and cities often have a 24-hour pharmacy.

SHOPS

Most shops are open Monday–Saturday 9–5:30 or 6. Once a week—normally Wednesday, Thursday, or Saturday—they close at 1 PM. These times do *not* apply to Dublin, where stores generally stay open later, and they can vary from region to region, so it's best to check locally. Larger shopping malls usually stay open late once a week—generally until 9 on Thursday or Friday.

Shops in Belfast are open weekdays 9–5:30, with a late closing on Thursday, usually at 9. Elsewhere in Northern Ireland, shops close for the afternoon once a week, usually Wednesday or Thursday; check locally. In addition, most smaller shops close for an hour or so at lunch. Airport shops are open daily.

CAMERAS AND PHOTOGRAPHY

Nature has blessed Ireland with spectacular landscapes, and it won't take long for something to capture the photographer's eye. In addition to cliffs, hills, and beaches, sunsets along the north and west coast can be particularly dramatic because of the variable cloud cover and the clarity of light. Take a step outside at dusk during your visit wherever you may be and see if you can catch a sunset. If you are looking for people, try to get to the horse market in Smithfield in Dublin the first Sunday of each month. The combination of children and horses will provide you with a few priceless candid shots. The *Kodak Guide to Shooting Great Travel Pictures* (available at bookstores everywhere) is loaded with tips.

➤ PHOTO HELP: **Kodak Information Center** (☎ 800/242–2424).

EQUIPMENT PRECAUTIONS

Don't pack film and equipment in checked luggage, where it is much more susceptible to damage. X-ray machines used to view checked luggage are becoming much more powerful and therefore are much more likely to ruin your film. Always **keep film and tape out of the sun.** Carry an extra supply of batteries, and **be prepared to turn on your camera or camcorder** to prove to security personnel that the device is real. Always **ask for hand inspection of film,** which becomes clouded after repeated exposure to airport X-ray machines, and **keep videotapes away from metal detectors.**

FILM AND DEVELOPING

Major brands of film are available throughout Ireland, although 24-hour developing is found only in larger cities. Advantix formula film and developing are widely available in larger centers. A roll of 36-exposure color film will cost between €6.35 and €7.60.

VIDEOS

Videotape is widely available, though the local tape standard is PAL. A standard 180-minute cassette will cost around €5.10.

CAR RENTAL

If you are renting a car in the Irish Republic and intend to visit Northern Ireland (or vice versa), make this clear when you get your car, and check that the rental insurance applies when you cross the border.

Renting a car in Ireland is far more expensive than organizing a rental before you leave the United States. Rates in Dublin for an economy car with a manual transmission and unlimited mileage begin at €34.30 a day, €177.75 a week (January–April and November–December 15); €44.45 a day, €222.20 a week (May–June and September–October); and €57.15 a day, €304.75 a week (July–August and December 16–31). This includes the Republic's 12½% tax on car rentals.

Rates in Belfast begin at U.K.£29 a day, U.K.£157 a week (January–June and September–December 15) and U.K.£33 a day, U.K.£190 a week (July–August and December 16–31). This does not include the 17½% tax on car rentals in the North.

Both manual and automatic transmissions are readily available, though automatics will cost a bit extra. Typical economy car models include the familiar Toyota Corolla, Ford Mondeo, and Nissan Micra. Luxury cars such as Mercedes or Alfa Romeos are available for about €190.45 a day, and four-wheel-drive vehicles such as a Jeep Cherokee can be rented for a price of €120.65 a day. Minivans are also available for about €127 a day. Argus Rent A Car and Dan Dooley have convenient locations at Dublin, Shannon, Belfast, and Belfast City airports as well as at ferry ports.

➤ MAJOR AGENCIES: **Alamo** (☎ 800/522–9696; 020/8759–6200 in the U.K., WEB www.alamo.com). **Avis**

(☎ 800/331–1084; 800/879–2847 in Canada; 02/9353–9000 in Australia; 09/526–2847 in New Zealand; 0870/606–0100 in the U.K.; WEB www.avis.com). **Budget** (☎ 800/527–0700; 0870/156–5656 in the U.K.; WEB www.budget.com). **Dollar** (☎ 800/800–6000; 0124/622–0111 in the U.K., where it's affiliated with Sixt; 02/9223–1444 in Australia; WEB www.dollar.com). **Hertz** (☎ 800/654–3001; 800/263–0600 in Canada; 020/8897–2072 in the U.K.; 02/9669–2444 in Australia; 09/256–8690 in New Zealand; WEB www.hertz.com). **National Car Rental** (☎ 800/227–7368; 020/8680–4800 in the U.K.; WEB www.nationalcar.com).

CUTTING COSTS

To get the best deal, **book through a travel agent who will shop around.** Also **price local car-rental companies,** although the service and maintenance may not be as good as those of a major player. Remember to ask about required deposits, cancellation penalties, and drop-off charges if you're planning to pick up the car in one city and leave it in another. If you're traveling during a holiday period, also make sure that a confirmed reservation guarantees you a car.

Do **look into wholesalers,** companies that do not own fleets but rent in bulk from those that do and often offer better rates than traditional car-rental operations. Payment must be made before you leave home.

➤ LOCAL AGENCIES: **Argus** (☎ 01/490–4444 in Dublin, WEB www.argus-rentacar.com). **Dan Dooley** (☎ 800/331–9301 in the U.S.; 0208/995–4551 in the U.K.; 062/53103 in Ireland, WEB www.dan-dooley.ie). **ECL Chauffeur Drive** (☎ 01/842–0249, WEB www.iol.ie~/ecl/ecl.html).

➤ WHOLESALERS: **Auto Europe** (☎ 207/842–2000 or 800/223–5555, FAX 207/842–2222, WEB www.autoeurope.com). **Destination Europe Resources** (✉ 9501 W. Devon Ave., Rosemont, IL 60018, ☎ 800/782–2424, WEB www.der.com). **Europe by Car** (☎ 212/581–3040 or 800/223–1516, FAX 212/246–1458, WEB www.europebycar.com). **Kemwel Holiday Autos** (☎ 800/678–0678, FAX 207/842–2124 or 800/576–1590, WEB www.kemwel.com).

INSURANCE

When driving a rented car you are generally responsible for any damage to or loss of the vehicle. Before you rent, see what coverage your personal auto-insurance policy and credit cards provide.

Before you buy collision coverage, check your existing policies—you may already be covered. However, collision policies that car-rental companies sell for European rentals usually do not include stolen-vehicle coverage.

REQUIREMENTS AND RESTRICTIONS

In Ireland your own driver's license is acceptable. An International Driver's Permit is a good idea; it's available from the American or Canadian Automobile Association and, in the United Kingdom, from the Automobile Association or Royal Automobile Club. These international permits are universally recognized, and having one in your wallet may save you a problem with the local authorities.

Most rental companies require you to be over 23 to rent a car in Ireland (a few will rent to those over 21) and to have had a license for more than a year. Some companies also refuse to rent to visitors over 70.

Children under 12 years of age are not allowed to ride in the front seat unless in a properly fitted child seat.

SURCHARGES

Before you pick up a car in one city and leave it in another, **ask about drop-off charges or one-way service fees,** which can be substantial. Note, too, that some rental agencies charge extra if you return the car before the time specified in your contract. To avoid a hefty refueling fee, **fill the tank just before you turn in the car,** but be aware that gas stations near the rental outlet may overcharge.

Drivers between the ages of 21 to 25 and 70 to 75 who wish to rent cars should be able to, though they will be subject to an insurance surcharge. An additional driver will add about €3.80 a day to your car rental, and a child seat costs about €19 for the rental and will require 24-hour advance notice.

CAR TRAVEL

A car journey on Ireland's many back roads and byways is the ideal way to explore the country's predominantly rural attractions. Roads are generally good, although four-lane, two-way roads are the exception rather than the rule. Most National Primary Routes (designated by the letter N) have two lanes with generous shoulders on which to pass. Brand-new divided highways, or motorways—designated by blue signs and the letter M—take the place of some N roads. They are the fastest way to get from one point to another, but use caution: they sometimes end as abruptly as they begin. In general, traffic is light, especially off the national routes, although Dublin is always very congested in rush hour and on weekend evenings. It's also wise to **slow down on the smaller, often twisty roads** and **watch out for cattle and sheep;** they may be just around the next bend. Reckless driving, such as speeding, is not uncommon in the countryside, so stay alert and use caution. Speed limits are 96 kph (60 mph) on the open road, 112 kph (70 mph) on the motorways, and 48 kph (30 mph) in urban areas. However, because roads are generally winding and pass through many towns, expect to average about 64 kph (40 mph).

Road signs are generally in both Irish (Gaelic) and English; in the northwest and Connemara, most are in Irish only, so **make sure you have a good road map.** On the new green signposts distances are in kilometers; on the old white signposts they're given in miles. Because of the coexistence of both old and new signs, the route number is not always referred to on the signpost, particularly on National Secondary Roads (also called N-numbered routes) and Regional roads (R-numbered routes). On such roads, knowing the name of the next town on your itinerary is more important than knowing the route number: neither the small local signposts nor the local people refer to roads by official numbers. At unmarked intersections, a good rule of thumb is to **keep going straight if there's no sign directing you to do otherwise.**

Traffic signs are the same as in the rest of Europe, and roadway markings are standard. Note that a continuous white line down the center of the road prohibits passing. Barred markings on the road and flashing yellow beacons indicate a crossing, where pedestrians have right of way. At a junction of two roads of equal importance, the driver to the right has right of way.

The road network in Northern Ireland is excellent and, outside Belfast, uncrowded. Road signs and traffic regulations conform to the British system. Speed limits are 48 kph (30 mph) in towns, 96 kph (60 mph) on country roads, and 112 kph (70 mph) on two-lane roads and motorways.

All ferries on both principal routes to the Irish Republic—Holyhead–Dublin and Fishguard/Pembroke–Rosslare— take cars. Fishguard and Pembroke are relatively easy to reach by road. The car trip to Holyhead, on the other hand, is sometimes difficult: delays on the A55 North Wales coastal road are not unusual.

Car ferries to Belfast leave from the Scottish port of Stranraer and the English city of Liverpool; those to Larne leave from Stranraer and Cairnryan.

EMERGENCY SERVICES

Membership in a breakdown service is definitely advisable if you're using your own car in Ireland. The Automobile Association of Ireland is a sister organization of its English counterpart and is highly recommended.

➤ CONTACTS: **Automobile Association of Ireland** (☎ 01/617–9999, WEB www.aaireland.ie).

GASOLINE

You'll find gas stations along most roads. Self-service is the norm in larger establishments. Major credit cards and traveler's checks are usually accepted. Prices are near the lower end for Europe with unleaded gas priced around €.85 a liter, or more than double the gasoline costs in the U.S. Prices tend to vary significantly from station to station, so it is worth driving around the block.

ROAD CONDITIONS

Most roads are paved and make for easy travel. Watch for traffic at rush hours in Dublin, Cork, Limerick, Belfast, and Galway. Roads are classified as M, N, or R. M are the new double-lane divided highways with paved shoulders, and N routes will generally be undivided highways with shoulders. R, or regional, roads tend to be very narrow and twisty, and if you are not accustomed to driving on the left-hand side, try to avoid them.

Rush hour in Dublin starts at about 7 AM until 9:30 AM and 5 PM to 7 PM; special events such as football or soccer games in Dublin will tie up traffic around the city.

In Dublin especially, there are plenty of pedestrians, and jaywalking is common, so be careful—particularly through intersections. In the winter, fog and black ice can be a problem. Fog lights on cars are handy for dealing with fog. For winter driving, keep an eye on the temperature, and reduce speeds when traveling over bridges or in shaded areas where ice is likely to accumulate.

ROAD MAPS

Road maps can be found at most gas stations and bookstores.

RULES OF THE ROAD

The Irish, like the British, **drive on the left-hand side of the road.** Safety belts must be worn by the driver and all passengers, and children under 12 must travel in the back unless riding in a car seat. It is compulsory for motorcyclists and their passengers to wear helmets.

Drunk-driving laws are strict. The legal limit is 80 mgof alcohol per 100 ml of blood. Ireland has a Breathalyzer test, which the police can administer anytime. If you refuse to take it, the odds are you'll be prosecuted anyway. As always, the best advice is **don't drink if you plan to drive.**

Despite the relatively light traffic, parking in towns can be a problem. Signs with the letter P indicate that parking is permitted; a stroke through the P warns you to stay away or you'll be liable for a fine of €19.05–€63.50; however, if you get towed, the fine is €190.45. In Dublin and Cork, parking lots are your best bet, but check the rate first in Dublin; they can vary wildly.

In Northern Ireland there are plenty of parking lots in the towns (usually free except in Belfast), and you should use them. In Belfast, you cannot park your car in some parts of the city center, more because of congestion than security problems.

Army checkpoints are a thing of the past between the North and the South, though there are some border checkpoints for cattle (in an effort to contain BSE-contaminated livestock).

CHILDREN IN IRELAND

The Irish go to great lengths to make children welcome. Many hotels offer baby-sitting services, and most will supply a cot if given advance notice. Hotel and pub restaurants often have a children's menu and can supply a high chair if necessary. Unlike in Great Britain, Irish licensing laws allow children under 14 into pubs—although they may not consume alcohol on the premises until they are 18, and they are expected to leave by about 5:30 PM (although they may be allowed to stay until 7 PM, depending on how busy the pub gets). This is a boon if you are touring by car, because pubs are perfect for lunch or tea stops.

While most attractions and bus and rail journeys offer a rate of half price or less for children, **look for "family tickets,"** which may be cheaper and usually cover two adults and up to four children. The Irish Tourist Board (ITB) publishes "A Tour of Favorite Kids' Places," which covers a week's worth of sights around the country.

Be sure to plan ahead and **involve your youngsters** as you outline your trip. When packing, include things to keep them busy en route. On sightseeing days try to schedule activities of special interest to your children.

Places that are especially appealing to children are indicated by a rubber duckie icon (⏾) in the margin.

There are plenty of attractions in Dublin to amuse children, including castles, museums, and zoos. Child-friendly attractions are a little more difficult to find outside major centers, but keep an eye on the weather. If you happen upon a good day, children can amuse themselves for hours at one of the many beaches. A sampling of theater productions for children can also be found at local playhouses around the country. Listings of upcoming events are published in the *Irish Times* (€1.27) each Wednesday.

If you are renting a car, don't forget to **arrange for a car seat** when you reserve. For general advice about traveling with children, consult *Fodor's FYI: Travel with Your Baby* (available in bookstores everywhere).

➤ LOCAL INFORMATION: **Dublin Tourism** (☎ 01/605–7700, WEB www.visitdublin.com). *Irish Times* (WEB www.ireland.com).

FLYING

If your children are two or older, **ask about children's airfares.** As a general rule, infants under two not occupying a seat fly at greatly reduced fares or even for free. When booking, **confirm carry-on allowances** if you're traveling with infants. In general, for babies charged 10% of the adult fare you are allowed one carry-on bag and a collapsible stroller; if the flight is full, the stroller may have to be checked or you may be limited to less.

Experts agree that it's a good idea to use safety seats aloft for children weighing less than 40 pounds. Airlines set their own policies: U.S. carriers usually require that the child be ticketed, even if he or she is young enough to ride free, since the seats must be strapped into regular seats. Do **check your airline's policy about using safety seats during takeoff and landing.** And since safety seats are not allowed everywhere in the plane, get your seat assignments early.

When reserving, **request children's meals or a freestanding bassinet** if you need them. But note that bulkhead seats, where you must sit to use the bassinet, may lack an overhead bin or storage space on the floor.

FOOD

Most of the food will feel familiar to children, from the traditional bacon-and-eggs breakfast to fish-and-chips. Pubs are your best bet if you want to be guaranteed children will recognize what they're eating.

In the larger centers fast-food chains such as McDonald's, KFC, and Pizza Hut are quite common. Some smaller towns do not have such familiar names, and you may need to search for the local equivalent.

LODGING

Most hotels in Ireland allow children under a certain age to stay in their parents' room at no extra charge, but others charge for them as extra adults; be sure to **find out the cutoff age for children's discounts.** Family-friendly hotels at all levels will offer cots, cribs, and baby-sitting services, though for an additional charge. Only more expensive hotels are likely to have swimming pools. Accommodation guides published by the ITB list family-friendly facilities in hotels across the country.

SUPPLIES AND EQUIPMENT

Items for babies and children are available in every town and village; check the supermarket or family grocery store. Familiar brands are available for all baby supplies. A 400-g (14.29-oz) box of powdered baby formula will cost around €5.10 and 600 ml of premixed formula is about €7.60. Disposable diapers will cost between €5.10 and €6.35 for a package of 26.

TRANSPORTATION

Children under 16 years of age ride the train for half price and infants ride for free. Car seats are permitted, though bassinets are not available for infants. Buses operate under the same system.

Car seats are readily available at car rental firms, but most do require 24 hours' advance notice. Children under 12 years of age are not permitted to ride in the front seat unless in a car seat.

COMPUTERS ON THE ROAD

If you're traveling with a laptop, carry a spare battery and adapter. Most laptops will work at both 120V and 220V, but you will need an adapter so the plug will fit in the socket.

CONSUMER PROTECTION

Whenever shopping or buying travel services in Ireland, **pay with a major credit card**, if possible, so you can cancel payment or get reimbursed if there's a problem. If you're doing business with a particular company for the first time, **contact your local Better Business Bureau and the attorney general's offices** in your state and (for U.S. businesses) the company's home state as well. Have any complaints been filed? Finally, if you're buying a package or tour, always **consider travel insurance** that includes default coverage (☞ Insurance).

➤ BBBs: **Council of Better Business Bureaus** (✉ 4200 Wilson Blvd., Suite 800, Arlington, VA 22203, ☎ 703/276–0100, FAX 703/525–8277, WEB www.bbb.org).

CRUISE TRAVEL

Cruise travel in Ireland consists of traveling the inland waterways. The Shannon River system provides a great alternative to traveling overland to see the interior of the country. In some cases bicycles can be rented so you can drop anchor and explore.

➤ CRUISE LINES: **Ireland Line Cruisers** (✉ Killaloe, ☎ 061/375011). **Leisure Afloat Ltd.** (✉ Shellumsrath House, Kilkenny, ☎ 056/64395, WEB www.leisureafloat.com). **Riversdale Barge Holidays** (✉ Ballinamore, ☎ 078/44122). **Shannon Castle Line** (✉ Williamstown Harbor, Whitegate, ☎ 061/927042). **Silver Line Cruisers** ✉ (The Marina, Banagher, ☎ 0509/51112, WEB www.silverlinecruisers.com). **Waveline Cruisers** (✉ Quigley's Marina, Killinure Point, Glassan, ☎ 0902/85711, WEB www.waveline.ie).

CUSTOMS AND DUTIES

When shopping, **keep receipts** for all purchases. Upon reentering the country, **be ready to show customs officials what you've bought.** If you feel a duty is incorrect or object to the way your clearance was handled, note the inspector's badge number and ask to see a supervisor. If the problem isn't resolved, write to the appropriate authorities, beginning with the port director at your point of entry.

IN AUSTRALIA

Australian residents who are 18 or older may bring home $A400 worth of souvenirs and gifts (including jewelry), 250 cigarettes or 250 grams of tobacco, and 1,125 ml of alcohol (including wine, beer, and spirits). Residents under 18 may bring back $A200 worth of goods. Prohibited items include meat products. Seeds, plants, and fruits need to be declared upon arrival.

➤ INFORMATION: **Australian Customs Service** (Regional Director, ✉ Box 8, Sydney, NSW 2001, Australia, ☎ 02/9213–2000 or 1300/363263; 1800/020504 quarantine-inquiry line, FAX 02/9213–4000, WEB www.customs.gov.au).

IN CANADA

Canadian residents who have been out of Canada for at least seven days may bring home C$500 worth of goods duty-free. If you've been away fewer than seven days but more than 48 hours, the duty-free allowance drops to C$200; if your trip lasts 24–48 hours, the allowance is C$50. You may not pool allowances with family members. Goods claimed under the C$500 exemption may follow you by mail; those claimed under the lesser exemptions must accompany you. Alcohol and tobacco products may be included in the seven-day and 48-hour exemptions but not in the 24-hour exemption. If you meet the age requirements of the province or territory through which you reenter Canada, you may bring in, duty-free, 1.14 liters (40 imperial ounces) of wine or liquor *or* 24 12-ounce cans or bottles of beer or ale. If you are 16 or older you may bring in, duty-free, 200 cigarettes and 50 cigars. Check ahead of time with Revenue Canada or the Department of Agriculture for policies regarding meat products, seeds, plants, and fruits.

You may send an unlimited number of gifts worth up to C$60 each duty-free to Canada. Label the package UNSOLICITED GIFT—VALUE UNDER $60. Alcohol and tobacco are excluded.

➤ INFORMATION: **Canada Customs and Revenue Agency** (✉ 2265 St. Laurent Blvd. S, Ottawa, Ontario K1G 4K3, Canada, ☎ 204/983–3500, 506/636–5064, 800/461–9999, WEB www.ccra-adrc.gc.ca/).

IN IRELAND

Clearing customs at major gateway airports is a fairly quick and easy procedure. Duty-free allowances have been abolished for those traveling between countries in the European Union (Austria, Belgium, Denmark, Finland, France, Germany, Greece, Ireland, Italy, Luxembourg, the Netherlands, Portugal, Spain [but not the Canary Islands], Sweden, the United Kingdom, but not the Channel Islands or Gibraltar).

For goods purchased outside the EU, you may import duty-free: (1) 200 cigarettes or 100 cigarillos or 50 cigars or 250 grams of smoking tobacco; (2) 2 liters of wine, and either 1 liter of alcoholic drink over 22% volume or 2 liters of alcoholic drink under 22% volume (sparkling or fortified wine included); (3) 50 grams (60 mls) of perfume and ¼ liter of toilet water; and (4) other goods (including beer) to a value of €180.30 per person (€92.70 per person for travelers under 15 years of age).

Goods that cannot be freely imported to the Irish Republic include firearms, ammunition, explosives, illegal drugs, indecent or obscene books and pictures, oral smokeless tobacco products, meat and meat products, poultry and poultry products, plants and plant products (including shrubs, vegetables, fruit, bulbs, and seeds), meat and meat products, and hay or straw even used as packing. Domestic cats and dogs from outside the United Kingdom and live animals from outside Northern Ireland must be quarantined for six months.

No animals or pets of any kind may be brought into Northern Ireland without a six-month quarantine. Other items that may not be imported include fresh meats, plants and veg-

etables, controlled drugs, and firearms and ammunition.

➤ INFORMATION: **Customs and Excise** (✉ Irish Life Building, 2nd floor, Middle Abbey St., Dublin 1, ☎ 01/878–8811, WEB www.revenue.ie).

IN NEW ZEALAND

Homeward-bound residents 17 or older may bring back $700 worth of souvenirs and gifts. Your duty-free allowance also includes 4.5 liters of wine or beer; one 1,125-ml bottle of spirits; and either 200 cigarettes, 250 grams of tobacco, 50 cigars, or a combination of the three up to 250 grams. Prohibited items include meat products, seeds, plants, and fruits.

➤ INFORMATION: **New Zealand Customs** (Head office: ✉ The Custom House, 17–21 Whitmore St., Box 2218, Wellington, ☎ 09/300–5399 or 0800/428–786, WEB www.customs.govt.nz).

IN THE U.K.

If you are a U.K. resident and your journey was wholly within the European Union (EU), you won't have to pass through customs when you return to the United Kingdom. If you plan to bring back large quantities of alcohol or tobacco, check EU limits beforehand. In most cases, if you bring back more than 200 cigars, 800 cigarettes, 10 liters of spirits, and/or 90 liters of wine, you have to declare the goods upon return.

➤ INFORMATION: **HM Customs and Excise** (✉ Portcullis House, 21 Cowbridge Rd. E, Cardiff CF11 9SS, ☎ 029/2038–6423 or 0845/010–9000, WEB www.hmce.gov.uk).

IN THE U.S.

U.S. residents who have been out of the country for at least 48 hours may bring home, for personal use, $400 worth of foreign goods duty-free, as long as they haven't used the $400 allowance or any part of it in the past 30 days. This exemption may include 1 liter of alcohol (for travelers 21 and older), 200 cigarettes, and 100 non-Cuban cigars. Family members from the same household who are traveling together may pool their $400 personal exemptions. For fewer than 48 hours, the duty-free allowance drops to $200, which may include 50 cigarettes, 10 non-Cuban cigars, and 150 milliliters of alcohol (or perfume containing alcohol). The $200 allowance cannot be combined with other individuals' exemptions, and if you exceed it, the full value of all the goods will be taxed. Antiques, which the U.S. Customs Service defines as objects more than 100 years old, enter duty-free, as do original works of art done entirely by hand, including paintings, drawings, and sculptures.

You may also send packages home duty-free, with a limit of one parcel per addressee per day (except alcohol or tobacco products or perfume worth more than $5). You can mail up to $200 worth of goods for personal use; label the package PERSONAL USE and attach a list of its contents and their retail value. If the package contains your used personal belongings, mark it PERSONAL GOODS RETURNED to avoid paying duties. You may send up to $100 worth of goods as a gift; mark the package UNSOLICITED GIFT. Mailed items do not affect your duty-free allowance on your return.

➤ INFORMATION: **U.S. Customs Service** (for inquiries, ✉ 1300 Pennsylvania Ave. NW, Washington, DC 20229, WEB www.customs.gov, ☎ 202/354–1000; for complaints, ✉ Customer Satisfaction Unit, 1300 Pennsylvania Ave. NW, Room 5.5A, Washington, DC 20229; for registration of equipment, ✉ Office of Passenger Programs, 1300 Pennsylvania Ave. NW, Room 5.4D, Washington, DC 20229; ☎ 202/927–0530).

DINING

It wasn't so long ago that people shared jokes about the stodgy, overcooked, slightly gray food they were served in Ireland. But in the last decade there have been changes in all aspects of Irish life, including food and drink. The country is going through a culinary renaissance, and Dublin chefs are leading the charge. They're putting nouvelle spins on traditional Irish favorites. And, spurred on by a wave of new immigration, ethnic eateries of all types have sprung up in most major towns and cities.

The restaurants we list are the cream of the crop in each price category. They are indicated in the text by ✗ . Establishments denoted by ✗▥ stand out equally for their restaurants and their rooms. For information about restaurants beyond those reviewed in our guide, look for dining guides available from the Irish Tourist Board (ITB) or the Northern Ireland Tourist Board (NITB).

CATEGORY	THE REPUBLIC*	NORTHERN IRELAND*
$$$$	over €29	over U.K. £18
$$$	€22–€29	U.K.£13– U.K.£18
$$	€13–€21	U.K.£7– U.K.£12
$	under €13	under U.K. £7

Per person for a main course at dinner

MEALS AND SPECIALTIES

A postmodern renaissance in Irish cuisine has lead to a pursuit for authenticity in traditional Irish food. Many of the finer restaurants in Dublin, Cork, and Galway now offer a couple of dishes that are variations on a traditional theme. *Coddle,* a boiled stew of bacon, sausage, and smoked meats, is an old Dublin favorite.

A typical Irish breakfast includes fried eggs, bacon, black and white puddings, sausage, and a pot of tea. A typical lunch might feature a hearty sandwich; dinner meals usually include meat and two vegetables. Some of the best food is found at family bed-and-breakfasts and in inexpensive cafés.

Fresh fish and seafood are at the heart of many specialties. Irish smoked salmon—usually served on brown soda bread with plenty of butter—is among the finest in the world, and many a wondrous dish has been created around the humble cockle and mussel, abundant in the clear Atlantic waters. Galway and the West are rapidly becoming famous for their top-class oyster beds.

Of course there's the omnipresent potato, too. The Irish have many words for the humble spud, which is like snow to the Eskimo, and they have invented plenty of ways to serve it up. The best of these is *boxty,* a traditional pancake of once- and twice-cooked potatoes: it makes the perfect bed for a beef-and-Guinness stew, or the equally hearty lamb casserole.

MEALTIMES

Breakfast is served from 7 to 10, lunch runs from 1 to 2:30, and dinners are usually mid-evening occasions.

Pubs are generally open Monday and Tuesday 10:30 AM–11:30 PM and Thursday–Saturday 10:30 AM–12:30 AM. The famous Holy Hour, which required city pubs to close from 2:30 to 3:30, was abolished in 1988, and afternoon opening is now at the discretion of the owner or manager; few bother to close. On Sunday, pubs are open 12:30 PM–12:30 AM or later on certain Sundays. All pubs close on Christmas Day and Good Friday, but hotel bars are open for guests.

Pubs in Northern Ireland are open 11:30 AM–11 PM Monday–Saturday and 12:30 PM–2:30 PM and 7 PM–10 PM on Sunday. Sunday opening is at the owner's or manager's discretion.

Unless otherwise noted, the restaurants listed in this guide are open daily for lunch and dinner.

PAYING

Traveler's checks and credit cards are widely accepted, although it's cash-only at smaller pubs and take-out restaurants.

RESERVATIONS AND DRESS

Reservations are always a good idea: we mention them only when they're essential or not accepted. Book as far ahead as you can, and reconfirm as soon as you arrive. We mention dress only when men are required to wear a jacket or a jacket and tie.

WINE, BEER, AND SPIRITS

All types of alcoholic beverages are available in Ireland. Beer and wine are sold in shops and supermarkets, and you can get drinks "to go" at some bars, although at inflated prices. Stout (Guinness, Murphy's, Beamish)

is the Irish beer; whiskey comes in many brands and is smoother and more blended than Scotch.

DISABILITIES AND ACCESSIBILITY

Ireland has only recently begun to provide facilities such as ramps and accessible toilets for people with disabilities. Public transportation also lags behind. However, visitors with disabilities will often find that the helpfulness of the Irish makes up for the lack of amenities.

➤ LOCAL RESOURCES: **Disability Action** (✉ 2 Annadale Ave., Belfast, ☎ 028/9029–7880, WEB www.disabilityaction. org). **National Disability Resource Center** (✉ 44 N. Great George's St., Dublin, ☎ 01/874–7503).

LODGING

In the $$$$ category of hotels in Dublin, the Conrad Dublin International has some of the best amenities for people using wheelchairs. It has a ramped entrance, access to all floors, and bedrooms with adapted bathroom. For the $$$ range in Dublin, try the Doyle Burlington, though be warned that it has limited access and that many people using wheelchairs will need assistance in relation to the toilet facilities. In the $ category, offering the best services in any price range is Jurys Christchurch Inn or Jurys Customs House Inn. Both of these hotels are fully accessible to people using wheelchairs. In Belfast the Belfast Hilton ($$$$) is fully accessible.

RESERVATIONS

When discussing accessibility with an operator or reservations agent, **ask hard questions.** Are there any stairs, inside *or* out? Are there grab bars next to the toilet *and* in the shower/tub? How wide is the doorway to the room? To the bathroom? For the most extensive facilities meeting the latest legal specifications, **opt for newer accommodations.** If you reserve through a toll-free number, consider also calling the hotel's local number to confirm the information from the central reservations office. Get confirmation in writing when you can.

TRANSPORTATION

Dublin airport is accessible for people using wheelchairs. Assistance will be needed at other airports.

The suburban rail system in Dublin (DART) is also accessible to most people using wheelchairs, but not all stations are accessible, so it is advisable to have some assistance present. The national rail system cars do not permit wheelchairs to move through the aisles, though accommodation can be made in the vestibule area of the carriage, which is spacious and air-conditioned. However, the passenger using a wheelchair will be isolated from fellow travelers.

People using wheelchairs will have difficulty on buses, as very few are equipped for wheelchairs; however, there are several taxi companies that operate wheelchair-accessible cars. Hand-controlled cars are no longer available for rent in Ireland due to the high cost of insurance.

Travelers with disabilities who display the wheelchair sign on their cars can park free of charge at parking meters in Dublin and in designated parking spaces. The Orange Badge issued to people with disabilities in the United Kingdom can be used while visiting Ireland.

➤ COMPLAINTS: **Aviation Consumer Protection Division** (☞ Air Travel) for airline-related problems. **Departmental Office of Civil Rights** (for general inquiries, ✉ U.S. Department of Transportation, S-30, 400 7th St. SW, Room 10215, Washington, DC 20590, ☎ 202/366–4648, FAX 202/366–3571, WEB www.dot.gov/ost/docr/index.htm). **Disability Rights Section** (✉ NYAV, U.S. Department of Justice, Civil Rights Division, 950 Pennsylvania Ave. NW, Washington, DC 20530; ☎ ADA information line 202/514–0301, 800/514–0301, 202/514–0383 TTY, 800/514–0383 TTY, WEB www.usdoj.gov/crt/ada/adahom1.htm).

TRAVEL AGENCIES

In the United States, the Americans with Disabilities Act requires that travel firms serve the needs of all travelers. Some agencies specialize in working with people with disabilities.

➤ TRAVELERS WITH MOBILITY PROBLEMS: **Access Adventures** (✉ 206 Chestnut Ridge Rd., Scottsville, NY 14624, ☎ 716/889–9096, dltravel@prodigy.net), run by a former physical-rehabilitation counselor. **CareVacations** (✉ 5-5110 50th Ave., Leduc, Alberta T9E 6V4, Canada, ☎ 780/986–6404 or 877/478–7827, FAX 780/986–8332, WEB www.carevacations.com), for group tours and cruise vacations. **Flying Wheels Travel** (✉ 143 W. Bridge St., Box 382, Owatonna, MN 55060, ☎ 507/451–5005, FAX 507/451–1685, WEB www.flyingwheelstravel.com).

➤ TRAVELERS WITH DEVELOPMENTAL DISABILITIES: **New Directions** (✉ 5276 Hollister Ave., Suite 207, Santa Barbara, CA 93111, ☎ 805/967–2841 or 888/967–2841, FAX 805/964–7344, WEB www.newdirectionstravel.com).

DISCOUNTS AND DEALS

Tourists should take advantage of the Heritage Service Heritage Card. The card will give travelers access to 65 Heritage sites for €19.05 or €45.70 for a family pass. Cards are sold in Ireland at all Heritage Service sites.

Be a smart shopper and **compare all your options** before making decisions. A plane ticket bought with a promotional coupon from travel clubs, coupon books, and direct-mail offers may not be cheaper than the least expensive fare from a discount ticket agency. And always keep in mind that what you get is just as important as what you save.

DISCOUNT RESERVATIONS

To save money, **look into discount reservations services** with toll-free numbers, which use their buying power to get a better price on hotels, airline tickets, even car rentals. When booking a room, always **call the hotel's local toll-free number** (if one is available) rather than the central reservations number—you'll often get a better price. Always ask about special packages or corporate rates.

When shopping for the best deal on hotels and car rentals, **look for guaranteed exchange rates,** which protect you against a falling dollar. With your rate locked in, you won't pay more, even if the price goes up in the local currency.

➤ AIRLINE TICKETS: ☎ 800/AIR–4LESS.

➤ HOTEL ROOMS: **Hotel Reservations Network** (☎ 800/964–6835, 🕸 www.hoteldiscount.com). **Players Express Vacations** (☎ 800/458–6161, 🕸 www.playersexpress.com). **Steigenberger Reservation Service** (☎ 800/223–5652, 🕸 www.srs-worldhotels.com). **Travel Interlink** (☎ 800/888–5898, 🕸 www.travelinterlink.com). **Turbotrip.com** (☎ 800/473–7829, 🕸 www.turbotrip.com).

PACKAGE DEALS

Don't confuse packages and guided tours. When you buy a package, you travel on your own, just as though you had planned the trip yourself. Fly-drive packages, which combine airfare and car rental, are often a good deal. If you **buy a rail-drive pass,** you may save on train tickets and car rentals. All Eurail- and Europass holders get a discount on Eurostar fares through the Channel Tunnel.

ELECTRICITY

To use your U.S.-purchased electric-powered equipment, **bring a converter and adapter.** The electrical current in Ireland is 220 volts, 50 cycles alternating current (AC); wall outlets take plugs with three prongs.

If your appliances are dual-voltage, you'll need only an adapter. Don't use 110-volt outlets marked FOR SHAVERS ONLY for high-wattage appliances such as blow dryers. Most laptops operate equally well on 110 and 220 volts and so require only an adapter.

EMBASSIES

➤ AUSTRALIA: (✉ Fitzwilton House, Wilton Terr., Dublin 2, ☎ 01/676–1517).

➤ CANADA: (✉ 65 St. Stephen's Green, Dublin 2, ☎ 01/478–1988).

➤ NEW ZEALAND: (✉ New Zealand House, The Haymarket, London SW1Y 4TQ, ☎ 44/20/7930–8422).

➤ UNITED KINGDOM: (✉ 29 Merrion Rd., Dublin 4, ☎ 01/205–3700).

➤ UNITED STATES: (✉ 42 Elgin Rd., Ballsbridge, Dublin 4, ☎ 01/668–7122).

EMERGENCIES

The only emergency number you have to know in Ireland is 999. Wherever you are, this number will connect you with local police, ambulance, and fire services. All three services are very professional, and you can expect a prompt response to your call.

➤ CONTACTS: **Ambulance, fire, police** (☎ 999).

ETIQUETTE AND BEHAVIOR

The Irish are a casual, comfortable lot who aren't too particular about points of etiquette. Handshakes are more common than hugs, although public displays of affection—in moderation—are often seen. Two things to note, though, are the great respect of the younger Irish for their elders and the great respect of all churchgoers for the sermon (hence, no talking during the service).

GAY AND LESBIAN TRAVEL

In 1993 the Republic of Ireland began to replace virulently homophobic laws (inherited from British rule and enforced up to the 1970s) with some of the most gay-progressive statutes in the EU. Homosexual acts have been decriminalized, and hate crimes and discrimination in the workplace and public accommodation are now illegal. Leading these efforts was Ireland's progressive president, Mary Robinson, the first woman to hold this office. (She was named United Nations High Commissioner for Human Rights in June 1997.)

This enlightened legal environment, however, doesn't readily translate into the same public lesbian and gay presence you find in U.S. and other European cities. Outside the Republic's major cities—Dublin, Cork, and Galway—signs of gay life can be difficult to find, and even in these cities you're likely to find them only in small pockets: a pub here, a café there. If you do encounter any difficulties as a gay traveler, it's likely to be with lodging establishments. Proprietors at even some of the most upscale places may resist letting a room with one bed to same-sex couples; at other establishments, no one may so much as raise an eyebrow. Test the waters in advance: be explicit about what you want when you make your reservation.

➤ GAY- AND LESBIAN-FRIENDLY TRAVEL AGENCIES: **Different Roads Travel** (⊠ 8383 Wilshire Blvd., Suite 902, Beverly Hills, CA 90211, ☎ 323/651–5557 or 800/429–8747, FAX 323/651–3678, lgernert@tzell.com). **Kennedy Travel** (⊠ 314 Jericho Turnpike, Floral Park, NY 11001, ☎ 516/352–4888 or 800/237–7433, FAX 516/354–8849, WEB www.kennedytravel.com). **Now Voyager** (⊠ 4406 18th St., San Francisco, CA 94114, ☎ 415/626–1169 or 800/255–6951, FAX 415/626–8626, WEB www.nowvoyager.com). **Skylink Travel and Tour** (⊠ 1006 Mendocino Ave., Santa Rosa, CA 95401, ☎ 707/546–9888 or 800/225–5759, FAX 707/546–9891), serving lesbian travelers.

CORK

Ireland's second-largest city has the country's only lesbian and gay community center and a decade-old gay bar. The Cork Film Festival (☞ Festivals and Seasonal Events), held in October, incorporates the Irish Lesbian and Gay Film Festival.

The Lesbian and Gay Line operates Wednesday 7 PM–9 PM and Saturday 3 PM–5 PM; it functions as a lesbian hot line Thursday 8 PM–10 PM. Loafers is Cork's main gay bar. The Other Place, a lesbian and gay community center, houses a bookstore and café and hosts Friday- and Saturday-night dances.

➤ CORK CONTACTS: **Cork Lesbian Line** (☎ 021/425–4710). **Gay Information Cork** (☎ 021/427–1087). **Loafers** (⊠ 26 Douglas St., ☎ 021/311612). **The Other Place** (⊠ 8 S. Main St., ☎ 021/278470).

DUBLIN

By far, Dublin has more accessible lesbian and gay life than any other city in Ireland. Consult the *Gay Community News,* Ireland's free monthly lesbian and gay newspaper, and *In Dublin* for current information about what's going on in the community. The Gay Switchboard

Dublin operates Sunday–Friday 8 PM–10 PM and Saturday 3:30 PM–6 PM. The George is the city's main gay bar, with a mainly male crowd, while Out on the Liffey draws both men and women.

➤ DUBLIN CONTACTS: *Gay Community News* (GCN; ☎ 01/671–9076 or 01/671–0939, WEB www.gcn.ie). **Gay Switchboard Dublin** (☎ 01/872–1055). **The George** (⊠ 89 S. Great George's St., ☎ 01/478–2983). *In Dublin* (⊠ 3–7 Camden Pl., ☎ 01/478–4322).

GALWAY

A young populace, a progressive university, and a few outstanding theater companies help make Ireland's bohemian left-coast city one of the country's most gay-friendly places. Zulu's Bar is Galway's first specifically gay bar. The Attic has gay nights on Friday and Sunday.

➤ GALWAY CONTACTS: **The Attic @ Liquid** (⊠ Salthill, ☎ 091/522715). **Galway Gay Helpline** (☎ 091/566134) operates Tuesday and Thursday 8 PM–10 PM. **Galway Lesbian Helpline** (☎ 091/564611) operates Wednesday 8 PM–10 PM. **Zulu's Bar** (⊠ Raven's Terr., ☎ 091/581204).

GUIDEBOOKS

Plan well and you won't be sorry. Guidebooks are excellent tools—and you can take them with you. You may want to check out color-photo-illustrated guides such as *Fodor's Exploring Ireland,* which is thorough on culture and history, and *Fodor's Escape to Ireland,* which highlights unique experiences. Pocket-size *Citypack Dublin* includes a foldout map. All are available at on-line retailers and bookstores everywhere.

HEALTH

Ireland is a very safe country for travel, with virtually no risk of health problems from food, drink, or insects. The weather, however, is another story; be sure to dress for the cold and rain or you may find yourself plagued by a constant cough and sniffles.

HOLIDAYS

Irish national holidays in 2003 are as follows: January 1 (New Year's Day);

March 17 (St. Patrick's Day); April 18 (Good Friday); April 21 (Easter Monday); May 5 (May Day); June 2 and August 4 (summer bank holidays); October 27 (autumn bank holiday); and December 25–26 (Christmas and St. Stephen's Day). If you plan to visit at Easter, remember that theaters and cinemas are closed for the last three days of the preceding week.

INSURANCE

The most useful travel-insurance plan is a comprehensive policy that includes coverage for trip cancellation and interruption, default, trip delay, and medical expenses (with a waiver for preexisting conditions).

Without insurance you will lose all or most of your money if you cancel your trip, regardless of the reason. Default insurance covers you if your tour operator, airline, or cruise line goes out of business. Trip-delay covers expenses that arise because of bad weather or mechanical delays. Study the fine print when comparing policies.

If you're traveling internationally, a key component of travel insurance is coverage for medical bills incurred if you get sick on the road. Such expenses are not generally covered by Medicare or private policies. U.K. residents can buy a travel-insurance policy valid for most vacations taken during the year in which it's purchased (but check preexisting-condition coverage).

Always **buy travel policies directly from the insurance company**; if you buy them from a cruise line, airline, or tour operator that goes out of business you probably will not be covered for the agency or operator's default, a major risk. Before making any purchase, **review your existing health and home-owner's policies** to find what they cover away from home.

➤ TRAVEL INSURERS: In the U.S.: **Access America** (✉ 6600 W. Broad St., Richmond, VA 23230, ☎ 804/285–3300 or 800/284–8300, FAX 804/673–1491 or 800/346–9265, WEB www.accessamerica.com). **Travel Guard International** (✉ 1145 Clark St., Stevens Point, WI 54481, ☎ 715/345–0505 or 800/826–1300, FAX 800/955–8785, WEB www.travelguard.com).

➤ INSURANCE INFORMATION: In the U.K.: **Association of British Insurers** (✉ 51–55 Gresham St., London EC2V 7HQ, U.K., ☎ 020/7600–3333, FAX 020/7696–8999, WEB www.abi.org.uk). In Canada: **RBC Travel Insurance** (✉ 6880 Financial Dr., Mississauga, Ontario, L5N 7Y5, Canada, ☎ 905/791–8700; 800/668–4342 in Canada, FAX 905/816–2498, WEB www.royalank.com). In Australia: **Insurance Council of Australia** (✉ Level 3, 56 Pitt St., Sydney NSW 2000, ☎ 03/9614–1077, FAX 03/9614–7924). In New Zealand: **Insurance Council of New Zealand** (✉ Level 7, 111–115 Customhouse Quay, Box 474, Wellington, New Zealand, ☎ 04/472–5230, FAX 04/473–3011, WEB www.icnz.org.nz).

LANGUAGE

Irish (also known as Gaelic)—a Celtic language related to Scots Gaelic, Breton, and Welsh—is the official national language. Though English is technically the second language of the country, it is, in fact, the everyday tongue of 95% of the population. Nowadays all Irish speakers are fluent in English.

Irish-speaking communities are found mainly in sparsely populated rural areas along the western seaboard, on some but not all islands, and in pockets in West Cork and County Waterford. Irish-speaking areas are known as Gaeltacht (pronounced *gale*-taukt). Although most road signs in Ireland are given in both English and Irish, within Gaeltacht areas the signs are often in Irish only. A good touring map will give both Irish and English names to places within the Gaeltacht. You really need only know two Irish words: *fir* (men) and *mná* (women)—useful vocabulary for a trip to a public toilet.

LODGING

Accommodations in Ireland range from deluxe renovated castles and stately homes to thatched cottages and farmhouses. Room standards are rising all the time, especially in the middle and lower price ranges. Pressure on hotel space reaches a peak from June to September, but it's always a good idea to **reserve in advance.** Many Irish hotels can be booked directly from the United States. Ask your travel agent.

The Irish Tourist Board (ITB) has an official grading system and publishes a list of "approved accommodations," which includes hotels, guest houses, bed-and-breakfasts, farmhouses, hostels, and camping parks. For each accommodation, the list gives a maximum charge that no hotel may exceed without special authorization. Prices must be displayed in every room, so if the hotel oversteps its limit, do not hesitate to complain to the hotel manager and/or the ITB. The ITB and the NITB (Northern Ireland Tourist Board) also distribute five accommodation guides, covering various kinds of lodgings, which are free if obtained in the United States (☞ Visitor Information).

Ideally, visitors should **sample a range of accommodations.** The very expensive country-house hotels and renovated castles offer a unique combination of luxury and history. Less impressive, but equally charming, are the provincial inns and country hotels with simple but adequate facilities. Many visitors seeking to meet a wide cross section of Irish people prefer a different B&B every night. Others enjoy the simplicity of self-catering for a week or two in a thatched cottage. ITB-approved guest houses and B&Bs display a green shamrock outside and are usually considered more reputable than those without. Hotels and other accommodations in Northern Ireland are similar to those in the Republic of Ireland.

The lodgings we list are the cream of the crop in each price category. We always list the facilities that are available, but we don't specify whether they cost extra; when pricing accommodations, always ask what's included and what costs extra. Lodgings are assigned price categories based on the range from their least-expensive standard double room at high season (excluding holidays) to the most expensive. Lodgings marked ✕🏠 are lodgings whose restaurants warrant a special trip.

Assume that hotels operate on the **European Plan** (EP, with no meals) unless we specify otherwise.

CATEGORY	DUBLIN*	ELSEWHERE IN THE REPUBLIC*
$$$$	over €280	over €230
$$$	€230–€280	€178–€230
$$	€178–€230	€127–€178
$	under €178	under €127

All prices are for two people in a double room, including VAT and a service charge (often applied in larger hotels).

CATEGORY	NORTHERN IRELAND*
$$$$	over U.K.£120
$$$	U.K.£90–U.K.£120
$$	U.K.£60–U.K.£90
$	under U.K.£60

All prices are for two people in a double room, including 17.5% local sales tax and a service charge (often applied in larger hotels).

RESERVATIONS

The Irish Tourist Board, known as Bord Fáilte, and Dublin Tourism operate a credit-card central reservations service for hotels and other accommodations, including guest houses, B&Bs throughout Ireland, and self-catering facilities. There's a booking fee of €3.80 plus a charge of 10% of the cost of the accommodations.

➤ CONTACT INFORMATION: **Bord Fáilte** (☎ 800/223–6470 in the U.S. and Canada; 800/0397000 in the U.K.; 02/9299–6177 in Australia; 09/379–8720 in New Zealand, WEB www.irelandvacations.com). **Dublin Tourism** (☎ 01/605–7700 or 01/602–4129, FAX 01/605–7787; 01/475–8046 for non–credit card accommodation inquiries, WEB www.visitdublin.com).

APARTMENT AND VILLA RENTALS

If you want a home base that's roomy enough for a family and comes with cooking facilities, **consider a furnished**

rental. These can save you money, especially if you're traveling with a group. Home-exchange directories sometimes list rentals as well as exchanges.

➤ INTERNATIONAL AGENTS: **At Home Abroad** (✉ 405 E. 56th St., Suite 6H, New York, NY 10022, ☎ 212/421–9165, ℻ 212/752–1591, ™ www.athomeabroadinc.com). **Hideaways International** (✉ 767 Islington St., Portsmouth, NH 03801, ☎ 603/430–4433 or 800/843–4433, ℻ 603/430–4444, ™ www.hideaways.com; membership $129). **Hometours International** (✉ Box 11503, Knoxville, TN 37939, ☎ 865/690–8484 or 800/367–4668, ™ thor.he.net/~hometour/). **Interhome** (✉ 1990 N.E. 163rd St., Suite 110, N. Miami Beach, FL 33162, ☎ 305/940–2299 or 800/882–6864, ℻ 305/940–2911, ™ www.interhome.com). **Villas and Apartments Abroad** (✉ 1270 Avenue of the Americas, 15th floor, New York, NY 10020, ☎ 212/897–5045 or 800/433–3020, ℻ 212/897–5039, ™ www.ideal-villas.com). **Villas International** (✉ 950 Northgate Dr., Suite 206, San Rafael, CA 94903, ☎ 415/499–9490 or 800/221–2260, ℻ 415/499–9491, ™ www.villasintl.com).

BED-AND-BREAKFASTS

B&Bs are classified by the ITB as either town homes, country homes, or farmhouses. Town and country B&Bs are listed in the ITB's "Quality Approved Irish Homes Accommodation Guide." Many now have at least one bedroom with a bathroom, but don't expect this as a matter of course. B&Bs often charge an extra €.60–€1.30 for a bath or shower. If this is located in the family bathroom, you should ask first whether you can use the facility. Many travelers do not bother booking a B&B in advance. They are so plentiful in rural areas that it's often more fun to leave the decision open, allowing yourself a choice of final destinations for the night. For B&B reservation services, *see* Reservations.

CAMPING

This is the cheapest way of seeing the country, and facilities for campers and caravaners are improving steadily. An abundance of coastal campsites compensates for the shortage of inland ones. All are listed in *Caravan and Camping Ireland* available from the ITB. Rates start at about €5.10 per tent, €7.60 per caravan overnight.

COTTAGES

In more than 100 locations there are clusters of holiday cottages for rent. Although often built in the traditional style, they have central heating and all the other modern conveniences. A three-bedroom cottage equipped for six adults is around €380 per week in mid-season. It is essential to reserve in advance. The ITB's publication *Self-Catering* lists individual properties and clusters of traditional cottages available by the week. For cottage reservation services, *see* Reservations.

FARM VACATIONS

Many Irish farms offer holidays with part board or full board on a weekly basis. These are listed in the ITB's illustrated publication *Farmhouse Accommodation.* You will notice at once from the booklet that very few are picturesque: they are more likely to be modern bungalows or undistinguished two-story houses than creeper-clad Georgian mansions—though exceptions do exist. Room and part board—breakfast and an evening meal—start at €267 per week. For farm reservation services, *see* Reservations.

GUEST HOUSES

To qualify as a guest house, establishments must have at least five bedrooms, but in major cities they often have many more. Some guest houses are above a bar or restaurant; others are part of a family home. As a rule, they're cheaper (some include an optional evening meal) and offer fewer amenities than hotels. But often that's where the differences end. Most have high standards of cleanliness and hospitality. Some even have a bathroom, a TV, and a direct-dial phone in each room. For guest house reservations services, *see* Reservations.

HOME EXCHANGES

If you would like to exchange your home for someone else's, **join a home-**

exchange organization, which will send you its updated listings of available exchanges for a year and will include your own listing in at least one of them. It's up to you to make specific arrangements.

➤ EXCHANGE CLUBS: **HomeLink International** (✉ Box 47747, Tampa, FL 33647, ☎ 813/975–9825 or 800/638–3841, FAX 813/910–8144, WEB www.homelink.org; $106 per year). **Intervac U.S.** (✉ 30 Corte San Fernando, Tiburon, CA 94920, ☎ 800/756–4663, FAX 415/435–7440, WEB www.intervacus.com; $90 yearly fee for a listing, on-line access, and a catalog; $50 without catalog).

HOSTELS

No matter what your age, you can **save on lodging costs by staying at hostels.** In some 4,500 locations in more than 70 countries around the world, Hostelling International (HI), the umbrella group for a number of national youth-hostel associations, offers single-sex, dorm-style beds and, at many hostels, rooms for couples and family accommodations. Membership in any HI national hostel association, open to travelers of all ages, allows you to stay in HI-affiliated hostels at member rates; one-year membership is about $25 for adults (C$35 for a two-year minimum membership in Canada, £13 in the U.K., A$52 in Australia, and NZ$40 in New Zealand); hostels run about $10–$30 per night. Members have priority if the hostel is full; they're also eligible for discounts around the world, even on rail and bus travel in some countries.

For hostel reservation services, *see* Reservations.

➤ ORGANIZATIONS: **Hostelling International—American Youth Hostels** (✉ 733 15th St. NW, Suite 840, Washington, DC 20005, ☎ 202/783–6161, FAX 202/783–6171, WEB www.hiayh.org). **Hostelling International—Canada** (✉ 400–205 Catherine St., Ottawa, Ontario K2P 1C3, ☎ 613/237–7884 or 800/663–5777, FAX 613/237–7868, WEB www.hihostels.ca). **Youth Hostel Association of England and Wales** (✉ Trevelyan House, Dimple Rd., Matlock, Derbyshire DE4 3YH, U.K., ☎ 0870/870–8808, FAX 0169/592–702, WEB www.yha.org.uk). **Youth Hostel Association Australia** (✉ 10 Mallett St., Camperdown, NSW 2050, ☎ 02/9565–1699, FAX 02/9565–1325, WEB www.yha.com.au). **Youth Hostels Association of New Zealand** (✉ Level 3, 193 Cashel St., Box 436, Christchurch, ☎ 03/379–9970, FAX 03/365–4476, WEB www.yha.org.nz).

HOTELS

Standard features in most hotels include private bath, air-conditioning, two twin beds (you can usually ask for a king-size instead), TV (often with VCR), free parking, and no-smoking rooms. There is usually no extra charge for these services. All hotels listed have private bath unless otherwise noted.

➤ TOLL-FREE NUMBERS: **Best Western** (☎ 800/528–1234, WEB www.bestwestern.com). **Choice** (☎ 800/424–6423, WEB www.choicehotels.com). **Clarion** (☎ 800/424–6423, WEB www.choicehotels.com). **Comfort Inn** (☎ 800/424–6423, WEB www.choicehotels.com). **Forte** (☎ 800/225–5843, WEB www.forte-hotels.com). **Four Seasons** (☎ 800/332–3442, WEB www.fourseasons.com). **Hilton** (☎ 800/445–8667, WEB www.hilton.com). **Holiday Inn** (☎ 800/465–4329, WEB www.sixcontinentshotels.com). **Marriott** (☎ 800/228–9290, WEB www.marriott.com). **Le Meridien** (☎ 800/543–4300, WEB www.lemeridien-hotels.com). **Quality Inn** (☎ 800/424–6423, WEB www.choicehotels.com). **Radisson** (☎ 800/333–3333, WEB www.radisson.com). **Ramada** (☎ 800/228–2828; 800/854–7854 international reservations, WEB www.ramada.com or www.ramadahotels.com). **Westin Hotels & Resorts** (☎ 800/228–3000, WEB www.starwood.com/westin).

MAIL AND SHIPPING

Letters take a week to 10 days to reach the United States and Canada, 3 to 5 days to reach the United Kingdom.

POSTAL RATES

Airmail rates to the United States and Canada from the Irish Republic are €.60 for letters and postcards. Mail to all European countries goes by air automatically, so airmail stickers or envelopes are not required. Rates are €.40 for letters and postcards.

Rates from Northern Ireland are 43p for letters and 37p for postcards (not over 10 grams). To the rest of the United Kingdom and the Irish Republic, rates are 26p for first-class letters and 20p for second class.

RECEIVING MAIL

Mail can be held for collection at any post office free of charge for up to three months. It should be addressed to the recipient "c/o Poste Restante." In Dublin, use the General Post Office.

➤ CONTACT: **General Post Office** (✉ O'Connell St., Dublin 1, ☎ 01/705–8833).

MEDIA

NEWSPAPERS AND MAGAZINES

In Ireland, there are three national daily broadsheet newspapers, the *Irish Times* and the *Irish Independent*—both Dublin based—and the *Examiner* (formerly the *Cork Examiner*), which is published in Cork. The *Irish Times* is the most authoritative and esteemed of the three; the *Irish Independent* is the most popular; and the *Examiner* is widely read in the southern counties. The British *Daily Star* and the *Sun* also have Irish editions.

The *Evening Herald* is the only nationwide evening newspaper. The *Evening Echo* is published by the Examiner group and sold in the Cork region. There are five Irish Sunday newspapers: the very popular and opinion-focused *Sunday Independent*; the more intellectual *Sunday Tribune*; the business-oriented *Sunday Business Post*; the popular tabloid, *Sunday World*; and *Ireland on Sunday*. Regional weekly newspapers are published in almost every county. In Northern Ireland, the main dailies are the *Belfast Telegraph* and the *Belfast Newsletter*. The British broadsheet and tabloid dailies and Sunday newspapers are widely available throughout Ireland.

RADIO AND TELEVISION

Radio Telefis Éireann (RTÉ) is Ireland's national television and radio network. There are two television channels—RTÉ 1, which concentrates on news and documentaries; and Network 2, which carries more feature films and light entertainment shows. TV3 is a private channel with a lot of American and British soaps and situation comedies. TG4 is an Irish-language channel (with English subtitles). The British television channels (BBC 1, BBC 2, UTV, Channel 4) and many satellite channels—including SkyNews, SkyMovies, SkySports, CNN, MTV, and TV5 Europe—are also widely available.

There are two 24-hour national radio stations in Ireland—Radio 1 (mainly talk shows) and the popular music-dominated station, 2FM. FM3 is a classical music station that is broadcast in the early mornings and evenings on the same wavelength as the daytime Irish-language radio station, Raidio Na Gaeltachta. There are more than 25 local commercial radio stations whose broadcasting standards vary from county to county. All the BBC radio channels are also available.

MONEY MATTERS

A modest hotel in Dublin costs about €127 a night for two; this figure can be reduced to under €90 by staying in a registered guest house or inn, and reduced to less than €45 by staying in a suburban B&B. Lunch, consisting of a good one-dish plate of bar food at a pub, costs around €7.60; a sandwich at the same pub, about €2.55. In Dublin's better restaurants, dinner will run around €25.40–€38.10 per person, excluding drinks and tip. Theater and entertainment in most places are inexpensive—about €17.80 for a good seat, and double that for a big-name, pop-music concert. For the price of a few drinks and (in Dublin and Killarney) a small entrance fee of about €1.90, you can spend a memorable evening at a *seisun* (pronounced *say-shoon*) in a music pub. Entrance to most public galleries is free, but stately homes and similar attractions normally charge about €3.80 per person. Just about everything is more expensive in Dublin, so add at least 10% to these sample prices: cup of coffee, €1; pint of beer, €3.15; soda, €1.30; and 2-km (1-mi) taxi ride, €5.10. Travelers from the United Kingdom and, to a lesser extent, the United States will find value when visiting Ireland. Due to the exchange rate, Canadians, Australians, and New Zealanders will find Ireland a little pricey when they convert costs to their home currency.

Hotels and meals in Northern Ireland are less expensive than in the United Kingdom and the Republic of Ireland. Also, the lower level of taxation makes dutiable goods such as gasoline, alcoholic drinks, and tobacco cheaper.

Prices throughout this guide are given for adults. Substantially reduced fees are almost always available for children, students, and senior citizens. For information on taxes, *see* Taxes.

ATMS

ATMs are found in all major towns. Most major banks are connected to CIRRUS or PLUS systems; there is a four-digit maximum for your PIN.

CREDIT CARDS

Throughout this guide, the following abbreviations are used: **AE**, American Express; **DC**, Diners Club; **MC**, MasterCard; and **V**, Visa.

➤ REPORTING LOST CARDS: **American Express** (☎ 0353/1205–5111). **Diners Club** (☎ 0353/661–1800). **MasterCard** (☎ 1800/557378). **Visa** (☎ 1800/558002).

CURRENCY

The Irish Republic is a member of the European Monetary Union (EMU), and since January 1, 2002, the euro has become legal tender replacing the pound or punt, pronounced *poont*.

Euro notes come in denominations of €500, €200, €100, €50, €20, €10 and €5. The euro is divided into 100 cents, and coins are available as €2 and €1 and 50, 20, 10, 5, 2, and 1 cents. The euro can be used in 11 other European countries: Austria, Belgium, Finland, France, Germany, Greece, Italy, Luxembourg, the Netherlands, Portugal, and Spain.

The British pound is the currency of Northern Ireland; in this guide it is written U.K.£.

CURRENCY EXCHANGE

Dollars and British pounds are accepted only in large hotels and shops geared to tourists. Elsewhere you will be expected to use the euro.

At press time, the euro stood at around U.S.$.88, Canadian $1.43, U.K.£.61, Australian $1.72, and New Zealand $2.09; however, these rates will inevitably change both before and during 2003. Keep a sharp eye on the exchange rate.

For the most favorable rates, **change money through banks.** Although ATM transaction fees may be higher abroad than at home, ATM rates are excellent because they are based on wholesale rates offered only by major banks. You won't do as well at exchange booths in airports or rail and bus stations, in hotels, in restaurants, or in stores. To avoid lines at airport exchange booths, **get a bit of local currency before you leave home.**

➤ EXCHANGE SERVICES: **International Currency Express** (☎ 888/278–6628 orders). **Thomas Cook Currency Services** (☎ 800/287–7362 orders and retail locations, WEB www.us.thomascook.com).

TRAVELER'S CHECKS

Do you need traveler's checks? It depends on where you're headed. If you're going to rural areas and small towns, go with cash; traveler's checks are best used in cities. Lost or stolen checks can usually be replaced within 24 hours. To ensure a speedy refund, buy your own traveler's checks—don't let someone else pay for them: irregularities like this can cause delays. The person who bought the checks should make the call to request a refund.

OUTDOORS AND SPORTS

BICYCLING

Ireland is made for the cyclist. In general it's flat with some gently rising hills; it's never too far from one town to the next; repair and support services are good; and the scenery is unparalleled. In summer cycle traffic is at its peak, as winter and early spring tend to be too wet for even the most avid bicycle fan. For information on bike rentals, *see* Bike Travel.

FISHING

New salmon and sea trout restrictions were introduced in 2002, limiting your catch to one of either variety per day between January and May. The best period for sea trout is from June to late September. Permits are necessary for salmon and sea-trout fishing on privately owned waters or club waters. Besides the permit for the use of a certain stretch of water, those who wish to fish for salmon and sea trout by rod and line must also have a state license. In the Irish Republic, these licenses (€31.75 annually, or €12.70 for 21 days) are available in some tackle shops or from the Central Fisheries Board. No license is required for brown trout, rainbow trout, or coarse fish, including pike. Sea angling is available on rocks and piers around the coast.

To game-fish in Northern Ireland, you need a rod license; Foyle Fisheries Commission (FFC) distributes licenses for game fishing in the Foyle area and the Fisheries Conservancy Board (FCB) handles all other regions. A license costs approximately U.K.£10 for eight days. You must also obtain a permit from the owner of the waters in which you plan to fish. Most of the waters in Northern Ireland are owned by the Department of Agriculture, which charges about U.K.£15 for a 15-day permit, U.K.£3.50 for a 3-day one. If you plan to fish outside the jurisdiction of the Department of Agriculture, you must obtain a permit from one of the local clubs. For more information, and for Department of Agriculture permits and FFC and FCB rod licenses, contact the NITB (☞ Visitor Information).

➤ INFORMATION: **Central Fisheries Board** (✉ Balngowan House, Mobhi Boreen, Glasnevin, Dublin 9, ☎ 01/837–9206, WEB www.cfb.ie). **Department of Agriculture** (✉ Fisheries Division, Dundonald House, Upper Newtownards Rd., Belfast BT4 3SB, ☎ 028/9052–4999, WEB www.dardni.gov.uk). **Fisheries Conservancy Board** (✉ FCB, 1 Mahon Rd., Portadown, BT62 3EE, ☎ 028/3833–4666). **Foyle Fisheries Commission** (✉ 22 Victoria Rd., Derry BT47 2AB, ☎ 028/7134–2100).

GOLF

What makes Irish golf so great—and increasingly popular—is quite simply the natural architecture. The wild, wonderful coastline seems to be made for links golf. Most famous of these, of course, is the celebrated Ballybunion. Fortunately, links courses can be played year-round—an asset in a rainy country like Ireland. Pack plenty of sweaters and rain gear, and make sure you're in good shape: electric cars are only available at the most expensive courses. Golf clubs and bags can be rented almost anywhere. With the exception of the ancient Royal Belfast, all golf clubs in Ireland are happy to have visitors (and charge well for the privilege). For details on specific courses, *see* Chapter 10.

➤ INFORMATION: **Golfing Union of Ireland** (✉ 81 Eglington Rd., Donnybrook Dublin 1, ☎ 01/269–4111, WEB www.gui.ie).

HIKING

Hikers from all over the world spend weeks on the almost 30 major and countless minor trails covering the country. As with biking, the relatively flat landscape, stunning scenery, and nearness of towns to each other make hiking a relatively carefree activity. A tent is always a good idea, but you can certainly plan any walk so that you reach civilization every night. Pack for wind and rain, as there will always be some. A good ordinance survey map is also useful.

The most famous of Ireland's walks is the classic Wicklow Way, a 137-km (85-mi) trail that begins in the Dublin suburbs before winding its way through the Wicklow mountains. Much of the route lies above 1,600 ft and follows rough sheep tracks, forest firebreaks, and old bog roads. Whether you're a novice or veteran hiker, Wicklow's gentle hills are a terrific place to begin an Irish walking vacation. Consider participating in one of the Wicklow walking festivals held at Easter, in May, and in autumn. Other popular hiking options include the Kerry Way, which starts and ends in Killarney, and the Donegal Walk across the center of wild, rugged County Donegal.

HORSEBACK RIDING

There are plenty of opportunities for horseback riding throughout the country. You're never more than a few miles from a riding center, and the variety of riding possibilities is one of Ireland's major attractions. Short gallops or weeklong guided trips are available. Terrains include beaches, mountain tracks, forests, and flat farmland ideal for cantering. Dublin's environs have excellent horseback riding. Stables on the city's outskirts give immediate access to suitable riding areas. In the city itself, Phoenix Park has superb, quiet riding conditions away from the busy main road that bisects the park. About 20 riding stables in the greater Dublin area have horses for hire by the hour or the day, for novices and experienced riders. A few also operate as equestrian centers and give lessons. Prices vary a great deal, but expect to pay around €19 an hour.

SPECTATOR SPORTS

The Irish are sports mad, and for an island of only 5 million people they have achieved notable success on the global stage with Olympic champions, World Cup qualifiers, and some of the finest Thoroughbreds on the planet. The natives love watching sports almost as much as taking part in them. Horse racing has long been a favorite pastime, with courses ringing Dublin and spread throughout the rest of the country. At Curragh Racecourse, in Dublin's environs, the Irish Derby and other international horse races are run. The capital city is home to two dog racing tracks: Harolds Cross and Shelbourne Park. Soccer has increased in popularity over the last two decades with the dramatic successes of the Republic of Ireland team; most of the major towns and cities have a semiprofessional club in the National League that runs from August to May every year. For a truly Irish sports experience you should try to attend one of two Gaelic games, either football or hurling; the first is played with a soccer-type ball that is kicked out of the hands, and the second with a wooden stick and a hard ball very much like a baseball. The speed and skill on display in both games can be breathtaking. An inter-county championship takes place from May through September.

➤ INFORMATION: **Curragh Racecourse** (✉ Kildare, ☎ 045/441205, WEB www.curragh.ie). **Football Association of Ireland** (✉ 80 Merrion Sq., Dublin 2, ☎ 01/676–6864, WEB www.fai.ie). **Gaelic Athletic Association** (✉ Croke Park, Dublin 4, ☎ 01/836–3222, WEB www.gaa.ie). **Harolds Cross** (✉ Harolds Cross, Dublin 6, ☎ 01/497–3439, WEB www.igb.ie). **Shelbourne Park** (✉ Shelbourne Park, Dublin 4, ☎ 01/668–3502, WEB www.shelbournepark.com).

PACKING

In Ireland you can experience all four seasons in a day, so pack accordingly. Even in July and August, the hottest months of the year, a heavy sweater and a good waterproof coat or umbrella are essential. You should **bring at least two pairs of walking shoes:** it can and does rain at any time of the year, and shoes can get soaked in minutes.

The Irish are generally informal about clothes. In the more expensive hotels and restaurants most people dress formally for dinner, and a jacket and tie may be required in bars after 7 PM, but very few places operate a strict dress policy. Younger travelers should note that old or tattered blue jeans and running shoes are forbidden in certain bars and dance clubs.

In your carry-on luggage, **pack an extra pair of eyeglasses or contact lenses** and **enough of any medication you take** to last a few days longer than the entire trip. You may also ask your doctor to write a spare prescription using the drug's generic name, since brand names may vary from country to country. In luggage to be checked, **never pack prescription drugs or valuables.** To avoid customs delays, carry medications in their original packaging. And don't forget to carry with you the addresses of offices that handle refunds of lost traveler's checks. Check *Fodor's How to Pack* (available in bookstores everywhere) for more tips.

CHECKING LUGGAGE

How many carry-on bags you can bring with you is up to the airline.

Most allow two, but not always, so make sure that everything you carry aboard will fit under your seat or in the overhead bin, and get to the gate early. Note that if you have a seat at the back of the plane, you'll probably board first, while the overhead bins are still empty.

If you are flying internationally, note that baggage allowances may be determined not by piece but by weight—generally 88 pounds (40 kilograms) in first class, 66 pounds (30 kilograms) in business class, and 44 pounds (20 kilograms) in economy.

Airline liability for baggage is limited to $1,250 per person on flights within the United States. On international flights it amounts to $9.07 per pound or $20 per kilogram for checked baggage (roughly $640 per 70-pound bag) and $400 per passenger for unchecked baggage. You can buy additional coverage at check-in for about $10 per $1,000 of coverage, but it excludes a rather extensive list of items, shown on your airline ticket.

Before departure, **itemize your bags' contents** and their worth, and label the bags with your name, address, and phone number. (If you use your home address, cover it so potential thieves can't see it readily.) Inside each bag, **pack a copy of your itinerary.** At check-in, **make sure that each bag is correctly tagged** with the destination airport's three-letter code. If your bags arrive damaged or fail to arrive at all, file a written report with the airline before leaving the airport.

PASSPORTS AND VISAS

When traveling internationally, **carry your passport** even if you don't need one (it's always the best form of I.D.) and **make two photocopies of the data page** (one for someone at home and another for you, carried separately from your passport). If you lose your passport, promptly call the nearest embassy or consulate and the local police.

ENTERING IRELAND

All U.S., Canadian, Australian, and New Zealand citizens, even infants, need a valid passport to enter Ireland for stays of up to 90 days. Citizens of the United Kingdom, when traveling on flights departing from Great Britain, do not need a passport to enter Ireland. Passport requirements for Northern Ireland are the same as for the Republic.

PASSPORT OFFICES

The best time to apply for a passport or to renew is in fall and winter. Before any trip, check your passport's expiration date, and, if necessary, renew it as soon as possible.

➤ AUSTRALIAN CITIZENS: **Australian Passport Office** (☎ 131–232, WEB www.passports.gov.au).

➤ CANADIAN CITIZENS: **Passport Office** (to mail in applications: ✉ Department of Foreign Affairs and International Trade, Ottawa, Ontario K1A 0G3; ☎ 800/567–6868 toll-free in Canada or 819/994–3500, WEB www.dfait-maeci.gc.ca/passport).

➤ NEW ZEALAND CITIZENS: **New Zealand Passport Office** (☎ 0800/ 22–5050 or 04/474–8100, WEB www. passports.govt.nz).

➤ U.K. CITIZENS: **London Passport Office** (☎ 0870/521–0410, WEB www. passport.gov.uk).

➤ U.S. CITIZENS: **National Passport Information Center** (☎ 900/225–5674, 35¢ per minute for automated service or $1.05 per minute for operator service, WEB www.travel.state.gov).

SAFETY

The theft of car radios, mobile phones, cameras, video recorders, and other items of value from cars is common in Dublin and other major cities and towns. Never leave any valuable items on car seats or in the foot space between the back and front seats or in the glove compartments. In fact, never leave anything whatsoever in sight in your car—even if you're leaving it for only a short time. You should also think twice about leaving valuables in your car while visiting tourist attractions anywhere in the country.

SENIOR-CITIZEN TRAVEL

To qualify for age-related discounts, **mention your senior-citizen status up front** when booking hotel reservations (not when checking out) and before you're seated in restaurants (not when paying the bill). When renting a car, ask about promotional car-rental discounts, which can be cheaper than senior-citizen rates.

➤ EDUCATIONAL PROGRAMS: **Elderhostel** (✉ 11 Ave. de Lafayette, Boston, MA 02111-1746, ☎ 877/426–8056, FAX 877/426–2166, WEB www. elderhostel.org). **Interhostel** (✉ University of New Hampshire, 6 Garrison Ave., Durham, NH 03824, ☎ 603/862–1147 or 800/733–9753, FAX 603/862–1113, WEB www.learn.unh.edu).

SHOPPING

Once a destination rich only in tales of leprechauns and fairies, Ireland has experienced an economic revival that has created a wealth of new shopping opportunities. From the souvenir shop selling the local woolen goods, linens, and crystal to internationally known retailers, the country has something for everyone's taste.

KEY DESTINATIONS

On a weekend, trying to navigate Grafton Street, Dublin's pedestrian shopping promenade, is not unlike being caught in rush-hour traffic. This is the heart of shopping in the country. Upscale department stores filled with designer labels can be found on the main strip, and fine boutiques await discovery just off the beaten path, making Dublin a great shopping destination.

Other major cities, such as Belfast, Cork, and Galway, will also have a wide variety of stores, including a few large department stores. The West is the place for those chunky Aran sweaters and hand-knitted knitwear of all types. Donegal is famous for its tweed, of course, and for crystal you can choose between world-famous Waterford and slightly less expensive Cavan. Northern Ireland, especially Belfast, has a long tradition of producing fine Irish linens.

STUDENTS IN IRELAND

To save money, **look into deals available through student-oriented travel agencies.** To qualify you'll need a bona fide student ID card. Members of international student groups are also eligible.

➤ IDs AND SERVICES: **STA Travel** (☎ 212/627–3311 or 800/781–4040, FAX 212/627–3387, WEB www.sta.com). **Travel Cuts** (✉ 187 College St., Toronto, Ontario M5T 1P7, Canada, ☎ 416/979–2406 or 888/838–2887, FAX 416/979–8167, WEB www. travelcuts.com).

TAXES

VALUE-ADDED TAX

When leaving the Irish Republic, U.S. and Canadian visitors **get a refund** of the value-added tax (VAT), which currently accounts for a hefty 20% of the purchase price of many goods and 12.5% of those that fall outside the luxury category. Apart from clothing, most items of interest to visitors, right down to ordinary toilet soap, are rated at 20%. Most crafts outlets and department stores operate a system called Cashback, which enables U.S. and Canadian visitors to collect VAT rebates in the currency of their choice at Dublin or Shannon Airport on departure. Otherwise, refunds can be claimed from individual stores after returning home. Forms for the refunds must be picked up at the time of purchase, and the form must be stamped by customs before leaving Ireland (including Northern Ireland). Most major stores deduct VAT at the time of sale if goods are to be shipped overseas; however, there is a shipping charge. VAT is not refundable on accommodation, car rental, meals, or any other form of personal services received on vacation.

When leaving Northern Ireland, U.S. and Canadian visitors can also get a refund of the 17.5% VAT by the over-the-counter and the direct-export methods. Most larger stores provide these services upon request and will handle the paperwork. For the over-the-counter method, you must spend more than U.K.£75 in one store. Ask the store for Form VAT 407 (you must have identification—passports are best), to be given to customs when you leave the country. The refund will be forwarded to you in about eight weeks (minus a small service charge) either in the form of a sterling check or as a credit to your charge card. The direct-export method, where the goods are shipped directly to your home, is more cumbersome. VAT Form 407/1/93 must be certified by customs, police, or a notary public when you get home and then sent back to the store, which will refund your money.

Global Refund is a VAT refund service that makes getting your money back hassle-free. The service is available Europe-wide at 130,000 affiliated stores. In participating stores, **ask for the Global Refund refund form** (called a Shopping Cheque). Have it stamped like any customs form by customs officials when you leave the European Union (be ready to show customs officials what you've bought). Then take the form to one of the more than 700 Global Refund counters—conveniently located at every major airport and border crossing—and your money will be refunded on the spot in the form of cash, check, or a refund to your credit-card account (minus a small percentage for processing).

➤ VAT REFUNDS: **Global Refund** (✉ 99 Main St., Ste. 307, Nyack, NY 10960, ☎ 800/566–9828, ℻ 845/ 348–1549, WEB www.globalrefund. com).

TELEPHONES

Ireland's telephone system is up to the standards of the United Kingdom and the United States. Direct-dialing is common; local phone numbers have five to eight digits. You can make international calls from most phones, and some cell phones also work here, depending on the carrier.

Do not make calls from your hotel room unless it's absolutely necessary. Practically all hotels add 200% to 300% to the cost of a call.

AREA AND COUNTRY CODES

The country code for Ireland is 353; for Northern Ireland, which is part of the United Kingdom telephone system, 44. The local area code for Northern Ireland is 028. However, when dialing Northern Ireland from the Republic you can simply dial 048 without using the U.K. country code. When dialing an Irish number from abroad, drop the initial 0 from the local area code. The country code is 1 for the United States and Canada, 61

for Australia, 64 for New Zealand, and 44 for the United Kingdom.

DIRECTORY AND OPERATOR ASSISTANCE

If the operator has to connect your call, it will cost at least one-third more than direct dial.

➤ DIRECTORY INFORMATION: **Republic of Ireland** (☎ 11811 for directory inquiries in the Republic and Northern Ireland; 11818 for U.K. and international numbers; 114 for operator assistance with international calls; 10 for operator assistance for calls in Ireland, Northern Ireland, and the U.K.). **Northern Ireland and the U.K.** (☎ 192 for directory inquiries in Northern Ireland and the U.K.; 153 for international directory inquiries, which includes the Republic; 155 for the international operator; 100 for operator assistance for calls in the U.K. and Northern Ireland.).

INTERNATIONAL CALLS

International dialing codes can be found in all telephone directories. The international prefix from Ireland is 00. For calls to Great Britain, dial 0044 before the exchange code, and drop the initial zero of the local code. For the United States and Canada dial 001, for Australia 0061, and for New Zealand 0064.

LOCAL CALLS

To make a local call just dial the number direct. Public phones take either coins (€.25 for a call) or cards, but not both. At coin phones just pick up the receiver and deposit the money before you dial the number. At card phones pick up the receiver, wait until the display tells you to insert the card, then dial. In the Republic, €.25 will buy you a three-minute local call; around €1 is needed for a three-minute long-distance call within the Republic. In Northern Ireland, a local call costs 10p.

LONG-DISTANCE CALLS

To make a long-distance call, just dial the area code, then the number.

The local code for Northern Ireland is 028, unless you are dialing from the Republic. If you are dialing Northern Ireland from the Republic, dial 048 or

Smart Travel Tips A to Z

4428, followed by the eight-digit number.

LONG-DISTANCE SERVICES

AT&T, MCI, and Sprint access codes make calling long distance relatively convenient, but you may find the local access number blocked in many hotel rooms. First ask the hotel operator to connect you. If the hotel operator balks, ask for an international operator, or dial the international operator yourself. One way to improve your odds of getting connected to your long-distance carrier is to travel with more than one company's calling card (a hotel may block Sprint, for example, but not MCI). If all else fails, call from a pay phone.

➤ ACCESS CODES: **AT&T Direct** (☎ 1800/550000 from the Republic of Ireland; 0500/890011 from Northern Ireland). **MCI WorldPhone** (☎ 1800/ 551001 from the Republic of Ireland; 0800/890222 from Northern Ireland using BT; 0500/890222 using C&W). **Sprint International Access** (☎ 1800/ 552001 from the Republic of Ireland; 0800/890877 from Northern Ireland using BT; 0500/890877 using C&W).

PHONE CARDS

"Callcards" are sold in all post offices and at most newsagents. These come in denominations of 10, 20, and 50 units and range in price from about €2.55 for 10 calls to €20.30 for 100 calls. Card phones are now more popular than coin phones.

PUBLIC PHONES

Public pay phones are in all towns and villages. They can be found in street booths and in restaurants, hotels, bars, and shops, some of which display a sign saying YOU CAN PHONE FROM HERE. There are currently at least three different models of pay phones in operation; read the instructions or ask for assistance.

TIME

Dublin is 5 hours ahead of New York, 8 hours ahead of Los Angeles and Vancouver, 9 hours ahead of Auckland, and 10 hours ahead of Sydney and Melbourne.

TIPPING

In some hotels and restaurants a service charge of around 10%—rising to 15% in a few plush spots—is added to the bill. If in doubt, ask whether service is included. In places where it is included, tipping is not necessary unless you have received particularly good service. But if there is no service charge, add a minimum of 10% to the total.

Tip taxi drivers about 10% of the fare displayed by the meter. Hackney cabs, who make the trip for a prearranged sum, do not expect tips. There are few porters and plenty of baggage trolleys at airports, so tipping is usually not an issue; if you use a porter, €.65 is the minimum. Tip hotel porters about €.65 per large suitcase. Hairdressers normally expect about €1.30. You don't tip in pubs, but for waiter service in a bar, a hotel lounge, or a Dublin lounge bar, leave about €.65. It is not customary to tip for concierge service.

TOURS AND PACKAGES

Because everything is prearranged on a prepackaged tour or independent vacation, you'll spend less time planning—and often get it all at a good price.

BOOKING WITH AN AGENT

Travel agents are excellent resources. But it's a good idea to collect brochures from several agencies, as some agents' suggestions may be influenced by relationships with tour and package firms that reward them for volume sales. If you have a special interest, **find an agent with expertise in that area**; the American Society of Travel Agents (ASTA; ☞ Travel Agencies) has a database of specialists worldwide.

Make sure your travel agent knows the accommodations and other services of the place being recommended. Ask about the hotel's location, room size, beds, and whether it has a pool, room service, or programs for children, if you care about these. Has your agent been there in person or sent others whom you can contact?

Do some homework on your own, too: local tourism boards can provide information about lesser-known and small-niche operators, some of which may sell only direct.

BUYER BEWARE

Each year consumers are stranded or lose their money when tour operators—even large ones with excellent reputations—go out of business. So **check out the operator.** Ask several travel agents about its reputation, and try to **book with a company that has a consumer-protection program.** (Look for information in the company's brochure.) In the United States, members of the National Tour Association and the United States Tour Operators Association are required to set aside funds to cover your payments and travel arrangements in the event that the company defaults. It's also a good idea to choose a company that participates in the American Society of Travel Agents' Tour Operator Program (TOP); ASTA will act as mediator in any disputes between you and your tour operator.

Remember that the more your package or tour includes the better you can predict the ultimate cost of your vacation. Make sure you know exactly what is covered, and **beware of hidden costs.** Are taxes, tips, and transfers included? Entertainment and excursions? These can add up.

➤ TOUR-OPERATOR RECOMMENDATIONS: **American Society of Travel Agents** (ASTA; ✉ 1101 King St., Suite 200, Alexandria, VA 22314, ☎ 800/965–2782 24-hr hot line, FAX 703/739–3268, WEB www.astanet.com). **National Tour Association** (NTA; ✉ 546 E. Main St., Lexington, KY 40508, ☎ 859/226–4444 or 800/682–8886, WEB www.ntaonline.com). **United States Tour Operators Association** (USTOA; ✉ 342 Madison Ave., Suite 1522, New York, NY 10173, ☎ 212/599–6599 or 800/468–7862, FAX 212/599–6744, WEB www.ustoa.com).

TRAIN TRAVEL

The Irish Republic's train services are generally reliable, reasonably priced, and comfortable. All the principal towns are easily reached from Dublin, though services between provincial cities are roundabout. To reach Cork City from Wexford, for example, you have to go via Limerick Junction. It is often quicker, though perhaps less comfortable, to take a bus. Most mainline trains have one standard class. Round-trip tickets are usually cheapest.

In Northern Ireland, Northern Ireland Railways has three main rail routes, all operating out of Belfast's Central Station. These are north to Derry, via Ballymena and Coleraine; east to Bangor along the shores of Belfast Lough; and south to Dublin and the Irish Republic. Note that Eurailpasses are not valid in Northern Ireland.

CUTTING COSTS

To save money, **look into rail passes.** But be aware that if you don't plan to cover many miles you may come out ahead by buying individual tickets.

Ireland (excluding Northern Ireland) is one of 17 countries in which you can **use Eurailpasses,** which provide unlimited first-class rail travel, in all of the participating countries, for the duration of the pass. If you plan to rack up the miles, get a standard pass. These are available for 15 days ($572), 21 days ($740), one month ($918), two months ($1,298), and three months ($1,606). If your plans call for only limited train travel, **look into a Europass,** which costs less money than a Eurailpass. Unlike with Eurailpasses, however, you get a limited number of travel days, in a limited number of countries, during a specified time period. For example, a two-month pass ($360) allows 5 days of rail travel but costs $200 less than the least expensive Eurailpass; 15 days of travel in two months costs $710. Keep in mind, however, that the Europass is good only in France, Germany, Italy, Spain, and Switzerland, and the number of countries you can visit is further limited by the type of pass you buy. For example, the basic two-month pass allows you to visit only three of the five participating countries.

In addition to standard Eurailpasses, **ask about special rail-pass plans.** Among these are the Eurail Youthpass (for those under age 26), the Eurail Saverpass (which gives a discount for two or more people traveling together), a Eurail Flexipass (which allows a certain number of travel days within a set period), the Euraildrive Pass and the Europass Drive (which combines travel by train and rental car). Whichever pass you choose, remember that you must **purchase your pass before you leave** for Europe.

The Irish Explorer Rail & Bus Pass, for use on Ireland's railroads, bus system, or both, covers all the state-run and federal railways and bus lines throughout the Republic of Ireland. It does not apply to the North or to transportation within the cities. An 8-day ticket for use on buses *and* trains during a 15-day period is €127, €63.50 for children. Contact Irish Rail International for details.

The Emerald Isle Card offers unlimited bus and train travel anywhere in Ireland and Northern Ireland, valid within cities as well. An 8-day pass gives you eight days of travel over a 15-day period; it costs €146, €73.65 for children. A pass for 15 days of travel over a 30-day period costs €253.95, €127 for children. Irish Rail International provides details on this card as well.

In Northern Ireland, Rail Runabout tickets, entitling you to seven days' unlimited travel on scheduled rail services April–October, are available from main Northern Ireland Railway stations. They cost U.K.£35 for adults, U.K.£18 for children under 16 and senior citizens. Interrail tickets are also valid in Northern Ireland.

➤ INFORMATION AND PASSES: **CIE Tours International** (✉ 100 Hanover Ave., Box 501, Cedar Knolls, NJ 07927, ☎ 800/243–8687, WEB www. cietours.com). **DER Travel Services** (✉ 9501 W. Devon Ave., Rosemont, IL 60018, ☎ 888/337–7350, FAX 800/ 282–7474 or 847/692–4165, WEB www.dertravel.com). **Rail Europe** (✉ 44 S Broadway, No. 11, White Plains, NY 10601, ☎ 800/438–7245, FAX 800/432–1329, WEB www.raileurope. com; ✉ 2087 Dundas E, Suite 105, Mississauga, Ontario L4X 2V7, ☎ 800/361–7245, FAX 905/602–4198).

➤ TRAIN INFORMATION: In the Irish Republic: **Irish Rail** (Iarnrod Éireann; ☎ 01/836–6222, WEB www.irishrail. ie), the rail division of CIE. In Northern Ireland: **Northern Ireland Railways** (☎ 028/9089–9411, WEB www.translink.co.uk).

RESERVATIONS

Many travelers assume that rail passes guarantee them seats on the trains they wish to ride. Not so. You need to **book seats ahead even if you are using a rail pass**; seat reservations are required on some European trains, particularly high-speed trains, and are a good idea on trains that may be crowded—particularly in summer on popular routes. You will also need a reservation if you purchase sleeping accommodations.

TRANSPORTATION AROUND IRELAND

Ireland is small and relatively flat, so negotiating your way around the island should not be difficult. In the past, many of the more remote areas were only accessible by tiny, winding roads—usually in dire condition. A prolonged program of road building and improvement, financed by European grants, has drastically improved driving throughout Ireland. With long-distance public transport somewhat unreliable and sketchy, a car is the best way to see the country. But the new prosperity and improved roads mean more traffic, which has had a dual effect of increasing noise and pollution in the countryside and giving rise to traffic jams in the cities.

If public transport is your only option, the trains are comfortable, but they only connect major cities and towns and tend to be overpriced. Buses go to more destinations and are better value, but they don't always go frequently, and you might find yourself stuck in a small town overnight.

TRAVEL AGENCIES

A good travel agent puts your needs first. Look for an agency that has been in business at least five years, emphasizes customer service, and has someone on staff who specializes in your destination. In addition, **make sure the agency belongs to a profes-**

sional trade organization. The American Society of Travel Agents (ASTA)—the largest and most influential in the field, with more than 24,000 members in some 140 countries—maintains and enforces a strict code of ethics and will step in to help mediate any agent-client disputes if necessary. ASTA (whose motto is "without a travel agent, you're on your own") also maintains a Web site that includes a directory of agents. (If a travel agency is also acting as your tour operator, *see* Buyer Beware *in* Tours & Packages.)

➤ LOCAL AGENT REFERRALS: **American Society of Travel Agents** (ASTA; ⊠ 1101 King St., Suite 200, Alexandria, VA 22314, ☎ 800/965–2782 24-hr hot line, FAX 703/739–3268, WEB www.astanet.com). **Association of British Travel Agents** (⊠ 68–71 Newman St., London W1T 3AH, ☎ 020/7637–2444, FAX 020/7637–0713, WEB www.abtanet.com). **Association of Canadian Travel Agents** (⊠ 130 Albert St., Suite 1705, Ottawa, Ontario K1P 5G4, ☎ 613/237–3657, FAX 613/237–7052, WEB www.acta.ca). **Australian Federation of Travel Agents** (⊠ Level 3, 309 Pitt St., Sydney, NSW 2000, ☎ 02/9264–3299, FAX 02/9264–1085, WEB www.afta.com.au). **Travel Agents' Association of New Zealand** (⊠ Level 5, Tourism and Travel House, 79 Boulcott St., Box 1888, Wellington 6001, ☎ 04/499–0104, FAX 04/499–0827, WEB www.taanz.org.nz).

VISITOR INFORMATION

For information on travel in the Irish Republic, contact the Irish Tourist Board (ITB), known as Bord Fáilte (pronounced board *fal*-cha); its Web site is www.ireland.travel.ie. Information on travel in the North is available from the Northern Ireland Tourist Board (NITB) office; its Web site is www.discovernorthernireland.com.

➤ ITB: **Ireland** (⊠ Baggot St. Bridge, Dublin 2, ☎ 01/602–4000, 669/792083, or 1850/230330 [within Ireland], FAX 01/602–4100). **U.K.** (⊠ Ireland House, 150 New Bond St., London W1Y 0AQ, ☎ 020/7493–3201, FAX 020/7493–9065). **U.S.** (⊠ 345 Park Ave., New York, NY 10154, ☎ 212/418–0800 or 800/223–6470, FAX 212/371–9052).

➤ NITB: **Northern Ireland** (⊠ 59 North St., Belfast BT1 1NB, ☎ 028/9023–1221, FAX 028/9024–0960). **Canada** (⊠ 2 Bloor St. W, Suite 1501, Toronto, Ontario M4W 3E2, ☎ 416/925–6368, FAX 416/925–6033). **U.K.** (⊠ 24 Haymarket, London SW1 4DG, ☎ 020/7766–9920 or 08701/555–250 info line, FAX 020/7766–9929). **U.S.** (⊠ 551 5th Ave., Suite 701, New York, NY 10176, ☎ 212/922–0101 or 800/326–0036, FAX 212/922–0099).

➤ U.S. GOVERNMENT ADVISORIES: **U.S. Department of State** (⊠ Overseas Citizens Services Office, Room 4811, 2201 C St. NW, Washington, DC 20520, ☎ 202/647–5225 interactive hot line or 888/407–4747, WEB www.travel.state.gov); enclose a business-size SASE.

WEB SITES

Do check out the World Wide Web when planning your trip. You'll find everything from weather forecasts to virtual tours of famous cities. Be sure to **visit Fodors.com** (www.fodors.com), a complete travel-planning site. You can research prices and book plane tickets, hotel rooms, rental cars, vacation packages, and more. In addition, you can post your pressing questions in the Travel Talk section. Other planning tools include a currency converter and weather reports, and there are loads of links to travel resources.

For a comprehensive directory of sites on Ireland, visit www.irishabroad.com. Some of the most popular sites (note that their log-on addresses are subject to change) are as follows: Best of Ireland (www.iol.ie/~discover/welcome.htm); Every Celtic Thing on the Web (www.og-man.net); and Heritage Ireland (www.heritageireland.ie). In addition, many of the leading newspapers of Ireland (☞ Media) have their own Web sites, which can be gold mines of timely information about special events, the latest restaurants, and newest cultural happenings. Track down these newspaper Web sites using a search engine.

WHEN TO GO

Summer remains the most popular time to visit Ireland, and for good reason. The weather is pleasant, the days are long (daylight lasts until after 10 in late June and July), and the countryside is green and beautiful. But there will be crowds in popular holiday spots, and prices for accommodations are at their peak. As British and Irish school vacations overlap from late-June to mid-September, families, backpacking students, and other vacationers descend on popular coastal resorts in the South, West, and East. Unless you are determined to enjoy the short (July and August) swimming season, you would be well advised to **take your vacation in Ireland outside peak travel months.**

Fall and spring are good times to travel (late September can often be dry and warm, although the weather can be unpredictable). Seasonal hotels, restaurants, and accommodations usually close from early or mid-November until mid-March or Easter. During this off-season, prices are considerably lower than in summer, but your selection of hotels and restaurants is limited, and many minor attractions also close. St. Patrick's Week in March gives a focal point to a spring visit, but some American visitors may find the saint's-day celebrations a little less enthusiastic than the ones back home. Dublin, however, welcomes American visitors on March 17 with a weekend-long series of activities, including a parade and the Lord Mayor's Ball. If you're planning an Easter visit, don't forget that most theaters close from Thursday to Sunday of Holy Week (the week preceding Easter), and all bars and restaurants, except those serving hotel residents, close on Good Friday.

If you want to feel like the only tourist in town, **try a winter visit.** Many hotels arrange special Christmas packages with entertainment and outdoor activities; horse races and hunting trips abound. Mid-November to mid-February is either too cold or too wet for all but the keenest golfers, but some of the coastal links courses are playable in almost any weather.

DUBLIN

Jan.	47F	8C	May	59F	15C	Sept.	63F	17C
	34	1		43	6		49	9
Feb.	47F	8C	June	65F	18C	Oct.	58F	14C
	36	2		49	9		43	6
Mar.	50F	10C	July	68F	20C	Nov.	50F	10C
	38	3		52	11		40	4
Apr.	56F	13C	Aug.	67F	20C	Dec.	47F	8C
	40	4		52	11		38	3

CORK

Jan.	49F	9C	May	61F	16C	Sept.	65F	18C
	36	2		45	7		50	10
Feb.	49F	9C	June	67F	19C	Oct.	58F	14C
	38	3		50	10		45	7
Mar.	52F	11C	July	68F	20C	Nov.	52F	11C
	40	4		54	12		40	4
Apr.	56F	13C	Aug.	68F	20C	Dec.	49F	9C
	41	5		54	12		38	3

BELFAST

Jan.	43F	6C	May	59F	15C	Sept.	61F	16C
	36	2		43	6		49	9
Feb.	45F	7C	June	65F	18C	Oct.	56F	13C
	36	2		49	9		45	7
Mar.	49F	9C	July	65F	18C	Nov.	49F	9C
	38	3		52	11		40	4
Apr.	54F	12C	Aug.	65F	18C	Dec.	45F	7C
	50	4		52	11		38	3

There are cheerful open fires in almost all hotels and bars, and, with extra time on their hands, people tend to take an added interest in visitors.

CLIMATE

What follows are average daily maximum and minimum temperatures for some major cities in Ireland.

➤ FORECASTS: **Weather Channel Connection** (☎ 900/932–8437), 95¢ per minute from a Touch-Tone phone.

FESTIVALS AND SEASONAL EVENTS

In both the Republic and Northern Ireland, festivals devoted to the arts, literature, sports, harvests, and animals fill up the calendar year-round. The Republic's Bord Fáilte and the Northern Ireland Tourist Board jointly produce an annual 80-page Calendar of Events (€1.30; ☞ Visitor Information). A horse race is run practically every day of the year in Ireland; the **Irish Horse Racing Authority**'s marketing and promotions department (☎ 01/289–2888, WEB www.iha.ie) is a good source for information.

➤ EARLY MAR.: **Castleward Opera** (☎ 028/9066–1090, WEB www.castlewardopera.faithweb.com) performs at Belfast's Grand Opera House. The annual **Arklow Music Festival** (☎ 0402/32732) includes orchestra, choir, solo singing, drama, and verse-speaking competitions.

➤ MAR.: For three weeks on either side of St. Patrick's Day, the **Celtic Spring Festival** (☎ 028/7136–5151) brings theatrical and rock music performances, an Irish-language festival, and a parade to **Derry City,** County Derry.

➤ MID-MAR.: At the **Roaring '20s Festival** (☎ 064/35757) in **Killarney,** County Kerry, which leads up to St. Patrick's Day, revelers turn out in Great Gatsby outfits to enjoy afternoon teas, cocktail parties, and live music. Bands of every stripe and size march in step and blow their horns in the annual **Limerick International Band Festival** (☎ 061/410777), which immediately follows the city's St. Patrick's Day celebrations. The **Adare Jazz Festival** (☎ 061/396118) in County Limerick fills the town's

pubs with great jazz. **St. Patrick's Day** celebrations throughout the country get under way three days before the climactic day itself, March 17. Ireland's major St. Patrick's event is the **Dublin Festival and Parade** (☎ 01/676–3208), more elaborate every year, which includes a huge fireworks show and guest bands from the United States; there's also a festival of traditional Irish music, the Dublin Feis Ceoil. For 10 days, the **Dublin Film Festival** (☎ 01/679–2937) presents an eclectic mix of the best independent and feature films from Ireland and around the world, plus lectures, seminars, and other events for cineastes.

➤ APR.: With Easter arrives one of the biggest events of the racing calendar, the two-day **Fairyhouse Easter Racing Festival,** County Meath (☎ 01/825–6167), about 19 km (12 mi) north of Dublin. **Easter walking festivals** also get visitors and locals tootling around on foot at various venues throughout the country, including Rathdrum, County Wicklow (☎ 0404/46262); Glencar, County Kerry (☎ 066/60101); and Kenmare, County Kerry (☎ 064/41034, WEB www.kenmare.com). Contact **Walking World Ireland** (☎ 01/492–3030) for details on walking festivals throughout the year.

➤ LATE APR.: The Punchestown Racecourse, just outside **Naas,** hosts the **Punchestown National Hunt Festival** (☎ 045/897704). The **Antiques and Collectibles Fair** (☎ 01/670–8295) brings dealers from all parts of Ireland to Dublin.

➤ EARLY MAY: Sixty-plus traditional music sessions take place over the first weekend in May at **Kinvara's Cuckoo Fleadh** (☎ 091/637145).

➤ MAY: Twenty-one days of concerts, competitions, and exhibitions take place during the **Belfast Civic Festival** (☎ 028/9027–0466); festivities kick off with the **Lord Mayor's Show,** a parade. Part of the Belfast Civic Festival, the **Belfast Marathon** (☎ 028/9027–0345, WEB www.belfastcity.gov.uk/marathon) fills the streets in early May with 6,000 runners.

➤ MID-MAY: The **Murphy's International Mussel Fair** (☎ 027/50064, WEB www.bantrymusselfair.ie) in **Bantry,**

County Cork, celebrates the peak of the harvest season for this delicacy *na mara* ("of the sea" in Irish). Heritage properties and private gardens open to the public during the **County Wicklow Garden Festival** (☎ 0404/66058, WEB www.wicklow.ie).

➤ LATE MAY: The **Galway Early Music Festival** (☎ 091/528166) in **Galway City** fills the city with the sounds of pre-Baroque Irish and European music. The **Fleadh Nua** (☎ 065/684–2988, WEB www.comhaltas.com), the annual festival of traditional Irish music, song, and dance, takes place in **Ennis**, County Clare. Fifteen guided hikewalks around West Cork and parts of Kerry make up the **Kenmare Whit Walking Festival** (☎ 064/41034). Theater, literary readings, and plenty of music fill the calendar of the **Sligo Arts Festival** (☎ 071/69802), which continues into early June.

➤ EARLY JUNE: **Listowel Writers' Week** (☎ 068/21074), one of Ireland's leading literary festivals, brings writers, poets, and lovers of literature together in this County Kerry town. Cartoonists congregate in the Wicklow village of **Rathdrum** for the annual **Guinness International Cartoon Festival** (☎ 0404/46811). **Carlow** celebrates the arts in its annual **Éigse Carlow Arts Festival** (☎ 0503/40491). The **Weavers' Fair and Vintage Weekend** (☎ 075/41262) comes to **Ardara** in County Donegal in early June, although today the fair has as much to do with music, dance, and having fun as it does with selling homespun.

➤ JUNE: Pick up some decorating tips while you're swooning over Schubert at the **AIB Music Festival in Great Irish Homes** (☎ 01/278–1528), which puts on classical-music concerts in some of Ireland's finest country houses.

➤ MID-JUNE: **Ballycastle** puts on its own lively three-day music and dance folk festival, the **Fleadh Amhrán agus Rince** (☎ 028/2563–5575). Devoted Joyceans celebrate the fictional wanderings of *Ulysses*'s Leopold and Molly Bloom and Stephen Daedalus on June 16 (the day the novel was set, in 1904) in **Dublin** with **Bloomsday** (☎ 01/878–8547, WEB www.

jamesjoyce.ie); readings, dramatizations, and pilgrimages take place around the city.

➤ LATE JUNE: The **Budweiser Irish Derby** (☎ 045/441205) at the **Curragh Racecourse**, County Kildare, is the biggest race event of the year. The Borodin Quartet and other chamber groups perform at the annual **West Cork Chamber Music Festival** (☎ 027/52788), held at Bantry House in **Bantry,** County Cork.

➤ EARLY JULY: The **Coalisland International Music Festival** (☎ 028/8774–8052) attracts traditional and folk bands from all over Europe to County Tyrone. The **Eagle Wing Festival** (☎ 028/9127–8051) at **Groomsport** in County Down celebrates 300 years of links with America; it has music, line dancing, history lectures, and American food. **Castlebar,** County Mayo, is the venue for the **International Four-Day Walking Festival** (☎ 094/24102, WEB www.castlebar4dayswalks.com). **Murphy's Irish Open Golf Championship** (☎ 01/269–4111, WEB www.gui.ie) will be held on one of Ireland's premier links courses.

➤ MID-JULY: On July 12 **Belfast** and other towns throughout the North commemorate the historic 1690 **Battle of the Boyne** (☎ 028/9032–2801). Bachelors from throughout the country strut their stuff in **Mullingar** for the **Guinness International Bachelor Festival** (☎ 044/44044). Galway is jam-packed for the two-week **Galway Arts Festival** (☎ 091/565577, WEB www.galwayartsfestival.com), the West's premier arts event, which includes theater, film, music of all kinds, art exhibits, and a not-to-be-missed kickoff parade. The **James Joyce Summer School** (☎ 01/706–8480) draws academics and aficionados from all over the world to **University College Dublin.** Also in **Dublin,** the streets and pubs of Temple Bar resound day and night to jazz and blues music for the annual **Temple Bar Blues Festival** (☎ 01/497–0381). **Kilmore Quay** hosts a two-week-long **Seafood Festival** (☎ 053/29922) that runs through to the end of the month.

➤ JULY 28: On the last Sunday in July, thousands of pilgrims, some in bare feet, climb the rocky slopes of **Croagh Patrick** (2,500 ft) in County Mayo to honor St. Patrick.

➤ LATE JULY–EARLY AUG.: The **Galway Races** (☎ 091/753870, WEB www.iol.ie/galway-races) start the day after Galway's Arts Festival ends for a week of revelry. **Boyle,** County Roscommon, hosts the **Boyle Arts Festival** (☎ 079/64069), one of the best performing and visual-arts festivals in the region. Would-be beauty queens come to **Dungloe,** County Donegal, from as far away as Australia and New Zealand to compete in the **Mary of Dungloe International Festival** (☎ 075/21254). Across the whole of **County Derry** the best of the country's musicians take part in the **Festival of Popular Irish Music** (☎ 028/7126–7284).

➤ EARLY AUG.: You have even more festivals than usual to choose from at this time of year. The **Ballyshannon Folk and Traditional Music Festival** (☎ 072/51088, WEB www.donegalbay.ie) in County Donegal is one of the best of the season. Everyone's got the beat at the **Waterford Spraoi** (☎ 051/841808, WEB www.spraoi.com), an international rhythm festival. The two-week **Yeats International Summer School** (☎ 071/42693, WEB www.yeats-sligo.com) in **Sligo Town** celebrates its 44th anniversary in 2003.

➤ MID-AUG.: **Kinvara,** County Galway, hosts its long-standing sailing event, **Cruinniú na mBád** ("Festival of the Gathering of the Boats"; ☎ 091/637579), in which traditional brown-sailed Galway hookers laden with turf race across Galway Bay. The **Kerrygold Dublin Horse Show** (☎ 01/668–0866) attracts a fashionable set to watch the best in Irish bloodstock. Aeronautical enthusiasts should check out the **Abbeyshrule Fly-in Festival and Air Show** (☎ 044/57424) in County Longford. The three-day **Puck Fair** (☎ 066/976–2366) in **Killorglin,** County Kerry, one of the country's oldest and more mythical festivals, retains vestiges of old pre-Christian fertility rites, like the garlanding with flowers of a large billy goat to signify his being crowned king.

➤ LATE AUG.: **Kilkenny** hosts **Kilkenny Arts Week** (☎ 056/63663,

WEB www.kilkennyarts.ie), a marvelous assemblage of classical music, art exhibits, and theater. The highlight of the traditional music calendar is the **Fleadh Cheoil na hEireann** (pronounced *flah kee'yo na erin* ☎ 01/280–0295, WEB www.fleadhcheoil.com). The world-famous **Rose of Tralee International Festival** (☎ 066/712–1322, WEB www.roseoftralee.ie) selects a "Rose of Tralee" from an international lineup of young women of Irish descent and packs this County Kerry town in the process. The competition coincides with the **Tralee Races.** On the third Thursday of the month, the **Connemara Pony Show** (☎ 095/21863) brings Ireland's finest yearlings and stallions to **Clifden,** County Galway.

If you're in the neighborhood of **Ballycastle,** County Antrim, don't miss Ireland's oldest fair, **Oul' Lammas Fair** (☎ 028/2076–2024), held every year since 1606 on the last Monday and Tuesday in August. It's a modern version of the ancient Celtic harvest festival of Lughnasa (Irish for "August").

➤ SEPT.: Single people of all ages from throughout Ireland and beyond flock to County Clare for the **Lisdoonvarna Matchmaking Festival** (☎ 065/707–4005, WEB www.matchmakerireland.com) in the hopes of finding a spouse—or at least a date. The **Appalachian and Bluegrass Music Festival** (☎ 028/8224–3292) traces the roots of Appalachian music back to Ireland at the Ulster American Folk Park in **Omagh,** County Tyrone. The hugely popular **Hurling and Gaelic Football Finals** (☎ 01/836–3222) are played in Croke Park Stadium in **Dublin.**

➤ LATE SEPT.: Indulge in the "food of the gods" at the start of the oyster season at the **Galway International Oyster Festival** (☎ 091/522066); the season lasts from September to April. Farmers compete in the **All Ireland Ploughing Championships** (☎ 0507/25125, WEB www.npa.ie); they are usually held in different locations around the country. **Opera Northern Ireland** (☎ 028/9032–2338) kicks off its autumn season in the Grand Opera House in **Belfast.** Troupes from all over Europe compete at **Waterford's**

Theatre Royal during the annual **International Festival of Light Opera** (☎ 051/375437), which continues into early October.

➤ OCT.: The **Dublin Theatre Festival** (☎ 01/677–8439) puts on 10 visiting international productions, 10 Irish plays (most of them new), a children's festival, and a fringe of 60-plus plays. The beautiful coastal Cork town of **Kinsale** opens its best restaurants for the **International Gourmet Festival** (☎ 021/477–4026).

➤ MID-OCT.: One of Ireland's premier film events, the **Cork Film Festival** (☎ 021/427–1711) shows new feature-length films, documentaries, and short films—a specialty of the festival. Amateur and professional runners fill the streets of **Dublin** in the **Dublin City Marathon** (☎ 01/626–3757).

➤ LATE OCT.: The **Cork Jazz Festival** (☎ 021/278979, WEB www.corkjazzfestival.com) draws jazz lovers from Ireland and beyond.

➤ LATE OCT.–EARLY NOV.: The **Wexford Opera Festival** (☎ 053/22400, WEB www.wexfordopera.com) brings in major international stars to stage and perform three rarely heard opera gems in a tiny Georgian theater.

➤ NOV.: The three-day **Millstreet Indoor International Horse Show** (☎ 029/70800) brings out-of-season equestrian enthusiasts to this County Cork town. The **Belfast Festival at Queen's University** (☎ 028/9066–7687, WEB www.belfastfestival.com) is the city's preeminent arts festival, with hundreds of musical, film, theater, and ballet performances.

➤ NOV.: The **Irish Rugby Football season** gets under way in **Dublin** with games between Ireland and nations *not* in the Six Nations group (Scotland, Wales, England, France, Italy, and Ireland). A limited number of tickets are available through the Irish Rugby Football Union (☎ 01/647–3800, WEB www.irfu.ie).

➤ MID-DEC.: The yearling, foal, and breeding stock sale at **Goff's Bloodstock Sales** (☎ 045/886600), **Kill,** County Kildare, gives visitors a peek at how the rich and famous buy and sell their prized horses.

➤ DEC. 26: On **St. Stephen's Day,** the traditional Wren Boys in blackface and fancy dress still wander the streets of some rural towns asking for money and singing (these days much of the money goes to charity); by far the most extravagant celebration of this ancient folktale takes place on Sandymount Green in **Dublin** from about 11 AM.

1 DESTINATION: IRELAND

Eire Apparent

What's Where

Pleasures and Pastimes

Fodor's Choice

Great Itineraries

EIRE APPARENT

IF YOU FLY INTO IRELAND, your descent will probably be shrouded by gray clouds. As your plane breaks through the mists, you'll see the land for which the famed Emerald Isle was named: a lovely patchwork of rolling green fields speckled with farmhouses, cows, and sheep. Shimmering lakes, meandering rivers, narrow roads, and stone walls add to the impression that rolled out before you is a luxurious welcome carpet, one knit of the legendary "forty shades of green." (If you're lucky you may even see a rainbow—something you'll see again and again if you travel the countryside.) This age-old view of misty Ireland may be exactly what you imagined. Travelers still arrive expecting Eire to be the land of leprechauns, shillelaghs, shamrocks, and mist. Be warned, however—the only known specimens of leprechauns or shillelaghs are those in souvenir shop windows; shamrock only blooms on St. Patrick's Day or around the borders of Irish linen handkerchiefs and table cloths; and the mists, in reality a soft, apologetic rain, can envelop the entire country, cities and towns included, in a matter of minutes.

The Celtic Tiger

The real Ireland is two-faced, like the Janus-stones and sheela-na-gigs of its pre-Christian past. It's a complex place where the mystic lyricism of Yeats, the hard Rabelaisian passions of Joyce, and the spare, aloof dissections of Beckett grew not only from a rich and ancient culture but also from 20th-century upheavals, few of which have been as dramatic as the transformation that has been changing Ireland for the past decade. Consider the evidence: more than 150 years since the apocalyptic Great Famine, Ireland's economy—christened the "Celtic Tiger"—is now the fastest-growing in the industrialized world. Ireland is the second-largest exporter of computer software in the world, after the United States. Unemployment, which was 11.5% in 1996, fell to 3.8% in 2002, and 41% of Ireland's populace are under the age of 25, with 24% under 15, making it the youngest nation in Europe. Not to mention a 98% literacy rate. Most

telling, however, is the fact that, in a profound demographic shift, Ireland's net emigration has reversed. There has been major immigration in each of the last three years—beginning in 2001 with 15,000—and that trend shows every sign of continuing. The young who once left for London and New York are now staying, and more college graduates are returning than are leaving.

The foreign capital that has flowed into the country since it joined the Common Market (now the European Union) in 1973 has been crucial to this regeneration. But money alone doesn't guarantee culture, and Irish culture is thriving. Take just a few examples from literature: In January 2000, after winning Ireland's fourth Nobel Prize for literature (in 1995), Seamus Heaney won the prominent Whitbread Book of the Year Award for his verse translation of the epic Anglo-Saxon poem *Beowulf. Angela's Ashes,* Frank McCourt's memoir of his early life in Limerick, found millions of readers and won every major American literary prize. You name it—food, music, movies, literature, poetry, theater, art, fashion—and something innovative is afoot among the Irish at home and abroad. If you've been moved by seeing *Riverdance* or *Lord of the Dance* or hearing the Corrs, Enya, Van Morrison, U2, The Irish Tenors, or any of the hundreds of other prominent Irish musicians, you're likely to feel the spirit that touched you more palpably in Ireland itself as you meet its people and witness them imagining—and creating—the Irish spirit anew.

A Friendly People

Liam Neeson, Kenneth Branagh, Daniel Day-Lewis, Neil Jordan, and the Cranberries are just a few of the envoys extraordinaire for Irish culture around the world. To find the real Ireland, however, you must venture down its back roads. You'll quickly discover that hospitality is counted among the greatest of Irish virtues, a legacy from Celtic times when anyone not offering the traveler food and drink was shamed. "You are welcome," people say in greeting the moment you cross the threshold of the smallest cottage, while total strangers will take you home for tea or supper and strike up conversations with ease and curiosity, entertaining you perhaps with an account of their second cousin's memorable fortnight in America (a fortnight's worth of stories if you have the time).

Time, in fact, is one of the greatest luxuries in Ireland—outside fast-forward Dublin, that is. On a fine day, along a lushly green country lane, you may pass a bicycle abandoned against a tree; looking for its owner, you'll find him reclining in the feathery hedgerows or on the long grass, contemplating fast-moving clouds like some philosopher-king. "Oh the dreaming, the dreaming, the heart-scalding bitter, maddening dreaming," cried the playwright George Bernard Shaw, but to knowing travelers in the stressed and industrialized world, this haven of dreamers is a pearl of great price, sought after and kept secret. Forget America's car culture—Ireland has cow culture. You'll find the moo-cows own the country lanes, staring haughtily and curiously at interloping motorists, lazily drooping timothy from their soft maws. In the end, with persuasion from harried livery, equipped with frisky dogs and long-knobbed sticks, they'll share the road—but on *their* schedule.

This may explain why Ireland is what some anthropologists call a "lived" culture, one that doesn't put all its stock in the outward monuments of achievement; where the most potent history is oral, where storytelling is an art, and where people will travel for miles for the "craic," the Irish term for a rousing good time. Ireland teaches you patience, reminds you of the rhythms of the natural world, and convinces you, reassuringly, of the essential well-being of humanity.

This is nowhere more the case than in the local pub, the center of social life in Ireland. Even a small town such as Dingle in County Kerry (population 1,000) boasts 52 watering holes, open day and night. Protocol dictates that you enter and greet everyone, taking a seat alone until invited (as you inevitably are) to join a table. Then the ancient custom of rounds begins, with the newcomer offering to buy the first set of drinks, and when the pints are barely half full, another imbiber stands the round, and so on, in turn. Dark village pubs, with their scratched wooden counters, dusty tiled floors, and yeasty smell of

Guinness, exude a feeling of sanctity and remove from worldly cares. Sit awhile and enjoy your stout, but know also that wit also flows untapped. Nuance and irony are the law—anything less would be considered flat-footed. Irish expertise in double-think and the witty tongue makes for a universally acknowledged aptitude for legal affairs, a gift for words of imagination and persuasiveness that you can find in the crossroads *shebeen* (pub) much as in Dublin's Leinster House, where the Irish Dáil (legislature) sits.

WHAT'S WHERE

You are never very far from anywhere in Ireland, but each of its 32 counties has its special character and history, and fierce loyalty from its sons and daughters. Below we give a preview of Ireland's cities and counties—organizing our discussion using the same groupings we use in this guide.

Dublin
Dublin—Europe's most intimate capital—is the jewel in Mother Eire's crown. Today it is a graceful mix of elegant Georgian buildings, a lively waterfront, wrought-iron canals and bridges, an army of booksellers, 800-odd pubs, and a booming cultural life. Ireland chooses to exempt artists from taxes, designating them national resources of sorts, and filmmakers, painters, and writers are part of the local scenery, along with the "rale Dubs," or "jackeens"—the breezy natives born in the heart of the city between the Grand and Royal canals that divide North and South Dublin into two worlds. Here, on both sides of the Liffey, are famous sights that nearly encompass the city's entire history—let's not forget that Dublin has been, in sequence, a Celtic settlement by the ford of the River Liffey, a Norse encampment for raiding Viking and Danish pirates, and finally the citadel-seat of the British colonizers' power for centuries. A small Whitman's Sampler of must-sees includes St. Patrick's Cathedral, the Gate Theatre, the National Gallery of Ireland, St. Stephen's Green, Trinity College, Merrion and Fitzwilliam squares, and the James Joyce Cultural Centre. But although Dublin can be a sophisticated city, with sushi bars, bold theater, some of Europe's finest restaurants (and some of its

worst), it hasn't lost any of its simple plea-sures, like waking to the tinkling of glass bottles with round silver caps, delivered to the stoop by a milkman dressed all in white; afternoon tea at Bewley's with scones slathered with Kerry Gold butter; soda farls heaped with clouds of whipped cream; waitresses in black dress and starched aprons; or breakfast "the likes of which you'll never see again," your landlady will promise (though everywhere in Ireland seems to be competing in this category). Now added to these ageless pleasures is Dublin's amazing new economic and cul-tural renaissance. Today, the city is a boom-town—the soul of the new Ireland in the throes of what is easily its most dramatic period of transformation since the Geor-gian era. Whether you're out to enjoy old or new Dublin, you'll find it a colossally entertaining city, all the more astonishing considering its intimate size.

Dublin Environs

The counties that surround Dublin constitute the Pale, the area most strongly influenced by English rule from Norman times onward. Here (as in other parts of Ireland), the an-cestral homes of the dwindling members of the Anglo-Irish ascendancy dot the land-scape, and lords and baronets down on their luck have turned hoteliers and welcome guests to castle holidays with adaptable grace. The gorgeous Wicklow Mountains—to some tastes Ireland's finest—lie tantalizingly close to the capital on its southern edge. Wicklow's evocative monastic settlement at Glendalough, many later abbeys and churches, castles, and several of Ireland's grandest houses and gardens are dotted amid hidden, scenic wooded valleys. Some of the country's most fascinating Neolithic ruins—including the famous passage graves at Newgrange—lie to the north in the Boyne Valley, where layer upon layer of his-tory penetrates down into earlier, un-knowable ages.

The Midlands

These small, watery counties form the ge-ographical heart of Ireland, yet are usu-ally portrayed as places to get *through* on the way to somewhere more interesting. However, closer exploration of these un-sung plains reveal historic towns, abbey ruins, grand houses, and a gamut of out-door activities—including some of the finest fishing in Europe. County Tipper-ary's rolling green flatlands and Galtee mountains are known for champion grey-hounds and the stud farms that have turned out winners for generations. The Midlands are home to fine cultural sites, including Strokestown House, Birr Cas-tle Gardens, Emo Court and Gardens, and the magnificent monastic ruins of Clonmacnoise. Delightfully, here you'll also find you're welcomed with true hos-pitality—without anyone haranguing you to buy sweaters or shamrock table linen.

The Southeast

In sharp contrast to the scenic wildness often associated with Ireland, the landscape of the Southeast is mostly low-lying and docile. Rich pastureland watered by brim-ming rivers extends gently to a quiet coast-line of estuarial mudflats of wading birds; low cliffs that fringe deep bays; and long, sandy beaches which, owing to the re-gion's climate—sunnier and drier than elsewhere in Ireland—draw families in summer. The coast of County Wexford was the original beachhead of Ireland named by the Vikings after the consort of their one-eyed god Odin; it still bears the stamp of its fearless, seagoing settlers in its steep pathways and fine seafood. Wex-ford is a quick trip to Kilkenny, the finest medieval city in Ireland and one known for its artisans. Also nearby is Waterford City, where the crystal of the same name is produced, at the confluence of three great rivers—the Nore, the Barrow, and the Suir. Waterford City has one of the oldest forts in Ireland, Reginald's Tower, built in 1003 and named for the Viking warrior who founded the city. Ireland's most fer-tile farmland lies in Tipperary's Golden Vale. The Rock of Cashel, seat of the Kings of Munster for 700 years (where St. Patrick said his first mass in Ireland) is here, along with Cahir Castle, one of the few places that managed to resist Cromwell's hordes, now restored to its former impressiveness.

The Southwest

With their striking scenery, charming towns, mild climate, and deep-rooted his-tory, the southwestern counties of Cork and Kerry are perennially popular. Long called "The Rebel County" (if you saw Neil Jordan's 1996 film *Michael Collins,* you know why), Cork is a Venice-like port city of canals and bridges, and a bustling mer-cantile center. It was once home to writ-ers Sean O'Faolain and Frank O'Connor, and is today a city of sport. Its team is always in the championship finals of hurling, that fast and furious ancient game that makes soccer look like kick-the-can, and the city is one of the few places where they still play the traditional 2,000-year-old game of bowls at which the Irish giant Cuchulainn used to excel. If your taste runs to less athletic entertainment, head for the exquisitely quaint village and historically significant seaside village of Kinsale. Just to the north of Cork, summer travelers have been thrilling to Kerry's surfeit of natural beauty for centuries, as they've gazed down from the heights of Killarney, or the black rocks and green waves glistening at Slea Head on the Dingle Peninsula, or at the Blasket Islands, where St. Brendan the Navigator was said to have set sail in a wooden curragh to discover the Americas in the 7th century. Seabirds reel and wild donkeys graze among the fuschia hedges awash in crimson velvet flowers, and the fields explode with deep yellow gorse, may-blossom, and honeysuckle against a dark-blue sky. To the north of Kerry, County Limerick is famed as horse country.

The West
Within the three counties of Clare, Galway, and Mayo lies a colossal variety of landscapes and natural sights—from the barren limestone Burren to the majestic Cliffs of Moher to the looming Twelve Bens. The West's largest city, Galway is the fastest-growing place in Ireland—a buzzing, youthful university town and the favorite getaway city for many native Irish. It's also the departure point for the Aran Islands, celebrated by playwright J. M. Synge in *Riders to the Sea* and Robert Flaherty in his classic documentary film *Man of Aran*. Just to the west of Galway City lies the wild and rugged coast and mountains of Connemara, loved by painters, who flock there in summer, by writers (from Yeats to Gogarty to Joyce), and by all seekers of silence and beauty. It, too, is a Gaeltacht (Irish-speaking area), celebrated for its simplicity of lifestyle and genuinely warm natives. Connemara is also known for its ponies, descendants of the Andalusian horses that swam to shore from the Spanish fleet and bred with the local Celtic stock (direct descendants of the original Ice Age horse of 20,000 BC). To the north, Mayo is quieter and less popular, although its peaceful scenery has always appealed to a discerning minority.

The Northwest
County Donegal, in the far northwest, is among the wildest, most ruggedly beautiful places in the world, with its long, rocky coastline, white beaches, turbulent surf, and forlorn, windswept mountains and plateaus, full of legendary lore of giants and witches, and fairies known as *pishogues*. Irish is widely spoken here, and the music is famous; traditional groups, such as Clannad and De Dannaan, named after the prehistoric followers of the goddess Dana, are local heroes. When Enya, daughter of local musicians, hit the top of the charts in Europe and the United States with her Irish–New Age instrumentals, the roof flew off Leo's pub in Gweedore, where spontaneous sessions for the music-loving community are regular happenings.

Northern Ireland
The ancient provinces of Munster, Leinster, and Connaught constitute the Irish Republic, plus three of the nine counties of Ulster; the other six remained part of Britain in 1921. ("One of Ireland's four green fields is still in strangers' hands," as a song goes.) Today Northern Ireland, thriving in its newfound era of peace, is definitely worth a trip: here you have the beauty of the Antrim Coast from Carncastle to Bushmills; the Giant's Causeway, glorious as every other great geologic accident; the rich farmlands and lake lands of Fermanagh; and the austere beauty of the Mourne Mountains. People are as friendly and helpful here as they are in the Republic, and, probably because of their history, perhaps even often a little sharper and wittier. Northern Ireland is also fascinating for any follower of history and politics, for you get an unforgettable glimpse of the winds of time changing, a scene not unlike the last days of the Raj, as Britain's first colony erodes to be her last.

PLEASURES AND PASTIMES

Dining
Ireland is in the throes of a food revolution. Venture out of Dublin and you'll see some of the reasons why: livestock grazing in impossibly green fields, immaculately

clear waters where fish easily spawn, and acres of produce thriving in the temperate climate. But above all it's Ireland's chefs who are the movers and shakers here. Many are young and widely traveled, and have absorbed the best influences of Europe, North America, and the Pacific Rim, and are producing a Pan-European, postmodern cuisine. This new Irish cuisine—sometimes referred to as *cuisine Irlandaise*—has moved beyond the heavy traditional roast beef and Yorkshire pudding styles of the old Anglo-Irish country houses. An innovative, indigenous style is emerging. Chefs are taking simple, traditional dishes—Clonakilty black pudding, Clare nettle soup, Galway oysters, Cong wild salmon—and sprucing them up with more exotic, complicated preparations. The result: smart, unusual combinations of the best local, often organic, ingredients.

Diehard traditionalists, however, will still find many examples of old Celtic cooking, particularly in bars serving lunches of Irish stew, boiled bacon and cabbage, or steamed mussels. The national drink, Guinness, is a pitch-black, malted stout—one of the great beers of the world. With raw oysters and Tabasco, it is a blissful marriage of opposites.

Regional cooking is a strength of Irish cuisine, and some of the best restaurants are tucked away in small fishing villages or remote locations. Hotel dining rooms vary in quality, but the best country-house hotels offer some of the finest dining in Europe (and most will take reservations for meals only).

Literary Haunts

Ireland has produced a disproportionately large number of internationally famous authors for a country of its size: four Nobel Prize winners, George Bernard Shaw, William Butler Yeats, Samuel Beckett, and Seamus Heaney head the list, one that's studded with world-famous names—Oscar Wilde, Sean O'Casey, Sean O'Faolain, Brian Friel, Edna O'Brien. Ireland's literary heritage is evident everywhere you go—in Dublin you will find James Joyce's Liffey, Dean Swift's cathedral, and Trinity College, alma mater of the 18th-century Anglo-Irish writers. An anthology of Irish verse is a travel guide in itself: Yeats opens up the country of Sligo; the Aran Islands were the inspiration of J. M. Synge; there's Frank O'Connor's Cork; and

Castletownshend, home of Somerville and Ross; Oliver Goldsmith's Lissoy; and Frank McCourt's Limerick. Irish writing developed its distinctive traits largely because of the country's physical isolation (not even Julius Caesar wanted to conquer Ireland; centuries later, Ireland remained the only country in Europe uninfluenced by the cultural excitement of the Renaissance). In the end, it came to produce a literature that conquered distant shores, partly through its grand dramatic tradition. The famous Abbey Theatre is still a potent symbol of Ireland's great playwrights Boucicault, Wilde, Shaw, Synge, and Behan. In any event, sit a while in Dublin's Davy Byrne's pub, order a glass of Burgundy and a Gorgonzola sandwich (as Joyce's Leopold Bloom once did), and spend an hour studying a map of Ireland. Thanks to the beguiling names you'll find on it—Ballyvourney, Labasheeda, Toorenamblath, Clonmacnoise—it may fire your poetic imagination, too.

Music

Ireland is the land of *ceol agus craic,* which, loosely translated, means "music and merriment." Wherever you go in Ireland, you'll hear a musical air to accompany the scenery, and every town buzzes with its own individual blend of styles and sounds. The traditional music scene, far from becoming fossilized as a permanent tourist fixture, has evolved with each generation, remaining lively and contemporary while still cherishing the craft and skill of its past exponents. Young traditional musicians are also unafraid to experiment with the music of other cultures, and it's not unusual to discover exciting mixtures of trad, folk, African rhythms, jazz improvisations, and even Appalachian mountain music. The deep-rooted musical tastes of the Irish are reflected in the live music scene in pubs, clubs, and theaters; a check of local event guides will turn up a wealth of live entertainment from rock to folk to traditional, and it's often possible to go into a small local venue and find a world-class artist in performance, whose talents are unsung outside a small circle of knowledgeable friends and fans.

Outdoors and Sports
BICYCLING
The combination of numerous side roads and very light traffic makes Ireland a ter-

rific destination for cyclists. The less energetic can concentrate their itinerary on the relatively flat central area of the country; those who brave the mountains of the West and Southwest will be rewarded by magnificent scenery and a wonderfully varied coastline.

CRUISING

Fully equipped boats are rented by the week on the Shannon and the Grand Canal. It's a simple and relaxing holiday, allowing you to explore lesser-known, but beautiful, corners of Ireland. Boats can accommodate up to eight people and have toilets, showers, and well-equipped galleys. Prices start at about £190 per week.

FISHING

Ireland is well known as a game-angling resort: Wild Atlantic salmon, wild brown trout, and sea trout abound in the rivers, lakes, and estuaries; and offshore is the deep-sea challenge. Coarse fishing (for all fish that are not trout or salmon) is also available.

GAELIC GAMES

Gaelic football and hurling are played in most parts of the Republic. Gaelic football is an extremely fast and rough form of football (closer to rugby than American football), which involves two teams of 15 who kick and run around a field with a round, soccerlike ball. The rules are complicated, but the skill and speed of the players make it exciting and impressive to watch, even if you don't quite understand what is going on. Hurling, considered by many to be the fastest field game in the world, also involves two teams of 15 who use a 3-ft wooden stick with a broad base to aggressively catch and hurl a leather-covered ball toward goalposts; a typical game produces several injuries. Gaelic games are organized by the Gaelic Athletic Association (GAA) and can be observed free of charge at local GAA fields and sports centers around the Republic. Interprovincial games and All-Ireland finals are played in July and August at the GAA stadiums in Cork and Dublin. Croke Park in Dublin is usually where the annual All-Ireland finals are held. Tickets for these matches can be hard to obtain, but the events are televised.

GOLF

There are more than 360 golf courses in Ireland—including Northern Ireland—from world-famous championship links courses to scenic nine-holers. About 50 of these courses have opened in the last two years. Choose between the challenging links of the Atlantic coast, the more subtle layouts on the eastern seaboard, and the mature parklands of the inland courses. (Chapter 10 details Ireland's best golf courses.)

HIKING

Bord Fáilte (the Irish Tourist Board) provides free information sheets on long-distance paths, set up throughout the country over the last few years with the consent of local landowners. Routes are indicated by trail markers and signposts. Most are between 30 and 60 km/18 and 37 mi in length, with the exception of the Wicklow Way, the first to be opened and still one of the best, which is 137 km/85 mi long. Alternatively, you can plan your own walks with the help of a good touring map: Ireland is an excellent walking country, with its mild climate and virtually traffic-free byroads. In Northern Ireland, there is the challenge of the 790-km/491-mi Ulster Way, a footpath that travels through spectacular coastal scenery.

HORSE RACING

There is a horse race somewhere in Ireland almost every day of the year. The flat season runs from March to November; steeplechases are held throughout the year. Several courses—there are some 28 in all—are within easy reach of Dublin. Irish classics are run at the Curragh in County Kildare, and the Irish Grand National is at Fairyhouse in County Meath. Some of the best meetings are held in the summer at smaller courses: Killarney in mid-July, Galway in late July–early August, Tramore in mid-August, Tralee in late August, and Listowel at the end of September.

The Pub

Just how important is an Irish pub? Irish Pub, a Dublin-based company, has shipped more than 1,000 of its five styles of "ready-to-pour" pubs—Victorian Dublin, Gaelic, Irish Brewery Pub, Irish Pub Shop, and Irish Country Cottage—to more than 35 countries around the world, at about $300,000 a pop. Back on their home turf, pubs are still among the pillars of Irish social life—places where you can chat, listen, learn, and gossip about everything from horse racing to music to philosophy. Pubs have diversified in the last few years, owing partly to increasingly strict drunk-driving laws. Many now serve food at lunchtime and could be mistaken for restaurants between the hours of 12:30 and 2; many but not quite all also serve tea and coffee during daylight hours. Especially in rural areas they can be an important source of local information. If you're stuck for a meal or a bed for the night, ask a friendly publican if he knows of anyone who can solve your problem. A word about music in pubs: If it's in the main bar of a pub, you'll seldom have to pay a cover charge. However, if you're really enjoying the *craic*, as it's called, it is good form to buy a pint for the performers. Dancing to a fully amplified band in a room adjacent to the bar costs anywhere from £1.50 to £8.

Shopping

Few visitors leave Ireland without purchasing a tweed hat or a hand-knit Aran sweater, a linen tablecloth or a piece of Waterford crystal. Dublin is the country's political *and* shopping capital—especially if you're looking for antiques, books, and the most *au courant* European and Irish fashions. Cork City offers less choice but quite a few surprises, and Galway has its share of galleries, bookstores, and offbeat boutiques. Most crafts shops sell a mix of goods from all over the country. If you're after something a little different, keep an eye open for signs indicating "craft workshops"—there are at least 20 around the country—where independent craftspeople sell directly from their studios.

ANTIQUES

Top-quality antiques shops are concentrated around Dublin's Francis Street area, but it's still possible to pick up modestly priced pieces of 18th- and 19th-century silver, 19th-century pewter, and antique period furniture elsewhere—try Cork City, Castlecomer, Kilkenny, Galway City, and Limerick.

CRYSTAL

Irish lead crystal is justifiably world famous. The best known of all, Waterford glass, is on sale all over Ireland in department stores and crafts shops. The demand is so great that substantial export orders can take weeks or even months to fill. Check out the lesser-known crystals—Cork, Dublin, Kinsale, Tipperary, Tyrone, and Galway crystal—and the less formal, uncut glass from Jerpoint and Stoneyford.

DRINKABLES

Irish whiskey has an altogether different taste from Scotch whisky, and a different spelling, too. Well-known brands include Powers, Paddy, Jameson, and Bushmills. There are also two excellent Irish liqueurs: Irish Mist, which contains whiskey and honey, and Bailey's Irish Cream, a concoction of whiskey and cream, sometimes drunk on ice as an aperitif.

FOOD

Smoked salmon can vary greatly in taste and quality. Make sure it's wild salmon, not farmed; and if the label tells you what sort of wood it was smoked over, opt for oak chips. A cheaper but also delicious alternative is smoked trout. Or go for whole farmhouse cheeses like St. Killian's—a Camembert-like pasteurized cheese. More exotic and more expensive are the handmade farmhouse cheeses, each from an individual herd of cows. Milleens, Durrus, and Gubbeen are all excellent, though strong when ripe. A milder alternative is the Gouda-like Coolea cheese, found in most duty-free shops.

JEWELRY

Dublin and Cork City are the best spots for antique jewelry, but don't despair if the prices there are beyond your resources. Beautiful modern reproductions of such Celtic treasures as the Tara brooch are on sale for a fraction of the antique price. Other good buys include Claddagh friendship rings (Galway City is a particularly good place to shop for these) and beautiful pieces made by modern silversmiths using polished Connemara marble.

KNITWEAR

Aran sweaters were developed by the women of the Aran Isles to provide a working garment that was warm, comfortable, and weatherproof. The religious symbols and folk motifs woven into distinctive patterns once enabled local people to identify one another's families and localities. Even today, no two Arans are alike: if you want to buy a hand-knit, take your time and wait till you find one that really strikes your fancy. Cheaper and less durable Arans are referred to as "hand-loomed," which is another way of saying "machine-made." Other types of sweaters include classic, blue, fisherman's rib sweaters; homespun, hand-dyed hand-knits; picture sweaters; and sophisticated mohair garments.

LINEN

A pure linen blouse, like an Aran sweater, can last forever. Designs are classic, so they won't become dated. Linen handkerchiefs for men make useful gifts. Damask tablecloths and crocheted-linen place mats make ideal wedding gifts. Most Irish linen is made in Northern Ireland.

TWEEDS

The best selection of traditional tweeds is still found in the specialist tweed shops of Counties Galway and Donegal. Weavers can also be found at work in Kerry, Dublin, Wicklow, Cork, and elsewhere in Connemara. Tweeds vary a good deal in type, from rugged-looking garments to clothes with jewel-like colors that have been popularized by Avoca Handweavers.

FODOR'S CHOICE

With so many special places in Ireland, Fodor's writers and editors have their favorites. Here are a few that stand out. For detailed information about each entry, refer to the appropriate chapter.

Quintessential Ireland

Ballyhack Village from Passage East, Waterford. Join the many admirers of lovely Ballyhack, an old-world scene of thatched cottages and an imposing 16th-century castle surrounded by green hills.

Blasket Islands from Slea Head, near Dingle. Slea Head's towering cliffs, above a beautiful and treacherous coastline, are a marvelous place from which to view these rugged, uninhabited islands.

Dusk over Killarney's Lower Lake from Aghadoe. Even Queen Victoria was overwhelmed by the vista. This enchanting, island-studded lake glowers under the expansive evening sky.

Georgian squares on a Sunday, Dublin. Surrounded by a charming Georgian streetscape and dotted with sculpture and meandering paths is tranquil, evergreen Merrion Square. Also popular is the 27-acre St. Stephen's Green, with festive flower gardens and expansive lawns.

Glendalough Valley, County Wicklow. A tranquil, lush valley is a splendid backdrop to this once-flourishing monastic center founded by St. Kevin in the 6th century. This important, evocative site is studded with ancient ruins: abbeys, churches, and graveyards with hundreds of intricately carved Celtic crosses.

Historic Buildings and Monuments

Castletown House, Co. Kildare. Ireland's largest and most splendid Palladian-style house is one of the country's architectural glories. Interestingly, the American poet Robert Lowell lived here in the sixties.

Clonmacnoise, Co. Offaly. This isolated monastery at the confluence of two rivers was famous throughout Europe as a center for learning. It's also a royal burial ground.

Crown Liquor Saloon and Grand Opera House, Belfast. A tunnel is said to join these two great edifices of the city's baroque Victorian splendor, allowing "stage-door Johnnies" to entertain, discreetly, the chorus girls of one in the private snugs of the other.

Glenveagh Castle, Co. Donegal. Prepare to be oddly charmed by this flamboyant 19th-century estate—a grand, turreted, and luxurious folly, with acres and acres of gardens.

Newgrange, Co. Meath. It's older than Stonehenge and is built with 250,000 tons of stones. Come in the morning during winter solstice, when 20 brief minutes of light illuminate the interior of this spectacular prehistoric tomb.

Rock of Cashel, Co. Tipperary. A cluster of ruins—a cathedral, chapel, and round tower—crown this circular, mist-shrouded rock that rises dramatically above the plain.

Trinity College, Dublin. Ireland's oldest university, founded by Queen Elizabeth to "civilize" Dublin, provided 40 acres of stomping grounds for the greats—Beckett, Wilde, Stoker—and houses one of the Anglo Saxon world's most masterfully illuminated manuscripts, the *Book of Kells*.

Dining

Ballymaloe House, Shanagarry, Co. Cork. Myrtle Allen continues to revolutionize and refine Irish cooking at her elegant inn. The justly famous cooking school here turns out Ireland's top chefs. *$$$$*

Longueville House, Mallow, Co. Cork. If you don't come for the wild duck and wood cock shoot in the fall, come to Longueville for William O'Callaghan's elegant Irish-French dishes, which use produce from the family farm, garden, and river. $$$$

Patrick Guilbaud, Dublin. Flawless food, impeccable service. Don't even think about skipping this place—created by Dublin's culinary savant—or Guilbaud's specialty, Chalons duck à l'orange. As for the plate of five hot and cold chocolate desserts, life is short. (And the wine list is long, it spans 70 pages.) $$$$

Peacock Alley, Dublin. Chef-owner Conrad Gallagher cooks with great brio and style—for celebrities staying at the Fitzwilliam, and, if you're lucky, you. Unusual, at times strikingly inventive, the food is on par with any of the best you've indulged, and the wine list is quite good. $$$$

Rathsallagh House, Dunlavin, Co. Wicklow. Think enthusiastic country-house cooking with an internationalist edge—produce from their organic gardens, game in season, seafood specialties. $$$$

Shanks, Bangor, Northern Ireland. Robbie Millar *hand-picks* his scallops from the sea. In his piquant, exciting dishes (European techniques, Asian spicing) he uses local ingredients—game reared on his estate, Irish seafood, artisan cheeses—and imports what he can't find from Paris. It's a 15-min drive from Belfast. $$$$

The Vintage, Kinsale. Irishness abounds in Federic Pastorino's inspired dishes—seafood from the West Cork Sea, and oxtail, veal, and deer from Ireland's lush fields, forests, and mountains. It's worth the jaunt to the seaside town of Kinsale for Lobster Dublin Lawyer (with mustard-whiskey sauce) alone. $$$–$$$$

Cromleach Lodge, Castlebaldwin, Co. Sligo. Outstanding views *and* food from a self-taught chef. Expect fantastically quirky dishes with multi-dimensional flavors. $$$

Casino House, Timoleague, Co. Cork. Traditional farmhouse turned restaurant, Casino House gives Irish country cooking an elegant edge with flavors full of verve. $$–$$$

Deane's, Belfast. Eclectic, Thai-influenced Michael Deane concocts innovative east-west dishes—squab with quail eggs, squab with rabbit. (Squab is a specialty.) Subtle spicing adds spirit-enhancing gusto to the meal. $$–$$$

Erriseask House, Ballyconneely, Co. Galway. David Ryan's contemporary, witty send-ups of local foods are the rage here—think monktail, black sole, oak-smoked salmon, Connemara lamb. $$–$$$

Wineport, Athlone, the Midlands. The energetic, imaginative food in this informal and wonderful waterside restaurant range in season from braised lamb shank and Irish Angus beef to crab claws and tiger prawns. Try the inimitable Baileys marshmallow cheesecake or the blood-orange mousse in a chocolate cup. $$–$$$

Lodging

Ardtara House, Upperlands, Northern Ireland. This gorgeously furnished 19th-century country house is the finest in the North. The village, with a working mill, is the last surviving reminder of a once-thriving linen industry. $$$$

Kildare Hotel and Country Club, Straffan, Co. Kildare. The lush Arnold Palmer-designed golf course and a multitude of activities (clay target shooting, game fishing) make this sumptuous mansion a splendid, if lavish, indulgence. $$$$

Merrion, Dublin. Splurge on these four luxurious Georgian town houses that make up one of Dublin's more traditional grand hotels. Besides intricate stucco plasterwork, a fine art collection, meandering gardens, a spa, and marvelous marble bathrooms, there's a bar in the wine vaults. $$$$

Mount Juliet, Thomastown, Co. Kilkenny. *Another* Georgian mansion on a 1,500-acre estate? This one has a championship golf course, extensive riding trails, and a slew of other old-world sports activities (archery, angling, clay target shooting). $$$$

Park Hotel, Kenmare, Co. Kerry. At this magnificent stone château, one of Ireland's premier country-house hotels, you can take views of the Caha Mountains and terraced lawns sweeping down to the bay. It's a stunning base for exploring the Ring of Kerry and historic Kenmare. $$$$

St. Ernan's House, Donegal Town, Co. Donegal. Talk about hideaways. Imagine a 19th-century country house on its own wooded, tidal island in Donegal Bay, with handsome, beautifully lit rooms, and the term *unwind* takes on new meaning. *$$$$*

Ballynahinch Castle, Recess, Co. Galway. This river's-edge hotel in rugged Connemara has long been a favorite retreat of statesmen and stars. Persian rugs, leather chesterfields, elegant rooms, fabulous fishing, and 350 wooded acres are why. *$$–$$$$*

Ash-Rowan Guest House, Belfast. Former restaurateurs Sam and Evelyn Hazlett own and run this outstanding B&B, the former home of Thomas Andrews, designer of the ill-fated *Titanic.* Sit in the lovely reading lounge and devour the many books scattered around the house, not to mention the first-rate breakfasts and dinners. *$$$*

Barberstown Castle, Straffan, Co. Kildare. Spanning 750 years of history, this unusual country-house hotel began as a medieval castle and expanded, with Elizabethan and Georgian wings, over the years. Rooms and food are creative and sumptuous. *$$–$$$*

Delphi Lodge, Leenane, Co. Mayo. This comfortable, lakeside Georgian sporting lodge is ensconced among wildly beautiful mountains-and-lakes scenery. *$$*

Ballymakeigh House, Youghal, Co. Cork. In lush dairy country, this is the sort of creeper-clad Irish farmhouse you dream of discovering. *$*

GREAT ITINERARIES

Highlights of Dublin, the East, and the South

5 to 7 days

Dublin's literary charm and Georgian riches, rugged County Wicklow, and the historic Meath plains are all just a few hours' drive apart. In the south you'll find fishing towns and bustling markets, coastal panoramas, and stunning mountain-and-lake scenery.

Dublin *1 to 3 days.* James Joyce's Dublin holds treasures for all sorts. Literary types: explore Trinity College, Beckett's stomping grounds, and its legendary *Book of Kells.* Visit key Joyce sights, the Dublin Writers Museum, and indulge in the *Dublin Literary Pub Crawl.* Joyce fanatics: arrive a week before Bloomsday (June 16) for Bloomstime celebrations. Literary or not, spend some time strolling around the city center and take in the elegant Georgian architecture around St. Stephen's Green, the austere Dublin Castle, and the national treasures in the museums around Merrion Square and pedestrian Grafton Street. Check out Temple Bar, Dublin's hip zone, and by all means join locals in this city-of-1,000-pubs for a foamy pint in the late afternoon. Pay your respects by taking a tour of the ever-popular Guinness Brewery and Storehouse. Night options: catch a show at W. B. Yeats's old stomping grounds, the Abbey Theatre; see some Victorian music hall at the Olympia Theatre; or listen to traditional or alternative music at any number of pubs or other venues. Spend as much time as you can muster in pubs—the real center of Dublin activity. Last-call arrives early, even here, so if you're still revved, go to Lesson Street and hit the nightclubs. For a dose of unmitigated Irish enthusiasm, join the roaring crowds at Croke Park and see some traditional Gaelic football and hurling. ☞ Exploring Dublin in Chapter 2.

Boyne Valley and County Wicklow *2 days.* Rent a car or join an organized tour and head out to the Boyne Valley, a short trip north of the capital. Spend the morning walking among the Iron Age ruins of the rolling Hill of Tara. After a picnic lunch on top of the hill, drive through ancient Kells and then to Newgrange, one of Europe's most spectacular prehistoric tombs. One thousand years older than Stonehenge, the great white-quartz structure merits two or three hours. Spend the rest of your day driving through the low hills and valleys of verdant County Meath and on to the Georgian village of Slane. Dominating the town are elegant Slane Castle and 500-ft Slane Hill. On the following day, drive through the County Wicklow mountains. You might want to get out of your car in one of the small, quiet towns along the Wicklow Way, Ireland's premier hiking trail, and go for a short hike. Drive on to stately Powerscourt House, whose grounds are perhaps the finest in the country. On the way to Glendalough and the medieval monastery of the hermit St. Kevin, stop for a bite in Round-wood, Ireland's highest village. ☞ North of Dublin in the Boyne Valley, and County Wicklow's Coast and Mountains in Chapter 3.

West Cork and Kerry 2 *days*. Head south to Cork City, perfect for half a day of walk-ing. Drive directly south to Kinsale, an old fishing town turned resort, with many good restaurants. A slow three- or four-hour drive along the coast and up through the small towns of West Cork takes you through the kind of lush landscape that inspired Ireland's nickname, the Emer-ald Isle. Spend the night in the market town of Skibbereen. Next morning, cross into County Kerry and head straight for pop-ular, bustling Killarney, right at the cen-ter of a scattering of azure lakes and heather-clad mountains. It's a good base for exploring your pick of three great At-lantic-pounded peninsulas: the Beara Peninsula, the Ring of Kerry, and the Din-gle Peninsula. All offer stunning ocean views, hilly landscapes, and welcoming towns with good B&Bs. The five-hour drive back to Dublin takes you through Limerick City and the lakes of the Mid-lands. ☞ Cork City, Kinsale to Glengar-riff via Bantry Bay, the Ring of Kerry, Killarney and Environs, the Dingle Penin-sula, and North Kerry and Shannonside in Chapter 6.

Highlights of Ireland: The West and the North

6 to 7 days

"To hell or to Connaught" was the choice given the native population by Cromwell, and indeed the harsh, barren landscape of parts of the west and north might appear cursed to the eye of an uprooted farmer. But there is an appeal in the very wildness of counties Clare, Galway, Mayo, Sligo, and Donegal—their stunning, steep coast-lines hammered and shaped for aeons by the Atlantic. Here, in isolated communi-ties, you'll hear locals speaking Irish as they go about their everyday lives. To the east, in the lusher pastures of long-suffering Northern Ireland, the arrival of peace has opened a treasure trove of gems for trav-elers.

Galway and Clare 2 *days*. A three-hour drive west from Dublin leads straight to the 710-ft Cliffs of Moher, perhaps the sin-gle most impressive sight in Ireland. Using the waterside village of Ballyvaughan as your base, spend a day exploring the lunar landscape of the harsh, limestone Bur-ren. In spring it becomes a mighty rock garden of exotic colors. The next morn-ing head north out of Ballyvaughan toward Galway City. On the way you'll pass 2-million-year-old Ailwee Cave and pic-ture-perfect Kinvara. Galway City, spectacularly overlooking Galway Bay, is rapidly growing, vibrant, and packed with culture and history. If time allows, drive west to Ros an Mhil (Rossaveal) and take a boat to the fabled Aran Islands. Spend the night in Galway City. ☞ The Burren and Beyond—West Clare to South Galway, and Galway City and the Aran Islands in Chapter 7.

Connemara, Mayo, Sligo, and Donegal 2 *days*. Northwest of Galway City is tiny Clifden, with some of the country's best Atlantic views. From here, head east through one of the most beautiful stretches of road in Connemara—through Kyle-more Valley, home of Kylemore Abbey, a huge Gothic Revival castle. After seeing the castle and its grounds, head north through tiny Leenane (the setting of the hit Broadway play, *The Beauty Queen of Leenane*) and on to the most attractive town in County Mayo, Westport. It's the per-fect spot to spend the night: the 18th-century planned town is on an inlet of Clew Bay, and some of the west coast's finest beaches are nearby. Your drive north leads right through the heart of Yeats Country in Sligo. Just north of cozy Sligo Town is the stark outline of a great hill, Ben Bul-ben, in whose shadow poet Yeats wanted to be buried. South of town, follow the signposted Yeats Trail around woody, gorgeously scenic Lough Gill. Continuing north, you pass Yeats's simple grave in unas-suming Drumcliff, a 3000 BC tomb in Creevykeel, and small Donegal Town. Head north through Letterkenny on the tight, meandering roads, into the windswept mountains and along the jagged coastline of northern Donegal. A trip on a fishing boat to one of the many islands off the coast is a must, as is a slow drive along the coast from the Gweedore Headland, cov-ered with heather and gorse, to the for-mer plantation village of Dun Fionnachaid (Dunfanaghy), heart of Donegal's Gaelic-speaking Gaeltacht region and a friendly place to spend the night. ☞ Through Connemara and County Mayo in Chapter 7, Yeats Country—Sligo Town and Environs, Around Donegal Bay, and Northern Donegal in Chapter 8.

Northern Ireland *2 days.* Begin exploring the province in historic, divided Derry City (called Londonderry by Unionists), Northern Ireland's second city. A few hours is sufficient to take in the views from the old city walls and the fascinating murals of the Catholic Bogside district. Continue on to two of the region's main attractions, the 13th-century Norman fortress of Dunluce Castle and the Giant's Causeway, shaped from volcanic rock some 60 million years ago. Heading south, sticking to coastal roads for the best scenery, you'll soon pass through the Glens of Antrim, whose green hills roll down into the sea. Tucked away in the Glens are a number of small, unpretentious towns with great hotels. Early in the morning, head straight to Northern Ireland's capital, Belfast. The old port city, gray and often wet, is a fascinating place recovering from years of strife. A morning of driving through its streets will have to suffice before you head west through the rustic, pretty countryside to Lough Neagh, the largest lake in the British Isles. It's time to head back to Dublin, but if you're ahead of schedule, take the longer route that passes though the glorious Mountains of Mourne and around icy-blue Carlingford Lough. ☞ Around Counties Antrim and Derry, and Belfast in Chapter 9.

2 · DUBLIN

Ask any Dubliner what's happening and you may hear echoes of one of W. B. Yeats's oft-quoted lines: "All changed, changed utterly." You can practically hear the roar as Western Europe's most intimate capital transforms itself into its fastest-growing urban tourist destination. Nowhere are the changes more apparent than in Temple Bar, the cobblestoned arts and culture quarter. But the city's pleasures are uncontainable: historic Georgian buildings, 1,000-odd pubs, buzzing cafés and restaurants, museums of quiet glory, lovely green parks, and, best of all, the easy friendliness of the people.

I **N HIS INIMITABLE,** irresistible way, James Joyce immortalized Dublin in his *Ulysses, Dubliners,* and *A Portrait of the Artist as a Young Man,* filling his works with the people he knew, with their own words, and with not a few of his own. As it turns out, he became one of Dublin's most famous exiles. Disappointed with the city's provincial outlook and small-town manners, he departed in 1902, at the age of 20 (his famed peers Sean O'Casey and Samuel Beckett soon followed). If, however, Joyce was to return to his genteel hometown today and take an extended, quasi-Homeric odyssey through the city (as he does so famously in *Ulysses*), would he even recognize Dublin as his "Dear Dirty Dumpling, foostherfather of fingalls and dotthergills"?

Updated by
Anto Howard

What would he make of Temple Bar—the city's erstwhile down-at-heels neighborhood now crammed with restaurants and stylish hotels in its reborn state as Dublin's "Left Bank"? Or the old market area of Smithfield, whose makeover has seen it "Cinderelled" into an impressive plaza and summer venue for big-name concerts? Or of the new Irishness, where every aspect of Celtic culture is red-hot: from Frank McCourt's *Angela's Ashes,* which dominated best-seller lists in the United States (the movie version was shot in the city and elsewhere around the country), to *Riverdance,* the old Irish mass-jig gone global? Plus, the returned Joyce would be stirred by the songs of U2, fired up by the films of Neil Jordan, and moved by the poems of Nobel laureate Seamus Heaney. In short, Irish is way in. As for Ireland's capital, elegant shops and hotels, galleries, art-house cinemas, coffeehouses, and a stunning variety of restaurants are springing up on almost every street in Dublin, transforming the genteel capital that once suffocated Joyce into a city almost as cosmopolitan as the Paris to which he fled.

Forget the Vikings and the English. Fast-forward to the new Dublin, where the army of invaders landing at the intersection of O'Connell Street and Temple Lane are London lads on a wild bachelor night, Europeans in search of a chic weekend getaway, and representatives from the United States of the "FBI"—or foreign-born Irish. Thanks to "the Celtic Tiger"—the nickname given to the roaring Irish economy—this most intimate capital city in Western Europe has become a boomtown.

Dublin's popularity has provoked a goodly number of its citizens to protest that the rapid transformation of their heretofore tranquil city is forever changing its spirit and character. Some observers view the openings of the 400-seat Sports Bar in Temple Bar as signs of the corporatization of Ireland's fair city. With the first hints of a slowdown in the economy felt in late 2001, these skeptics await the outcome of "Dublin: The Sequel"—can the "new Dublin" get beyond the rage stage and recover its rate of phenomenal growth or will it, like London, have to suffer recession and crisis to rediscover its soul?

Happily, enough of the old Dublin remains to enchant. After all, it's the fundamentals—the Georgian elegance of Merrion Square, the Norman drama of Christ Church Cathedral, a foamy pint at an atmospheric pub—that still gratify. Fittingly, some of the more recent developments hark back to the earliest. Two multimedia shows in the downtown area remind us that Norsemen (various neighborhood names, such as Howth, Leixlip, and Dalkey, echo their historic presence) were responsible for the city's original boom. In ancient days, more than 1,500 years ago, Dublin had been little more than a crossroads—albeit a critical one—of four of the main thoroughfares that traversed the country. Then, it had two names: Baile Atha Cliath, meaning City of the Hurdles, which was bestowed by Celtic traders in the 2nd century AD and which you can still see on buses and billboards throughout the city, and Dubhlinn, or "dark pool" (the murkiness of the water was caused by peat), which is believed to have been where Dublin Castle now stands.

In 837, Norsemen from Scandinavia carried out the first invasion on Dublin, only to be followed by other waves of warriors staking their claim to the city—from the 12th-century Anglo-Normans to Oliver Cromwell in 1651. Not until the 18th century did Dublin reach a period of glory, when a golden age of enlightened patronage by wealthy nobles turned the city into one of Europe's most prepossessing capitals. Streets and squares, such as Merrion and Fitzwilliam squares, were constructed with neoclassic dignity and Palladian grace. If, today, Dublin is still redolent in parts of the elegance of the 18th century, it is due to the eminently refined Georgian style of art and architecture, which flowered in the city between 1714 and 1820 during the English reigns of the three Georges. To satisfy the taste for luxury of the oftentitled, unusually wealthy members of society, lemon-color chintz borders, gilded Derbyshire pier tables, and Adamesque wood paneling were installed in the salons of town houses. The arts also flourished: Handel, the German-born English composer, wrote much of his great oratorio *Messiah* here, where it was first performed in 1742. But the aura of "the glorious eighteenth" was short-lived; in 1800, the Act of Union brought Ireland and Britain together in a common United Kingdom, and political power moved from Dublin to London. Dublin quickly lost its cultural and social sparkle as many members of the nobility moved to the new power center, turning Ireland practically overnight into "the Cinderella of all nations," in historian Maurice Craig's words.

The 19th century proved to be a time of political turmoil and agitation, although Daniel O'Connell, the first Catholic lord mayor of Dublin (his statue dominates O'Connell Street), won early success with the introduction of Catholic emancipation in 1829. During the late 1840s, Dublin escaped the worst effects of the famine, caused by potato blight, that ravaged much of southern and western Ireland. As an emerging Victorian middle class introduced an element of genteel snobbery to the city, Dublin began a rapid outward expansion to the new suburban enclaves of Ballsbridge, Rathgar, and Rathmines on the southside and Clontarf and Drumcondra on the northside.

The city entered a period of cultural ferment in the first decade of the 20th century—an era that had its political apotheosis in the Easter Uprising of 1916. A war aimed at winning independence from Britain began in County Tipperary in 1919 and lasted for three years. During the Civil War, which followed the setting up of the Irish Free State in December 1921, the Four Courts and the Custom House both came under fire and were severely damaged. The capital had to be rebuilt during the 1920s. After the Civil War was over, Dublin entered a new era of political and cultural conservatism, which continued until the late 1970s. Amazingly, the major turning point in Dublin's fortunes occurred in 1972, when Ireland, emerging from 40 years of isolationism, joined the European Economic Community. In the 1980s, while the economy remained in the grasp of recession, Dublin and Ireland once again turned to the cultural sphere to announce themselves to the rest of the world. Irish musicians stormed the American and British barricades of rock-and-roll. Bob Geldof and the Boomtown Rats ("I Don't Like Mondays") and Chris de Burgh were among the most prominent of the musicians who found audiences well beyond their native shores, but it was U2, that climbed to the topmost heights of rock-and-roll stardom, that forged a permanent place in international popular culture for Irish musicians.

Sinéad O'Connor, the Cranberries, and the Corrs have since followed, and more are on the fast track.

If the 1980s saw the ascent of Irish rock stars, the 1990s and the new century were truly the boom years—a decade of broadly improved economic fortunes, major capital investment, declining unemployment, and reversing patterns of immigration—all set in motion to a great extent by Ireland's participation in the EEC (now the European Union, or EU). When Ireland overwhelmingly approved the new EU treaty in 1992, it was one of the poorest European nations; it qualified for EU grants of all kinds. Since then, money has, quite simply, *poured* into Ireland—nowhere more so than in Dublin. The International Financial Services Centre, gleaming behind the two-centuries-old Custom House, is one of the most overt signs of the success the city has had in attracting leading multinational corporations, particularly those in telecommunications, software, and service industries. In 2000 the government announced that Ireland was the world's biggest exporter of software. In the spring of 1998, the Irish overwhelmingly voted in favor of membership in the single European currency; since January 2002, Ireland's main currency has been the euro and the pound has been withdrawn from circulation. The recent downturn in the global economy has slowed the Celtic Tiger to crawling pace and economists argue over the future prospects for a country so dependent on exports.

Today, roughly half of the Irish Republic's population of 3.6 million people live in Dublin and its suburbs. It's a city of young people—astonishingly so. Students from all over Ireland attend Trinity College and the city's dozen other universities and colleges. On weekends, their counterparts from Paris, London, and Rome fly in, swelling the city's youthful contingent, crowding its pubs and clubs to overflowing. After graduating, more and more young people are sticking around rather than emigrating to New York or London, filling the raft of new jobs set up by multinational corporations and contributing to the hubbub that's evident everywhere.

All this development has not been without growing pains; with London-like house prices, increased crime, and major traffic problems, Dubliners are at last suffering the woes so familiar to city dwellers around the world. An influx of immigrants has caused resentment among some of the otherwise famously hospitable Irish. "Me darlin' Dublin's dead and gone," so goes the old traditional ballad, but the rebirth, at times difficult and a little messy, has been a spectacular success.

Pleasures and Pastimes

Literary Dublin

Dublin packs more literary punch per square foot than practically any other spot on the planet—largely because of the ferment that took hold at the end of the 19th century, when two main cultural movements emerged. In 1893, Douglas Hyde, a Protestant and later the first president of Ireland, founded the Gaelic League (Conradh na Gaelige), with a goal of preserving the Irish language and Gaelic traditions. The poet W. B. Yeats also played a pivotal role in the Irish literary renaissance. With funding from his patron Annie Horniman, Yeats and Lady Gregory founded the **Abbey Theatre** in 1903 (it opened in 1904), to develop and produce a decidedly Irish repertoire. With this new venue, and the growing prominence of such playwrights as Sean O'Casey and J. M. Synge, Irish literature thrived. The **Dublin Writers Museum** gives a terrific introduction to this story and to the more than two dozen major writers Ireland subsequently produced (at least the dead ones—living legends have to wait to be included). To go further back in literary history, head for **Trinity College,** where you can see a few pages of the legendary 9th-century *Book of Kells* and stroll through the hallowed campus where Samuel Beckett studied and where a theater now bears his name. If you're an Oscar Wilde fan, you can pay homage to him at 1 Merrion Square. The Close-Up: "ReJoyce! A Walk through James Joyce's Dublin and *Ulysses*" guides you through some key sites connected with Joyce and *Ulysses*. And if you want to stock up on anecdotes about the relationship between the pint and the pen, check out the *Dublin Literary Pub Crawl* or take a guided tour of literary pubs.

Musical Dublin

Music fills Dublin's streets (especially Grafton Street) and its pubs, where *talk* of music is as popular as the tunes themselves. Dubliners are obsessed with music of every kind and will happily discuss anything from Elvis's earliest recordings (remember Jimmy's father in *The Commitments*?) to U2's latest incarnation. The city has been the stomping ground of so many big-league rock and pop musicians that Dublin Tourism has created a "Rock 'n Stroll" Trail, which covers 16 sites, most of them in the city center and Temple Bar. It includes spots like **Bewley's Oriental Café,** where Bob Geldof and the other members of the Boomtown Rats hung out, and the Bad Ass Café, where Sinéad O'Connor once worked. You're forgiven if you think some connections between the trail sites and the musicians seem hokey, but you're not if you don't seek out Dublin's lively, present-day music scene. A number of small pubs and larger halls host live music, but the best places are midsize venues—such as the **Olympia Theatre** and the **Temple Bar Music Centre**—where you can hear well-established local acts *and* leading international artists (including world-renowned Irish musicians) playing everything from traditional and folk rock to jazz-funk and "Dubcore," a term coined to describe the city's many noisy alternative bands. Traditional Irish music (or "Trad"), very much a child of rural Ireland, is alive and kicking in the urban sprawl of Dublin. Scores of city bars are home to impromptu "sessions" and professional gigs. **The Cobblestone** in lively Smithfield is one of the most famous and atmospheric venues.

A Thousand Pubs

Even if you order only a Ballygowan (the Irish Evian), a visit to an Irish pub (or two or three) is a must. The Irish public house is a national institution—down to the spectacle, at some pubs, of patrons standing at closing time to the playing of Ireland's national anthem. Samuel Beckett would often repair to one, believing a glass of Guinness stout was the best way to ward off depression. Indeed, Dublin is for the stout of heart—the city has one pub for every 450 of its 500,000 adults. There are actor's pubs, sports pubs, even pubs for "less famous literary types" (Grogan's on South William Street). And any occasion—be it "ordinations, liquidations, cremations," as one storefront puts it—is the right occasion. Today, Irish pubs are being exported at an unprecedented rate all around the world, but in Dublin it's a different story altogether. Here, surprisingly, modern, European-style café-bars are fast replacing the capital's traditional drinking spots. The extraordinary prices being offered for the old pubs by new entrepreneurs have proven hard to resist for the longtime owners. In the city center you'll now find high-concept designer pubs with bright, arty facades and a pervasive scent of affluence. To be sure, in the City of 1,000 Pubs, you're still certain of finding a good, old-fashioned watering hole. And if you do find yourself in a new spot, surrounded by the trappings of European chic, you'll soon discover that Dubliners still enjoy good *craic*—quintessentially Irish friendly chat and lively, irony-laced conversation. Wherever you go, remember that when you order a Guinness, the barman first pours it three-quarters of the way, lets it settle, then tops it off and brings it over to the bar. You should then wait again until the top-up has settled, at which point the brew turns a deep black. The mark of a perfect pint? As you drink the glass down, the brew will leave thin rings to mark each mouthful.

EXPLORING DUBLIN

In Dublin's fair city—"where the girls are so pretty" went the centuries-old ditty. Today, parts of the city—particularly the vast, uniform housing projects of the northern suburbs—may not be fair or pretty. But even if you're not conscious of it while you're in the city center, Dublin is in a beautiful setting: it loops around the edge of Dublin Bay and on a plain at the edge of the gorgeous, green Dublin and Wicklow mountains, rising softly just to the south. From the famous Four Courts building in the heart of town, the sight of the city, the bay, and the mountains will take your breath away. From the city's noted vantage points, such as the South Wall, which stretches far out into Dublin Bay, or from choice spots in the suburbs of south and north County Dublin, you can nearly get a full measure of the city. From north to south, Dublin stretches 16 km (10 mi). From its center, immediately adjacent to the port area and the River Liffey, the city spreads westward for an additional 10 km (6 mi); in total, it covers 28,000 acres. But its heart is far more compact than these numbers indicate. As in Paris, London, and Florence, and as in so many other cities throughout the world, a river runs right through Dublin. The River Liffey divides the capital into the "northside" and the "southside," as everyone calls the two principal center-city areas, and almost all the major sights in the area are well within less than an hour's walk of one another.

Coverage is organized into eight walks of the city center and the areas immediately surrounding it, and two excursions into County Dublin—the first to the southern suburbs, the latter to the northern. The first two walks—The Center City: Around Trinity College and The Georgian Heart of Dublin—cover many of the southside's major sites: Trinity College, St. Stephen's Green, Merrion Square, and Grafton Street. It makes sense to do these walks first, as they will quickly orient you to a good portion of the southside. The third walk—Temple Bar: Dublin's "Left Bank"—takes you through this revived neighborhood, which is the hottest, hippest zone in the capital. The fourth walk—Dublin West: From Dublin Castle to the Four Courts—picks up across the street from Temple Bar and gets you to the Guinness Brewery and Storehouse, the city's most popular attraction. The fifth walk—The Liberties—takes you on a brief stroll through working-class Dublin, a historic but often overlooked part of the city. A word about these five walks: although we've split the southside into five, you'll soon realize that the distance between the areas in all these walks is not very great. The sixth walk—North of the Liffey—moves to the northside of the city center and covers all the major cultural sites there, including the James Joyce Cultural Centre, Gate Theatre, Dublin Writers Museum, and Hugh Lane Municipal Gallery of Modern Art. It also includes the rapidly developing Smithfield district, which locals are already hailing as the future "Temple Bar of the northside." The seventh walk—Along the Grand Canal—covers noteworthy sites along the canal, beginning in the northeast part of the city and ending in the southwest. Phoenix Park and Environs, at the western fringe of the northside city center, is the main focus of the eighth Dublin walk.

If you're visiting Dublin for more than two or three days, you'll probably want to explore farther afield. There's plenty to see and do a short distance from the center city—in the suburbs of both north and south County Dublin—but since you need either a car or public transportation to reach these destinations, we cover them in our Side Trips section.

Because of its compact size and traffic congestion (brought on in the last few years by an astronomical increase in the number of new vehicles), *pedestrian* traffic—especially on the city center's busiest streets during commute hours—is astonishing. Watch where you stop to consult your map or you're liable to be swept away by the ceaseless flow of the bustling crowds.

Numbers in the text correspond to numbers in the margin and on the Dublin City Center, Dublin West, County Dublin–Southside, and County Dublin–Northside maps.

Great Itineraries

It will take you about a week to cover almost all of our Dublin Exploring suggestions, including the Side Trips. But in three or even two days, you can see many city-center sites and probably come away with a greater familiarity of the city than you could establish in a similar length of time in any of Europe's other capitals.

IF YOU HAVE 1 DAY

Touring the largest city in Ireland in the space of a single day sounds like an impossible goal, but if you're determined you can do it in the span of a single sunrise-to-sunset day. Think Dublin 101. South of the Liffey are graceful squares and fashionable terraces from Dublin's elegant Georgian heyday; interspersed with some of the city's leading sights, this area is perfect for an introductory city tour. You might begin at O'Connell Bridge—as Dublin has no central focal point, most natives have, traditionally, regarded it as the city's Piccadilly Circus or Times Square. Then head south down Westmoreland Street on your way to view one of Dublin's most spectacular buildings, James Gandon's 18th-century Parliament House, now the Bank of Ireland building. To fuel up for the walk ahead, first stop at 12 Westmoreland Street and go into Bewley's Oriental Café, an institution that has been supplying Dubliners with coffee and buns since 1842. After you drink in the grand colonnade of the Bank of Ireland building, head west to the genteel, elegant campus of Trinity College—the oldest seat of Irish learning. Your first stop should be the Library, to see the staggering Long Room and Ireland's greatest art treasure, the *Book of Kells,* one of the world's most famous—and most beautiful—illuminated manuscripts.

Leave the campus and take a stroll along Grafton Street, Dublin's ritziest shopping street and—"Who will buy my beautiful roses?"—open-air flower market. Appropriately enough, one of the city's favorite relaxation spots, the lovely little park of St. Stephen's Green, is nearby. Head over to the northeast corner of the park to find ground zero for the city's cultural institutions. Here, surrounding the four points of Leinster House (built by the Duke of Kildare, Ireland's first patron of Palladianism), are the National Museum, replete with artifacts and exhibits dating back to prehistoric times; the National Gallery of Ireland (don't miss the Irish collection and the Caravaggio *Taking of Christ*); the National Library; and the Natural History Museum. Depending on your interests, pick one to explore, and then make a quick detour westward to Merrion Square—among Dublin's most famous Georgian landmarks.

For a lovely lunch, head back to Stephen's Green and the Victorian Shelbourne Méridien Hotel—the lobby salons glow with Waterford chandeliers and blazing fireplaces. From Stephen's Green head west to pay your respects to St. Paddy—St. Patrick's Cathedral. If, instead, the Dublin of artists and poets is more your speed, hop a double-decker bus and head north of the Liffey to the Dublin Writers Museum. End the day with a performance at the nearby Gate Theatre, another Georgian eye-knocker, or spend the evening exploring the cobbled streets, many cafés, and shops of Dublin's bohemian quarter, the compact Temple Bar area. Because you couldn't fit in a stop at the Guinness Brewery and Storehouse, top the evening off with a pint at the Norseman pub. By the time the barman says "Finish your pints" to announce closing time at 11 PM, you'll agree that although this day was a lightning tour of the city's main sights, it has left an indelible impression of what Dublin is all about.

IF YOU HAVE 3 DAYS

The above tour is the grand curtain-raiser for this itinerary. Dedicate your second day to the north and west of the city center. In the morning, cross the Liffey via O'Connell Bridge and walk up O'Connell Street, the city's widest thoroughfare, stopping to visit the General Post Office—the besieged headquarters of the 1916 rebels—on your way to the Dublin Writers Museum and the Hugh Lane Municipal Gallery of Modern Art. Be sure to join the thousands of Dubliners strolling down Henry, Moore, and Mary streets, the northside's pedestrian shopping area. In the afternoon, head back to the Liffey for a quayside walk by Dublin's most imposing structure, the Custom House; then head west to the Guinness Brewery and Storehouse. Hop a bus or catch a cab back into the city and a blow-out dinner at the glamorous Tea Room in the Temple Bar's Clarence hotel. Spend the evening on a literary pub crawl to see where the likes of Beckett and Behan held court, perhaps joining a special guided tour. On the third day tour the northern outskirts of Dublin from Glasnevin Cemetery and the National Botanic Gardens across to the sublime Marino Casino in Marino and the quaint fishing village of Howth. Back in the city, have tea at Bewley's and catch a musical performance at the Olympia Theatre or a play at the Abbey Theatre.

IF YOU HAVE 5 DAYS

Follow the two itineraries above and then start your fourth day at Dublin's dawn—a living history of Dublin can be seen at medieval Dublinia, across the street from ancient Christ Church Cathedral, whose underground crypt is Dublin's oldest structure. Head north, jumping across the Liffey to the Four Courts, James Gandon's Georgian masterpiece and the home of the Irish judiciary. Continue northward to visit the Royal Kilmainham Hospital—the home of the Irish Museum of Modern Art—and Kilmainham Gaol, where the leaders of the Easter Rising were executed following their capture. Return via Dublin Castle, residence of British power in Ireland for nearly 800 years, and now the home of the Chester Beatty Library, containing Chinese and Turkish exhibits. On your fifth and final day explore the southern outskirts of the city, accessible by DART train, including the suburban areas of Dalkey and Sandycove (where you can visit the James Joyce Martello Tower), and the busy ferry port of Dun Laoghaire. Before returning to the city center, take a stroll along the 5-km (3-mi) beach of Sandymount Strand—that is, if Irish skies are smiling.

The Center City: Around Trinity College

The River Liffey provides a useful aid to orientation, flowing as it does through the direct middle of Dublin. If you ask a native Dubliner for directions—from under an umbrella, as it will probably be raining—he or she will most likely reply in terms of "up" or "down," up meaning away from the river or down toward it. Dublin's center of gravity had traditionally been O'Connell Bridge, a diplomatic landmark in that it avoided locating the center to the north or south of the river—strong local loyalties still prevailed among "northsiders" (who live to the north of the river) and "southsiders," and neither would ever accept that the city's center lay on the other's side of the river. The economic boom, however, has seen diplomacy go by the wayside—Dublin's heart now beats loudest southward across the Liffey, due in part to a large-scale refurbishment and pedestrianization of Grafton Street, which made this already upscale shopping address *the* street to shop, stop, and be seen. At the foot of Grafton Street is the city's most famous and recognizable landmark, Trinity College; at the top of it is Dublin's most popular strolling retreat, St. Stephen's Green, a 27-acre landscaped park with flowers, lakes, bridges, and Dubliners enjoying a time-out.

A Good Walk
Numbers in the text correspond to numbers in the margin and on the Dublin City Center map.

Start at **Trinity College** ①, exploring the quadrangle as you head to the Old Library to see the *Book of Kells*. If you want to see modern art, visit the collection housed in the Douglas Hyde Gallery, just inside the Nassau Street entrance to the college. If you're interested in the Georgian era, try to view the Provost's House and its salon, the grandest in Ireland. Trinity can easily eat up at least an hour or more, so when you come back out the front gate, you can either stop in at the **Bank of Ireland** ②, a neoclassic masterpiece that was once the seat of the Irish Parliament, or make an immediate left and head up **Grafton Street** ③, the pedestrian spine of the southside. The **Dublin Tourism** ④ office is just off Grafton Street, on the corner of Suffolk Street. If Grafton Street's shops whet your appetite for more browsing and shopping, turn right down Wicklow Street, then left up South William Street to **Powerscourt Townhouse Centre** ⑤, where a faux-Georgian atrium (very dubiously set within one of Dublin's greatest 18th-century mansions) houses high-priced shops and pleasant cafés. The **Dublin Civic Museum** ⑥ is next door to Powerscourt, across the alley on its south flank. If you're doing well on time and want to explore the shopping streets farther east, jog via the alley one block east to Drury Street, from which you can access the Victorian **George's Street Arcade** ⑦. Whether or not you make this excursion, you should head back to Grafton Street, where **Bewley's Oriental Café** ⑧, a Dublin institution, is another good place for a break. Grafton Street ends at the northwest corner of **St. Stephen's Green** ⑨, Dublin's most popular public gardens; they absolutely require a stroll-through. **Newman House** ⑩ is on the south side of the green. Amble back across the green, exiting onto the northeast corner, at which sits the grand **Shelbourne Méridien Hotel** ⑪, a wonderful place for afternoon tea or a quick pint at one of its two pubs. The **Huguenot Cemetery** ⑫ is just down the street from the hotel, on the same side. If you want to see more art, make a detour to the **RHA Gallagher Gallery** ⑬.

TIMING

Dublin's city center is so compact you could race through this walk in an hour, but in order to gain full advantage of what is on offer, set aside at least half a day—if you can—to explore the treasures of Trinity College and amble up and around Grafton Street to Stephen's Green.

Sights to See
❷ **Bank of Ireland.** Across the street from the west facade of **Trinity College** stands one of Dublin's most striking buildings, now the Bank of Ireland but formerly the original home of the Irish Parliament. Sir Edward Lovett Pearce designed the central section in 1729; three other

architects would ultimately be involved in the building's construction. A pedimented portico fronted by six massive Corinthian columns dominates the grand facade, which follows the curve of Westmoreland Street as it meets College Green, once a Viking meeting place and burial ground. Two years after the Parliament was abolished in 1801 under the Act of Union, which brought Ireland under the direct rule of Britain, the building was bought for €50,790 by the Bank of Ireland. Inside, stucco rosettes adorn the coffered ceiling in the pastel-hue, colonnaded, clerestoried **main banking hall,** at one time the Court of Requests, where citizens' petitions were heard. Just down the hall is the original **House of Lords,** with tapestries depicting the Battle of the Boyne and the Siege of Derry, an oak-paneled nave, and a 1,233-piece Waterford glass chandelier; ask a guard to show you in. Visitors are welcome during normal banking hours; the Dublin historian and author Éamonn Mac Thomáis conducts a brief guided tour every Tuesday at 10:30, 11:30, and 1:45. Accessed via Foster Place South, the small alley on the bank's east flank, the **Bank of Ireland Arts Center** frequently exhibits contemporary Irish art and has a permanent exhibition devoted to "The Story of Banking." ⊠ *2 College Green, City Center,* ☎ *01/677–6801; 01/671–1488 arts center.* ⊡ *€3.80.* ⊙ *Mon.– Wed. and Fri. 10–4, Thurs. 10–5; Arts Center Tues.–Fri. 10–4, Sat. 2– 5, Sun. 10–1.*

❽ Bewley's Oriental Café. The granddaddies of the capital's cafés, Bewley's has been serving coffee and buns to Dubliners since it was founded by Quakers in 1842, and now has four locations. Bewley's trademark stained-glass windows were designed by Harry Clarke (1889–1931), Ireland's most distinguished early 20th-century artist in this medium. All the branches are fine places in which to observe Dubliners of all ages and occupations. The aroma of coffee is irresistible, and the dark interiors—marble-top tables, bentwood chairs, and mahogany trim— evoke a more leisurely Dublin. The food is overpriced and not particularly good, but people-watching here over a cup of coffee or tea is a quintessential Dublin experience. (If you're interested in a more modern cup of coffee, check out the Metro Café, nearby at 43 South William Street—it's one of Dublin's best haunts for the caffeine-addicted and its staff is devoid of the devil-may-care, pseudo-existential inefficiency that seems to plague so many other Dublin cafés.) ⊠ *78 Grafton St., City Center,* ☎ *01/677–6761 (for all locations);* ⊙ *Sun.– Thurs. 7:30 AM–1 AM, Fri.–Sat. 7:30 AM–4 AM.* ⊠ *12 Westmoreland St., City Center;* ⊙ *Mon.–Sat. 7:30 AM–9 PM, Sun. 9:30 AM–9 PM.* ⊠ *40 Mary St., North of the Liffey;* ⊙ *Mon.–Wed. and Fri.–Sat. 7 AM– 6 PM, Thurs. 7 AM–9 PM.* ⊠ *Jervis Shopping Centre, Jervis and Mary Sts., North of the Liffey;* ⊙ *Mon.–Wed. and Fri. 9 AM–6 PM, Thurs. 9 AM–9 PM, Sun. noon–6 PM.*

❻ Dublin Civic Museum. Built between 1765 and 1771 as an exhibition hall for the Society of Artists, this building later was used as the City Assembly House, precursor of City Hall. The museum's esoteric collection includes Stone Age flints, Viking coins, old maps and prints of the city, and the sculpted head of British admiral Horatio Nelson, which used to top Nelson's Pillar, beside the General Post Office on O'Connell Street; the column was toppled by an explosion in 1966 on the 50th anniversary of the Easter Uprising. The museum holds exhibitions relating to the city. ⊠ *58 S. William St., City Center,* ☎ *01/ 679–4260.* ⊡ *Free.* ⊙ *Tues.–Sat. 10–6, Sun. 11–2.*

❹ Dublin Tourism. Churches are not just for prayers, as this deconsecrated medieval church proves. Resurrected as a visitor center, St. Andrew's, fallen into ruin after years of neglect, now houses Dublin Tourism, a

Abbey Presbyterian
Church. 55
The Ark 27
Arthouse 30
Bambrick's 71
Bank of Ireland 2
Bewley's Oriental
Café 8
Central Bank 33
Custom House. 64
Dublin Civic
Museum. 6
Dublin Tourism 4
Dublin Writers
Museum. 56
GAA Museum. 62
Gallery of
Photography 31
Garden of
Remembrance 58
Gate Theatre 54
Genealogical Office . . 22
General Post Office
(GPO) 53
George's Street Arcade . . 7
Government Buildings . . 16
Grafton Street 3
Ha'penny Bridge. . . . 26
Hot Press Irish Music
Hall of Fame. 51
Hugh Lane Municipal
Gallery of Modern Art . . 57
Huguenot Cemetery. . 12
Irish Film Centre (IFC) . . 28
Irish Jewish Museum . . 70
James Joyce
Cultural Centre 59
Leinster House. 18
Mansion House 23
Meeting House
Square. 29
Merrion Square. 14
Mount Street Bridge . . 67
Mountjoy Square. . . . 60
National Gallery of
Ireland 19
National Library 20
National Museum . . . 21
Natural History
Museum. 17
Newman House 10
Number
Twenty–Nine. 15
O'Connell Street 52
Olympia Theatre 32
Powerscourt
Townhouse Centre . . . 5
Pro-Cathedral 63
RHA Gallagher
Gallery 13
Rotunda Hospital. . . . 65
Royal Irish Academy . . 24
St. Ann's Church 25
St. Francis Xavier
Church. 61
St. Stephen's Green . . . 9
Scruffy Murphy's. . . . 68
Shaw Birthplace 72
Shelbourne
Méridien Hotel 11
Statue of Patrick
Kavanagh 69
Trinity College 1
Waterways
Visitors Centre 66

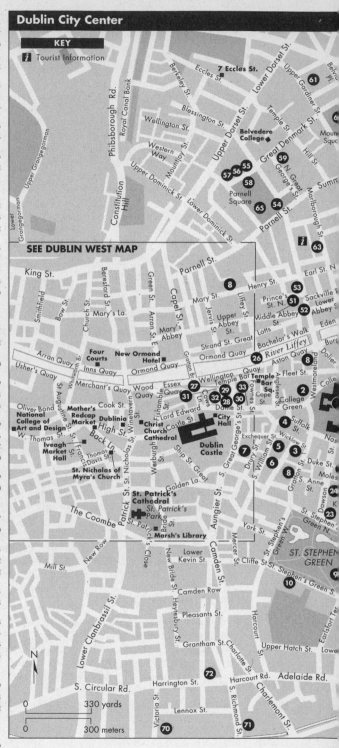

Dublin City Center

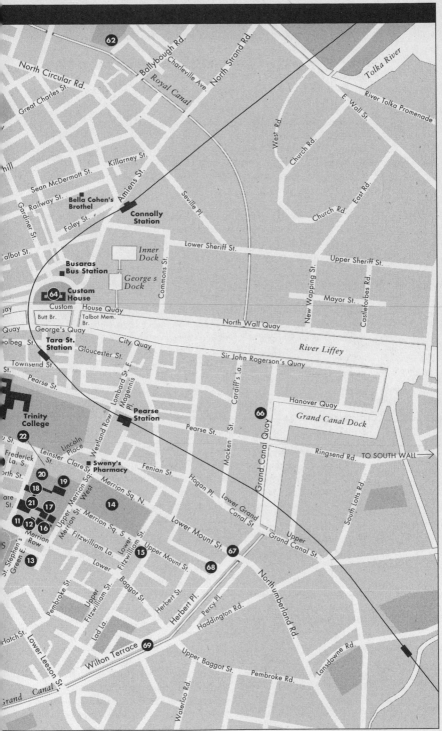

North Circular Rd.

Great Charles St.

...hill

Sean McDermott St.

Railway St.

Gardiner St.

Killarney St.

Amiens St.

Bella Cohen's Brothel

Foley St.

...albot St.

Busaras Bus Station

Custom House

Custom

Talbot Mem. Br.

Butt Br.

George's Quay

...olbeg St.

Tara St. Station

Townsend St.

Pearse St.

Trinity College

Frederick La. S.

...orth St.

...are St.

Leinster St.

Lincoln Place

Clare St.

Sweny's Pharmacy

Fenian St.

Merrion Sq. West

Upper Merrion Sq.

Merrion Sq. N.

Merrion Sq. S.

Lower Fitzwilliam St.

Upper Mount St.

Lower Mount St.

Merrion Row

St. Stephen's Green E.

Pembroke St.

Upper Fitzwilliam St.

Lower Fitzwilliam St.

Baggot St.

Herbert St.

Herbert Pl.

Lad La.

Lower Leeson St.

Wilton Terrace

Upper Baggot St.

...rand Canal

Waterloo Rd.

Pembroke Rd.

Percy Pl.

Haddington Rd.

Northumberland Rd.

Lansdowne Rd.

Ballybough Rd.

Charleville Ave.

North Strand Rd.

Royal Canal

Seville Pl.

Connolly Station

Inner Dock

George's Dock

Commons St.

Lower Sheriff St.

House Quay

North Wall Quay

City Quay

Gloucester St.

Westland Row

Lombard St. E.

Magennis Pl.

Pearse Station

Pearse St.

Hogan Pl.

Macken St.

Cardiff's ...a.

Sir John Rogerson's Quay

River Liffey

Upper Sheriff St.

New Wapping St.

Mayor St.

Castleforbes Rd.

Hanover Quay

Grand Canal Dock

Grand Canal Quay

Ringsend Rd.

TO SOUTH WALL →

Lower Grand Canal St.

Upper Grand Canal St.

South Lotts Rd.

Tolka River

River Tolka Promenade

West Rd.

Church Rd.

East Wall St.

East Rd.

Church Rd.

62

64

22

20

19

18

21

17

11

12

16

14

15

68

67

69

66

13

private concern that offers the most complete information on Dublin's sights, restaurants, and hotels; you can even rent a car here. The office provides reservations facilities for all Dublin hotels, as well as guided tours, a plethora of brochures, and a gift shop (beware the exorbitant prices). Upstairs is a pleasant café serving sandwiches and drinks. ⊠ *St. Andrew's Church, Suffolk St., City Center,* ☎ *01/605–7700; 1850/ 230330 (in Ireland).* ⊘ *July–Sept., Mon.–Sat. 8:30–6, Sun. 11–5:30; Oct.–June, daily 9–6.*

❼ George's Street Arcade. This Victorian covered market fills the block between Drury Street to the west and South Great George's Street to the east. You'll find two dozen or so stalls selling books, prints, clothing (mostly secondhand), exotic foodstuffs, and trinkets. ⊠ *S. Great George's St., City Center* ⊘ *Mon.–Sat. 9–6.*

NEED A BREAK?   In one of Dublin's most ornate traditional taverns, the **Long Hall Pub** (⊠ 51 S. Great George's St., City Center, ☎ 01/475–1590) you'll find Victorian lamps, a mahogany bar, mirrors, chandeliers, and plasterwork ceilings, all more than 100 years old. The pub serves sandwiches and an excellent pint of Guinness.

★ ❸ Grafton Street. It's no more than 200 yards long and about 20 ft wide, but brick-lined Grafton Street, open only to pedestrians, can make a claim to be the most humming street in the city, if not in all of Ireland. It is one of Dublin's vital spines: the most direct route between the front door of Trinity College and Stephen's Green, and the city's premier shopping street, home to Dublin's two most distinguished department stores, **Brown Thomas** and **Marks & Spencer.** Both on Grafton Street itself and in the smaller alleyways that radiate off it, you'll also find dozens of independent stores, a dozen or so colorful flower sellers, and some of Dublin's most popular watering holes. In summertime, buskers from all over the country and the world line both sides of the street, pouring out the sounds of drum, whistle, pipe, and string.

⓬ Huguenot Cemetery. One of the last such burial grounds in Dublin, this cemetery was used in the late 17th century by French Protestants who had fled persecution in their native land. The cemetery gates are rarely open, but you can view the grounds from the street—it's on the northeast corner across from the square. ⊠ *27 St. Stephen's Green N, City Center.*

⓾ Newman House. One of the greatest glories of Georgian Dublin, Newman House is actually two imposing town houses joined together. The earlier of the two, No. 85 St. Stephen's Green (1738), was designed by Richard Castle, favored architect of Dublin's rich and famous, and features a winged Palladian window on the Wicklow granite facade. Originally known as Clanwilliam House, it has two landmarks of Irish Georgian style: the Apollo Room, decorated with stuccowork depicting the sun god and his muses; and the magnificent Saloon, "the supreme example of Dublin Baroque," according to scholars Jacqueline O'Brien and Desmond Guinness, crowned with an exuberant ceiling aswirl with cupids and gods, created by the Brothers Lafranchini, the finest *stuccadores* (plasterworkers) of 18th-century Dublin. Next door at No. 86 (1765), the staircase, on pastel-color walls, is one of the city's most beautiful rococo examples—with floral swags and musical instruments picked out in cake-frosting white. Catholic University (described by James Joyce in *A Portrait of the Artist as a Young Man*) was established in this building in 1850, with Cardinal John Henry Newman as its first rector. At the back of Newman House lie **Iveagh Gardens,** a delightful hideaway with statues and sunken gardens that remains one of Dublin's best-kept secrets (you can enter via Earlsfort Terrace and Harcourt Street). The Commons Restaurant is in the basement. ⊠ *85–86 St. Stephen's Green, City Center,* ☎ *01/475-7255.* 🖃 *House and garden* €*3.80.* ⊙ *June–Aug. (guided tours only), Tues.–Fri. at noon, 2, 3, and 4; Sat. at 2, 3, and 4; Sun. at 11, noon, and 1.*

❺ Powerscourt Townhouse Centre. Lucky man, this Viscount Powerscourt. In the mid-18th century, not only did he build Ireland's most spectacular country house, in Enniskerry, County Wicklow (which bears the family name), but he also decided to rival that structure's grandeur with one of Dublin's largest stone mansions. Staffed with 22 servants and built of granite from the viscount's own quarry in the Wicklow Hills, Powerscourt House was a major statement in the Palladian style designed by Robert Mack in 1774—a massive, Baroque-style edifice that towers over the little street it sits on (note the top story, framed by massive volutes, that was once intended as an observatory). The interior decoration runs from rococo salons by James McCullagh to Adamesque plasterwork by Michael Stapleton to—surprise—an imaginative shopping atrium, installed in and around the covered courtyard. The stores here include high-quality Irish crafts shops and numerous food stalls. The mall exit leads to the Carmelite **Church of St. Teresa's** and **Johnson's Court.** Beside the church, a pedestrian lane leads onto Grafton Street. ⊠ *59 S. William St., City Center,* ☎ *01/679–4144.* ⊙ *Mon.–Fri. 10–6, Thurs. 10–8, Sat. 9–6, Sun. noon to 6 limited shops open.*

⓭ RHA Gallagher Gallery. The Royal Hibernian Academy, an old Dublin institution, is housed in a well-lit building, one of the largest exhibition spaces in the city. The gallery holds adventurous exhibitions of the best in contemporary art, both from Ireland and abroad. ⊠ *15 Ely Pl., off St. Stephen's Green, City Center,* ☎ *01/661–2558.* 🖃 *Free.* ⊙ *Mon.–Wed. and Fri.–Sat. 11–5, Thurs. 11–8, Sun. 2–5.*

★ ⓫ Shelbourne Méridien Hotel. The ebullient, redbrick, white-wood-trimmed facade of the Shelbourne has commanded "the best address in Dublin" from the north side of St. Stephen's Green since 1865. In 1921 the Irish Free State's constitution was drafted here in a first-floor suite. The most financially painless way to soak up the hotel's old-fashioned luxury and genteel excitement is to step past the entrance—note the statues of Nubian princesses and attendant slaves—for afternoon tea (€17.15 per person, including sandwiches and cakes) in the green-wallpapered **Lord Mayor's Lounge** or for a drink in one of its two bars, the **Shelbourne Bar** and the **Horseshoe Bar,** both of which are thronged with businesspeople and politicos after the workday ends. Elizabeth Bowen, famed novelist, wrote her novel *The Hotel* about this very place. ⊠ *27 St. Stephen's Green, City Center,* ☎ *01/676–6471,* 🌐 *www. shelbourne.ie.*

★ ❾ St. Stephen's Green. Dubliners call it simply Stephen's Green, and green it is (year-round)—a verdant, 27-acre city-center square that was an open common used for the public punishment of criminals until 1664. After a long period of decline, it became a private park in 1814—the first time in its history that it was closed to the general public. Its fortunes changed again in 1880, when Sir Arthur Guinness, later Lord Ardiluan (a member of the Guinness brewery family), paid for it to be laid out anew. Flower gardens, formal lawns, a Victorian bandstand, and an ornamental lake with lots of waterfowl are all within the park's borders, connected by paths guaranteeing that strolling here or just passing through will offer up unexpected delights (palm trees). Among the park's many statues are a memorial to Yeats and another to Joyce by Henry Moore, and the *Three Fates,* a dramatic group of bronze female figures watching over man's destiny. In the 18th century the walk on the north side of the green was referred to as the Beaux Walk because most of Dublin's gentlemen's clubs were in town houses here. Today it is dominated by the **Shelbourne Méridien Hotel.** On the south side is the alluring Georgian-gorgeous Newman House. 🖼 *Free.* ⊘ *Daily sunrise–sunset.*

★ ❶ **Trinity College.** Founded in 1592 by Queen Elizabeth I to "civilize" (Her Majesty's word) Dublin, Trinity is Ireland's oldest and most famous college. The memorably atmospheric campus is a must; here you can enjoy tracking the shadows of some of the more noted alumni, such as Jonathan Swift (1667–1745), Oscar Wilde (1854–1900), Bram Stoker (1847–1912), and Samuel Beckett (1906–89). Trinity College, Dublin (familiarly known as TCD), was founded on the site of the confiscated Priory of All Hallows. For centuries Trinity was the preserve of the Protestant church. A free education was offered to Catholics—provided that they accepted the Protestant faith. As a legacy of this condition, until 1966 Catholics who wished to study at Trinity had to obtain a dispensation from their bishop or face excommunication. Today more than 70% of Trinity's students are Catholics, an indication of how far away those days seem to today's generation.

Trinity's grounds cover 40 acres. Most of its buildings were constructed in the 18th and early 19th centuries. The extensive **West Front,** with a classical pedimented portico in the Corinthian style, faces College Green and is directly across from the **Bank of Ireland**; it was built between 1755 and 1759, and is possibly the work of Theodore Jacobsen, architect of London's Foundling Hospital. The design is repeated on the interior, so the view is the same both from outside the gates and from the quadrangle inside. On the lawn in front of the inner facade are **statues** of orator Edmund Burke (1729–97) and dramatist Oliver Goldsmith (1728–74), two other alumni. Like the West Front, **Parliament Square** (commonly known as Front Square), the cobblestoned quadrangle that lies just beyond this first patch of lawn, also dates from the 18th century. On the right side of the square is Sir William Chambers's **theater,** or **Examination Hall,** dating from the mid-1780s, which contains the college's most splendid Adamesque interior (designed by Michael Stapleton). The hall houses an impressive organ retrieved from an 18th-century Spanish ship and a gilded oak chandelier from the old House of Commons; concerts are sometimes held here. The **chapel,** which stands on the left of the quadrangle, has stucco ceilings and fine woodwork. Both the theater and the chapel were designed by Scotsman William Chambers in the late 18th century. The looming **Campanile,** or bell tower, is the symbolic heart of the college; erected in 1853, it dominates the center of the square. To the left of the campanile is the **Graduates Memorial Building,** or GMB. Built in 1892, the slightly Gothic building is now home to both the Philosophical and Historical Societies, Trinity's ancient and fiercely competitive debating groups. At the back of the square stands old redbrick **Rubrics,** looking rather ordinary and out of place among the gray granite and cobblestones. Rubrics, now used as rooms for students and faculty, dates from 1690, making it the oldest building still standing.

Ireland's largest collection of books and manuscripts is housed in **Trinity College Library.** Its principal treasure is the *Book of Kells,* generally considered the most striking manuscript ever produced in the Anglo-Saxon world and one of the greatest masterpieces of early Christian art. Once thought to be lost—the Vikings looted the book in 1007 for its jeweled cover but ultimately left the manuscript behind—the book is a splendidly illuminated version of the Gospels. In the 12th century,

Guardius Cambensis declared that the book was made by an angel's hand in answer to a prayer of St. Bridget; in the 20th century, scholars decided instead that the book originated on the island of Iona in Scotland, where followers of St. Colomba lived until the island came under siege in the early to mid-9th century. They fled to Kells, County Meath, bringing the book with them. The 680-page work was rebound in four volumes in 1953, two of which are usually displayed at a time, so you typically see no more than four original pages. (Some wags have taken to calling it the "Page of Kells.") However, such is the incredible workmanship of the *Book of Kells* that one folio contains the equivalent of many other manuscripts. On some pages, it has been determined that within a quarter inch, no fewer than 158 interlacements of a ribbon pattern of white lines on a black background can be discerned—little wonder some historians feel this book contains all the designs to be found in Celtic art. Note, too, the extraordinary colors, some of which were derived from shellfish, beetles' wings, and crushed pearls. The most famous page shows the "XPI" monogram (symbol of Christ), but if this page is not on display, you can still see a replica of it, and many of the other lavishly illustrated pages, in the adjacent exhibition—dedicated to the history, artistry, and conservation of the book—through which you must pass to see the originals.

Because of the fame and beauty of the *Book of Kells,* it is all too easy to overlook the other treasures in the library. They include the *Book of Armagh,* a 9th-century copy of the New Testament that also contains St. Patrick's Confession, and the legendary *Book of Durrow,* a 7th-century Gospel book from County Offaly. You may have to wait in line to enter the library; it's less busy early in the day.

The **Old Library,** aptly known as the Long Room, is one of Dublin's most staggering sights. It's 213 ft long and 42 ft wide, and contains in its 21 alcoves approximately 200,000 of the 3 million volumes in Trinity's collection. Originally the room had a flat plaster ceiling, but in 1859–60 the need for more shelving resulted in a decision to raise the level of the roof and add the barrel-vaulted ceiling and the gallery bookcases. Since the 1801 Copyright Act, the college has received a copy of every book published in Britain and Ireland, and a great number of these publications must be stored in other parts of the campus and beyond. Of note are the carved Royal Arms of Queen Elizabeth I, above the library entrance—the only surviving relic of the original college buildings—and, lining the Long Room, a grand series of marble busts, of which the most famous is Roubiliac's portrait of Jonathan Swift. The Trinity College Library Shop sells books, clothing, jewelry, and postcards. *City Center,* ☎ *01/608–2308,* WEB *www.tcd.ie.* ✉ *€5.70 for the Long Room.* ☉ *June–Sept., Mon.–Sat. 9:30–5, Sun. 9:30–4:30; Oct.– May, Mon.–Sat. 9:30–5, Sun. noon–4:30.*

Trinity College's stark, modern Arts and Social Sciences Building, with an entrance on Nassau Street, houses the **Douglas Hyde Gallery of Modern Art,** which concentrates on contemporary art exhibitions and has its own bookstore. Also in the building, down some steps from the gallery, there's a snack bar with coffee, tea, sandwiches, and students willing to talk about life in the old college. ☎ *01/608–1116.* ✉ *Free.* ☉ *Mon.–Wed. and Fri. 11–6, Thurs. 11–7, Sat. 11–4:45.*

The **New Berkeley Library,** the main student library at Trinity, was built in 1967 and named after the philosopher and alumnus George Berkeley. The small open space in front of the library contains a spherical brass sculpture designed by Arnaldo Pomodoro. The library is not open to the general public. ✉ *College Green,* ☎ *01/677–2941.* ☉ *Grounds daily 8 AM–10 PM.*

In the Thomas Davis Theatre in the arts building, the **"Dublin Experience,"** a 45-minute audiovisual presentation, explains the history of the city over the last 1,000 years. ☎ *01/608–1688.* 🖃 *€3.80; in conjunction with Old Library, €7.60.* ⊙ *Late-May–Oct., daily 10–5; shows every hr on the hr.*

The Georgian Heart of Dublin

If there's one travel poster that signifies "Dublin" more than any other, it's the one that pictures 50 or so Georgian doorways—door after colorful door, all graced with lovely fanlights upheld by columns. A building boom began in Dublin in the early 18th century as the Protestant ascendancy constructed town houses for themselves and civic structures for their city in the style that came to be known as Georgian, for the four successive British Georges who ruled from 1714 through 1830. The Georgian architectural rage owed much to architects like James Gandon and Richard Castle. They and others were influenced by Andrea Palladio (1508–80), whose *Four Books of Architecture* were published in the 1720s in London and helped to precipitate the revival of his style, which swept through England and its colonies. Never again would Dublin be so "smart," so filled with decorum and style, nor its visitors' book so full of aristocratic names. Note that while Dublin's southside is a veritable shop window of the Georgian style, there are many other period sights to be found northside—for instance, the august interiors of the Dublin Writers Museum and Belvedere College, or James Gandon's great civic structures, the Custom House and the Four Courts, found quayside. These, and other Georgian goodies, are described in the Exploring sections of Dublin West and North of the Liffey.

A Good Walk
Numbers in the text correspond to numbers in the margin and on the Dublin City Center map.

When Dublin was transformed into a Georgian metropolis, people came from all over to admire the new pillared and corniced city. Today, walking through Fitzwilliam Square or Merrion Street Upper, you can still admire vistas of calm Georgian splendor. Begin your Palladian promenade at the northeast corner of Stephen's Green—here, in front of the men's clubs, was the Beaux Walk, a favorite 18th-century gathering place for fashionable Dubliners. Chances are you won't bump into a duke on his way to a Handel concert or an earl on his way to a rout, ball, and supper, but then, you won't have to dodge pigs either, which used to dot the cityscape back then. Walk down Merrion Street to **Merrion Square** ⑭—one of Dublin's most attractive squares. The east side of Merrion Square and its continuation, Fitzwilliam Street, form what is known as "the Georgian mile," which, unlike some Irish miles, actually measures less than a kilometer. On a clear day the Dublin Mountains are visible in the distance and the prospect has almost (thanks to the ugly, modern office block of the Electricity Supply Board) been preserved to give an impression of the spacious feel of 18th-century Dublin. Walk down the south side of the square to **Number Twenty-Nine** ⑮. Cut back through the square to visit the refurbished **Government Buildings** ⑯, the **Natural History Museum** ⑰, **Leinster House** ⑱, and/or the **National Gallery of Ireland** ⑲. The last leg of this walk is up Kildare Street to the **National Library** ⑳, passing the back of Leinster House to the **National Museum** ㉑. Stop in at the **Genealogical Office** ㉒ if you're doing research about your ancestors. Walk back to Stephen's Green and down Harrington Street to Synge Street and the **Shaw Birthplace** ㉒. Return to the Green and go down Dawson Street, which runs parallel to Grafton Street. The **Mansion House** ㉓, **Royal Irish Academy** ㉔, and **St. Ann's Church** ㉕ are on the left as you walk down toward Trinity College's side entrance.

TIMING

Dublin is so compact you could race through this walk in two hours, if you don't linger anywhere or set foot in one of the museums. But the treasures at the National Gallery and the National Museum, and the green tranquillity of Merrion Square, may slow you down. Many of Dublin's finest sites along the way, and dozens of the city's most historic pubs, may also entice you. So, if you don't get too distracted, do this walk over the course of a half-day.

Sights to See

㉒ **Genealogical Office.** Are you a Fitzgibbon from Limerick, a Cullen from Waterford, or a McSweeney from Cork? This reference library is a good place to begin your ancestor-tracing efforts. If you're a total novice at genealogical research, you can meet with an advisor (€31.75 for an hour consultation) who can help get you started. It also houses the **Heraldic Museum,** where displays of flags, coins, stamps, silver, and family crests highlight the uses and development of heraldry in Ireland. Note that a map detailing the geographical origin of the hundred or so most common Irish surnames can be found at the back of this book. ✉ *2 Kildare St., City Center,* ☎ *01/661–4877,* WEB *www.nli.ie.* 🎫 *Free.* ☻ *Genealogical Office weekdays 10–12:30 and 2–4:30, Sat. 10–12:30; Heraldic Museum weekdays 10–8:30, Sat. 10–12:30. Guided tours by appointment.*

⑯ **Government Buildings.** The swan song of British architecture in the capital, this enormous complex was the last neoclassical edifice to be erected by the British government. A landmark of "Edwardian Baroque," it was designed by Sir Aston Webb (who did many of the similarly grand buildings in London's Piccadilly Circus) as the College of Science in the early 1900s. Following a major restoration, these buildings became the offices of the Department of the *taoiseach* (the prime minister, pronounced *tea*-shuck) and the *tánaiste* (the deputy prime minister, pronounced tawn-*ish*-ta). Fine examples of contemporary Irish furniture and carpets populate the offices. A stained-glass window, known as "My Four Green Fields," was originally made by Evie Hone for the 1939 World Trade Fair in New York. It depicts the four ancient provinces of Ireland: Munster, Ulster, Leinster, and Connacht. The government offices are accessible only via 45-minute guided tours given on Saturday (tickets are available on the day of the tour from the National Gallery), though they are dramatically illuminated every night. ✉ *Upper Merrion St., City Center,* ☎ *01/662–4888.* 🎫 *Free.* ☻ *Sat. 10:30–3:30.*

⑱ **Leinster House.** Commissioned by the Duke of Leinster and built in 1745, this residence almost single-handedly ignited the Georgian style that dominated Dublin for 100 years. It was not only the largest private home in the city but Richard Castle's first structure in Ireland (Castle, a follower of Palladio, designed some of the country's most important Palladian country houses). Inside, the grand salons were ornamented with coffered ceilings, Rembrandts, and Van Dycks, fitting settings for the parties often given by the duke's wife (and celebrated beauty), Lady Emily Lennox. The building has two facades: the one facing Merrion Square is designed in the style of a country house; the other, on Kildare Street, resembles that of a town house. This latter facade—if you ignore the ground-floor level—was a major inspiration for Irishman James Hoban's designs for the White House in Washington, D.C. Built in hard Ardbracan limestone, the house's exterior makes a cold

THE AGE OF ELEGANCE: DUBLIN'S GEORGIAN STYLE

EXTRAORDINARY DUBLIN!" sigh art lovers and connoisseurs of the 18th century. It was during the "gorgeous eighteenth" that this duckling of a city was transformed into a preening swan, largely by the Georgian style of art and architecture that flowered between 1714 and 1820 during the reigns of the three English Georges. Today, Dublin remains in good part a sublimely Georgian city, thanks to enduring grace notes: the commodious and uniformly laid out streets, the genteel town squares, the redbrick mansions accented with demilune fan windows. The great 18th-century showpieces are **Merrion, Fitzwilliam, Mountjoy,** and **Parnell squares. Merrion Square East,** the longest Georgian street in town, reveals scenes of decorum, elegance, polish, and charm, all woven into a "tapestry of rosy brick and white enamel," to quote the 18th-century connoisseur Horace Walpole. Setting off the facades are fan-lighted doors (often lacquered in black, green, yellow, or red) and the celebrated "patent reveal" window trims, thin plaster linings painted white to catch the light. These demilune fanlights—as iconic of the city as clock towers are of Zurich—are often in neoclassic Adamesque style.

Many exteriors appear severely plain, but don't be fooled: these town houses can be compared to bonbons whose sheaths of hard chocolate conceal deliciously creamy centers. Just behind their stately front doors are entry rooms and stairways aswirl with tinted rococo plasterwork, often the work of *stuccadores*, or plasterworkers imported from Italy (including the talented Lafranchini brothers). **Newman House,** one of the very finest of Georgian houses, is open to the public. **Belvedere College** (⊠ 6 Great Denmark St., North of the Liffey) is open by appointment only.

The Palladian style—as the Georgian style was then called—began to reign supreme in domestic architecture in 1745 when the Croesus-rich Earl of Kildare returned from an Italian Grand Tour and built a gigantic Palladian palace called **Leinster House** in the seedy section of town. "Where I go, fashion will follow," he declared, and indeed it did. By then, the Anglo-Irish elite had given the city London airs by building the **Parliament House** (now the Bank of Ireland), **Royal Exchange** (now City Hall), the **Custom House,** and the **Four Courts** in the new style. But this phase of high fashion came to an end with the Act of Union: according to historian Maurice Craig, "On the last stroke of midnight, December 31, 1800, the gaily caparisoned horses turned into mice, the coaches into pumpkins, the silks and brocades into rags, and Ireland was once again the Cinderella among the nations." It was nearly 150 years before the spotlight shone once again on 18th-century Dublin, thanks to the conservation efforts of the **Irish Georgian Society** (⊠ 74 Merrion Sq., South of the Liffey, ☎ 01/676–7053, ⓦⒺⒷ www.archerie.com/igs).

Close-Up

ANCESTOR-HUNTING

THE LATE PRESIDENT KENNEDY and former President Reagan are only two among many thousands of Americans who have been drawn to Ireland in an attempt to track down their ancestors. So popular has this become that Ireland today has numerous facilities for those in search of their past. However, before you begin some genealogical Sherlock Holmesing, you'll need some detailed information, not just the fact that your last name is Murphy, Kelly, or O'Donnell. The memories of elderly relatives about the place which they or their forebears emigrated, for example, is often a useful starting point. The county name is an aid, but the name of their village or town is even better. It can lead quickly to parish registers, often going back 200 years or more, which the local clergy will usually be very glad to let you see (keep in mind that many of these parish registers have been moved to regional town halls and government agencies). Best of all, however, is to organize some professional help. The Genealogical Office in Dublin is the best source of information on family names and family crests. Similarly, the Office of the Registrar General in Dublin's Custom House has details of many births, deaths, and marriages after 1864, and some marriages dating back to 1845 (a substantial part of their records were destroyed, however, in the Troubles of 1921). The Public Record Office at the Four Courts and the Registry of the Deeds in Henrietta Street, both in Dublin, are two other potentially useful sources of information. Of course, if your great-grandfather's name was Blarney Killakalarney, you should have an easy time sleuthing your family roots. Chances are, however, your name is one of the more prominent surnames in Ireland (☞ Irish Family Names, *in* Chapter 11), so you'll have a longer time tracking down your ancestors among all the Ahernes.

---

impression, and, in fact, the duke's heirs pronounced the house "melancholy" and fled. Today, the house is the seat of Dáil Éireann (the House of Representatives, pronounced dawl *e*-rin) and Seanad Éireann (the Senate, pronounced shanad *e*-rin), which together constitute the Irish Parliament. When the Dáil is not in session, tours can be arranged weekdays; when the Dáil is in session, tours are available only on Monday and Friday. The Dáil visitors' gallery is included in the tour, although it can be accessed on days when the Dáil is in session and tours are not available. To arrange a visit, contact the public relations office at the phone number provided. ⊠ *Kildare St., City Center,* ☎ *01/618–3000,* 🌐 *www.irlgov.ie.* 🎟 *Free*

㉓ **Mansion House.** The mayor of Dublin resides at the Mansion House, which dates from 1710. It was built for Joshua Dawson, who later sold the property to the government on condition that "one loaf of double refined sugar of six pounds weight" be delivered to him every Christmas. In 1919 the Declaration of Irish Independence was adopted here. Dawson Street (named for the house's original tenant) is the site of the annual and popular **August Antiques Fair.** The house is not open to the public. ⊠ *Dawson St., City Center.*

★ ⑭ **Merrion Square.** Created between 1762 and 1764, this tranquil square a few blocks to the east of St. Stephen's Green is lined on three sides by some of Dublin's best-preserved Georgian town houses, many of which have brightly painted front doors crowned by intricate fan-lights. Leinster House—Dublin's Versailles—and the Natural History Museum and National Gallery line the west side of the square. It's on the other sides, however, that the Georgian terrace streetscape comes into its own—the finest houses are on the north border. Even when its flower gardens are not in bloom, the vibrant, mostly evergreen grounds, dotted with sculpture and threaded with meandering paths, are worth a walk-through. The square has been the home of several distinguished Dubliners, including Oscar Wilde's parents, Sir William and "Speranza" Wilde (No. 1); Irish national leader Daniel O'Connell (No. 58); and authors W. B. Yeats (Nos. 52 and 82) and Sheridan LeFanu (No. 70). Walk past the houses and read the plaques on the house facades, which identify the former inhabitants. Until 50 years ago, the square was a fashionable residential area, but today most of the houses are offices. At the south end of Merrion Square, on Upper Mount Street, stands **St. Stephen's Church** (Church of Ireland). Known locally as the "pepper canister" church because of its cupola, the structure was inspired in part by Wren's churches in London. *South of the Liffey.* ☉ *Daily sunrise–sunset.*

★ ⑲ **National Gallery of Ireland.** Caravaggio's *The Taking of Christ* (1602), Reynolds's *First Earl of Bellamont* (1773), Vermeer's *Lady Writing a Letter with Her Maid* (ca. 1670) . . . you get the picture. The National Gallery of Ireland—the first in a series of major civic buildings on the west side of Merrion Square—is one of Europe's finest smaller art museums, with more than 3,000 works. Unlike Europe's largest art museums, which are almost guaranteed to induce Stendhal's syndrome, the National Gallery can be thoroughly covered in a morning or afternoon without inducing exhaustion. An 1854 Act of Parliament provided for the establishment of the museum, which was helped along by William Dargan (1799–1867), who was responsible for building much of Ireland's railway network in the 19th century (he is honored by a statue on the front lawn). The 1864 building was designed by Francis Fowke, who was also responsible for London's Victoria & Albert Museum.

A highlight of the museum is the major collection of paintings by Irish artists from the 17th through 20th centuries, including works by Roderic O'Conor (1860–1940), Sir William Orpen (1878–1931), William Leech (1881–1968), and Jack B. Yeats (1871–1957), the brother of W. B. Yeats and by far the best-known Irish painter of the 20th century. Yeats painted portraits and landscapes in an abstract expressionist style not unlike from that of the later Bay Area Figurative painters of the 1950s and 1960s. His *The Liffey Swim* (1923) is particularly worth seeing for its Dublin subject matter (the annual swim is still held, usually on the first weekend in September).

The collection also claims exceptional paintings from the 17th-century French, Dutch, Italian, and Spanish schools. Among the highlights that you should strive to see are those mentioned above (the spectacular Caravaggio made headlines around the world when it was found hanging undiscovered in a Jesuit house not far from the museum) and Rembrandt's *Rest on the Flight into Egypt* (1647), Poussin's *The Holy Family* (1649) and *Lamentation over the Dead Christ* (ca. 1655–60), and, somewhat later than these, Goya's *Portrait of Doña Antonia Zárate* (circa 1810). Don't forget to check out the portrait of the *First Earl of Bellamont,* by Reynolds; the earl was among the first to introduce the Georgian fashion to Ireland, and this portrait stunningly flaunts the extraordinary style of the man himself. The French Impressionists are represented with paintings by Monet, Sisley, and Pissarro. The northern wing of the gallery houses the British collection and the Irish National Portrait collection, and the amply stocked **gift shop** is a good place to pick up books on Irish artists. In January 2002, the spectacular new Millennium Wing, a standout of postmodern architecture in Dublin, opened. The wing also houses part of the permanent collection, and will be used to stage major international travelling shows. Free guided tours are available on Saturday at 3 PM and on Sunday at 2, 3, and 4. ⊠ *Merrion Sq. W, City Center,* ☎ *01/661–5133,* WEB *www.nationalgallery.ie.* ☒ *Free.* ☉ *Mon.–Wed. and Fri.–Sat. 9:30–5:30, Thurs. 9:30–8:30, Sun. 12–5:30.*

NEED A BREAK?

Fitzer's (⊠ Merrion Sq. W, South of the Liffey, ☎ 01/661–4496), the National Gallery's self-service restaurant, is a find—one of the city's best spots for an inexpensive, top-rate lunch. The 16 to 20 daily menu items are prepared with an up-to-date take on new European cuisine. It's open Monday–Saturday 10–5:30 (lunch is served noon–2:30), and Sunday 2–5.

㉐ National Library. Ireland is one of the few countries in the world where one can happily admit to being a writer. And few countries as geographically diminutive as Ireland have garnered as many recipients of the Nobel Prize for Literature. Along with works by W. B. Yeats (1923), George Bernard Shaw (1925), Samuel Beckett (1969), and Seamus Heaney (1995), the National Library contains first editions of every major Irish writer, including books by Jonathan Swift, Oliver Goldsmith, and James Joyce (who used the library as the scene of the great literary debate in *Ulysses*). In addition, of course, almost every book ever published in Ireland is kept here, as well as an unequaled selection of old maps and an extensive collection of Irish newspapers and magazines—more than 5 million items in all. The main **Reading Room** opened in 1890 to house the collections of the Royal Dublin Society. Beneath its dramatic domed ceiling, countless authors have researched and written their books over the years. ⊠ *Kildare St., City Center,* ☎ *01/661–8811,* WEB *www.nli.ie.* ☒ *Free.* ☉ *Mon.–Wed. 10–9, Thurs.–Fri. 10–5, Sat. 10–1.*

★ ㉑ National Museum. On the other side of Leinster House from the National Library, Ireland's National Museum houses a fabled collection of Irish artifacts, dating from 7000 BC to the present. The museum is organized around a grand rotunda and elaborately decorated, with mosaic floors, marble columns, balustrades, and fancy ironwork. It has the largest collection of Celtic antiquities in the world, including an array of gold jewelry, carved stones, bronze tools, and weapons. The Treasury collection, including some of the museum's most renowned pieces, is open on a permanent basis. Among the priceless relics on display are the 8th-century **Ardagh Chalice,** a two-handle silver cup with gold filigree ornamentation; the bronze-coated, iron **St. Patrick's Bell,** the oldest surviving example (5th–8th centuries) of Irish metalwork; the 8th-century **Tara Brooch,** an intricately decorated piece made of white bronze, amber, and glass; and the 12th-century bejeweled oak **Cross of Cong,** covered with silver and bronze panels. The Road to Independence Room is devoted to the 1916 Easter Uprising and the War of Independence (1919–21); displays here include uniforms, weapons, banners, and a piece of the flag that flew over the General Post Office during Easter Week, 1916. Upstairs, Viking Age Ireland is a permanent exhibit on the Norsemen, featuring a full-size Viking skeleton, swords, leather works recovered in Dublin and surrounding areas, and a replica of a small Viking boat. In contrast to the ebullient late-Victorian architecture of the main museum building, the design of the **National Museum Annexe** is purely functional; it houses temporary shows of Irish antiquities. The 18th-century **Collins Barracks**, near the Phoenix Park, houses a collection of glass, silver, furniture, and other decorative arts. ✉ *Kildare St.; Annexe: 7–9 Merrion Row, City Center;* ☎ *01/677–7444,* WEB *www.museum.ie.* 🖾 *Free.* ☉ *Tues.– Sat. 10–5, Sun. 2–5.*

⑰ Natural History Museum. The famed explorer of the African interior, Dr. Stanley Livingstone (recall the expression, "Dr. Livingstone, I presume?") inaugurated this museum when it opened in 1857. Today, it is little changed from Victorian times and remains a fascinating repository of mounted mammals, birds, and other flora and fauna. The Irish Room houses the most famous exhibits, skeletons of Ireland's extinct, prehistoric giant "Irish elk." The World Animals Collection includes a 65-ft whale skeleton suspended from the roof. Don't miss the very beautiful Blaschka Collection, finely detailed glass models of marine creatures, the zoological accuracy of which has never been achieved since. The museum is next door to the **Government Buildings.** ✉ *Merrion Sq. W, City Center,* ☎ *01/677–7444,* WEB *www.museum.ie.* 🖾 *Free.* ☉ *Tues.–Sat. 10–5, Sun. 2–5.*

⑮ Number Twenty-Nine. Everything in this carefully refurbished 1794 home, known simply as Number Twenty-Nine, is in keeping with the elegant lifestyle of the Dublin middle class between 1790 and 1820, the height of the Georgian period, when the house was owned by a wine merchant's widow. From the basement to the attic, in the kitchen, nursery, servant's quarters, and the formal living areas, the National Museum of Ireland has re-created the period's style with authentic furniture, paintings, carpets, curtains, paint, wallpapers, and even bellpulls. ✉ *29 Lower Fitzwilliam St., South of the Liffey,* ☎ *01/702–6165.* 🖾 *€3.15.* ☉ *Tues.–Sat. 10–5, Sun. 2–5.*

㉔ Royal Irish Academy. Adjacent to the **Mansion House,** the country's leading learned society houses important manuscripts in its 18th-century library, including a large collection of ancient Irish manuscripts, such as the 11th- to 12th-century *Book of the Dun Cow,* and the library of the 18th-century poet Thomas Moore. ✉ *19 Dawson St., City Center,* ☎ *01/676–2570,* WEB *www.ria.ie.* 🖾 *Free.* ☉ *Weekdays 9:30–5.*

㉕ St. Ann's Church. St. Ann's plain, neo-Romanesque granite exterior, built in 1868, belies the Church of Ireland's rich Georgian interior, which Isaac Wills designed in 1720. Highlights of the interior include polished-wood balconies, ornate plasterwork, and shelving in the chancel dating from 1723—and still in use for distributing bread to the parish's poor. ✉ *Dawson St., City Center,* ☎ *01/676–7727,* 🖾 *Free.* ☉ *Weekdays 10–4, Sun. for services.*

㊲ Shaw Birthplace. "Author of many plays" is the simple accolade to George Bernard Shaw on the plaque outside his birthplace. The Nobel laureate was born here in 1856 to a once prosperous family fallen on harder times. Shaw lived in this modest, Victorian terrace house until he was 10 and remembers it as having a "loveless" feel. The painstaking restoration of the little rooms highlights the cramped, claustrophobic atmosphere. All the details of a family home—wallpaper, paint, fittings, curtains, furniture, utensils, pictures, rugs—remain, and it appears as if the family has just gone out for the afternoon. You can almost hear one of Mrs. Shaw's musical recitals in the tiny front parlor. The children's bedrooms are dotted with photographs and original documents and letters that throw light on Shaw's career. ✉ *33 Synge St., South of the Liffey,* ☎ *01/475–0854.* 🖾 *€5.50.* ☉ *Apr.–Oct., Mon.–Sat. 10– 5, Sun. 11–5.*

Temple Bar: Dublin's "Left Bank"

More than any other neighborhood in Dublin, Temple Bar represents the dramatic changes (good and bad) and ascending fortunes of Dublin in the last 10 years. Named after one of the streets of its central spine, the area was targeted for redevelopment in 1991–92 after a long period of neglect, having survived widely rumored plans to turn it into a massive bus depot and/or a giant parking lot. Temple Bar took off *fast* into Dublin's version of New York's SoHo, Paris's Bastille, London's Notting Hill—a thriving mix of high and alternative culture distinct from that you'll find in every other part of the city. Dotting the area's narrow cobblestone streets and pedestrian alleyways are new apartment buildings (inside they tend to be small and uninspired, with sky-high rent), vintage-clothing stores, postage-stamp–size boutiques selling €250 sunglasses and other expensive gewgaws, art galleries galore, a hotel resuscitated by U2, hip restaurants, pubs, clubs, European-style cafés, and a smattering of cultural venues. Visit the Temple Bar Web site (www.temple-bar.ie) for information about events in the area.

Temple Bar's regeneration was no doubt abetted by that one surefire real estate asset: location, location, location. The area is bordered by Dame Street to the south, the Liffey to the north, Fishamble Street to the west, and Westmoreland Street to the east. In fact, Temple Bar is so perfectly situated between everywhere else in Dublin that it's difficult to believe this neighborhood was once largely forsaken. It's now sometimes called the "playing ground of young Dublin," and for good reason: on weekend evenings and daily in the summer it teems with young people—not only from Dublin but from all over Europe—who fly into the city for the weekend, drawn by its pubs, clubs, and lively craic. It has become a favorite of young Englishmen on "stag" weekends, 48-hour bachelor parties heavy on drinking and debauching. Some who have witnessed Temple Bar's rapid gentrification and commercialization complain that it's losing its artistic soul—*Harper's Bazaar* said it was in danger of becoming "a sort of pseudoplace," like London's Covent Garden Piazza or Paris's Les Halles. Over the next few years the planned Smithfield development may replace Temple Bar at the cutting edge of Dublin culture, but for the moment there's no denying that this is one of the best places to get a handle on the city.

A Good Walk

Numbers in the text correspond to numbers in the margin and on the Dublin City Center map.

Start at O'Connell Bridge and walk down Aston Quay, taking in the terrific view west down the River Liffey. Alleys and narrow roads to your left lead into Temple Bar, but hold off turning in until you get to **Ha'penny Bridge** ㉖, a Liffey landmark. Turn right and walk through Merchant's Arch, the symbolic entry into Temple Bar (see if you can spot the surveillance cameras up on the walls), which leads you onto the area's long spine, named Temple Bar here but also called Fleet Street (to the east) and Essex Street (both east and west, to the west). You're right at Temple Bar Square, one of the two largest plazas in Temple Bar. Just up on the right are two of the area's leading art galleries, the Temple Bar Gallery (at Lower Fownes Street) and, another block up, the Original Print Gallery and Black Church Print Studios. Turn left onto Eustace Street. If you have children, you may want to go to the **Ark** ㉗, a children's cultural center. Across the street from the Ark, stop in at the Temple Bar Information Centre and pick up a handy *Temple Bar Guide*. Farther down Eustace Street is the **Irish Film Centre** ㉘, Temple Bar's leading cultural venue and a great place to catch classic or new indie films. In summer, the IFC organizes Saturday-night outdoor screenings on **Meeting House Square** ㉙, behind the Ark, accessed via Curved Street. The street is dominated on one side by the **Arthouse** ㉚ and on the other by the Temple Bar Music Centre. Dublin's leading photography gallery, the **Gallery of Photography** ㉛, is also here. Walk a few steps west to the narrow, cobbled Sycamore Street, and then turn right and walk to Dame Street, where you'll find the **Olympia Theatre** ㉜. Farther down Dame Street, the ultramodern **Central Bank** ㉝ rises above the city. Head for the corner of Parliament Street, where you can stop for a break or begin the next walk.

TIMING

You can easily breeze through Temple Bar in an hour or so, but if you've got the time, plan to spend a morning or afternoon here, drifting in and out of the dozens of stores and galleries, relaxing at a café over a cup of coffee or at a pub over a pint, or maybe even watching a film, if you're looking for a change from sightseeing.

Sights to See

㉗ **The Ark.** If you're traveling with children and looking for something fun to do, stop by the Ark, Ireland's children's cultural center, housed in a former Presbyterian church. Its theater opens onto Meeting House Square for outdoor performances in summer. A gallery and workshop space host ongoing activities. ⊠ *Eustace St., Temple Bar,* ☎ *01/670–7788,* WEB *www.ark.ie.* ⊡ *Free.* ⊙ *Weekdays 9:30–5:30, weekends only if there is a show.*

㉚ **Arthouse.** If you're a fan of the art of the digital age, you'll love this place. If not, skip it. Arthouse is one of the first multimedia centers for the arts in the world. Its modern design—glass, metal, and painted concrete—is the work of architect Shay Cleary Doyle, who wanted the building to reflect the object glorified within: the computer. Inside are a training center, a performance venue, a creative studio, and an exhibition space that hosts art exhibitions. Pride of place, however, goes to the Art Information Bureau and the Artifact artist's database, which features the work of more than 1,000 modern Irish artists working in Ireland and abroad. This useful catalog is open to anyone who wants to buy or admire the work of the listed artists. You can search for work according to specific criteria—you press a few buttons and a list of artists and images of their work fitting your description will appear. ⊠ *Curved St., Temple Bar,* ☎ *01/605–6800,* WEB *www.arthouse.ie.* ⊡ *Free.* ⊙ *Weekdays 9–6.*

㉝ **Central Bank.** Everyone in Dublin seems to have an opinion on the Central Bank. Designed by Sam Stephenson in 1978, the controversial, ultramodern glass-and-concrete building suspends huge concrete slabs around a central axis. It was originally one floor taller, but that had to be lopped off as a hazard to low-flying planes. Skateboarders and in-line skaters have taken up residence on the little plaza in front of the building. ⊠ *Dame St., Temple Bar,* ☎ *01/671–6666,* WEB *www. centralbank.ie.* ⊡ *Free.* ⊙ *Weekdays 10–6.*

㉛ **Gallery of Photography.** Dublin's premier photography gallery has a permanent collection of early 20th-century Irish photography and also puts on monthly exhibits of contemporary Irish and international photographers. The gallery is an invaluable social record of Ireland. The bookstore is the best place in town to browse for photography books and pick up arty postcards. ⊠ *Meeting House Sq. S, Temple Bar,* ☎ *01/671–4654,* WEB *www.irish-photography.com.* ⊡ *Free.* ⊙ *Tues.–Sat. 11–6.*

㉖ **Ha'penny Bridge.** Every Dubliner has a story about meeting someone on this cast-iron Victorian bridge, a heavily trafficked footbridge that crosses the Liffey at a prime spot—Temple Bar is on the south side, and the bridge provides the fastest route to the thriving Mary and Henry Street shopping areas to the north. Until early in the 20th century, a half-penny toll was charged to cross it. Yeats was one among many Dubliners who found this too high a price to pay—more a matter of principle than of finance—and so made the detour via O'Connell Bridge. Congestion on the Ha'penny has been relieved with the opening of the Millennium Footbridge a few hundred yards up the river. In a major renovation in 2001 the old bridge was cleaned and returned to its original sparkling white.

㉘ Irish Film Centre (IFC). The opening of the IFC in a former Quaker meetinghouse helped to launch the revitalization of Temple Bar. It has two comfortable art-house cinemas showing revivals and new independent films, the Irish Film Archive, a bookstore for cineastes, and a popular bar and restaurant/café, all of which makes this one of the neighborhood's most vital cultural institutions and *the* place to be seen. ✉ *6 Eustace St., Temple Bar,* ☎ *01/679–5744,* WEB *www.fii.ie.* ✉ *Free.* ⊙ *Weekdays 9:30–late, weekends 11–late.*

NEED A BREAK? | The trendy **Irish Film Centre Café** (✉ 6 Eustace St., Temple Bar, ☎ 01/ 679–5744) is a pleasant place for a lunchtime break. Sandwiches are large and healthful, with plenty of nonmeat choices, and the people-watching is nonpareil.

㉙ Meeting House Square. Behind the Ark and accessed via Curved Street, the square gets its name from a nearby Quaker meetinghouse. Now it's something of a gathering place for Dublin's youth and artists. A variety of summer events—classic movies (every Saturday night), theater, games, and family programs—take place here. (Thankfully, seats are installed.) The Square is also a favorite site for the continuously changing street sculpture that pops up all over Temple Bar (artists commissioned by the city sometimes create oddball pieces, such as a half of a Volkswagon protruding from a wall). But year-round, the Square is a great spot to sit, people-watch, and take in the sounds of the buskers (street musicians) who swarm to the place. There's also an organic food market here every Saturday morning.

★ **㉜ Olympia Theatre.** One of the best places anywhere in Europe to see live musical acts, the Olympia is Dublin's second oldest and one of its busiest theaters. Built in 1879, this classic Victorian music hall has a gorgeous red wrought-iron facade. Conveniently, you'll find two pubs here—through doors directly off the back of the theater's orchestra section. The Olympia's long-standing Friday and Saturday series, "Midnight at the Olympia," has brought a wide array of musical performers to Dublin, and the theater has also seen many notable actors strut on its stage, including Alec Guinness, Peggy Ashcroft, Noël Coward, and even Laurel and Hardy. Big-name performers like Van Morrison often choose the intimate atmosphere of the Olympia over a larger venue. It's really a hot place to see some fine performances, so if you have a chance, by all means go. ✉ *72 Dame St., Temple Bar,* ☎ *01/677–7744.*

NEED A BREAK? | The creamiest, frothiest coffees in all of Temple Bar can be had at the **Joy of Coffee/Image Gallery Café** (✉ 25 E. Essex St., Temple Bar, ☎ 01/679–3393); the wall of windows floods light onto the small gallery with original photographs adorning the walls.

Dublin West: From Dublin Castle to the Four Courts

This section of Dublin takes you from the 10th-century crypt at Christ Church Cathedral—the city's oldest surviving structure—to the modern plant of the Guinness Brewery and its Storehouse museum. It also crosses the Liffey for a visit to Smithfield, the old market area being billed as the next hot location in the city. Dublin is so compact, however, that to separate out the following sites from those covered in the two other city-center southside walks is potentially to mislead—by suggesting that this area is at some remove from the heart of the city center. In fact, this tour's starting point, City Hall, is just across the street from Thomas Read's, and Christ Church Cathedral is a very short walk farther west. The westernmost sites covered here—notably the Royal Hospital and Kilmainham Gaol—*are*, however, at some distance, so if you're not an enthusiastic walker, you may want to drive or catch a cab or a bus out to them.

A Good Walk

Numbers in the text correspond to numbers in the margin and on the Dublin West map.

Begin with a brief visit to **City Hall** ㉞, and then walk up Cork Hill to the Castle Street entrance to **Dublin Castle** ㉟, whose highlights—the grand salons that show off Viceregal Dublin at its most splendid—are only visitable via a guided tour. In the castle you'll also find the **Chester Beatty Library** ㊱, a world-renowned collection of Oriental art and manuscripts. Leave via the same gate, turn left, and walk up Castle Street to the ancient, picturesque **Christ Church Cathedral** ㊲, on one of the city's few hills. At the southeast corner of the cathedral, connected via an utterly beguiling Victorian-era bridge, **Dublinia** ㊳ gives you a chance to experience life in medieval Dublin. Just down Nicholas Street is— begorrah!—**St. Patrick's Cathedral** ㊴. If you're eager to venture back to the 17th century or love old books, visit the quaint **Marsh's Library** ㊵, next door to St. Patrick's. You can then stroll through the old artisan redbrick dwellings in the Liberties, home to the heaviest concentration of the city's antiques stores, to Thomas Street and—just follow your nose—the **Guinness Brewery and Storehouse** ㊶, where you can keep your spirits up in more ways than one. At this point, if you want to see more architecture and modern art, proceed farther west to the Irish Museum of Modern Art in the elegant 18th-century **Royal Hospital Kilmainham** ㊷, and the **Kilmainham Gaol** ㊸. If you don't elect to head this way, turn back down Thomas Street, crossing the Liffey at Bridge Street, which on its north side becomes Church Street. On your left is the **Four Courts** ㊹. A little farther up on the left is **St. Michan's Church** ㊺ and the beginning of the Smithfield area. A quick jog over to Bow Street (via Mary's Lane) brings you to the **Old Jameson Distillery** ㊻—here you'll learn all there is to learn about Irish whiskey. End your walk with a thrilling ride up the glass elevator to the top of **The Chimney** ㊼.

TIMING

Allow yourself a few hours, especially if you want to include the Guinness Brewery and Storehouse and the Irish Museum of Modern Art at the Royal Hospital. Keep in mind that if you want to cover the easternmost sites—Dublin Castle, City Hall, Christ Church Cathedral, and environs—you can easily append them to a tour of Temple Bar.

Sights to See

★ ㊱ **Chester Beatty Library.** After Sir Alfred Chester Beatty (1875–1968), a Canadian mining millionaire, assembled one of the most significant collections of Islamic and Far Eastern art in the Western world, he donated these to Ireland. Housed in the gorgeous clock tower building of **Dublin Castle,** it's one of Dublin's real hidden gems. Among the library's exhibits are clay tablets from Babylon dating from 2700 BC, Japanese color wood-block prints, Chinese jade books, and Turkish and Persian paintings. The second floor, dedicated to the great religions,

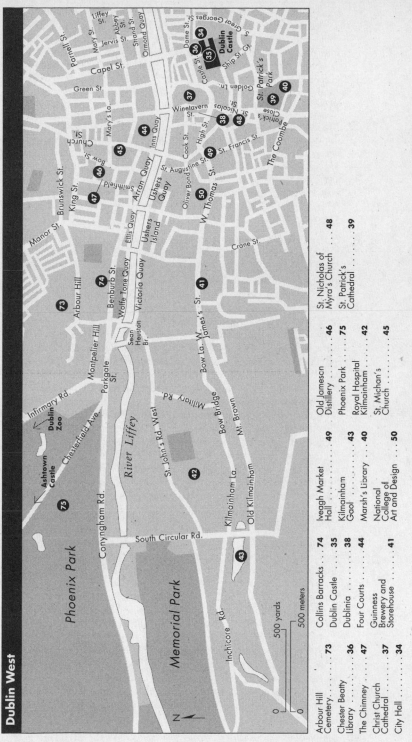

Dublin West

St. Nicholas of
Myra's Church ... **48**
St. Patrick's
Cathedral **39**

Old Jameson
Distillery **46**
Phoenix Park **75**
Royal Hospital
Kilmainham **42**
St. Michan's
Church **45**

Iveagh Market
Hall **49**
Kilmainham
Gaol **43**
Marsh's Library .. **40**
National
College of
Art and Design ... **50**

Collins Barracks ... **74**
Dublin Castle **35**
Dublinia **38**
Four Courts **44**
Guinness
Brewery and
Storehouse **41**

Arbour Hill
Cemetery **73**
Chester Beatty
Library **36**
The Chimney **47**
Christ Church
Cathedral **37**
City Hall **34**

houses 250 manuscripts of the Koran from across the Muslim world, as well as one of the earliest gospels. Life size Buddhas from Burma and rhino cups from China are among the other curios on show. Guided tours of the library are available on Tuesday and Saturday at 2:30 PM. On sunny days you'll find the garden is one of the most tranquil places in central Dublin. ⊠ *Castle St., Dublin West,* ☎ *01/407–0750,* WEB *www. cbl.ie.* 🎫 *Free.* ⊙ *May–Oct., Mon.–Fri. 10–5, Sat. 11–5, Sun. 1–5; Nov.–Apr. Tues.–Fri. 10–5, Sat. 11–5, Sun. 1–5.*

🐾 **㊼** **The Chimney.** Just in front of the Chief O'Neill hotel you'll see one of the original brick chimneys of the Old Jameson Distillery, which has been turned into into a 185-ft observation tower with the first 360-degree view of Dublin. Built in 1895, the redbrick chimney now has a two-tiered, glass-enclosed platform at the top. The ride up in the glass elevator is just as thrilling as the view. ⊠ *Smithfield Village, Dublin West,* ☎ *01/817–3820,* WEB *www.chiefoneills.com.* 🎫 €6.35. ⊙ *Mon.–Sat. 10–5:30, Sun. 11–5:30.*

★ **㊲** **Christ Church Cathedral.** You'd never know from the outside that the first Christianized Danish king built a wooden church at this site in 1038; thanks to the extensive 19th-century renovation of its stonework and trim, the cathedral looks more Victorian than Anglo-Norman. Construction on the present Christ Church—the flagship of the Church of Ireland and one of two Protestant cathedrals in Dublin (the other is St. Patrick's just to the south)—was begun in 1172 by Strongbow, a Norman baron and conqueror of Dublin for the English crown, and went on for 50 years. By 1875 the cathedral had deteriorated badly; a major renovation gave it much of the look it has today, including the addition of one of Dublin's most charming structures: a Bridge of Sighs–like affair that connects the cathedral to the old Synod Hall, which now holds the Viking extravaganza, Dublinia. Remains from the 12th-century building include the north wall of the nave, the west bay of the choir, and the fine stonework of the transepts, with their pointed arches and supporting columns. Strongbow himself is buried in the cathedral beneath an impressive effigy. The vast, sturdy **crypt,** with its 12th- and 13th-century vaults, is Dublin's oldest surviving structure and the building's most notable feature. At 6 PM on Wednesday and Thursday you can enjoy the glories of a choral evensong. ⊠ *Christ Church Pl. and Winetavern St., Dublin West,* ☎ *01/677–8099,* WEB *www. cccdub.ie.* 🎫 €2.55. ⊙ *Daily 9:45–5.*

㉞ **City Hall.** Facing the Liffey from Cork Hill at the top of Parliament Street, this grand Georgian municipal building (1769–79), once the Royal Exchange, marks the southwestern corner of Temple Bar. Today it's the seat of the Dublin Corporation, the elected body that governs the city. Thomas Cooley designed the building with 12 columns that encircle the domed central rotunda, which has a fine mosaic floor and 12 frescoes depicting Dublin legends and ancient Irish historical scenes. The 20-ft-high sculpture to the right is the "Liberator" Daniel O'Connell. He looks like he's about to begin the famous speech he gave here in 1800. The building houses a multimedia exhibition—with artifacts, kiosks, graphics, and A/V presentations—tracing the evolution of Ireland's 1,000-year-old capital. ⊠ *Dame St., Dublin West,* ☎ *01/672–2204,* WEB *www.dublincity.ie/cityhall/home.htm.* 🎫 €3.80. ⊙ *Mon.–Sat 10–5:15, Sun. 2–5.*

㉟ **Dublin Castle.** Neil Jordan's film *Michael Collins* captured Dublin Castle's near indomitable status well: seat and symbol of the British rule of Ireland for 7½ centuries, the castle figured largely in Ireland's turbulent history early in the 20th century. It's now, however, mainly used for Irish and EU governmental purposes. The sprawling **Great Court-**

yard is the reputed site of the Black Pool (Dubh Linn, pronounced *dove-lin*) from which Dublin got its name. In the Lower Castle Yard, the **Record Tower,** the earliest of several towers on the site, is the largest remaining relic of the original Norman buildings, built by King John between 1208 and 1220. The clock tower building now houses the **Chester Beatty Library.** Guided tours are available around the principal **State Apartments** (on the southern side of the Upper Castle Yard), formerly the residence of the English viceroys. Now used by the president of Ireland to host visiting heads of state and EU ministers, the State Apartments are lavishly furnished with rich Donegal carpets and illuminated by Waterford glass chandeliers. The largest and most impressive of these chambers, **St. Patrick's Hall,** with its gilt pillars and painted ceiling, is used for the inauguration of Irish presidents. The **Round Drawing Room,** in Bermingham Tower, dates from 1411 and was rebuilt in 1777; a number of Irish leaders were imprisoned in the tower, from the 16th century to the early 20th century. The blue oval **Wedgwood Room** contains Chippendale chairs and a marble fireplace. The **Castle Vaults** now holds an elegant little patisserie and bistro.

Carved oak panels and stained glass depicting viceroys' coats of arms grace the interior of the **Church of the Holy Trinity** (formerly called Chapel Royal), on the castle grounds. The church was designed in 1814 by Francis Johnston, who also designed the original General Post Office building on O'Connell Street. Once you're inside, look up—you'll see an elaborate array of fan vaults on the ceiling. Make sure you also see the more than 100 carved heads that adorn the walls outside. St. Peter and Jonathan Swift preside over the north door, St. Patrick and Brian Boru over the east. One-hour guided tours of the castle are available every half hour, but the rooms are closed when in official use, so phone first. The church is on the castle grounds; the easiest way into the castle is through the **Cork Hill Gate,** just west of City Hall. ⊠ *Castle St., Dublin West,* ☎ *01/677–7129,* WEB *www.dublincastle.ie.* 🎫 *State Apartments €4, including tour.* ⊘ *Weekdays 10–5, weekends 2–5.*

🖑 ❸ **Dublinia.** Dublin's Medieval Trust has set up an entertaining and informative reconstruction of everyday life in medieval Dublin. The main exhibits use high-tech audiovisual and computer displays; there's also a scale model of what Dublin was like around 1500, a medieval maze, a life-size reconstruction based on the 13th-century dockside at Wood Quay, and a fine view from the tower. For a more modern take on the city, check out the James Malton series of prints of 18th-century Dublin, hanging on the walls of the coffee shop. Dublinia is in the old Synod Hall (formerly a meeting place for bishops of the Church of Ireland), attached via a covered stonework Victorian bridge to Christ Church Cathedral. ⊠ *St. Michael's Hill, Dublin West,* ☎ *01/679–4611,* WEB *www.dublinia.ie.* 🎫 *Exhibit €5.* ⊘ *Apr.–Sept., daily 10–5; Oct.–Mar., Mon.–Sat. 11–4, Sun. 10–4:30.*

❹ **Four Courts.** The stately Corinthian portico and the circular central hall warrant a visit here, to the seat of the High Court of Justice of Ireland. The distinctive copper-covered dome on a colonnaded rotunda makes this one of Dublin's most instantly recognizable buildings; the view from the rotunda is terrific. Built between 1786 and 1802, the Four Courts are James Gandon's second Dublin masterpiece—close on the heels of his **Custom House,** downstream on the same side of the River Liffey. In 1922, during the Irish Civil War, the Four Courts was almost totally destroyed by shelling—the adjoining Public Records Office was gutted, and many priceless legal documents, including innumerable family records, destroyed. Restorations took 10 years. There is no tour of the building, but you are welcome to sit in while the courts are in ses-

sion. ⊠ *Inns Quay, Dublin West,* ☎ *01/872–5555,* WEB *www.courts.ie.* ⊙ *Daily 10–1 and 2:15–4.*

★ ㊶ **Guinness Brewery and Storehouse.** Founded by Arthur Guinness in 1759, Ireland's all-dominating brewer—at one time the largest stout-producing brewery in the world—spans a 60-acre spread west of Christ Church Cathedral. Not surprisingly, it's the most popular tourist destination in town—after all, the Irish national drink is Guinness stout, a dark brew made with roasted malt. The brewery itself is closed to the public, but the **Guinness Storehouse** is a spectacular attraction, designed to woo you with the wonders of the "dark stuff." Located in a 1904, cast-iron–and–brick warehouse, the museum display covers six floors built around a huge central glass atrium. Beneath the glass floor of the lobby you'll see Arthur Guinness's original lease on the site, for a whopping 9,000 years. The exhibition elucidates the brewing process and its history, with antique presses and vats, a look at bottle and can design through the ages, a history of the Guinness family, and a fascinating archive of Guinness advertisements. You might think it's all a bit much (it's only a drink, after all), and parts of the exhibit do feel a little over-the-top. The star attraction is undoubtedly the top-floor **Gravity Bar,** with 360-degree floor-to-ceiling glass walls that offer a nonpareil view out over the city at sunset while you sip your free pint. One of the bar's first clients was one William Jefferson Clinton. ⊠ *St. James' Gate, Dublin West,* ☎ *01/408–4800,* WEB *www. guinness.com.* ⊡ *€12.* ⊙ *Daily 9:30–5.*

㊸ **Kilmainham Gaol.** Leaders of the 1916 Easter Uprising, including Pádrig Pearse and James Connolly, were held in this grim, forbidding structure before being executed in the prison yard. Other famous inmates included the revolutionary Robert Emmet and Charles Stewart Parnell, a leading politician. You can visit the cells, a chilling sight, while the guided tour and a 30-minute audiovisual presentation relate a graphic account of Ireland's political history over the past 200 years—from a Nationalist viewpoint. You can only visit the prison as part of a guided tour, which leaves every hour on the hour. You'll find a small tearoom on the premises. ⊠ *Inchicore Rd., Dublin West,* ☎ *01/453–5984,* WEB *www.heritageireland.ie.* ⊡ *€4.40.* ⊙ *Mon.–Sat. 9:30–5, Sun. 10–5.*

㊵ **Marsh's Library.** When Ireland's first public library was founded and endowed in 1701 by Narcissus Marsh, the Archbishop of Dublin, it was open to "All Graduates and Gentlemen." The two-story brick Georgian building has been practically unchanged inside since then. It houses a priceless collection of 250 manuscripts and 25,000 15th- to 18th-century books. Many of these rare volumes are locked inside cages, as are the readers who wish to peruse them. The cages were to discourage students who, often impecunious, may have been tempted to make the books their own. The library has been restored with great attention to its original architectural details, especially in the book stacks. The library is a short walk west from St. Stephen's Green and accessed through a charming little cottage garden. ⊠ *St. Patrick's Close off Patrick St., Dublin West,* ☎ *01/454–3511,* WEB *www.kst.dit.ie/marsh.* ⊡ *€2.50.* ⊙ *Mon. and Wed.–Fri. 10–12:45 and 2–5, Sat. 10:30–12:45.*

㊻ **Old Jameson Distillery.** Founded in 1791, this distillery produced one of Ireland's most famous whiskeys for nearly 200 years, until 1966 (at that point, local distilleries merged to form Irish Distillers and moved to a purpose-built, ultramodern distillery in Middleton, County Cork). Part of the complex was converted into the group's head office, and the distillery itself became a museum. There's a short audiovisual history of the industry, which had its origins 1,500 years ago in Middle Eastern perfume making. You can also tour the old distillery, and learn about the distilling of whiskey from grain to bottle, or view a reconstruction of a former warehouse, where the colorful nicknames of former barrel makers are recorded. There's a 20-minute audiovisual show about the making of whiskey at Jameson's distillery, a 40-minute tour, and a complimentary tasting (remember: Irish whiskey is best drunk without a mixer—try it straight or with water); four attendees are invited to taste different brands of Irish whiskey and compare them against bourbon and Scotch. If you have a large group and everyone wants to do this, phone in advance to arrange it. ⊠ *Bow St., Dublin West,* ☎ *01/807–2355,* WEB *www.irish-whiskey-trail.com.* ⊠ *€6.50.* ☉ *Daily 9–5:30; tours every ½ hr.*

★ ㊷ **Royal Hospital Kilmainham.** This replica of Les Invalides in Paris is regarded as the most important 17th-century building in Ireland. Commissioned as a hospice for disabled and veteran soldiers by James Butler—the Duke of Ormonde and Viceroy to King Charles II—the building was completed in 1684, making it the first building built in Dublin's golden age. It survived into the 1920s as a hospital, but after the founding of the Irish Free State in 1922, the building fell into disrepair. Over the last 15 years or so, the entire edifice has been restored to what it once was.

The structure's four galleries are arranged around a courtyard; there's also a grand dining hall—100 ft long by 50 ft wide. The architectural highlight is the hospital's Baroque **chapel,** distinguished by its extraordinary plasterwork ceiling and fine wood carvings. "There is nothing in Ireland from the 17th century that can come near this masterpiece," raved cultural historian John FitzMaurice Mills. The Royal Hospital also houses the **Irish Museum of Modern Art.** The museum displays works by non-Irish, 20th-century greats, including Picasso and Miró, and regularly hosts touring shows from major European museums. They do concentrate, however, on the work of Irish artists: Richard Deacon, Richard Gorman, Dorothy Cross, Sean Scully, Matt Mullican, Louis Le Brocquy, and James Colman are among the contemporary artists represented. The Café Musée has soups, sandwiches, etc. The hospital is a short ride by taxi or bus from the city center. ⊠ *Kilmainham La., Dublin West,* ☎ *01/612–9900,* WEB *www.modernart.ie.* ⊠ *Royal Hospital free; individual shows may have separate charges; Museum of Modern Art permanent collection free, small charge for special exhibitions.* ☉ *Royal Hospital Tues.–Sat. 10–5:30, Sun. noon–5:30, tours every ½ hr; Museum of Modern Art Tues.–Sat. 10–5:30, Sun. noon–5:30; tours Wed. and Fri. at 2:30, Sat. at 11:30.*

㊺ **St. Michan's Church.** However macabre, St. Michan's main claim to fame is down in the vaults, where the totally dry atmosphere has preserved a number of corpses in a remarkable state of mummification. They lie in open caskets. Most of the preserved bodies are thought to have been Dublin tradespeople (one was, they say, a religious crusader). Except for its 120-ft-high bell tower, this Anglican church is architecturally undistinguished. The church was built in 1685 on the site of an 11th-century Danish church (Michan was a cannonized Danish saint). Another reason to come is to see the 18th-century organ, which Handel supposedly played for his first performance of the *Messiah.* Don't forget to check out the Stool of Repentance—the only one still in existence in the city. Parishioners judged to be "open and notoriously naughty livers" used it to do public penance. ⊠ *Lower Church St., Dublin West,* ☎ *01/872–4154.* ⊠ *€2.55.* ☉ *Apr.–Oct., weekdays 10– 12:45 and 2–4:45, Sat. 10–12:45, Sun. service at 10* AM*; Nov.–Mar., weekdays 12:30–3:30, Sat. 10–12:45, Sun. service at 10* AM.

㊴ **St. Patrick's Cathedral.** The largest cathedral in Dublin and also the national cathedral of the Church of Ireland, St. Patrick's is the second of the capital's two Protestant cathedrals. (The other is Christ Church, and the reason Dublin has two cathedrals is because St. Patrick's originally stood outside the walls of Dublin, while its close neighbor was within the walls and belonged to the see of Dublin.) Legend has it that in the 5th century St. Patrick baptized many converts at a well on the site of the cathedral. The original building, dedicated in 1192 and early English Gothic in style, was an unsuccessful attempt to assert supremacy over Christ Church Cathedral. At 305 ft, it's the longest church in the country, a fact Oliver Cromwell's troops—no friends to the Irish—found useful as they made the church's nave into their stable, in the 17th century. They left the building in a terrible state; its current condition is largely due to the benevolence of Sir Benjamin Guinness—of the brewing family—who started financing major restoration work in 1860.

Make sure you see the gloriously heraldic **Choir of St. Patrick's,** hung with colorful medieval banners, and find the tomb of the most famous of St. Patrick's many illustrious deans, Jonathan Swift, immortal author of *Gulliver's Travels,* who held office from 1713 to 1745. **Swift's tomb** is in the south aisle, not far from that of his beloved "Stella," Mrs. Esther Johnson. Swift's epitaph is inscribed over the robing-room door. Yeats—who translated it thus: "Swift has sailed into his rest; Savage indignation there cannot lacerate his breast"—declared it the greatest epitaph of all time. Other memorials include the 17th-century **Boyle Monument,** with its numerous painted figures of family members, and the **monument to Turlough O'Carolan,** the last of the Irish bards and one of the country's finest harp players. Immediately north of the cathedral is a small park, with statues of many of Dublin's literary figures and **St. Patrick's Well.** "Living Stones" is the cathedral's permanent exhibition celebrating St. Patrick's place in the life of the city. If you're a music lover, you're in for a treat; matins (9:45 AM) and evensong (5:35 PM) are still sung on most days. ⊠ *Patrick St., Dublin West,* ☎ *01/453–9472,* ⌨ *www.stpatrickscathedral.ie.* ⊠ *€3.45.* ☼ *May and Sept.–Oct., weekdays 9–6, Sat. 9–5, Sun. 10–11 and 12:45– 3; June–Aug., weekdays 9–6, Sat. 9–4, Sun. 9:30–3 and 4:15–5:15; Nov.– Apr., weekdays 9–6, Sat. 9–4, Sun. 10–11 and 12:45–3.*

The Liberties

A stroll through the Liberties puts you in square working-class Dublin, past and present, good and bad. The name derives from Dublin of the Middle Ages, when the area south and west of Christ Church Cathedral was outside the city walls and free from the jurisdiction of the city rulers. A certain amount of freedom, or "liberty," was enjoyed by those who settled here, which attracted people on the fringes of society, especially the poor.

A Good Walk

Numbers in the text correspond to numbers in the margin and on the Dublin West map.

Start on Patrick Street, in the shadow of St. Patrick's Cathedral. Look down the street toward the Liffey and take in the glorious view of Christ Church. Go right on Dean Street, where you'll find John Fallons pub. Take a right off Dean Street onto Francis Street and walk uphill. A number of quality antiques shops line both sides of the thoroughfare. Halfway up Francis Street, on the right, behind hefty wrought-iron gates, you'll discover one of Dublin's most-overlooked treasures: **St. Nicholas of Myra's Church** ㊽. Continue up Francis Street and take the next right onto Thomas Davis Street (named after a famous patriot and revolutionary—the Liberties has long had a close association with Irish Nationalism). The street is full of classic, two-story redbrick houses. The area, once the heart of "Darlin' Dublin" and the holy source of its distinctive accent, is rapidly becoming yuppified. Back on Francis Street, in an old factory building with its chimney stack intact, you'll find an exciting market, **Iveagh Market Hall** ㊾. At the top of Francis Street turn left onto Thomas Street. Across the road, on your right side, stands the wonderfully detailed exterior of St. Augustine and St. John, with its grandiose spire stretching above it. You'll notice churches all over the Liberties; the bishops thought it wise to build holy palaces in the poorest areas of the city as tall, shining beacons of comfort and hope. Farther up Thomas Street in another converted factory is the **National College of Art and Design** ㊿.

TIMING

Unless you intend on doing some serious antiques shopping, this is a relatively quick stroll—perhaps two hours—as the Liberties is a compact area of small, winding streets.

Sights to See

㊾ **Iveagh Market Hall.** One of numerous buildings bestowed upon the city of Dublin by Lord Iveagh of the Guinness family, the cavernous, Victorian, redbrick-and-granite Iveagh Market Hall holds an eclectic market—with books, vintage clothes, records, and jewelry—from Tuesday to Saturday. ⊠ *Francis St., Dublin West.* ▭ *Free.* ⊘ *Tues.– Sat. 9–5.*

㊿ **National College of Art and Design.** The delicate welding of glass and iron onto the redbrick Victorian facade of this onetime factory makes this school worth a visit. Walk around the cobblestone central courtyard, where there's always the added bonus of viewing some of the students working away in glass, clay, metal, and stone. ⊠ *Thomas St., Dublin West,* ☎ *01/671–1377,* WEB *www.ncad.ie.* ▭ *Free.* ⊘ *Weekdays 9–7.*

㊽ **St. Nicholas of Myra's Church.** A grand Neoclassical style characterizes this church, completed in 1834. The highly ornate chapel inside includes ceiling panels of the 12 apostles, and a pietà raised 20 ft above the marble altar, guarded on each side by angels sculpted by John Hogan while he was in Florence. The tiny nuptial chapel to the right has a small Harry Clarke stained-glass window. ⊠ *St. Nicholas St., Dublin West.* ▭ *Free.* ⊘ *Hrs vary.*

North of the Liffey

If you stand on O'Connell Bridge or the pedestrian-only Ha'penny span, you'll get excellent views up and down the Liffey, in Gaelic known as the *abha na life,* which James Joyce transcribed phonetically as Anna Livia in *Finnegan's Wake.* Here, framed with embankments just like those along Paris's Seine, the river nears the end of its 128-km (80-mi) journey from the Wicklow Mountains into the Irish Sea. And near the the bridges, you begin a pilgrimage into James Joyce Country—north of the Liffey, in the center of town—and the captivating sights of Dublin's northside, a mix of densely thronged shopping streets and recently refurbished genteel homes.

The northside *absolutely* warrants a walk, for three reasons: major cultural institutions (the Gate Theatre, the James Joyce Cultural Centre, the Dublin Writers Museum, and the Hugh Lane Municipal Gallery of Modern Art), sites of historical significance with ties to Irish Republicanism, and vibrant, busy streets.

During the 18th century, most of the upper echelons of Dublin society lived in the Georgian houses in the northside—around Mountjoy Square—and shopped along Capel Street, which was lined with stores selling fine furniture and silver. But southside development—Merrion Square in 1764, the Georgian Leinster House in 1745, and Fitzwilliam Square in 1825—permanently changed the northside's fortunes. The city's fashionable social center crossed the Liffey, and although some of the northside's illustrious inhabitants stuck it out, this area gradually became more run-down. The northside's fortunes have changed, however. Once-derelict swaths of houses, especially on and near the Liffey, have been rehabilitated, and large new shopping centers have opened on Mary and Jervis streets. A huge shopping mall and entertainment complex are planned for O'Connell Street, right where the defunct Cartlon Cinema stands. Precisely because the exciting redevelopment that transformed Temple Bar is still in its early stages here—*because* it's a place on the cusp of transition—the northside is an intriguing part of town to visit.

A Good Walk
Numbers in the text correspond to numbers in the margin and on the Dublin City Center map.

Begin at O'Connell Bridge—if you look closely at it you will notice that it is wider than it is long—and head north up **O'Connell Street** ㉜. Stop to admire the monument to Daniel O'Connell, "The Liberator," erected as a tribute to the great orator's achievement in securing Catholic Emancipation in 1829 (note the obvious scars from the fighting of 1916 on the figures). A quick trip down middle Abbey Street takes you to the brand-new **Hot Press Irish Music Hall of Fame** �, a museum dedicated to Irish pop music. Then continue north to the **General Post Office** ㉝, a major site in the Easter Uprising of 1916. O'Connell leads to the southeastern corner of Parnell Square. Heading counterclockwise around the square, you'll pass in turn the **Gate Theatre** ㉞ and **Abbey Presbyterian Church** ㉟ before coming to the **Dublin Writers Museum** ㊱ and the **Hugh Lane Municipal Gallery of Modern Art** ㊲, both on the north side of the square and both housed in glorious neoclassic mansions; these are the two sites where you should plan to spend most of your time on the northside. Either before you go in or after you come out, you might also want to visit the solemn yet serene **Garden of Remembrance** ㊳.

From here, you have two choices: to continue exploring the cultural sights that lie to the northeast of Parnell Square and east of O'Connell Street or to head to Moore, Henry, and Mary streets for a flavor of middle-class Dublin that you won't get on the spiffier southside. If you decide to continue your cultural explorations, jump two blocks northeast of Parnell Square to the **James Joyce Cultural Centre** ㊴, and then head farther northeast to the once glamorous **Mountjoy Square** ㊵. Half a mile east of Mountjoy Square is Croke Park, gaelic football stadium and home to the Gaelic Athletic Association's **GAA Museum** ㊷. Return to Mountjoy Square and turn south, stopping in at the **St. Francis Xavier Church** ㊶ on Gardiner Street. Head back west to Marlborough Street (parallel to and between Gardiner and O'Connell streets) to visit the **Pro-Cathedral** ㊽. Continue down to the quays and jog a block east to the **Custom House** ㊾. If you decide to shop with the locals, leave Parnell Square via the southwestern corner, stopping first to check out the chapel at the **Rotunda Hospital** ㊿; Moore Street is your first left off Parnell Street and leads directly to Henry Street.

TIMING

The northside has fewer major attractions than the southside and, over-all, is less picturesque. As a result, you're unlikely to want to stroll as leisurely here. If you zipped right through this walk, you could be done in less than two hours. But the two major cultural institutions—the Dublin Writers Museum and the Hugh Lane Municipal Gallery of Mod-ern Art—easily deserve several hours each, so it's worth doing this walk only if you have the time to devote to them. Also, a number of addi-tional sights connected with James Joyce and *Ulysses*—covered in "ReJoyce! A Walk through James Joyce's Dublin and *Ulysses*"—are in the vicinity, so if you're a devoted Joycean, consult the Close-Up box before setting out on this walk.

Sights to See

⑤⑤ Abbey Presbyterian Church. A soaring spire marks the exterior of this church, popularly known as Findlater's Church—after Alex Findlater, a noted Dublin grocer who endowed it. Completed in 1864, the church stands on the northeast corner of Parnell Square; the inside has a stark Presbyterian mood, despite stained-glass windows and ornate pews. For a bird's-eye view, take the small staircase that leads to the balcony. ⊠ *Parnell Sq., North of the Liffey,* ☎ *01/837–8600.* ☞ *Free.* ☉ *Hrs vary.*

⑥④ Custom House. Seen at its best reflected in the waters of the Liffey dur-ing the short interval when the high tide is on the turn, the Custom House is the city's most spectacular Georgian building. Extending 375 ft on the north side of the river, this is the work of James Gandon, an English architect who arrived in Ireland in 1781, when construction commenced (it continued for 10 years). Crafted from gleaming Port-land stone, the central portico is linked by arcades to the pavilions at either end. Unfortunately, the dome is on the puny side and out of pro-portion. A statue of Commerce tops the copper dome; statues on the main facade are based on allegorical themes. Note the exquisitely carved lions and unicorns supporting the arms of Ireland at the far ends of the facade. Republicans set the building on fire in 1921, but it was completely restored and now houses government offices. The build-ing opened to the public in mid-1997 after having been closed for many years, and with it came a new visitor center tracing the building's his-tory and significance, and the life of Gandon. ⊠ *Custom House Quay, North of the Liffey,* ☎ *01/878–7660.* ☞ *€1.27.* ☉ *Mid-Mar.–Oct., weekdays 10–5:30, weekends 2–5:30; Nov.–Feb., Wed.–Fri. 10–5, Sun. 2–5:30.*

★ **⑤⑥ Dublin Writers Museum.** "If you would know Ireland—body and soul—you must read its poems and stories," wrote Yeats in 1891. Further investigation into the Irish way with words can be found here at this unique museum, in a magnificently restored 18th-century town house on the north side of Parnell Square. Once the home of John Jameson (of the Irish whiskey family), the mansion centers on an enormous draw-ing room, gorgeously decorated with paintings, Adamesque plaster-work, and a deep Edwardian lincrusta frieze. Rare manuscripts, diaries, posters, letters, limited and first editions, photographs, and other me-mentoes commemorate the life and works of the nation's greatest writ-ers (and there are *many* of them, so leave plenty of time), including Joyce, Shaw, J. M. Synge, Lady Gregory, Yeats, Beckett, and many others. On display are an 1804 edition of Swift's *Gulliver's Travels,* an 1899 first edition of Bram Stoker's *Dracula,* and an 1899 edition of Wilde's *Ballad of Reading Gaol.* There's even a special "Teller of Tales" ex-hibit showcasing Behan, O'Flaherty, and O'Faolan. Readings are pe-riodically held. The bookshop and café make this an ideal place to spend a rainy afternoon. If you lose track of time and stay until the closing hour, you might want to dine at Chapter One, a highly regarded restaurant in the basement, which would have had Joyce ecstasizing about its currant-sprinkled scones. ✉ *18 Parnell Sq. N, North of the Liffey*, ☎ *01/872-2077*, WEB *www.visitdublin.com.* ⬚ *€5.50.* ⊘ *June–Aug., Mon.–Fri. 10–6, Sat. 10–5, Sun. 11–5; Sept.–May, Mon.–Sat. 10–5, Sun. 11–5.*

62 **GAA Museum.** In the bowels of Croke Park, the main stadium and headquarters of the GAA (Gaelic Athletics Association), this museum gives you a great introduction to native Irish sport. The four Gaelic games (football, hurling, camogie, and handball) are explained in detail, and if you're brave enough you can have a go yourself. High-tech displays take you through the history and highlights of the games. *National Awakening* is a really smart, interesting short film reflecting the key impact of the GAA on the emergence of the Irish Nation and the forging of a new Irish identity. The exhilarating *A Day in September* captures the thrill and passion of All Ireland finals day—the annual denouement of the inter-county hurling and Gaelic football—every bit as important to the locals as the Superbowl is in the US. ✉ *New Stand, Croke Park, North County Dublin*, ☎ *01/855–8176,* WEB *www.gaa.ie;* ⬚ *€5.00;* ⊘ *May–Sept., daily 9:30–5; Oct.–Apr., Tues.–Sat. 10–5, Sun. noon–5*

58 **Garden of Remembrance.** Opened in 1966, 50 years after the Easter Uprising of 1916, the garden in Parnell Square commemorates those who died fighting for Ireland's freedom. At the garden's entrance you'll find a large plaza; steps lead down to the fountain area, graced with a sculpture by contemporary Irish artist Oisín Kelly, based on the mythological Children of Lír, who were turned into swans. The garden serves as an oasis of tranquillity in the middle of the busy city. ✉ *Parnell Sq., North of the Liffey.* ⊘ *Daily 9–5.*

54 **Gate Theatre.** The Gate has been one of Dublin's most important theaters since its founding in 1929 by Micháel MacLiammóir and Hilton Edwards (who also founded Galway City's An Taibhdhearc as the national Irish-language theater). The theatre stages many innovative productions by Irish playwrights, as well as by foreign playwrights—and plenty of foreign actors have performed here, including Orson Welles (his first paid performance) and James Mason (early in his career). Shows here begin as soon as you walk into the auditorium—a Georgian masterwork designed by Richard Johnston in 1784 as an assembly room for the Rotunda Hospital complex. Today the theater plays it safe with a major repertory of European and North American drama and new plays by established Irish writers. ✉ *Cavendish Row, North of the Liffey,* ☎ *01/874-4045.* ⊘ *Shows Mon.–Sat.*

53 **General Post Office.** Known as the GPO, it is one of the great civic buildings of Dublin's Georgian era, but it's famous because of the role it played in the Easter Uprising. It has an impressive facade in the neoclassical style, and was designed by Francis Johnston and built by the British between 1814 and 1818 as a center of communications. This gave it great strategic importance—and was one of the reasons why it was chosen by the insurgent forces in 1916 as a headquarters. Here, on Easter Monday, 1916, the Republican forces, about 2,000 in number and under the guidance of Pádrig Pearse and James Connolly, stormed the building and issued the Proclamation of the Irish Republic. After a week of shelling, the GPO lay in ruins; 13 rebels were ultimately executed (including Connolly, who was dying of gangrene from a leg shattered in the fighting and had to be propped up in a chair before the firing squad). Most of the original building was destroyed, though the facade survived (you can still see the scars of bullets on its pillars). Rebuilt and subsequently reopened in 1929, it became a working post office—with an attractive two-story main concourse. A bronze sculpture depicting the dying Cuchulainn, a leader of the Red Branch Knights in Celtic mythology, sits in the front window. The 1916 Proclamation and the names of its signatories are inscribed on the green marble plinth. ⊠ *O'Connell St., North of the Liffey*, ☎ *01/872–8888*, WEB *www.anpost.ie*. ☎ *Free.* ☉ *Mon.–Sat. 8–8, Sun. 10:30–6.*

51 Hot Press Irish Music Hall of Fame. A few years ago Ireland's flagship music magazine had the clever idea of opening a museum dedicated to Irish rock and pop music. Ireland has had a large impact on the world music scene, and the Hall of Fame is like a garage sale for the greats of Irish pop music: Van Morrison's big hat, Bob Geldof's cheap guitar, Sinéad O'Connor's self-mutilated jeans, the Corrs' infinitesimally small dresses, and, of course, Bono's superfly Zooropa shoes—all neatly piled in chronological order. The self-guided audio tour takes you through the highs and lows of this musical journey, from the Beat bands of the '60s; '70s punk bands with rockin' names like Stiff Little Fingers; the 1980s, when U2 was the world's most popular band; through to the boy bands and diva-driven (Sinéad, Andrea Corr, Delores O'Riordian of the Cranberries) '90s scene. Favorite items include Sinéad O'Connor's first royalty check from Island records for £13.66. It's uncashed. ⊠ *57 Middle Abbey St., North of the Liffey*, ☎ *01/878–3345*, WEB *www.imhf.com*. ☎ *€5.70.* ☉ *Apr.–Sept., daily 10–6; Oct.–Mar., daily 11–5.*

★ **57 Hugh Lane Municipal Gallery of Modern Art.** Built originally as a town house for the Earl of Charlemont in 1762, this residence was so grand its Parnell Square street was nicknamed "Palace Row" in its honor. Designed by Sir William Chambers (who also built the Marino Casino for Charlemont) in the best Palladian manner, its delicate and rigidly correct facade, extended by two demilune arcades, was fashioned from the "new" white Ardmulcan stone (now seasoned to gray). Charlemont was one of the cultural locomotives of 18th-century Dublin—his walls were hung with Titians and Hogarths, and he frequently dined with Oliver Goldsmith and Sir Joshua Reynolds—so he would undoubtedly be delighted that his home is now the Hugh Lane Gallery, named after a nephew of Lady Gregory (Yeats's aristocratic patron). Lane collected both Impressionist paintings and 19th-century Irish and Anglo-Irish works. A complicated agreement with the National Gallery in London (reached after heated diplomatic dispute) stipulates that a portion of the 39 French paintings amassed by Lane shuttle back and forth between London and here. You can see Pissarro's *Printemps*, Manet's *Eva Gonzales*, Morisot's *Jour d'Été*, and, the jewel of the collection, Renoir's *Les Parapluies*.

In something of a snub to the British art establishment, the late Francis Bacon's partner donated the entire contents of the artist's studio to the Hugh Lane Gallery. The studio of Britain's arguably premier 20th-century artist has been reconstructed in all its gaudy glory in Dublin. It gives you, however, a unique opportunity: to observe the working methods of the artist responsible for such masterpieces as *Study After Velázquez 1950* and the tragic splash-and-crash *Triptych*. The reconstructed studio will remain on permanent display, along with Bacon's diary (that should be worth a read), books, and anything else they picked up off his floor.

Between the collection of Irish paintings in the **National Gallery of Ireland** and the superlative works on view here, you can quickly become familiar with Irish 20th-century art. Irish artists represented include

Roderic O'Conor, well known for his views of the West of Ireland; William Leech, including his *Girl with a Tinsel Scarf* (ca. 1912) and *The Cigarette*; and the most famous of the group, Jack B. Yeats (W. B.'s brother). The museum has a dozen of his paintings, including *Ball Alley* (ca. 1927) and *There Is No Night* (1949). There is also strikingly displayed stained-glass work by early 20th-century Irish master artisans Harry Clarke and Evie Hone. ✉ *Parnell Sq. N, North of the Liffey,* ☎ *01/874–1903,* WEB *www.hughlane.ie.* 🎫 *Free (Bacon Studio €7.50).* ☉ *Tues.–Thurs. 9:30–6, Fri.–Sat. 9:30–5, Sun. 11–5.*

59 **James Joyce Cultural Centre.** Everyone in Ireland has at least *heard* of James Joyce—especially since a copy of his censored and suppressed *Ulysses* was one of the top status symbols of the early 20th century. Joyce is of course now acknowledged as one of the greatest modern authors, and his *Dubliners, Finnegan's Wake,* and *A Portrait of the Artist as a Young Man* can even be read as quirky "travel guides" to Dublin. Open to the general public, this restored 18th-century Georgian town house, once the dancing academy of Professor Denis J. Maginni (which many will recognize from *Ulysses*), is a center for Joycean studies and events related to the author. It has an extensive library and archives, exhibition rooms, a bookstore, and a café. The collection includes letters from Beckett, Joyce's guitar and cane, and a celebrated edition of *Ulysses* illustrated by Matisse. Along with housing the **Joyce Museum** in Sandycove, the center is the main organizer of "Bloomstime," which marks the week leading up to June 16's Bloomsday celebrations. (Bloomsday, June 16, is the single day *Ulysses* chronicles, as Leopold Bloom winds his way around Dublin in 1904.) ✉ *35 N. Great George's St., North of the Liffey,* ☎ *01/878–8547,* WEB *www.jamesjoyce.ie.* 🎫 *€5.50.* ☉ *Apr.–Oct., Mon.–Sat. 10–1 and 2–6, Sun. 2–6; Nov.–Mar. by appointment only.*

60 **Mountjoy Square.** Built over the two decades before 1818, this square was once surrounded by elegant, terraced houses. Today only the northern side remains intact. The houses on the once derelict southern side have been converted into apartments. Irishman Brian Boru, who led his soldiers to victory against the Vikings in the Battle of Clontarf in 1014, was said to have pitched camp before the confrontation on the site of Mountjoy Square. Playwright Sean O'Casey once lived here at No. 35 and used the square as a setting for *The Shadow of a Gunman.*

52 **O'Connell Street.** Dublin's most famous thoroughfare, 150 ft wide, was previously known as Sackville Street, but its name was changed in 1924, two years after the founding of the Irish Free State. After the devastation of the 1916 Easter Uprising, the street had to be almost entirely reconstructed, a task that took until the end of the 1920s. The main attraction of the street, **Nelson's Pillar,** a Doric column towering over the city center and a marvelous vantage point, was blown up in 1966, the 50th anniversary of the Easter Uprising. The large **monument** at the south end of the street is dedicated to Daniel O'Connell (1775–1847), "The Liberator," and was erected in 1854 as a tribute to the orator's achievement in securing Catholic Emancipation in 1829. Seated winged figures represent the four Victories—courage, eloquence, fidelity, and patriotism—all exemplified by O'Connell. Ireland's four ancient provinces—Munster, Leinster, Ulster, and Connacht—are identified by their respective coats of arms. Look closely and you'll notice that O'Connell is wearing a glove on one hand, as he did for much of his adult life, a self-imposed penance for shooting a man in a duel. Alongside O'Connell is another noted statue, a modern rendition of Joyce's **Anna Livia,** seen as a lady set within a waterfall and now nicknamed

REJOYCE! A WALK THROUGH JAMES JOYCE'S DUBLIN AND ULYSSES

JAMES JOYCE'S GENIUS for fashioning high art out of his day-to-day life brought him literary immortality and makes him, even today and possibly for all time, the world's most famous Dubliner. He set all of his major works—*Dubliners, A Portrait of the Artist as a Young Man, Ulysses,* and *Finnegan's Wake*—in the city where he was born and spent the first 22 years of his life, and although he spent the next 36 in self-imposed exile, he never wrote about anywhere else. Joyce knew and remembered Dublin in such detail that he claimed that if the city were destroyed, it could be rebuilt in its entirety from his written works.

Joyceans flock to Dublin annually on June 16 to commemorate **Bloomsday,** the day in 1904 on which Leopold Bloom wanders through the city in *Ulysses.* Why *this* day? It had been an important one for Joyce—when he and his wife-to-be, Nora Barnacle, had their first date. Today Bloomsday has evolved into "Bloomstime," with events taking place in the days leading up to the 16th, then all day and well into the night. Even if you don't make it to Dublin on Bloomsday, you can still roam its streets, sniffing out Bloom's—and Joyce's—haunts.

Begin in the heart of the northside, on **Prince's Street,** next to the **GPO,** where the office of the old and popular *Freeman's Journal* newspaper (published 1763–1924) was located before it was destroyed during the 1916 Easter Uprising. Bloom was a newspaper advertisement canvasser for the *Journal.* Leopold and Molly Bloom's fictional home stood at **7 Eccles Street,** north of Parnell Square. On Great

Denmark Street, **Belvedere College** (☎ 01/874–3974) is housed in a splendid 18th-century mansion. Between 1893 and 1898, Joyce studied here under the Jesuits. A few steps away, the **James Joyce Cultural Centre** is the hub of Bloomsday celebrations. Also on the northside is the site of **Bella Cohen's Brothel** (✉ 82 Railway St., North of the Liffey), in an area that in Joyce's day contained many such houses of ill repute. Across town on the western edge of the northside, the **New Ormond Hotel** (✉ Upper Ormond Quay, North of the Liffey, ☎ 01/872–1811) was an afternoon rendezvous spot for Bloom.

Across the Liffey, walk up Grafton Street to **Davy Byrne's Pub** and then proceed to the **National Library**—where Bloom has a near meeting with Blazes Boylan, his wife's lover, and looks for a copy of an advertisement—via **Molesworth Street.** No establishment mentioned by Joyce has changed less since his time than **Sweny's Pharmacy** (✉ Lincoln Pl., South of the Liffey), at the back of Trinity College, which still has its black-and-white exterior and an interior crammed with potions and vials.

A number of key Joyce sites lie outside the city center. On February 2, 1882, Joyce was born in the genteel southern suburb of Rathgar, at **41 Brighton Square,** where he spent the first two years of his life. (Bus 15A and Bus 15B make the 5-km [3-mi] journey.) Other sites are covered elsewhere in our guide: **Sandymount Strand,** the **James Joyce Martello Tower,** and **One Martello Terrace.**

by the natives the "floozy in the Jacuzzi." **O'Connell Bridge,** the main bridge spanning the Liffey (wider than it is long), marks the street's southern end.

NEED A
BREAK?

On the northside you'll find a number of good places to take a break. One of Dublin's oldest hotels, the **Gresham** (⌂ Upper O'Connell St., North of the Liffey, ☎ 01/874–6881) is a pleasant, old-fashioned spot for a morning coffee or afternoon tea. **Conway's** (⌂ Parnell St. near Upper O'Connell St., North of the Liffey, ☎ 01/873–2687), founded in 1745, is reputed to be Dublin's second-oldest pub. It's unpretentious and has great pub-grub. For a real Irish pub lunch, stop in at **John M. Keating** (⌂ 14 Mary St., North of the Liffey, ☎ 01/873–1567), at the corner of Mary and Jervis streets; head upstairs, where you can sit at a low table and chat with locals.

⑥³ Pro-Cathedral. Dublin's principal Catholic cathedral (also known as St. Mary's) is a great place to hear the best Irish male voices—a Palestrina choir, in which the great Irish tenor John McCormack began his career, sings in Latin here every Sunday at 11. The cathedral, built between 1816 and 1825, has a classical church design—one that's on a suitably epic scale. The church's facade, with a six-Doric-pillared portico, is based on the Temple of Theseus in Athens; the interior is modeled after the Grecian-Doric style of St-Philippe du Roule in Paris. But the building was never granted full cathedral status, nor has the identity of its architect ever been discovered; the only clue is in the church ledger, which lists a "Mr. P." as the builder. ⌂ *Marlborough St., North of the Liffey,* ☎ *01/874–5441,* WEB *www.procathedral.ie.* ☐ *Free.* ☉ *Daily 8 AM–6 PM.*

⑥⁵ Rotunda Hospital. Founded in 1745 as the first maternity hospital in Ireland or Britain, the Rotunda was designed on a grand scale by architect Richard Castle (1690–1751), with a three-story tower and a copper cupola. It's now most worth a visit for its **chapel,** with elaborate plasterwork executed by Bartholomew Cramillion between 1757 and 1758, appropriately honoring motherhood. The **Gate Theatre,** in a lavish Georgian assembly room, is also part of the complex. The public is not allowed inside. ⌂ *Parnell St., North of the Liffey,* ☎ *01/873–0700.*

⑥¹ St. Francis Xavier Church. One of the city's finest churches in the classical style, the Jesuit St. Francis Xavier's was begun in 1829, the year of Catholic Emancipation, and was completed three years later. The building is designed in the shape of a Latin cross, with a distinctive Ionic portico and an unusual coffered ceiling. The striking, faux-marble high altarpiece, decorated with lapis lazuli, came from Italy. The church appears in James Joyce's story "Grace." ⌂ *Upper Gardiner St., North of the Liffey,* ☎ *01/836–3411.* ☐ *Free.* ☉ *Daily 7 AM–8:30 PM.*

Along the Grand Canal

At its completion in 1795, the 547-km (342-mi) Grand Canal was celebrated as the longest in Britain and Ireland. It connected Dublin to the River Shannon, and horse-drawn barges carried cargo (mainly turf) and passengers to the capital from all over the country. By the mid-19th century the train had arrived and the great waterway slowly fell into decline, until the last commercial traffic ceased in 1960. But the 6-km (4-mi) loop around the capital is ideal for a leisurely stroll.

A Good Walk

Numbers in the text correspond to numbers in the margin and on the Dublin City Center map.

Begin by walking down the Pearse Street side of Trinity College until you arrive at the Ringsend Road Bridge. Raised on stilts above the canal is the **Waterways Visitors Centre** ⑥⑥. Head west along the bank until you reach the **Mount Street Bridge** ⑥⑦. On the southside is Percy Place, a street with elegant, three-story, terraced houses. On the northside, a small lane leads up to the infamous **Scruffy Murphy's** ⑥⑧ pub. Taking a little detour at the next right, you'll pass a road that leads up to St. Stephen's. Another right takes you into Powerscourt, a classic, inner-city estate of two-up, two-down terraced houses. Return to the canal and continue your walk along Herbert Place. You can get really close to the dark green water here as it spills over one of the many wood-and-iron locks (all still in working order) that service the canal. James Joyce lost his virginity to a prostitute on the next stretch of the Canal, around Lower Baggot Street Bridge, but these banks belong to the lonesome ghost of another writer, Patrick Kavanagh. A life-size **statue of Patrick Kavanagh** ⑥⑨ sits here, contemplative, arms folded, legs crossed on a wooden bench. Less than 2 km (1 mi) past Kavanagh's statue the canal narrows as it approaches Richmond Bridge. Just beyond the bridge is the **Irish Jewish Museum** ⑦⓪. To finish your walk in style, take a right onto Richmond Street, past a few antiques stores, until you arrive at **Bambrick's** ⑦①, a public house in the best tradition of Dublin.

TIMING

You could walk this section of the canal in half an hour if you hurried, but a leisurely pace best suits a waterside walk, so give yourself a couple of hours to visit the Jewish Museum and explore the old streets off the canal.

Sights to See

⑦① **Bambrick's.** This is a pub in the best Irish tradition: a long, dark-wood bar, half-empty, frequented mostly by men over 50, and with a staff whose sharp, grinning humor verges on rudeness. ⊠ *11 Richmond St. South, South of the Liffey,* ☎ *01/475–4402.* ⌷ *Free.* ⊙ *Daily 11 AM–midnight.*

⑦⓪ **Irish Jewish Museum.** Roughly 5,000 European Jews fleeing the pogroms of Eastern Europe arrived in Ireland in the late 19th century and early 20th century. Today the Jewish population hovers around 1,800. The museum, opened in 1985 by Israeli president Chaim Herzog (himself Dublin-educated), includes a restored synagogue and a display of photographs, letters, and personal memorabilia culled from Dublin's most prominent Jewish families. Exhibits trace the Jewish presence in Ireland back to 1067. In homage to Leopold Bloom, the Jewish protagonist of Joyce's *Ulysses,* every Jewish reference in the novel has been identified. The museum is a 20-minute walk or so from St. Stephen's Green. ⊠ *3–4 Walworth Rd., South of the Liffey,* ☎ *01/453–1797.* ⌷ *Free.* ⊙ *Oct.–Apr., Sun. 10:30–2:30; May–Sept., Tues., Thurs., and Sun. 11–3:30; also by appointment.*

⑥⑦ **Mount Street Bridge.** The bridge has a wooden lock on either side and is the perfect spot to watch these original gateways to the canal in operation. On the southwest corner of the bridge a small stone monument commemorates the battle of Mount Street Bridge in 1916 and the Irish Volunteers who died on this spot.

⑥⑧ **Scruffy Murphy's.** Many a backroom deal by the country's political power brokers has been made in the back room of this classy wood-and-brass pub. It's the perfect spot for a pint and a snack. ⊠ *Lower Mount St., South of the Liffey,* ☎ *01/661–5006.* ⌷ *Free.* ⊙ *Daily 11 AM–midnight.*

⑥⑨ **Statue of Patrick Kavanagh.** Patrick Kavanagh—Ireland's great rural poet who in 1942 published his best-known poem, "The Great Hunger," about farming and poverty—spent the later years of his life sitting on a bench here writing about the canal, which flowed from his birthplace in the Midlands to the city where he would die. In one such poem he tells those who outlive him, "O commemorate me with no hero-coura-geous tomb, just a canal-bank seat for the passerby." Acknowledging Kavanagh's devotion to this spot, his friends commissioned a life-size bronze of the poet here. ⊠ *Canal bank along Wilton Terr., South of the Liffey.*

66 **Waterways Visitors Centre.** In the airy, wood-and-glass building you can learn about the history of Irish rivers and canals through photos, videos, and models. ⊠ *Grand Canal Quay, South of the Liffey,* ☎ *01/ 677–7501.* ☜ *€2.55.* ⊙ *June–Sept., daily 9:30–5:30; Oct.–May, Wed.– Sun. 12:30–5:30.*

Phoenix Park and Environs

Far and away Dublin's largest park, Phoenix Park (the name is an an-glicization of the Irish *Fionn Uisce,* meaning clear water) is a vast, green arrowhead-shaped oasis north of the Liffey, a 20-or-so-minute walk from the city center. Dubliners flock here to "take it aisy." It remains the city's main lung, escape valve, sports center (cricket, soccer, Gaelic games, and polo), and home to the noble creatures of the Dublin Zoo. A handful of other cultural sites near the park are also worth visiting, but to combine a visit to any of them with any of our other walks would be a bit difficult. Smithfield and the Old Jameson Distillery, at the end of the Dublin West walk, are the sites closest (the Guinness Brewery and Storehouse, across the river, is also fairly close). So if you do make it to any of those, think about whether you have enough time to ap-pend a visit to one or another of these sites. Otherwise, plan to make a special trip out here—walk if you're up to it, or take a car or cab.

A Good Walk

Numbers in the text correspond to numbers in the margin and on the Dublin West map.

Beginning at the Custom House, walk down the quays on the north side of the Liffey until you come to Blackhall Place. Walk up to Ar-bour Hill and turn left: the **Arbour Hill Cemetery** 73 will be on your left. Directly across Arbour Hill are the **Collins Barracks** 74, now a branch of the National Museum (the main entrance is on Benburb Street on the south side). On its east side Benburb becomes Parkgate Street, and it's just a short stroll farther down to the main entrance of **Phoenix Park** 75.

TIMING
Phoenix Park is *big*; exploring it on foot could easily take the better part of a day. If you're looking for a little exercise, head here: jogging, horseback riding, and bicycling are the ideal ways to explore the park more quickly than you can simply by strolling.

Sights to See

73 **Arbour Hill Cemetery.** All 14 Irishmen executed by the British follow-ing the 1916 Easter Uprising are buried here, including Pádrig Pearse, who led the rebellion; his younger brother Willie, who played a minor role in the uprising; and James Connolly, a socialist and labor leader wounded in the battle. Too weak from his wounds to stand, Connolly was tied to a chair and then shot. The burial ground is a simple but formal area, with the names of the dead leaders carved in stone beside an inscription of the proclamation they issued during the uprising. ⊠ *Arbour Hill, Dublin West.* ☜ *Free.* ⊙ *Mon.–Sat. 9–4:30, Sun. 9:30– noon.*

74 Collins Barracks. The huge Collins Barracks (named for the assassinated republican leader Michael Collins) houses a section of the National Museum—their collection of glass, silver, furniture, and other decorative arts; exhibitions on Irish military history; and an exhibition of 200 years of Irish costumes and jewelry. A prize exhibit is a 2,000-year-old Japanese ceremonial bell. ⊠ *Benburb St., Dublin West,* ☎ *01/677-7444,* WEB *www.museum.ie.* 🎫 *Free.* ⊙ *Tues.–Sat. 10–5, Sun. 2–5.*

★ ☼ **75 Phoenix Park.** Europe's largest public park, which extends about 5 km (3 mi) along the Liffey's north bank, encompasses 1,752 acres of verdant green lawns, woods, lakes, and playing fields. It's a jogger's paradise. Sunday is the best time to visit: games of cricket, soccer, polo, baseball, hurling—a combination of lacrosse, baseball, and field hockey—and Irish football are likely to be in progress. Old-fashioned gas lamps line both sides of **Chesterfield Avenue,** the main road that bisects the park for 4 km (2½ mi), which was named for Lord Chesterfield, a lord lieutenant of Ireland, who laid out the road in the 1740s. To the right as you enter the park, you'll see the **People's Garden,** a colorful flower garden designed in 1864.

Among the park's major monuments are the **Phoenix Column,** erected by Lord Chesterfield in 1747, and the **198-ft obelisk,** built in 1817 to commemorate the Duke of Wellington, the Irish general who defeated Napoléon for the British. (Wellington was born in Dublin but, true to the anti-Irish prejudice so prevalent in 19th-century England, balked at the suggestion that he was Irish: "If a man is born in a stable, it doesn't mean he is a horse," he is reputed to have said.) A tall **white cross** marks the spot where Pope John Paul II addressed more than a million people during his 1979 visit to Ireland. Wild deer can be seen grazing in the many open spaces of the park, especially near here.

You're guaranteed to see wildlife at the **Dublin Zoo,** the third-oldest public zoo in the world, founded in 1830, and just a short walk beyond the People's Garden. The place looks a little dilapidated, but the government has allocated money for a five-year renovation that is now under way. Animals from tropical climes are kept in barless enclosures, and Arctic species swim in the lakes close to the reptile house. Interestingly, the zoo is one of the few places in the world where lions will breed in captivity. Some 700 lions have been bred here since the 1850s, one of whom became familiar to movie fans the world over when MGM used him for its trademark. (As they will tell you at the zoo, he is in fact yawning in that familiar shot: an American lion had to be hired to roar and the "voice" was dubbed.) An African Plains area houses the zoo's larger species. The Pets Corner and City Farm has goats, guinea pigs, and lambs. In summer the Lakeside Café serves ice cream and drinks. ⊠ *Phoenix Park, Dublin West,* ☎ *01/677–1425,* WEB *www.dublinzoo.ie.* 🎫 *€9.80.* ⊙ *Mar.–Oct., Mon.–Sat. 9:30–6, Sun. 10:30–6; Nov.–Feb., Mon.–Sat. 9:30–5, Sun. 10:30–5.*

Both the president of Ireland and the U.S. ambassador have official residences in the park (the president's is known as Aras an Uachtarain), but neither building is open to the public. Also within the park is a **visitor center,** in the 17th-century fortified Ashtown Castle; it has information about the park's history, flora, and fauna. ⊠ *Phoenix Park, Dublin West,* ☎ *01/677–0095,* WEB *www.heritageireland.ie.* 🎫 *€2.55.* ⊙ *Apr.–May, daily 9:30–5:30; June–Sept., daily 10–6; Oct., daily 10–5; Nov.–mid-Mar., weekends 9:30–4:30; mid–end Mar., daily 9:30–5.*

NEED A BREAK? Just before the entrance to Phoenix Park, **Ryan's Pub** (⊠ 28 Parkgate St., Dublin West, ☎ 01/677–6097) is one of Dublin's last remaining genuine, late-Victorian-era pubs.

DINING

Revised by
Muriel Bolger
and Graham
Bolger

Dining out has become something of a national pastime in Ireland. With the blossoming economy of the past seven or eight years, now 30 percent of all food eaten is consumed outside the home—a trend that's not confined to Dublin. The dining *experience,* too, has exploded to new levels. Ireland has always been ranked high for its pub culture—world-renowned Guinness and Irish whiskies, and good, wholesome pub grub—but now it's fast becoming a serious contender on the international restaurant scene.

The renaissance in Irish dining is due in no small way to the wave of talented young chefs who are cooking with new levels of imagination and innovation. Chefs have become celebrities on the Irish circuit, many having trained in the best kitchens at home and the world over. They have put a new blas (Irish for gloss) on traditional ingredients. You'll still find the humble Irish spud (potato) featured in all sorts of ways, accompanying wild salmon and other seafood, tender lamb, beef and pork. You'll also find them in potato cakes and boxty, as well as in colcannon, a traditional Irish dish—with bacon and corned beef—that's a must.

Being an agricultural country, Ireland benefits from a copious supply of freshly grown produce, as well as a pure water supply. Meats are plentiful: you'll find lots of excellent Irish beef, pork, ham, and lamb. Keep an eye out, too, for seasonal specials, such as wild and farmed quail and pheasant. And, of course, there are rich and delicious seafood harvests. Consequently, you can expect to find fresh and smoked salmon, oysters, mussels, and shellfish in many guises vying with tender cuts of meat and an appetizing selection of quality vegetables on most menus. Excellent dairy products are also essential to Irish cuisine—dollops of fresh cream with home-baked desserts promise some exciting conclusions to these feasts. Have no doubt, however, that the native cheeses are the finale. Don't miss out on these. You'll find mature cheddars and blue cheeses, the slightly sweet Dubliner, St. Tola goat's cheese from Clare, and Carrigburne Brie from Wexford—only a few of the many fine artisan cheeses produced around the country.

Being an isolated island nation, the Irish love to travel aboard—foreign holidays are now the norm for most of the population. The wonderful thing is that such travel has broadened the tastes and culinary preferences of the nation, and these changes are reflected in the choice of eateries that now abound both in the capital and in other cities.

If you want ethnic food, you'll have no problem finding an establishment to suit your pocket and palette. There are elegant restaurants, stylish bistros, relaxed hideaways, and late-night eateries from which to choose. Indulge in superb French or Italian food one day, and fusion the next—you'll find that menus are influenced by Asian, Mediterranean, and other cultures. Vegetarian dishes are becoming more varied with each passing year.

The Irish dine later than Americans. They stay up later, too, so bookings are usually not taken before 6:30 or 7 PM and are made until around 11 PM. Lunch goes from 12:30 to 2:30. Pubs often serve food all day—until 8:30 or 9 PM. The Irish are an informal bunch, so smart casual dress is typical. The more select restaurants, however, do expect you to wear a jacket and tie. Shorts and sneakers are out. Check when booking if unsure.

Included here are some of the city's best addresses for a hearty pub lunch, which is where you'll now find a lot of Dubliners dining. Soups and sandwiches, hot pots, salmon, salads, and carvery joints are the usual bill of fare—along with the ubiquitous roast, mash, or chips. And while you're in Dublin, do indulge, at least once, in the traditional Irish breakfast (often served until lunchtime). It includes rashers (bacon), sausages, black and white pudding (a type of sausage), mushrooms, tomato, and a fried egg—with lots of traditional homemade brown and soda breads and the famous Irish creamery butter.

Prices

Value Added Tax (VAT)—a 12.5% tax on food and a government excise tax on drinks—will automatically be added to your bill. Before paying, check to see whether service has been included. If it has been included, you can pay it with a credit card; but if it has not, it's more considerate to the staff to leave the tip in cash (10% to 15%) if paying the main bill by credit card.

A word of warning—you will pay for your dining pleasure here: high overheads and staffing costs have pushed up prices, especially in upscale places. The good news is that, while Dublin doesn't have Starbucks, there are scores of local cafés serving excellent coffee, often with a good sandwich. Small bakeries are beginning to spring up, borrowing trends from all around the world, offering inexpensive pizzas, focaccia, pitas, tacos, and wraps (taking over from the sandwich as the favorite snack).

It's worthwhile to see if the restaurant of your choice offers an early-bird and/or pre- or post-theater menu, with significantly lower set prices at specific times, often from 6 to 7:30 PM.

CATEGORY	THE REPUBLIC*
$$$$	over €29
$$$	€22–€29
$$	€13–€21
$	under €13

Per person for a main course at dinner

City Center (Southside)

AMERICAN

$$$–$$$$ ✕ **Shanahans.** Dublin's first American-style steak house, in an elegant Georgian building, proves to be a huge success. It's an old-style place—think large fireplaces, gilt mirrors, a deep carpet, and elegant chandeliers. Certified Irish Angus beef is the star dish, though seafood and lamb are also prized. The basement bar—the Oval Office—is full of Americana and presidential paperwork. ⊠ *119 St. Stephen's Green, City Center,* ☎ *01/407–0939. Reservations essential. AE, DC, MC, V. No lunch.*

CONTEMPORARY

$$$$ ✕ **Peacock Alley.** This elegant, modern restaurant with a large, airy
★ 120-seat room commands a spectacular view over St. Stephen's Green at one end and the white-tiled open kitchen at the other. Strikingly inventive dishes include smoked salmon with basmati rice, pear, preserved ginger, soy sauce, and quesadilla; deep-fried crab cakes with *katafi* (shredded phyllo pastry); and daube of pot-roasted beef. Service is excellent, and there's a strong wine list—well-suited to the type of food served here. ⊠ *Fitzwilliam Hotel, St. Stephen's Green, City Center,* ☎ *01/478–7015. Reservations essential. AE, DC, MC, V. Closed Tues.*

$$$ ✕ **Cooke's Café.** Johnny Cooke's Mediterranean bistro is a cool spot for visiting movie stars. Sit out in summer under an awning and people-watch while you enjoy elegantly presented dishes—on huge, white

60

Bad Ass Café **18**
Beaufield Mews **47**
Belgo **8**
Brownes Brasserie . .**36**
Bruno's **7**
Burdock's **14**
Chapter One **1**
The Commons
Restaurant **43**
Cooke's Café **29**
Diep le Shaker **38**
Dish **9**
Dobbins **39**
Eden **11**
Elephant & Castle **6**
Ernie's Restaurant . .**48**
Halo **3**
Harbour Master **22**
Il Primo **44**
Jaipur **28**
Khyber Tandoori **30**
Kilkenny Kitchen **27**
La Stampa **35**
Lemon Crêpe and
Coffee Co. **24**
Les Frères Jacques . .**10**
Locks **45**
Mao **25**
Mermaid Cafe **15**
Milano **34**
Nude **23**
O'Connells **49**
Old Dublin **13**
One Pico **33**
Osteria Romano **12**
Pasta Fresca **32**
Patrick Guilbaud . . .**37**
Peacock Alley **41**
Shanahans **42**
Soup Dragon **2**
101 Talbot **21**
The Steps of Rome . . .**31**
The Tea Room **5**
Thornton's **46**
Yamamori **16**
Wagamama **40**

Pub Food
Davy Byrne's **26**
Old Stand **17**
O'Neill's **20**
Stag's Head **19**
Zanzibar **4**

Dublin Dining

KEY

DART Railway
Station

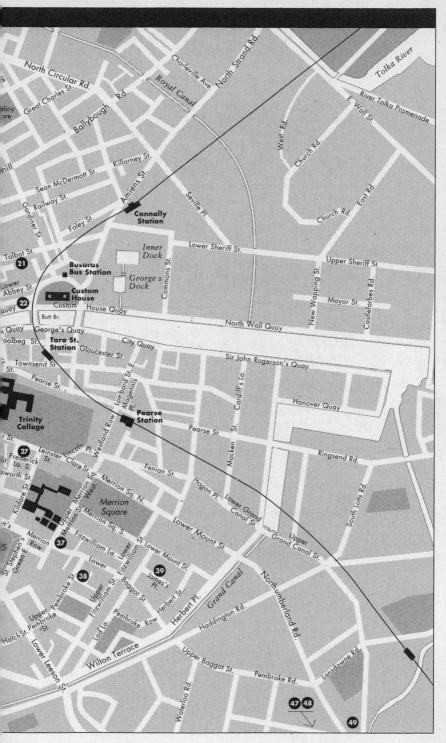

North Circular Rd.

Great Charles St.

Ballybough Rd.

Charleville Ave.

North Strand Rd.

Royal Canal

Tolka River

River Tolka Promenade

West Rd.

Church Rd.

E. Wall St.

Church Rd.

East Rd.

Sean McDermott St.

Killarney St.

Amiens St.

Seville Pl.

Railway St.

Gardiner St.

Foley St.

Connolly Station

Lower Sheriff St.

Upper Sheriff St.

Talbot St.

21

Busáras Bus Station

Inner Dock

Commons St.

New Wapping St.

Mayor St.

Castleforbes Rd.

Lower Abbey St.

22

Custom House

George's Dock

Custom House Quay

Butt Br.

North Wall Quay

George's Quay

Coolbeg St.

City Quay

Tara St. Station

Gloucester St.

Sir John Rogerson's Quay

Townsend St.

Pearse St.

Lombard St. E.

Magennis Pl.

Cardiff's La.

Hanover Quay

Trinity College

Westland Row

Pearse Station

Pearse St.

Macken St.

Ringsend Rd.

27

Leinster St.

Lincoln Pl.

Clare St.

Frederick La. S.

Kildare St.

Fenian St.

Hogan Pl.

Lower Grand Canal St.

South Lotts Rd.

Merrion St. West

Merrion Sq. N.

Merrion Square

Merrion St.

Merrion Sq. S.

Lower Mount St.

Upper Grand Canal St.

37

Merrion Row

Fitzwilliam La.

Lower St.

Lower Mount St.

38

Upper Fitzwilliam St.

Baggot St.

James's Pl.

39

St. Stephen's Green E.

Lower Fitzwilliam St.

Pembroke Row

Herbert Pl.

Herbert St.

Grand Canal

Northumberland Rd.

Upper Pembroke St.

Lad La.

Pembroke Row

Hatch St.

Lower Leeson St.

Wilton Terrace

Upper Baggot St.

Haddington Rd.

Lansdowne Rd.

Waterloo Rd.

Pembroke Rd.

47 **48**

49

Wedgwood plates. Favorites include pasta with a rich, bubbling Gorgonzola sauce; lobster simply grilled with garlic-herb butter; salad with pieces of tender roast duck; and crab salad with spinach, coriander, mango salsa, and lime dressing. Don't come if you're in a hurry, because the service, through charming, is slow. ⊠ *14 S. William St., City Center,* ☎ *01/679–0536. Reservations essential. AE, DC, MC, V. Closed Sun.–Mon.*

$–$$$ ✕ **La Stampa.** It's one of the most dramatic dining rooms in Dublin, with huge gilt mirrors and elaborate candelabra that are gloriously over the top. This gives even the simplest meal a sense of fun and occasion. The menu changes frequently, and reflects the restaurant's eclectic, international style. Get rack of organic lamb with braised beans, tomatoes, and rosemary jus; roast scallops with artichoke mash and a tomato vinaigrette; or giant prawns served with garlic or mango mayonnaise. Expect brisk but friendly service. ⊠ *35 Dawson St., City Center,* ☎ *01/677–8611. AE, DC, MC, V.*

CONTINENTAL

$$$–$$$$ ✕ **Locks.** A genuinely warm welcome awaits you at Claire Douglas's town-house restaurant, which overlooks the Grand Canal. The dining room is comfortable and old-fashioned, with banquette seating and starched table linens. Hearty portions are served on antique ironstone plates. Classic starters include Locks's special potato skins—dished up with prawns, tomato, and spinach with a fabulous hollandaise sauce—and excellent smoked salmon. Choose your main course from the traditional fish dishes, Irish lamb, and venison. ⊠ *1 Windsor Terr., Portobello, South of the Liffey,* ☎ *01/454–3391. Reservations essential. AE, DC, MC, V. Closed Sun.*

$$–$$$ ✕ **Brownes Brasserie.** Go to this Georgian town house, now a boutique hotel on St. Stephen's Green, if you're looking for a lovely spot in which to share an intimate meal. Huge mirrors reflect the light from crystal chandeliers onto the jewel-colored walls and upholstery. The rich and heartwarming food includes such classics as pan-seared scallops and black pudding on beet-root marmalade. Treat yourself to the lavender-scented crème brûlée. ⊠ *22 St. Stephen's Green, City Center,* ☎ *01/ 638–3939. Reservations essential. AE, DC, MC, V. No lunch Sat.*

ETHNIC

$$ ✕ **Khyber Tandoori.** Take a short walk from St. Stephen's Green to this gem of a restaurant. It specializes in Pakistani cuisine, but also serves a broad range of Indian dishes. Try the shami (Syrian) kebabs—dainty, spiced patties of minced lamb and lentils—or *kabuli chicken tikka shashlik,* marinated, diced chicken with onions and red and green peppers, which comes bright red and sizzling on an iron platter. Settle in and admire the richly embroidered wall hangings and the great gusts of steam coming from the tandoori oven in the glassed-in area. ⊠ *44–45 S. William St., City Center,* ☎ *01/670–4855. AE, DC, MC, V. No lunch Sun.*

$–$$ ✕ **Jaipur.** A spacious room with a sweeping staircase and contemporary furnishings reflect the modern, cutting-edge approach to Indian cooking. Mixed with more traditional dishes, such as chicken tikka masala, you'll find the more unusual *matka gosdh* (lamb dish) on offer. Dishes can be toned down (or spiced up) to suit your palate, and service is courteous and prompt. The wine list is well thought out. ⊠ *41 S Great George's St., City Center,* ☎ *01/677–0999. Reservations essential. AE, MC, V.*

FRENCH

$$$$ ✕ **Patrick Guilbaud.** Expect superb cooking and impeccable service at
★ this fine restaurant with a marvelously lofty dining room hung with

paintings from the owners' private collection. The best dishes here are simple—and flawless. Try the house specialty, Chalons duck à l'orange. Follow that, if you can, with the *assiette au chocolat* (a plate of five hot and cold chocolate desserts). ✉ *21 Upper Merrion St., South of the Liffey,* ☎ *01/676–4192. Reservations essential. AE, DC, MC, V. Closed Sun.–Mon.*

$$$$ ✗ **Thornton's.** If you are passionate about food, this place is manda-
★ tory—owner Kevin Thornton has forged a reputation as one of the very best chefs in Ireland. The upstairs dining room is simply decorated—there's little to distract you from the exquisite food. Thornton's cooking style is light, and his dishes are small masterpieces of structural engineering. In season, he marinates legs of partridge, then debones and reforms the bird, with the breasts shaped into a crown. Desserts range from banana ice cream to fig tartlet. Sheridans of Dublin supplies the enormous selection of cheeses. ✉ *1 Portobello Rd., South of the Liffey,* ☎ *01/454–9067. Reservations essential. AE, DC, MC, V. Closed Sun.–Mon. No lunch Tues.–Thurs.*

$ ✗ **Lemon Crêpe and Coffee Co.** They've got the best crêpes in town, and hungry Dubliners know it. The space is compact, white, and minimalist. A few pavement tables—complete with an outdoor heater—make this a great spot for a tasty snack while you watch Dublin saunter by. To really indulge, follow up savory pancakes with sugar-sweet crêpes. Takeout service is swift. ✉ *66 S. William St., City Center,* ☎ *01/672–9044. No credit cards.*

IRISH

$$$$ ✗ **The Commons Restaurant.** This large, elegant dining room is in the basement of Newman House. The patio doors open onto a paved courtyard—ideal for for summer aperitifs and alfresco lunches. Typical dishes include ravioli of artichoke with truffles and asparagus. If you have time, take a stroll in the nearby Iveagh Gardens, an enclosed park that's one of Dublin's best-kept secrets. ✉ *85–86 St. Stephen's Green, City Center,* ☎ *01/478–0530. Reservations essential. AE, DC, MC, V. No lunch Sat. Closed Sun..*

$$–$$$ ✗ **Dobbins.** Don't be deceived by the sawdust on the floor and the simple furnishings. The combination of cozy booth seating, friendly service, and classic bistro food make Dobbins popular with businesspeople. Owner John O'Byrne presides over an impressive cellar with hundreds of wines from around the world. Tempura of prawns is a popular starter; boned brace of quail, with black pudding (sausage with dried pig's blood) and foie gras stuffing is a typical entrée. There's valet parking, and the staff are expert at summoning taxis. ✉ *15 Stephens La., off Mount St., City Center,* ☎ *01/676–4679. Reservations essential. AE, DC, MC, V. Closed Mon.*

$$–$$$ ✗ **One Pico.** Not only is the design sophisticated and modern, but Eamonn O'Reilly's cooking is decidedly contemporary. Dishes such as fresh chicken and kale-and-bacon mashed potato demonstrate a savvy use of Irish ingredients. Follow this with the baked chèvre cheesecake with praline chocolate and orange confit. Service is excellent, and the top-class cooking makes this good value for the money. ✉ *5–6 Moleswotrh Place, Schoolhouse Lane, South of the Liffey,* ☎ *01/676–0300. Reservations essential. AE, DC, MC, V. No lunch weekends.*

$ ✗ **Burdock's.** Join the inevitable queue at Dublin's famous take-out fish-and-chips shop, right next door to the Lord Edward. Eat in the gardens of St. Patrick's Cathedral, a five-minute walk away. ✉ *21 Werburgh St., City Center,* ☎ *01/454–0306. No credit cards.*

$ ✗ **Kilkenny Kitchen.** Take a break from shopping and sightseeing at this big self-service restaurant on the upper floor of the Kilkenny Shop. Homemade soup, casseroles, cold meats, and salads are arranged on a long buffet, along with lots of tasty breads and cakes. Try to get a table by the window overlooking the playing fields of Trinity College. Lunchtime is busy, but it's very pleasant for morning coffee or afternoon tea. ⊠ *5–6 Nassau St., City Center,* ☎ *01/677–7066. AE, DC, MC, V.*

$ ✕ **Soup Dragon.** This tiny café and take-out soup shop serves an astonishing array of fresh soups daily. Soups come in three sizes, and you can get vegetarian soup or soups with meat- or fish-based broth. Favorites include red pepper, tomato, and goat cheese soup; fragrant Thai chicken soup; and hearty mussel, potato, and leek soup. The friendly staff make fine coffee and delicious smoothies. The cost of soup includes bread and a piece of fruit for dessert—an excellent value. ⊠ *168 Capel St., North of the Liffey,* ☎ *01/872–3277. No credit cards. No dinner. Closed Sun.*

ITALIAN

$–$$$ ✕ **Il Primo.** Old wooden tables and chairs give this place a casual feel, and the friendly, if cramped, surroundings attracts a devoted clientele. The Irish-Italian cuisine is both imaginative and reassuring. Among the main courses, a delicious chicken ravioli in white wine cream, with Parma ham and wild mushrooms, is a standout. There's a very long wine list specializing in Italian wines. ⊠ *Montague St., off Harcourt St., South of the Liffey,* ☎ *01/478–3373. AE, DC, MC, V. No lunch weekends.*

$–$$$ ✕ **Pasta Fresca.** This stylish little Italian restaurant and deli off Grafton Street squeezes a surprising number of people into a fairly small space. Antipasto *misto* (assorted sliced Italian meats) makes a good appetizer— or go for carpaccio *della casa* (wafer-thin slices of beef filet, with fresh Parmesan, olive oil, lemon juice, and black pepper). The main courses consist of Pasta Fresca's own very good versions of well-known dishes, such as spaghetti *alla Bolognese,* cannelloni, and lasagna *al forno.* The pasta is freshly made each day. Lines form at lunchtime. ⊠ *3–4 Chatham St., City Center,* ☎ *01/679–2402. AE, DC, MC, V.*

$ ✕ **Milano.** The big open kitchen at this bright, cheerful place turns out a wide array of tasty, flashy pizzas, with combinations like tomato and mozzarella, ham and eggs, Cajun with prawns and Tabasco, spinach and egg, or ham and anchovies. There are also simple salads, such as tomato and mozzarella with dough balls, and some baked pasta dishes. This is a good place to dine late, with last orders at midnight. Two other branches have opened up, one in Temple Bar and another on Bachelors Walk along the Quays. ⊠ *38 Dawson St., City Center,* ☎ *01/670– 7744;* ⊠ *18 Essex St. E, Temple Bar,* ☎ *01/670–3384;* ⊠ *38–39 Lower Ormond Quay, North of the Liffey,* ☎ *01/872–0003. AE, DC, MC, V.*

$ ✕ **The Steps of Rome.** Just a few steps from Grafton Street, it's perfect for a late-night bite or quick lunch (or takeout). Slices of delicious, thin base, homemade pizza, with all the traditional toppings, are the main attraction. The mushroom pizza *(fungi)* is particularly good. The handful of tables is usually full, but it's worth waiting for the classic Italian pasta dishes—pasta parmigiano or pesto, and good, fresh salads with focaccia. Follow it up with ice cream or tiramisu, and good, strong espresso. ⊠ *1 Chatham Ct., City Center,* ☎ *01/670–5630. No credit cards.*

JAPANESE

$–$$ ✕ **Yamamori.** The first of many Ramen noodle bars to open in Ireland, this is one of the best. The meals-in-a-bowl are a splendid slurping experience, and although you will be supplied with a small Chinese-style soup spoon, the best approach is with chopsticks. You can also get sushi and sashimi, and delicious chicken teriyaki. ⊠ *71–72 S. Great George's St., City Center,* ☎ *01/475–5001. AE, MC, V.*

$ ✕ **Wagamama.** Modeled on a Japanese canteen, the long wooden tables and benches ensure a unique communal dining experience. This low-ceilinged basement noodle bar is constantly packed, but service is swift. Formal courses aren't acknowledged—food is served as soon as it's ready, and appetizers and main courses arrive together. Choose from filling bowls of Cha Han (fried rice with chicken, prawns, and vegetables) or chili beef Ramen, and wash it down with fresh fruit or vegetable juices. ✉ *S. King St., City Center,* ☎ *01/478–2152. AE, DC, MC, V.*

PAN-ASIAN

$–$$$ ✕ **Diep le Shaker.** Slightly off the beaten track, on a narrow lane off Pembroke Street, this big, flamboyant Thai food spot was an instant success when it opened. Comfortable high-back chairs, pristine table linen, and elegant stemware make it a lovely, and posh, place to dine. Know in advance that it's a place where half the reason for going is to see and be seen. Try the steamed scallops and ginger, or lobster in garlic pepper and Thai herbs. Don't be surprised to see people ordering champagne to go with their meal—there's a permanent party feel here, which attracts Ireland's wealthy in droves. ✉ *55 Pembroke La., City Center,* ☎ *01/661–1829. AE, DC, MC, V. Closed Sun.*

$–$$ ✕ **Mao.** Everything is Asian fusion at this bustling café, from the little Andy Warhol pastiche of Chairman Mao on the washroom door to the eclectic mix of dishes on the menu, which combine influences of Thai, Vietnamese, and other Southeast Asian cuisines. Favorites are the Malaysian chicken and the *Nasi Goreng* (Indonesian fried rice with chicken and shrimp). Reservations aren't accepted, so go early to be sure of a seat. There's another branch in Dun Laoghaire, a 20-minute taxi ride from the city center. ✉ *2 Chatham Row, City Center,* ☎ *01/ 670–4899;* ✉ *The Pavilion, Dun Laoghaire, South County Dublin,* ☎ *01/214–8090. MC, V.*

RUSSIAN

$$–$$$ ✕ **Old Dublin.** This brasserie-style restaurant near St. Patrick's Cathedral specializes in Russian and Scandinavian food. In the evening, glowing fires warm the cozy-but-elegant low-ceilinged rooms; tables are candlelit. You'll find familiar dishes: blini, borscht, chicken Kiev, and beef Stroganoff, but also a few Irish staples, such as roast lamb and fresh baked salmon. One fine surprise on the menu is planked sirloin Hussar, a steak baked between two oak planks, served on an oak platter with salad and sweet pickle. ✉ *90–91 St. Francis St., City Center,* ☎ *01/454–2028. AE, DC, MC, V. Closed Sun. No lunch Mon., Tues., Sat.*

VEGETARIAN

$ ✕ **Nude.** This sleek fast-food café was such a good idea that owner Norman Hewson—brother of U2's Bono—has opened another branch for takeout only. The menu is mostly vegetarian, and everything on it is made with organic and free-range ingredients. Choose from homemade soups and vegetable wraps, smoothies, and fresh-squeezed juices. ✉ *21 Suffolk St., City Center,* ☎ *01/677–4804. AE, DC, MC, V.*

Temple Bar

AMERICAN/CASUAL

$–$$$ ✕ **Belgo.** It's part of a Belgian chain of restaurants, and perfect if you want a large serving of comfort food and are prepared to be adventurous with what you drink. They have dozens of beers, and the french fries, served alongside omelets, burgers, *saucissons* (large, flavored Belgian sausages), and steaks, are the best you'll eat in Temple Bar. ✉ *17–19 Sycamore St., Temple Bar,* ☎ *01/672–7554. AE, DC, MC, V.*

$–$$$ ✕ **Elephant & Castle.** One of Temple Bar's most popular and established eateries, Elephant & Castle serves traditional American food—charcoal-grilled burgers, salads, omelets, sandwiches, and pasta. Sunday brunch is always packed. When the service is good, the turnover tends to be quick, although you may be inclined to linger. Generous portions of unfussy and well-prepared food, and the casual environment, make this a Dublin standout. New Yorkers take note: yes, this is a cousin of the restaurant of the same name in Greenwich Village. ⊠ *18 Temple Bar,* ☎ *01/679–3121. Reservations not accepted. AE, DC, MC, V.*

$–$$ ✕ **Bad Ass Café.** Sinéad O'Connor used to wait tables at this lively café in a converted warehouse between the Central Bank and Ha'penny Bridge. (A "Rock 'n Stroll" tour plaque notes O'Connor's past here.) Old-fashioned cash shuttles whiz around the ceiling of the barnlike space, with bare floors and painted in primary colors inside and out. You can indulge in some great people-watching behind the wall of glass here. The food—mainly pizzas and burgers—is unexceptional, but the Bad Ass can be a lot of fun and appetites of all ages love it. ⊠ *9–11 Crown Alley, Temple Bar,* ☎ *01/671–2596. AE, MC, V.*

CONTEMPORARY

$$$$ ✕ **The Tea Room.** If you have something to celebrate or you're hoping to spot some celebrities, this is a good bet. It's part of the Clarence hotel, where the stars of stage and screen stay when they're in town. The bright, lofty dining room has spectacular flower arrangements and elegant, modern table settings. The food is adventurous and consistently good. Typically mouthwatering entrées include risotto of mussels and courgettes with parsley and garlic. ⊠ *Clarence hotel, 6–8 Wellington Quay, Temple Bar,* ☎ *01/407–0813. Reservations essential. AE, DC, MC, V.*

$$–$$$ ✕ **Eden.** The young owners of several of Dublin's café-style bars, in-
★ cluding the Front Lounge and the Globe, have followed those successes with a popular brasserie-style restaurant with an open kitchen and high wall of glass looking out onto one of Temple Bar's main squares. Patio-style doors lead to an outdoor eating area—a major plus in a city with relatively few al fresco dining spots. Have no doubt: Eden is a happening, trendy place, hip with fashion and media types. Standout dishes include duck leg confit with lentils, and mustard-crusted braised hock of ham served with *champ* (creamy, buttery mashed potatoes with scallions). Desserts include rhubarb crème brûlée and homemade ice creams and sorbets. ⊠ *Meeting House Sq., Temple Bar,* ☎ *01/670–5372. Reservations essential. AE, DC, MC, V.*

$$–$$$ ✕ **Mermaid Café.** One of the chef-owners dabbles in fine art, and his tastes in this area are reflected in his artistic and decorative style of bistro cooking. It's not cheap, but the food is quite good. Lunch is an exceptional value—piquant crab cakes, hearty seafood casseroles, venison sausage, or radicchio and melted goat's cheese. Good attention to detail and a thoughtful wine list make this modest restaurant with tall windows looking onto busy Dame Street one of the most popular eateries in Temple Bar. ⊠ *69 Dame St., Temple Bar,* ☎ *01/670–8236. MC, V.*

$–$$ ✕ **Dish.** Clever cuisine, a relaxed dining room, and pleasant staff have secured Dish a loyal following. The large white room with sanded floorboards, oversized mirrors, and industrial piping is a wonderfully stylish space in which to enjoy Gerard Foote's confident cooking. Dishes range from grilled Clonakilty black pudding with roast red pepper and borlotti beans to roast monkfish with bacon, savoy cabbage, beetroot, and cream. The focus is on Irish ingredients. It's popular for Sunday brunch, and the midweek lunch is also an excellent value. ⊠ *2 Crow St., Temple Bar,* ☎ *01/671–1248. Reservations essential. AE, DC, MC, V.*

FRENCH

$$$–$$$$ ✕ **Les Frères Jacques.** It brings a little bit of Paris to Temple Bar: old
★ prints of Paris and Deauville hang on the green-papered walls, and the
French waiters, dressed in white Irish linen and black bow ties, exude
a Gallic charm without being excessively formal. Expect traditional
French cooking that nods to the seasons. Seafood is a major attrac-
tion, and lobster, fished right from the tank, is a specialty—it's typi-
cally roasted and flambéed with Irish whiskey. Also recommended are
the meat and game specialties, when in season. A piano player performs
Friday and Saturday evenings and the occasional weeknight. ⊠ *74 Dame
St., Temple Bar,* ☎ *01/679–4555. Reservations essential. AE, MC, V.
Closed Sun. No lunch Sat.*

ITALIAN

$$–$$$ ✕ **Osteria Romano.** Members of the Italian community congregate in
the evenings at this cheerful eatery, which serves authentic Roman cui-
sine. Specialties include *melanzane parmigiani,* a delicious dish of
baked eggplant and cheese, and the excellent cream-based pastas, such
as spaghetti Alfredo and carbonara. Beware of finishing the meal with
too many flaming *sambucas* (anise-flavored, semisweet Italian liqueur).
The best table, by the window, overlooks the street. ⊠ *5 Crow St., Tem-
ple Bar,* ☎ *01/670–8662. AE, DC, MC, V.*

MEDITERRANEAN

$$–$$$ ✕ **Bruno's.** Experienced French-born restaurateur Bruno Berta has a
hit on his hands with his French-Mediterranean bistro on one of the
busiest corners in Temple Bar. Simple but stylish dishes range from starters
like feuilleté of crab meat and saffron sauce to main dishes of roast
scallops with Jerusalem artichoke purée and warm smoked bacon and
walnut dressing. The friendly service and relaxed surroundings make
this one of the area's best bets. ⊠ *30 Essex St. E, Temple Bar,* ☎ *01/
670–6767. AE, DC, MC, V. Closed Sun.*

South City Center: Ballsbridge, Donnybrook, and Stillorgan

CONTEMPORARY

$$ ✕ **O'Connells.** Fresh Irish produce and baked goods are the emphasis
in this vast, modern space with sleek timber paneling and floor-to-ceil-
ing windows. Go for the spit-roasted chicken or anything baked in the
huge clay oven. Other tasty dishes include a warm salad of kidneys
with greens and oyster mushrooms, and monkfish with a lively pepper, tomato, and coriander salsa. A tremendous array of fresh breads
is on display in the open kitchen, which turns into a buffet for breakfast and lunch. ⊠ *Merrion Rd., Ballsbridge, South County Dublin,* ☎
01/647–3304. AE, DC, MC, V.

CONTINENTAL

$$–$$$ ✕ **Beaufield Mews.** The original cobbled courtyard and the 18th-cen-
tury coach house, with stables, wonderfully, remain. The place is even
said to be haunted by a friendly monk. Inside it's all black beams, old
furniture, and bric-a-brac. The more desirable tables overlook the
courtyard or the garden or are, less predictably, "under the nun" (the
nun in question is a 17th-century portrait). While the main attraction
is the surroundings, the food, based on fresh ingredients, will keep you
coming back—old favorites include roast duckling à l'orange and
grilled wild-salmon steaks. The restaurant is a 10-mi taxi ride from the
city center. ⊠ *Woodlands Ave., Stillorgan, South County Dublin,* ☎
*01/288–0375. Reservations essential. AE, DC, MC, V. No dinner Sun.,
closed Mon.*

IRISH

$$$–$$$$ ✕ **Ernie's Restaurant.** High-quality ingredients, attention to detail, and consistency are the hallmarks of this long-established and welcoming restaurant, built around a large tree and fountain. Blue Irish linen and sparkling crystal decorate the tables. The seasonal menu always has a variety of catches of the day—grilled sole with spring onion and thyme butter, or poached wild salmon on a bed of creamed potato. You can also expect four or five meat and poultry entrées, such as roasted rack of Wicklow lamb with a caramelized onion tart. Ernie's is only a few minutes by taxi from the city center. ⊠ *Mulberry Gardens, Donnybrook, South County Dublin,* ☎ *01/269–3300. AE, DC, MC, V. Closed Sun.–Mon. and 1 wk at Christmas. No lunch weekends.*

City Center (Northside)

CONTEMPORARY

$$$ ✕ **Chapter One.** In the vaulted, stone-walled basement of the Dublin Writers Museum, just down the street from the Hugh Lane Municipal Gallery of Modern Art, is one of the most notable restaurants in northside Dublin. Try the roast venison with mustard and herb lentils, pancetta, and chestnut dumpling, and roast beetroot. The rich bread-and-butter pudding is a stellar dessert. ⊠ *18–19 Parnell Sq., North of the Liffey,* ☎ *01/873–2266. Reservations essential. AE, DC, MC, V. Closed Sun.–Mon. No lunch Sat.*

$$–$$$ ✕ **Halo.** This restaurant in the chic Morrison hotel has been an instant hit with the fashion crowd and lawyers from the nearby Four Courts. The dramatic dining room with a soaring ceiling and minimalist decor, devised by fashion designer John Rocha, looks moody and mysterious by night, and a little forbidding by day. The emphasis is on complex dishes that look as good as they taste: seared, cured salmon on creamed spinach, and *pomme vapour* (mashed potatoes) with coriander are among the specialties. Desserts are miniature works of art on enormous China platters. ⊠ *Morrison hotel, Ormond Quay, North of the Liffey,* ☎ *01/887–2421. AE, DC, MC, V.*

$–$$ ✕ **Harbour Master.** The main attraction of this big, airy restaurant and bar in the Irish Financial Services Centre north of the Liffey is its setting: it overlooks a canal basin. At lunch the place is packed with stockbrokers and lawyers; dinner is more subdued. You can dine bistro-style at the cavernous bar, but it's better to head for the more spacious—and relaxing—newly built section, which serves hearty prawn linguine with cashews, and beef and Guinness stew. ⊠ *Custom House Docks, North of the Liffey,* ☎ *01/670–1688. AE, DC, MC, V.*

MEDITERRANEAN

$–$$ ✕ **101 Talbot.** Popular with Dublin's artistic and literary set, and conveniently close to the Abbey and Gate theaters, this comfortable upstairs restaurant showcases an ever-changing exhibition of local artists' work. The creative, contemporary food—with Mediterranean and Middle Eastern influences—uses fresh, local ingredients. Try the roast pork fillet marinated in orange, ginger, and soy, and served with fried noodles. The cashew and red-pepper rissoles with chili and ginger jam, served with wild and basmati rice, also impresses. Healthy options and several vegetarian choices make this a highly versatile restaurant. ⊠ *101 Talbot St., North of the Liffey,* ☎ *01/874–5011. Reservations essential. AE, DC, MC, V. Closed Sun.–Mon.*

Pub Food

Most pubs serve food at lunchtime, some throughout the day. Food ranges from hearty soups and stews to chicken curries, smoked-salmon salads, and sandwiches, and much of it is surprisingly good. Expect to pay €6–€10 for a main course. Some of the larger, more popular pubs may take credit cards.

✕ **Davy Byrne's.** James Joyce immortalized this pub in *Ulysses*. Nowadays it's more akin to a cocktail bar than a Dublin pub, but it's good for fresh and smoked salmon, salads, and a hot daily special. ⊠ *21 Duke St., City Center,* ☎ *01/671–1298.*

✕ **Old Stand.** It's conveniently close to Grafton Street, and serves grilled food, including steaks. ⊠ *37 Exchequer St., City Center,* ☎ *01/ 677–7220.*

✕ **O'Neill's.** This fine pub, a stone's throw from Trinity College, has the best carvery of any pub in the city. (Immensely popular in Ireland, a carvery is meat cut to order—you pick the joint, they carve for you as much of it as you can eat. It comes with vegetables or potatoes and gravy.) A hearty lunch, served between noon and 2:30, costs about €6.35–€7.60. ⊠ *2 Suffolk St., City Center,* ☎ *01/670–5755.*

✕ **Stag's Head.** Serving one of Dublin's best pub lunches, this place is a favorite among both Trinity students and businesspeople. ⊠ *1 Dame Ct., City Center,* ☎ *01/679–3701.*

✕ **Zanzibar.** This spectacular, immense bar on the north side of the Liffey looks as though it might be more at home in downtown Marrakesh. Laze away an afternoon in one of the wicker chairs and enjoy hearty, freshly made sandwiches, salads, and cocktails. ⊠ *34–35 Lower Ormond Quay, North of the Liffey,* ☎ *01/878–7212.*

LODGING

"An absolute avalanche of new hotels" is how the *Irish Times* characterized Dublin's hotel boom. New lodgings have sprung up all over the city, including the much-talked-about Chief O'Neill's in Smithfield, and a few in Ballsbridge, an inner "suburb" that's a 20-minute walk from the city center. Demand for rooms means that rates are still high at the best hotels by the standards of any major European or North American city (and factoring in the exchange rate means a hotel room can take a substantial bite out of any traveler's budget). The recent slump in tourist travel, however, has caused a few hotels to cut their prices considerably. Service charges range from 15% in expensive hotels to zero in moderate and inexpensive ones. Be sure to inquire when you make reservations.

Many hotels have a weekend, or "B&B," rate that's often 30%–40% cheaper than the ordinary rate; some hotels also have a midweek special that provides discounts of up to 35%. These rates are available throughout the year but are harder to get in high season. Ask about them when booking a room (they are available only on a prebooked basis), especially if you plan a brief or weekend stay. If you've rented a car and you're not staying at a hotel with secure parking facilities, it's worth considering a location out of the city center, such as Dalkey or Killiney, where the surroundings are more pleasant and you won't have to worry about parking on city streets.

Dublin has a decent selection of less-expensive accommodations—including many moderately priced hotels with basic but agreeable rooms. As a general rule of thumb, lodgings on the north side of the river tend to be more affordable than those on the south. Many B&Bs, long the mainstay of the economy end of the market, have upgraded their facilities and now provide rooms with private bathrooms or showers, as well as multichannel color televisions and direct-dial telephones, for around €46 a night per person. B&Bs tend to be in suburban areas—generally a 15-minute bus ride from the center of the city. This is not in itself a great drawback, and savings can be significant.

CATEGORY	DUBLIN*
$$$$	over €280
$$$	€230–€280
$$	€178–€230
$	under €178

All prices are for two people in a double room, including VAT and a service charge (often applied in larger hotels).

City Center (Southside)

$$$$ 🏨 **Conrad Dublin International.** In a seven-story redbrick and smoked-glass building just off St. Stephen's Green, the Conrad, owned by the Hilton Group, firmly aims for international business travelers. Gleaming, light marble graces the large, formal lobby. Rooms are rather cramped and have uninspiring views of the adjacent office buildings, but are nicely outfitted with natural wood furnishings, painted in sand colors and pastel greens, and have Spanish marble in the bathrooms. A note to light sleepers: the air-conditioning/heating system can be noisy. The hotel has two restaurants: the informal Plurabelle and the plusher Alexandra Room. ⊠ *Earlsfort Terr., South of the Liffey,* ☎ *01/676–5555,* ℻ *01/676–5424,* ⬛ *www.conradinternational.ie. 182 rooms with bath, 9 suites. 2 restaurants, room service, in-room data ports, in-room safes, minibars, cable TV, in-room VCRs, gym, bar, concierge, business services, meeting rooms, free parking; no-smoking rooms, no-smoking floor. AE, DC, MC, V.*

$$$$ 🏨 **Fitzwilliam Hotel.** It has been dubbed a "designer" hotel for its impeccable decor: everything from light fixtures to luggage racks to staff uniforms is smartly designed. The modern glass building has a large roof garden and overlooks St. Stephen's Green. The spacious rooms are furnished in a contemporary, comfortable style. Conrad Gallagher, one of Ireland's most acclaimed chefs, presides over the rooftop restaurant. ⊠ *St. Stephen's Green, City Center,* ☎ *01/478–7000,* ℻ *01/478–7878,* ⬛ *www.fitzwilliamh.com. 128 rooms with bath, 2 suites. Restaurant, room service, cable TV, in-room VCRs, in-room data ports, gym, bar, laundry service, business services, meeting rooms; no-smoking rooms. AE, DC, MC, V.*

$$$$ 🏨 **Le Méridien Shelbourne.** Paris has the Ritz, New York has the Plaza,
★ and Dublin has the Shelbourne. Waterford chandeliers, gleaming old masters on the wall, and Irish Chippendale chairs invite you to linger in the lobby. Each guest room has fine, carefully selected furniture and luxurious drapes, with splendid antiques in the older rooms. Those in front overlook St. Stephen's Green, but rooms in the back, without a view, are quieter. The Lord Mayor's Lounge, off the lobby, is a perfect rendezvous spot and offers a lovely afternoon tea—a real Dublin tradition. ⊠ *27 St. Stephen's Green, City Center,* ☎ *01/663–4500; 800/543–4300 in the U.S.,* ℻ *01/661–6006,* ⬛ *www.shelbourne.ie. 181 rooms with bath, 9 suites. 2 restaurants, room service, indoor pool, health club, hot tub, sauna, 2 bars, free parking; no-smoking rooms. AE, DC, MC, V.*

$$$$ 🏨 **Merrion.** The home of the Duke of Wellington, hero of the Battle
★ of Waterloo, is one of the four exactingly restored Georgian town houses that make up this luxurious hotel. The stately rooms are appointed in classic Georgian style—from the crisp linen sheets to the Carrara marble bathrooms. Some are vaulted with delicate Adamesque plasterwork

ceilings, and others are graced with magnificent, original marble fire-places. Rooms in the old house are more expensive than those in the new extension. You know this place must be special, because leading Dublin restaurateur Patrick Guilbaud has moved his eponymous restaurant here. ✉ *Upper Merrion St., South of the Liffey,* ☎ *01/603–0600,* FAX *01/603–0700,* WEB *www.merrionhotel.com. 225 rooms with bath, 45 suites. 2 restaurants, room service, in-room data ports, in-room safes, minibars, cable TV, in-room VCRs, indoor pool, hair salon, massage, steam room, 2 bars, dry cleaning, laundry service, concierge, business services, meeting rooms, free parking; no-smoking rooms, no-smoking floor. AE, DC, MC, V.*

$$$$ 🏨 **Westbury.** This comfortable, modern hotel is in the heart of southside Dublin, right off the city's buzzing shopping mecca: Grafton Street. Join elegantly dressed Dubliners for afternoon tea in the spacious mezzanine-level main lobby, which is furnished with antiques. Alas, the utilitarian rooms—painted in pastels—don't share the lobby's elegance. More inviting are the suites, which combine European stylings with tasteful Japanese screens and prints. The flowery Russell Room serves formal lunches and dinners; the downstairs Sandbank, a seafood restaurant and bar, looks like a turn-of-the-20th-century establishment. ✉ *Grafton St., City Center,* ☎ *01/679–1122,* FAX *01/679–7078,* WEB *www.jurysdoyle.com. 204 rooms with bath, 8 suites. 2 restaurants, room service, minibars, cable TV, in-room VCRs, bar, dry cleaning, laundry service, free parking; no-smoking rooms. AE, DC, MC, V.*

$$$ 🏨 **Davenport.** The gorgeous, bright-yellow neoclassic facade of this hotel behind Trinity College was originally built in the 1860s to front a church. Tasteful, deep colors and functional furnishings characterize the reasonably spacious rooms and larger suites. The hotel restaurant, Lanyon's, serves breakfast, lunch, and dinner amid traditional Georgian surroundings. In the comfortable President's Bar, see how many heads of state you can identify in the photos covering the walls. ✉ *Merrion Sq., South of the Liffey,* ☎ *01/661–6800; 800/327–0200 in the U.S.,* FAX *01/661–5663,* WEB *www.ocallaghanhotels.ie. 118 rooms with bath, 2 suites. Restaurant, room service, minibars, cable TV, in-room VCRs, bar, dry cleaning, laundry service, concierge, business services, meeting rooms, free parking; no-smoking rooms. AE, DC, MC, V.*

$$–$$$ 🏨 **Westin Dublin.** Reconstructed from three 19th-century landmark buildings across the road from Trinity College, the Westin is all about location. The public spaces re-create a little of the splendor of yesteryear: marble pillars, tall mahogany doorways, blazing fireplaces, and period detailing on the walls and ceilings. The bedrooms, on the other hand, are functional and small, with the crisp, white Indian linen and custom-made beds the only luxurious touches. The rooms that overlook Trinity are a little more expensive, but the engaging view makes all the difference. ✉ *College Green, South of the Liffey,* ☎ *01/645–1000,* FAX *01/645–1234,* WEB *www.westin.com. 141 rooms with bath, 22 suites. Restaurant, room service, minibars, cable TV, 2 bars, dry cleaning, laundry service, concierge, business services, meeting rooms, free parking; no-smoking rooms. AE, DC, MC, V.*

$$ 🏨 **Clarion Stephen's Hall Hotel & Suites.** Dublin's only all-suite hotel occupies a tastefully modernized Georgian town house just off Stephen's Green. The suites, considerably larger than the average hotel room, include one or two bedrooms, a separate sitting room, a fully equipped kitchen, and bath. They are comfortably equipped with quality modern furniture. Top-floor suites have spectacular city views, and ground-floor suites have private entrances. Morel's Restaurant serves breakfast, lunch, and dinner. ✉ *14–17 Lower Leeson St., South of the Liffey,* ☎ *01/661–0585,* FAX *01/661–0606,* WEB *www.premgroup.ie. 34 suites.*

Restaurant, room service, cable TV, 2 bars, meeting rooms, free parking; no-smoking rooms. AE, DC, MC, V.

$–$$ ⌂ **Drury Court Hotel.** This small hotel, a two-minute walk from Grafton Street, is just around the corner from some of the city's best restaurants. Rooms are done in subtle greens, golds, and burgundies. In the parquet-floored rathskeller dining room you can get breakfast and dinner; lunch is served in the casual Digges Lane Bar, frequented by many young Dubliners. ⊠ *28–30 Lower Stephens St., City Center,* ☎ *01/ 475–1988,* FAX *01/478–5730,* WEB *www.indigo.ie/~druryct/. 30 rooms with bath, 2 suites. Restaurant, room service, bar, dry cleaning, laundry service, meeting room. AE, DC, MC, V.*

$–$$ ⌂ **Number 31.** Two Georgian mews strikingly renovated in the early '60s as the private home of Sam Stephenson, Ireland's leading modern architect, are now connected via a small garden to the grand town house they once served. Together they form a marvelous guest house a short walk from St. Stephen's Green. Owners Deirdre and Noel Comer serve made-to-order breakfasts at refectory tables in the balcony dining room. The white-tiled sunken living room, with its black leather sectional sofa and modern artwork that includes a David Hockney print, will make you think you're in California. ⊠ *31 Leeson Close, South of the Liffey,* ☎ *01/676–5011,* FAX *01/676–2929,* WEB *www.number31.ie. 21 rooms with bath. Dry cleaning, laundry service, free parking; no-smoking rooms. AE, MC, V.*

$ ⌂ **Avalon House.** Many young, independent travelers rate this cleverly restored redbrick Victorian building the most appealing of Dublin's hostels. A 2-minute walk from Grafton Street and 5–10 minutes from some of the city's best music venues, the hostel has a mix of dormitories, rooms without bath, and rooms with bath. The dorm rooms and en-suite quads all have loft areas that offer more privacy than you'd typically find in a multibed room. The Avalon Café serves food until 10 PM but is open as a common room after hours. ⊠ *55 Aungier St., City Center,* ☎ *01/475– 0001,* FAX *01/475–0303,* WEB *www.avalon-house.ie. 35 4-bed rooms with bath, 5 4-bed rooms without bath, 4 twin rooms with bath, 4 single rooms without bath, 22 twin rooms without bath, 5 12-bed dorms, 1 10-bed dorm, 1 26-bed dorm. Café, bar; no room TVs. AE, MC, V.*

$ ⌂ **Central Hotel.** Established in 1887, this grand, old-style redbrick hotel is in the heart of the city center, steps from Grafton Street, Temple Bar, and Dublin Castle. Rooms are small but have high ceilings and practical but tasteful furniture. Adjacent to the hotel is Molly Malone's Tavern, a lively hotel-bar with plenty of regulars who come for the atmosphere and the live, traditional Irish music on Friday and Saturday nights. The restaurant and Library Bar—one of the best spots in the city for a quiet pint—are on the first floor. ⊠ *1–5 Exchequer St., City Center,* ☎ *01/ 679–7302,* FAX *01/679–7303,* WEB *www.centralhotel.ie. 67 rooms with bath, 3 suites. Restaurant, room service, 2 bars, dry cleaning, laundry service, concierge, business services, meeting rooms. AE, DC, MC, V.*

$ ⌂ **Jurys Christchurch Inn.** Expect few frills at this functional budget hotel, part of a Jurys minichain that offers a low, fixed room rate for up to three adults or two adults and two children. (The **Jurys Custom House Inn** [⊠ Custom House Quay, South of the Liffey Dublin 1, ☎ 01/607–5000, FAX 01/829–0400], at the International Financial Services Centre, operates according to the same plan.) The biggest plus is the pleasant location, facing Christ Church Cathedral and within walking distance of most city-center attractions. The rather spartan rooms are decorated in pastel colors and utilitarian furniture. ⊠ *Christ Church Pl., Dublin West,* ☎ *01/454–0000,* FAX *01/454–0012,* WEB *www.jurysdoyle.com. 182 rooms with bath. Restaurant, bar, parking (fee); no-smoking rooms. AE, DC, MC, V.*

$ ⊞ **Kilronan House.** A five-minute walk from St. Stephen's Green, this large, late-19th-century terraced house with a white facade has been carefully converted into a guest house. The furnishings are updated each year. Richly patterned wallpaper and carpets decorate the guest rooms, and orthopedic beds (rather rare in Dublin hotels, let alone guest houses) help to guarantee a restful night's sleep. ⊠ *70 Adelaide Rd., South of the Liffey,* ☎ *01/475–5266,* FAX *01/478–2841,* WEB *www.dublinn.com. 15 rooms with bath. Free parking; no-smoking room. MC, V.*

Temple Bar

$$$$ ⊞ **The Clarence.** You might well bump into celebrity friends of co-owners Bono and the Edge of U2 at this contemporary hotel, understated to the point of austerity. The Octagon Bar and the Tea Room Restaurant are popular Temple Bar watering holes. Guest rooms are decorated in a mishmash of earth tones accented with deep purple, gold, cardinal red, and royal blue. With the exception of those in the penthouse suite, rooms are small. The laissez-faire service seems to take its cue from the minimalist style, so if you like to be pampered, stay elsewhere. ⊠ *6–8 Wellington Quay, Temple Bar,* ☎ *01/407–0800,* FAX *01/ 407–0820,* WEB *www.theclarence.ie. 47 rooms with bath, 3 suites. Restaurant, minibars, cable TV, bar, dry cleaning, laundry service, meeting rooms, free parking; no-smoking rooms. AE, DC, MC, V.*

$–$$ ⊞ **Parliament.** Although the Parliament is in one of Dublin's finest Edwardian buildings, its interior is very much functional, if tidy, and appeals to mainly a business clientele—drawn by the location near the Central Bank and Trinity College. Rooms are a good size, with a simple, slightly monotonous beige and off-white color scheme. The Senate Restaurant and Forum Bar keep up the democratic theme with reliable selections. ⊠ *Lord Edward St., Temple Bar,* ☎ *01/670–8777,* FAX *01/ 670–8787,* WEB *www.regencyhotels.com. 63 rooms with bath. Restaurant, bar, cable TV; no-smoking rooms. AE, DC, MC, V.*

$–$$ ⊞ **Temple Bar.** The hotel's delightful Art Deco lobby has a large, old-fashioned cast-iron fireplace, natural-wood furniture, and lots of plants. Off the lobby are a small cocktail bar and the bright, airy, glass-roofed Terrace Restaurant, which serves sandwiches, pastas, omelets, and fish all day. Mahogany furnishings and autumn green and rust colors characterize the guest rooms, nearly all of which have double beds (this makes them more than a little cramped). The Boomerang nightclub on the premises is open both to guests and the public. The hotel is in a former bank building, around the corner from Trinity College. ⊠ *Fleet St., Temple Bar,* ☎ *01/677–3333,* FAX *01/677–3088,* WEB *www.towerhotelgroup. ie/templebar. 133 rooms with bath, 2 suites. Restaurant, cable TV, 2 bars, nightclub, parking (fee). AE, DC, MC, V.*

$ ⊞ **Paramount.** At the heart of modern Temple Bar, this medium-size hotel has opted to maintain its classy Victorian facade. The foyer continues this theme of solid elegance, with incredibly comfortable leather couches, bleached-blond oak floors, and Burgundy red curtains. The bedrooms are decorated in dark woods and subtle colors—very 1930s (you just know if Bogart and Bacall ever came to Dublin they'd have to stay here). If you're fond of a tipple, try the hotel's Art Deco Turks Head Bar and Chop House. ⊠ *Parliament St. and Essex Gate, Temple Bar,* ☎ *01/417–9900,* FAX *01/417–9904,* WEB *www.paramounthotel.ie. 70 rooms with bath. Restaurant, cable TV, in-room data ports, bar, laundry service; no-smoking rooms. AE, DC, MC, V.*

South City Center—Ballsbridge

$$$$ ⊞ **Berkeley Court.** The most quietly elegant of Dublin's large modern hotels, Berkeley Court has a glass-and-concrete exterior that's de-

signed in a modern, blocklike style, and is surrounded by verdant grounds. The vast white-tiled and plushly carpeted lobby has roomy sofas and antique planters. The large rooms are decorated in golds, yellows, and greens, with antiques or reproductions of period furniture; bathrooms are tiled in marble. There are five luxury suites. The Berkeley Room restaurant has table d'hôte and à la carte menus; the more informal Conservatory Grill, with large windows, serves grilled food and snacks. ⊠ *Lansdowne Rd., South County Dublin,* ☎ *01/660–1711; 800/550–0000 in the U.S.,* ℻ *01/661–7238,* ᴡᴇʙ *www.jurysdoyle.com. 158 rooms with bath, 29 suites. 2 restaurants, room service, cable TV, gym, hair salon, some hot tubs, bar, shops, dry cleaning, laundry service, business services, meeting rooms, free parking; no-smoking rooms. AE, DC, MC, V.*

$$$$ 🖭 **Four Seasons.** Much controversy surrounds the brash, postmodern architecture of this hotel. The six-floor building mixes a Victorian and Georgian design with modern glass and concrete. The impressive landscaping makes the hotel seem like an oasis; a big effort has been made to ensure that a bit of greenery can be seen from most rooms. Rooms are spacious, with large windows that allow the light to flood in. A selection of landscapes on the walls gives the place a more human feel. ⊠ *Simmonscourt Rd., South County Dublin,* ☎ *01/665–4000,* ℻ *01/ 665–4099,* ᴡᴇʙ *www.fourseasons.com. 192 rooms with bath, 67 suites. Restaurant, cable TV, coffee shop, indoor pool, hot tub, bar, shop, dry cleaning, laundry service, business services, meeting rooms, free parking; no-smoking rooms. AE, DC, MC, V.*

$$$$ 🖭 **Herbert Park Hotel.** Adjacent to a park of the same name, and beside the River Dodder, the hotel's large lobby has floor-to-ceiling windows and a slanted glass roof. The spacious bar, terrace lounge, and restaurant are Japanese-inspired minimalist in style. Relaxing shades of blue and cream predominate in the nicely sized rooms; all have individually controlled air-conditioning, a large desk, and two telephone lines. Some look onto the park. Two of the suites have large balconies with views of the park or the leafy suburbs. The restaurant has a terrace where you can dine in warm weather. ⊠ *Ballsbridge, South County Dublin,* ☎ *01/ 667–2200,* ℻ *01/667–2595,* ᴡᴇʙ *www.herbertparkhotel.ie. 150 rooms with bath, 3 suites. Restaurant, cable TV, gym, bar, business services, free parking; no-smoking rooms. AE, DC, MC, V.*

$$$$ 🖭 **Jurys Ballsbridge and the Towers.** These adjoining seven-story hotels, popular with businesspeople, have more atmosphere than most comparable modern hotels. The Towers has an edge over its older, larger, less-expensive companion, Jurys Ballsbridge. The Towers' rooms are decorated in blue and gold with built-in, natural-wood furniture; the large beds and armchairs are comfortable. Jurys Ballsbridge, on the other hand, has large, plainly decorated rooms with light walls and brown drapes; furnishings are functional but uninspired. ⊠ *Jurys Ballsbridge: Pembroke Rd.; The Towers: Lansdowne Rd., Ballsbridge, South County Dublin,* ☎ *01/660–5000,* ℻ *01/679–7078,* ᴡᴇʙ *www.jurysdoyle.com. Jurys Ballsbridge: 300 rooms with bath, 3 suites; the Towers: 100 rooms with bath, 4 suites with kitchenettes. 2 restaurants, coffee shop, indoor-outdoor pool, hot tub, bar, cabaret (May–Oct.), shop, dry cleaning, laundry service, business services, meeting rooms, free parking. AE, DC, MC, V.*

$$$ 🖭 **Doyle Burlington.** In high contrast to the hotel's impersonal, 1972 glass-and-concrete facade, the staff are friendly and attentive. Public rooms, especially the large bar, have mahogany counters and hanging plants that enhance the conservatory-style setting. The generous-size rooms, in the usual modern minimalism (neutral tones), have large pic-

ture windows. At night, Annabel's nightclub and the seasonal (summer) Irish cabaret are both lively spots. The Burlington has no sports and health facilities but the Doyle hotel group, which runs it, has an arrangement that allows you to use the RiverView Sports Club in nearby Clonskeagh for €6.35 a visit. ⊠ *Upper Leeson St., South County Dublin,* ☎ *01/660–5222,* FAX *01/660–8496,* WEB *www.jurysdoyle. com. 523 rooms with bath. 2 restaurants, room service, cable TV, 3 bars, cabaret (May–Oct.), nightclub, shops, dry cleaning, laundry service, business services, meeting rooms, free parking; no-smoking room. AE, DC, MC, V.*

$$–$$$ ⊞ **Hibernian.** This early 20th-century Edwardian nurses' home designed
★ by Albert E. Murray—one of the architects of the Rotunda Hospital—is now a small luxury hotel. One of the city's most elegant and intimate hotels, it retains the distinctive red-and-amber brick facade and has smallish rooms, nicely done in pastels, with deep-pile carpets and comfortable furniture. The public rooms, in cheerful chintz and stripes, include a period-style library and a sun lounge—both comfortable spaces to relax before or after a dinner in the hotel's intimate restaurant, the Patrick Kavanagh Room. Amid all this Victorian elegance, the owners haven't forgotten the warming touches. ⊠ *Eastmoreland Pl. off Upper Baggot St., South County Dublin,* ☎ *01/668–7666 or 800/414243,* FAX *01/660–2655,* WEB *www.hibernianhotel.com. 40 rooms with bath. Restaurant, bar, parking (fee). AE, DC, MC, V.*

$–$$ ⊞ **Mount Herbert Hotel.** The Loughran family's sprawling accommodation includes a number of large, Victorian-era houses. It overlooks some of Ballsbridge's fine rear gardens and is right near the main rugby stadium; the nearby DART will have you in the city center in seven minutes. The simple rooms are painted in light shades and contain little besides beds; all have bathrooms and 10-channel TVs. The lounge is a good place to relax. The restaurant, which overlooks the English-style back garden (floodlit at night) and children's play area, serves three meals a day; at dinner you can get steaks and stews. ⊠ *7 Herbert Rd., South County Dublin,* ☎ *01/668–4321,* FAX *01/660– 7077,* WEB *www.mountherberthotel.ie. 200 rooms with bath. Restaurant, cable TV, sauna, bar, shop, business services, meeting rooms, free parking; no-smoking rooms. AE, DC, MC, V.*

$ ⊞ **Ariel Guest House.** This redbrick 1850 Victorian guest house in a
★ tree-lined suburb is one of Dublin's finest, just a few steps from a DART stop and a 15-minute walk from St. Stephen's Green. Restored rooms in the main house are lovingly decorated with Victorian and Georgian antiques, Victoriana, and period wallpaper and drapes. The 13 rooms at the back of the house are more spartan, but all are immaculate. A Waterford-crystal chandelier hangs over the comfortable leather and mahogany furniture in the gracious, fireplace-warmed drawing room. Owner Michael O'Brien is an extraordinarily helpful and gracious host. ⊠ *52 Lansdowne Rd., South County Dublin,* ☎ *01/668–5512,* FAX *01/ 668–5845,* WEB *www.ariel-house.com. 40 rooms with bath. Free parking. MC, V.*

$ ⊞ **Lansdowne.** The cozy, Georgian-style rooms in this small Ballsbridge
★ hotel have delightful floral-pattern furnishings. Photos of sports personalities hang on the walls of the Green Blazer bar in the basement, a popular haunt for local businesspeople and fans of the international rugby matches held at nearby Lansdowne Road; you can get a bite to eat here all day. Next to the bar is Parker's Restaurant, which specializes in seafood and grilled steaks. ⊠ *27 Pembroke Rd., South County Dublin,* ☎ *01/668–2522,* FAX *01/668–5585,* WEB *www.lansdownehotel. com. 38 rooms with bath, 2 suites. Restaurant, bar, free parking. AE, DC, MC, V.*

Ariel
Guest House **36**

Arlington Hotel **11**

Avalon House **21**

Berkeley Court **35**

Bewleys at
Newlands Cross . . **8**

Central Hotel **16**

Charleville Lodge **3**

Chief O'Neill's **7**

The Clarence **10**

Clarion Hotel IFSC . . **6**

Clarion
Stephen's Hall
Hotel & Suites **26**

Conrad Dublin
International **25**

Davenport **22**

Doyle Burlington . . **29**

Drury Court Hotel . . **19**

Fitzpatrick Castle
Dublin **39**

Fitzwilliam Hotel . . **20**

Four Seasons **33**

Globetrotters
Tourist Hostel **5**

Great Southern
Hotel **2**

Herbert Park
Hotel **32**

Hibernian **30**

Holiday Inn
Dublin Airport **2**

Jurys Christchurch
Inn **17**

Jurys Ballsbridge and
The Towers **34**

Jurys Skylon **1**

Jurys Tara **38**

Kilronan House **27**

Lansdowne **31**

Le Méridien
Shelbourne **23**

Merrion **24**

The Morrison **9**

Mount Herbert
Hotel **37**

Number 31 . . . . . . **28**

Paramount **14**

Parliament **15**

Royal Dublin
Hotel **4**

Royal Marine **40**

Temple Bar **12**

Westbury **18**

Westin Dublin **13**

Dublin Lodging

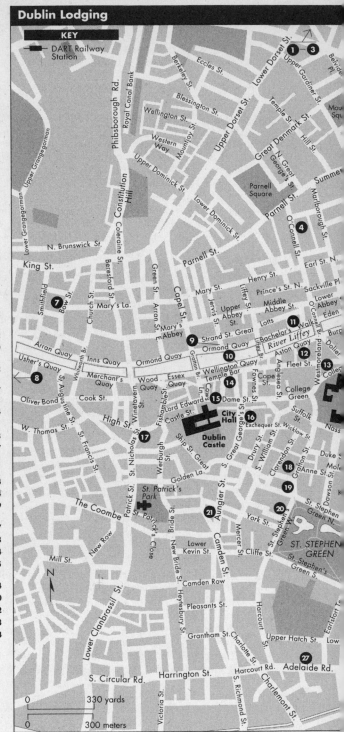

KEY

DART Railway
Station

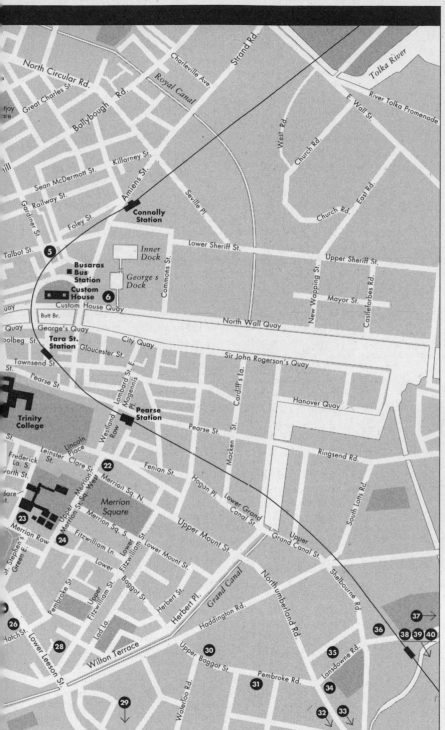

City Center (Northside)

$$$$ 🏨 **The Morrison.** Halfway between the Ha'penny and Capel Street bridges, it's no more than a 10-min walk to Trinity College. The highly modern interior—designed by John Rocha, Ireland's most acclaimed fashion designer—can be a bit cold. He had the last word on every-thing down to the toiletries and staff uniforms. Rooms have unfussy modern furnishings and are high-tech, with top-of-the-line entertainment units, satellite TV, and ISDN lines. The Halo restaurant has an Asian fusion theme. ⊠ *Ormond Quay, North of the Liffey,* ☎ *01/887–2400,* FAX *01/878–3185,* WEB *www.morrisonhotel.ie. 88 rooms with bath, 7 suites. 2 restaurants, room service, in-room data ports, minibars, cable TV, in-room VCRs, 2 bars, dry cleaning, laundry service, concierge, business services, meeting rooms, free parking; no-smoking rooms. AE, DC, MC, V.*

$$–$$$ 🏨 **Chief O'Neill's.** Named after a 19th-century Corkman who became chief of police in Chicago, this hotel is by far the largest building in Smith-field Village. Smallish, high-tech rooms all have ISDN lines and look thoroughly up-to-date—with chrome fixtures and minimalist furnishings. Top-floor suites have delightful roof-top gardens with views of the city on both sides of the Liffey. The café-bar has live traditional music and contemporary Irish food, and Asian cuisine is available in Kelly & Ping, a bright, airy restaurant off Duck Lane, a shopping arcade that's part of the hotel complex. ⊠ *Smithfield Village, North of the Liffey,* ☎ *01/817–3838,* FAX *01/817–3839,* WEB *www.chiefoneills.com. 70 rooms with bath, 3 suites. Restaurant, room service, in-room data ports, minibars, cable TV, in-room VCRs, gym, bar, shops, dry cleaning, laundry service, free parking; no-smoking rooms. AE, DC, MC, V.*

$$–$$$ 🏨 **Clarion Hotel IFSC.** Smack in the middle of the International Financial Services Centre, the Clarion—with an office-block-like exterior—is indistinguishable from many of the financial institutions that surround it. The public spaces are bright and cheery, if a little uninspired, and the bedrooms are all straight lines and contemporary light-oak furnishings. Shades of blue and taupe create a calm environment. Try get a room at the front with great views out over the Liffey. They mainly cater to the business traveller, so weekend bargains are a definite possibility—make sure you ask for them. ⊠ *IFSC, North of the Liffey,* ☎ *01/433–8800,* FAX *01/433–8811,* WEB *www.clarionhotelifsc.com. 147 rooms with bath, 13 suites. Restaurant, room service, in-room data ports, minibars, cable TV, indoor pool, gym, health club, massage, bar, dry cleaning, laundry service, free parking; no-smoking rooms. AE, DC, MC, V.*

$$ 🏨 **Royal Dublin Hotel.** O'Connell Street is not what it once was, but this renovated, upmarket hotel has just about a perfect location at the top of the old thoroughfare. All of the northside's major attractions are nearby, and you can walk south to Trinity College in 10 minutes. The public spaces are well-lit, and decorated in glass and brass. Rooms are spacious, and the hotel has built a solid reputation for extra-friendly service. The Georgian Room and Raffles bar try to put on posh English airs (think crisp linen), but the casual warmth of the staff undoes the stuffiness. ⊠ *O'Connell St., North of the Liffey,* ☎ *01/873–3666,* FAX *01/873–3120,* WEB *www.royaldublin.com. 117 rooms with bath, 3 suites. Restaurant, room service, in-room data ports, minibars, cable TV, in-room VCRs, bar, dry cleaning, laundry service; no-smoking rooms. AE, MC, V.*

$–$$ 🏨 **Arlington Hotel.** A converted auction house on the quays is the setting for this privately owned boutique hotel. The rooms have a Georgian style, with soothing pastel yellow or lavender walls; spreads and drapes are awash in golds, rusts, and blues, and have patterns and details evocative of tapestries. The bar, boisterous and echo-filled, is more mead hall than cozy pub. Rich upholstery, romantic lighting, and hearty Irish fare (full breakfast is included in the rates) make the restaurant more intimate, however. The hotel has limited off-street parking. ✉ *23–25 Bachelor's Walk, O'Connell Bridge, North of the Liffey,* ☎ *01/804–9100,* FAX *01/804–9112,* WEB *www.arlington.ie. 115 rooms with bath, 6 suites. Restaurant, cable TV, in-room data ports, bar, dance club, baby-sitting, laundry service, meeting rooms, free parking; no-smoking rooms. AE, DC, MC, V.*

$ 🖬 **Charleville Lodge.** It's worth the short commute to the city center (the No. 10 bus takes five minutes and it's a great walk in good weather) to enjoy the luxury (and great-value) of the Charleville Lodge. It's part of a row of beautifully restored Victorian terraced houses in the historic Phibsborough area of Dublin's northside. The dramatically lit residents' lounge, with a working fireplace, is a great spot to chat with other travelers who have dared to stray off the beaten path. Rooms are brightly colored and spacious. ✉ *268–272 N. Circular Rd., North of the Liffey,* ☎ *01/838–6633,* FAX *01/838–5854,* WEB *www.charlevillelodge.ie. 30 rooms with bath. Free parking; no-smoking rooms. MC, V.*

$ 🖬 **Globetrotters Tourist Hostel.** Globetrotters is a giant step up from many Dublin hostels, with a pleasant outdoor courtyard; clean, locking dorm rooms with en-suite showers; a turf fire; comfortable bunk beds (with lamps for late-night reading); and a delicious all-you-can-eat breakfast. Plus, you're within walking distance of the city center, one block from the bus station, and two blocks from the train station. They also own the Town House, a cute bed-and-breakfast in the same building. ✉ *46 Lower Gardiner St., North County Dublin,* ☎ *01/873–5893,* FAX *01/878–8787,* WEB *www.townhouse.ie. 94 dorm beds, 38 double rooms with bath. Restaurant. MC, V.*

South County Dublin Suburbs

$$–$$$ 🖬 **Royal Marine.** This 1870 seaside hotel has comfortable, capacious rooms with contemporary furnishings. The lofty ceilings from the original building are preserved in the suites, with four-poster beds and sitting rooms. Ask for a room at the front of the hotel, facing Dun Laoghaire harbor. ✉ *Marine Rd., South County Dublin, Dun Laoghaire,* ☎ *01/280–1911,* FAX *01/280–1089,* WEB *www.ryan-hotel.com. 95 rooms with bath, 8 suites. Restaurant, room service, 2 bars, business services, free parking; no-smoking rooms. AE, DC, MC, V.*

$$ 🖬 **Fitzpatrick Castle Dublin.** For its sweeping views over Dun Laoghaire
★ and Dublin Bay, the Fitzpatrick is worth the 15-km (9-mi) drive from the city center. The original part of the hotel is an 18th-century stone castle, with a substantial modern addition housing rooms; many are furnished with antiques and four-poster beds, and have large bathrooms. The hotel is convenient to golfing, horseback riding, and fishing; the fitness facilities include an 82-ft heated pool. The views from Killiney Hill, behind the hotel, are spectacular; the seaside village of Dalkey and Killiney Beach are both within walking distance. ✉ *South County Dublin, Killiney,* ☎ *01/230–5400,* FAX *01/230–5466,* WEB *www.fitzpatricks.com. 113 rooms with bath. Restaurant, cable TV, indoor pool, health club, bar, meeting rooms, free parking. AE, DC, MC, V.*

$ 🖬 **Bewleys at Newlands Cross.** Stay at this four-story hotel on the southwest outskirts of the city if you're planning to head out of the city early (especially to points in the Southwest and West) and don't want to deal with morning traffic. The hotel is emulating the formula popularized by Jurys Inns, in which rooms—here each has a double bed, a single bed, and a sofa bed—are a flat rate for up to three adults or two adults and two children. ✉ *Newlands Cross, Naas Rd., South County Dublin,* ☎ *01/464–0140,* FAX *01/464–0900,* WEB *www.bewleyshotels.com. 256 rooms with bath. Café, free parking; no-smoking rooms. AE, MC, V.*

$ 🖭 **Jurys Tara.** On the main coast road 10–15 minutes from the Dun Laoghaire ferry terminal and 6½ km (4 mi) from the city center, you'll find this unpretentious, informal seven-story hotel. It's also near the Booterstown Marsh Bird Sanctuary. The best rooms are in the original section and face Dublin Bay; rooms in the addition have slightly more modern furnishings. The restaurant serves grilled fish, steaks, and omelets. The hotel staff is very personable. ✉ *Merrion Rd., South County Dublin,* ☎ *01/269–4666,* FAX *01/269–1027,* WEB *www.jurysdoyle.com. 114 rooms with bath. Restaurant, bar, dry cleaning, laundry service, free parking; no-smoking rooms. AE, DC, MC, V.*

Dublin Airport

$$–$$$ 🖭 **Holiday Inn Dublin Airport.** You'll find basic but spacious rooms at the Holiday Inn, a low-rise redbrick structure with a plain exterior. The Bistro Restaurant serves both fish and meat entrées and vegetarian dishes; Sampans serves Chinese cuisine at dinner only. There's live music in the bar on weekends. Guests have access to a nearby health club. ✉ *Dublin Airport, North County Dublin,* ☎ *01/808–0500,* FAX *01/844– 6002,* WEB *www.forte-hotels.com. 250 rooms with bath. 2 restaurants, room service, bar, free parking; no-smoking rooms. AE, DC, MC, V.*

$ 🖭 **Great Southern Hotel.** *Within* the airport complex, near the main terminal, and next to the main road into the city center you'll find a modern five-story hotel that's part of one of Ireland's most respected chains. The accommodation itself is spacious and comfortable, if a little unexciting, but the service is exceptional. ✉ *Dublin Airport, North County Dublin,* ☎ *01/844–6000,* FAX *01/844–6001,* WEB *www.dubairport.gsh.ie. 147 rooms with bath. Restaurant, room service, bar, free parking. AE, DC, MC, V.*

$ 🖭 **Jurys Skylon.** On the main road into Dublin city center from the airport is a modern five-story hotel with a concrete-and-glass facade and generous-size rooms, plainly decorated in cool pastels. Rooms have double beds and a pair of easy chairs are almost the only furniture. A glass-fronted lobby with a large bar and the Rendezvous Room restaurant dominate the public areas. The cooking is adequate but uninspired, with dishes such as grilled steak, poached cod, and omelets. ✉ *Upper Drumcondra Rd., North County Dublin,* ☎ *01/837–9121,* FAX *01/ 837–2778,* WEB *www.jurysdoyle.com. 88 rooms with bath. Restaurant, bar, free parking. AE, DC, MC, V.*

NIGHTLIFE AND THE ARTS

Long before Stephen Daedalus's excursions into nighttown (read Joyce's *A Portrait of the Artist as a Young Man*), Dublin was proud of its lively after-hours scene, particularly its thriving pubs. Lately, however, with the advent of Irish rock superstars (think U2, the Cranberries, Sinéad O'Connor, Bob Geldof) and the resurgence of Celtic music (think *Riverdance*, the sound track to *Titanic*), the rest of the world seems to have discovered that Dublin is one of the most happening places in the world. Most nights the city's pubs and clubs overflow with young cell phone–toting Dubliners and Europeans who descend on the capital for weekend getaways. The city's 900-plus pubs are its main source of entertainment; many public houses in the city center have live music—from rock to jazz to traditional Irish.

Theater has always been taken seriously in the city that was home to O'Casey, Synge, Yeats, and Beckett. Today Dublin has eight major theaters that reproduce the Irish "classics," and newer fare from the likes of Martin Macdonagh and Conon Macpherson. At long last, the Gaiety Theatre has given long-overlooked opera a home in Dublin. If you're a movie buff, you'll appreciate the two dozen cinema screens in the city center. There are also a number of large, multiscreen cinema complexes in the suburbs, which show current releases made in Ireland and abroad.

The visual arts have always been the poor cousin in the Dublin cultural family. In recent years, small galleries have sprung up all over the city, and the development of Temple Bar Galleries has encouraged a whole new generation of painters, photographers, and sculptors.

Check the following newspapers for informative listings: the *Irish Times* publishes a daily guide to what's happening in Dublin and in the rest of the country, and has complete film and theater schedules. The *Evening Herald* lists theaters, cinemas, and pubs with live entertainment. *In Dublin* and the *Big Issue* are weekly guides to all film, theater, and musical events around the city. You'll find the *Event Guide,* a weekly free paper that lists music, cinema, theater, art shows, and dance clubs, in pubs and cafés around the city. In peak season, consult the free Bord Fáilte leaflet "Events of the Week."

The Arts

Art Galleries

The Bridge. This restored 18th-century Georgian house on the river houses an impressive, open-plan gallery. An internal bridge leads from the gallery shop to the big space at the back where you'll find exhibits of established and rising Irish artists in all media. ⊠ *6 Upper Ormond Quay, North of the Liffey,* ☎ 01/872–9702. ☯ *Mon.–Sat. 10–6, Sun. 2–5.*

5th. This is the gallery every Irish artist wants to be shown in. The location is spectacular: it's on the fifth floor of the impressive Guinness Storehouse. Regularly changing exhibits include painting and sculpture, but there is an emphasis on innovative installation and web art from all over the world. ⊠ *St. James Gate, Dublin West,* ☎ 01/408–4800. ☯ *Daily 9–5:30.*

Green on Red Galleries. It's strange that this rather unprepossessing gallery, near the back of Trinity College, is one of Dublin's best. Exhibitions are constantly changing—they feature the work of some of the country's—and Britain's—most promising up-and-coming artists. ⊠ *26–28 Lombard St. E, South of the Liffey,* ☎ 01/671–3414. ☯ *Weekdays 11–6, Sat. 11–5.*

Kerlin Gallery. Perhaps Dublin's most important commercial gallery, this large space behind Grafton Street exhibits the work of many of Ireland's important contemporary artists, including such internationally recognized figures as New York–based Sean Scully, Kathy Prendergast, Paul Seawright, and Stephen McKenna. ⊠ *Anne's La., S. Anne St., City Center,* ☎ 01/670–9093. ☯ *Weekdays 10–5:45, Sat. 11–4:30.*

National Photographic Archive. It's a treasure trove of Irish photographs from the late 19th and early 20th centuries. The Archive also hosts exhibits of work from contemporary Irish photographers—North and South. ⊠ *Temple Bar,* ☎ 01/603–0200. ☯ *Weekdays 10–5, Sat. 10–2.*

Original Print Gallery. An ultramodern building by the same prominent Dublin architect who designed Temple Bar Gallery, this place specializes in handmade limited editions of prints by Irish artists. Also in the building, the **Black Church Print Studio** (☎ 01/677–3629) exhibits prints. ⊠ *4 Temple Bar,* ☎ *01/677–3657.* ☾ *Tues.–Fri. 10:30–5:30, Sat. 11–5, Sun. 2–6.*

Rubicon Gallery. A second-floor gallery overlooking St. Stephen's Green, Rubicon holds a number of yearly exhibitions. They exhibit work in all media. ⊠ *10 St. Stephen's Green, City Center,* ☎ *01/670–8055.* ☾ *Mon.–Sat. 11–5:30.*

Solomon Gallery. Although not exactly a risk taker, the Solomon has slowly developed a reputation as one of Dublin's leading fine-art galleries. ⊠ *Powerscourt Townhouse Centre, S. William St., City Center,* ☎ *01/679–4237.* ☾ *Mon.–Sat. 10–5:30.*

Temple Bar Gallery. At this flagship of the Temple Bar redevelopment project, expect to see the work of emerging Irish photographers, painters, sculptors, and other artists. Shows are on monthly rotating schedules. ⊠ *5–9 Temple Bar,* ☎ *01/671–0073.* ☾ *Mon.–Sat. 11–6, Sun. 2–6.*

Classical Music and Opera

The **Bank of Ireland Arts Center** (⊠ Foster Pl. S, City Center, ☎ 01/671–1488) is great at lunchtime, when classical music and opera recitals take place.

National Concert Hall (⊠ Earlsfort Terr., South of the Liffey, ☎ 01/475–1666), just off St. Stephen's Green, is Dublin's main theater for classical music of all kinds, from symphonies to chamber groups. It houses the National Symphony Orchestra of Ireland.

Opera Ireland (⊠ John Player House, 276–288 S. Circular Rd., South of the Liffey, ☎ 01/453–5519) performs at the Gaiety Theatre; call to find out what's on and when.

Opera Theatre Company (⊠ Temple Bar Music Centre Curved Street, Temple Bar, ☎ 01/679–4962) is Ireland's only touring opera company. They perform at venues in Dublin and throughout the country.

Royal Hospital Kilmainham (⊠ Military Rd., Dublin West, ☎ 01/671–8666) presents frequent classical concerts in its magnificent 17th-century interior.

St. Stephen's Church (⊠ Merrion Sq., South of the Liffey, ☎ 01/288–0663) stages a regular program of choral and orchestral events under its glorious "pepper canister" cupola.

Film

Irish Film Centre (⊠ 6 Eustace St., Temple Bar, ☎ 01/677–8788) shows classic and new independent films.

Savoy Cinema (⊠ O'Connell St., North of the Liffey, ☎ 01/874–6000), just across from the General Post Office, is a four-screen theater with the largest screen in the country.

Screen Cinema (⊠ 2 Townsend St., City Center, ☎ 01/671–4988), between Trinity College and O'Connell Street Bridge, is a popular three-screen art-house cinema.

UGC Multiplex (⊠ Parnell Center, Parnell St., North of the Liffey, ☎ 01/872–8400), a 12-screen theater just off O'Connell Street, is the city center's only multiplex movie house; it shows the latest commercial features.

Rock and Contemporary Music

The **Ambassador** (⊠ 1 Parnell Sq., North of the Liffey, ☎ 01/889–9403)was once a cinema attached to the Gate Theatre. The plush interior and seats have been removed, and the stripped-down venue now houses visiting bands and "school-disco" nights with music from the '70s and '80s.

HQ (✉ 57 Middle Abbey St., North of the Liffey, ☎ 01/889–9403) is a very comfortable 500-seat venue, located at the Hot Press Irish Music Hall of Fame, that attracts international big-name acts. It's fun to watch performances from the balcony here; there's also a restaurant.

The **International Bar** (✉ Wicklow St., City Center, ☎ 01/677–9250) has a long-established, tiny, get-close-to-the band venue upstairs. It hosts theater in the afternoons.

Olympia Theatre (✉ 72 Dame St., Temple Bar, ☎ 01/677–7744) puts on its "Midnight from the Olympia" shows every Friday and Saturday from midnight to 2 AM, with everything from rock to country.

The **Point** (✉ Eastlink Br., North of the Liffey, ☎ 01/836–3633), a 6,000-capacity arena about 1 km (½ mi) east of the Custom House on the Liffey, is Dublin's premier venue for internationally renowned acts. Call or send a self-addressed envelope to receive a list of upcoming shows; tickets can be difficult to obtain, so book early.

Temple Bar Music Centre (✉ Curved St., Temple Bar, ☎ 01/670–0533) is a music venue, rehearsal space, television studio, and pub rolled into one. It buzzes with activity every day of the week. Live acts range from rock bands to ethnic music to singer-songwriters.

Whelan's (✉ 25 Wexford St., City Center, ☎ 01/478–0766), just off the southeastern corner of St. Stephen's Green, is one of the city's best—and most popular—music venues. You'll find well-known performers playing everything from rock to folk to traditional.

Theater

Abbey Theatre (✉ Lower Abbey St., North of the Liffey, ☎ 01/878–7222), the home of Ireland's national theater company, stages mainstream, mostly Irish traditional, plays. Its sister theater at the same address, the **Peacock**, offers more experimental drama. In 1904 W. B. Yeats and his patron, Lady Gregory, opened the theater, which became a major center for the Irish literary renaissance—the place that first staged works by J. M. Synge and Sean O'Casey, among many others. The original theater burned down in 1951, but it reopened with a modern design in 1966.

Andrew's Lane Theatre (✉ 9–11 Andrew's La., City Center, ☎ 01/679–5720) presents experimental productions.

Gaiety Theatre (✉ S. King St., City Center, ☎ 01/677–1717) is the home of Opera Ireland when it's not showing musical comedy, drama, and revues.

Gate Theatre (✉ Cavendish Row, Parnell Sq., North of the Liffey, ☎ 01/874–4045), an intimate 371-seat theater in a jewel-like Georgian assembly hall, produces the classics and contemporary plays by leading Irish writers.

New Project Arts Centre (✉ 39 E. Essex St., Temple Bar, ☎ 01/671–2321) is a theater and performance space right in the center of Temple Bar. Fringe and mainstream theater, contemporary music, and experimental art have all found a home here.

Olympia Theatre (✉ 72 Dame St., Temple Bar, ☎ 01/677–7744) is Dublin's oldest and premier multipurpose theatrical venue. In addition to its high-profile musical performances, it has seasons of comedy, vaudeville, and ballet.

Samuel Beckett Centre (✉ Trinity College, City Center, ☎ 01/608–2266) is home to Trinity's Drama Department, as well as visiting groups from around Europe. Dance is often performed here by visiting troupes.

Tivoli (✉ 135–138 Francis St., Dublin West, ☎ 01/454–4472) brings culture to the heart of old working-class Dublin, the Liberties. Comedy-based shows and the occasional Shakespeare play are favored.

Nightlife

Dubliners have always enjoyed a night out, but in the last decade or so they have turned the pleasure into a work of art. The city has undergone a major nightlife revolution and now, for better or worse, bears more than a passing resemblance to Europe's nightclub hotspot, London. Internationally known dance clubs, where style and swagger rule, have replaced the old-fashioned discos, once the only alternative for late-night entertainment. The streets of the city center, once hushed after the pubs had closed, are the scene of what appears to be a never-ending party—you're as likely to find crowds at 2 AM on a Wednesday as you are at the same time on a Saturday. Although the majority of clubs cater to an under-30 crowd of trendy students and young professionals eager to sway to the rhythmic throb of electronic dance music, there are plenty of alternatives, including a number of nightclubs where the dominant sounds range from soul to salsa. While jazz isn't a big part of the nightlife here, a few regular venues do draw the best of local and international talent. And if you're looking for something more mellow, the city doesn't disappoint: there are brasseries, bistros, cafés, and all manner of other late-night eateries where you can sit, sip, and chat until 2 AM or later.

In another trend, some of Dublin's old classic pubs—arguably some of the finest watering holes in the world—have been "reinvented" as popular spots, with modern interiors and designer drinks to attract a younger, upwardly mobile crowd. Beware Dublin Tourism's "Official Dublin Pub Guide 2002," which has a tendency to recommenced many of these bland spots. Despite the changes, however, the traditional pub has steadfastly clung to its role as the primary center of Dublin's social life. The city has nearly 1,000 pubs ("licensed tabernacles," writer Flann O'Brien calls them). And while the vision of elderly men enjoying a chin wag over a creamy pint of stout has become something of a rarity, there are still plenty of places where you can enjoy a quiet drink and a chat. Last drinks are called as late as 12:30 AM Monday to Saturday and 11 PM on Sunday; some city-center pubs even have extended opening hours from Thursday through Saturday and don't serve last drinks until 1:45 AM.

A word of warning: although most pubs and clubs are extremely safe, the lads can get lively—public drunkenness is very much a part of Dublin's nightlife. While this is for the most part seen as the Irish form of unwinding after a long week (or, well, day), it can sometimes lead to regrettable incidents (fighting, for instance). In an effort to keep potential trouble at bay, bouncers and security men maintain a visible presence in all clubs and many pubs around the city. At the end of the night, the city center is full of young people trying to get home, which makes for extremely long lines at taxi stands and late-night bus stops, especially on weekends. The combination of drunkenness and impatience can sometimes lead to trouble, so act cautiously. If you need late-night transportation, try to arrange it with your hotel before you go out.

Jazz

JJ Smyth's (✉ 12 Aungier St., City Center, ☎ 01/475–2565) is an old-time jazz venue where Louis Stewart, the granddaddy of Irish jazz, is a regular visitor.

Jurys Ballsbridge (✉ Pembroke Rd., Ballsbridge, South of the Liffey, ☎ 01/660–5000) attracts the country's top jazz musicians and voices to its lively Sunday evening sessions.

Pendulum Club (✉ The Norseman, at Eustace and E. Essex Sts., Temple Bar, ☎ 01/671–5135) is the place to go for good jazz. Some of Ireland's top acts play here; internationally recognized musicians occasionally make guest appearances.

Pubs

SOUTH CITY CENTER

Byrnes (✉ Galloping Green, Stillorgan, South County Dublin, ☎ 01/288–7683) has the airy atmosphere of an old-fashioned country pub, even though it's only 8 km (5 mi) from the city center. It's one of the few suburban pubs that haven't been renovated or yuppified.

Dubliner Pub (✉ Jurys hotel, Pembroke Rd., Ballsbridge, South County Dublin, ☎ 01/660–5000) has been remade—from a hotel bar—into an old-fashioned Irish pub; it's a busy meeting place at lunch and after work.

John Fallons (✉ 129 Dean St., Dublin West), a classy public house in the Liberties, has one of the finest snugs in the city and great photos of old Dublin.

Kiely's (✉ Donnybrook Rd., South County Dublin, ☎ 01/283–0208) appears at first glance to be just another modernized pub, but go up the side lane and you'll find a second pub, Ciss Madden's, in the same building. This is an absolutely authentic and convincing reconstruction of an ancient Irish tavern, right down to the glass globe lights and old advertising signs.

Kitty O'Shea's (✉ Upper Grand Canal St., South of the Liffey, ☎ 01/660–9965) has Pre-Raphaelite–style stained glass, lots of sports paraphernalia on the walls, and is popular with sports fans of all types. Its sister pubs are in Brussels and Paris; this is the original.

O'Brien's (✉ Sussex Terr., South County Dublin, ☎ 01/668–2594), beside the Doyle Burlington hotel, is a little antique gem of a pub, scarcely changed in 50 years, with traditional snugs.

CITY CENTER

Brazen Head (✉ Bridge St., Dublin West, ☎ 01/677–9549), Dublin's oldest pub (the site has been licensed since 1198), has stone walls and open fires—it has hardly changed over the years. The pub is renowned for traditional-music performances and lively sing-along sessions on Sunday evenings. On the south side of the Liffey quays, it's a little difficult to find—turn down Lower Bridge Street and make a right into the old lane.

Cassidy's (✉ 42 Lower Camden St., South of the Liffey, ☎ 01/475–1429) is a quiet neighborhood pub with a pint of stout so good that former president Bill Clinton dropped in for one during a visit to Dublin.

The **Cellar Bar** (✉ 24 Upper Merrion St., South of the Liffey, ☎ 01/603–0600) at the Merrion Hotel, is located in a stylish 18th-century wine vault, with bare brick walls and vaulted ceilings. It tends to draw a well-heeled crowd.

Chief O'Neill's (⊠ Smithfield Village, Dublin West, ☎ 01/817–3838), a Dublin hotel, has a large bar-café that's open and airy; it often hosts traditional Irish sessions.

The **Cobblestone** (⊠ N. King St., Dublin West, ☎ 01/872–1799) is a glorious house of ale in the best Dublin tradition. Popular with Smithfield market workers, its chatty imbibers and live traditional music are attracting a wider, younger crowd from all over town.

Davy Byrne's (⊠ 21 Duke St., City Center, ☎ 01/671–1298) is a pilgrimage stop for Joyceans. In *Ulysses,* Leopold Bloom stops in here for a glass of burgundy and a Gorgonzola cheese sandwich. He then leaves the pub and walks to Dawson Street, where he helps a blind man cross the road. Unfortunately, the pub is unrecognizable from Joyce's day, but it still serves some fine pub grub.

Dockers (⊠ 5 Sir John Rogerson's Quay, South of the Liffey, ☎ 01/677–1692), a trendy quayside spot east of city center, is just around the corner from Windmill Lane Studios—where U2 and other noted bands record. At night the area is a little dicey, so come during the day.

Doheny & Nesbitt (⊠ 5 Lower Baggot St., South of the Liffey, ☎ 01/676–2945), a traditional spot with snugs, dark wooden furnishings, and smoke-darkened ceilings, has hardly changed over the decades.

Doyle's (⊠ 9 College St., City Center, ☎ 01/671–0616), a small, cozy pub, is a favorite with journalists from the *Irish Times,* just across the street.

The **Globe** (⊠ 11 S. Great George's St., City Center, ☎ 01/671–1220), one of the hippest café-bars in town, draws arty, trendy Dubliners who sip espresso drinks by day and pack the place at night. There's live jazz on Sunday.

Grogans (⊠ 15 S. William St., City Center, ☎ 01/677–9320), also known as the Castle Lounge, is a small place packed with creative folk.

Hogan's (⊠ 35 Great St. George's St., City Center, ☎ 01/6677–5904), a huge floor space on two levels, gets jammed most nights, but the old place maintains its style through it all and the beer is top class.

Horseshoe Bar (⊠ Shelbourne Méridien Hotel, 27 St. Stephen's Green, City Center, ☎ 01/676–6471) is a popular meeting place for Dublin's businesspeople and politicians, though around the semicircular bar there's comparatively little space for drinkers.

Kehoe's (⊠ 9 S. Anne St., City Center, ☎ 01/677–8312) is popular with Trinity students and academics. The tiny back room is cozy.

McDaid's (⊠ 3 Harry St., City Center, ☎ 01/679–4395) attracted boisterous Brendan Behan and other leading writers in the 1950s; its wild literary reputation still lingers, although the bar has been discreetly modernized and the atmosphere is altogether quieter.

Modern Green Bar (⊠ 31 Wexford St., South of the Liffey, ☎ 01/470–0583) offers not only some of Dublin's top DJs but also a wide selection of imported beers. The result: a young, hip crowd who like to dance.

Mother Redcap's Tavern (⊠ Back La., Dublin West, ☎ 01/453–8306) is an authentic re-creation of a 17th-century Dublin tavern, with stone walls from an old flour mill, beams, and old prints of the city.

Mulligan's (⊠ 8 Poolbeg St., City Center, ☎ 01/677–5582) is synonymous in Dublin with a truly inspirational pint of Guinness. Until a few years ago no women were admitted. Today journalists, locals, and students of both genders flock here for the perfect pint.

Dublin Pubs

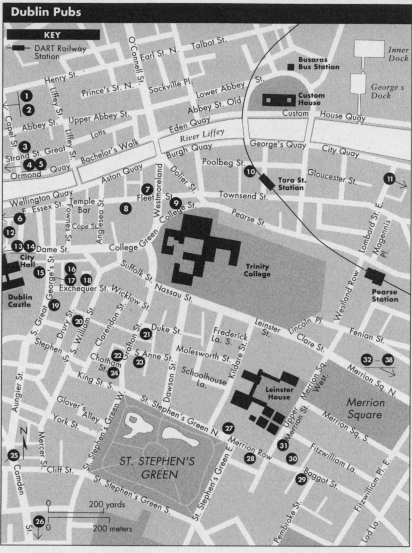

KEY

DART Railway Station

Brazen Head	6	
Byrnes	32	
Cassidy's	26	
The Cellar Bar	31	
Chief O'Neill's	1	
The Cobblestone	2	
Davy Byrne's	21	
Dockers	11	
Doheny & Nesbitt	30	
Doyle's	9	
Dubliner Pub	33	
The Front Lounge	14	
The George	15	
The Globe	17	
Grogans	20	
GUBU	3	
Hogan's	19	
Horseshoe Bar	27	
John Fallons	38	
Johnnie Fox's	34	
Kehoe's	23	
Kiely's	35	
Kitty O'Shea's	36	
McDaid's	22	
Modern Green Bar	25	
Mother Redcap's Tavern	13	
Mulligan's	10	
Neary's	24	
O'Brien's	37	
O'Donoghue's	28	
The Old Stand	18	
Oliver St. John Gogarty	8	
Out on the Liffey	4	
Palace Bar	7	
The Porterhouse	12	
Ryan's Pub	5	
Stag's Head	16	
Toner's	29	

Neary's (⊠ 1 Chatham St., City Center, ☎ 01/677–7371), with an exotic Victorian-style interior, was once the haunt of music-hall artists and a certain literary set, including Brendan Behan. Join the actors from the adjacent Gaiety Theatre for a good pub lunch.

O'Donoghue's (⊠ 15 Merrion Row, South of the Liffey, ☎ 01/676–2807), a cheerful, smoky hangout, has impromptu musical performances that often spill out onto the street.

The Old Stand (⊠ 37 Exchequer St., South of the Liffey, ☎ 01/677–7220), one of the oldest pubs in the city, is named after the old stand at Landsdowne Road, home to Irish Rugby and Soccer. The place is renowned for great pints and fine steaks.

Ryan's Pub (⊠ 28 Parkgate St., Dublin West, ☎ 01/677–6097) is one of Dublin's last genuine, late-Victorian-era pubs, and has changed little since its last (1896) remodeling.

Stag's Head (⊠ 1 Dame Ct., City Center, ☎ 01/679–3701) dates from 1770 and was rebuilt in 1895; theater people from the nearby Olympia, journalists, and Trinity students turn up around the unusual counter, fashioned from Connemara red marble.

Toner's (⊠ 139 Lower Baggot St., South of the Liffey, ☎ 01/676–3090), though billed as a Victorian bar, actually goes back 200 years, with an original flagstone floor to prove its antiquity, as well as wooden drawers running up to the ceiling—a relic of the days when bars doubled as grocery shops. Oliver St. John Gogarty accompanied W. B. Yeats here, in what was purportedly the latter's only visit to a pub.

COUNTY DUBLIN—SOUTHSIDE

Johnnie Fox's (⊠ South County Dublin Glencullen, Co. Dublin, ☎ 01/295–5647), 12 km (8 mi) from the city center, sits 1,000 ft up in the Dublin Mountains, making it the highest licensed premises in Ireland. You approach it by a winding and steeply climbing road that turns off the main Dublin–Enniskerry road at Stepaside. Refusing to bow to the whims of modernization, it has steadfastly maintained its traditional character—oak tables, rough-stone floor flags strewn with sawdust, and ancient bric-a-brac, including copper kettles, crockery, old prints, and guns—and appears very much as it did in the early 19th century, when Daniel O'Connell used it as a safe house for his seditious meetings. You can get lunch and dinner here; the specialty is seafood, and it alone is worth the journey. In the evenings expect to hear traditional Irish music.

TEMPLE BAR

The **Front Lounge** (⊠ 33 Parliament St., Temple Bar, ☎ 01/679–3988), a modern pub, caters to a mixed crowd of young professionals, both gay and straight.

Oliver St. John Gogarty (⊠ 57 Fleet St., Temple Bar, ☎ 01/671–1822) is a lively bar that attracts all ages and nationalities, and which overflows in summer. On most nights there is traditional Irish music upstairs.

Palace Bar (⊠ 21 Fleet St., Temple Bar, ☎ 01/677–9290), scarcely changed over the past 60 years, is tiled and rather barren looking, but is popular with journalists and writers. (The *Irish Times* is nearby.) The walls are hung with cartoons drawn by the illustrators who used to spend time here.

The Porterhouse (⊠ 16–18 Parliament St., Temple Bar, ☎ 01/679–8847) is one of the few bars in Ireland that brews its own beer. The Plain Porter won the best stout at the "Brewing Oscars" beating out the mighty Guinness. The tasteful interior is all dark woods and soft lighting.

Gay and Lesbian Pubs

The **George** (⊠ 89 S. Great George's St., City Center, ☎ 01/478–2983), Dublin's two-floor main gay pub, draws an almost entirely male crowd; its nightclub stays open until 2:30 AM nightly except Tuesday. The "alternative bingo night," with star drag act Miss Shirley Temple Bar, is a riot of risqué fun.

GUBU (⊠ Capel St., North of the Liffey, ☎ 01/874–0710) is the newest venture north of the river by the hugely successful owners of the Globe. It draws a mixed crowd. The pool table downstairs is a bonus.

Out on the Liffey (⊠ 27 Ormond Quay, Dublin West, ☎ 01/872–2480) is Dublin's second gay pub; it draws a mixed gay and straight crowd—both men and women.

Irish Cabaret

BALLSBRIDGE/SOUTH CITY CENTER

Doyle Burlington hotel (⊠ Upper Leeson St., South of the Liffey, ☎ 01/660–5222) has a high-class lounge featuring a well-performed Irish cabaret—with dancing, music, and song.

Jurys hotel (⊠ Pembroke Rd., Ballsbridge, South of the Liffey, ☎ 01/660–5000) stages a traditional Irish cabaret.

CITY CENTER

Castle Inn (⊠ Christ Church Pl., Dublin West, ☎ 01/475–1122) is really just a huge pub that has traditional Irish music and dancing with dinner in a medieval-style banquet hall.

COUNTY DUBLIN—NORTHSIDE

Abbey Tavern (⊠ North County Dublin Howth, ☎ 01/839–0307) has a rip-roaring cabaret with rousing traditional Irish songs.

Clontarf Castle (⊠ Castle Ave., North County Dublin Clontarf, ☎ 01/833–2321) is a spectacular setting for a traditional night of song and comedy.

Irish Music and Dancing

SOUTH DUBLIN

Comhaltas Ceoltóiri Éireann (⊠ 35 Belgrave Sq., South County Dublin Monkstown, ☎ 01/280–0295) is the place to come for a boisterous summer evening of Irish music and dancing.

Harcourt Hotel (⊠ Harcourt St., South of the Liffey, ☎ 01/478–3677) is where some of the best traditional musicians gather for wild jam sessions.

Nightclubs

The dominant sound in Dublin's nightclubs is electronic dance music, and the crowd that flocks to them every night of the week is of the trendy, under-25 generation. At a few pubs, however, you're more likely to hear tango than techno—such as the weekend nightclub at the Gaiety Theatre, Thursday night at the Pod, and Sunday night at Lillie's Bordello.

CITY CENTER

Leeson Street—just off St. Stephen's Green, south of the Liffey, and known as "the strip"—is a main nightclub area that starts at pub closing time and lasts until 4 AM. It has lost its gloss since the turn of the millennium, however, as a number of lap-dancing establishments have opened. The dress code at Leeson Street's dance clubs is informal, but jeans and sneakers are not welcome. Most of these clubs are licensed only to sell wine, and the prices can be exorbitant (up to €26 for a mediocre bottle); the upside is that most don't charge to get in.

Lillie's Bordello (✉ Grafton St., City Center, ☎ 01/679–9204) is a popular spot for a trendy, professional crowd, as well as for rock and film stars. On Sunday night, the strict dress code—shirt and jacket, no trainers, no jeans (unless you're famous)—is relaxed for a night of live music and DJs.

The **Pod** (✉ Harcourt St., South of the Liffey, ☎ 01/478–0166), also known as the "Place of Dance," qualifies as Dublin's most-renowned dance club, especially among the younger set. Whether you get in depends as much on what you're wearing as on your age. It helps to look stylish or rich, except on Thursday night, when the club hosts a no-frills, no-nonsense night of dance-floor jazz and funk.

The **Red Box** (✉ Old Harcourt St. Station, Harcourt St., South of the Liffey, ☎ 01/478–0166), adjacent to the Pod and the Chocolate Bar, can pack in more than 1,000 people and surround them with state-of-the-art sound and light. It regularly hosts Irish and international rock acts, and celebrity DJs from Europe and the United States. It has full bar facilities.

At **Renards** (✉ St. Fredrick St., South of the Liffey, ☎ 01/677–5876) you'll find thirtysomethings who like to let their hair down. The music can be a bit predictable; the jazz-and-supper-club is a better option.

Rí Ra (✉ Dame Ct., City Center, ☎ 01/677–4835) is part of the hugely popular Globe bar. The name means "uproar" in Irish, and on most nights the place does go a little wild. It's one of the best spots in Dublin for fun, no-frills dancing. Upstairs is more low-key.

TEMPLE BAR

The **Kitchen** (✉ E. Essex St., Temple Bar, ☎ 01/677–6359) is in the basement of the Clarence hotel. Its popularity, mainly with an under-30s crowd, owes much to its owners, Bono and the Edge of U2.

Viper Room (✉ 5 Aston Quay, Temple Bar, ☎ 01/672–5566), decorated in rich reds and purples, is a delightfully decadent late-night club that plays funky, chart, and rhythm n' blues. Downstairs you'll find live jazz and salsa.

OUTDOOR ACTIVITIES AND SPORTS

Health clubs have really caught on in Dublin, and seem to be sprouting up in every corner of the city (especially at hotels). But Dublin has no dearth of opportunities for getting out and moving about. You can explore a beach, horseback-ride, or bike through Phoenix Park, among other options.

Beaches

To the north of Dublin city you'll find **North Bull Island,** created over years by the action of the tides. The fine sand here stretches for almost 3 km (2 mi). Bus 130 from Lower Abbey Street stops by the walkway to the beach. **Malahide,** a charming village on the northside DART line, has a clean and easily accessible beach, though the current can be strong. The main beach for swimming on the south side of Dublin is at **Killiney** (✉ 13 km [8 mi] south of the city center, South County Dublin), a 3-km-long (2-mi-long) shingle (pebbly) beach. The DART train station is right by the beach; get off at Killiney. Near Dublin city center, **Sandymount Strand** is a long expanse of fine sand where the tide goes out nearly 3 km (2 mi), but it's not suitable for swimming or bathing because the tide races in so fast. The strand can be reached easily by the DART train.

Participant Sports

Bicycling

Unless you're nutty, don't ride bicycles in the city center—traffic is heavy and most roads don't have shoulders, much less bike lanes. Phoenix Park and some suburbs (especially Ballsbridge, Clontarf, and Sandymount), however, are pleasant once you're off the main roads. You'll find plenty of challenging terrain immediately south of the city, in the Dublin and Wicklow mountains. Don't forget to secure your bicycle if you leave it unattended.

You can rent bicycles for about €57.15 a week; an equivalent amount will be charged for deposit. Nearly 20 companies in the Dublin region rent bicycles; Tourist Information Offices (TIOs) have a full list. **McDonald's** (⊠ 38 Wexford St., City Center, ☎ 01/475–2586) is a centrally located bike repair and rental shop. **Mike's Bike Shop** (⊠ Dun Laoghaire Shopping Center, South County Dublin, ☎ 01/280–0417) is a long-established bike outfit in the southside surburbs of Dublin. **Tracks Cycles** (⊠ 8 Botanic Rd., Glasnevin, North County Dublin, ☎ 01/873–2455) has an established reputation for being trustworthy in repairs, sales, and rentals of all types of bikes.

Bowling

Bowling is a popular sport in Dublin; two kinds are played locally. The sedate, exclusive, outdoor variety known as crown-green bowling is played at a number of locations in the suburbs. Dublin also has six indoor 10-pin bowling centers. **Herbert Park** (⊠ Ballsbridge, South County Dublin, ☎ 01/660–1875) has a splendid, baby-soft bowling green. **Kenilworth Bowling Club** (⊠ Grosvenor Sq., South County Dublin, ☎ 01/497–2305) welcomes paying visitors, and lessons are available. The green is half the size of a soccer pitch, and smooth as a carpet. **Bray Leisure Bowl** (⊠ Quinsboro Rd., South County Dublin, ☎ 01/286–4455), an indoor bowling center, serves the area near the Wicklow border. **Leisureplex Coolock** (⊠ Malahide Rd., North County Dublin, ☎ 01/848–5722; ⊠ Village Green Center, Tallaght, South County Dublin, ☎ 01/459–9411) is popular with bowlers from both sides of the city, as it has plenty of lanes and is easy to get to. **Metro Bowl** (⊠ 149 N. Strand Rd., North County Dublin, ☎ 01/855–0400) tends to attract the more serious bowlers. **Stillorgan Bowl** (⊠ Stillorgan, South County Dublin, ☎ 01/288–1656) is the oldest 10-pin center in Ireland. **Superdome** (⊠ Palmerstown, South County Dublin, ☎ 01/626–0700) draws big crowds of teenage and family bowlers.

Golf

Think idyllic. The Dublin region is a great place for golfers—it has 32 18-hole courses and 16 9-hole courses, and several more 18-hole courses on the way. Below are only some of the major 18-hole courses around Dublin. **Deer Park** (⊠ North County Dublin Howth, ☎ 01/832–6039) is a top-quality parkland golf course. **Edmonstown** (⊠ South County Dublin Rathfarnham, ☎ 01/493–2461), a beautiful golf course, serves an upmarket clientele. **Elm Park** (⊠ South County Dublin Donnybrook, ☎ 01/269–3438) welcomes visiting golfers and beginners. **Foxrock** (⊠ Torquay Rd., South County Dublin, ☎ 01/289–3992) is a tough golf course with a gorgeous location in the southside suburbs. **Hermitage** (⊠ North County Dublin Lucan, ☎ 01/626–4781) is one of the city's more difficult golf courses. **Newlands** (⊠ South County Dublin Clondalkin, ☎ 01/459–2903) attracts golfers from the northside of the city. **Sutton** (⊠ South County Dublin Sutton, ☎ 01/832–3013) golf course is as exclusive and as pricey as everything else in this wealthy suburb. **Woodbrook** (⊠ South County Dublin Bray, ☎ 01/282–4799) is worth the trip out of the city for a day's golf by the sea.

At the **Golf D2** (⊠ Cow St., Temple Bar, ☎ 01/672–6181) in Temple Bar you can practice even if it's raining. You strike a real ball with a real club against a huge screen, which tracks the virtual course of your shot. It's a cool idea, and it works. You can play 34 of the world's most famous courses, including St. Andrews and Pebble Beach. It costs €19.05 for a half hour, and you must book ahead.

Health Clubs

The **Iveagh Fitness Club** (⊠ Christ Church St., Dublin West Dublin 8, ☎ 01/454–6555) is next to Christ Church Cathedral, in a complex of beautiful old redbrick buildings. It has a pool, sauna, and full weight room. Just off Grafton Street, the **Jackie Skelly Fitness Centre** (⊠ 41–42 Clarendon St., City Center Dublin 2, ☎ 01/677–0040) is perfect if you're staying in a city-center hotel without a gym. In Rathgar village, the **Orwell Club** (⊠ 75 Orwell Rd, South County Dublin, ☎ 01/492–3146) is not far away from many of the southside hotels.

Horseback Riding

Stables on the outskirts of the city give you immediate access to some excellent riding areas—Counties Dublin, Kildare, Louth, Meath, and Wicklow all have unspoiled country territory. In the city itself, you'll find superb, quiet riding conditions at Phoenix Park, away from the busy main road that bisects the park. About 20 riding stables in the greater Dublin area have horses for hire by the hour or day, both for novices and for experienced riders; a few also operate as equestrian centers and offer lessons. Outside Dublin, **Brittas Lodge Riding Stables** (⊠ Brittas, South County Dublin, ☎ 01/458–2726) has fantastic facilities and, wonderfully, is right next to one of the nicest beaches on the East Coast. Horseback riders at the **Deerpark Riding Center** (⊠ Castleknock Rd., Castleknock, North County Dublin, ☎ 01/820–7141) canter in Dublin's massive Phoenix Park.

Jogging

Traffic in Dublin, heavy from early morning until late at night, is getting worse, so if you jog here, expect to dodge vehicles and stop for lights. (Remember *always* to look to your right *and* your left before crossing a street.) If you're staying in Temple Bar or on the western end of the city and you can run 9 km (5½ mi), head to Phoenix Park, easily the nicest place in the city for a jog. If you're on the southside, Merrion Square, St. Stephen's Green, and Trinity College are all good places for short jogs, though be prepared to dodge pedestrians; if you're looking for a longer route, ask your hotel to direct you to the Grand Canal, which has a pleasant path you can run along as far east as the Grand Canal Street Bridge.

Swimming

One of the best of Dublin's 12 public pools is **Townsend Street** (⊠ Townsend St., City Center, ☎ 01/677–0503). **Williams Park** (⊠ Rathmines, South County Dublin, ☎ 01/496–1275) is a quality public pool on the southside. **Dundrum Family Recreation Center** (⊠ Meadowbrook, Dundrum, South County Dublin, ☎ 01/298–4654), a private pool, is open to the public for a small fee. **St. Vincent's** (⊠ Navan Rd., North County Dublin, ☎ 01/838–4906) is a public pool on the northside of the city. **Terenure College** (⊠ Templeogue Rd., South County Dublin, ☎ 01/490–7071) is a high school with a pool that's open to the public when school's not in session and competitions aren't taking place. For a hardy dip, there's year-round sea swimming at the **Forty Foot Bathing Pool,** a traditional bathing area—in use for more than a century—in Sandycove.

Tennis

Tennis is one of Dublin's most popular participant sports. Some public parks have excellent tennis facilities open to the public. **Bushy Park** (✉ Terenure, South County Dublin, ☎ 01/490–0320) has well-maintained public tennis courts. Thanks to its excellent facilities, **Herbert Park** (✉ Ballsbridge, South County Dublin, ☎ 01/668–4364) attracts some serious tennis players. **St. Anne's Park** (✉ Dollymount Strand, North County Dublin, ☎ 01/833–8898) has quality tennis courts within sniffing distance of the ocean. **Kilternan Tennis Centre** (✉ Kilternan Golf and Country Club Hotel, Kilternan, South County Dublin, ☎ 01/295–3729) has everything the tennis player could want—lessons, serving machines, racket stringing—at a price. **Lansdowne Lawn Tennis Club** (✉ Londonbridge Rd., South County Dublin, ☎ 01/668–0219) is as much about the social gathering as it is about the game itself. Dress appropriately. **West Wood Lawn Tennis Club** (✉ Leopardstown Racecourse, Foxrock, South County Dublin, ☎ 01/289–2911) is popular with young, serious-minded players. For more information about playing tennis in Dublin, contact **Tennis Ireland** (✉ 22 Argyle Sq., Donnybrook, South County Dublin, ☎ 01/668–1841).

Spectator Sports

Gaelic Games

The traditional games of Ireland, Gaelic football and hurling, attract a huge following, with roaring crowds cheering on their county teams. Games are held at Croke Park, the national stadium for Gaelic games, just north of the city center. For details of matches, contact the **Gaelic Athletic Association (GAA)** (✉ Croke Park, North County Dublin, ☎ 01/836–3222).

Greyhound Racing

As elsewhere in the world, greyhound racing is a sport in decline in Ireland. But the track can still be one of the best places to see Dubliners at their most passionate, among friends, and full of wicked humor. **Harolds Cross** (✉ Harolds Cross, South County Dublin, ☎ 01/497–1081) is a dilapidated greyhound racing track but serves its purpose. **Shelbourne Park** (✉ Shelbourne Park, South County Dublin, ☎ 01/668–3502) is a relatively stylish place to watch greyhound racing. You can book a table in the restaurant that overlooks the track.

Horse Racing

Horse racing—from flat to hurdle to steeplechase—is one of the great sporting loves of the Irish. The sport is closely followed and betting is popular, but the social side of attending racing is equally important to Dubliners. The main course in Dublin is **Leopardstown** (☎ 01/289–3607), an ultramodern course on the southside and home of the Hennessey Gold Cup in February, Ireland's most prestigious steeplechase. **Fairyhouse** (✉ North County Dublin, Co. Meath, ☎ 01/825–6167) hosts the Grand National, the most popular steeplechase of the season, every Easter Monday. The **Curragh** (☎ 045/441–205), southwest of Dublin, hosts the five Classics, the most important flat races of the season, which are run from May to September. **Punchestown** (☎ 045/897–704), outside Naas, County Kildare, is home of the ever-popular Punchestown National Hunt Festival in April.

Rugby

International rugby matches run during the winter and spring at the vast **Lansdowne Road Stadium** (✉ 62 Lansdowne Rd., South County

Dublin, ☎ 01/668–4601). Local matches are also played every week-end during that time. For details about rugby in Ireland, contact the **Irish Rugby Football Union** (☎ 01/647–3800, WEB www.irfu.ie/comp/6nats/asp.

Football

Soccer—called football in Europe—is very popular in Ireland, largely due to the euphoria resulting from the national team's successes throughout the late 1980s and early 1990s. However, the places where you can watch it aren't ideal—they tend to be small and out-of-date. **Lansdowne Road,** the vast rugby stadium, is the main center for in-ternational matches. League of Ireland matches take place throughout the city every Sunday from September to May. For details, contact the **Football Association of Ireland** (⌧ 80 Merrion Sq. S, South of the Lif-fey, ☎ 01/676–6864).

SHOPPING

The only known specimens of leprechauns or shillelaghs in Ireland are those in souvenir-shop windows, and shamrocks mainly bloom around the borders of Irish linen handkerchiefs and tablecloths. But today you'll find way more than kitschy designs. There's a tremendous variety of stores in Dublin, many of which are quite sophisticated—as a walk through Dublin's central shopping area, from O'Connell to Grafton Street, will prove. Department stores stock internationally known fashion-designer goods and housewares, and small (and often pricey) boutiques sell Irish crafts and other merchandise. But don't expect too many bargains here. And be prepared, if you're shopping in central Dublin, to push through crowds—especially in the afternoons and on weekends. Most large shops and department stores are open Monday–Saturday 9–6. Although nearly all department stores are closed on Sun-day, some smaller specialty shops stay open. Those with later closing hours are noted below. You're particularly likely to find sales in Jan-uary, February, July, and August.

Shopping Streets

Dublin's dozen or so main shopping streets each have a different char-acter. Visit them all to appreciate the wide a range of items for sale here. The main commercial streets north of the river have both chain and department stores that tend to be less expensive (and less design-con-scious) than their counterparts in the city center on the other side of the Liffey.

City Center (Northside)
Henry Street. Cash-conscious Dubliners shop on Henry Street, which runs westward from O'Connell Street. Arnotts department store is the anchor; smaller, specialty stores sell CDs, footwear, and clothing. Henry Street's continuation, Mary Street, has a branch of Marks & Spencer and the Jervis Shopping Centre.

O'Connell Street. One of Dublin's largest department stores, Clery's, faces the GPO across the city's main thoroughfare—more downscale than southside city streets (such as Grafton St.) but still worth a walk. On the same side of the street as the post office is Eason's, a large book, magazine, and stationery store.

City Center (Southside)
Dawson Street. Just east of Grafton Street between Nassau Street to the north and St. Stephen's Green to the south, you'll find the city's

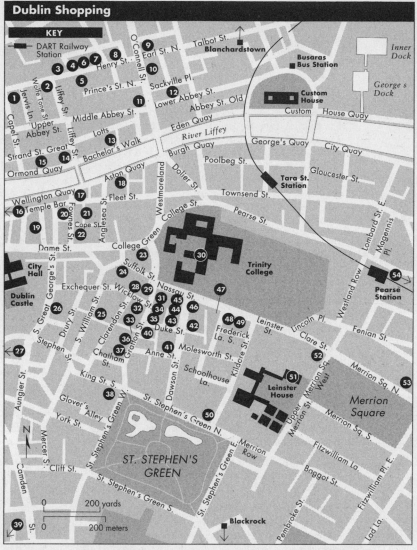

Dublin Shopping

Arnotts **5, 29**

An Táin **17**

A-Wear **8, 40**

Blarney
Woollen Mills **47**

Books Upstairs **23**

Brown Thomas . . . **32**

Cathach Books **43**

Celtic Note **48**

China Showrooms . . **12**

Claddagh
Records **20**

Cleo Ltd. **50**

Clery's **10**

Conlon Antiques . . . **39**

Crafts Centre of
Ireland **38**

Crannóg **19**

Designyard **16**

Dublin Bookshop . . **36**

Dublin
Woollen Mills **14**

Dunnes Stores . . . **7, 38**

Eason's **11**

Eason's/Hanna's . . **48**

Flip **22**

Flying Pig
Bookshop **21**

Gael Linn **53**

Greene's **52**

Ha'penny Bridge
Galleries **13**

HMV **6, 37**

Hodges Figgis . . . **44**

House of Ireland . . . **45**

Hughes &
Hughes **38**

Ilac Center **3**

Jenny Vander **26**

Jervis Shopping
Centre **1**

Kevin and
Howlin **46**

Kilkenny Shop **49**

Marks &
Spencer **2, 35**

McCullogh
Piggott **24**

McDowell **9**

Monaghan's **34**

National Gallery of
Ireland Shop **51**

National Museum
Shop **51**

O'Sullivan
Antiques **27**

Powerscourt
Townhouse
Centre **25**

Roches Stores **4**

Royal Hibernian
Way **41**

St. Stephen's
Green Centre **38**

Tierneys **38**

Tower Design
Centre **54**

Tower Records **28**

Trinity College
Library Shop **30**

Virgin
Megastore **18**

Waterstone's **42**

Weir & Sons **31**

Westbury Mall . . . **33**

Winding Stair **15**

primary bookstore avenue. Waterstone's and Hodges Figgis face each other on different sides of the street.

Francis Street. The Liberties, the oldest part of the city, is the hub of Dublin's antiques trade. This street and surrounding areas, such as the Coombe, have plenty of shops where you can browse. If you're looking for something in particular, dealers will gladly recommend the appropriate store to you.

Grafton Street. Dublin's bustling pedestrian-only main shopping street has two upscale department stores: Marks & Spencer and Brown Thomas. The rest of the street is taken up by smaller shops, many of them branches of international chains, such as the Body Shop and Bally, and many British chains. This is also the spot to buy fresh flowers, available at reasonable prices from a number of outdoor stands. On the smaller streets off Grafton Street, especially Duke Street, South Anne Street, and Chatham Street, you'll find worthwhile crafts, clothing, and designer housewares shops.

Nassau Street. Dublin's main tourist-oriented thoroughfare has some of the best-known stores selling Irish goods, but you won't find many locals shopping here. Still, if you're looking for classic Irish gifts to take home, you should be sure at least to browse along here.

Temple Bar. Dublin's hippest neighborhood is dotted with small, precious boutiques—mainly intimate, quirky shops that traffic in a small selection of *très* trendy goods, from vintage wear to some of the most avant-garde Irish clothing you'll find anywhere in the city.

Shopping Centers

City Center (Northside)

Ilac Center (✉ Henry St., North of the Liffey) was Dublin's first large, modern shopping center, with two department stores, hundreds of specialty shops, and several restaurants. The stores are not as exclusive as at some of the other centers, but there's plenty of free parking.

The slightly high-end **Jervis Shopping Centre** (✉ Jervis and Mary Sts., North of the Liffey, ☎ 01/878–1323) has some of the major British chain stores. It has a compact design and plenty of parking space.

City Center (Southside)

Powerscourt Townhouse Centre (✉ 59 S. William St., City Center), the former town home of Lord Powerscourt, built in 1771, has an interior courtyard that has been refurbished and roofed over; a pianist often plays on the dais at ground-floor level. Coffee shops and restaurants share space with a mix of antiques and crafts stores, including the **HQ Gallery**, the main showcase of the Irish Craft Council and one of the finest places in Dublin to buy contemporary crafts. You can also buy original Irish fashions here by young designers, such as Gráinne Walsh.

Royal Hibernian Way (✉ off Dawson St. between S. Anne and Duke Sts., City Center, ☎ 01/679–5919) is on the former site of the two-centuries-old Royal Hibernian Hotel, a coaching inn that was demolished in 1983. The pricey, stylish shops—about 20 or 30, many selling fashionable clothes—are small in scale and include a branch of Leonidas, the Belgian chocolate firm.

St. Stephen's Green Centre (✉ northwest corner of St. Stephen's Green, City Center, ☎ 01/478–0888), Dublin's largest and most ambitious shopping center, resembles a giant greenhouse, with ironwork in the Victorian style. On three floors overlooked by a vast clock, the 100 mostly small shops sell a variety of crafts, fashions, and household goods.

Tower Design Centre (✉ Pearse St., City Center, ☎ 01/677–5655), east of the heart of the city center (near the Waterways Visitor Centre), has more than 35 separate crafts shops in a converted 1862 sugar-refinery tower. On the ground floor, you can stop at workshops devoted to heraldry and Irish pewter; the other six floors have stores that sell hand-painted silks, ceramics, hand-knit items, jewelry, and fine-art cards and prints.

Westbury Mall (✉ Westbury Hotel, off Grafton St., City Center) is an upmarket shopping mall. Here you'll find designer jewelry, antique rugs, and decorative goods.

County Dublin Suburbs

Blackrock (✉ Blackrock, Co. Dublin, South County Dublin, ☎ 01/283–1660), to the south, is technically outside of Dublin's city center, but it deserves special mention as one of the most customer-friendly shopping centers around. It's built on two levels, looking onto an inner courtyard, with the giant Superquinn Foodstore, cafés, and restaurants. Blackrock can be reached conveniently on the DART train line; it has its own stop.

Blanchardstown (✉ Blanchardstown, North County Dublin Dublin 15, ☎ 01/822–1356) is the biggest shopping center in the country; you'll find plenty of families shopping here, as it's a good spot for bargains. The No. 39 bus from Lower Abbey Street goes to Blanchardstown.

Department Stores

Arnotts (✉ Henry St., North of the Liffey, ☎ 01/872–1111), on three floors, stocks a wide variety of clothing, household, and sporting goods. The smaller Grafton Street branch (✉ Grafton St., City Center, ☎ 01/872–1111) sells new fashion and footwear.

A-Wear (✉ Grafton St., City Center, ☎ 01/671–7200; ✉ Henry St., North of the Liffey, ☎ 01/872–4644) specializes in fashion for men and women. Many of the items are seasonal and closely follow the ever-changing trends. Leading Irish designers, including John Rocha, supply A-Wear with a steady stream of clothing.

Brown Thomas (✉ Grafton St., City Center, ☎ 01/679–5666), Dublin's most exclusive department store, stocks the leading designer names in clothing and cosmetics, and lots of stylish accessories. You'll also find clothing by Irish designers.

Clery's (✉ O'Connell St., North of the Liffey, ☎ 01/878–6000), once the city's most fashionable department store, is still worth a visit. You'll find all kinds of merchandise—from fashion to home appliances—on its four floors. Note that goods sold here reflect a distinctly modest, traditional sense of style.

Dunnes Stores (✉ St. Stephen's Green Centre, City Center, ☎ 01/478–0188; ✉ Henry St., North of the Liffey, ☎ 01/872–6833; ✉ Ilac Shopping Center, Mary St., North of the Liffey, ☎ 01/873–0211) is Ireland's largest chain of department stores. All stores stock fashion, household, and grocery items, and have a reputation for value and variety.

Eason's (✉ O'Connell St., North of the Liffey, ☎ 01/873–3811; ✉ Ilac Shopping Center, Mary St., North of the Liffey, ☎ 01/872–1322) is known primarily for its wide variety of books, magazines, and stationery; its larger O'Connell Street branch sells tapes, CDs, records, videos, and other audiovisual goodies.

Marks & Spencer (✉ Grafton St., City Center, ☎ 01/679–7855; ✉ Henry St., North of the Liffey, ☎ 01/872–8833), perennial competitor to Brown

Thomas, stocks everything from fashion (including lingerie) to tasty, unusual groceries. The Grafton Street branch even has its own bureau de change, which doesn't charge commission.

Roches Stores (✉ Henry St., North of the Liffey, ☎ 01/873–0044) is where sensible Dubliners have shopped for generations. Household goods are the specialty, but you'll also find great value on clothes.

Outdoor Markets

You'll find a number of open-air markets in Dublin. Outside the city center, weekend markets take place in Blackrock and Dun Laoghaire. **Moore Street,** behind the Ilac center, is open Monday–Saturday 9–6. Stalls, which line both sides of the street, sell fruits and vegetables; this is also a good spot to come to buy shoes and boots. Moore Street vendors are known for their sharp wit, so expect the traditional Dublin repartee when you're shopping. You'll find bric-a-brac at the **Liberty Market** on the north end of Meath Street, open on Friday and Saturday 10–6, Sunday noon–5:30. At the outdoor **Meeting House Square Market,** held Saturday mornings at the heart of Temple Bar, you can buy homemade food stuffs: breads, chocolate, and organic veggies.

Specialty Shops

Antiques

Dublin is one of Europe's best cities in which to buy antiques, largely due to a long and proud tradition of restoration and high-quality craftsmanship. The Liberties, Dublin's oldest district, is, fittingly, the hub of the antiques trade, and is chock-a-block with shops and traders. Bachelor's Walk, along the quays, also has some decent shops. It's quite a seller's market, but bargains are still possible.

Antiques and Collectibles Fairs (☎ 01/670–8295) take place at Newman House (✉ 85–86 St. Stephen's Green, City Center) every second Sunday throughout the year.

Conlon Antiques (✉ 21 Clanbrassil St., Dublin West, ☎ 01/453–7323) sells a diverse selection of antiques, from sideboards to fanlights.

Ha'penny Bridge Galleries (✉ 15 Bachelor's Walk, North of the Liffey, ☎ 01/872–3950) has four floors of curios, with a particularly large selection of bronzes, silver, and china.

O'Sullivan Antiques (✉ 43–44 Francis St., Dublin West, ☎ 01/454–1143 or 01/453–9659) specializes in 18th- and 19th-century furniture and has a high-profile clientele, including Mia Farrow and Liam Neeson.

Books

You won't have any difficulty weighing down your suitcase with books. Ireland, after all, produced four Nobel literature laureates in just under 75 years. If you're at all interested in modern and contemporary literature, be sure to leave yourself time to browse through the bookstores, as you're likely to find books available here you can't find back home. Best of all, thanks to an enlightened national social policy, there's no tax on books, so if you only buy books, you don't have to worry about getting VAT slips.

Books Upstairs (✉ 36 College Green, City Center, ☎ 01/679–6687) carries an excellent range of special-interest books, including gay and feminist literature, psychology, and self-help books.

Cathach Books (✉ 10 Duke St., City Center, ☎ 01/671–8676) sells first editions of Irish literature and many other books of Irish interest, plus old maps of Dublin and Ireland.

Dublin Bookshop (✉ 24 Grafton St., City Center, ☎ 01/677–5568) is an esteemed, family-owned store that sells mass market books.

Eason's/Hanna's (✉ 29 Nassau St., City Center, ☎ 01/677–1255) sells secondhand and mass market paperbacks and hardcovers, and has a good selection of works on travel and Ireland.

Flying Pig Bookshop (✉ 17 Crow St., Temple Bar, ☎ 01/679–5099) stocks Ireland's largest selection of secondhand science fiction and fantasy books.

Greene's (✉ Clare St., City Center, ☎ 01/676–2544) carries an extensive range of secondhand volumes and new educational and mass market books.

Hodges Figgis (✉ 56–58 Dawson St., City Center, ☎ 01/677–4754), Dublin's leading independent, stocks 1½ million books on three floors; there's a pleasant café on the first floor.

Hughes & Hughes (✉ St. Stephen's Green Centre, City Center, ☎ 01/478–3060) has strong travel and Irish-interest sections. There is also a store at Dublin Airport.

Waterstone's (✉ 7 Dawson St., City Center, ☎ 01/679–1415), a large branch of the British chain, features, on two floors, a fine selection of Irish and international books.

Winding Stair (✉ 40 Ormond Quay, North of the Liffey, ☎ 01/873–3292) is a charming new- and used-book store overlooking the Liffey. The little upstairs café is the perfect spot for an afternoon of reading.

China, Crystal, Ceramics, and Jewelry

Ireland is *the* place to buy Waterford crystal, which is available in a wide range of products, including relatively inexpensive items. Other lines are now gaining recognition, such as Cavan, Galway, and Tipperary crystal. **Brown Thomas** is the best department store for crystal; top specialty outlets are listed below.

Blarney Woollen Mills (✉ 21–23 Nassau St., City Center, ☎ 01/671–0068) is one of the best places for Belleek china, Waterford and Galway crystal, and Irish linen.

China Showrooms (✉ 32/33 Lower Abbey St., North of the Liffey, ☎ 01/878–6211), which is more than 60 years old, carries all the top brand names in fine china, including Aynsley, Royal Doulton, and Belleek. It also stocks Waterford, Tyrone, and Tipperary cut hand-cut crystal.

Crafts Centre of Ireland (✉ Stephen's Green Centre, City Center, ☎ 01/475–4526) carries an impressive inventory of Ireland's most famous contemporary designers, including Michael Kennedy and Diane McCormick (ceramics), Glen Lucas (wood turning), and Jerpoint Glass (glassworks).

Crannóg (✉ Crown Alley, Temple Bar, ☎ 01/671–0805), in Temple Bar, specializes in ceramics and contemporary Irish jewelry, especially silver pendants and rings.

Designyard (✉ E. Essex St., Temple Bar, ☎ 01/677–8453) carries beautifully designed Irish and international tableware, lighting, small furniture, and jewelry.

House of Ireland (✉ 37–38 Nassau St., City Center, ☎ 01/671–6133) has an extensive selection of crystal, jewelry, tweeds, sweaters, and other upscale goods.

Kilkenny Shop (⊠ 5–6 Nassau St., City Center, ☎ 01/677–7066) specializes in contemporary Irish-made ceramics, pottery, and silver jewelry, and regularly holds exhibits of exciting new work by Irish craftspeople.

McDowell (⊠ 3 Upper O'Connell St., North of the Liffey, ☎ 01/874–4961), a jewelry shop popular with Dubliners, has been in business for more than 100 years.

Tierneys (⊠ St. Stephen's Green Centre, City Center, ☎ 01/478–2873) carries a good selection of crystal and china. Claddagh rings, pendants, and brooches are popular.

Weir & Sons (⊠ 96 Grafton St., City Center, ☎ 01/677–9678), Dublin's most prestigious jewelers, sells not only jewelry and watches, but also china, glass, lamps, silver, and leather.

Museum Stores

National Gallery of Ireland Shop (⊠ Merrion Sq. W, South of the Liffey, ☎ 01/678–5450) has a terrific selection of books on Irish art, plus posters, postcards, note cards, and lots of lovely bibelots.

National Museum Shop (⊠ Kildare St., South of the Liffey, ☎ 01/677–7444 ext. 327) carries jewelry based on ancient Celtic artifacts in the museum collection, contemporary Irish pottery, a large selection of books, and other gift items.

Trinity College Library Shop (⊠ Old Library, Trinity College, City Center, ☎ 01/608–2308) sells Irish-theme books, *Book of Kells* souvenirs, and clothing, jewelry, and lovely Irish-made items.

Music

Irish-recorded material—including traditional folk music, country-and-western, rock, and even a smattering of classical music—is increasingly available in Dublin.

Celtic Note (⊠ 12 Nassau St., City Center, ☎ 01/670–4157) is aimed at the tourist market, with a lot of compilations and greatest hits formats.

Claddagh Records (⊠ 2 Cecilia St., Temple Bar, ☎ 01/679–3664) has a good selection of traditional and folk music.

Gael Linn (⊠ 26 Merrion Sq., South of the Liffey, ☎ 01/676–7283) specializes in traditional Irish-music and Irish-language recordings; it's where the aficionados go.

HMV (⊠ 65 Grafton St., City Center, ☎ 01/679–5334; ⊠ 18 Henry St., North of the Liffey, ☎ 01/872–2095) is one of the larger record shops in town.

McCullogh Piggott (⊠ 25 Suffolk St., City Center, ☎ 01/677–3138) is the best place in town for instruments, sheet music, scores, and books about music.

Tower Records (⊠ 6–8 Wicklow St., City Center, ☎ 01/671–3250) is the best-stocked international chain.

Virgin Megastore (⊠ 14–18 Aston Quay, City Center, ☎ 01/677–7361) is Dublin's biggest music store and holds in-store performances by Irish bands.

Sweaters and Tweeds

Don't think Irish woolens are limited to Aran sweaters and tweed jackets. You'll be pleasantly surprised by the range of hats, gloves, scarves, blankets, and other goods here. If you're traveling outside of Dublin, you may want to wait to make purchases elsewhere, but if Dublin is it, you still have plenty of good shops to choose from. The tweed on sale in Dublin comes from two main sources: Donegal and Connemara. Labels inside the garments guarantee their authenticity. Following are the largest retailers of traditional Irish woolen goods in the city.

An Táin (⊠ 13 Temple Bar Sq. N, Temple Bar, ☎ 01/679–0523) carries hyperstylish handmade Irish sweaters, jackets, and accessories.

Blarney Woollen Mills (⊠ 21–23 Nassau St., City Center, ☎ 01/671–0068) carries a good selection of tweed, linen, and woolen sweaters in all price ranges.

Cleo Ltd. (⊠ 18 Kildare St., South of the Liffey, ☎ 01/676–1421) sells hand-knit sweaters and accessories made only from natural fibers; it also carries its own designs.

Dublin Woollen Mills (⊠ Metal Bridge Corner, North of the Liffey, ☎ 01/677–5014) at Ha'penny Bridge has a good selection of hand-knit and other woolen sweaters at competitive prices.

Kevin and Howlin (⊠ 31 Nassau St., City Center, ☎ 01/677–0257) specializes in handwoven tweed men's jackets, suits, and hats, and also sells tweed fabric.

Monaghan's (⊠ Grafton Arcade, 15–17 Grafton St., City Center, ☎ 01/677–0823) specializes in cashmere.

Vintage

Flip (⊠ 4 Upper Fownes St., Temple Bar, ☎ 01/671–4299), one of the original stores in Temple Bar, sells vintage and retro clothing from the '50s, '60s, and '70s.

Jenny Vander (⊠ Georges Street Arcade, City Center, ☎ 01/677–0406) is the most famous name in Irish vintage and retro clothing. Just browsing through her collection is a pleasure.

SIDE TRIPS

Dubliners are undeniably lucky. Few populaces enjoy such glorious—and easily accessible—options for day trips. Just outside the city, you'll find some of the region's most unique sights, including Joyce Tower, the Marino Casino, and Malahide Castle. Once you cross over the Grand Canal, which defines the southern border of the city center, you enter exclusive Ballsbridge and other southern areas of the city and its suburbs. If you do set out for points south and you don't have time to see everything, plan to begin in Ballsbridge. If you have a car, then head to Rathfarnham, directly south of the city. Alternatively, head east and follow the coast road south to Dun Laoghaire (and points even farther south, covered in Chapter 3). Beyond Ballsbridge, these areas are too spread out to cover on foot, and either a car or public transportation (the bus or DART) is the only way to get around. Traveling to and from each of the suburbs will take up most of a day, so you need to pick and choose the excursions you prefer.

County Dublin—Southside

Dublin's southside suburbs are home to its more affluent and well-heeled citizens. As is usually the case, the wealthy folk have chosen some of the most scenic parts of the city, with the beautiful coastline to the east and Wicklow and its mountains to the south.

Numbers in the text correspond to numbers in the margin and on the County Dublin–Southside map.

Rathfarnham

Bus 47A from Hawkins St. in the city center goes to both parks in Rathfarnham. Or drive, leaving the city center via Nicholas St. just west of Christ Church Cathedral and following it south through Terenure.

Two parks lie in the suburb of Rathfarnham, due south of the city at the edge of the Dublin Mountains. The 18th-century house in ❶ **St. Enda's National Historic Park** has been turned into the **Pearse Museum,** commemorating Pádrig Pearse, leader of Dublin's 1916 Easter Uprising. In the early 20th century, the house was a Irish-language boys' school, which Pearse and his brother Willie founded. The museum preserves Pearse family memorabilia, documents, and photographs. A lake and nature trails are also on the park's 50-acre grounds, and guides are available for tours of the park or simply for information. ✉ *Grange Rd.,* ☎ *01/493–4208.* 🎫 *Free.* ⏲ *Park daily 8:30–dusk. Museum May–Aug., daily 10–1 and 2–5:30; Sept.–Apr., daily 10–1 and 2–4.*

❷ To get to **Marlay Park,** leave St. Enda's Park via Grange Road and walk up the hill for about 1 km (½ mi), turning left at the T junction and continuing another ½ km (¼ mi). The park marks the start of the **Wicklow Way,** a popular walking route that crosses the Wicklow Mountains for 137 km (85 mi), through some of the most rugged landscapes in Ireland. In addition to its woodlands and nature walks, the 214-acre park has a cobbled courtyard, home to brightly plumaged peacocks. Surrounding the courtyard are crafts workshops, where you're welcome to observe bookbinding, jewelry making, and furniture making in process. Every Saturday from 3 to 5, kids can take a free ride on the model steam railway. ✉ *Grange Rd.,* ☎ *01/493–4059.* 🎫 *Free.* ⏲ *Nov.–Jan., daily 10–5; Feb.–Mar., daily 10–6; Apr. and Sept., daily 10–8; May–Aug., daily 10–9; Oct., daily 10–7.*

Ballsbridge

Take the DART train to Sidney Parade, or Bus 7 or Bus 8 from Burgh Quay (on the south bank of the Liffey, just east of O'Connell Bridge).

You'll find many of Dublin's best hotels and restaurants in the northern reaches of Ballsbridge, a leafy suburb directly across the Grand Canal from the city center. Its major cultural sites, however, are considerably farther south—a bit too far to reach on foot unless you're really an ambitious walker.

❸ **Sandymount Strand,** which stretches for 5 km (3 mi) from Ringsend to Booterstown, can be accessed a few blocks west of the Sydney Parade DART station. It was cherished by James Joyce and his beloved from Galway, Nora Barnacle, and it figures as one of the settings in *Ulysses.* (The beach is "at the lacefringe of the tide," as Joyce put it.) When the tide recedes, the beach extends for 1½ km (1 mi) from the foreshore, but the tide sweeps in again very quickly. A sliver of a park lies between the main Strand Road and the beach.

OFF THE BEATEN PATH

SOUTH WALL – East of the city is the South Wall, a long breakwater that stretches 1½ km (1 mi) out into Dublin Bay from the Ringsend power station. The wall is punctuated at its end by **Poolbeg Lighthouse.** On a nice day, it's a wonderful place for a walk; here you can get stunning views of North Bull Island to the north, Dublin to the west, and the entirety of the bay. It's too far to walk to the wall from the city center, and public transportation runs sporadically, so your best bet is to come by car.

Booterstown

Take the DART local train from either Tara St. or Pearce St. Or take R118 from the corner of Lower Merrion St. and Merrion Sq.

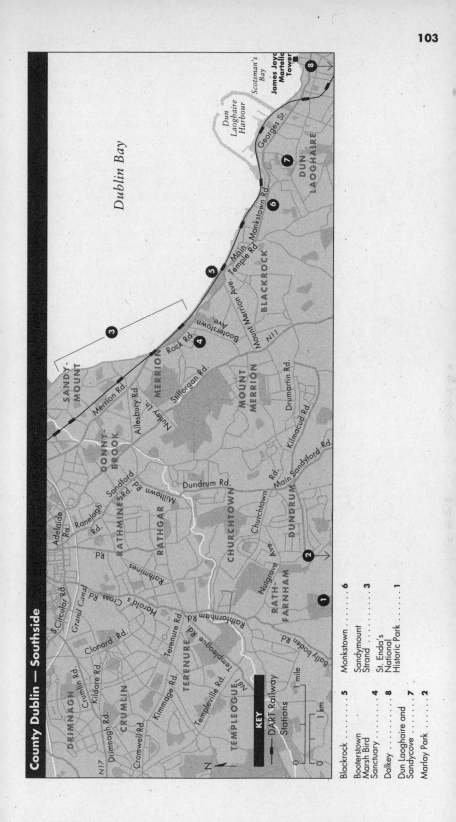

County Dublin — Southside

Dublin Bay

Scotsman's Bay

James Joyce Martello Tower 8

Dun Laoghaire Harbour

Georges St.

DUN LAOGHAIRE 7

6 Monkstown Rd.

Main Temple Rd. 5

BLACKROCK

Mount Merrion Ave.

Booterstown Ave.

N11

SANDY-MOUNT 3

MERRION

Rock Rd. 4

Stillorgan Rd.

Merrion Rd.

Ailesbury Rd.

Nutley Ln.

MOUNT MERRION

Drumartin Rd.

Kilmacud Rd.

DONNY-BROOK

Sandford Rd.

Milltown Rd.

Dundrum Rd.

Main Sandyford Rd.

Adelaide Rd.

Ranelagh Rd.

Rd.

Rathmines

RATHMINES

RATHGAR

CHURCHTOWN

Churchtown Rd.

DUNDRUM

Nutgrove Ave.

2

S. Circular Rd.

Grand Canal

Harold's Cross Rd.

Clonard Rd.

Terenure Rd.

Templeogue Rd.

Rathfarnham Rd.

RATH-FARNHAM

1

Ballyboden Rd.

DRIMNAGH

Crumlin Rd.

Kildare Rd.

Drimnagh Rd.

Cromwell Rd.

CRUMLIN

Kimmage Rd.

TERENURE

Templeville Rd.

N81

TEMPLEOGUE

N17

N

KEY

DART Railway
Stations

0   1 mile

0   1 km

Blackrock 5

Booterstown
Marsh Bird
Sanctuary 4

Dalkey 8

Dun Laoghaire and
Sandycove 7

Marlay Park 2

Monkstown 6

Sandymount
Strand 3

St. Enda's
National
Historic Park 1

Booterstown stretches along Dublin Bay south of Sandymount. The ❹ **Booterstown Marsh Bird Sanctuary** is the largest wildlife preserve in the Dublin area. Curlews, herons, kingfishers, and other fairly rare migratory species come to nest here; information boards along the road describe the birds for visitors. Also on this main road you'll pass **Glena,** the house where Athlone-born John McCormack, one of the best and most popular tenors in the first quarter of the 20th century, died on September 16, 1945. ✉ *Between the DART line and Rock Rd.,* ☎ *01/454–1786.*

Blackrock
❺ *3 km (2 mi) south of Booterstown. Take the DART line from the city center to Blackrock.*

Fine sea views, swimming, and a major shopping center draw Dubliners down to Blackrock, a bedroom community where James Joyce's parents lived with their large brood for most of 1892. Above the Blackrock DART station, at **Idrone Terrace**—lined with restored, old-fashioned lamps—you'll get a lovely view across the bay to Howth Peninsula.

Monkstown
❻ *3 km (2 mi) south of Blackrock on R119. Take the DART train from the city center to the Monkstown and Seapoint stations.*

One of Dublin's most exclusive suburbs, Monkstown is known for its two architectural curiosities. John Semple, the architect of Monkstown's **Anglican parish church,** was inspired by two entirely different styles, the Gothic and the Moorish, which he joined into an unlikely hybrid of towers and turrets. Built in 1833 in the town's main square, the church is only open during Sunday services. The well-preserved ruins of **Monkstown Castle** lie about 1 km (½ mi) south of the suburb; it's a 15th-century edifice with a keep, a gatehouse, and a long wall section, all surrounded by greenery. The **Lambert Puppet Theatre** (✉ Clifton La., ☎ 01/280–0974), which stages regular puppet shows, houses a puppetry museum.

Dun Laoghaire and Sandycove
❼ *2½ km (1½ mi) beyond Monkstown along R119, the Monkstown Crescent.*

After the British monarch King George IV disembarked for a brief visit in 1821, Dun Laoghaire (pronounced dun *lear*-ee) was renamed Kingstown, but it reverted to its original Irish name 99 years later. Its Irish name refers to Laoghaire, the High King of Tara who in the 5th century permitted St. Patrick to begin converting Ireland to Christianity. The town was once a Protestant stronghold of the old ruling elite; in some of the neo-Georgian squares and terraces behind George's Street, the main thoroughfare, a little of the community's former elegance can still be felt.

Dun Laoghaire has long been known for its great harbor, enclosed by two piers, each 2½ km (1½ mi) long. The harbor was constructed between 1817 and 1859, using granite quarried from nearby Dalkey Hill; the west pier has a rougher surface and is less favored for walking than the east pier, which has a bandstand where musicians play in summer. The workaday business here includes passenger-ship and freight-services sailings to Holyhead in north Wales, 3½ hours away. Dun Laoghaire is also a yachting center, with the members-only Royal Irish, National, and Royal St. George yacht clubs, all founded in the 19th century, lining the harbor area.

West of the harbor and across from the Royal Marine Hotel and the People's Park, the **National Maritime Museum** is in the former Mariners' church. Its nave makes a strangely ideal setting for exhibits like the French longboat captured during an aborted French invasion at Bantry, County Cork, in 1796. A particularly memorable exhibit is the old optic from the Baily Lighthouse on Howth Head, across Dublin Bay; the herringbone patterns of glass reflected light across the bay until several decades ago. ⊠ *Haigh Terr.,* ☎ *01/280–0969.* 🖼 *€1.90.* ☉ *May–Sept., Tues.–Sun. 1–5.*

From the harbor area Marine Parade leads alongside Scotsmans Bay for 1¼ km (¾ mi), as far as the **Forty Foot Bathing Pool,** a traditional bathing area that attracts mostly nude older men. Women were once banned from here, but now hardy swimmers of both genders are free to brave its cold waters.

A few steps away from the Forty Foot Bathing Pool stands the **James Joyce Martello Tower.** Originally built in 1804 when Napoléon's invasion seemed imminent, it was demilitarized in the 1860s along with most of the rest of the 34 Martello towers that ring Ireland's coast. (Martello towers were originally Italian and were constructed to protect the Italian coastline against the possibility of a Napoleonic naval invasion. In Ireland, they were built by the British to protect Irish shores from the same threat and were remarkable for their squat and solid construction, rotating cannon at the top, and—most importantly—their proximity to one another, so that each one is within visible range of the one next to it. In 1904, this tower was rented to Oliver St. John Gogarty, a medical student who was known for his poetry and ready wit, for £8 a year. He wanted to create a nurturing environment for writers and would-be literati. Joyce spent a week here in September 1904 and described it in the first chapter of *Ulysses,* using his friend as a model for the character Buck Mulligan. The tower now houses the **Joyce Museum,** founded in 1962 thanks to Sylvia Beach, the Paris-based first publisher of *Ulysses.* The exhibition hall contains first editions of most of Joyce's works. Joycean memorabilia include his waistcoat, embroidered by his grandmother, and a tie that he gave to Samuel Beckett (who was Joyce's onetime secretary). The gunpowder magazine stores the Joyce Tower Library, including a death mask of Joyce taken on January 13, 1941. ⊠ *Sandycove,* ☎ *01/280–9265,* 🌐 *www.visitdublin.com.* 🖼 *€5.50.* ☉ *Apr.–Oct., Mon.–Sat. 10–1 and 2–5, Sun. 2–6; Nov.–Mar. by appointment.*

DINING

$$–$$$ ✕ **Brasserie Na Mara.** Chef Derek Breen serves Irish dishes with a modern twist in this brasserie—*na mara* means "of the sea" in Gaelic, and although he kept the name, he jettisoned the strict emphasis on seafood. Fish, is, nonetheless, one specialty, and baked monkfish tops the list. The building has an unusual history: the first railway in Ireland, opened in 1834, was built from Westland Row (now Pearse Station) in Dublin to Dun Laoghaire. Much of the original station's entrance and ticketing area has been converted into this restaurant—now tall Georgian windows overlook the busy Dun Laoghaire ferryport. Reservations are essential on weekends. ⊠ *Dun Laoghaire Harbour,* ☎ *01/280–6767. AE, DC, MC, V. No lunch Sat. No dinner Sun.*

$$ ✕ **Duzy's Café.** This stylish restaurant sits above the Eagle House pub on the north side of Dun Laoghaire. The summery Mediterranean colors, striking paintings—large and specially commissioned—create a dashing impression. The panfried scallops in a sesame and lime dressing is terrific. ⊠ *18 Glasthule Rd.,* ☎ *01/230–0210. AE, DC, MC, V. No lunch Sat.*

$$ ✕ **Caviston's.** Stephen Caviston and his family have been dispensing fine food for years from their fish counter and delicatessen in Sandycove. The fish restaurant next door is an intimate place. Typical entrées include panfried scallops served in the shell with a Thermidor sauce, and steamed Dover sole with mustard sauce. You can also get a halved lobster with a simple butter sauce for an exceptionally good price. ⊠ *58–59 Glasthule Rd.,* ☎ *01/280–9120. MC, V. Closed Sun.–Mon. and late Dec.–early Jan. No dinner.*

Dalkey Village

⑧ *From the James Joyce Tower in Sandycove, it's an easy walk or quick drive 1 km (½ mi) south to Dalkey. Or take the DART line from the city center to Dalkey.*

Along Castle Street, the town's main thoroughfare, you'll find the substantial stone remains, resembling small, turreted castles, of two 15th- and 16th-century fortified houses. From the mainland's Vico Road, beyond Coliemore Harbour, are astounding bay views as far as Bray in County Wicklow. On Dalkey Hill is **Torca Cottage,** home of the Nobel Prize–winning writer George Bernard Shaw from 1866 to 1874. You can return to Dalkey Village by Sorrento Road. The **Heritage Centre** attached to Dalkey Castle has exhibits on local history with a script written by playwright and local resident Hugh Leonard.

In summer, small boats make the 15-minute crossing from Coliemore Harbour to **Dalkey Island,** covered with long grass and uninhabited except for a herd of goats, and graced with its own Martello tower—and an excellent bird sanctuary. The 8th-century ruins of **St. Begnet's** church sit right beside the bird sanctuary.

County Dublin—Northside

Dublin's northern suburbs remain predominantly working class and largely residential, but there are a few places worth the trip. As with most other suburban areas, walking may not be the best way to get around. It's good, but not essential, to have a car. Buses and trains service most of these areas, the only drawback is that to get from one suburb to another by public transportation you have to backtrack through the city center. Even if you're traveling by car, visiting all these sights will take a full day, so plan your trip carefully before setting off.

Glasnevin

Drive from the north city center by Lower Dorset St., as far as the bridge over the Royal Canal. Turn left, go up Whitworth Rd., by the side of the canal, for 1 km (½ mi); at its end, turn right onto Prospect Rd. and then left onto the Finglas road, N2. You may also take Bus 40 or Bus 40A from Parnell St., next to Parnell Sq., in the north city center.

⑨ **Glasnevin Cemetery,** on the right-hand side of the Finglas road, is the best-known burial ground in Dublin. Here you'll find the graves of many distinguished Irish leaders, including Eamon De Valera, a founding father of modern Ireland and a former Irish *taoiseach* (prime minister) and president, and Michael Collins, the celebrated hero of the Irish War of Independence. Other notables interred here include late-19th-century poet Gerard Manley Hopkins and Sir Roger Casement, an Irish rebel hanged for treason by the British in 1916. The large column to the right of the main entrance is the tomb of "The Liberator" Daniel O'Connell, perhaps Ireland's greatest historical figure, renowned for his nonviolent struggle for Catholic rights and emancipation, which he achieved in 1829. The cemetery is freely accessible all day.

⑩ On the northeastern flank of Glasnevin Cemetery, the **National Botanic Gardens** date from 1795 and have more than 20,000 different varieties of plants, a rose garden, and a vegetable garden. The main

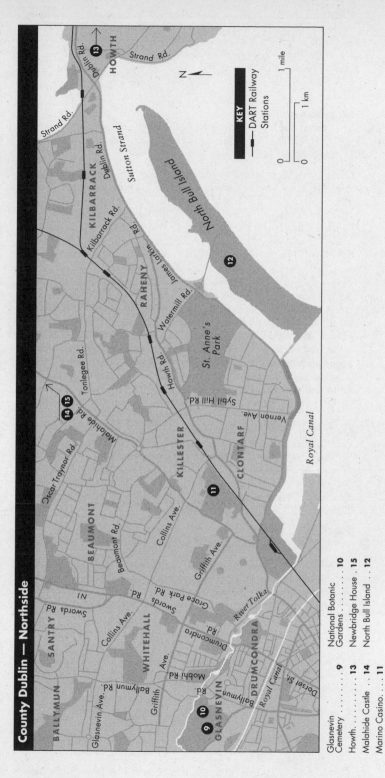

County Dublin — Northside

KEY
DART Railway Stations

1 mile
1 km

HOWTH
Strand Rd.
Dublin Rd.
Sutton Strand
North Bull Island
KILBARRACK
Kilbarrack Rd.
Dublin Rd.
Strand Rd.
RAHENY
James Larkin Rd.
Watermill Rd.
Howth Rd.
St. Anne's Park
Sybil Hill Rd.
Tonlegee Rd.
Malahide Rd.
Oscar Traynor Rd.
KILLESTER
CLONTARF
Vernon Ave.
BEAUMONT
Beaumont Rd.
Collins Ave.
Griffith Ave.
Royal Canal
SANTRY
BALLYMUN
N1
Swords Rd.
Collins Ave.
Glasnevin Ave.
WHITEHALL
Griffith Ave.
Mobhi Rd.
Ballymun Rd.
Grace Park Rd.
Swords Rd.
Drumcondra Rd.
River Tolka
DRUMCONDRA
GLASNEVIN
Ballymun Rd.
Royal Canal
Dorset St.

Glasnevin Cemetery 9
Howth 13
Malahide Castle . . . 14
Marino Casino 11
National Botanic Gardens 10
Newbridge House . 15
North Bull Island . . 12

attraction is the **Curvilinear Range,** 400-ft-long greenhouses designed and built by a Dublin ironmaster, Richard Turner, between 1843 and 1869. The Palm House, with its striking double dome, was built in 1884 and houses orchids, palms, and tropical ferns. ✉ *Glasnevin Rd.,* ☎ *01/837–4388.* 🎟 *Free.* ☉ *Apr.–Sept., Mon.–Sat. 10–6, Sun. 11–6; Oct.–Mar., Mon.–Sat. 10–4:30, Sun. 11–4:30.*

Marino Casino

⓫ *Take the Malahide road from Dublin's north city center for 4 km (2½ mi). Or take Bus 20A or Bus 24 to the Casino from Cathal Brugha St. in the north city center.*

One of Dublin's most exquisite, yet also most underrated, architectural landmarks, the Marino Casino (the name has nothing to do with gambling—it means "little house by the sea") is a small-scale, Palladian-style Greek temple, built between 1762 and 1771 from a plan by Sir William Chambers. Often compared to the Petit Trianon at Versailles, it was commissioned by the great Irish grandee, Lord Charlemont, as a summerhouse. It overlooks Dublin harbor. While the grand mansion on Charlemont's estate was tragically demolished in 1921, this sublime casino was saved and has now been lovingly restored (thankfully, Sir William's original plans survived). Inside, highlights are the china-closet boudoir, the huge golden sun set in the ceiling of the main drawing room, and the signs of the zodiac in the ceiling of the bijou-size library. When you realize that the structure has, in fact, 16 rooms—there are bedrooms upstairs—Sir William's sleight-of-hand is readily apparent: from its exterior, the structure seems to contain only one room. The tricks don't stop there: the freestanding columns on the facade are hollow so they can drain rainwater, while the elegant marble urns on the roof are chimneys. Last but not least, note the four stone lions on the outside terrace—they were carved by Joseph Wilson, who created the famous British royal coronation coach back in London. All in all, this remains, to quote Desmond Guinness, "one of the most exquisite buildings in Europe." It makes a good stop on the way to Malahide, Howth, or North Bull Island. ✉ *Malahide Rd., Marino,* ☎ *01/833–1618,* 🌐 *www.heritageireland.ie.* 🎟 *€2.55.* ☉ *Feb.–Mar. and Nov., Sun. and Thurs. noon–4; Apr., Sun. and Thurs. noon–5; May and Oct., daily 10–5; June–Sept., daily 10–6.*

North Bull Island

⓬ *From Dublin's north city center, take the Clontarf road for 4 km (2½ mi) to the causeway.*

A 5-km-long (3-mi-long) island created in the 19th century by the action of the tides, North Bull Island is one of Dublin's wilder places—it's a nature conservancy with vast beach and dunes. The island is linked to the mainland via a wooden causeway that leads to **Bull Wall,** a 1½-km (1-mi) walkway that stretches as far as the **North Bull Lighthouse.** The island is also accessible via a second, northerly causeway, which takes you to **Dollymount Strand.** (The two routes of entry don't meet at any point on the island.) You can reach it from the mainland via James Larkin Road. The small **visitor center** here largely explains the island's bird life. ✉ *Off the northerly causeway,* ☎ *01/833–8341.* 🎟 *Free.* ☉ *Mar.–Oct., Mon.–Wed. 10:15–1 and 1:30–4, Thurs. 10:15–1 and 1:30–3:45, Fri. 10:15–1 and 1:30–2:30, weekends 10–1 and 1:30–5:30; Nov.–Feb., Mon.–Wed. 10:15–1 and 1:30–4, Thurs. 10:15–1 and 1:30–3:45, Fri. 10:15–1 and 1:30–2:30, weekends 10–1 and 1:30–4:30.*

On the mainland directly across from North Bull Island is **St. Anne's Park,** a public green with extensive rose gardens (including many prize hybrids) and woodland walks. ⊠ *James Larkin Rd. and Mt. Prospect Ave.*

Howth

★ ⑬ *From Dublin, take the DART train, which takes about 30 mins; Bus 31B from Lower Abbey St. in the city center; or, by car, take the Howth road from the north city center for 16 km (10 mi).*

A fishing village at the foot of a long peninsula, Howth (derived from the Norse *hoved,* meaning head; it rhymes with "both") was an island inhabited as long ago as 3250 BC. Between 1813 and 1833, Howth was the Irish terminus for the sea crossing to Holyhead in north Wales, but it was then superseded by the newly built harbor at Kingstown (now Dun Laoghaire). Today, its harbor, which supports a large fishing fleet, includes a marina. Both arms of the harbor pier form extensive walks. Separated from Howth Harbour by a channel nearly 1½ km (1 mi) wide, **Ireland's Eye** has an old stone church on the site of a 6th-century monastery and an early 19th-century Martello tower. In calm weather, local boatmen make the crossing to the island.

At the King Sitric restaurant on the East Pier, a 2½-km (1½-mi) cliff walk begins, leading to the white **Baily Lighthouse,** built in 1814. In some places, the cliff path narrows and drops sheerly to the sea, but the views out over the Irish Sea are terrific. Some of the best views in the whole Dublin area await from the parking lot above the lighthouse, looking out over the entire bay as far south as Dun Laoghaire, Bray, and the north Wicklow coast. You can also see quite a bit of Dublin.

Until 1959, a tram service ran from the railway station in Howth, over Howth Summit, and back down to the station. One of the open-topped ☺ Hill of Howth trams that plied this route is now the star at the **National Transport Museum,** a short, 800-yard walk from Howth's DART station. Volunteers have spent several years restoring the tram, which stands alongside other unusual vehicles, including old horse-drawn bakery vans. ☎ *01/848–0831 or 01/847–5623. ⊡ €2.50. ☺ June–Aug., daily 10–5:30; Oct.–May, weekends 2–5.*

Next door to the Transport Museum and accessible from the Deer Park Hotel, the **Howth Castle Gardens** were laid out in the early 18th century. The many rare varieties of its fine rhododendron garden are in full flower April–June; there are also high beech hedges. The rambling castle, originally built in 1654 and considerably altered in the intervening centuries, is not open to the public, but you can access the ruins of a tall, square 16th-century castle and a Neolithic dolmen. ⊠ *Deer Park Hotel, ☎ 01/832–2624. ⊡ Free. ☺ Daily 8–dusk.*

DINING

$$$–$$$$ ✕ **King Sitric.** This well-known seafood restaurant is one of Howth's main attractions. It's in a Georgian house on the harborfront, with the yacht marina and port on one side and with sea views from the upstairs seafood bar, where informal lunches are served in summer. A house specialty is black sole meunière, grilled and finished with a nut-brown butter sauce, but lobster, caught just yards away in Balscadden Bay, is the big treat—it's best at its simplest, in butter sauce. Crab is equally fresh, dressed with mayonnaise or Mornay sauce. ⊠ *East Pier, ☎ 01/ 832–5235. AE, DC, MC, V. Closed Sun. No lunch Sat.*

$$–$$$$ ✕ **Abbey Tavern.** The original stone walls, flagged floors, blazing turf fires, and old gaslights of the ancient building that houses this old-world tavern all make you feel like you're back in an old-world environment. The upstairs restaurant serves traditional Irish and Continental cuisine, and specializes in fish dishes. Sole Abbey (filleted and stuffed with prawns, mushrooms, and herbs) is a house specialty, and fresh Dublin Bay prawns can be cooked to order. Traditional Irish music is performed in a different part of the building. The restaurant is a five-minute walk from the DART station; call for directions. ⊠ *Abbey St.,* ☎ *01/839–0307. Reservations essential. AE, DC, MC, V. No dinner Sun.*

Malahide

To get here by car, drive from the north city center on R107 for 14½ km (9 mi). Or catch the hourly train from Connolly Station, which takes about 20 mins. Or board Bus 42 to Malahide, which leaves from Beresford Pl. behind the Custom House (service runs every 15 mins; the ride takes about 40 mins).

★ Ⅽⅰⅰ ⑭ Malahide is chiefly known for **Malahide Castle,** a picture-book castle occupied by the Anglo-Irish and aristocratic Talbot family from 1185 until 1976, when it was sold to the Dublin County Council. The great expanse of parkland around the castle includes a botanical garden with more than 5,000 species and varieties of plants, all clearly labeled. The castle itself is a combination of styles and periods; the earliest section, the three-story tower house, dates from the 12th century. The medieval great hall is the only one in Ireland that is preserved in its original form, while the National Portrait Gallery has many fine paintings of the Talbot family and 18th- and 19th-century Irish notables. Other rooms are well furnished with authentic 18th-century pieces. Also in the castle is the **Fry Model Railway Museum,** with rare, handmade models of the Irish railway. Children always marvel at one of the world's largest miniature railways, which covers an area of 2,500 square ft. The castle's self-service restaurant serves good homemade food all day. ⊠ *10 km (6 mi) north of Howth on the Coast Road,* ☎ *01/846–2184,* W̅E̅B̅ *www.malahide.ie.* ⧉ €5.50. ☉ *Apr.–Sept., Mon.–Sat. 10–5, Sun. 2–6.*

Ⅽⅰⅰ ⑮ **Newbridge House,** in nearby Donabate, was built between 1740 and 1760 for Charles Cobbe, Archbishop of Dublin. Newbridge was owned by the Cobbe family until 1985, when it, along with most of its furnishings, was purchased by the state. One of the finest Georgian interiors in Ireland, the **Red Drawing Room** is hung with dozens of paintings and decorated with many fine antiques. The **kitchens** of the house still have their original utensils. Crafts workshops and some examples of old-style transportation, such as coaches, are in the courtyard. Beyond the walled garden are 366 acres of parkland and a restored 18th-century animal farm. **Tara's Palace,** a dollhouse that was made to raise funds for children's charities, is also here; it has 25 rooms, all fully furnished in miniature. The exterior of the dollhouse is based on the facades of three great Irish houses—Carton, Castletown, and Leinster. The **coffee shop** is renowned for the quality and selection of its homemade goods. You can travel from Malahide to Donabate by train, which takes about 10 minutes. From the Donabate train station, the walk to the Newbridge House grounds takes 15 minutes. ⊠ *Donabate, 8 km (5 mi) north of Malahide, signposted from N1,* ☎ *01/843–6534.* ⧉ €5.50. ☉ *Apr.–Sept., Tues.–Sat. 10–5, Sun. 2–6; Oct.– Mar., weekends 2–5.*

DINING

$$$–$$$$ ✕ **Bon Appetit.** The striking floral decor creates a cozy, traditional atmosphere, an impression heightened by the staff of black-jacketed waiters. Owner-chef Patsy McGuirk's traditional Continental menu includes such entrées as warm salad of Dublin Bay king prawns with pine nuts, prawn oil, and shavings of Parmesan and a generous selection of desserts. Especially fine is sole McGuirk—filleted, stuffed with prawns and turbot, and baked with white wine and cream. ⊠ *9 James's Terr.,* ☎ *01/845–0314. AE, DC, MC, V. Closed Sun. No lunch Sat.*

DUBLIN A TO Z

To research prices, get advice from other travelers, and book travel arrangements, visit www.fodors.com.

AIR TRAVEL TO AND FROM DUBLIN

There are daily services to Dublin from all major London airports. Flights to Dublin also leave from Birmingham, Bristol, East Midlands, Liverpool, Luton, Manchester, Leeds/Bradford, Newcastle, Edinburgh, and Glasgow. Prices vary a great deal between companies and at different seasons. You'll also find there are numerous flights from Europe and North America.

CARRIERS

From the United Kingdom, six airlines now serve destinations in Ireland: Aer Lingus, Ryanair, City Jet, Go, British Airways, and British Midland Airways. Aer Lingus operates 12 flights from Heathrow and Gatwick Airports. British Airways has a regular schedule out of Heathrow. British Midland operates 10 flights to Dublin from Heathrow. Ryanair operates several no-frills, low-price flights from Luton and Stanstead airports. City Jet flies from the very central London City Airport. Go flies from Edinburgh. Ryanair is known for being the cheapest, but this means cutting back on comfort and services.

Major European carriers, such as Air France, Lufthansa, Sabena, SAS, and Alitalia, run direct services to Dublin from most European capital cities and major regional airports, especially those in Germany.

Three airlines have regularly scheduled flights from the United States to Dublin. Aer Lingus flies direct from New York, Boston, Los Angeles, and Chicago to Dublin and Shannon. Continental flies from New York (Newark Airport) to Dublin and Shannon. Delta flies from Atlanta to Dublin via New York.

Within Ireland, Aer Lingus operates flights from Dublin to Belfast, Cork, Derry, Kerry, Shannon, Galway, Knock in County Mayo, Donegal, and Sligo. Ryanair flies to Belfast.

➤ AIRLINES AND CONTACTS: **Aer Lingus** (☎ 01/844–4747). **British Airways** (☎ 800/626–747). **British Midland** (☎ 01/283–8833). **City Jet** (☎ 01/844–5566). **Go** (☎ 1890/923–922). **Continental** (☎ 1890/925–252). **Delta** (☎ 01/844–4166 or 01/676–8080). **Ryanair** (☎ 01/844–4411).

AIRPORTS AND TRANSFERS

Dublin Airport, 10 km (6 mi) north of the city center, serves international and domestic airlines.

➤ AIRPORT INFORMATION: **Dublin Airport** (☎ 01/844–4900).

TRANSFERS

Dublin Bus operates a shuttle service between Dublin Airport and the city center with departures outside the arrivals gateway; pay the driver inside the coach. The single fare is €4.50. Service runs from 5:45 AM to 11:30 PM, at intervals of about 20 minutes (after 8 PM buses run every hour), to as far as Dublin's main bus station (Busaras), behind the Custom House on the northside. Journey time from the airport to the city center is normally 30 minutes, but it may be longer in heavy traffic. If you have time take a regular bus for €1.30.

A taxi is a quicker alternative than the bus to get from the airport to Dublin center. A line of taxis waits by the arrivals gateway; the fare for the 30-minute journey to any of the main city-center hotels is about €15.25 to €17.80 plus tip (tips don't have to be large but they are increasingly expected). Ask about the farè before leaving the airport.

➤ TAXIS AND SHUTTLES: **Busaras** (☎ 01/830–2222). **Dublin Bus** (☎ 01/873–4222).

BOAT AND FERRY TRAVEL

Irish Ferries has a regular car and passenger service directly into Dublin port from Holyhead in Wales. Stena Sealink docks in Dublin port (3½-hour service to Holyhead) and in Dun Laoghaire (High Speed Service, known as "HSS," which takes 99 minutes). Prices and departure times vary according to season, so call to confirm. In summer, reservations are strongly recommended. Dozens of taxis wait to take you into town from both ports, or you can take DART or a bus to the city center.

➤ BOAT AND FERRY INFORMATION: **Irish Ferries** (✉ Merrion Row, South of the Liffey, ☎ 01/661–0511). **Stena Sealink** (✉ Ferryport, South County Dublin Dun Laoghaire, ☎ 01/204–7777).

BUSINESS HOURS

Dublin is gradually becoming a 24-hour city, even though the bus and DART train services close down for the night at 11:30. (A few lines run until dawn on the weekends, and late buses go until 3 AM.) Many taxis run all night, but the demand, especially on weekends, can make for long lines at taxi stands. Many clubs on the Leeson Street strip and elsewhere stay open until 4 AM or later.

Banks are open weekdays 10–4 and remain open on Thursday until 5. All stay open at lunchtime. Most branches have ATMs that accept bank cards and MasterCard and Visa credit cards.

Museums are normally open Tuesday–Saturday and Sunday afternoon.

Stores are open Monday–Saturday 9–5:30 or 9–6, except on Thursday when they're open until 8. Smaller city-center specialty stores open on Sunday as well, usually 10–6. Most department stores are closed on Sunday.

Most pubs are open Monday–Saturday at 10:30 AM and 12:30 PM on Sunday. They must stop serving at 11:30 PM Monday–Wednesday, 12:30 AM Thursday–Saturday, and 11 PM on Sunday, but take another hour to empty out. A number of bars in the center of the city have permission to serve until 2 AM on weekend nights.

BUS TRAVEL TO AND FROM DUBLIN

Busaras is Dublin's main bus station, just behind the Custom House on the northside.

➤ BUS INFORMATION: **Busaras** (☎ 01/830–2222).

BUS TRAVEL WITHIN DUBLIN

Dublin has an extensive network of buses, most of which are green double-deckers. Some bus services run on cross-city routes, including the smaller "Imp" buses, but most buses start in the city center. Buses to the north of the city begin in the Lower Abbey Street–Parnell Street area, while those to the west begin in Middle Abbey Street and in the Aston Quay area. Routes to the southern suburbs begin at Eden Quay and in the College Street area. A number of services are links to DART stations, and another regular bus route connects the two main provincial railway stations, Connolly and Heuston. If the destination board indicates AN LÁR, that means that the bus is going to the city center. Late-night buses run Monday to Saturday to 3 AM on all major routes; the fare is €3.80.

Museumlink is a shuttle service that links up the Natural History Museum, National Museum, and Collins Barracks. You can catch it outside any of the three museums.

FARES AND SCHEDULES

Timetables (€3.20) are available from Dublin Bus, staffed weekdays 9–5:30, Saturday 9–1. Fares begin at 55p and are paid to the driver, who will accept inexact fares, but you'll have to go to the central office in Dublin to pick up your change as marked on your ticket. Change transactions and the city's heavy traffic can slow service down considerably.

➤ BUS INFORMATION: **Dublin Bus** (✉ 59 Upper O'Connell St., North of the Liffey, ☎ 01/873–4222).

CAR RENTAL

Renting a car in Dublin is very expensive, with high rates and a 12½% local tax. Gasoline is also expensive by U.S. standards, at around €1 a liter. Peak-period car-rental rates begin at around €260 a week for the smallest stick models, like a Ford Fiesta. Dublin has many car-rental companies, and it pays to shop around and to avoid "cowboy" outfits without proper licenses.

A dozen car-rental companies have desks at Dublin Airport; all the main national and international firms also have branches in the city center. Some reliable agencies are listed below.

➤ LOCAL AGENCIES: **Avis** (✉ 1 Hanover St. E, South of the Liffey, ☎ 01/677–5204; ✉ Dublin Airport, North County Dublin, ☎ 01/844–5204). **Budget** (✉ 151 Lower Drumcondra Rd., North County Dublin, ☎ 01/837–9802; ✉ Dublin Airport, North County Dublin, ☎ 01/844–5919). **Dan Dooley** (✉ 42–43 Westland Row, South of the Liffey, ☎ 01/677–2723; ✉ Dublin Airport, ☎ 01/844–5156). **Hertz** (✉ Leeson St. Bridge, South of the Liffey, ☎ 01/660–2255; ✉ Dublin Airport, North County Dublin, ☎ 01/844–5466). **Murray's Rent-a-Car** (✉ Baggot St. Bridge, South of the Liffey, ☎ 01/668–1777; ✉ Dublin Airport, North County Dublin, ☎ 01/844–4179).

CAR TRAVEL

Traffic in Ireland has increased exponentially in the last few years, and nowhere has the impact been felt more than in Dublin, where the city's complicated one-way streets are congested not only during the morning and evening rush hours but often during much of the day. If possible, avoid driving a car except to get in and out of the city (and be sure to ask your hotel or guest house for clear directions to get you out of town).

COMPUTERS

INTERNET CAFÉS

In the city center are a number of Internet cafés, which all charge between €3.50 and €7 an hour. Betacafe serves coffee and sandwiches. Cyberia is very popular with students, who tend to spend hours playing computer games. Planet Cyber Café is the city's best, with top-notch computers and a good coffee bar. You'll find some of the cheapest places on Thomas Street, as it's not smack in the center of town.

➤ ADDRESSES: **Betacafe** (✉ Arthouse, Curved St., Temple Bar, ☎ 01/671–5717). **Cyberia** (✉ The Granary, Temple La. S, Temple Bar, ☎ 01/679–7607). **Planet Cyber Café** (✉ 13 Andrews St., City Center, ☎ 01/670–5182).

EMBASSIES

Embassies are open weekdays 9–1 and 2–5.

➤ AUSTRALIA: (✉ Fitzwilton House, Wilton Terr., South of the Liffey, ☎ 01/676–1517).

➤ CANADA: (✉ 65 St. Stephen's Green, South of the Liffey, ☎ 01/478–1988).

➤ SOUTH AFRICA: (✉ Earlsfort Centre, South of the Liffey, ☎ 01/661–5553).

➤ UNITED KINGDOM: (✉ 29 Merrion Rd., South of the Liffey, ☎ 01/205–3700).

➤ UNITED STATES: (✉ 42 Elgin Rd., South of the Liffey, ☎ 01/668–8777).

EMERGENCIES

Call Dublin's Eastern Help Board for the names of doctors. The Dublin Dental Hospital has emergency facilities and lists of dentists who offer emergency care. Hamilton Long, a Dublin pharmacy, is open Monday–Wednesday and Saturday 8:30–6, Thursday 8:30–8, and Friday 8:30–7. Temple Bar Pharmacy is open Monday–Wednesday and Friday–Saturday 9–7, Thursday 9–8.

➤ DOCTORS AND DENTISTS: **Dublin Dental Hospital** (✉ 20 Lincoln Pl., South of the Liffey, ☎ 01/662–0766). **Eastern Help Board** (☎ 01/679–0700).

➤ EMERGENCY SERVICES: **Gardai (police), ambulance, fire** (☎ 999).

➤ HOSPITALS: **Beaumont** (✉ Beaumont Rd., North County Dublin, ☎ 01/837–7755). **Mater** (✉ Eccles St., North of the Liffey, ☎ 01/830–1122). **St. James's** (✉ 1 James St., Dublin West, ☎ 01/453–7941). **St. Vincent's** (✉ Elm Park, South County Dublin, ☎ 01/269–4533).

➤ LATE-NIGHT PHARMACIES: **Hamilton Long** (✉ 5 Upper O'Connell St., North of the Liffey, ☎ 01/874–8456). **Temple Bar Pharmacy** (✉ 20 E. Essex St., Temple Bar, ☎ 01/670–9751).

LODGING

BED-AND-BREAKFASTS

For a small fee, the Irish Tourist Board, known as Bord Fáilte, will book accommodations anywhere in Ireland through a central reservations system. B&Bs can be booked at local visitor information offices when they are open; however, even these reservations will go through the central system.

➤ CONTACT INFORMATION: **Bord Fáilte** (☎ 800/223–6470 in the U.S. and Canada; 800/039–7000 in the U.K.; 02/9299–6177 in Australia; 09/379–8720 in New Zealand, WEB www.irelandvacations.com, www.ireland.travel.ie).

MAIL AND SHIPPING

Post offices are open weekdays 9–1 and 2–5:30, Saturday 9–12:30. Main post offices are open Saturday afternoons, too (look for green signs that say "An Post"). The General Post Office (GPO) on O'Connell Street, which has foreign exchange and general delivery facilities, is open Monday–Saturday 8–8, Sunday 10:30–6:30.

SAFETY

What crime there is in Dublin is often drug-related. Sidestreets off O'Connell Street can be dangerous, especially at night. When you park your car, *do not* leave any valuables inside, even under a raincoat on the backseat or in the trunk; be especially careful parking around the Guinness Brewery and the Old Jameson Distillery.

TAXIS

Official licensed taxis, metered and designated by roof signs, do not cruise. You'll find taxi stands beside the central bus station, and at train stations, O'Connell Bridge, St. Stephen's Green, College Green, and near major hotels; the Dublin telephone directory has a complete list. The initial charge is €2.30 with an additional charge of about €2 a kilometer thereafter. The fare is displayed on a meter (make sure it's on). You may, instead, want to phone a taxi company and ask for a cab to meet you at your hotel, but this may cost up to €2.55 extra. Hackney cabs, which also operate in the city, have neither roof signs nor meters and will sometimes respond to hotels' requests for a cab. Negotiate the fare before your journey begins. Although the taxi fleet in Dublin is large, the cabs are nonstandard and some cars are neither spacious nor in pristine condition. Cab Charge has a reliable track record. Metro is one of the city's biggest but also the busiest. VIP Taxis usually has a car available for a longer trip.

➤ TAXI COMPANIES: **Cab Charge** (☎ 01/677–2222). **Metro** (☎ 01/668–3333). **VIP Taxis** (☎ 01/478–3333).

TOURS

BUS TOURS

Dublin Bus has three- and four-hour tours of the city center that include Trinity College, the Royal Hospital Kilmainham, and Phoenix Park. The one-hour City Tour, with hourly departures, allows you to hop on and off at any of the main sites. Tickets are available from the driver or Dublin Bus. There's also a continuous guided open-top bus tour (€10), run by Dublin Bus, which allows you to hop on and off the bus as often as you wish and visit some 15 sights along its route. The company also conducts a north-city coastal tour, going to Howth, and a south-city tour, traveling as far as Enniskerry.

Gray Line Tours runs city-center tours that cover the same sights as the Dublin Bus itineraries. Bus Éireann organizes day tours out of Busaras, the main bus station, to country destinations such as Glendalough.

➤ FEES AND SCHEDULES: **Bus Éireann** (☎ 01/836–6111). **Dublin Bus** (☎ 01/873–4222). **Gray Line Tours** (☎ 01/670–8822).

TRAIN AND CARRIAGE TOURS

Guided tours of Dublin using the DART system are organized by Views Unlimited. Horse-drawn carriage tours are available around Dublin and in Phoenix Park. For tours of the park, contact the Department of the Arts, Culture and the Gaeltacht. Carriages can be hired at the Grafton Street corner of St. Stephen's Green, without prior reservations.

➤ FEES AND SCHEDULES: **Department of the Arts, Culture and the Gaeltacht** (☎ 01/661–3111). **Views Unlimited** (✉ 8 Prince of Wales Terr., South County Dublin Bray, ☎ 01/286–0164 or 01/285–6121).

PUB AND MUSICAL TOURS

Dublin Tourism (☞ Visitor Information) has a booklet to its self-guided "Rock 'n Stroll" Trail, which covers 16 sites with associations to such performers as Bob Geldof, Christy Moore, Sinéad O'Connor, and U2. Most of the sites are in the city center and Temple Bar. The Traditional Musical Pub Crawl begins at Oliver St. John Gogarty's and moves on to other famous Temple Bar pubs. Led by two professional musicians who perform songs and tell the story of Irish music, the tour is given May–October, daily at 7:30 PM; the cost is €9. The Comedy Coach is a nightly hop-on, hop-off tour of Dublin pubs, clubs, and restaurants. There is nonstop entertainment on the bus—musicians and comics keep everyone happy between pints. A ticket costs around €15.

Colm Quilligan arranges highly enjoyable evening walks of the literary pubs of Dublin, where "brain cells are replaced as quickly as they are drowned." The *Dublin Literary Pub Crawl* is a 122-page guide to those Dublin pubs with the greatest literary associations; it's widely available in Dublin bookstores.

➤ Fees and Schedules: **Colm Quilligan** (☎ 01/454–0228). **Music and Comedy Coach** (☎ 01/280–1899). **Oliver St. John Gogarty's** (✉ Fleet St., Temple Bar). **Traditional Musical Pub Crawl** (✉ Discover Dublin, 20 Lower Stephens St., City Center, ☎ 01/478–0191).

WALKING TOURS

At the same time historical and hilarious, two well-know Dublin actors adopt a host of characters in HonestDublin's inventive two-hour walking tour of Dublin's major sites. A favorite scenario is the "drunken guide." The tours run from June to September, Monday to Friday at 11 AM and weekends at 11 AM and 3 PM. Meet at the front gates of Dublin Castle. The cost is €10 and it's worth every cent. Historical Walking Tours of Dublin, run by Trinity College history graduate students, are excellent two-hour tour introductions to Dublin. The Bord Fáilte–approved tour assembles from May to September at the front gate of Trinity College, daily at 11 AM and 3 PM, with an extra tour on Saturday and Sunday at noon, October to April on Friday to Sunday at noon. It costs €9. A Georgian/Literary Walking Tour leaves from Bewley's Oriental Café June–September daily at 11; each tour lasts approximately two hours and costs €9. Trinity Tours organizes walks of the Trinity College campus on weekends from March 17 (St. Patrick's Day) through mid-May and from mid-May to September daily; the half-hour tour costs €7.60 and includes admission to the *Book of Kells*; tours start at the college's main gate. If you choose the Zozimus Experience you'll get an enjoyable walking tour of Dublin's medieval past, with a particular focus on the seedy, including great escapes, murders, and mythical happenings. Led by a guide in costume, tours are by arrangement only and run from the main gate of Dublin Castle from 6:45 PM; it costs €9 per person. (Prepare yourself for a surprise.)

➤ Fees and Schedules: **Georgian/Literary Walking Tour** (☎ 01/496–0641). **Historical Walking Tours of Dublin** (☎ 01/878–0227). **HonestDublin Walking Tours** (☎ 01/672–9971). **Trinity Tours** (☎ 01/608–2320). **Zozimus Experience** (☎ 01/661–8646).

TRAIN TRAVEL

Dublin has two main train stations. Connolly Station provides train services to and from the east coast, Belfast, the north, and northwest. Heuston Station is the place for trains to and from the south and west. Pearse Station is for Bray and connections via Dun Laoghaire to the Liverpool-Holyhead ferries. Contact the Irish Rail Travel Centre for information.

An electric railway system, the DART (Dublin Area Rapid Transit), connects Dublin with Howth to the north and Bray to the south on a fast, efficient line. There are 25 stations on the route, which is the best means of getting to seaside destinations, such as Howth, Blackrock, Dun Laoghaire, Dalkey, Killiney, and Bray. Train services run from Heuston Station to Kildare Town west of Dublin via Celbridge, Sallins, and Newbridge. From Connolly Station you can catch a train to more distant locations like Malahide, Maynooth, Skerries, and Drogheda to the north of Dublin and Wicklow and Arklow to the south.

FARES AND SCHEDULES

DART service starts at 6:30 AM and runs until 11:30 PM; at peak periods, 8–9:30 AM and 5–7 PM, trains arrive every five minutes. At other times of the day, the intervals between trains are 15 to 25 minutes. Call ahead to check precise departure times (they do vary, especially on bank holidays). Tickets can be bought at stations, but it's also possible to buy weekly rail tickets, as well as weekly or monthly "rail-and-bus" tickets, from the Irish Rail Travel Centre. Individual fares begin at €.85 and range up to €1.65. You'll pay a heavy penalty for traveling the DART without a ticket. For the Railways and DART Lost and Found, contact the Irish Rail Travel Centre.

➤ Train Information: **Connolly Station** (✉ Amiens St., North of the Liffey). **DART** (☎ 01/836–6222). **Heuston Station** (✉ end of Victoria Quay, Dublin West). **Irish Rail Travel Centre** (✉ 35 Lower Abbey St., North of the Liffey, ☎ 01/836–6222). **Pearse Station** (✉ Westland Row, South of the Liffey).

TRANSPORTATION AROUND DUBLIN
Traveling around Dublin by public transportation is comparatively easy, although a car is useful for getting to the outlying suburbs. If you're just planning to visit city-center Dublin, do it without a car.

TRAVEL AGENCIES
➤ Local Agents: **American Express** (✉ 116 Grafton St., City Center, ☎ 01/677–2874). **Thomas Cook** (✉ 118 Grafton St., City Center, ☎ 01/677–1721).

VISITOR INFORMATION
The main Dublin Tourism center on Suffolk Street is open July–September, Monday–Saturday 8:30–6, Sunday 11–5:30, and October–June, daily 9–6; at Dublin Airport, daily 8 AM–10 PM; and at the Ferryport, Dun Laoghaire, daily 10–9. Bord Fáilte, the Irish Tourist Board, has its own visitor information offices in the entrance hall of its headquarters at Baggot St. Bridge and is open weekdays 9:15–5:15. A suburban tourist office in Tallaght is open March–December, daily 9:30–5. The Temple Bar Information Centre produces the easy-to-use, annually updated *Temple Bar Guide,* which provides complete listings of the area's stores, pubs, restaurants, clubs, galleries, and other cultural venues.

➤ Tourist Information: **Bord Fáilte** (✉ Baggot St. Bridge, South of the Liffey, ☎ 01/602–4000; 1850/230330 [within Ireland], FAX 01/602–4100, WEB www.ireland.travel.ie). **Dublin Tourism** (✉ Suffolk St., off Grafton St., City Center, ☎ 01/605–7700; 1850/230330 [within Ireland], FAX 01/605–7787, WEB www.visitdublin.com). **Temple Bar Information Centre** (✉ 18 Eustace St., Temple Bar, ☎ 01/671–5717, FAX 01/677–2525).

3 DUBLIN ENVIRONS

THE BOYNE VALLEY AND COUNTIES WICKLOW AND KILDARE

The Pale—the counties north, south, and west of Dublin—holds glory and grandeur. Here, you'll find some of the richest treasure houses in the land: Castletown, Russborough, and Powerscourt Houses. But the region has more than just 18th-century Palladian porticoes. Celtic crosses, historic churches, the ancient passage graves at Newgrange, and the "monastic city" of Glendalough await—all time-burnished sites that still guard the roots of Irishness.

Oe **NE OF THE LOVELIEST REGIONS** in Ireland, the Pale—the counties immediately north, south, and west of Dublin—is a kind of open-air museum filled with legendary Celtic sites, grand gardens, and elegant Palladian country estates. France has its châteaux of the Loire Valley, England the treasure houses of Kent and Sussex, Germany its castles of the Rhine, but the grand estates of the Pale rank pretty darn high in the galaxy of stately style.

Updated by
Anto Howard

Dublin environs include three basic geographical regions: County Wicklow's coast and mountains, the Boyne Valley, and County Kildare. Lying tantalizingly close to the south of Dublin stretches the mountainous county of Wicklow, which contains some of the most *et-in-arcadia-ego* scenery in the Emerald Isle. Here, the gently rounded Wicklow Mountains—to some tastes Ireland's finest—contain the evocative monastic settlement at Glendalough, many later abbeys and churches, and such noted 18th-century estates as Powerscourt and Russborough. Nearby is an impressive eastern coastline that stretches from Counties Wicklow to Louth, punctuated by delightful harbor towns and fishing villages. The coast is virtually unspoiled for its entire length.

North of Dublin lies the Boyne Valley, with its abundant ruins of Celtic Ireland stretching from Counties Meath to Louth. Some of the country's most evocative Neolithic ruins—including the famous passage graves at Newgrange—are nestled into this landscape, where layer upon layer of history penetrates down into earlier, unknowable ages. It was west of Drogheda—a fascinating town settled by the Vikings in the early 10th century—that the Tuatha De Danann, onetime residents of Ireland, went underground when defeated by the invading Milesians and became, it is said, "the good people" or fairies of Irish legend. In pagan times this area was the home of Ireland's high kings, and the center of religious life. In those days, all roads led to Tara, the fabled Hill of Kings, the royal seat and the place where the national assembly was once held. Today, time seems to stand still there—and you should do so, too, for it is almost sacrilegious to introduce a note of urgency.

Southwest of Dublin you'll find the flat pastoral plains of County Kildare; the plains stretch between the western Midlands and the foothills of the Dublin and Wicklow mountains—both names actually refer to one mountain, but each marks its county's claim to the land. Kildare is the flattest part of Ireland, a playing field for the breeding, training, and racing of some of the world's premier Thoroughbreds.

Of all the artistic delights that beckon both north and south of Dublin, few enchant as much as the imposing country estates of County Wicklow. Here, during the "glorious eighteenth," great Anglo-Irish estates were built by Irish "princes of Elegance and Prodigality." Only an hour or two from Dublin, these estates were profoundly influenced by the country villas of the great Italian architect Andrea Palladio, who erected the estates of the Venetian aristocracy only a short distance from the city on the lagoon. As in other parts of Ireland, the ancestral homes of the dwindling members of the Anglo-Irish ascendancy dot the landscape in the Pale. Today, lords and baronets down on their luck have turned into hoteliers who welcome guests to castle holidays with adaptable grace.

Pleasures and Pastimes

Dining

Dining out in the area is still essentially a casual affair, but the innovations and experimentation of Dublin's top restaurateurs are influencing the cooking—and the prices—at the finer establishments outside the capital. As in the Southwest, chefs hereabouts have a deep respect for fresh, locally grown and raised produce. You'll find everything from Continental-style meals to hearty ploughman's lunches.

CATEGORY	THE REPUBLIC*
$$$$	over €29
$$$	€22–€29
$$	€13–€21
$	under €13

Per person for a main course at dinner

Lodging

In Counties Wicklow and Kildare you'll find excellent accommodations, even if the choice may not be vast. If you have only a night or two outside Dublin, try to stay at least one night in one of the area's country-house or manor-house hotels, where some of Ireland's finest hosts welcome you into sometimes glorious, sometimes rustic, but almost invariably comfortable homes. Old-style hotels in Counties Meath and Louth are showing signs of improvement and are becoming ever more popular. Bed-and-breakfasts, as elsewhere in Ireland, are always a delightful option.

CATEGORY	THE REPUBLIC*
$$$$	over €230
$$$	€178–€230
$$	€127–€178
$	under €127

All prices are for two people in a double room, including VAT and a service charge (often applied in larger hotels).

Prehistoric and Monastic Sites

The Boyne Valley, which straddles the county of Louth and runs through the flat heartland of Meath, is home to 10% of all prehistoric monuments in Ireland. Foremost among these is Neolithic Newgrange, passage graves built between 2800 and 2400 BC. The Hill of Tara, one of the focal points for the ancient high kings of Ireland, was where disputes between clans were settled, new laws were passed, and, eventually, Christianity was proclaimed from the summit by St. Patrick. The advent of Christianity led to the construction of County Wicklow's Glendalough monastery, founded by one of St. Patrick's followers, St. Kevin. Later in the 12th century, the first Cistercian house in Ireland, the monastery of Mellifont, was founded. North of Mellifont are the ruins of Monasterboice, another monastic site where one of the finest high crosses in Ireland stands in the shadow of a 9th-century round tower.

Walking, Hiking, and Biking

Whether you're a novice or veteran hiker, Wicklow's gentle, rolling hills are a terrific place to begin an Irish walking vacation. Devoted hikers come from all over the world to traverse the 137-km (85-mi) Wicklow Way, the first long-distance trail to open in Ireland and one of the best. Beginning in Marlay Park (see Side Trips in Chapter 2), just a few miles south of Dublin, much of the route lies above 1,600 ft and follows rough sheep tracks, forest firebreaks, and old bog roads; rain gear, windproof clothing, and sturdy footwear are essential. Consider participating in one of the walking festivals held at Easter, in May, and in autumn. Biking is also an excellent way to see the area.

Exploring Dublin Environs

All of the towns and sites in the Dublin environs region can be visited on a day trip from the city. This chapter is organized into three different sections, each of which makes a reasonable day trip. Keep in mind that it's easy to lose an hour or so making detours, chatting with locals, and otherwise enjoying the unexpected. The itineraries below cover the area's highlights; if you have fewer than three days, use parts of each day's suggested itinerary to plan your excursion. A car is essential for visiting most sights—and don't plan on visiting both the north and south of Dublin in the same day. You can also reach some points of interest by public transport: bus tours from Dublin cover County Wicklow as far as Glendalough in the southwest and the Boyne Valley to the north; suburban bus services reach into the foothills of the Dublin Mountains; and Bus Éireann services take in the outlying towns. Some popular sites have direct connections to Dublin, including Enniskerry and Powerscourt House, Gardens, and Waterfall, which can be reached by taking the No. 44 bus from the Dublin quays area.

Numbers in the text correspond to numbers in the margin and on the Dublin Environs map.

Great Itineraries

IF YOU HAVE 3 DAYS

Begin your first day by traveling southward along N11 to **Powerscourt House, Gardens, and Waterfall** ⑲, the opulent Palladian mansion and garden estate, set under the great Sugar Loaf. Keep your spirits up, literally, by taking the road to **Roundwood** ⑳, the highest village in Ireland. Move on to the early Christian monastic settlement of **Glendalough** ㉑, set amid the tranquil Wicklow Mountains' forests. Follow R752 south to Rathnew and proceed to **Avoca** ㉕, where you can browse for wool fabric and apparel at Ireland's oldest mill. End your day in 🏨 **Wicklow Town** ㉓, north of Avoca on R754; or, if you want to remain Dublin based, return to the capital via N11.

Begin your second day with a visit to one of Ireland's grandest mansions, **Castletown House** ㉗ near Celbridge, easily reached via N4, with a left turn at Leixlip, followed by an 8-km (5-mi) drive down R403. Continue south and turn left at Clane until you reach **Naas** ㉙, where you turn left along R410 and go the short distance to Sir Alfred Beit's sumptuous **Russborough House** ㉚—a feast of old master paintings, Regency armoires, and Georgian stuccowork. Or, continue west toward **Kildare Town** ㉝, an elegant, prosperous town surrounded by the broad, flat plains of the **Curragh** ㉜. The **National Stud and Japanese Gardens**, just outside Kildare Town, are the real highlight of the area. If you spent your first night in Wicklow, return to Glendalough and proceed onward toward Kildare via the wonderfully scenic Wicklow Gap, a maze of winding roads that take you through the villages of Granabeg, Hollywood (no relation to its American namesake), and Kilcullen. Spend your second night either in nearby 🏨 **Straffan** ㉘ or back in 🏨 **Dublin.**

On your third day, head north of Dublin to Counties Meath and Louth via N3, which will take you to the **Hill of Tara** ②, one of Ireland's most important Celtic sites and home of the Irish kings just after the birth of Christ. Travel back another 2,000 years in time with a visit to **Newgrange** ⑤, home to the most important Neolithic passage tombs in Europe. On your way north to **Monasterboice** ⑩, where one of the finest high crosses in all of Ireland awaits, be sure to visit the small Georgian village of **Slane** ⑥. Make a stop along N51 at **King William's Glen** ⑦, site of the Battle of the Boyne in 1690 between the Catholic forces of

King James II and the Protestant army of King William of Orange—a battle that shaped the course of Irish history. Return to Dublin via N2.

IF YOU HAVE 5 DAYS

Five days should give you ample opportunity to "take it aisy"—or, at least, to take it as easy as you can, considering the array of beautiful sights found in this part of the country. Make a stop in the coastal town of Bray ⑱, a Victorian seaside resort founded in the 1850s, before heading south toward **Powerscourt House, Gardens, and Waterfall** ⑲, **Roundwood** ⑳, and on to **Glendalough** ㉑. (If you haven't already explored the towns along Dublin Bay north of Bray but south of Dublin, consult the Side Trips section in Chapter 2 to decide whether to visit the County Dublin sights we cover in that section on your way farther south.) For a taste of more recent history, follow N11 a few miles south to Rathnew and drive inland on R752 until you reach **Avondale House and Forest Park** ㉔, the home of the 19th-century Irish leader Charles Stewart Parnell. Stay overnight in ⛼ **Wicklow Town** ㉓, which dates back to Viking days, or near the ⛼ **Poulaphouca Reservoir** ㉛, home of the wonderful Rathsallagh House. If you have time, you may want to visit the seaside resort of **Arklow** ㉖ or the **Mount Usher Gardens** ㉒ northwest of Wicklow Town, off N11 beyond Rathnew. Spend your second day visiting the broad flatland of County Kildare, venturing as far south as **Ballytore** ㉟ and **Castledermot** ㊱ before spending the night in ⛼ **Straffan** ㉘. On your third day, set off for the Celtic and prehistoric sights of County Meath. Be sure to visit the 12th-century remains of **Mellifont Abbey** ⑨ near **Slane** ⑥, and the town of **Kells** ④, where Ireland's greatest treasure was unearthed from a bog. You can spend the night in historic ⛼ **Drogheda** ⑧. The following morning, travel north to ⛼ **Dundalk** ⑭, the border town of **Omeath** ⑰, and **Inniskeen** ⑬, home of poet Patrick Kavanagh. After lunch, take the **Cooley Peninsula Drive** ⑮ and visit the medieval fishing town of **Carlingford** ⑯, which should take up most of the afternoon. If possible, spend the night in Drogheda, returning to Dublin the next day via the ancient town of **Louth** ⑫ and the market town of **Ardee** ⑪.

When to Tour the Dublin Environs

The wild mountains of Wicklow and the flat pasturelands of Kildare are at their best in spring and summer. However, the rainfall is often higher in March and April. If you're planning to tour the towns and historic sites, come in winter to avoid the crush. Bring warm clothing and boots, and be prepared for light snow on the hills.

NORTH OF DUBLIN IN THE BOYNE VALLEY

The great prehistoric, pagan, and Celtic monuments of the wide arc of fertile land known as the Boyne Valley invariably evoke a grand sense of wonder. As you'll discover, you don't have to be an archaeologist to be awed by Newgrange, Knowth, and Dowth—all set beside the River Boyne—or the sites of the Hill of Tara, Mellifont Abbey, and the high cross of Monasterboice. You might, as we suggest here, begin at Trim, the locale closest to Dublin, and work your way north. Keep in mind that Omeath and the scenic Cooley Peninsula at the end of this section are on the border of Northern Ireland. (If you make it this far north, consult Chapter 9, particularly our coverage of the Mountains of Mourne, which are just across Carlingford Lough.)

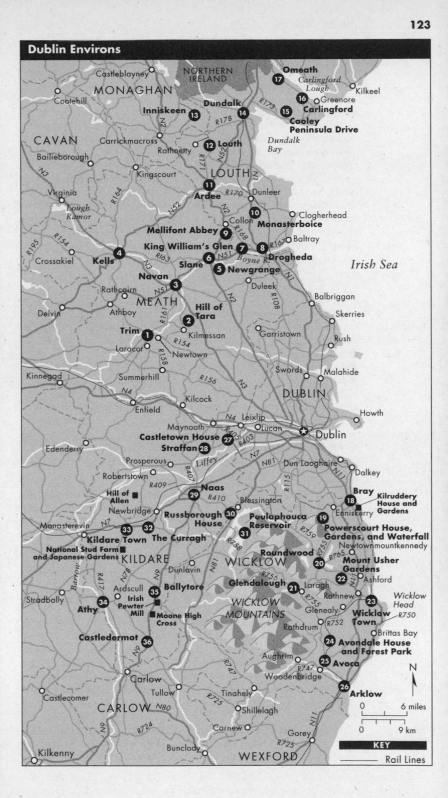

Dublin Environs

Castleblayney

NORTHERN IRELAND

Omeath 17

Carlingford Lough

Greenore • Kilkeel

MONAGHAN

Coatehill

Inniskeen **Dundalk**

13 **Dundalk** 14

R173 16 **Carlingford** 15

Cooley Peninsula Drive

CAVAN

Bailieborough

Carrickmacross

Rathnetty

12 **Louth**

N52

Dundalk Bay

Virginia

Kingscourt

LOUTH

Lough Ramor

R164

11

Ardee

R170 • Dunleer

Crossakiel

Kells 4

N3

10

Collon

Clogherhead

Mellifont Abbey 9

Monasterboice

King William's Glen 7

8 R167 • Baltray

Navan

6 N51 *Boyne R.* **Drogheda**

Slane

5 **Newgrange**

3

Duleek

MEATH

Rathcairn

Hill of Tara

2

Balbriggan

Delvin

Athboy

Kilmessan

Garristown

Skerries

Trim 1

Laracor

R154

Newtown

Swords

Rush

Kinnegad

Summerhill

R156

N3

Malahide

N4

Kilcock

DUBLIN

Enfield

Maynooth

Leixlip

Lucan

Howth

Castletown House 27

Straffan 28

Edenderry

Prosperous

Liffey

N7

Dun Laoghaire

Dalkey

Robertstown

R409

Naas

29 R410

Blessington

Bray 18 **Kilruddery House and Gardens**

Hill of Allen

Newbridge

30 **Russborough House**

Poulaphouca Reservoir

19 Enniskerry

Powerscourt House, Gardens, and Waterfall

Monasterevin

N7

33 32 **The Curragh**

Kildare Town

31

WICKLOW

20 **Roundwood** Newtownmountkennedy

Mount Usher Gardens

National Stud Farm and Japanese Gardens

KILDARE

Dunlavin

Glendalough

22 Ashford

Stradbally

34

35

Ardscull

Ballytore

21 Laragh

Rathnew

23 *Wicklow Head*

Athy

Irish Pewter Mill

WICKLOW MOUNTAINS

Glenealy

Wicklow Town

Moone High Cross

Rathdrum

R752

Brittas Bay

Castledermot 36

24 **Avondale House and Forest Park**

25 **Avoca**

Carlow

Aughrim

Woodenbridge

Castlecomer

Tullow

26 **Arklow**

N

CARLOW N80

Tinahely

Shillelagh

0 6 miles

0 9 km

Kilkenny

Carnew

Bunclody

WEXFORD

Gorey

KEY

— Rail Lines

Irish Sea

Trim

❶ *51 km (32 mi) northwest of Dublin via N3 to R154.*

The heritage town of Trim, on the River Boyne, contains some of the finest medieval ruins in Ireland. In 1359, on the instructions of King Edward III, the town was walled and its fortifications strengthened; in the 15th century several parliaments were held here. Oliver Cromwell massacred most of its inhabitants when he captured the town in 1649. **Trim Castle,** the largest Anglo-Norman fortress in Ireland, dominates present-day Trim from its 2½-acre site, which slopes down to the river's placid waters. Built by Hugh de Lacy in 1173, the castle was soon destroyed and then rebuilt from 1190 to 1220. The ruins include an enormous keep with 70-ft-high turrets flanked by rectangular towers. The outer castle wall is almost 500 yards long, and five D-shape towers survive. The admission price includes a tour. ⊠ *Trim, Co. Meath,* ☎ *041/982–4488,* 🌐 *www.heritageireland.ie.* ⊠ *Keep and grounds €3.10, grounds only €1.20.* ◷ *May–Oct., daily 10–6.*

Facing the river is the **Royal Mint,** a ruin that illustrates Trim's political importance in the Middle Ages.

The **Yellow Steeple** overlooks Trim from a ridge opposite the castle. The structure was built in 1368 and is a remnant of the 13th-century Augustinian abbey of St. Mary's, which itself was the sight of a great medieval pilgrimage to a statue of the Blessed Virgin. Much of the tower was destroyed in 1649 to prevent its falling into Cromwell's hands, and today only the striking, 125-ft-high east wall remains. The Church of Ireland **St. Patrick's Cathedral** (⊠ Loman St.) dates from the early 19th century, but the square tower belongs to an earlier structure built in 1449. The Trim **visitor center's** "The Power and the Glory" audiovisual display tells the story of the arrival of the Normans and of medieval Trim. ⊠ *Mill St. Co. Meath,* ☎ *046/37227,* 🌐 *www.meathtourism.ie.* ⊠ *€3.50.* ◷ *Mon.–Sat. 10–5, Sun. noon–5:30.*

If your ancestors are from County Meath, take advantage of the family-history tracing service at the **Meath Heritage and Genealogy Center.** ⊠ *Castle St., Co. Meath,* ☎ *046/36633.* ⊠ *Free.* ◷ *Mon.–Thurs. 9–1 and 1:30–5, Fri. 9–2.*

You may want to check out several places east and south of Trim as well. At **Newtown,** 1¼ km (¾ mi) east of Trim on the banks of the River Boyne, are the ruins of what was the largest cathedral in Ireland, built beginning in 1210 by Simon de Rochfort, the first Anglo-Norman bishop of Meath. At **Laracor,** 3 km (2 mi) south of Trim on R158, a wall to the left of the rectory is where Jonathan Swift (1667–1745), the satirical writer, poet, and author of *Gulliver's Travels,* was rector from 1699 until 1714, when he was made dean of St. Patrick's Cathedral in Dublin. Nearby are the walls of the cottage where Esther Johnson, the "Stella" who inspired much of Swift's writings, once lived. One of the most pleasant villages of south County Meath, **Summerhill,** 8 km (5 mi) southeast of Laracor along R158, has a large square and a village green with a 15th-century cross. South of Summerhill is **Cnoc an Linsigh,** an attractive area of forest walks with picnic sites, ideal for a half day's meandering. Many of the lanes that crisscross this part of County Meath provide delightful driving between high hedgerows and afford occasional views of the lush, pastoral countryside.

En Route From Trim, follow R154 12 km (7½ mi) northwest. A few miles before Athboy you will enter **Rathcairn,** the only Gaeltacht (Irish-speaking) region in Leinster. Thanks to a 1930s social experiment, a number of Connemara Irish-speaking families were transported to this fertile part of County Meath. They flourished, and Rathcairn is proud to be the only expanding Gaeltacht area. Spend a few hours in the sleepy town and the surrounding land, where, charmingly, everything is conducted in Irish.

Hill of Tara

❷ *14½ km (9 mi) east of Trim, 33 km (21 mi) northwest of Dublin on N3.*

At the meeting point of the five ancient roads of Ireland and known in popular folklore as the seat of the High Kings of Ireland, the Hill of Tara is one of the country's most important historical sites. The 19th-century ballad by Thomas Moore, "The Harp That Once Through Tara's Halls," was a factor in the long over-romanticized view of Tara. Systematic excavation by 20th-century archaeologists has led to the less exciting conclusion that the remains are those of an Iron Age fort that had multiple ring forts, some of which were ruined in the 19th century by religious zealots from England who believed they would find the Ark of the Covenant here. The "Mound of the Hostages," a Neolithic passage grave, most likely gave the place its sacred character. During the hill's reign as a royal seat, which lasted to the 11th century, a great *feis* (national assembly) was held here every three years, when laws were passed and tribal disputes were settled. Tara's decline was predicted one eventful Easter Eve in the 5th century on a night when, according to the Druid religion, no fires could be lit. Suddenly on a hillside some miles away, flames were spotted. "If that fire is not quenched now," said a Druid leader, "it will burn forever and will consume Tara." The fire seen by the court at Tara was lit by St. Patrick at Slane to celebrate the Christian rites of the Paschal. Tara's influence waned with the arrival of Christianity; the last king to live here was Malachy II, who died in 1022.

But like so many of the most prominent sites of the pagan, pre-Christian era, Christianity remade Tara in its own image. Today a modern statue of St. Patrick stands here, as does a pillar stone that may have been the coronation stone (it was reputed to call out in approval when a king was crowned). In the graveyard of the adjacent Anglican church, you'll find a pillar with the worn image of a pagan god and a Bronze Age stone standing on end. However, the main attraction is the Hill of Tara's height: it rises more than 300 ft above sea level, and from its top on a clear day you can see across the flat central plain of Ireland, with the mountains of east Galway rising nearly 160 km (100 mi) away. In the mid-19th century, the nationalist leader Daniel O'Connell staged a mass rally that supposedly drew more than a million people—nearly a third of Ireland's current population. In an old Church of Ireland church on the hillside, the **Interpretative Center** tells the story of Tara and its legends. This can be truly informative, for without expert assistance, it is difficult to identify many of the earthworks at Tara. ⊠ *Hill of Tara, Co. Meath,* ☎ *046/25903.* ☜ *€1.90.* ☉ *May–mid-June and mid-Sept.–Oct., daily 10–5; mid-June–mid-Sept., daily 9:30–6:30.*

Navan

❸ *10 km (6 mi) northwest of the Hill of Tara on N3, 48 km (30 mi) north of Dublin on N3.*

A busy market and mining town with evidence of prehistoric settlements, Navan lies at the crucial juncture of the Rivers Blackwater and Boyne. It took off in the 12th century, when Hugh de Lacy, Lord of Trim, had the place walled and fortified, making it a defensive stronghold of the English Pale in eastern Ireland. It is now the administrative center of Meath. At **St. Mary's Church,** built in 1839, you'll find a late-18th-century wood carving of the Crucifixion, the work of a local artist, Edward Smyth—who at the time was the greatest sculptor Ireland had produced since the Middle Ages. On Friday, the **Fair Green,** beside the church, is the site of a bustling outdoor market. ⊠ *Trimgate St. Co. Meath* ⌷ *Free.* ⊙ *Daily 8–8.*

The best views of town and the surrounding area are from the top of the **Motte of Navan,** a grassy mound said to be the tomb of Odhbha, the deserted wife of a Celtic king who, the story goes, died of a broken heart. D'Angulo, the Norman baron, adapted it into a motte and bailey (a type of medieval Norman castle).

Dining and Lodging

$–$$ ✕⌷ **Mountainstown House.** A real gem at a great price, this restored Queen Anne and Georgian house and courtyard has been in the Pollock family since 1796. Eight hundred acres of parkland surround the grand old manor, with horses, donkeys, poultry, and peacocks all basking in the rolling landscape. The six rooms all face south, and the three with in-suite bathrooms are very large. The splendidly ornamental restaurant serves a wonderful, set-menu meal, which changes every night but always involves local meats and produce. ⊠ *Castletown, Navan, Co. Meath,* ☎ *046/54154,* ⌷AX *046/54154. 6 rooms, 3 with bath. Restaurant, bar. AE, MC, V.*

Kells

④   *16 km (10 mi) northwest of Navan on N3.*

In the 9th century, a group of monks from Iona in Scotland took refuge at Kells (Ceanannus Mór) after being expelled by the Danes. St. Columba had founded a monastery here 300 years earlier, and while some historians think the indigenous monks wrote and illustrated the *Book of Kells*—the Latin version of the four Gospels and one of Ireland's greatest medieval treasures—most scholars now believe that the Scottish monks brought it with them. Reputed to have been fished out of a watery bog at Kells, the legendary manuscript was removed for safekeeping during the Cromwellian wars to Trinity College, Dublin, where it remains. A large exhibit is now devoted to it in the college's Old Library, where a few of the original pages at a time are on view. A copy of the *Book of Kells* is on display in the Church of Ireland **St. Columba's,** in Kells. Four elaborately carved high crosses stand in the church graveyard; you'll find the stump of a fifth in the marketplace—during the 1798 uprising against British rule it was used as a gallows.

St. Colmcille's House, a small, two-story, 7th-century church measuring about 24 ft square and nearly 40 ft high, with a steeply pitched stone roof, is similar in appearance to St. Kevin's Church at Glendalough and Cormac's Chapel at Cashel. Adjacent to St. Colmcille's House, the nearly 100-ft-high **round tower,** which dates prior to 1076, is in almost perfect condition. Its top story has five windows, each facing an ancient entrance to the medieval town.

Lodging

$ ⌷ **Lennoxbrook.** This fine, 200-year-old-plus farmhouse is run by Pauline Mullan, whose children are the fifth generation of the family to occupy the home. A casual, friendly mood prevails throughout the house. Upstairs, the four rooms are decorated with finely patterned wallpaper and period furniture. Lamb and produce are typical dinner entrées (€20 extra). The house, 5 km (3 mi) north of Kells on N3, is convenient to Newgrange. The prehistoric forts, passage graves, and other remains dating from 2000 BC on the Loughcrew Hills are a 15-minute drive away. ✉ *Co. Meath,* ☎ *046/45902. 4 rooms with bath. Dining room. MC, V.*

Newgrange

★ ⑤ *11⅓ km (7 mi) east of Navan on N51, 24 km (15 mi) east of Kells.*

Expect to see no less than one of the most spectacular prehistoric tombs in Europe when you come to Newgrange. Built in the 4th millennium BC—which makes it roughly 1,000 years older than Stonehenge—Newgrange was constructed with some 250,000 tons of stones, much of which is from the Wicklow Mountains south of Dublin. How the people who built this tumulus transported the stones here remains a mystery. The mound above the tomb measures more than 330 ft across and reaches a height of 36 ft at the front. White quartz stones—somehow hauled the 80 km (50 mi) from the mountains of Wicklow to the south—were used for the retaining wall, while egg-shape gray stones were studded at intervals. The passage grave may have been the world's earliest observatory. It was so carefully constructed that, for five days on and around the winter solstice, the rays of the rising sun still hit a roof box above the lintel at the entrance to the grave. The rays then shine for about 20 minutes down the main interior passageway to illuminate the burial chamber. The site was restored in 1962 after years of neglect and quarrying. A visit to the passage grave during the winter solstice is considered to be the most memorable experience of all, in part due to the luck needed to witness the illumination. You'll have to get on the nine-year waiting list to reserve one of the 24 places available on each of the five mornings (December 19–23). And even if you have a place, there's no guarantee that clouds won't be obscuring the sun. But if you visit the interior of this Bronze Age tomb you can see the effect artificially re-created. The geometric designs on some stones at the center of the burial chamber continue to baffle experts.

The prehistoric sites of nearby Dowth and Knowth have been under excavation since 1962, and although Dowth is still closed to the public, the partially excavated site at **Knowth** is open between May 1 and October 31. It is far larger and more diversified than the more famous Newgrange tomb, with a huge central mound and 17 smaller ones. About one-third of the site has been excavated, and you can watch archaeologists at work on the rest of the site. The earliest tombs and carved stones date from the Stone Age (3000 BC), although the site was in use until the early 14th century. In the early Christian era (4th–8th centuries AD) it was the seat of the High Kings of Ireland. Access to Newgrange and Knowth is solely via **Brú na Bóinne** ("palace of the Boyne"), the Boyne Valley visitor center. Arrive early if possible, because Newgrange often sells out. ✉ *Donore, Co. Meath, off N2, signposted from Slane,* ☎ *041/982–4488,* WEB *www.heritageireland.ie.* ✆ *Newgrange and interpretive center €5; Knowth and interpretive center €3.80; Newgrange, Knowth, and interpretive center €8.* ☉ *Newgrange May, daily 9:30–6:30; June–mid-Sept., daily 9:30–7; mid-Sept.–Feb., daily 10–4:30; Mar.–Apr., daily 10–5. Knowth June–mid-Sept., daily 9–7; May and mid-Sept.–end of Sept., daily 9–6:30; Mar., Apr., and Oct., daily 9:30–5:30; Nov.–Feb., daily 9:30–5.*

Slane

⑥ *2½ km (1½ mi) north of Newgrange, 46 km (29 mi) northwest of Dublin on N2.*

Slane Castle is the draw at this small, Georgian village, built in the 18th century around a crossroads on the north side of the River Boyne. The

Conyngham Arms Hotel (☎ 041/988–4444), at the crossroads in Slane, is an agreeable, family-run establishment that serves a buffet from noon to 3 and a bar menu throughout the day. The 16th-century building known as the **Hermitage** was constructed on the site where St. Erc, a local man who was converted to Christianity by St. Patrick, led a hermit's existence. All that remains of his original monastery is the faint trace of the circular ditch that surrounded it. **Slane Castle,** beautifully situated overlooking a natural amphitheater, was badly damaged in a fire and is now closed to the public. Back in 1981, the castle's owner, Anglo-Irish Lord Henry Mountcharles, staged the first of what have been some of Ireland's largest rock concerts; U2, still only one album old, had second billing to Thin Lizzy that year. Most of rock's greatest names have performed here since, including Bob Dylan, Bruce Springsteen, David Bowie, U2, and the Rolling Stones—REM's show holds the record for attendance, with 70,000.

North of Slane town is the 500-ft-high **Slane Hill,** where St. Patrick proclaimed the arrival of Christianity in 433 by lighting the Paschal Fire. From the top, you have sweeping views of the Boyne Valley. On a clear day, the panorama stretches from Trim to Drogheda, a vista extending 40 km (25 mi).

Two mi east of Slane on the N51, farmer Willie Redhouse has opened up the fully functioning arable and livestock **Newgrange Farm** to tourists. The two-hour tour includes feeding the ducks, bottle-feeding the lambs, a tour of the aviaries with their exotic birds, and a donkey ride for the kids. Demonstrations of sheepdog work, threshing, and horseshoeing are given. Every Sunday at 3 PM the weekly "Sheep Derby" takes place, with teddy bears tied to the animals in the place of jockeys. Visiting children are made "owners" of individual sheep for the duration of the race. ⊠ *Slane, Co. Meath,* ☎ *041/982–4119.* ⚹ €5. ◷ *Easter–Aug., daily 10–5.*

King William's Glen

❼ *7½ km (4½ mi) east of Slane on N51.*

On the northern bank of the River Boyne, King William's Glen is where a portion of King William's Protestant army hid before the Battle of the Boyne in 1690. They won by surprising the Catholic troops of James II, who were on the southern side, but many of the Protestant-Catholic conflicts in present-day Northern Ireland can be traced to the immediate aftermath of this battle. The site is marked with an orange and green sign, while part is also incorporated in the nearby, early 19th-century **Townley Hall Estate,** which has forest walks and a nature trail.

Drogheda

❽ *6½ km (4 mi) east of King William's Glen on N51, 45 km (28 mi) north of Dublin on N1.*

One of the most enjoyable and historic towns—a setting for one of the most tragic events in Irish history—on the east coast of Ireland, Drogheda (pronounced draw-*hee*-da) was colonized in 911 by the Danish Vikings. Two centuries later, the town was taken over by Hugh de Lacy, the Anglo-Norman lord of Trim, who was responsible for fortifying the towns along the River Boyne. At first, two separate towns existed on the northern and southern banks of the river. In 1412, already heavily walled and fortified, Drogheda was unified, making it the largest English town in Ireland. Today, large 18th-century warehouses line the northern bank of the Boyne. In the center of the town, around West Street, you'll find the historic heart of Drogheda. Towering over the river is the long **railway viaduct.** Built around 1850 as part of the railway line from Dublin to Belfast, it is still used and is a splendid example of Victorian engineering. Because of its height above the river, the viaduct remains Drogheda's most prominent landmark.

The bank building on the corner of West and Shop streets, called the **Tholsel,** is an 18th-century square granite edifice with a cupola. **St. Laurence's Gate,** one of the two surviving entrances from Drogheda's original 11 gates in its town walls, has two four-story drum towers and is one of the most perfect examples in Ireland of a medieval town gate. **Butler's Gate,** near the Millmount Museum, predates St. Laurence's Gate by 50 years or more.

The Gothic Revival, Roman Catholic **St. Peter's Church** (⊠ West St.) houses the preserved head of St. Oliver Plunkett. Primate of all Ireland, he was martyred in 1681 at Tyburn in London; his head was pulled from the execution flames. A severe, 18th-century church within an enclosed courtyard, the Anglican **St. Peter's** (⊠ Fair St.) is rarely open except for Sunday services. It's worth a peek for its setting and the fine views over the town from the churchyard.

Off the Dublin road (N1) south of Drogheda, the **Millmount Museum and Martello Tower** shares space in a renovated British Army barracks with crafts workshops, including a pottery and picture gallery and studio. Relics of eight centuries of Drogheda's commercial and industrial past are on display, including painted banners of the old trade guilds; a circular willow and leather coracle (the traditional fishing boat on the River Boyne); and many instruments and utensils from domestic and factory use. You can also see mementos of the most infamous episode in Drogheda's history, the 1649 massacre of 3,000 people by Oliver Cromwell. During the attack, Sir Arthur Aston, the town garrison leader and a staunch royalist, was beaten to death with his own wooden leg. In the summer of 2000, a newly restored Martello Tower was opened adjacent to the museum. The exhibit inside focuses on the military history of Drogheda. ⊠ *Millmount, Co. Louth,* ☎ *041/983–3097.* ⊠ *Museum €3, tower €1.20.* ☉ *Mon.–Sat. 10–5:30, Sun. 2:30–5:30.*

Dining and Lodging

$$ ✕ **Buttergate.** Expect traditional Irish dishes both at lunch and dinner; tasty "light bites" are available throughout the day. Pork, beef, and lamb dishes are all cooked to old local recipes, but the specialty is seafood and the stuffed wild salmon is a favorite. ⊠ *Millmount, Co. Louth,* ☎ *041/983–4759. MC, V.*

$-$$ ✕▥ **Boyne Valley Hotel and Country Club.** Once owned by a Drogheda brewing family, this 19th-century mansion sits on 16 acres and is approached via a 1-km (½-mi) drive. The newer wing of the hotel has double rooms, all with contemporary furnishings. A large conservatory houses a bar and overlooks the grounds, while a large hall is decorated with antiques and comfy chairs. The Cellar Restaurant specializes in fresh fish. ⊠ *Dublin Rd., Co. Louth,* ☎ *041/983–7737,* ℻ *041/983–9188,* WEB *www.boyne-valley-hotel.ie/. 37 rooms with bath. Restaurant, 18-hole golf course, 2 tennis courts, indoor pool, health club, bar. AE, DC, MC, V.*

En Route From Drogheda's center, follow R167 north along the northern bank of the River Boyne for 11 km (7 mi) to **Baltray,** a fishing village that still looks much like it did in the 18th century. From here, continue north another 8 km (5 mi) to the fishing village of **Clogherhead.** Take a walk above the local harbor to the heights of Clogher Head for outstanding views north to the Mountains of Mourne and south to Skerries.

Mellifont Abbey

❾ *11 km (7 mi) north of Newgrange on N2, 8 km (5 mi) west of Drogheda on R168.*

On the eastern bank of the River Mattock, which creates a natural border between Counties Meath and Louth here, lie the remains of Mellifont Abbey, the first Cistercian monastery in Ireland. Founded in 1142 by St. Malachy, Archbishop of Armagh, it was inspired by the formal structure around a central courtyard of St. Bernard of Clairvaux's monastery, which St. Malachy had visited. Among the substantial ruins are the two-story chapter house, built in 12th-century English-Norman style and once a daily meeting place for the monks; it now houses a collection of medieval glazed tiles. Four walls of the 13th-century octagonal lavabo, or washing place, still stand, as do some arches from the Romanesque cloister. At its peak Mellifont presided over almost 40 other Cistercian monasteries throughout Ireland, but all were suppressed by Henry VIII in 1539 after his break with the Catholic Church. Adjacent to the car park is a small **architectural museum** depicting the history of the abbey and the craftsmanship that went into its construction. ⊠ *Near Collon, Co. Louth,* ☎ *041/982–6459.* ⊠ *€1.90.* ⊘ *May–mid-June and mid-Sept.–Oct., daily 10–5; mid-June–mid-Sept., daily 9:30–6:30.*

Dining

$$–$$$ ✕ **Forge Gallery Restaurant.** In a converted forge in Collon, north of Slane on N2, this well-established restaurant is decorated in warm rose and plum tones and antique furnishings, and an old fireplace creates a comforting warmth and light. The cuisine mixes French Provençale with a strong hint of traditional Irish cooking. Try two popular specialties: salmon and crab in phyllo pastry, and prawns and scallops in a cream and garlic sauce. Make sure you try one of the seasonal homemade soups. Paintings in the reception area, by local artists, are for sale. Reservations are essential on weekends. ⊠ *Collon, Co. Louth,* ☎ *041/982–6272. AE, DC, MC, V. Closed Sun.–Mon. and second wk in Jan.*

Monasterboice

❿ *8 km (5 mi) northeast of Mellifont Abbey on N1, 17 km (11 mi) northeast of Slane.*

Ireland has more carved-stone high crosses than any other European country, and an outstanding collection is in the small, secluded village of Monasterboice. Dating back to AD 923, the **Muireadach Cross** stands nearly 20 ft high and is considered to be the best-preserved example of a high cross anywhere in Ireland. Its elaborate panels depict biblical scenes, including Cain slaying Abel, David and Goliath, and a centerpiece of the Last Judgment. (Figurative scenes are not a characteristic of earlier high crosses, such as those found in Ahenny, County Clare, which are elaborately ornamented but without figures.) From the adjacent, 110-ft-high **round tower,** the extent of the former monastic settlement at Monasterboice is apparent. The key to the tower door is held at the nearby gate lodge.

Ardee

⓫ *14½ km (9 mi) north of Monasterboice on N2.*

In this market town, formerly at the northern edge of the Pale, you'll find two 13th-century castles: Ardee Castle and Hatch's Castle. The town of Ardee (Baile Átha Fhirdia or Ferdia's Ford), interestingly, was named after the ford where the mythical folk hero Cuchulainn fought his foster brother Ferdia. There's a statue depicting this battle at the start of the riverside walk. **Ardee Castle** (the one with square corners) was converted into a courthouse in the 19th century. The castle faces north—built to protect the Anglo-Irish Pale from the Celtic Tribes beyond. **Hatch's Castle** (with rounded corners) is a private residence and not open to the public. **St. Mary's Church of Ireland** on Main Street incorporates part of a 13th-century Carmelite church burned by Edward Bruce in early 1316.

Dining

$$ ✕ **Gables House and Restaurant.** At this family-run spot off N2, not far from the Dundalk junction, expect generous portions, a French-influenced cooking style, and a fine catch of the day—often monkfish, halibut, or sole. The restaurant has lush, traditional-style furnishings: antique mahogany furniture, deep-burgundy velvet curtains, and oil paintings by local artists. Polished tables, silver cutlery, linen napkins, lace coasters, and gleaming leaded-crystal glasses add an elegant touch. For dessert, satisfy your sugar craving with the Gables Medley: cheesecake, profiteroles, and homemade ice cream. ⊠ *Dundalk Rd., Co. Louth,* ☎ *041/985–3789. MC, V.*

Louth

⑫ *11½ km (7 mi) north of Ardee on R171.*

Louth warrants a visit, if only for the splendidly preserved oratory here. St. Patrick, Ireland's patron saint, was reputed to have built his first church (which is no longer there) in this hilltop village in the 5th century. He also made St. Mochta (d. 534) the first bishop of Louth. Standing at the center of the village is the excellently preserved **St. Mochta's House,** an oratory dating from the 11th century, which has a steeply pitched stone roof that can be reached by a stairway. The house is freely accessible—but watch out for cattle in the surrounding field.

Inniskeen

⑬ *6½ km (4 mi) north of Louth.*

On the road to Dundalk and just over the Louth county boundary in Monaghan, you'll find Inniskeen, a small farming town that doubles as a social hearth for the area's far-flung community. Patrick Kavanagh (1906–69), the area's most famous poet, is commemorated at the **Inniskeen Folk Museum,** housed in a converted church next to a round tower. Born and raised here, Kavanagh immortalized the town in his early poem "Inniskeen Road"—where as a child he spied on young lovers and their "wink and elbow language of delight"—before becoming one of Ireland's leading poets. He was brought back to the village for burial. ☎ *042/937–8109. ⊡ Donations accepted. ⊘ May–Sept., Sun. 3–6, or by appointment.*

Dundalk

⑭ *14½ km (9 mi) east of Inniskeen, 80 km (50 mi) north of Dublin on N1.*

Dundalk is a thriving, if uninspiring, frontier town—only 9½ km (6 mi) from the Northern Ireland border—with some fine historic buildings. It's the main town of County Louth (Ireland's smallest county), and it dates from the early Christian period, around the 7th century. The area near the town is closely connected with Cuchulainn (pronounced **coo**-lain)—"a greater hero than Hercules or Achilles," as

Frank McCourt, in *Angela's Ashes*, recalls his father claiming. Cuchulainn, the warrior-hero of the old Irish epic *Táin Bó Cuailnge* (Cattle Raid of Cooley), was the hero of ancient Ulster—which then included the Dundalk area—and defended her borders and interests against newcomers. On Mill Street, the **bell tower** of a Franciscan monastery with Gothic windows dates from the 13th century. The Market House, the Town Hall, and the **Courthouse** are examples of the town's 19th-century heritage; the Courthouse is the most impressive of the three, built in the 1820s in a severe Greek Revival style, with Doric columns supporting the portico. It stands north of St. Patrick's Cathedral.

The Catholic **St. Patrick's Cathedral** was built between 1835 and 1847, when the Gothic Revival was at its height. It is modeled on the 15th-century King's College Chapel (at Cambridge, England), with its buttresses and mosaics lining the chancel and the side chapel walls. The fine exterior was built in Newry granite, and the high altar and pulpit are of carved Caen stone. ⊠ *Town center.* ☼ *Daily 8–6.*

The **Dundalk County Museum** is dedicated to preserving the history of the dying local industries, such as beer brewing, cigarette manufacturing, shoe and boot making, and railway engineering. Other exhibits deal with the history of Louth from 7500 BC to the present. ⊠ *Joycelyn St., Co. Louth,* ☎ *042/932–7056,* WEB *www.louthcoco.ie.* ⊡ *€3.80.* ☼ *May–Sept., Mon.–Sat. 10:30–5:30, Sun. 2–6; Oct.–Apr., Tues.–Sat. 10:30–5:30, Sun. 2–6.*

OFF THE BEATEN PATH
ARDGILLAN DEMESNE – Across the Louth border in County Dublin, 18 km (13 mi) south of Dundalk, you'll find Ardgillan Demesne, one of the prettiest parks along the coast. Its 194 acres consist of rolling pastures, mixed woodland, and gardens overlooking the Bay of Drogheda, with splendid views of the coastline. The **castle,** built in 1738 for a landowning family, rises two stories; ground-floor rooms are decorated in Georgian and Victorian styles; first-floor rooms house a permanent display of 17th-century maps, and host an annual program of exhibitions. ⊠ *Balbriggan, Co. Dublin,* ☎ *01/849–2212,* WEB *www.fingalcountycouncil. ie.* ⊡ *€3.80.* ☼ *Apr.–June and Sept., Tues.–Sun. 11–6; Oct.–Mar., Tues.–Sun. 11–4:30.*

Dining and Lodging

$$–$$$ ✕⌂ **Ballymascanlon House Hotel.** On 130 acres on the scenic Cooley Peninsula just north of Dundalk, you'll find this converted Victorian mansion with a reputation for comfort and good cuisine. Rooms are large, and furnished with reproduction period pieces. The restaurant serves a set menu of Irish and French cuisine; it specializes in fresh seafood, such as lobster in season. Vegetarian plates are also available. ⊠ *Dundalk, Co. Louth,* ☎ *042/937–1124,* FAX *042/937–1598,* WEB *www. globalgolf.com. 74 rooms with bath. Restaurant, 18-hole golf course, 2 tennis courts, indoor pool, health club, 2 bars. AE, DC, MC, V.*

Cooley Peninsula Drive

⑮ *Beginning in Dundalk, 80 km (50 mi) north of Dublin, 35 km (22 mi) north of Drogheda.*

If you have a car and three or four free hours, go for a scenic drive around the Cooley Peninsula and indulge some of the finest views of the east coast of Ireland. This is a 64-km (40-mi) round-trip beginning and ending in Dundalk. Beyond the Carlingford Lough on the north side of the peninsula, the Mountains of Mourne rise in the distance. From **Gyles Quay,** a small coastal village with a clean, safe beach, you'll get excellent views southward along the County Louth coast to Clogher

Head. A road winds east around the Cooley Peninsula to **Greenore,** a town built in Victorian times as a ferryboat terminal. Today it's a port for container traffic.

Carlingford

⑯ *6½ km (4 mi) south of Omeath on R173, 21 km (13 mi) from Dundalk.*

The small, medieval fishing town of Carlingford appeals for its natural setting, as well as its striking whitewashed, thatched cottages. The mountains of the Cooley Peninsula back right up to the town, the Carlingford Lough lies at its feet, and the Mountains of Mourne rise only 5 km (3 mi) away across the lough.

Some remnants from the area's medieval days include a tower from the town wall and one of its gates, which later became the town hall; the 15th-century **Mint Tower House,** with mullioned windows; and Taaffe's Castle, a 16th-century fortified town house. A massive, 13th-century fortress that rises up over the entrance to Carlingford Lough, **King John's Castle** has an unusual feature: its west gateway is only wide enough to admit one horseman.

The **Holy Trinity Heritage Centre** is in a former church. The highlight is a mural depicting the village at the height of the Middle Ages. An audiovisual display focuses on village history and the efforts to preserve Carlingford's medieval heritage. ✉ *Churchyard Rd., Carlingford, Co. Louth,* ☎ *042/937-3888.* 🎟 *€2.* ⊙ *May–Sept., daily 9:30–4:30; Oct.–Apr., weekdays 9:30–4:30.*

Omeath

⑰ *6½ km (4 mi) northwest of Carlingford on R173.*

This northernmost town on Cooley Peninsula is blessed not only with a stunning landscape, but also with the distinction of having unusual pictures—stations of the cross—that Catholics pray before in a solemn procession every Good Friday. Omeath was the last main Gaeltacht (Irish-speaking) village in this part of Ireland (most extant Gaeltacht villages are in the Southwest and the West). There's a narrow road that climbs the mountains behind Omeath. As you ascend, the views become ever more spectacular, stretching over the Mountains of Mourne in the north and as far south as Skerries, 32 km (20 mi) north of Dublin. This narrow road leads back to Dundalk. On the eastern side of the Omeath, on the outside of a shrine, you'll find open-air **stations of the cross**—the 14 pictures of the key moments during Christ's last days—at the monastery of the Rosminian Fathers. Jaunting cars (traps pulled by ponies) take visitors to the site from the quayside—at which, daily from June to September—you'll see stalls selling all kinds of shellfish, including oysters and mussels, from the nearby lough. A ferry service runs daily until 6 PM in July and August; the journey from the quay to Warrenpoint, across the lough in Northern Ireland, takes five minutes.

COUNTY WICKLOW'S COAST AND MOUNTAINS

Make your way to the fourth or fifth story of almost any building in Dublin that faces south and you'll see off in the distance—amazingly, though, not *that* far off in the distance—the green, smooth hills of the Dublin and Wicklow mountains. On a clear day the mountains are even visible from some streets in and around the city center. If your idea of solace is green hills, and your visit to Ireland is otherwise limited to Dublin, County Wicklow—or Cill Mhantain (pronounced kill **wan**-tan), as it is known in Irish—should be on your itinerary.

Not that the secret isn't out: rugged and mountainous with dark, wooded forests, central Wicklow, known as the "garden of Ireland," is a popular picnic area among Dubliners. It has some of Ireland's grandest 18th-century mansions, and cradles one of the country's earliest Christian retreats: Glendalough. Nestled in a valley of dense woods and placid lakes, Glendalough and environs can seem (at least during the off-season) practically untouched since their heyday 1,000 years ago. The same granite mountains that have protected Glendalough all these years run into the sea along the east coast, which is home to several popular sandy beaches. Journey from Dublin down to Arklow, sticking to the east side of the Wicklow Mountains. A quick note about getting here: it takes stamina to extract yourself from the unmarked maze of the Dublin exurbs (your best bet is to take N11, which becomes M11, and then again N11), but once you've accomplished that feat, this gorgeous, mysterious terrain awaits.

Bray

🔞 *22 km (14 mi) south of Dublin on N11, 8 km (5 mi) east of Enniskerry on R755.*

One of Ireland's oldest seaside resorts, Bray is a trim village known for its dilapidated summer cottages and sand-and-shingle beach, which stretches 2 km (1 mi). When the trains first arrived from Dublin in 1854, Bray became the number one spot for urban vacationers and subsequently took on the appearance of an English oceanfront town. Some Dubliners still flock to the faded glory of Bray's boardwalk to push baby carriages and soak up the sun. It's the terminus of the DART train from Dublin, so it's easy to get here without a car. Opposite the Royal Hotel, in the old courthouse, is the **heritage center.** Downstairs you'll find a re-created castle dungeon with a 1,000-years-of-Bray exhibition. Upstairs is a huge model railway and a display about modern Bray. ⊠ *Lower Main St., Co. Wicklow,* ☎ *01/286–6796,* WEB *www.bray.ie.* 🎫 *€3.80.* ⊙ *May–Sept., weekdays 9–5, Sat. 10–3, Sun. noon–5; Oct.–Apr., weekdays 9:30–4:30, Sat. 10–4:30.*

One Martello Terrace (☎ 01/286–8407), at the harbor, is Bray's most famous address. James Joyce (1882–1941) lived here between 1887 and 1891 and used the house as the setting for the Christmas dinner in *A Portrait of the Artist as a Young Man.* Today the house is privately owned by an Irish Teachta Dála (member of Parliament, informally known as a "TD"). The phone number listed above rings at her constituency office; someone there should be able to help scholars and devotees arrange a visit. Call on a Thursday 10 AM–1 PM. Although the residence has been renovated, the dining room portrayed in Joyce's novel still maintains the spirit of his time.

☾ **National Sealife** is an aquarium and museum dedicated to the creatures of the sea, with an emphasis on those that occupy the waters around Ireland. Besides massive sea tanks that contain all manner of swimming things, there's a major conservation project with captive breeding of sea horses. FinZone is an undersea adventure trail perfect for kids, with puzzles to solve. Touch-screen computers and video games give the whole thing a high-tech feel. In winter, check opening times before visiting. ⊠ *Strand Rd., Co. Wicklow,* ☎ *01/286–6939,* WEB *www.sealife.ie.* 🎫 *€7.50.* ⊙ *Apr.–Oct., daily 10–6; Nov.–Mar., weekends 10–5.*

At **Killruddery House** you'll find 17th-century formal gardens, precisely arranged, with fine beech hedges, Victorian statuary, and a parterre of lavender and roses. The Brabazon family, the Earls of Meath, have lived here continuously since 1618. In 1820 they hired William Morris to remodel the house as a revival Elizabethan mansion. The estate also has a Crystal Palace conservatory modelled on those at the botanic gardens in Dublin. ⊠ *Killruddery, Co. Wicklow, off the Bray–Greystones Rd., 3 km (2 mi) south of Bray,* ☎ *01/286–2777.* ⊞ *House and gardens €5.70, gardens only €3.80.* ☉ *Gardens Apr.–Sept., daily 1–5; house May–June and Sept., daily 1–5; by appointment at other times.*

Dining

$$–$$$ ✕ **Tree of Idleness.** This Greek-Cypriot restaurant, a 10-minute walk
★ from Bray's DART train station, is a pleasant dining spot on the ground floor of a Victorian house along the seafront. It specializes in classic dishes, such as moussaka (eggplant and meat) and *keftedes* (meatballs). Expect tasty, hearty portions, and get the excellent roast suckling pig with caramelized apples. The extensive wine list includes Greek and Cypriot house wines, as well as plenty of French, Italian, and New World wines. ⊠ *Seafront, Co. Wicklow,* ☎ *01/286–3498. AE, MC, V. Closed Mon., last wk in Aug., and 1st wk in Sept. No lunch.*

$ ✕ **Poppies Country Cooking.** Following the success of their remark-
★ able restaurant in Enniskerry, the owners of Poppies decided to open a second restaurant with the same name in Greystones, an old-fashioned seaside resort only a couple of miles south of Bray along the coast. The ceilings are high, the space is airy and bright, and the food tastes absolutely delicious. If you can, dine here in summer, when you can avail yourself of the sun-drenched garden terrace. ⊠ *1 Trafalgar Sq., Greystones, Co. Wicklow,* ☎ *01/287–4228. No credit cards.*

Outdoor Activities and Sports

Uncrowded hiking and mountain-bike trails criss-cross the mountains bordering Bray to the south. One of the best is a well-marked path leading from the beach to the 10-ft-tall cross that crowns the spiny peak of Bray Head, a rocky outcrop that rises 791 ft from the sea. The semi-difficult, one-hour climb affords stunning views of Wicklow Town and Dublin Bay.

Powerscourt House, Gardens, and Waterfall

★ ♨ ⑲ *25 km (16 mi) south of Dublin on R117, 22 km (14 mi) north of Glendalough on R755.*

Within the shadow of the famous Sugar Loaf mountain and one of the prettiest villages in Ireland, **Enniskerry** is built around a sloping central triangular square and surrounded by the wooded Wicklow Mountains. The main reason to visit the area around Enniskerry is the **Powerscourt Estate.** The grounds were originally granted to Sir Richard Wingfield, the first viscount of Powerscourt, by King James I of England in 1609. Richard Castle, the architect of Russborough House, designed Powerscourt House in a grand Palladian style, and it was constructed between 1731 and 1743. The original ballroom on the first floor—once "the grandest room in any Irish house," according to historian Desmond Guinness—still gives a sense of the house's former life.

Powerscourt Gardens, considered among the finest in Europe, were first laid out from 1745 to 1767 following the completion of the house—and then were radically redesigned in the Victorian style, from 1843 to 1875. The redesign was the work of the eccentric, boozy Daniel Robertson, who liked to be tootled around the gardens-in-progress in a wheelbarrow while nipping at his bottle of sherry. The Villa Butera in Sicily inspired him—which is why you'll find, in the gardens, sweeping terraces, antique sculptures, and a circular pond and fountain flanked by winged horses. There's a celebrated view of the Italianate patterned ramps, lawns, and pond across the beautiful, heavily wooded Dargle Valley, which stair-steps to the horizon and the noble profile of Sugar Loaf mountain. The grounds include many specimen trees (plants grown for exhibition), an avenue of monkey puzzles, a parterre of brightly colored summer flowers, and a Japanese garden. The kitchen gardens, with their modest rows of flowers, are a striking antidote to the classical formality of the main sections. A self-serve restaurant, crafts center, garden center, and a children's play area are also on the grounds. (From Dublin you can get to Enniskerry directly, by taking the No. 44 bus from the Dublin quays area.) ⊠ *Enniskerry, Co. Wicklow,* ☎ *01/ 204–6000,* WEB *www.powerscourt.ie.* ⌂ *House €2.50, gardens €6.* ☉ *Mar.–Oct., daily 9:30–5:30; Nov.–Feb., daily 9:30–dusk.*

One of the most inspiring sights to the writers and artists of the Romantic generation, the 400-ft **Powerscourt Waterfall,** 5 km (3 mi) south of the gardens, is the highest in the British Isles. ⊠ *Enniskerry, Co. Wicklow.* ⌂ *€3.50.* ☉ *Mar.–Oct., daily 9:30–7; Nov.–Feb., daily 10:30–dusk. Closed 2 wks before Christmas.*

Dining

$ ✕ **Poppies Country Cooking.** It's so charming it seems a bit like some-
★ thing out of a fairy tale. Cozy Poppies is a great café for breakfast, lunch, or late-afternoon tea. It has a low, pine-paneled ceiling, floral wallpaper and matching cloth lamp shades, and pine farmhouse furniture. Expect potato cakes, shepherd's pie, lasagna, vegetarian quiche, house salads, and soup. Terrific homemade desserts include caramel squares, lemon meringue pie, and Pavlova. You'll be tempted to sit here for hours writing postcards and daydreaming. ⊠ *The Square, Enniskerry, Co. Wicklow,* ☎ *01/282–8869. No dinner. No credit cards.*

Roundwood

⑳ *18 km (13 mi) south of Enniskerry on R755.*

At 800 ft above sea level, Roundwood is the highest village in Ireland. It's also surrounded by some pretty spectacular scenery. The Sunday-afternoon market in the village hall, where cakes, jams, and other homemade goods are sold, livens up what is otherwise a sleepy place. From the broad main street, by the Roundwood Inn, a minor road leads west for 8 km (5 mi) to two lakes, **Lough Dan** and **Lough Tay,** lying deep between forested mountains like Norwegian fjords.

Dining

$$–$$$ ✕ **Roundwood Inn.** Definitely check out this 17th-century inn, furnished
★ in a traditional style, with wooden floors, dark furniture, and diamond-shape windows. It's best known for its good, reasonably priced bar food—eaten at sturdy tables beside an open fire. The restaurant offers a combination of Continental and Irish cuisines, reflecting the traditions of the German proprietor, Jurgen Schwalm, and his Irish wife, Aine. The separate bar and lounge also serve an excellent menu that includes a succulent seafood platter of salmon, oysters, lobster, and shrimp. ⊠ *Main St., Roundwood village center, Co. Wicklow,* ☎ *01/ 281–8107. Reservations essential. AE, MC, V. Restaurant closed Sun. dinner and Mon. and Tues.*

Glendalough

★ ㉑ *54 km (34 mi) south of Dublin on R117 and R755, 9½ km (6 mi) south-west of Roundwood.*

Nestled in a lush, quiet valley deep in the rugged Wicklow Mountains, among two lakes, evergreen and deciduous trees, and acres of windswept heather, Glendalough is one of Ireland's premier monastic sites. It flourished as a monastic center from the 6th century until 1398, when English soldiers plundered the site, leaving the ruins that you see today. (The monastery survived earlier 9th- and 10th-century Viking attacks.) St. Kevin (Coemghein, or "fair begotten" in Irish), a descendant of the royal house of Leinster, founded Glendalough; St. Kevin renounced the world and came here to live as a hermit before opening the monastery in 550. Note that in high season, hordes of visitors to Glendalough make it difficult to appreciate the quiet solitude that brought Kevin to this valley. The visitor center is a good place to orient yourself and pick up a useful pamphlet. Many of the ruins are clumped together beyond the visitor center, but some of the oldest surround the Upper Lake, where signed paths direct you through spectacular scenery absent of crowds. Most ruins are open all day and are freely accessible.

Probably the oldest building on the site, presumed to date from St. Kevin's time, is the Teampaill na Skellig (Church of the Oratory), on the south shore of the Upper Lake. A little to the east is St. Kevin's Bed, a tiny cave in the rock face, about 30 ft above the level of the lake, where St. Kevin lived his hermit's existence. It is not easily accessible; you approach the cave by boat, but climbing the cliff to the cave can be dangerous so it isn't a great idea. At the southeast corner of the Upper Lake is Reefert Church, also dating from the 11th century, with the ruins of a nave and a chancel. The saint also lived in the adjoining, ruined beehive hut with five crosses, which marked the original boundary of the monastery. You get a superb view of the valley from here.

The ruins by the edge of the Lower Lake are the most important of those at Glendalough. The gateway, beside the Glendalough Hotel, is the only surviving entrance to an ancient monastic site anywhere in Ireland. An extensive graveyard lies within, with hundreds of elaborately decorated crosses, as well as a perfectly preserved six-story round tower. Built in the 11th or 12th century, it stands 100 ft high, with an entrance 25 ft above ground level.

The largest building at Glendalough is the substantially intact 7th- to 9th-century cathedral, where you'll find the nave (small for a large church, only 30 ft wide by 50 ft long), chancel, and ornamental oolite limestone window, which may have been imported from England. South of the cathedral is the 11-ft-high Celtic St. Kevin's Cross. Made of granite, it is the best-preserved such cross on the site. St. Kevin's Church is an early barrel-vaulted oratory with a high-pitched stone roof.

A note about getting here directly from Dublin: you can take the St. Kevin's bus service. If you're driving from Dublin, consider taking the scenic route along R155, which includes awesome, austere mountaintop passes. Don't drive this route if you're in a hurry, and don't look for a lot of signage—just concentrate on the glorious views. ☎ 0404/45325, WEB *www.heritageireland.ie.* ☞ €2.50. ☉ *Mid-Mar.–mid-Oct., daily 9:30–6; mid-Oct.–mid-Mar., daily 9:30–5; last admission 45 mins before closing.*

Dining and Lodging

$$ ✕☷ **Glendalough Hotel.** Purists object to how close this old-fashioned, early 19th-century hotel is to the ruins at Glendalough, but to others it's a convenience. Some of the bedrooms, decorated in pastel colors, overlook the monastery and the wooded mountain scenery; others face the grounds. The burble of running water from the Glendassan River audibly enhances the experience. The restaurant also has views

of the lawn. The menu is simple but portions are hearty, and the pub
is the only one for miles around. ☒ *Co. Wicklow,* ☎ *0404/45135,* FAX
*0404/45142. 40 rooms with bath. Restaurant, fishing, bar. AE, DC,
MC, V. Closed Dec. and Jan.*

Mount Usher Gardens

㉒ *14½ km (9 mi) southeast of Roundwood on R764, 13 km (8 mi) east
of Glendalough.*

Settled into more than 20 acres on the banks of the River Vartry,
Mount Usher Gardens were first laid out in 1868 by textile magnate
Edward Walpole. Succeeding generations of the Walpole family further planted and maintained the grounds, which today have more
than 5,000 species. The gardener has made the most of the riverside
locale by planting eucalypti, azaleas, camellias, and rhododendrons.
The river is visible from nearly every place in the gardens; miniature
suspension bridges bounce and sway underfoot as you cross the river.
You'll find a cluster of crafts shops, including a pottery workshop, as
well as a bookstore and self-service restaurant, at the entrance. The
twin villages of Ashford and Rathnew are to the south and east, and
Newtownmountkennedy is to the north.☒ *Ashford, Co. Wicklow,* ☎
0404/40205, WEB *www.mount-usher-gardens.com.* ☒ €5.50. ☉ *Mid-
Mar.–Oct., daily 10:30–6.*

Dining and Lodging

$$$–$$$$ ✕▥ **Tinakilly House.** William and Bee Power have beautifully restored
this Victorian-Italianate mansion, built in the 1870s by Captain Robert
Halpin (1836–94). The lobby has mementos of Captain Halpin and
his nautical exploits, including paintings and ship models; Victorian
antiques fill the house. Some bedrooms have four-poster beds, sitting
areas, and views of the Wicklow landscape, the Irish Sea, or the lovely
gardens on the 7-acre grounds. In the dining room, expect to be served
French-influenced Irish cuisine, with fresh vegetables from the garden.
Brown and fruit breads are baked daily. ☒ *Rathnew, Co. Wicklow,* ☎
0404/69274, FAX *0404/67806,* WEB *www.tinakilly.ie. 45 rooms with
bath, 6 suites. Restaurant, some hot tubs, tennis court, bar. AE, DC,
MC, V.*

$$$ ✕▥ **Hunter's Hotel.** You'll find one of Ireland's oldest coaching inns—
first opened in the early 1700s—in a lovely rural setting on the banks
of the River Vartry, only 1 km (½ mi) east of Rathnew Village. Locals
and guests both tend to love the old-world surroundings: period prints,
beams, and antiques. All bedrooms have delicate flower-print wallpaper and are beautifully furnished with Victorian-style pieces. The fine
restaurant serves a set five-course menu; in the summer, afternoon tea,
with homemade scones and jams, is served in the magnificent garden
that stretches down to the river. ☒ *Rathnew, Co. Wicklow,* ☎ *0404/
40106,* FAX *0404/40338,* WEB *indigo.ie/~hunters. 16 rooms with bath.
Restaurant, bar. AE, DC, MC, V.*

Wicklow Town

㉓ *26 km (16 mi) east of Glendalough on R763, 51 km (32 mi) south of
Dublin on N11.*

At the entrance to the attractive, tree-lined Main Street of Wicklow
Town—its name, from the Danish *wyking alo,* means "Viking
meadow"—sprawl the extensive ruins of a 13th-century Franciscan friary. The **friary** was closed down during the 16th-century dissolution
of the monasteries in the area, but its ruins are a reminder of Wicklow's stormy past, which began with the unwelcome reception given

to St. Patrick on his arrival in AD 432. Inquire at the nearby priest's house (⊠ Main St., ☎ 0404/67196) to see the ruins.

The old town jail, just above Market Square, has been converted into a museum and **heritage center,** where visitors can trace their genealogical roots in the area. Using computer displays and life-size models, the gruesome history of the jail is told, from the local rebellion in 1798 right up to the late 19th century. ⊠ *Market Sq., Co. Wicklow,* ☎ *0404/61599,* WEB *www.wicklow.ie.* ⊡ *€5.50.* ◷ *Mar. 17–Dec., daily 10–5.*

The **harbor** is Wicklow Town's most appealing area. Take Harbour Road down to the pier; a bridge across the River Vartry leads to a second, smaller pier, at the northern end of the harbor. From this end, follow the shingle beach, which stretches for 5 km (3 mi); behind the beach is the broad lough, a lagoon noted for its wildfowl. Immediately south of the harbor, perched on a promontory that has good views of the Wicklow coastline, you'll find the ruin of the **Black Castle.** This structure was built in 1169 by Maurice Fitzgerald, an Anglo-Norman lord who arrived with the English invasion of Ireland. The ruins (freely accessible) extend over a large area; with some difficulty, you can climb down to the water's edge.

Between one bank of the River Vartry and the road to Dublin stands the Protestant **St. Lavinius Church,** which incorporates a variety of unusual details: a Romanesque door, 12th-century stonework, fine pews, and an atmospheric graveyard. The church is topped off by a copper, onion-shape cupola, added as an afterthought in 1771. ⊡ *Free.* ◷ *Daily 10–6.*

Dining and Lodging

$ ✕ **Pizza del Forno.** Take advantage of this great vantage point for people-watching on Main Street. The place has red-and-white-check tablecloths, low lighting, and a pizza oven blazing away. The inexpensive pizzas, pasta, steaks, and vegetarian dishes appeal to a wide array of appetites. ⊠ *Main St., Co. Wicklow,* ☎ *0404/67075. AE, MC, V. Closed Christmas–mid-Feb.*

$$ ⌂ **Wicklow Head Lighthouse.** Just south of town on Wicklow Head you'll see the old lighthouse, right next to the new, automated one. The 95-ft-high stone tower—first established in 1781—once supported an eight-sided lantern, and has been renovated by the Irish Landmark Trust. It sleeps four to six people in two delightfully quirky octagonal bedrooms and one double sofa bed in the sitting room. The kitchen-dining room at the top has stunning views out over the coast. Don't forget anything in the car; it's a long way down. You must book for at least two nights. ⊠ *Wicklow Head, Co. Wicklow,* ☎ *01/670–4733,* FAX *01/670–4887. Sleeps 4–6, 2 baths. MC, V.*

$ ⌂ **Old Rectory Country House.** Once a 19th-century rectory, this charming Greek Revival country house—only open in the summer—is perched on a hillside just off the main road from Dublin on the approach to Wicklow Town. Black-and-white marble fireplaces, bright colors, original oil paintings, and antique and contemporary furniture decorate the house; the light, spacious guest rooms are decorated in white and pastel shades, and have antique Victorian and country-house furniture. ⊠ *Wicklow Town, Co. Wicklow,* ☎ *0404/67048,* FAX *0404/69181. 8 rooms with bath. AE, MC, V. Closed Sept.–May.*

Avondale House and Forest Park

㉔ *17 km (11 mi) southwest of Wicklow Town on R752.*

Outside the quaint village of Rathdrum, on the west bank of the Avondale River, you'll find the 523-acre **Avondale Forest Park.** It was, in

1904, the first forest in Ireland to be taken over by the state, and part of a then-burgeoning movement to preserve and expand the Irish forests. There's a fine 5½-km (3½-mi) walk along the river, as well as pine and exotic-tree trails. **Avondale House,** on the grounds of the park, resonates with Irish history. The house was the birthplace and lifelong home of Charles Stewart Parnell (1846–91), "The Uncrowned King of Ireland," the country's leading politician of the 19th century and a wildly popular campaigner for democracy and land reform. His career came to a halt after he fell in love with a married woman, Kitty O'Shea—her husband started divorce proceedings and news of the affair ruined Parnell's political career. He died a year later. (Joyce dramatized the controversy, in *A Portrait of the Artist as a Young Man,* as a keenly contested argument during the Daedalus family dinner.) Parnell's house, built in 1779, has been flawlessly restored—except for the reception and dining rooms on the ground floor, which are filled with Parnell memorabilia, including some of his love letters to Kitty O'Shea and political cartoons portraying Parnell's efforts to secure home rule for Ireland. ☎ 0404/46111, WEB *www.coillte.ie.* ✆ €4.45, parking €5. ☼ Mid-Mar.–Oct., daily 11–6.

Avoca

🔵 6½ km (4 mi) south of Avondale Forest Park on R754.

Don't miss a visit to the small, lovely hamlet of Avoca, surrounded by heavily forested hills, at the confluence of the Rivers Avonbeg and Avonmore. Beneath a riverside tree here, the Irish Romantic poet Thomas Moore (1779–1852) composed his 1807 poem, "The Meeting of the Waters." There are some pleasant forest walks nearby, with scenic views of the valley. The oldest hand-weaving mill in Ireland, **Avoca Handweavers,** offers a short tour of the mill, which is still operating. The store sells a wide selection of its own superb fabrics and woven and knit apparel, some of which is difficult to find elsewhere. ☎ 0402/ 35105. ✆ Free. ☼ Shop Mid-Mar.–Oct. daily 9:30–6, Nov.–mid-Mar. daily 9:30–5:30; mill mid-Mar.–Oct. daily 8–4:30, Nov.–mid-Mar. weekdays 8–4:30.

Arklow

🔵 11 km (7 mi) southeast of Avoca on R754.

An ideal point to access the intensely pastoral Vale of Avoca, the small beach town of Arklow is wrapped around an old port. If you love bread and have a sweet tooth, stop in at **Stone Oven Bakery** (✉ 65 Lower Main St., ☎ 0402/39418) at the bottom of the hill. The German-born baker, Egon Friedrich, prepares sourdough breads and delicious sweet treats, including hazelnut-chocolate triangles; at the shop you can also get simple cheese and bread sandwiches to go—or you can eat in the tiny, slightly haphazard café. The **Maritime Museum,** in the public library building near the railway station, traces Arklow's distinguished seafaring tradition. Exhibits include old photographs, some original boats, and the logs of long-dead captains. To get here, take a left at St. Peter's Church as you're heading out of town in the direction of Gorey and Wexford. ✉ St. Mary's Rd., Co. Wicklow, ☎ 0402/32868. ✆ €5. ☼ May–Sept., Mon.–Sat. 10–1 and 2–5; Oct.–Apr., weekdays 10–1 and 2–5.

☾ Immediately north of Arklow is **Brittas Bay,** an expanse of white sand, quiet coves, and rolling dunes—perfect for adventurous kids. In summer it's popular with vacationing Dubliners.

COUNTY KILDARE AND WEST WICKLOW

Horse racing is a passion in Ireland—you'll notice every little town has at least one betting shop—and County Kildare is the country's horse capital. Nestled between the basins of the River Liffey to the north and the River Barrow to the east, its gently sloping hills and grass-filled plains are perfect for breeding and racing Thoroughbreds. For first-time visitors, the National Stud just outside Kildare Town offers a fascinating glimpse into the world of horse breeding. The Japanese Gardens, adjacent to the National Stud, are among Europe's finest, while Castletown House, in Celbridge to the north, is one of Ireland's foremost Georgian treasures. We make Dublin your starting point, but you may want to pick up this leg from Glendalough. The spectacular drive across the Wicklow Gap, from Glendalough to Hollywood, makes for a glorious entrance into Kildare. One last note: Consult Chapter 5, the Southeast, if you make it as far south as Castledermot (the southern-most point in this section) because Carlow and environs are only 10 km (6 mi) farther south.

Castletown House

★ ㉗ *24 km (15 mi) southwest of Dublin via N7 to R403, 6½ km (4 mi) south of Maynooth.*

In the early 18th century, a revival of the architectural style of Andrea Palladio (1508–80) swept through England. Architects there built dozens of houses reinterpreting that style. The rage took hold of Ireland's Anglo-Irish aristocracy as well. Arguably the largest and finest example of an Irish Palladian-style house is Castletown, begun in 1722 for William Conolly (1662–1729), the Speaker of the Irish House of Commons and then the country's wealthiest man. Conolly hired the Italian architect Alessandro Galilei, who designed the facade of the main block; in 1724, the young Irish architect Sir Edward Lovett Pearce completed the house by adding the colonnades and side pavilions. Conolly's death brought construction to a halt; it wasn't until his great-nephew, Thomas Conolly, and his wife, Lady Louisa (née Lennox), took up residence in 1758 that work on the house picked up again. Today Castletown is the largest house built as a private residence. (The American poet Robert Lowell lived here for a time in the 1960s.) The house was rescued in 1967 by Desmond Guinness—of the brewing family—and then the president of the Irish Georgian Society. Now the Irish state owns the property. It's also the headquarters of the Irish Georgian Society and contains many pieces of the original furniture.

Inside the house you'll find hall plasterwork by the Lafranchini brothers, Swiss-Italian craftsmen who worked in Dublin in the mid-18th century. The ground-floor **Print Room** is the only 18th-century example in Ireland of this elegant fad—like oversize postage stamps in a giant album, black-and-white prints were glued to the walls by fashionable young women. Upstairs at the rear of the house, the **Long Gallery**, almost 80 ft by 23 ft, is the most notable of the public rooms—it's decorated in Pompeian style and has three Venetian Murano glass chandeliers. ⊠ *Celbridge, Co. Kildare,* ☎ *01/628–8252,* WEB *www. heritageireland.ie.* ㊑ *€4.* ☉ *Apr.–Sept., weekdays 10–6, weekends 1–6; Oct., weekdays 10–5, Sun. 1–5; Nov., Sun. 1–5.*

OFF THE BEATEN PATH | **MAYNOOTH** – Before heading to Castletown House, make a quick detour slightly farther west to Maynooth, a tiny Georgian town 24 km (15 mi) west of Dublin. **St. Patrick's College,** once a center for the training of Catholic priests, is one of Ireland's most important lay universities. The visitor center chronicles the college's history and that of the Catholic Church in Ireland. Stroll through the university gardens—the Path of Saints or the Path of Sinners. ☎ 01/628-5222, WEB www.may.ie. ☉ May–Sept., Mon.–Sat. 11–5, Sun. 2–6; guided tours every hr.

At the entrance to St. Patrick's College you'll find the ruins of **Maynooth Castle,** the ancient seat of the Fitzgerald family. The Fitzgeralds' fortunes changed for the worse when they led the rebellion of 1536 (it failed). The castle keep, which dates from the 13th century, and the great hall, are still in decent condition. Mrs. Saults at 9 Parson Street has the key. ☒ Free.

Dining and Lodging

$$$–$$$$ ✕☷ **Moyglare Manor.** Owner Nora Devlin has exuberantly decorated this majestic Georgian manor house with her renowned antiques collection. Velvet chairs, oil paintings, and thickly draped windows furnish the drawing room, and the grand bedrooms have four-poster canopy beds, roomy wardrobes, marble fireplaces, and comfortable, chintz-covered armchairs. Lamp-shaded wall sconces add a romantic touch to the formal dining room, where a traditional French five-course set menu is served. The manor, which occupies 16 pastoral acres dotted with sheep and cows, is 29 km (18 mi) west of Dublin. ☒ Maynooth, Co. Kildare, ☎ 01/628-6351, FAX 01/628-5405, WEB www.moyglaremanor.ie. 16 rooms with bath. Restaurant, 2 bars. AE, DC, MC, V.

Straffan

㉘ 5 km (3 mi) southwest of Castletown House on R403, 25½ km (16 mi) southwest of Dublin.

Its attractive location on the banks of the River Liffey, its unique butterfly farm, and the Kildare Hotel and Country Club—where Arnold Palmer designed the K Club, one of Ireland's most renowned 18-hole golf courses—are what make Straffan so appealing. The only one of its kind in Ireland, the **Straffan Butterfly Farm** has a tropical house with exotic plants, butterflies, and moths. Mounted and framed butterflies are for sale. ☎ 01/627-1109. ☒ €4. ☉ May–early-Aug., daily noon–5:30.

The **Steam Museum** covers the history of Irish steam engines, handsome machines used both in industry and agriculture—churning butter, threshing corn. There's also a fun collection of model locomotives. Engineers are present on "live steam days"; phone in advance to confirm. ☒ Lodge Park, Co. Kildare, ☎ 01/627-3155. ☒ Live steam days €5.10, other times €3.80. ☉ Easter–May and Sept., Tues.–Sun. 2–6; June–Aug., Mon.–Sat. 2–6, Sun. 2:30–5:30.

Dining and Lodging

$$$$ ✕☷ **Kildare Hotel and Country Club.** Manicured gardens and the
★ renowned Arnold Palmer–designed K Club golf course surround this mansard-roofed county mansion. The spacious, comfortable guest rooms are each uniquely decorated with antiques, and have large windows that overlook either the Liffey or the golf course. (The rooms in the old house are best.) The hotel also has a leasing agreement with several privately owned cottages on the property. Chef Michel Flamme serves an unashamedly French menu—albeit with the hint of an Irish flavor—at the Byerly Turk Restaurant (named after a famous racehorse). ☒ Co. Kildare, ☎ 01/601-7200, FAX 01/601-7299, WEB www.kclub.ie.

45 rooms with bath, 20–30 apartments. 2 restaurants, 18-hole golf course, 4 tennis courts, indoor pool, hair salon, fishing, horseback riding, squash, 3 bars. AE, DC, MC, V.

\$\$–\$\$\$ ✕🖼 **Barberstown Castle.** With a 13th-century castle keep at one end,
★ an Elizabethan central section, and a large Georgian country house at the other, Barberstown represents 750 years of Irish history. Turf fires blaze in ornate fireplaces in the three sumptuously decorated lounges. Bedrooms are furnished with reproduction pieces; some have four-poster beds. The restaurants—one Georgian, one medieval (the latter on the ground floor of the castle keep)—serve creatively prepared food. ✉ *Co. Kildare,* ☎ *01/628–8157,* FAX *01/627–7027,* WEB *www.barberstowncastle.com. 22 rooms with bath. Restaurant, bar. AE, DC, MC, V.*

En Route County Kildare has two major canal systems that connect Dublin with the Rivers Shannon and Barrow and the interior Lakelands. Sixteen km (10 mi) southwest of Straffan, **Robertstown** sits on the **Grand Canal** (the other major canal is the **Royal**, which heads to the northeast from Dublin), where you can take scenic walks and, during the summer, barge trips. Built in the early 19th century to accommodate passengers on the canal, the **Grand Canal Hotel** (☎ 045/870–005) offers candlelit dinners and musical entertainment.

Naas

🕙 *13 km (8 mi) south of Straffan on R407, 30 km (19 mi) southwest of Dublin on N7.*

The seat of County Kildare and a thriving market town in the heartland of Irish Thoroughbred country, Naas (pronounced nace) is full of pubs with high stools where short men (trainee jockeys) discuss the merits of their various stables. Naas has its own small racecourse, but **Punchestown Racecourse** (✉ 3 km/2 mi from Naas) has a wonderful setting amid rolling plains, with the Wicklow Mountains a spectacular backdrop. Horse races are held regularly here, but the most popular event is the Punchestown National Hunt Festival in April.

Russborough House

🕥 *16 km (10 mi) southeast of Naas on R410.*

One of the highlights of the western part of County Wicklow, Russborough House is among the finest of the many Palladian-style villas built in Ireland by the Anglo-Irish ascendancy in the first half of the 18th century. (Castletown House, Emo Court, and Castle Coole are the other stars in this constellation.) In 1741, a year after Joseph Leeson inherited a vast fortune from his father, a successful Dublin brewer, he commissioned Richard Castle (architect of Leinster House and Powerscourt) to build this palatial house, and he worked on it until his death (after which Francis Bindon took over). They pulled out all the stops to create a confident, majestic house with a silver-gray Wicklow granite facade that extends for more than 700 ft and encompasses a seven-bay central block, off which radiate two semicircular loggias connecting the flanking wings.

Baroque exuberance reigns in the house's main rooms, especially in the lavishly ornamented plasterwork ceilings executed by the Lafranchini brothers (they also worked at Castletown House). After a long succession of owners, Russborough was bought in 1952 by Sir Alfred Beit, the nephew of the German cofounder (with Cecil Rhodes) of the De Beers diamond operation, and it now belongs to Lady Beit, his widow. In 1988, after two major robberies, the finest works in the Beits' art collection were donated to the National Gallery of Ireland in Dublin. However, works by Gainsborough, Guardi, Reynolds, Rubens, and Murillo remain, as well as bronzes, silver, and porcelain. The views from Russborough's windows take in the foothills of the Wicklow Mountains and a small lake in front of the house; the extensive woodlands on the estate are open to visitors. ⊠ *Blessington, off N81, Co. Kildare,* ☎ *045/865–239.* 🖻 *€5.50, upstairs bedrooms €3.50.* ☉ *May–Sept., daily 10:30–5:30; Apr. and Oct., Sun. 10:30–5:30.*

Poulaphouca Reservoir

㉛ *33 km (21 mi) west of Glendalough on R758 via R756, 3 km (2 mi) southeast of Russborough House.*

Known locally as the **Blessington Lakes,** Poulaphouca (pronounced pool-a-*fook*-a) Reservoir is a large, meandering artificial lake that provides Dublin's water supply minutes from Russborough House. You can drive around the entire perimeter of the reservoir on minor roads; on its southern end lies Hollywood Glen, a particularly beautiful natural spot.

The small market town of **Blessington,** with its wide main street lined on both sides by tall trees and Georgian buildings, and on the western shore of the lakes, is one of the most charming villages in the area. It was founded in the late 17th century, and was a stop on the Dublin–Waterford mail-coach service in the mid-19th century. Until 1932, a steam train ran from here to Dublin.

Beyond the southern tip of the Poulaphouca Reservoir, 13 km (8 mi) south of Blessington on N81, you'll spot a small sign for the **Piper's Stones,** a Bronze Age stone circle that was probably used in a ritual connected with worship of the sun. It's just a short walk from the road.

Dining and Lodging

$$$–$$$$ ✕🏠 **Rathsallagh House.** Low-slung, ivy-covered Queen Anne sta-
★   bles—at the end of a long drive that winds through a golf course, and set in 530 acres of parkland—were converted to a farmhouse in 1798. Two drawing rooms are furnished with enveloping couches and chairs, fresh flower arrangements, large windows, fireplaces, and lots of lamps. Kay's outstanding haute Irish dinner menu changes daily. Specialties include paupiette of herb-filled salmon with onion and chive beurre blanc. ⊠ *Dunlavin, Co. Wicklow,* ☎ *045/403–112,* 🖷 *045/403–343,* 🕸 *www.rathsallagh.com. 29 rooms with bath. Restaurant, 18-hole golf course, tennis court, indoor pool, massage, sauna, croquet, bar, meeting rooms. AE, DC, MC, V.*

Outdoor Activities and Sports

Prepare yourself for splendid views of the Blessington Lakes from the top of **Church Mountain,** which you reach via a vigorous walk through **Woodenboley Wood,** at the southern tip of Hollywood Glen. Follow the main forest track for about 20 minutes and then take the narrow path that heads up the side of the forest to the mountaintop.

The Curragh

㉜ *8 km (5 mi) southwest of Naas on M7, 25½ km (16 mi) west of Poulaphouca Reservoir.*

The broad plain of the Curragh, bisected by the main N7 road, is the biggest area of common land in Ireland, encompassing about 31 square km (12 square mi) and devoted mainly to grazing. It's Ireland's major racing center, where you'll find **Curragh Racecourse** (☎ 045/441–205); the Irish Derby and other international horse races are run here.

The **Curragh Main Barracks,** a large camp where the Irish Army trains, has a small museum. One of its prize relics is the armored car once used by Michael Collins, the former head of the Irish Army—in December 1921, Collins signed the Anglo-Irish Treaty, designating a six-county North to remain in British hands, in exchange for complete independence for Ireland's remaining 26 counties. The car can be seen with permission from the commanding officer. ☎ *045/445–161; ask for the command adjutant.*

Kildare Town

③③ *5 km (3 mi) west of the Curragh on M7, 51 km (32 mi) southwest of Dublin via N7 and M7.*

Horse breeding is the cornerstone of Kildare County's thriving economy, and Kildare Town is the place to come if you're crazy about horses. Right off Kildare's main market square, the **Silken Thomas** (☎ 045/ 522–232) pub re-creates an old-world atmosphere with open fires, dark wood decor, and leaded lights; it's a good place to stop for lunch before exploring the sights here.

St. Brigid's Cathedral (Church of Ireland) is where the eponymous saint founded a religious settlement in the 5th century. The present cathedral, with its stocky tower, is a restored 13th-century structure. It was partially rebuilt about 1686, but restoration work wasn't completed for another 200 years. The stained-glass west window of the cathedral depicts three of Ireland's greatest saints: Brigid, Patrick, and Columba. In pre-Christian times druids gathered around a sacred oak that stood in the grounds and from which Kildare (*Cill Dara*) or the "Church of the Oak" gets it's name. Also within the grounds is a restored fire pit reclaimed from the time of Brigid, when a fire was kept burning—by a chaste woman—in a female-only fire temple. Interestingly, Brigid started the place for women, but it was she who asked monks to move here as well. ⊠ *Off Market Sq.* ☒ €.80. ⊘ *Daily 10–6.*

The 108-ft-high **round tower,** in the graveyard of St. Brigid's Cathedral, is the second highest in Ireland. It dates from the 12th century. Extraordinary views across much of the Midlands await you if you're energetic enough to climb the stairs to the top. ☎ *045/521–229.* ☒ €2.55. ⊘ *May–Sept., daily 10–1 and 2–5.*

If you're a longtime horse aficionado, or even just curious, check out the **National Stud Farm,** a main center of Ireland's racing industry. The Stud was founded in 1900 by brewing heir Colonel William Hall-Walker, and transferred to the Irish state in 1945. It's here that breeding stallions are groomed, exercised, tested, and bred. Spring and early summer, when mares will have new foals, are the best times to visit. Besides being crazy about horses, Walker may just have been crazy—he believed in astrology, so new foals had their charts done. Those with unfavorable results were sold right away. He even built the stallion boxes with lantern roofs that allow the moon and stars to work their magic on the occupants. The **National Stud Horse Museum,** also on the grounds, recounts the history of horses in Ireland. Its most outstanding exhibit is the skeleton of Arkle, the Irish racehorse that won major victories in Ireland and England during the late 1960s. The museum also contains medieval evidence of horses, such as bones from 13th-century Dublin, and some early examples of equestrian equipment. ⊠ *South of Kildare Town about ½ km (⅓ mi), Co. Kildare,* ☎ *045/521– 617,* WEB *www.irish-national-stud.ie.* ☒ €8 *(includes entry to the Japanese Gardens).* ⊘ *Mid-Feb.–mid-Nov., daily 9:30–6.*

★ Adjacent to the National Stud Farm, the **Japanese Gardens** were created between 1906 and 1910 by the Stud's founder, Colonel Hall-Walker, and laid out by a Japanese gardener, Tassa Eida, and his son Minoru. The gardens are recognized as among the finest in Europe, although they're more of an East-West hybrid rather than authentically Japanese. The Scots pine trees, for instance, are an appropriate stand-in for traditional Japanese pines, which signify long life and happiness. The gardens symbolically chart the human progression from birth to death, although the focus is on the male journey. A series of landmarks are situated on a meandering path: the Tunnel of Ignorance (No. 3) represents a child's lack of understanding; the Engagement and Marriage bridges (Nos. 8 and 9) span a small stream; and from the Hill of Ambition (No. 13), you can look back over your joys and sorrows. It ends with the Gateway to Eternity (No. 20), beyond which lies a Buddhist meditation sand garden. It's a worthwhile destination any time of the year, though it's particularly glorious in spring and fall. ⊠ *South of Kildare Town about 2½ km (1½ mi), clearly signposted to left of market square, Co. Kildare,* ☎ *045/521–617,* WEB *www.irish-national-stud.ie.* ☞ *€8 (includes entry to the National Stud).* ⊙ *Mid-Feb.–mid-Nov., daily 9:30–6.*

Athy

34 *24 km (15 mi) south of Kildare Town on R417, 33½ km (21 mi) south of Naas.*

The River Barrow widens considerably at the industrial town of Athy, whose designation as a heritage town has spiffed things up—especially the 18th century town houses and the castle here. Overlooking the river, by the bridge, 16th-century **White's Castle,** now a private house (that's not accessible), was built by the earl of Kildare to defend this strategic crossing.

The modern pentagonal **Catholic church** (1963–65) in the middle of town has a striking interior with statues, a crucifix by local artist Brid ni Rinn on the high altar, and stations of the cross by the well-known painter and member of the R.H.A., George Campbell (d. 1979). ☞ *Free.* ⊙ *Daily 8–6.*

Ballytore

35 *8 km (5 mi) east of Athy, 26 km (16 mi) south of Naas on N9.*

In the 18th and 19th centuries, Ballytore was a Quaker settlement—one of few in Ireland—and the place where the Irish philosopher and man of letters Edmund Burke was educated. An old schoolhouse is now a small **Quaker Museum.** Among the pupils at the school was Edmund Burke (1729–97), the orator and political philosopher who was close to Samuel Johnson and Sir Joshua Reynolds. ☎ *045/431–109.* ☞ *Free.* ⊙ *Tues.–Fri. 11–6, Sat. 11–1.*

An old mill was converted into the **Crookstown Heritage Centre,** a museum of the flour-milling and baking industries with a functioning water mill. Built in 1840, the center helped reduce the effects of the Great Famine in this area. You can get a quick bite in its coffee shop. ☎ *0507/ 23222.* ☞ *€3.20.* ⊙ *Apr.–Sept., daily 10–7; Oct.–Mar., Sun. 2–5:30.*

Dining

$ ✕ **Moone High Cross Inn.** A cornucopia of local artifacts, newspaper clippings, and old photographs decorate this old pub, which makes for fascinating browsing while you nosh on the bar food—steak, salmon, and bacon and cabbage. Save room for the homemade apple pie. On sunny days, you can sit outside and admire the old signs in the beer garden. The inn's down the road from the Moone High Cross, about 7½ km (5 mi) south of Ballymote. ⊠ *Bolton Hill, Moone, Co. Kildare,* ☎ *0507/24112. MC, V.*

En Route From Ballytore take the main N9 road south for 3 km (2 mi) to Timolin, where the **Irish Pewter Mill** pays splendid tribute to an old Irish craft with its showrooms, factory, and museum. Jugs, plates, and other pewter items are for sale. ☎ *0507/24164.* ⊙ *May–Sept., weekdays 9:30–5, weekends 11–4.*

You'll find several well-preserved high crosses, among monastic ruins, in South Kildare. On N9, 1½ km (1 mi) beyond Timolin, take the signposted right turn at the Moone Post Office and continue for 3 km (2 mi) to the **Moone High Cross,** an ancient Celtic cross that stands 17½ ft high—its 51 sculptured panels showing scriptural scenes.

Castledermot

③⑥ *13 km (8 mi) south of Ballytore on N9.*

On the left side of the village of Castledermot, you'll find an almost perfectly preserved 10th-century **round tower** together with two 10th-century **high crosses,** equally well preserved, on the grounds of the local church. From the church gate, you can walk back to the main road along the footpath, which is totally enclosed by trees. It's a splendid, serene walk. On the right side of the road in the village, you'll find the substantial ruins of a Franciscan friary, mostly dating from the 14th century.

Dining and Lodging

$$$–$$$$ ✕🗏 **Kilkea Castle.** Built in 1180 as a defensive Anglo-Norman castle, this is a wonderfully elegant and old-world place to stay. The castle is seeped in history and populated with the ghosts of a great Irish family. The castle was the longtime home of the FitzGerald family, though it was later modified and restored. The eleven rooms in the castle itself are more luxuriously furnished than the rooms that surround the adjacent courtyard. The restaurant is in what was the great hall of the castle. Dishes are based on fresh, seasonal produce, some of it from the old, walled gardens below. The hotel has an extensive sports complex, including a golf course and clubhouse. ⊠ *Castledermot, Co. Kildare, near Athy,* ☎ *0503/45156,* 🅵🅰🆇 *0503/45187. 36 rooms with bath. Restaurant, 18-hole golf course, 2 tennis courts, indoor pool, health club, fishing, archery, 2 bars. AE, DC, MC, V.*

DUBLIN ENVIRONS A TO Z

To research prices, get advice from other travelers, and book travel arrangements, visit www.fodors.com.

BUS TRAVEL

Bus services link Dublin with main and smaller towns in the environs. All bus services for the region depart from Busaras, the central bus station, at Store Street. For bus inquiries, contact Bus Éireann. St. Kevin's, a private bus service, runs daily from Dublin (outside the Royal College of Surgeons on St. Stephen's Green) to Glendalough, stopping off at Bray, Roundwood, and Laragh en route. Buses leave Dublin daily at 11:30 AM and 6 PM (7 PM on Sunday); buses leave Glendalough weekdays at 7:15 AM and 4:15 PM (9:45 AM and 4:15 PM on Saturday; 9:45 AM and 5:30 PM on Sunday). One-way fare is €8; round-trip, €13.

➤ Bus Information: **Bus Éireann** (☎ 01/836–6111). **St. Kevin's** (☎ 01/281–8119).

CAR TRAVEL

The easiest and best way to tour Dublin's environs is by car, because many sights are not served by public transportation, and what service there is, especially to outlying areas, is infrequent. (☞ If you need to rent a car, see Car Rental in Dublin A to Z in Chapter 2.) To visit destinations in the Boyne Valley, follow N3, along the east side of Phoenix Park, out of the city and make Trim and Tara your first stops. Alternatively, leave Dublin via N1/M1 to Belfast. Try to avoid the road during weekday rush hours (8 AM–10 AM and 5 PM–7 PM); stay on it as far as Drogheda and start touring from there.

To reach destinations in County Kildare, follow the quays along the south side of the Liffey (they are one-way westbound) to St. John's Road West (N7); in a matter of minutes, you're heading for open countryside. Avoid traveling this route during the evening peak rush hours, especially on Friday, when Dubliners are themselves making their weekend getaways.

To reach destinations in County Wicklow, N11/M11 is the fastest and most clearly marked route. The two more scenic routes to Glendalough are R115 to R759 to R755, or R177 to R755.

EMERGENCIES

➤ CONTACTS: **Police, fire, ambulance** (☎ 999).

LODGING

BED-AND-BREAKFASTS

For a small fee, the Irish Tourist Board, known as Bord Fáilte, and Dublin Tourism, will book accommodations anywhere in Ireland through a central reservations system. B&Bs can be booked at local visitor information offices when they are open; however, even these reservations will go through the central reservations system.

➤ CONTACT INFORMATION: **Bord Fáilte** (☎ 800/223–6470 in the U.S. and Canada; 800/039–7000 in the U.K.; 02/9299–6177 in Australia; 09/379–8720 in New Zealand, WEB www.irelandvacations.com). **Dublin Tourism** (☎ 01/605–7700 or 01/602–4129, FAX 01/605–7787; 01/475–8046 for non–credit card accommodation inquiries, WEB www.visitdublin.com).

OUTDOOR ACTIVITIES AND SPORTS

HORSEBACK RIDING

Wicklow Trail Rides takes experienced adult horseback riders on weeklong rides through the Wicklow Mountains (May–September), with overnight stays in country homes and guest houses. Instructional holidays for children and adults at the riding center are also available.

➤ CONTACTS: **Wicklow Trail Rides** (✉ Grainne Sugars, Calliaghstown Riding Center, Ratcoole, Co. Dublin, ☎ 01/458–9236, FAX 01/458–8171).

WALKING AND HIKING

The Wicklow Way is Ireland's most popular walking route, a 137-km (85-mi) trek through the Dublin and Wicklow mountains. The walk begins in Marlay Park, just south of Dublin city center, where there is a selection of different trails. County Wicklow also sponsors three annual walking festivals. The two-day Rathdrum Easter Walking Festival includes hill walks of varying lengths over Easter weekend. The first weekend of May, the Wicklow Mountains May Walking Festival is centered on Blessington. The Wicklow Mountains Autumn Walking Festival is based in the Glenmalure area.

➤ CONTACTS: **Rathdrum Easter Walking Festival** (☎ 0404/46262). **Wicklow Mountains Autumn Walking Festival** (☎ 0404/66058). **Wick-**

low Mountains May Walking Festival (☏ 0404/66058). Wicklow Way Information (☏ 01/493–4059).

TOURS
BUS TOURS

Bus Éireann runs guided bus tours to many of the historic and scenic locations throughout the Dublin environs daily during the summer. Visits include trips to Glendalough in Wicklow; Boyne Valley and Newgrange in County Louth; and the Hill of Tara, Trim, and Navan in County Meath. All tours depart from Busaras Station, Dublin; information is available by phone Monday–Saturday 8:30–7, Sunday 10–7. Gray Line, a privately owned touring company, also runs many guided bus tours throughout the Dublin environs between May and September. Wild Coach Tours has half- and full-day trips to Glendalough, Powerscourt House and Garden, and Malahide Castle in small Mercedes coaches. Prices start at €16.50.

➤ FEES AND SCHEDULES: **Bus Éireann** (☏ 01/836–6111). **Gray Line** (☏ 01/661–9666). **Wild Coach Tours** (☏ 01/280–1899).

TRAIN TRAVEL

Iarnród Éireann trains run the length of the east coast, from Dundalk to the north in County Louth to Arklow along the coast in County Wicklow. Trains make many stops along the way; there are stations in Drogheda, Dublin (the main stations are Connolly Station and Pearse Station), Bray, Greystones, Wicklow, and Rathdrum. From Heuston Station, the Arrow, a commuter train service, runs westward to Celbridge, Naas, Newbridge, and Kildare Town. Contact Iarnród Éireann for schedule and fare information.

➤ TRAIN INFORMATION: **Connolly Station** (✉ Amiens St.). **Heuston Station** (✉ Victoria Quay and St. John's Road W). **Iarnród Éireann** (✉ Irish Rail, ☏ 01/836–6222). **Pearse Station** (✉ Westland Row).

VISITOR INFORMATION

For information on travel in the Dublin environs and for help in making lodging reservations, contact one of the following Tourist Information Offices (TIOs): Dublin Tourism and Bord Fáilte; Dundalk; Mullingar; Trim; or Wicklow Town. Mullingar is the head office of tourism for Counties Louth, Meath, and Kildare; it can give you contact information for temporary TIOs in these areas. During the summer, temporary TIOs are open throughout the environs, in towns such as Arklow and Avoca in County Wicklow; Drogheda and Dundalk in County Louth; and Kildare Town in County Kildare.

➤ TOURIST INFORMATION: **Bord Fáilte** (☏ 1850/230–330 in Ireland, 800/223–6470 in the U.S. and Canada; 800/039–7000 in the U.K.; 02/9299–6177 in Australia; 09/379–8720 in New Zealand). **Dublin Tourism** (☏ 01/605–7700 or 01/602–4129, FAX 01/605–7725). **Dundalk** (☏ 042/933–5484, FAX 042/933–8070). **Mullingar** (☏ 044/48761, FAX 044/40413). **Trim** (☏ 046/37227, FAX 046/31595). **Wicklow Town** (☏ 0404/69117, FAX 0404/69118).

4 THE MIDLANDS

COUNTIES OFFALY, ROSCOMMON,
LONGFORD, CAVAN, MONAGHAN,
WESTMEATH, THE NORTH TIPPERARY,
LAOIS, AND THE SOUTH OF LEITRIM

Unspectacular and unsung, the flat plains
of the Midlands form the geographical
heart of Ireland. There's water at every
turn in this landscape of wide lakes and
fast rivers, including the mighty Shannon,
Ireland's central artery and the longest river
in the British Isles. Among the highlights are
Clonmacnoise, Ireland's most important
monastic ruins; historic towns with age-
old industries, such as lace-making and
crystal; the gardens of Birr Castle; and
some of Ireland's finest Anglo-Irish
houses—Strokestown House, Castle
Leslie, and Emo Court.

IRISH SCHOOLCHILDREN WERE ONCE TAUGHT to think of their country as a saucer, with mountains around the edge and a dip in the middle. The dip is the Midlands—or the Lakelands, as it is sometimes also referred to—and this often-overlooked region comprises seven counties: Cavan, Laois (pronounced leash), Westmeath, Longford, Offaly, Roscommon, Monaghan, and North Tipperary and Leitrim.

Updated by
Alannah
Hopkin

A fair share of Ireland's 800 bodies of water speckle this lush countryside. Many of the lakes formed by glacial action some 10,000 years ago are quite small, especially in Cavan and Monaghan. Anglers have learned to expect to have a lake to themselves. Because of all the water, much of the landscape lies under blanket bog, a unique ecosystem that's worth exploring. The River Shannon, one of the longest rivers in Europe and the longest in the British Isles, bisects the Midlands from north to south, piercing a series of loughs (lakes): Lough Allen, Lough Ree, and Lough Derg. The Royal Canal and the Grand Canal cross the Midlands from east to west, ending in the Shannon north and south of Lough Ree.

The main roads from Dublin to the south and the west cross the area—and these roads ultimately came to eclipse the Shannon and the canals as important transportation arteries—but there is also a network of minor roads linking the more scenic areas. You'll find more conventionally attractive hill and lake scenery in the forest parks of Killykeen and Lough Key. The towns themselves—including Nenagh, Roscommon, Athlone, Boyle, Mullingar, Tullamore, Longford, and Cavan—are not among Ireland's most distinctive, but they are likely to appeal to people hungry for a time when the pace of life was slower and every neighbor's face was familiar. A Midland town's main hotel is usually the social center, a good place from which to experience life as the locals do. Night owls and thrill seekers should head elsewhere.

The Midlands also house some of Ireland's most impressive heritage properties: Strokestown Park House, Birr Castle Gardens, Emo Court and Gardens, Castle Leslie, and the magnificent monastic ruins of Clonmacnoise on the banks of the Shannon.

Pleasures and Pastimes

Dining

Most restaurants are simple eateries, ranging in price from inexpensive ($) to moderate ($$), and are often attached to a family hotel. Mullingar, in the center of the Midlands, is the beef capital of Ireland, and the many lakes and rivers of the region provide an abundance of fresh salmon and trout. No place in Ireland is more than an hour and a half from the sea, so expect to find lots of fresh ocean fish.

CATEGORY	THE REPUBLIC*
$$$$	over €29
$$$	€22–€29
$$	€13–€21
$	under €13

*Per person for a main course at dinner

Lodging

There are some opulent country-house hotels in the region, but accommodations are for the most part modest affairs. The choice is usually between a small-town hotel offering a reasonable standard of basic comfort or a scenic country-house bed-and-breakfast.

CATEGORY	THE REPUBLIC*
$$$$	over €230
$$$	€178–€230
$$	€127–€178
$	under €127

*All prices are for two people in a double room, including VAT and a service charge (often applied in larger hotels).

Outdoor Activities and Sports

BICYCLING

An excellent way to immerse yourself in the Midlands is to tour the region on a bicycle. You may not find the spectacular scenery of the hilly coastal regions, but the level terrain means a less strenuous ride. The twisting roads are generally in good condition, and there are pleasant picnic spots in the many state-owned forests just off the main roads. Bord Fáilte recommends two long tours: one of the Athlone-Mullingar-Roscommon area and another of the Cavan-Monaghan-Mullingar region. Avoid the major trunk roads that bisect the region.

BOATING

One especially fine and unusual way to see the Midlands is by boat—after all, the region has 485 km (300 mi) of navigable rivers and numerous island-studded lakes. Several companies rent out charter boats of varying sizes for vacations on the water. Most of these vessels hold from six to eight people, and all are operated by the parties who rent them, meaning everyone can be captain for a day.

FISHING

The River Shannon and its system of lakes attract anglers from around the world. Beam, rudd, tench, roach, perch, and hybrids are the main varieties, while pike roam select waters. Monaghan, Cavan, Boyle, and the small lakes to the east and west of Lough Derg are the best coarse fishing areas, while brown-trout lakes and rivers can be found around Birr, Banagher, Mullingar, and Roscommon. For pike, you'll find the most fruitful areas around Cavan, Clones, Cootehill, Castleblaney, Kingscourt, Carrick-on-Shannon, Boyle, Belturbet, and Butlersbridge. The Midlands region hosts several angling festivals, with prize money and fringe events such as sing-alongs, dart games, and card competitions. Castleblaney has a tournament in March; Carrickmacross and Ballinsasloe, in May; Athlone, in July and October; and Cootehill, in September.

GOLF

Although the parkland courses of the Midlands may lack the spectacular challenge of Ireland's more famous scenic and coastal greens, they have a quiet charm all their own. On weekdays you shouldn't have any trouble booking a tee time. Many older courses are inexpensive, costing as little as €15; greens fees at newer courses are moderate at around €19–€40.

HIKING AND WALKING

The many forest park trails (at Killykeen, Lough Key, and Dun a Ri) and narrow country roads here are great for touring the Midlands on foot. An impressive walking trail to the east of Birr, called the Slieve Bloom Way, runs through the Slieve Bloom Mountains on a 50-km (30-mi) circular route—it has deep glens, rock formations, waterfalls, and great views from mountain peaks.

Exploring the Midlands

This chapter is organized into three sections: the Eastern Midlands; the Northern Midlands; and North Tipperary and the West Midlands. The first two areas can easily be covered in an extended visit to the Midlands, as they chart a course almost due north from the initial starting point in Portarlington, County Laois. Because the third section includes sights west of those in the first two, keep it in mind if you're flying into Shannon and beginning your explorations of Ireland in the western half of the country. In fact, because the Midlands border virtually every major county of Ireland, there are three places in this chapter where you should be alert to nearby locales covered in other chapters: the easternmost sites in the Midlands (Emo Court and Coolbanagher) are within a few miles of the westernmost sites in Dublin Environs; the westernmost sites in the Midlands (Boyle and Lough Key Forest Park) are just across the border from County Sligo; and the northernmost sites and towns of the Midlands are just across the border from Northern Ireland.

Numbers in the text correspond to numbers in the margin and on the Midlands map.

Great Itineraries

The Midlands is a relatively small region, but part of its attraction lies in the temptation to follow a loose itinerary and spend time off the beaten path. In 10 days you can leisurely explore the region by bicycle. In a car you'll cover the same route in five days, with plenty of time to improvise. Three days are enough to sample the central part, which is probably more sensible than driving long distances on small roads in an effort to see everything.

IF YOU HAVE 3 DAYS

Heading east from Shannon Airport, turn off the N7 Limerick–Dublin road for ⛭ **Birr** ㉑, a quiet Georgian town built around its magnificent castle and gardens. Then take the nearby **Bord na Mona Bog Rail Tour** ⑲ near Shannonbridge, a good introduction to the flora and fauna of Ireland's many bogs. While you're in the area, stop at **Clonmacnoise** ⑱, Ireland's most important monastic settlement, which overlooks the River Shannon, and return to Birr for the night. The next day head for **Strokestown** ⑮ and its namesake house, where a museum documents the causes and effects of the 1845–49 Great Famine. If you have time, drive east to **Longford** ⑦, and visit the nearby **Carrigglas Manor,** a romantic 1837 Tudor-Gothic house that has Jane Austen associations. If the weather is good, take some fresh air in **Lough Key Forest Park** near ⛭ **Boyle** ⑭, a good place to stay overnight. From here you'll be well positioned to explore the West or Northwest.

IF YOU HAVE 5 DAYS

Heading from Dublin or from points east in Wicklow and Kildare, start at **Portarlington** ①, making sure to visit the nearby **Emo Court and Gardens.** This is the only large-scale country house designed by James Gandon, the architect responsible for much of Georgian Dublin. Move north to the Gothic Revival Charleville Castle outside **Tullamore** ②, then to **Kilbeggan** ③, where you can learn about whiskey making at the Kilbeggan Distillery; if you have time, stop in at the beautiful **Belvedere House Gardens** to the north. Stay in or around ⛭ **Mullingar** ④ for the night. In the morning of day two, briefly explore Mullingar, and then head north on scenic R394 to **Castlepollard** ⑤ and the massive Tullynally Castle and Gardens. Crystal aficionados will want to stop in **Cavan** ⑨, while nature buffs can easily spend the afternoon exploring the nearby water-laced **Killykeen Forest Park.** Spend the night in ⛭ **Cootehill** ⑩, an old-fashioned, friendly County Cavan town popular with the many anglers who frequent this area. Begin your third day visiting ⛭ **Castle Leslie** ⑫, beautifully situated on the shores of Glaslough (the "green lake"). If you're ready for some downtime, you can extend your visit

The Midlands

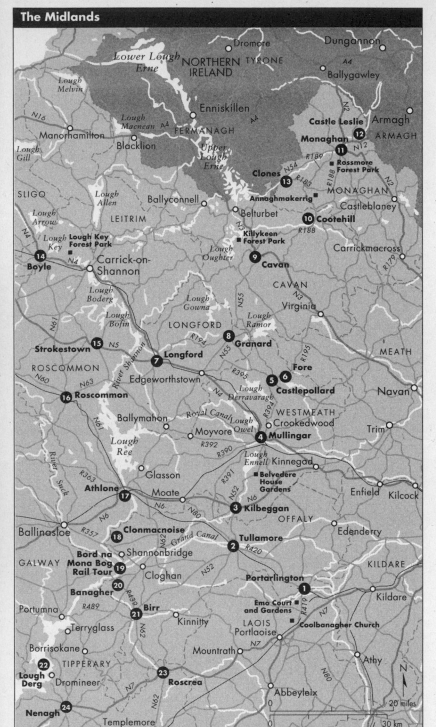

and stay the night (it's only accessible to guests, not to visitors). Alternatively, you can either jump across the border to explore the southernmost sights in Northern Ireland or head southwest, making a brief stop at **Rossmore Forest Park** on your way to the border town of **Clones** ⑬, a lace-making center. On your fourth day, return to Cavan and pick up the road to **Longford** ⑦. To the west lies **Strokestown** ⑮ and its namesake house. ⊡ **Athlone** ⑰ is a convenient place to spend the night—from here you're well positioned for an early morning visit to **Clonmacnoise** ⑱, the most important early Christian monastic site in Ireland. Stop at the **Bord na Mona Bog Rail Tour** ⑲ near Shannonbridge on your way to **Banagher** ⑳, where you can either take a two-hour Shannon cruise (a great trip in good weather) or drive around **Lough Derg** ㉒. Depending on your time, you can choose to end up in either ⊡ **Birr** ㉑, ⊡ **Roscrea** ㉓, or ⊡ **Nenagh** ㉔; from any of these towns you're not far from Shannon Airport and points to the west and southwest.

When to Tour the Midlands

The Midlands are a good year-round choice because, unlike those in the more popular destinations in the West and Southwest, the restaurants, accommodations, and major attractions stay open all year. The area is usually quiet, except at the boating resorts on the Shannon and its loughs, which are heavily booked by Irish vacationers in July and August.

THE EASTERN MIDLANDS

The eastern fringe of the Midlands is about an hour's drive from Dublin, and a visit to the area could easily be grafted onto a trip to the Dublin Environs. The route begins at Portarlington, the closest village to Dublin in the chapter, and move northwest to Castlepollard and environs, stopping just short of Longford, the jumping-off point for the Northern Midlands.

Portarlington

❶ *72 km (43 mi) southwest of Dublin.*

If you enjoy large-scale domestic architecture, head here. A quintessential landmark of Irish Palladian elegance lies just 7 km (4½ mi) south ★ of Portarlington: **Emo Court and Gardens,** one of the finest large-scale country houses near Dublin open to the public. If you elect to skip over much of the Midlands, at least try to tack on a visit to Emo, especially if you're in County Kildare or Wicklow. To come upon the house from the main drive, an avenue lined with magisterial Wellingtonia trees, is to experience one of Ireland's great treasure-house views. Begun in 1790 by James Gandon, architect of the Custom House and the Four Courts in Dublin, Emo (the name derives from the Italian version of the original Irish name Imoe) is thought to be Gandon's only domestic work on as grand a scale as his Dublin civic buildings. Construction continued on and off for 70 years, as family money troubles followed the untimely death of the Emo's first patron and owner, the first Earl of Portarlington.

In 1996, Emo's English-born owner, Mr. Cholmeley Dering Cholmeley-Harrison, donated the house to the Irish nation. The ground-floor rooms have been beautifully restored and decorated. Among the highlights are the **entrance hall,** with trompe l'oeil in the apses on each side, and the **library,** which has a carved Italian marble mantle with putti frolicking among grapevines. But the showstopper, and one of the finest rooms in Ireland, is the domed **rotunda**—in fact the work of one of Gandon's successors, the Irish architect William Caldbeck—inspired by the Roman Pantheon. The rotunda's blue-and-white coffered dome is supported by marble pilasters with gilded Corinthian capitals. Emo's 55 acres of grounds include a 20-acre lake, lawns planted with yew trees, a small garden (the Clocker) with Japanese maples, and a larger one (the Grapery) with rare trees and shrubs. ⌂ *Emo,* ☎ *0502/ 26573.* ⌨ *Gardens free, house €2.50.* ⊙ *Gardens daily 10:30–5:30; house mid-June–mid-Sept., Tues.–Sun. 10–6 (last tour at 5:15).*

Coolbanagher Church, the familiar name for the exquisite Church of St. John the Evangelist, was, like Emo Court and Gardens, designed by James Gandon. On view inside are Gandon's original 1795 plans; there's also an elaborately sculpted 15th-century font from an earlier church that once stood nearby, and adjacent is Gandon's mausoleum for Lord Portarlington, his patron at Emo. The church is open daily in the summer; during other months, ask around in the tiny village for a key, or call the rectory (☎ 0502/24143), a 10-minute drive away. ⌂ *8½ km (5½ mi) south of Portarlington on R419.* ⊙ *May–Oct., daily 9–6.*

Dining and Lodging

$ ✕⛶ **Preston House.** This ivy-clad Georgian schoolhouse on the main Cork–Dublin road is a popular lunch and coffee stop by day, renowned for home-baked goods, while in the evening the restaurant (closed Sunday and Monday) takes on a more formal aspect. Owner Allison Dowling prepares local beef and lamb in traditional Irish style—roast or grilled—and also offers lighter dishes, including baked cheese soufflé and warm chicken salad. The guest rooms are spacious, furnished with solid Victorian antiques, and all have working fireplaces. They also have views of the long back gardens and fields beyond. ⌂ *Main St., Abbeyleix, Co. Laois,* ☎ ᴦᴬˣ *0502/31432. 4 rooms with bath. Restaurant, pets permitted; no smoking. MC, V.*

$ ⛶ **Roundwood House.** Just off N7 in the Slieve Bloom Mountains, this
★ relaxed, classically beautiful 1730s house has a Palladian facade behind which you'll find a simple interior, with family antiques and Persian rugs. You can stay in one of the large rooms in the main house or in a smaller, cozy room in the original house, which dates from 1650 and is behind the herb garden. There are 18 acres of woodland, and hiking in the Slieve Blooms. Hosts Frank and Rosemarie Kennan often share your table at dinner (for residents only), which consists of a multicourse set menu of Continental cuisine. ⌂ *Mountrath, Co. Laois,* ☎ *0502/32120,* ᴦᴬˣ *0502/32711. 10 rooms with bath. Dining room; no room phones, no room TVs. AE, DC, MC, V.*

Tullamore

② *27 km (17 mi) northwest of Portarlington.*

Tullamore, the county seat of Offaly, is a big country town on the Grand Canal. The main reason to pass through is the **Charleville Forest Castle,** a castellated, Georgian–Gothic Revival manor house on about 30 acres of woodland walks and gardens. This magnificent building dates from 1812 and is a fine example of the work of architect Francis Johnston, who was responsible for many of Dublin's stately Georgian buildings. Look for the William Morris–designed dining room with its original wallpaper. Guided tours of the interior are available. ⌂ *1½ km (1 mi) outside Tullamore on N52 to Birr,* ☎ *0506/21279.* ⌨ *€5.* ⊙ *May, weekends 2–5; June–Sept., Wed.–Sun. 2–5; Oct.–Apr., groups of 4 or more by appointment.*

Outdoor Activities and Sports

BOATING

You can rent a river cruiser for a floating holiday from **Celtic Canal Cruisers Ltd.** (⊠ 24th Lock, ☎ 0506/21861).

GOLF

Esker Hills Golf & Country Club (☎ 0506/55999) is a challenging 18-hole, par-71 championship course with natural lakes and woodlands.

Tullamore Golf Club (⊠ Brookfield, ☎ 0506/21439) is an 18-hole, par-71 parkland course. It's a relatively straightforward course—not hugely challenging.

Kilbeggan

❸ *11 km (7 mi) north of Tullamore.*

Kilbeggan is known mainly for the **Locke's Distillery,** which was established in 1757 to produce a traditional Irish malt whiskey. It closed down in 1954 and was reopened in 1987 by Cooley Distillery, which now makes its whiskey in County Louth but brings it here to be matured in casks. The distillery has been restored as a museum of industrial archaeology illustrating the process of Irish pot-whiskey distillation and the social history of the workers' lives. ☎ *0506/32134,* WEB *www.lockesdistillerymuseum.com.* 🎫 *€4.20.* 🕙 *Apr.–Oct., daily 9–6; Nov.–Mar., daily 10–4.*

En Route **Belvedere House Gardens** occupies a beautiful spot: the northeast
ॐ shore of Lough Ennel. Access to this stately mid-18th-century house is through the Servants' Entrance—so you can see what life behind the scenes was like back then. In the gardens you'll find a Victorian glass house. The parkland beyond slopes down to the lake and provides a panoramic view of its islands. The estate contains a coffee shop, animal sanctuary, and children's play area. The Belvedere Tram (€1.30) tours the 160 acres of parkland and woodland trails. ⊠ *19 km (12 mi) north of Kilbeggan on N52,* ☎ *044/40861,* WEB *www.belvedere-house. ie.* 🎫 *€5.* 🕙 *Nov.–Mar., daily 10:30–4; Apr.–Aug., daily 10:30–7; Sept.–Oct., daily 10:30–6:30.*

Mullingar

❹ *24 km (15 mi) northeast of Kilbeggan.*

Irish farmers describe a good young cow as "beef to the ankle, like a Mullingar heifer." In this area of rich farmland, Mullingar is known as Ireland's beef capital. It's also County Westmeath's major town—a busy commercial and cattle-trading center on the Royal Canal, midway between two large, attractive lakes, Lough Owel and Lough Ennel. Buildings here date mostly from the 19th century.

Finely carved stonework decorates the front of the large, Renaissance-style Catholic **Cathedral of Christ the King.** Completed in 1939, the cathedral has a spacious interior with mosaics of St. Patrick and St. Anne by the Russian artist Boris Anrep. ⊠ *Mary St.,* ☎ *044/48391.* 🕙 *Daily 9–5:30.*

Mullingar Bronze and Pewter Centre offers free tours of its workshop, where the age-old craft of pewter making is still practiced. Sculptured bronze figures are also being made here—by Genesis Fine Art. You can purchase both pewter and bronze in the showroom. There's a coffee shop on the premises. ⊠ *Great Down, The Downs,* ☎ *044/44948.* 🎫 *Free.* 🕙 *Weekdays 9:30–5:30, Sat. 10–5:30.*

Dining and Lodging

$$ ✕🍴 **Temple.** The Fagan family will warmly welcome you into their superb Victorian farmhouse, surrounded by a 100 acres of parkland. The large rooms are furnished with modest antiques. This is a good place to stay if you have kids, as they can enjoy watching a working sheep farm while you indulge in a luscious relaxation program. The 24-hour inclusive rate includes spa treatments and the delicious, freshly prepared food from Bernadette Fagan's kitchen. Temple is along N6, almost equidistant from Mullingar, Tullamore, and Athlone. ⊠ *Horseleap, Moate, Co. Westmeath,* ☎ *0506/35118,* F̄Ā̄X̄ *0506/35008,* W̄Ē̄B̄ *www. templespa.ie/. 8 rooms with bath. Massage, sauna, spa, steam room, bicycles; no room phones, no room TVs, no smoking rooms. MC, V. Closed mid-Dec.–mid-Jan.*

$-$$ ✕🍴 **Crookedwood House.** This large rectory, more than 200 years old,
★ overlooks Lough Derravaragh. The nine spacious bedrooms are in a wing of the main house. The food here is a big draw: chef/owner Noel Kenny earned a reputation for his German-inspired take on modern Irish cuisine (he worked in the Black Forest, where he developed a love for game). In winter, get the Hunter's Plate—a selection of venison, pheasant, wild duck, and pigeon. The rack of lamb sells like crazy in springtime. Also irresistible is the trio of salmon, sole, and scallops with lobster sauce. Diehard foodies might want to try the unusual honey-roasted pork steak and salmon—wrapped in filo pastry, and baked with grapes. The house is 13 km (8 mi) north of Mullingar on R394 Castlepollard road. ⊠ *Mullingar, Co. Westmeath,* ☎ *044/72165,* F̄Ā̄X̄ *044/72166,* W̄Ē̄B̄ *www.crookedwoodhouse.com. 18 rooms with bath. Restaurant, cable TV. AE, DC, MC, V. Closed 2 wks in Nov., no dinner Mon.*

$$-$$$ 🍴 **Bloomfield House Hotel.** A rambling two-story former convent with a castellated roof on the shores of Lough Ennel has been converted into a comfortable hotel with an excellent fitness center. The style here is cheerful—modern furniture in warm shades of plaid. Rooms are spacious and all have peaceful country views. The Brinsley Restaurant has tall Georgian-style windows overlooking the lake, and serves local beef and seafood. The hotel is 3 km (2 mi) south of Mullingar on N52. ⊠ *Tullamore Rd., Mullingar, Co. Westmeath,* ☎ *044/40894,* F̄Ā̄X̄ *044/43767,* W̄Ē̄B̄ *www.bloomfieldhouse.com. 65 rooms with bath. Restaurant, bar, indoor pool, gym, hot tub, sauna, steam room, cable TV, meeting rooms. AE, DC, MC, V.*

Outdoor Activities and Sports

GOLF

Delvin Castle Golf Club (⊠ Delvin, ☎ 044/64315) is a 9-hole course. The **Heath Golf Club** (⊠ Portlaoise, ☎ 0502/46533) is a challenging 18-hole parkland course. **Mullingar Golf Club** (⊠ Belvedere, ☎ 044/48629) is an 18-hole parkland course.

HORSEBACK RIDING

Mullingar Equestrian Centre (⊠ Athlone Rd., ☎ 044/48331) has riding on the shores of Lough Derravaragh and lessons at all levels. The center also organizes residential riding holidays.

Castlepollard

⑤ *21 km (13 mi) north of Mullingar.*

Castlepollard is a pretty village of multihued, 18th- and 19th-century houses laid out around a large, triangular green. The biggest nearby attraction is **Tullynally Castle and Gardens,** the largest castle in Ireland still lived in as a family home. The total circumference of the building's masonry adds up to nearly ½ km (¼ mi)—an astonishing agglomeration of towers, turrets, and battlements that date from the first early fortified building, circa 1655, up through the mid-19th century, when additions in the Gothic Revival style went up one after another. Two wings designed by Sir Richard Morrison in 1840 that joined the main block to the stable court had dramatically different purposes: one was given over entirely to luxurious quarters for the Dowager Countess; the other housed 40 *indoor* servants. It was one of the first houses in the British Isles to have central heating.

Tullynally—the name, literally translated, means "Hill of the Swans"—has been the home of 10 generations of the literary Pakenham family and the seat of the earls of Longford. Among the living Pakenhams are the current earl of Longford, Frank Pakenham, the prison reformer and anti-pornography campaigner; wife Elizabeth and daughter Antonia Fraser, both historical biographers; and Antonia's brother Thomas, a historian. In addition to a fine collection of portraits and furniture, the house contains an immense kitchen furnished with many fascinating 19th-century domestic gadgets, including a marmalade cutter and an oversize contraption designed to take the buttermilk out of the freshly churned butter. The grounds also include a landscaped park and formal gardens. ⊠ *1½ km (1 mi) west of Castlepollard on the road to Granard (R395),* ☎ *044/61159.* ▣ *Castle and gardens €6.50; gardens only, €4.* ☉ *Gardens May–Aug., daily 2–6; castle rooms mid-June–July and mid-Sept.–end Sept., guided tours daily 2:30–6.*

Fore

❻ *5 km (3 mi) east of Castlepollard.*

Irish myths being what they are, the "seven wonders" of Fore are worth a fun walk to discover "the water that runs uphill" or "the stone raised by St. Fechin." The monk founded a monastery here, in the 7th century, and the village is now known not only for its legend, but for its medieval church and the remains (supposedly the largest in Ireland) of a Benedictine abbey. The remains of **Fore Abbey** dominate the simple village of Fore. **St. Fechin's Church,** dating from the 10th century, has a massive, cross-inscribed lintel stone. Nearby are the remains of a 13th-century Benedictine **abbey,** whose imposing square towers and loophole windows resemble a castle rather than an abbey.

THE NORTHERN MIDLANDS

This section starts in Longford and works its way north, leaving the ancient kingdom of Leinster for Ulster's two most southerly counties, Cavan and Monaghan. (Ulster's four other counties, which now constitute Northern Ireland, are covered in Chapter 9.) The land north of Cavan is characterized by small, round hills called drumlins and is known as "drumlin country."

Longford

❼ *37 km (24 mi) west of Castlepollard, 124 km (77 mi) northwest of Dublin.*

Longford, the seat of County Longford, is a typical little market-town community, and a draw for Jane Austen fans. If Jane Austen intrigues you, consider making a visit to **Carrigglas Manor.** The romantic Tudor-Gothic house, built in 1837 by Thomas Lefroy, offers a glimpse into gracious country living in 19th-century surroundings. Lefroy's descendants, who still live here, note that as a young man in England he was romantically involved with the novelist. Why they never married is a mystery, but it is believed that Austen based the character of Mr. Darcy in *Pride and Prejudice* on Mr. Lefroy. The house still has high-quality plasterwork and many of its original mid-19th-century furnishings. A magnificent stable yard, part of an earlier house on the site, was designed in 1790 by James Gandon, architect of Dublin's Custom House and Four Courts. Go into the stable yard and gardens to enter the small **costume museum,** which displays mostly 18th-century apparel found in the house. There's also an outdoor tea room in the plush period gardens. ✉ *5 km (3 mi) northeast of Longford on R194 to Granard,* ☎ *043/45165,* WEB *www.carrigglas.com.* ✉ *Stable yard, gallery, and shop free; gardens and museum €5.10.* ☉ *Stable yard, gardens, and museum daily 11–3; house, by appointment only, May–Sept., Mon.–Tues. and Fri.–Sat. 2–6.*

Granard

⑧ *18 km (11 mi) northeast of Longford.*

The market town and fishing center of Granard stands on high ground near the Longford-Cavan border. The **Motte of Granard** at the southwest end of town was once the site of a fortified Norman castle. In 1932, a statue of St. Patrick was erected here to mark the 15th centenary of his arrival in Ireland.

Outdoor Activities and Sports
County Longford Golf Club (✉ Glack, ☎ 043/46310) is an 18-hole parkland course.

Cavan

⑨ *30 km (19 mi) north of Granard, 114 km (71 mi) northwest of Dublin.*

A small, quiet, undistinguished town serving the local farming community, Cavan is also, increasingly, known for its crystal factory. There are two central streets: Main Street is like many others in similar Irish towns—it has pubs and shops; on Farnham Street you'll find Georgian houses, churches, and a courthouse. **Cavan Crystal** is an up-and-coming rival to Waterford in the cut-lead-crystal line; the company offers guided factory tours and access to its factory shop. This is a good opportunity to watch skilled craftspeople at work if you can't make it to Waterford. There is a major building attached to the factory, housing a visitor center, glass museum, restaurant, and coffee shop. ✉ *Dublin Rd.,* ☎ *049/433–1800,* WEB *www.cavancrystaldesign.com.* ✉ *Free.* ☉ *Guided tour weekdays at 9:30, 10:30, and 11:30.*

OFF THE
BEATEN PATH

KILLYKEEN FOREST PARK – This park is part of the beautiful, mazelike network of lakes called Lough Oughter. Within the park's 600 acres are a number of signposted walks and nature trails, stables offering horseback riding, and boats and bicycles for rent. Twenty-eight fully outfitted two- and three-bedroom cottages are available for weeklong, weekend, or midweek stays; everything is provided except towels. Rates vary according to season; call for details. ✉ *11 km (7 mi) north of Cavan,* ☎ *049/ 433–2541,* WEB *www.coillte.com.* ✉ *Free, parking €1.90.* ☉ *Feb.– Dec., daily 9–5.*

Dining and Lodging
$$$–$$$$ ✕🏠 **Slieve Russell Hotel and Country Club.** Take a convenient break,
★   on your Dublin–Sligo journey (the hotel is 26 km/16 mi west of Cavan) and stay at this palatial modern country hotel on 300 acres. The luxurious bedrooms have chunky, art deco–style furniture. The spa facilities are outstanding, but many guests come for the golfing and the excellent freshwater and trout fishing. You'll find white linens and wrought-iron chandeliers in the formal Conall Cearnach restaurant,

where the extensive menu includes traditionally prepared seafood dishes, such as black sole on the bone or salmon hollandaise. The Brackley Buttery restaurant is more informal. ✉ *Ballyconnell, Co. Cavan,* ☎ *049/952–6444,* ℻ *049/952–6474,* WEB *www.quinn-group.com. 141 rooms with bath, 10 suites. 2 restaurants, 2 bars, 9- and 18-hole golf courses, 4 tennis courts, 2 indoor pools, health club, sauna, fishing, horseback riding, Ping-Pong, squash, cable TV, in-room data ports, meeting rooms. AE, DC, MC, V.*

$$$ ✕🖬 **Cabra Castle.** This enormous gray-stone castle with its crenellated battlements and Gothic windows could have been designed in Hollywood. In fact, it was built in 1699 as the centerpiece of a 1,000-acre estate, most of which now belongs to the Dun a Ri National Park. For the full effect, ask for a "castle room," furnished with especially elaborate Victorian antiques. The Victorian-Gothic theme is carried through in the bar and the restaurant (fixed-price menu) with varying degrees of success. Don't miss the castle gallery, which has hand-painted ceilings and leaded-glass windows. ✉ *Kingscourt, Co. Cavan,* ☎ *042/966–7030,* ℻ *042/966–7039,* WEB *www.cabracastle.com. 29 rooms with bath. Restaurant, cable TV, 9-hole golf course, fishing, horseback riding, bar, meeting rooms. AE, DC, MC, V.*

$ ✕🖬 **MacNean House & Bistro.** Food lovers seeking the inspired cuisine of Neven Maguire make pilgrimages to this simple guest house and bistro tucked away on the Cavan-Fermanagh border. Seafood dishes include steamed turbot with buttered spinach in a basil-butter sauce, and game, including saddle of hare stuffed with chicken and pesto mousse on a parsnip purée and rosemary jus. Desserts are Neven's specialty—try the hazelnut nougat glacé. Given the remoteness of Blacklion, you might want to book a room when reserving a table. The 65-km (40-mi) detour makes sense if you are heading from Dublin to Sligo or Donegal. ✉ *Blacklion, Co. Cavan,* ☎ *072/53022. MC, V.*

Outdoor Activities and Sports

Visitors are welcome at the 18-hole **County Cavan Golf Club** (✉ Arnmore House, ☎ 049/433–1283). There are two golf courses at the **Slieve Russell Hotel** (✉ Ballyconnell, ☎ 049/952–6444), a 9-hole, par-3 parkland course and an 18-hole championship course.

Cootehill

🔟 *26 km (16 mi) northeast of Cavan.*

One of the most underestimated small towns in Ireland, Cootehill commands a lovely outpost on a wooded hillside in the heart of County Cavan. Its wide streets, with intriguing old shops, are always busy without being congested. Most who come here are anglers from Europe, the United Kingdom, and the rest of Ireland.

★ Only pedestrians are allowed through the gates of **Bellamont Forest.** After about a mile of woodlands, a trail leads to the exquisite, hilltop **Bellamont House,** designed in 1728 by Edward Lovett Pearce, architect of Dublin's Bank of Ireland. Small but perfectly proportioned, it has been virtually unaltered since it was built and is considered one of Ireland's finest Palladian-style houses. It's now a private home—but is occasionally opened to the public. If you're interested, inquire locally or at the Tourist Information Office (TIO) in Cavan. Walk up the main street of Cootehill to "the top of the town" (past the White Horse hotel), and you will see the entrance to the forest.

Dining and Lodging

$ ✕🖬 **Riverside House.** Both serious anglers and nonsporting types appreciate the genuine, old-fashioned Irish hospitality at Joe and Una

Smith's farm—and so will you. Their substantial Victorian house on 100 acres overlooks the River Annalee. All rooms have peaceful views and are individually decorated with modest antiques and family hand-me-downs. Bring your boots if you want to explore around this working dairy farm. The lodging is signposted 1 km (½ mi) outside town off R188. ✉ *Co. Cavan,* ☎ *049/555–2150,* 𝖥𝖠𝖷 *049/555–2150,* 𝖶𝖤𝖡 *www.irishfarmholidays.com/riverside-farmhouse.html. 6 rooms, 5 with bath. Dining room, boating, fishing; no room phones.* MC.

$ ✕▥ **The White Horse.** This typical market-town hotel serves as a lively gathering place for the community, and is particularly popular with visiting anglers. Some rooms in the rambling Victorian building are a bit small; all are plainly decorated, and the quieter ones are in the back. The restaurant, a softly lit room with mahogany furniture, is popular with town folk, who head here for generous portions and simply cooked dishes. ✉ *Market St., Co. Cavan,* ☎ *049/555–2124,* 𝖥𝖠𝖷 *049/ 555–2407. 30 rooms, 24 with bath. Restaurant, 2 bars.* MC, V.

Outdoor Activities and Sports

Rossmore Golf Club (✉ Rossmore Park, near Cootehill, ☎ 047/81316) is an 18-hole parkland course.

Monaghan

⓫ *24 km (15 mi) north of Cootehill.*

A former British garrison town, Monaghan is built around a central square known as the Diamond. The town's old **Market House,** elegantly constructed of limestone in 1792, is now the tourist office. The **County Museum** traces the history of Monaghan from earliest times to the present through archaeological finds, traditional crafts, artwork, and other historical artifacts. ✉ *Hill St., Co. Monaghan,* ☎ *047/82928.* ▥ *Free.* ☉ *June–Sept., Tues.–Sat. 11–5; Oct.–May, Tues.–Sat. 11–1 and 2–5.*

OFF THE BEATEN PATH   **ROSSMORE FOREST PARK –** Outside town (on R189 Newbliss road), you'll find fresh air in pleasant surroundings at this park with 691 acres of low hills, small lakes, and pleasant forest walks through rhododendron groves. Nature trails are signposted.

Dining and Lodging

$$$ ✕▥ **Nuremore Hotel and Country Club.** This Victorian country house, ★ now a luxury hotel, has excellent sporting facilities, including its own trout lake. Open fires blaze in the large lounge, which is furnished with plump armchairs and Victorian tables. The bedrooms are decorated with mahogany Victorian furniture. You'll happily discover, in the formal restaurant, a luxurious and rich French-Irish cuisine—Irish Angus beef, fresh foie gras, lobster, and classic desserts, including a pear and almond tart with fresh cream. Only 80 km (50 mi) from both Dublin and Belfast, Nuremore is a popular weekend retreat for city dwellers. ✉ *Carrickmacross, Co. Monaghan,* ☎ *042/966–1438,* 𝖥𝖠𝖷 *042/966– 1853,* 𝖶𝖤𝖡 *www.nuremore-hotel.ie. 65 rooms with bath, 5 suites. Restaurant, bar, 18-hole golf course, 2 tennis courts, indoor pool, health club, sauna, steam room, fishing, horseback riding, squash, cable TV, meeting rooms.* AE, DC, MC, V.

Castle Leslie

⓬ *11 km (7 mi) northeast of Monaghan.*

Castle Leslie, originally a medieval stronghold, has been the seat of the Leslie family since 1664. The castle sits on the shores of deep, beautiful **Glaslough** ("green lake"), whose waters are mirrorlike on sunny days. The present house was built around 1870 in a mix of Gothic and Italianate styles—Sir John Leslie, who built it, spent years in Italy and picked up many ideas there, including the colonnaded loggia, said to have been copied from Michelangelo's cloister at Santa Maria degli Angeli in Rome. The mildly eccentric Leslie family is known for its literary and artistic leanings—when Jonathan Swift stayed here, he wrote in the guest book: "Glaslough with rows of books upon its shelves/written by the Leslies about themselves." The family has many notable relations by marriage, including the Duke of Wellington and Sir Winston Churchill. Wellington's death mask is preserved at Castle Leslie, as is one of Churchill's baby dresses, along with an impressive collection of Italian works of art, including an Andrea della Robbia chimneypiece. The house is no longer open to the public, and the only way to visit it is to stay as a guest (see below).

Dining and Lodging

$$–$$$ ✕🏠 **Castle Leslie.** Samantha Leslie herself is usually on hand to host a memorable country-house experience. All of the furniture is original, some of it dating to 1660. The large bedrooms are decked out in Victorian splendor with a wealth of antiques; most beds are canopied, four-poster, or half-tester. Pre-dinner drinks are served by a roaring log fire. A four-course fixed-price dinner of Continental food is served by candlelight in the dining room, with waitresses in Victorian dress. Entrées may include braised partridge in season or salmon with sesame and ginger vinaigrette. ✉ *Glaslough, Co. Monaghan,* ☎ *047/88109,* FAX *047/88256,* WEB *www.castle-leslie.com. 14 rooms with bath. Dining room, boating, fishing; no room phones, no room TVs, no kids, no smoking. MC, V.*

Clones

⓭ *24 km (15 mi) southwest of Monaghan.*

Nowadays Clones, a small, agricultural market town 1 km (½ mi) from the Northern Ireland border, is one of two lace-making centers in County Monaghan (the other is Carrickmacross). It also has some ruins worth seeing. Clones (pronounced clo-*nez*) was the site, in early Christian times, of a monastery founded by St. Tighearnach, who died here in AD 458. An Augustinian abbey replaced the monastery in the 12th century, and its remains can still be seen near the 75-ft **round tower** on Abbey Street. A 10th-century Celtic **high cross,** with carved panels depicting scriptural scenes, stands in Clones's central diamond. In an attempt to bring in some income, local rectors' wives took up lace-making, which was introduced in the 19th century. Crochetwork and small raised dots are two hallmarks of Clones lace. A varied selection of Clones lace is on display around the town and can be purchased at the **Clones Lace Centre.** ✉ *Cara St.,* ☎ *047/52125.* ✉ *Free.* ◷ *Mon. and Wed.–Sat. 10–6.*

OFF THE BEATEN PATH

ANNAGHMAKERRIG – This small forest park with a lake is the site of An-naghmakerrig House, home of the Shakespearian stage director Sir Tyrone Guthrie until his death in 1971. He left it to the nation as a residential center for writers, artists, and musicians. It's not officially open to the public, but if you have a special interest in the arts or in its previous owner, do ask to be shown around. You can wander through and picnic on its grounds. ✉ *5 km (3 mi) southeast of Newbliss,* ☎ *047/54003,* WEB *www.tyrone.guthrie.ie.*

Lodging

$ ✦ **Hilton Park.** To find this stately Georgian mansion, look for large
★ black gates adorned with silver falcons 5 km (3 mi) outside Clones on
R183 Ballyhaise road. The 500-acre grounds include three lakes, a working sheep farm, and an organic market garden. Next door to Hilton
Park is Clones Golf Club. Johnny and Lucy Madden, the friendly
hosts, run their house with stylish informality. All rooms are individually decorated with antiques and have lovely views; some have four-
poster beds. Dinner of home-grown fruit and vegetables, combined with
local meat and fish, is available for guests only. ✉ *Clones, Co. Monaghan,* ☎ *047/56007,* FAX *047/56033,* WEB *www.hiltonpark.ie/. 6 rooms
with bath. Dining room, 9-hole golf course, lake, boating, fishing, croquet; no room phones, no room TVs, no kids under 8, no smoking.
MC, V. Closed Oct.–Mar.*

Outdoor Activities and Sports

Clones Golf Club (✉ Hilton Park, ☎ 047/56017) is a 9-hole course on
limestone that's dry year-round.

NORTH TIPPERARY AND THE WEST MIDLANDS

This section covers the area's western fringe, picking up in the town
of Boyle in County Roscommon. (If you do make it this far, be sure to
consult Chapter 9 for nearby locales.) It skirts the Lough Key, Lough
Ree, Lough Derg, and the River Shannon and, depending on how you
travel south, takes you through the hilly landscape of County Leitrim—
dappled with lakes and beloved of anglers for its fish-filled waters; it
is also almost uninhabited (though it has a liberal sprinkling of villages
and is the home of one of Ireland's leading writers, John McGahern).
Much of the land is bog. The towns are small and undistinguished, except Birr and Strokestown, both designed to complement the "big
houses" that share their names. The route then takes you southward,
to northern County Tipperary.

Boyle

⑭ *190 km (118 mi) northwest of Dublin.*

An old-fashioned town on the Boyle River midway between Lough Gara
and Lough Key, Boyle makes a good starting point for visits to the nearby
Curlew Mountains. A massive edifice in the center of town, **King
House** was built about 1730 by the local King family, who moved 50
years later to larger quarters at Rockingham in what is now Lough Key
Forest Park; that house burned down in 1957. The King family originally came from Staffordshire, England, and aggressively worked to
establish themselves as local nobility—Edward King, an ancestor of
the Kings who settled here, drowned in the Irish Sea in 1636; he was
the subject of Milton's poem "Lycidas." From 1788 to 1922 the house
was owned by the British Army and used as a barracks for the Connaught Rangers, known as the fiercest regiment of the British Army
(Wellington called them the "Devil's Own"). After extensive renovations, the house is now open to the public, with exhibits on the Connaught Rangers, the Kings of Connaught, and the history of the house.
A coffee shop, popular with locals, serves traditional Irish breakfasts
and hearty lunches, both with plenty of homemade baked goods on
the menu. ☎ 079/63242. 🎟 €3.80. ☉ *Apr.–mid-Oct., daily 10–6, weekends 10–6 (last tour at 5).*

The ruins of the **Cistercian abbey** reflect its long history. The church was founded in the late 12th century when the Romanesque style still prevailed, but as construction went on, the then-hot Gothic style made it to Ireland, evident in arches on the north side. A 16th- to 17th-century gatehouse, through which you enter the abbey, has a small exhibition. ⊠ *On N4,* ☎ *079/62604.* ☉ *Apr.–Oct., daily 9:30–6:30.*

OFF THE BEATEN PATH

LOUGH KEY FOREST PARK – Part of what was once the massive Rockingham Estate, this park is now a popular base for campers, backpackers, walkers, and anglers. It spans 840 acres on the shores of the lake, and contains a bog garden, deer enclosure, and cypress grove. Ruins from Rockingham days, including the remains of a stable block, church, icehouse, and temple, are also here. Boats can be hired on the lake, and there's also a restaurant. ⊠ *3 km (2 mi) northeast of Boyle off N4,* ☎ *079/62363.* ☜ *Parking €2.55.* ☉ *June–Sept.*

Lodging

$ ▦ **Royal Hotel.** The Royal has been at its town-center location for more than 250 years. Rooms vary in shape and size and are plainly but adequately furnished and well equipped. The chief reason to stay here, apart from good angling nearby, is to experience the slower pace of life of an old fashioned Irish small town. The restaurant overlooks a pretty stretch of river and serves both Chinese and Continental food. ⊠ *Bridge St., Co. Roscommon,* ☎ *079/62016,* FAX *079/62016. 16 rooms with bath. Restaurant, coffee shop, bar, in-room data ports, cable TV. AE, DC, MC, V.*

Outdoor Activities and Sports

Bikes can be rented from **Brendan Sheerin** (⊠ Main St., Boyle, ☎ 079/62010).

Strokestown

⑮ *28 km (17 mi) south of Boyle.*

Strokestown has the widest main street in Ireland—laid out to rival the Ringstrasse in Vienna—and the curious, Anglo-Irish Strokestown Park House. The town's main street leads to three Gothic arches that ★ mark the entrance to the grounds of **Strokestown Park House,** occupied by the Pakenham Mahon family from 1660 to 1979. The house once sat on 27,000 acres and was the second-largest estate in Roscommon, after the King family's Rockingham. To some degree, the complicated architectural history mirrors the histories of other Anglo-Irish houses. The oldest parts of the house date from 1696; Palladian wings were added in the 1730s to the original block; and the house was extended again in the early 19th century. Its contents are a rich trove specific to the site, as they were never liquidated in the auctions experienced by similar houses. The interior is full of curiosities, such as the gallery above the kitchen, which allowed the lady of the house to supervise domestic affairs from a safe distance. Menus were dropped from the balcony on Monday mornings with instructions to the cook for the week's meals. The 4-acre walled pleasure garden has the longest herbaceous border in Britain and Ireland. The **Irish Famine Museum,** in the stable yards, documents in detail the disastrous famine (1845–49) and the subsequent mass emigration. ⊠ *Co. Roscommon,* ☎ *078/33013,* WEB *www.strokestownpark.ie.* ☜ *House €5; house, museum, and garden €12.* ☉ *Apr.–Oct., daily 9:30–5:30; by appointment other times for groups.*

Roscommon

⑯ *43 km (27 mi) south of Boyle, 19 km (12 mi) south of Strokestown.*

Sheep- and cattle-raising are the main occupations here in the capital of County Roscommon. It's a pleasant little town with many solid stone buildings, including the Bank of Ireland, in the former courthouse, and the county jail. This large stone building in the town center has been transformed into a shopping mall—an unlikely venture that has to be seen to be believed. On the southern slopes of a hill in the lower part of town sit the remains of **Roscommon Abbey.** In the abbey's principal ruin, a church, are eight sculpted figures that represent gallowglasses (medieval Irish professional soldiers) and stand at the base of the choir. The ruins are freely accessible. To the north of Roscommon town are the weathered remains of **Roscommon Castle,** a large Norman stronghold first built in the 13th century.

Athlone

⑰ *29 km (18 mi) southeast of Roscommon, 127 km (79 mi) west of Dublin, 121 km (75 mi) east of Limerick.*

This is the main shopping hub for the surrounding area and an important road and rail junction. The introduction of a bypass has eased traffic congestion, and a local initiative highlighting the attractions of Athlone's "Left Bank" (behind the castle), where many of the buildings date from at least 200 years ago, have combined to make Athlone a more attractive destination.

Athlone Castle is the site most worth visiting in Athlone. Built in the 13th century, the castle lies beside the River Shannon, at the southern end of Lough Ree. After their defeat at the Battle of the Boyne in 1691, the Irish retreated to Athlone and made the river their first line of defense. The castle, a fine example of a Norman stronghold, houses a small museum of artifacts relating to Athlone's eventful past. Admission includes access to an interpretive center depicting the siege of Athlone in 1691, the flora and fauna of the Shannon, and the life of the tenor John McCormack (1884–1945), an Athlone native and perhaps the finest lyric tenor Ireland has ever produced. ⊠ *Town Bridge, Co. Westmeath,* ☎ *0902/92912.* 🎟 *€5.* ⊗ *May–Sept., daily 10–5; Oct.–Apr. by appointment.*

Dining and Lodging

$$–$$$ ✕ **Wineport Restaurant.** Once a wooden boathouse and headquarters
   ★   of the Lough Ree Yacht Club, this lakeside restaurant draws crowds for its imaginative cooking and the warm welcome you get when you arrive. The menu changes every eight weeks, but roast organic venison (from a nearby farm) served in a juniper marinade is a popular year-round main course. New Irish cuisine—smoked ham hocks with a sweet mustard-scallion (spring onion) béarnaise or braised lamb shank with a spicy butterbean cassoulet—is also featured. Bar food ($) is also available from 4 to 6 PM. Glasson is 5 km (3 mi) north of town on the shores of Lough Ree. ⊠ *Glasson, Co. Westmeath,* ☎ *0902/85466. AE, DC, MC, V. Closed Nov.–Easter and Thurs.–Sat.*

$$ ✕ **Le Château.** In Athlone's colorful Old Quarter, a former Presbyterian church now houses this romantic restaurant. The furniture may be ecclesiastical, but the decoration strikes a nautical note appropriate to the quayside location. The raised floors of the upstairs section are designed to resemble the deck of a galleon; the church theme is present in the original windows. Candlelit tables are set with large wine glasses and fine old bone china. Owner-chef Stephen Linehan's menu may include medallions of veal with smoked bacon, garlic, and herbs or roast

peppered monkfish with fresh herb sauce. For dessert try the lemon tart or, in summer, fresh strawberry vol-au-vents with homemade ice cream. ⊠ *St. Peter's Port, The Docks, Co. Westmeath,*☎ *0902/94517. AE, DC, MC, V. No lunch Mon.–Sat.*

$$$ ✕🍴 **Hodson Bay Hotel.** Head 4 km (2½ mi) out of town to this four-
★ story mansion—once an 18th-century family home—on the shores of Lough Ree. The hotel is adjacent to Athlone's golf course, and it has its own marina. All guest rooms are coordinated in deep pastel shades with art-deco style wooden furniture. L'Escale restaurant, a romantic, candlelit room, overlooks the lake. The menu offers imaginative Irish cooking with a French accent. To get to the hotel from Athlone, take the Athlone bypass–ring road to the N61 Roscommon road, from where the hotel is clearly signposted. ⊠ *Roscommon Rd., Athlone, Co. Westmeath,* ☎ *0902/80500,* FAX *0902/80520,* WEB *www.hodsonbayhotel. com. 133 rooms with bath, 7 suites. 2 restaurants, bar, 18-hole golf course, 2 tennis courts, indoor pool, health club, fishing, horseback riding, cable TV, meeting rooms. AE, DC, MC, V.*

Outdoor Activities and Sports

BICYCLING

Rent bikes from **M. R. Hardiman** (⊠ Irishtown, ☎ 0902/78669).

BOATING

The Viking is a riverboat that travels up the Shannon to nearby Lough Ree. ⊠ *The Strand,* ☎ *0902/79277.* 🎫 *€6.35.* ☉ *Sailings July–Sept., daily at 11, 2:30, and 4.*

A river cruiser for a floating holiday can be rented by the week from **Athlone Cruisers Ltd.** (⊠ Jolly Mariner Marina, ☎ 0902/72892).

GOLF

Athlone Golf Club (⊠ Hodson Bay, ☎ 0902/92073) is a lakeside 18-hole parkland course. **Glasson Golf & Country Club** (⊠ Glasson, ☎ 0902/ 85120) is an 18-hole parkland course bordered on three sides by Lough Ree and the River Shannon. **Mount Temple Golf Club** (⊠ Camp-field Lodge, Moate, ☎ 0902/81545) is an 18-hole parkland course 8 km (5 mi) east of Athlone.

Clonmacnoise

★ ⑱ *20 km (13 mi) south of Athlone, 93 km (58 mi) east of Galway.*

Many ancient sites dot the River Shannon, but Clonmacnoise is early Christian Ireland's foremost monastic settlement and, like Chartres, a royal site. The monastery was founded by St. Ciaran between 543 and 549 at a location that was not as remote as it now appears to be— near the intersection of two of what were then Ireland's most vital routes: the Shannon River, running north–south, and the Eiscir Riada, run-ning east–west. Like Glendalough, Celtic Ireland's other great monas-tic site, Clonmacnoise benefited from isolation; surrounded by bog, it is accessible only via one road or the Shannon.

The monastery was founded on an esker (natural gravel ridge) over-looking the Shannon and a marshy area known as the Callows, which today is protected habitat for the corncrake, a wading bird. Numer-ous buildings and ruins remain. The small **cathedral** dates as far back as the 10th century but has additions dating from the 15th century. It was the burial place of kings of Connaught and of Tara, and of Rory O'Conor, the last High King of Ireland, buried here in 1198. The two round towers include **O'Rourke's Tower,** which was struck by light-ning and subsequently rebuilt in the 12th century. There are **eight smaller churches.** The smallest is thought to be the burial place of St.

Ciaran; the only one not built within the monastery walls is the Nun's Church, about 1 km (½ mi) east. The **high crosses** have been moved into the visitor center to protect them from the elements (copies stand in their original places); the best preserved of these are the **Cross of the Scriptures,** also known as **Flann's Cross.** Some of the treasures and manuscripts originating from Clonmacnoise are now housed in Dublin; most are at the National Museum, while the 12th-century *Book of the Dun Cow* is at the Royal Irish Academy Library.

Clonmacnoise survived raids by feuding Irish tribes, Vikings, and Normans for almost 1,000 years, until 1552, when the English garrison from Athlone reduced it to ruin. Since then it has remained a prestigious burial place. Among the ancient stones are many other graves of local people dating from the 17th to the mid-20th century, when a new graveyard was consecrated on adjoining land. ⊠ *Near Shannonbridge,* ☎ *0905/74195,* WEB *www.heritageireland.ie.* 🎫 *€4.40.* ☉ *Mid-June–Sept., daily 9–7; Oct.–May, daily 10–6 or dusk.*

Bord na Mona Bog Rail Tour

★ ⑲ *10 km (6 mi) south of Clonmacnoise.*

As you pass through the small town of Shannonbridge, on either side of the road you'll notice vast stretches of chocolate-brown boglands and isolated industrial plants for processing this area's natural resource. Under the jurisdiction of Bord na Mona, the same government agency that makes commercial use of other boglands, the area is worth exploring. If you would like to have a close look at a bog, take a ride on the Bord na Mona Bog Rail Tour, which leaves from Uisce Dubh. A small, green-and-yellow diesel locomotive pulls one coach across the bog while the driver provides commentary on a landscape unchanged for millennia. There are more than 1,200 km (745 mi) of narrow-gauge bog railway, and the section on the tour, known as the Clonmacnoise and South Offaly Railway, is the only part accessible to the public. ⊠ *Uisce Dubh, near Shannonbridge,* ☎ *0905/74114,* WEB *www.bnm.ie.* 🎫 *€5.50.* ☉ *Tour Apr.–Oct., daily on the hr 10–5.*

Banagher

⑳ *21 km (13 mi) southeast of Shannonbridge.*

A small but lively village on the shores of the River Shannon, Banagher has a marina that makes the town a popular base for water-sports fans. Anthony Trollope, who came to Ireland as a post office surveyor in 1841, lived here while he wrote his first book, *The Macdermots of Ballycloran.* Charlotte Brontë spent her honeymoon here. **Flynn's** (⊠ Main St., ☎ 0509/51312), a light and spacious Victorian-style bar in the center of town, has a lunch menu of generously filled sandwiches, salad platters, a roast meat of the day, and chicken, fish, or burgers with chips.

If you happen to be in Banagher on a Thursday or a Sunday, consider taking a two-hour **Shannon cruise** on *The River Queen,* an enclosed launch that seats 54 passengers and has a full bar on board. ⊠ *Silver Line Cruisers Ltd., The Marina,* ☎ *0509/51112.* 🎫 *€8.* ☉ *Cruises June–mid-Sept., Thurs. at 3, Sun. at 2:30 and 4:30, weather permitting.*

Birr

㉑ *12 km (8 mi) southeast of Banagher, 130 km (80 mi) west of Dublin.*

This heritage town is a quiet, sleepy place with tree-lined malls and modest Georgian houses. The settlement's roots go back to the 6th century, but it was much later, in the mid-18th century, that Birr was given its modern-day appearance, as a Georgian building boom took hold.

★ All roads in Birr lead to the gates of **Birr Castle Demesne,** a Gothic Revival castle (built around an earlier 17th-century castle that was damaged by fire in 1823) that is still the home of the earls of Rosse. It's not open to the public, but you can visit the surrounding 150 acres of gardens. The present earl and countess of Rosse continue the family tradition of making botanical expeditions for specimens of rare trees, plants, and shrubs from all over the world. The formal gardens contain the tallest (32 ft) box hedges in the world and vine-sheltered hornbeam allees. In spring, check out the wonderful display of flowering magnolias, cherries, crab apples, and naturalized narcissi; in autumn, the maples, chestnuts, and weeping beeches blaze red and gold. The grounds are laid out around a lake and along the banks of two adjacent rivers; above one of these stands the castle. The grounds also contain **Ireland's Historic Science Centre,** an exhibition on astronomy, photography, botany, and engineering housed in the stable block. The giant (72-inch) reflecting telescope, built in 1845, remained the largest in the world for the next 75 years. Allow at least two hours to see everything. ⊠ *Rosse Row, Co. Offaly,* ☎ *0509/20336,* WEB *www.birrcastle. com.* ☑ €7. ⊙ *Nov.–Mar., daily 10–4; Apr.–Oct., daily 9–6.*

Dining and Lodging

$–$$ ✕ **The Thatch Bar.** It is worth venturing 2 km (1 mi) south of Birr, just off the N62 Roscrea road, into this thatched country pub and restaurant, which together serve a good selection of imaginative, freshly cooked Irish food. Inexpensive meals are available at the bar at lunchtime and early evening (until 7:30), while in the evening the restaurant offers a choice of a five-course dinner menu or à la carte. You may find local pigeon and rabbit terrines, sirloin steak with mushrooms in garlic, or roast loin of pork with a rhubarb compote on the changing menu. ⊠ *Crinkle, Co. Offaly,* ☎ *0509/206–822. DC, MC, V. Closed Mon. Oct.–Apr. and Sun.–Tues. May–Sept.*

$$$$ ✕▥ **Kinnitty Castle.** Venture over to the foot of the Slieve Bloom Mountains, 16 km (10 mi) east of Birr, to this exuberant, turreted, Gothic Revival edifice, rebuilt in 1927 of ashlar granite. Everything is on a large scale—bedrooms have large four-poster beds and intricately carved chairs, and heavy old beams are incorporated into the bathrooms in the old house. Accommodations in the new wing are smaller. The dining room has enormously tall windows and a dark wood floor. Typical main courses are panfried loin of lamb with its own sweetbreads or ragout of lobster from the tank, finished with sevruga caviar. ⊠ *Kinnitty, Birr, Co. Offaly,* ☎ *0509/37318,* FAX *0509/37284,* WEB *www.kinnittycastle. com. 37 rooms with bath. Restaurant, tennis court, fishing, horseback riding, Ping-Pong, bar, cable TV, meeting rooms. AE, DC, MC, V.*

$ ✕▥ **Dooly's.** You'll find this 250-year-old, black-and-white coaching inn tucked away in a corner of Birr's central square. A log fire burns in the front lobby, which is decorated in the Georgian style. Rooms have pastel colors, floral drapes and bedspreads, and plain, dark-pastel walls. The relaxed bar and coffee shop are busy all day; a more formal dining experience is in the Emmet Restaurant. The five-course table d'hôte dinner menu may include medallions of beef flambéed in whiskey and onions or fresh Corrib salmon steak poached in pink peppercorns and white wine. ⊠ *Emmet Sq., Co. Offaly,* ☎ *0509/20032,* FAX *0509/ 21332,* WEB *www.doolyshotel.com. 18 rooms with bath. Restaurant, coffee shop, fishing, horseback riding, bar, cable TV, meeting rooms. AE, DC, MC, V.*

$ ✕▥ **The Maltings.** In a picturesque riverside spot near Birr Castle, this beautiful cut-stone and brick malt house is a family-run accommodation. Spacious rooms have small windows, country pine furniture, and simple matching floral drapes and spreads. The cheerful, low-ceiling restaurant overlooks the river and offers good value in plain cooking. ⊠ *Castle St., Co. Offaly,* ☏ FAX *0509/21345. 13 rooms with bath. Restaurant. MC, V.*

Lough Derg

②② *16 km (10 mi) west of Birr on R489.*

Between Portland and Portumna the River Shannon widens into 32,000 acres of unpolluted water, known as Lough Derg, a popular center for water sports, including waterskiing, yachting, and motor cruising. Fishermen flock here as well for pike- and coarse-angling. There are excellent woodland walks around the shore of the Lough. (Be sure not to confuse this Lough Derg with the lake of the same name in County Donegal, a well-known pilgrimage site, covered in Chapter 8.) The well-signposted, scenic **Lough Derg Drive,** approximately 90 km (54 mi), encircles the lake, passing through a number of pretty waterside villages, from Portumna in the north to Killaloe in the south. **Terryglass,** on the eastern shore of Lough Derg and well signposted on R439 from Birr, is particularly popular with water-sports enthusiasts and anglers, as well as regular vacationers seeking an away-from-it-all destination; it is considered one of the prettiest villages in Ireland.

Lodging

$ ⊞ **Kylenoe.** The Moeran family's 200-year-old stone house stands on ℭ 150 acres of farm and woodland close to Lough Derg. Follow the lakeside road from Terryglass in the Ballinderry direction. The farm breeds racehorses and is a natural wildlife haven. Relax in front of the log fire, explore the countryside on foot or horseback, or enjoy water sports—all three are available nearby. Rooms are spacious, with modest antique furniture and family heirlooms. This is a nonsmoking, pet-friendly family home, where children are made welcome. Virginia Moeran's breakfasts have won awards, and she also cooks dinner (for guests only), which must be booked by 2:30 PM, from fresh local produce. ⊠ *Terryglass, Nenagh, Co. Tipperary,* ☏ *067/22015,* FAX *067/ 22275. 4 rooms, 2 with bath,. Dining room; no room phones, no smoking. MC, V.*

Outdoor Activities and Sports

Discerning golfers love the 18-hole parkland course at **Birr Golf Club** (⊠ The Glens, Birr, ☏ 0509/20082).

Roscrea

②③ *19 km (12 mi) south of Birr.*

The main Dublin–Limerick road (N7) passes through Roscrea, a charming town steeped in religious history, cutting right through a 7th-century monastery founded by St. Cronan. It also passes the west facade of a 12th-century Romanesque church that now forms an entrance gate to a modern Catholic church. Above the structure's round-headed doorway is a hood molding enclosing the figure of a bishop, probably St. Cronan.

With your back to St. Cronan's monastery, turn left and then right onto Castle Street to visit **Damer House,** a superb example of an early 18th-century town house on the grand scale. It was built in 1725 within the curtain walls of a Norman castle, at a time when homes were often constructed beside or attached to the strongholds they replaced. The house has a plain, symmetrical facade and a magnificent carved-pine staircase inside; on display are exhibits of local historical interest. The 13th-century stone castle is surrounded by a moat and consists of a gate tower, curtain walls, and two corner towers. The house also contains the **Roscrea Heritage Centre.** ⊠ *Castle St., Co. Tipperary,* ☏ *0505/21850,* WEB *www.heritageireland.ie.* ⊡ *€3.10.* ⊙ *May–Sept., daily 9:30–6; Oct.–Apr., weekends 10–5.*

Outdoor Activities and Sports

Roscrea Golf Club (⊠ Demyrale, ☏ 0509/21130) is an 18-hole parkland course with views of the Slieve Bloom Mountains.

Nenagh

❷ *35 km (21 mi) west of Roscrea, 35 km (21 mi) east of Limerick.*

Nenagh was originally a Norman settlement; it grew to a market town in the 19th century. Standing right in the center of Nenagh, the **Castle Keep** is all that remains of the original town. Once one of five round towers linked by a curtain wall, and measuring 53 ft across the base, it rises to 100 ft, with 19th-century castellations at the top. The gatehouse and governor's house of Nenagh's old county jail now form the **Nenagh Heritage Centre,** which has permanent displays of rural life before mechanization, as well as temporary painting and photography exhibits. ⊠ *Kickham St., Co. Tipperary,* ☏ *067/32633.* ⊡ *€2.55.* ⊙ *Easter–Oct., weekdays 9:30–5, Sun. 2:30–5; Nov.–Easter, weekdays 9:30–5.*

Dining and Lodging

$ ✕ **Country Choice.** Food lovers from all over Ireland seek out this well-stocked delicatessen or come to sample the home-cooked fare in the simple coffee shop at the back of the store. Owner Peter Ward is known as one of the best suppliers of Irish farmhouse cheese, and locally made cheese features on the menus of his wife, Mary. Specialties include a soup of broccoli and Cashel Blue (an Irish blue cheese), as well as slow-cooked meat dishes like lamb ragout or beef in Guinness casserole. Home-baked bread and pastries are made with local flour. ⊠ *25 Kenyon St., Co. Tipperary,* ☏ *067/32596. No credit cards.* ⊙ *Closed Sun. No dinner.*

$$–$$$ ✕⊡ **Waterman's Lodge.** Escape to this lovely lodge, an ideal rural retreat perched on a hilltop with bay windows overlooking the Shannon and distant County Clare. Open fires, piles of books, high ceilings, and timber floors create a relaxing country-house mood. Rooms have brass or cast-iron beds and modest antiques. The Courtyard Restaurant is renowned for its imaginative treatment of seasonal local produce. Try the roast rack of lamb with a parsley crust and lamb jus. ⊠ *Ballina, Killaloe, Co. Clare,* ☏ *061/376–333,* FAX *061/375–445,* WEB *www.watermanslodge.ie. 10 rooms with bath. Restaurant, fishing, horseback riding, in-room data ports. AE, DC, MC, V. Closed Christmas wk.*

$ ✕⊡ **Ashley Park House.** Experience informal country-house living in Margaret and P. J. Mounsey's 18th-century fishing lodge overlooking Lough Ourna. High ceilings, country views, and lots of antiques populate the large bedrooms. Formal gardens and 76 acres of beech woodland surround the house, and you can observe abundant wildlife—herons, swans, dabchicks, moorhens, and tufted ducks and mallards nesting in reed banks—from a rowboat. Dinners created from fresh local produce may include the trout you'll hopefully catch in the lake. ⊠ *Ardcroney, Co. Tipperary,* ☏ FAX *067/38223. 5 rooms, 2 with bath. Boating, fishing; no room phones, no room TVs. No credit cards.*

Outdoor Activities and Sports

BOATING

Shannon Sailing (✉ New Marina Complex, Dromineer, ☏ 067/24499) organizes cruises of scenic Lough Derg by water bus and also hires out cruisers and sailboards.

GOLF

Nenagh Golf Club (✉ Beechwood, ☏ 067/31476), 8 km (5 mi) outside of town, is a typical 18-hole, par-69 Midlands course: green, flat, and not too busy.

THE MIDLANDS A TO Z

To research prices, get advice from other travelers, and book travel arrangements, visit www.fodors.com.

AIRPORTS

Dublin Airport is the principal international airport that serves the Midlands; car-rental facilities are available here. Sligo Airport has daily flights from Dublin on Aer Lingus.

➤ AIRPORT INFORMATION: **Dublin Airport** (☏ 01/844–4900). **Sligo Airport** (☏ 071/68280).

BUS TRAVEL

Bus Éireann runs an express bus from Dublin to Mullingar in 1½ hours, with a round-trip fare of €12.05. Buses depart three times daily. A regular-speed bus, leaving twice daily, makes the trip in two hours. The express buses also make stops at Longford (2¼ hrs), Carrick-on-Shannon (3 hrs), Boyle (3¼ hrs), and Sligo (4¼ hrs). There is also a daily bus from Mullingar to Athlone and an express service connecting Galway, Athlone, Longford, Cavan, Clones, Monaghan, and Sligo. Details of all bus services are available from the Bus Éireann depots listed below.

➤ BUS INFORMATION: **Athlone Railway Station** (☏ 0902/72651). **Bus Éireann** (☏ 01/836–6111 in Dublin). **Cavan Bus Office** (☏ 049/433–1353). **Longford Railway Station** (☏ 043/45208). **Monaghan Bus Office** (☏ 047/82377). **Sligo Railway Station** (☏ 071/69888).

CAR RENTAL

➤ LOCAL AGENCIES: **Gerry Mullin** (✉ North Rd., Monaghan, ☏ 047/81396). **Hamill's Rent-a-Car** (✉ Dublin Rd., Mullingar, ☏ 044/44500). **O'Reilly & Sons/Euromobil** (✉ Dublin Rd., Longford, ☏ 043/46496).

CAR TRAVEL

Mullingar (the regional capital), Longford, and Boyle are on the main N4 route between Dublin and Sligo. It takes one hour to drive the 55 km (34 mi) from Dublin to Mullingar and two hours from Mullingar to Sligo (150 km [94 mi]). To get from Mullingar to the Southwest, you can take N52 to Nenagh, where it meets N7, and follow that into Limerick. R390 from Mullingar leads you west to Athlone, where it connects with N6 to Galway. The 120-km (75-mi) drive takes about 2½ hours.

ROAD CONDITIONS

Most of the winding roads in the Midlands are uncongested, although you may encounter an occasional animal or agricultural machine crossing the road. In Mullingar, the cattle-trading town, roads can become badly crowded, however. If you're driving in the north of Counties Cavan and Monaghan, be sure to avoid "unapproved" roads crossing the border into Northern Ireland. The approved routes into Northern Ireland connect the towns of Monaghan and Aughnacloy, Castlefinn and Castlederg, Swalinbar and Enniskillen, Clones and Newtownbutler, and Monaghan and Rosslea. Those driving a rented car should make sure it has been cleared for cross-border journeys.

EMERGENCIES

The general emergency number in the area is 999. For medical and ambulance service, contact Mullingar's General Hospital. Weir's Chemist is a pharmacy in Mullingar.

➤ CONTACTS: **Police, fire, ambulance** (☎ 999). **General Hospital** (☎ 044/40221). **Weir's Chemist** (✉ Market Sq., Mullingar, ☎ 044/48462).

LODGING

BED-AND-BREAKFASTS

For a small fee, the Irish Tourist Board, known as Bord Fáilte, will book accommodations anywhere in Ireland through a central reservations system. B&Bs can be booked at local visitor information offices when they are open; however, even these reservations will go through the central system.

➤ CONTACT INFORMATION: **Bord Fáilte** (☎ 800/223–6470 in the U.S. and Canada; 800/039–7000 in the U.K.; 02/9299–6177 in Australia; 09/379–8720 in New Zealand, WEB www.irelandvacations.com, www.ireland.travel.ie).

OUTDOOR ACTIVITIES AND SPORTS

FISHING

General information about fishing can be obtained in most hotels, B&Bs, and bars. Contact local TIOs or the Irish Tourist Board (see above) for more details on angling tournaments. For information on necessary licenses and permits, contact the Eastern Regional Fisheries Board.

➤ CONTACTS: **Eastern Regional Fisheries Board** (✉ Balnagowan Mobhi Boreen, Dublin 9, ☎ 01/837–9209).

TRAIN TRAVEL

A direct-rail service links Mullingar to Dublin (Connolly Station), with three trains every day making the 1½-hour journey. It costs €10.15 one-way and €17.80 round-trip. Contact Irish Rail for information. Trains from Mullingar, departing twice daily every weekday and Sunday, stop at Longford (35 mins), Carrick-on-Shannon (1 hr), Boyle (1¼ hrs), and Sligo (2 hrs).

➤ TRAIN INFORMATION: **Irish Rail** (☎ 01/836–6222).

VISITOR INFORMATION

Five Midlands Tourist Information Offices (TIOs) are open all year (not all have fax numbers): Carrick-on-Shannon, Cavan, Monaghan, Mullingar, and Portlaoise. The Mullingar TIO has information on Counties Westmeath, Offaly, Monaghan, Cavan, and Laois.

Another nine Midlands TIOs are open seasonally: Athlone (April–October); Birr (May–September); Boyle (April–September); Clonmacnoise (April–October); Longford (June–September); Nenagh (May–early September); Roscommon (mid-May–mid-September); Tipperary (May–October); and Tullamore (mid-June–mid-September). For off-season inquiries about Boyle and Roscommon, consult the Sligo TIO. For off-season inquiries about Tipperary, contact the Waterford City TIO.

➤ TOURIST INFORMATION: **Athlone** (✉ Church St., ☎ 0902/94630). **Birr** (✉ Rosse Row, ☎ 0509/20110). **Boyle** (✉ Bridge St., ☎ 079/62145). **Carrick-on-Shannon** (✉ The Marina, Co. Leitrim, ☎ 078/20170). **Cavan** (✉ Farnham St., Co. Cavan, ☎ 049/31942, WEB www.ireland-northwest.travel.ie). **Clonmacnoise** (✉ Clonmacnoise, ☎ 0905/74134). **Longford** (✉ Main St., ☎ 043/46566). **Monaghan** (✉ Market House, Co. Monaghan, ☎ 047/81122, WEB www.ireland-northwest. travel.ie). **Mullingar** (✉ Dublin Rd., Co. Westmeath, ☎ 044/48650, FAX 044/40413, WEB www.ecoast-midlands.travel.ie). **Nenagh** (✉ Connolly St., ☎ 067/31610). **Portlaoise** (✉ James Fintan Lawlor Ave., ☎ 0502/21178). **Roscommon** (✉ The Square, ☎ 0903/26342). **Sligo Town TIO** (✉ Temple and Charles Sts., Co. Donegal, ☎ 071/61201). **Tipperary** (✉ James St., ☎ 062/51457). **Tullamore** (✉ Bridge St., ☎ 0506/52617). **Waterford City TIO** (✉ 41 The Quay, Co. Waterford, ☎ 051/875823).

THE SOUTHEAST

COUNTIES WEXFORD, CARLOW, KILKENNY, TIPPERARY, AND WATERFORD

Known for having more sunshine than anywhere else in Ireland, the Southeast—especially Counties Wexford and Waterford—are leading holiday destinations for natives in the know. The landscape is diverse: white beaches and fishing villages with thatched cottages along the coast; Tipperary's verdant, picturesque Golden Vale; Kilkenny's cobbled Georgian streets and Tudor stone houses. There are plenty of intrinsically Irish things to offer here—most famously Waterford's hand-cut crystal. The region doesn't lack for culture, either: fans flock to Wexford for the world-renowned Opera Festival, which brings in top talent from around the world.

Updated by
Muriel and
Graham
Bolger

T HE IRISH LIKE TO PUT LABELS ON AREAS, and "Ireland's Sunny Southeast" is the tag they've taken to calling Counties Wexford, Carlow, Kilkenny, Tipperary, and Waterford. The moniker is by no means merely fanciful: the weather station on the coast at Rosslare reports that this region receives more hours of sunshine than anywhere else in the country. The Southeast, indeed, also has the driest weather in Ireland, with as little as 40 inches of rainfall per year—compared to an average of 80 inches on parts of the west coast. This is saying something in a country where seldom do more than three days pass without a shower of rain, which can vary from the finest light drizzle to a downpour that would convince Olympic swimmers they had never truly come to grips with the element of water. Little wonder the outdoor-loving Irish have made the Southeast's coast a popular vacation area. The whole area is Croesus-rich with natural beauty: not the rugged and wild wonders found to the north and west but an inland landscape of fertile river valleys and lush, undulating pastureland, with a coast that alternates between long, sandy beaches and rocky bays backed by low cliffs. Although the region is blessed with idyllic country sights and small and charming fishing villages, you'll find you never have to travel that far to find the bright lights—the cities of Kilkenny, Waterford, and Wexford.

The Southeast's coastal and inland areas both have a long, interesting history. The kings of Munster had their ceremonial center on the Rock of Cashel, which in the 7th century became an important monastic center and bishopric, and there were other thriving early Christian monasteries at Kilkenny, Ardmore, and Lismore. But the quiet life of early Christian Ireland was disrupted from the 9th century onward by a series of Viking invasions. The Vikings liked what they found here—a pleasant climate; rich, easily cultivated land; and a series of safe, sheltered harbors—so they stayed and founded the towns of Wexford and Waterford. (Waterford's name comes from the Norse Vadrefjord, Wexford's from Waesfjord.) Less than two centuries later, the same cities were conquered by Anglo-Norman barons and turned into walled strongholds. The Anglo-Normans and the Irish chieftains soon started to intermarry, but the process of integration came to a halt in 1366 with the Statutes of Kilkenny, based on English fears that if such intermingling continued they would lose whatever control over Ireland they had. The next great crisis was Oliver Cromwell's Irish campaign of 1650, which, in attempting to crush Catholic opposition to the English parliament, brought widespread woe.

Carlow Town, Kilkenny and Waterford cities, and Wexford Town together provide an introduction to Irish history. All have remnants of their successive waves of invaders—Celt, Viking, and Norman. The most beautiful is Kilkenny City, an important ecclesiastic and political center up to the 17th century and now a lively market town whose streets still contain many remains from medieval times, most notably St. Canice's Cathedral and a magnificent 12th-century castle that received in turn a sumptuous Victorian makeover. Wexford's narrow streets are built on one side of a wide estuary, and it has a delightful maritime atmosphere. Waterford, although less immediately attractive than Wexford, is also built on the confluence of two of the region's rivers, the Suir and the Barrow. It offers a rich selection of Viking and Norman remains, some attractive Georgian buildings, and also the world-renowned Waterford Glass Factory, open to visitors.

Beyond lies a tranquil countryside with more Edenic pleasures. The road between Rosslare and Ballyhack passes through quiet, atypical, flat countryside dotted with thatched cottages. Beyond Tramore, level, sandy beaches give way to rocky Helvick Head and the foothills of the Knockmealdown Mountains at Dungarvan. Among the inland riverside towns, Carrick-on-Suir and Clonmel each have a special, quiet charm. In the far southwest of County Waterford, near the Cork border, Ardmore presents early Christian remains on an exposed headland, while in the wooded splendor of the Blackwater Valley, the tiny cathedral town of Lismore has a hauntingly beautiful fairy-tale castle.

Anglers will scarcely believe the variety of fishing and scenery along the Rivers Barrow, Nore, and Suir and especially in the Blackwater Valley area. County Tipperary is the location of the Rock of Cashel, a vast, cathedral-topped rock rising above the plain and one of Ireland's most stunning historic sights. The ancient seat of the kings of Munster, Cashel is also, according to legend, where St. Patrick converted the High King of Ireland to Christianity.

Pleasures and Pastimes

Dining

The restaurants in this region are generally small and informal. Seafood—especially Wexford mussels, crab, and locally caught salmon—appears on most menus, along with local lamb, beef, and game in season. Food is usually prepared in a simple, country-house style, but be ready for some pleasant surprises, as there are a number of ambitious Irish chefs at work in the area in both restaurants and hotels.

CATEGORY	THE REPUBLIC*
$$$$	over €29
$$$	€22–€29
$$	€13–€21
$	under €13

Per person for a main course at dinner

Festivals and the Arts

There are two major arts festivals in the area: Kilkenny Arts Week, which is held in late August and features classical music, theater, and art exhibits; and the Wexford Opera Festival, during which each year in late October and early November three rare operas are given full-scale productions with internationally renowned casts.

Lodging

The coast is popular with Irish families during July and August, so if you are planning to come then, it is advisable to book in advance, especially at places right on the coast.

CATEGORY	THE REPUBLIC*
$$$$	over €230
$$$	€178–€230
$$	€127–€178
$	under €127

All prices are for two people in a double room, including VAT and a service charge (often applied in larger hotels).

Outdoor Activities and Sports

BICYCLING

The Southeast is a relatively unchallenging area for cyclists, with the only seriously hilly parts in the Knockmealdown and Comeragh mountains to the south of the region. If you enjoy bird life and sea vistas, try planning a coastal route—between Arklow and Wexford it's predominantly flat with expanses of sandy beaches. The Hook Peninsula between Wexford and Waterford has a network of small, quiet roads, many of them leading to tranquil fishing villages. If you travel from Waterford to Dungarvan via Dunmore East and Tramore you'll see a variety of scenery combining cliff-top rides with stretches of beachfront.

GOLF

Some of Ireland's best parkland courses can be found in the Southeast, and there is also a championship links course at Rosslare. Mount Juliet, near Kilkenny, has been publicly acclaimed by Nick Faldo as one of Europe's best. Expect to pay daily greens fees of about €110 on weekdays, €130 on weekends.

HIKING

Two hiking trails cross the region, and the scenery on both is interestingly varied with wooded hills, rich farmland, and several rivers. The South Leinster Way begins in the County Carlow town of Kildavin and makes its way southwest over Mt. Leinster and the River Barrow, terminating in Carrick-on-Suir. A second trail, the Munster Way, picks up where the first ends and leads through the Vee Gap in the Knockmealdown Mountains and on to Clogheen.

HORSEBACK RIDING

If you have any equestrian skills at all, you will probably want to ride some of the fine horses bred in this part of Ireland. Inland, the terrain is mainly arable farmland, while the long, sandy beaches of the coast are regularly used as gallops. Most establishments have riding for about €50 an hour—booking is generally essential—and many stables offer hunting packages to the more experienced rider; rates are available on request.

SPECTATOR SPORTS

The people of the Southeast are a sporting lot, and on any given day you're likely to find the stand at the races or the hurling matches overflowing. Greyhound racing is extremely popular here, and Irish dogs are considered to be among the best in the world. Races are held at night, and a bar and restaurant are usually within the stadium. Horse races are also held regularly in the area at small, informal meets. Ask locally about Gaelic football and hurling venues. These skillful and fast-moving games can often be watched for free or for the nominal entrance price at one of the seven Gaelic Athletic Association (GAA) stadia in the area.

Exploring the Southeast

The Southeast is geographically a large region, stretching from the town of Carlow near the border of County Wicklow in the north to Ardmore near the border of County Cork in the south. A car is essential for getting around here. Outside of the months of July and August, when the Irish head here for their own vacations, the region is relatively free of traffic, making it ideal for leisurely exploration. Wexford, Waterford, and Kilkenny all have compact town centers best explored on foot, and they also make good touring bases.

Numbers in the text correspond to numbers in the margin and on the Southeast, Kilkenny City, Wexford Town, and Waterford City maps.

Great Itineraries

IF YOU HAVE 3 DAYS

Three days is enough time for a greatest-hits itinerary of the Southeast, though it won't leave you much time for meandering along the back roads. Start in the south of the region by taking the main Cork–Wexford road (N25) and heading north to visit the popular seaside resort and cliff-top early Christian monuments at **Ardmore** ㊷. Stop in

the famed pubs of **Dungarvan** ⑩ for a *ceilí* (Irish dance); then head on
to **Lismore** ㊸, a small, pretty village on the Blackwater River, to tour
the gardens of the Duke of Devonshire's spectacular castle. From Lismore drive north along a scenic route known as the Vee Gap to visit
another great Irish castle at ⌖ **Cahir** ㊹. On the next day, spend the morning visiting that postcard icon, the awe-inspiring **Rock of Cashel** in the
market town of **Cashel** ㊻. Drive via Urlingford on the main N8 to
Kilkenny City ④–⑩, where you can wander the time-hallowed streets,
explore its medieval cathedral, and visit its Victorian baronial castle
seat. Head to **Leighlinbridge** ② for a salmon steak at the Lord Bagenal Inn, then down to the riverside village of ⌖ **Graiguenamanagh** ⑫
and its Duiske Abbey. On the following morning head for the coast
again and have a look at the still vibrant old Viking port of **Wexford
Town** ⑮–㉓. Drive on down this pretty stretch of coast through the waterside villages of **Kilmore Quay** ㉕ and **Ballyhack** ㉖ and cross by car
ferry to ⌖ **Waterford City** ㉗–㊲, another old Viking settlement on the
estuary of the Rivers Suir, Nore, and Barrow whose dazzling cut glass
has carried the city's name to the banquet halls of the world. Waterford is on the main Cork–Wexford road.

IF YOU HAVE 5 DAYS

Five days allows for a leisurely sampling of the different regions within
the Southeast, with time to get to know its three biggest towns,
Kilkenny, Wexford, and Waterford. Start in the north of the region,
approaching it through **Carlow Town** ①—a modern center but home
to several fascinating historical sights. Cross the River Barrow at **Leighlinbridge** ② and drive down to **Graiguenamanagh** ⑫, a hilly riverside
village with a nicely restored abbey. Continue on through **Thomastown**
⑪, a stone-built village on the River Nore with a ruined Cistercian
monastery that was in its time a masterpiece of Irish Romanesque style,
to ⌖ **Kilkenny City** ④–⑩, a lovely town with medieval coaching inns,
Tudor almshouses, Georgian streets, and alleyway "slips." Next morning you can explore the medieval city center with its castle and cathedral on foot. Drive on through Urlingford to the spectacular **Rock of
Cashel**, symbol of both Celtic and Christian Ireland, in the market town
of **Cashel** ㊻. If you continue to ⌖ **Cahir** ㊹ at the foot of the Galtee
Mountains, you can visit another kind of castle, this time of Norman
vintage, and inspect the town's numerous antiques shops.

Next day drive up through the scenic Vee Gap in the Knockmealdown
Mountains and detour to visit Mount Melleray Abbey, home to an order
of monks who welcome visitors. Continue to **Lismore** ㊸, which is the
Devonshire seat and has one of Ireland's prettiest castles. Then head
for the coast and the main road south, which leads to **Ardmore** ㊷, where
the early Christians built a cliff-top monastery and round tower. You
can spend the night either in ⌖ **Dungarvan** ⑩—a cheerful little fishing town—or inland among the sparsely populated Knockmealdown
Mountains in the ⌖ **Nire Valley** ㊶. Next day drive through the unspoiled
scenery of the pretty market town **Clonmel** ㊼, and follow the River Suir
through **Carrick-on-Suir** ㊽ to the port of **Waterford City** ㉗–㊲. Waterford, a center of local commerce, lures travelers with pedestrian malls
and historic exhibits, such as the large collection of Viking artifacts on
display over the tourist office near the Norman stronghold Reginald's
Tower. If you follow the River Nore north, you will reach **New Ross** ⑬,
a busy river port; signposts from here mark the way to the **John F.
Kennedy Arboretum**, which is near the cottage at Dunganstown where
the president's great-grandfather was born. Then you can pick up the
main road to **Wexford Town** ⑮–㉓, a Viking settlement on the estuary
of the River Slaney. Outside town, at Ferrycarrig, is the **Irish National**

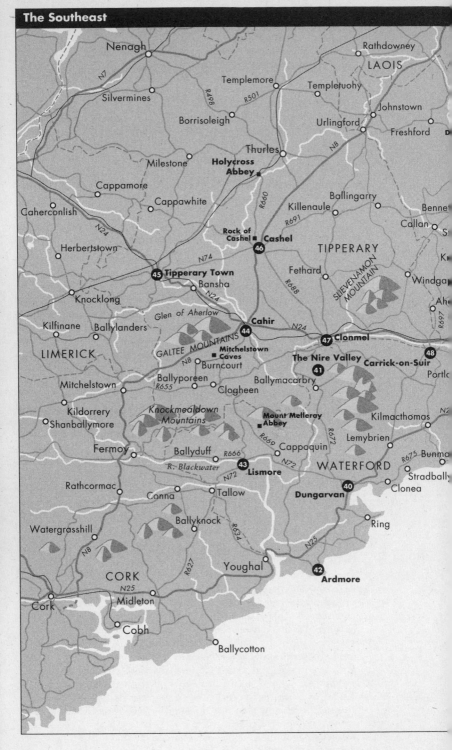

Castlecomer

Ballyragget

more Cave

R430

N9

R726

① **Carlow Town**

Tullow

WICKLOW

R725

Woodenbridge

Arklow

Shillelagh

Kildavin

R. Slaney

Old Leighlin ③ ②

N78

Leighlinbridge

Gorey

Muine Bheag (Bagenalstown)

Bunclody

Kilkenny City ④ — ⑩

N10

CARLOW

Ferns

Borris

N9

R703

Graiguenamanagh ⑫

R729

R. Barrow

Thomastown ⑪

R705

Inistioge

St. Mullins

Enniscorthy ⑭

R744

R741

R742

Jerpoint Abbey

ktopher

eyford

ridge

R700

R. Nore

Clonroche

N79

R. Slaney

N11

Blackwater

KILKENNY

N9

⑬ **New Ross**

N25

WEXFORD

Oilgate

Curracloe

Mullinavat

N25

Irish National Heritage Park

Wexford Town ⑮ — ㉓

John F. Kennedy Arboretum

Dunganstown

Wexford Harbour

St. George's Channel

R24

R733

Cheekpoint

Wellington Bridge

Piercetown

N25

R730

Rosslare ㉔

Rosslare Harbour

Waterford City ㉗ — ㊲

Passage East

⑯ **Ballyhack**

R733

Carrick

R736

Duncormick

Tomhaggard

TO WALES, FRANCE

Duncannonfort

Lady's Island

R675

R685

R684

㊳

Fethard-on-Sea

Forlorn Pt.

㉕ **Kilmore Quay**

㊴ **Tramore**

Dunmore East

Hook Peninsula

Churchtown

Saltee Islands

annestown

Waterford Harbour

Celtic Sea

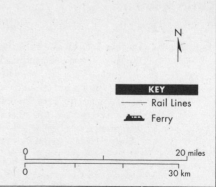

N

KEY

—— Rail Lines

⚓ Ferry

0   20 miles

0   30 km

Heritage Park. If wildlife interests you, don't miss **Curracloe Beach,** a 9-km (5½-mi) sandy beach to the north of the town.

On the next day, if you are heading north, take the N11 Dublin road via **Enniscorthy** ⑭, a historic town on the banks of the River Slaney dominated by its Norman castle. If you are heading south with time to spare, take the small coastal road through **Kilmore Quay** ㉕, past thatched cottages and narrow lanes, to **Ballyhack** ㉖, where you can take a car ferry across the harbor back to Waterford and the road south.

When to Tour the Southeast

The Southeast is a good area of Ireland to visit off-season. Restaurants and accommodations are open between November and March, months when many places in the more touristy western regions are closed. Beware Christmas Eve to at least mid-January, though, when many restaurateurs take their own holidays, and some lodgings and restaurants refurbish for the following season. Drier weather in the Southeast also makes it a good choice if you're visiting in the spring and autumn. Remember that in July and August, the Irish themselves descend on the coastal resorts, so if you plan to head for the beaches of the Southeast in the summer, be sure to reserve accommodations well in advance.

ON THE ROAD TO KILKENNY CITY AND WEXFORD TOWN

Many sights in this region—notably rich in historical and maritime attractions—make a visit here memorable. From Carlow Town's small county seat you travel through the farmlands of the Barrow Valley to Kilkenny City—which, from an architectural point of view, is among the most pleasing towns of inland Ireland. The historic city center is endowed with an old-world atmosphere, thanks to the country gentry who made their headquarters here in the 18th century, building themselves fine town houses in the Georgian style. From Thomastown, just outside Kilkenny, another cross-country drive follows the River Nore to New Ross, where it meets the River Barrow and proceeds to John F. Kennedy's ancestral home and the arboretum planted in his memory. You can then journey to the old Viking port of Wexford Town, now home to a celebrated opera festival, which presents rare works in the restored 18th-century Theatre Royal.

Carlow Town

❶ *83 km (52 mi) south of Dublin on N9.*

Carlow Town was established on the banks of the River Barrow by the Anglo-Normans in the 12th century. Its position on the border of the English Pale—the area around Dublin that was dominated by the English from Elizabethan times on—made it an important strategic center and hence the scene of many bloody battles and sieges. Today Carlow is a lively market town about an hour and a half from central Dublin. The presence of the large Institute of Technology here gives the town a lively buzz. It also has a thriving indigenous arts-and-crafts community.

The Roman Catholic **Cathedral of the Assumption** is one of Carlow Town's most prominent sights. Completed in 1883, the Gothic-style cathedral is notable for its stained-glass windows and a magnificently sculpted marble monument of its builder, Bishop James Doyle (1786–1834), a champion of Catholic emancipation; the monument was carved by the Irish sculptor John Hogan (1800–58). ⊠ *College St., Co. Carlow,* ☎ *0503/31227.* ⊠ *Free.* ◷ *Daily 7:30 AM–8 PM.*

The ruins of the 13th-century **Carlow Castle,** a strategically important fortification held by the English on the southeastern corner of the Pale, has imposing views of the River Barrow. This castle withstood a siege by Cromwell's troops in 1650, only to be destroyed accidentally in 1814 when a Dr. Philip Middleton attempted to renovate the castle for use as a mental asylum. While setting off explosives to reduce the thickness of the walls, he managed to demolish all but the west-side curtain wall and its two flanking towers.

One of the most poignant sites in Carlow town is the **Croppies Grave** (⊠ 98 St., off of Maryborough St.), a small memorial garden where the bodies of 640 United Irishmen—called "Croppies" because they cropped their hair to mark their allegiance to a free, independent Ireland—were buried in a mass grave, following the Battle of Carlow during the 1798 rebellion against English rule. Two trees planted by a widowed mother of three young men still stand; the third fell in a storm, and its two halves are inscribed with a testimonial to the courage of the Croppies.

The **County Museum** has a series of reconstructed interiors depicting life in Carlow during the early 20th century. Its more prestigious exhibit is the Jackson Collection, some 10,000 documents on the Grand Juries and Petty Juries—consisting of landlords who, from the early 18th through late 19th century, carried out the functions of local government in Ireland under English rule—put together in the 19th century by the quartermaster at Carlow Military Barracks. The museum is in the town hall, accessed from the old butter market. ⊠ *Centaur St., Co. Carlow,* ☎ *0503/40730.* ⊡ *€1.25.* ☉ *Tues.–Fri. 11–5, weekends 2–5.*

The famous **Browne's Hill Dolmen,** a stone monument dating from 2500 BC with a capstone weighing in at 100 tons, is one of the largest in Europe. The megalithic tomb, dating from the Stone Age (circa 3000–2000 BC), is thought to mark the burial place of a local king. The dolmen is reached via a pathway from the parking lot. ⊠ *Hacketstown Rd., 3 km (2 mi) outside Carlow Town (R726), Co. Carlow,* ⊡ *Free.*

Lodging

$ ⊡ **Barrowville Town House.** Sensitively restored by its owners, Randal and Marie Dempsey, this elegant Regency-style house is a blend of modern comfort and fine antique furnishings. Breakfast, which includes smoked salmon, an Irish-cheese board, and Irish breakfast fry, is served in a large conservatory overlooking the garden, under a grapevine that enjoys rude good health, despite the Irish weather. The hotel is minutes away from the center of Carlow Town. ⊠ *Kilkenny Rd., Co. Carlow,* ☎ *0503/43324,* FAX *0503/41953,* WEB *www.premier-guesthouses.ie. 7 rooms with bath. Croquet. AE, MC, V.*

Nightlife and the Arts

Started in 1979 as a weekend event to bring together arts, literature, and the Irish language, **Éigse,** Carlow's annual festival, takes over the town in June each year for 10 days. Drama, classical and pop music, and street entertainment vie with impressive visual arts exhibitions—including works by international artists—around the town. Irish music and dance play a prominent part in the celebrations. For information, contact the Éigse Festival Office (☎ 0503/40491).

Outdoor Activities and Sports

GOLF

Carlow Golf Club (⊠ Deerpark, Co. Carlow, ☎ 0503/31695), 3 km (2 mi) north of town on the Dublin road, is set in a wild deer park; the 18-hole course remains open all year.

Gaelic football and hurling are played at **Dr. Cullen Park GAA.**

Shopping

Carlow Craft Shop, in the same space as the TIO (⌧ Bridewell La., Co. Carlow), sells Ashling china made in Bagenalstown, as well as pottery, wood-turned pieces, and wrought-iron work, among other crafts.

Leighlinbridge

❷ *10 km (6 mi) south of Carlow Town on N9.*

In Leighlinbridge, the first bridge over the River Barrow was built in 1320 and is reputed to be one of the oldest functioning bridges in Europe. On the east bank of Leighlinbridge lie the ruins of **Black Castle,** built in 1181, one of the earliest Norman fortresses constructed in Ireland and the scene of countless battles and sieges over the centuries. A lone, ruined 400-year-old tower stands today.

Dining

$$$$ ✕ **Lord Bagenal Inn.** This famous old family pub beside the River Barrow is full of cozy nooks and warm, open fires. It even has a small playroom for children (open until 8 PM). Besides being a wine buff, owner James Kehoe is something of an art connoisseur, as the contemporary Irish art collection that lines the walls of the inn testifies. The restaurant's seasonal menu (prix fixe) is based on French country cooking and includes steak and poultry entrées, but it is renowned locally for its fresh seafood dishes. If you are interested in staying overnight in Leighlinbridge, inquire about the standard rooms ($). ⌧ *Main St., Co. Carlow,* ☎ *0503/21668,* WEB *www.lordbagenal.com. DC, V.*

Old Leighlin

❸ *5¼ km (3 mi) west of Leighlinbridge, signposted to the right off N9.*

The tiny village of Old Leighlin is the site of a monastery, founded in the 7th century by St. Laserian, that once accommodated 1,500 monks. It hosted the church synod in AD 630 at which the Celtic Church initially accepted the Roman date for the celebration of Easter (the date was officially accepted at the Synod of Whitby in AD 664); this decision marked the beginning of a move away from old Brehon Law and the deliberalization of the Church. The building was rebuilt in the 12th century as St. Laserian's Cathedral and enlarged in the 16th century. Guided tours are available. Carey's, the village pub, has been in the same family since 1542.

Kilkenny City

24 km (15 mi) southwest of Leighlinbridge on N10, 121 km (75 mi) southwest of Dublin.

One of Ireland's most alluring destinations, Kilkenny City demands to be explored by foot or bicycle, thanks to its easily circumnavigable town center. It's a lovely place that's filled with Georgian streets and Tudor stone houses—even the great town castle is a bewitching marriage of Gothic and Victorian styles. The city (population 20,000) is an impressively preserved, 900-year-old Norman citadel attractively situated on the River Nore, which forms the moat of its magnificently restored castle. In the 6th century, St. Canice (a.k.a. "the builder of churches") established a large monastic school here; the town's name reflects Canice's central role: Kil Cainneach means "Church of Canice." Kilkenny did not take on its medieval look for another 400 years, when the Anglo-Normans fortified the city with a castle, gates, and a brawny wall.

Kilkenny holds a special place in the history of Anglo-Irish relations. The infamous 1366 Statutes of Kilkenny, intended to strengthen English authority in Ireland by keeping the heirs of the Anglo-Norman invaders from becoming absorbed into the Irish way of life, was an attempt at apartheid. Intermarriage became a crime punishable by death. Irish cattle were barred from grazing on English land. Anglo-Norman settlers could lose their estates for speaking Irish, for giving their children Irish names, or for dressing in Irish clothes. The native Irish were forced to live outside town walls in shantytowns. Ironically, the process of Irish and Anglo-Norman assimilation was well under way when the statutes went into effect; perhaps if this intermingling had been allowed to evolve, Anglo-Irish relations in the 20th century might have been more harmonious.

By the early 17th century, the Irish Catholics had grown impatient with such repression; they tried to bring about reforms with the Confederation of Kilkenny, which governed Ireland from 1642 to 1648, with Kilkenny as the capital. Pope Innocent X sent money and arms. Cromwell responded in 1650 by overrunning the town and sacking the cathedral, which he then used to stable his horses.

The center city is small, and despite the large number of historic sights and picturesque streets—in particular, Butter Slip and High Street—it can easily be covered in less than three hours. One of the most pleasant cities south of Dublin (and one of the most popular in summer, when it can be swamped with visitors), Kilkenny City is a center for well-designed crafts, especially ceramics and sweaters; the premier venue is the Kilkenny Design Centre. The city is also home to more than 60 pubs, many of them on Parliament and High streets, which also support a lively music scene. Many of the town's pubs and shops have old-fashioned, highly individualized, brightly painted facades, created as part of the town's 1980s revival of this Victorian tradition.

4 In spite of Cromwell's defacements, **St. Canice's Cathedral** is still one of the finest cathedrals in Ireland, and it is the country's second-largest medieval church, after St. Patrick's Cathedral in Dublin. The bulk of the 13th-century structure (restored in 1866) was built in the early English style. Within the massive walls is an exuberant Gothic interior, given a somber grandeur by the extensive use of a locally quarried black marble. Many of the memorials and tombstone effigies represent distinguished descendants of the Normans, some depicted in full suits of armor. Look for a female effigy in the south aisle wearing the old Irish or Kinsale cloak; the 12th-century black marble font at the southwest end of the nave; and St. Ciaran's Chair in the north transept, also made of black marble, with 13th-century sculptures on the arms.

The biggest attraction on the grounds is the 102-ft **round tower,** which was built in 847 and is all that remains of the monastic development reputedly begun in the 6th century, around which the town arose. If you have the energy to climb the tower's 167 steps, the 360-degree view from the top is tremendous. Next door is **St. Canice's Library,** containing some 3,000 16th- and 17th-century volumes. ✉ *Dean St., Co. Kilkenny,* ☎ *056/64971.* ▣ *Cathedral €2 for prebooked groups, donations welcome from individuals; tower €2.* ☺ *Cathedral Easter–Oct., Mon.– Sat. 9–1 and 2–6, Sun. 2–6; Nov.–Easter, Mon.–Sat. 10–1 and 2–4, Sun. 2–4; tower access depends on weather.*

5 The 13th-century **Black Abbey** has been restored as a Dominican church by the order whose black capes gave the abbey its name. Nearby is the Black Freren Gate (14th century), the last remaining gateway to

186

Black
Abbey 5

Kilkenny
Castle 10

Kyteler's
Inn 7

Rothe
House 6

St. Canice's
Cathedral . . . 4

Tholsel
(Town Hall). . 8

Tourist
Information
Office
(Shee Alms
House). 9

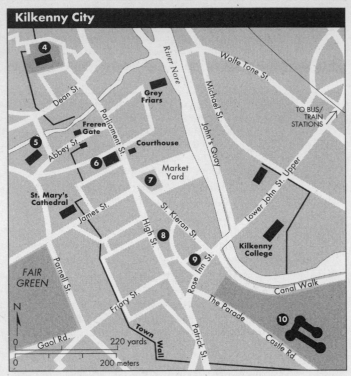

Kilkenny City

the medieval city. ⊠ *South of St. Canice's Cathedral.* ☎ *Free.* ⊙ *Daily 9–1 and 2–6.*

6 **Rothe House** is an example of a typical middle-class house of the Tudor period. Built by John Rothe between 1594 and 1610, it is owned by the **Kilkenny Archaeological Society** and houses a motley collection of Bronze Age artifacts, ogham stones, and period costumes. There's also a genealogical research facility that can help you trace your ancestors. ⊠ *Parliament St., Co. Kilkenny,* ☎ *056/22893.* ☎ *€2.50.* ⊙ *Apr.– Oct., Mon.–Sat. 10:30–5, Sun. 2–5; Nov.–Mar., Mon.–Sat. 1–5.*

7 **Kyteler's Inn** (⊠ *Kieran St.,* ☎ *056/21064*) the oldest in town, is notorious as the place where Dame Alice Kyteler, a member of a wealthy banking family and an alleged witch, was accused of poisoning her four husbands. The restaurant retains its medieval aura, thanks to its 14th-century stonework and exposed beams. Food and drink in this popular pub are as simple and plentiful as they would have been in Dame Alice's day—without her extra ingredients.

8 The **Tholsel,** or town hall, which was built in 1761 on Parliament Street, stands near the site of the medieval Market Cross.

9 The **Tourist Information Office (TIO)** is housed in the **Shee Alms House** (off the east side of High Street). The building was founded in 1582 by Sir Richard Shee as a hospital for the poor and served in that capacity until 1895. ⊠ *Rose Inn St., Co. Kilkenny,* ☎ *056/51500,* WEB *www.southeastireland.com.* ⊙ *Nov.–Mar., Mon.–Sat. 9–5; Apr. and Oct., Mon.–Sat. 9–6; May–June and Sept., Mon.–Sat. 9–6, Sun. 11–1 and 2–5; July–Aug., Mon.–Sat. 9–7, Sun. 11–1 and 2–5.*

★ **10** Founded in 1172 and dominating the south end of town, **Kilkenny Castle** served for more than 500 years, beginning in 1391, as the seat of the

Butler family—later designated earls and dukes of Ormonde—one of the more powerful clans in Irish history. In 1967 the sixth Marquess of Ormonde handed over the present building, which dates largely from 1820, to the state; since then it's been through a series of restorations. The graystone building, with two turreted wings and numerous chimneys poking over the battlements, stands amid rolling lawns beside the River Nore in 49 acres of landscaped parkland. Most impressive is the 150-ft-long, aptly named **Long Gallery,** a refined airy hall that contains a collection of family portraits, frayed tapestries, and a skylit, decorated ceiling of carved oak beams adjoined with Celtic lacework and adorned with brilliantly painted animal heads. The **Butler Gallery** houses a collection of modern art and frequently changing exhibitions. ⊠ *The Parade, Co. Kilkenny,* ☎ *056/21450,* WEB *www.heritageireland.ie.* ⊠ *Castle tour €4.40, grounds and Butler Gallery free.* ☉ *Apr.–May, daily 10:30–5; June–Sept., daily 10–7; Oct.–Mar., Mon.–Sat. 10:30–12:45 and 2–5, Sun. 11–12:45 and 2–5.*

Dining and Lodging

$$ ✕ **Café Sol.** Everything at this small, cheerful spot is homemade, except the pasta and baguettes. All dishes, ranging from steak to pasta to fish of the day, are cooked with attention to detail. The roasted pepper-and-parsnip soup is an excellent starter, followed by roast organic goose with potato-and-apple stuffing, and date-and-orange cake. Oilcloths cover the tables during the day; dinner settings appear in the evenings. ⊠ *William St., Co. Kilkenny,* ☎ *056/64987. MC, V. Closed Sun.*

$$ ✕ **Ristorante Rinuccini.** Kilkenny City's premier Irish-Italian restaurant occupies the basement of a Georgian town house opposite Kilkenny Castle. Owner-chef Antonio Cavaliere is intensely involved in preparing the luscious pasta dishes—tortelloni stuffed with ricotta cheese and spinach, served in a creamy Gorgonzola cheese sauce—as well as specialties of the house, such as organic Irish veal, and fresh seafood from Kilmore Quay. A splendid all-Italian wine list complements the menu, and there's a host of delicious homemade desserts. ⊠ *1 The Parade, Co. Kilkenny,* ☎ *056/61575,* WEB *www.rinuccini.com. Reservations essential. AE, DC, MC, V.*

$$ ✕🏠 **Langton's.** Imagine a country house hotel with a main building, two penthouses, tranquil gardens, and one of Ireland's most famous "eating pubs." It's a family-run establishment—a landmark since the 1940s—and a labyrinth of interconnected bars and restaurants. Most of the seating areas, with open fires, have different personalities—from the leather-upholstered gentlemen's club in the Horseshoe Bar to an attempt at art deco in the spacious dining room. Entrées include roast rack of lamb on eggplant and *capsicum frites* (fried peppers), traditional Irish stew, and a selection of steaks. ⊠ *69 John St., Co. Kilkenny,* ☎ *056/65133,* FAX *056/63693. 24 rooms with bath, 2 suites. AE, DC, MC, V.*

$$–$$$ 🏠 **Butler House.** This elegant Georgian house, with its magnificent plas-
★ tered ceilings and marble fireplaces, is an integral part of the Kilkenny Castle complex and once belonged to the Earls of Ormonde. All of the rooms are beautifully decorated; ask for one with a bay window overlooking the secluded gardens and Kilkenny Castle. ⊠ *16 Patrick St., Co. Kilkenny,* ☎ *056/65707,* FAX *056/65626,* WEB *www.butler.ie. 12 rooms with bath, 1 suite. Restaurant. AE, DC, MC, V.*

Nightlife and the Arts

The **Cat Laughs** is an early June festival with an international roster of stand-up comedians. **Kilkenny Arts Week** (☎ 056/63663) runs for nine days around the third week of August; classical music, film, theater, literary events, and visual-arts exhibits take place throughout Kilkenny.

Outdoor Activities and Sports

BICYCLING

Bikes for exploring the quiet countryside around Kilkenny can be rented through **J. J. Wall** (⊠ 88 Maudlin St., Co. Kilkenny, ☎ 056/21236).

GOLF

Kilkenny Golf Club (⊠ Glendine, Co. Kilkenny, ☎ 056/65400), 2 km (1 mi) northeast of town, is an 18-hole, par-71, mainly flat course.

SPECTATOR SPORTS

The 1366 Statutes of Kilkenny expressly forbade the ancient Irish game of hurling; today Kilkenny is considered one of the great hurling counties. Gaelic football and hurling matches are held at **Kilkenny GAA Grounds** (⊠ Nowlan Park, Co. Kilkenny). At **Kilkenny Greyhound Racetrack** (⊠ St. James's Park, Freshford Rd., Co. Kilkenny, ☎ 056/21214), evening meets are held each Wednesday and Friday where betting is the main attraction. **Gowran Park** (☎ 056/26126) holds horse races regularly.

Shopping

Kilkenny is a byword for attractive, original crafts that combine traditional arts with modern elements of design. You can see glass being blown at the **Jerpoint Glass Studio** (⊠ Stoneyford, Co. Kilkenny, ☎ 056/24350), where the glass is heavy, modern, uncut, and hand-finished. Their factory shop is a good place to pick up a bargain. The town's leading outlet, the **Kilkenny Design Centre** (⊠ Kilkenny Castle, Co. Kilkenny, ☎ 056/22118), in the old stable yard opposite the castle, sells ceramics, jewelry, sweaters, and handwoven textiles. **Murphy's Jewellers** (⊠ 85 High St., Co. Kilkenny, ☎ 056/21127) specializes in heraldic jewelry. At **Nicholas Mosse Pottery** (⊠ Bennettsbridge, Co. Kilkenny, ☎ 056/27505) you can buy attractive hand-crafted and decorated pottery—and see it made. **Rudolf Heltzel** (⊠ 10 Patrick St., Co. Kilkenny, ☎ 056/21497) is known for its striking, modern designs of gold and silver jewelry. **Stoneware Jackson Pottery** (⊠ Bennettsbridge, Co. Kilkenny, ☎ 056/27175) makes distinctive, hand-thrown tableware and lamps. The **Sweater Shop** (⊠ High St., Co. Kilkenny, ☎ 056/63405) carries a range of great sweaters.

Thomastown

⓫ *14½ km (9 mi) south of Kilkenny on R700 and N9.*

Thomastown is a pretty, stone-built village on the River Nore. **Jerpoint Abbey,** near Thomastown, is one of the most notable Cistercian ruins in Ireland, dating from about 1160. The church, tombs, and the restored cloisters—decorated with affecting human figures and fantastical mythical creatures—are a must for lovers of the Irish Romanesque. Guides are available from mid-June to mid-September. The last admission is 45 minutes before closing. ⊠ *2 km (1 mi) south of Thomastown, Co. Kilkenny,* ☎ *056/24623.* ⌑ *€2.50.* ☉ *Mar.–May and Oct.–mid-Nov., daily 10–5; June–Sept., daily 9:30–6:30.*

Dining and Lodging

$$$$ ✕▥ **Mount Juliet.** Within a walled 1,500-acre estate stands this imposing
★ three-story Georgian mansion. Bedrooms are large and individually decorated, with super-king-size beds, and original fireplaces. Sixteen rooms are available in Hunters Yard; 11 two-bedroom modern lodges are also available. Major activities here include horseback riding on the extensive trails within the estate and golfing on the Jack Nicklaus–designed course. The Lady Helen McAlmont Restaurant, its tables adorned with crystal, silverware, and fine linen, serves haute cuisine with con-

temporary Irish touches. ⊠ *Co. Kilkenny,* ☎ *056/73000,* FAX *056/ 73009,* WEB *www.mountjuliet.com. 70 rooms with bath. 2 restaurants, 18-hole golf course, tennis court, indoor pool, sauna, spa, fishing, archery, croquet, horseback riding, 3 bars. AE, DC, MC, V.*

$ ✕🛏 **Berryhill.** You'll find this warm, comfortable family home on a
★ working sheep farm. The charming, creeper-clad 1789 house is perched high on a ridge overlooking the River Nore and the picturesque village of Inistioge (southeast of Thomastown). You can enjoy the bright, airy drawing room, with its baby grand piano and a drinks trolley with an "honesty book." Rooms are decorated in animal themes of an elephant, a pig, and a frog; the last has a veranda. Breakfast, served at the dining-room table in front of a big open fire, often includes fresh trout. Prebooking for dinner, country-house style, is essential. ⊠ *Inistioge, Co. Kilkenny,* ☎ FAX *056/58434,* WEB *www.berryhillhouse.com. 3 suites. Fishing, croquet. MC, V. Closed Nov.–Apr.*

Outdoor Activities and Sports

GOLF

Visitors are welcome at **Mount Juliet Golf Course** (⊠ Mount Juliet Estate, Co. Kilkenny, ☎ 056/24455), the championship parkland course 19 km (11 mi) from Kilkenny Town. The course was designed by Jack Nicklaus and includes practice greens, a driving range, and a David Leadbetter golf academy.

HORSEBACK RIDING

The excellent facilities at **Mount Juliet** (⊠ Mount Juliet Estate, Co. Kilkenny, ☎ 056/73000) are open to nonresidents.

Graiguenamanagh

⑫ *15 km (9 mi) northeast of Thomastown on R703.*

The village of Graiguenamanagh (pronounced *gray*-gun-a-manna) sits on the banks of the River Barrow at the foot of Brandon Hill. This is good walking country; ask for directions to the summit of **Brandon Hill** (1,694 ft), a 7-km (4½-mi) hike. In the 13th century the early English-style church of **Duiske Abbey** was the largest Cistercian church in Ireland. The choir, the transept, and a section of the nave of the original abbey church are now part of a Catholic church. Purists will be disappointed by the modernization, carried out between 1974 and 1980, although medieval building techniques were used.

Dining and Lodging

$ ✕🛏 **Waterside.** All the rooms and the restaurant in this beautifully re-
★ stored 19th-century stone corn mill on the River Barrow have views of the water. The restaurant, which occupies the ground floor of the old mill building, has exposed pitch-pine beams and decorated windows; it serves Continental cuisine and has a good wine list. Located 27 km (17 mi) southeast of Kilkenny, Waterside is popular with hikers and those who value the nearby riding and golf. ⊠ *The Quay, Co. Kilkenny,* ☎ *0503/24246,* FAX *0503/24733,* WEB *www.watersideguesthouse.com. 10 rooms with bath. Restaurant, fishing. MC, V.*

New Ross

⑬ *17 km (11 mi) south of Graiguenamanagh on R705.*

New Ross is a busy inland port on the banks of the River Barrow. Even though it is one of the oldest towns in County Wexford, settled in the 13th century on an ancient monastic site, only the most dedicated history buffs will be tempted to stop and explore the steep, narrow streets above its unattractive docks. The major attraction in New Ross is a cruise up the River Barrow on the **Galley Cruising Restaurant** (☎ 051/421–723). You can take in the peaceful farmlands along the riverbank while sampling lunch, afternoon tea, or dinner. The emphasis is on fresh local produce and seafood. The restaurant is open Easter–October only.

The **John F. Kennedy Arboretum** is clearly signposted from New Ross on R733, which follows the banks of the Barrow southward for about 5 km (3 mi). The cottage where the president's great-grandfather was born is in Dunganstown; Kennedy relatives still live in the house. About 2 km (1 mi) down the road at Slieve Coillte you'll see the entrance to the arboretum, which has more than 600 acres of forest, nature trails, and gardens, and an ornamental lake. The grounds contain some 4,500 species of trees and shrubs, and serve as a resource center for botanists and foresters. Go to the top of the park to get fine panoramic views. ⊠ *Dunganstown, Co. Wexford,* ☎ *051/388–171.* 🎫 *€2.55.* ⊙ *Daily 10–dusk.*

Ballylane Farm, a 200-acre working farm, supplies maps and information sheets to guide you along a nature walk, where you can observe local wildlife, farm animals, and crops. A coffee shop–restaurant serves light meals when the nature walk is open to visitors. ⊠ *Signposted about 1 km (½ mi) past the turn to the Kennedy Arboretum (from Graiguenamanagh) on N25 New Ross–Wexford Rd., Co. Wexford,* ☎ *051/425–666.* 🎫 *€4.70.* ⊙ *May–Oct., daily 10–6; or by appointment.*

Enniscorthy

⑭ *32 km (20 mi) northeast of New Ross on N79.*

Enniscorthy, a thriving market town with a rich history, is on the main road between Dublin and Wexford, to the south of the popular resort of Gorey. Built on the steeply sloping banks of the River Slaney, the town is dominated by **Enniscorthy Castle,** built in the first quarter of the 13th century by the Prendergast family. The imposing Norman castle was the site of fierce battles against Oliver Cromwell in the 17th century and during the Uprising of 1798. Its square-towered keep now houses the **County Wexford Museum,** which contains thousands of historic items, including military memorabilia from the 1798 and 1916 uprisings. ⊠ *Castle Hill, Co. Wexford,* ☎ *054/35926.* 🎫 *€4.* ⊙ *May–Sept., Mon.–Sat. 10–6, Sun. 2–5:30.*

The **National 1798 Center** tells the tale of the United Irishmen and the ill-fated 1798 rebellion. ⊠ *Arnold's Cross, Co. Wexford,* ☎ *054/37596.* 🎫 *€6.* ⊙ *Mid-Mar.–Dec., Mon.–Sat. 9:30–5, Sun. 11–5.*

St. Aidan's Cathedral stands on a commanding site overlooking the Slaney. This Gothic Revival structure was built in the mid-19th century under the direction of Augustus Welby Pugin, the architect of the Houses of Parliament in London. ⊠ *Cathedral St., Co. Wexford* 🎫 *Free.* ⊙ *Daily 10–6.*

Outdoor Activities and Sports

GREYHOUND RACING

The **Showgrounds** (⊠ Co. Wexford, ☎ 054/33172) have greyhound racing on Monday and Thursday at 8 PM, with bar and catering facilities available.

Shopping

Carley's Bridge Pottery (⊠ Carley's Bridge, Co. Wexford, ☎ 054/33512), established in 1654, specializes in large terra-cotta pots. **Kiltrea Bridge Pottery** (⊠ Kiltrea Bridge, Caime, Co. Wexford, ☎ 054/35107) stocks garden pots, plant pots, and country kitchen crocks.

Wexford Town

24 km (15 mi) south of Enniscorthy on N11, 142 km (88 mi) south of Dublin.

From its appearance today, you would barely realize that Wexford is an ancient place—in fact, it was defined on maps by the Greek cartographer Ptolemy as long ago as the 2nd century AD. Its Irish name is Loch Garman, but the Vikings called it Waesfjord—the harbor of the mud flats—which became Wexford in English. Wexford became an English garrison town after it was taken by Oliver Cromwell in 1649. (The Anglo-Norman conquest of Ireland began in County Wexford in 1169, so the British presence has deep roots, and Wexford has been an English-speaking county for centuries.)

The River Slaney empties into the sea at Wexford Town. The harbor has silted up since the days when the Viking longboats docked here; nowadays only a few small trawlers fish from here. Wexford Town's compact center is set on the south bank of the Slaney, with its main street—the major shopping street of the town, with a pleasant mix of old-fashioned bakeries, butcher shops, stylish boutiques, and a share of Wexford's many pubs—running parallel to the quays on the riverfront. It can be explored on foot in an hour or two. Allow at least half a day in the area if you also intend to visit the Heritage Park at nearby Ferrycarrig, and a full day if you want to take in Johnstown Castle Gardens and its agricultural museum, or walk in the nature reserve at nearby Curracloe Beach. The town is at its best in late October and early November, when the Wexford Opera Festival creates a carnival atmosphere that permeates the town.

⑮ The **TIO** (✉ Crescent Quay, ☎ 053/23111) is a good place to start exploring Wexford Town on foot and to find out about guided walking tours organized by local historians.

⑯ Standing in the center of Crescent Quay, a large bronze **statue of Commodore John Barry** (1745–1803) commemorates the man who came to be known as the "Father of the American Navy." Born in 1745 in nearby Ballysampson, Barry settled in Philadelphia at age 15, became a brilliant naval fighter during the War of Independence (thus avenging his Irish ancestors), and trained many young naval officers who went on to achieve fame for themselves.

Rising above the town's rooftops are the graceful spires of two elegant examples of 19th-century Gothic architecture. These **twin churches** have identical exteriors, their foundation stones were laid on the same day, and their spires both reach a height of 230 ft. The **Church of the Immaculate Conception** is on Rowe Street. The **Church of the Assumption** is on Bride Street. The **Franciscan Church** (✉ School St.) has a ceiling worth noting for its fine, locally crafted stuccowork.

⑰
⑱
⑲

⑳ The **Wexford Bull Ring** (✉ Quay St., back toward the quays) was once the scene of bullbaiting, a medieval sport that was popular among the Norman nobility. Also in this arena, in 1649, Cromwell's soldiers massacred 300 panic-stricken townspeople who had gathered here to pray as the army stormed their town.

㉑ The red sandstone **Westgate Tower** (✉ Westgate) was the largest of five fortified gateways in the Norman and Viking town walls, and it is the only one remaining. The early 13th-century tower has been sensitively restored. Keep an eye out as you wander this part of town for other preserved segments of the old town walls.

㉒ The ruins of the 12th-century **Selskar Abbey** (✉ Selskar St., south of

192

Church of the
Assumption **18**

Church of the
Immaculate
Conception **17**

Franciscan
Church **19**

Selskar Abbey **22**

Statue of
Commodore
John Barry **16**

TIO (Tourist
Information
Office). **15**

Westgate Tower **21**

Wexford Bull Ring . . . **20**

Wexford Wildfowl
Reserve **23**

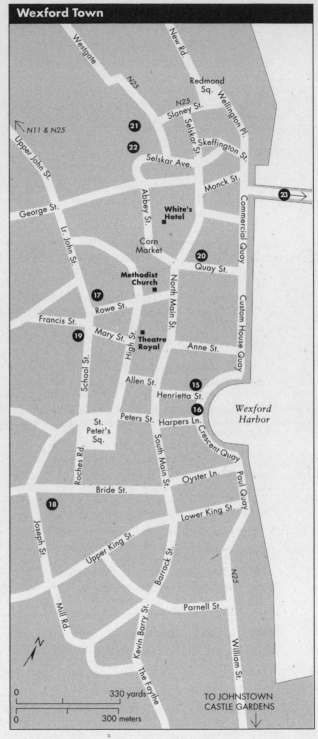

Wexford Town

Westgate Tower) still stand. Here the first treaty between the Irish and the Normans was signed in 1169.

❷ The **Wexford Wildfowl Reserve,** on the north bank of the Slaney, is a short walk across the bridge from the main part of town. One-third of the world's Greenland white-fronted geese—as many as 10,000—spend their winters on the mud flats, known locally as slobs, which also draw ducks, swans, and other waterfowl. Hides are provided for bird-watchers, and an audiovisual show and exhibitions are available at the visitor center. ⊠ *North Slob, Wexford Harbour,* ☎ *053/23129.* ▣ *Free.* ☉ *Mid-Apr.–Sept., daily 9–6; Oct.–mid-Apr., daily 10–5.*

★ ☾ The **Irish National Heritage Park** is one of Ireland's most successful and enjoyable family attractions. This 35-acre, open-air theme park beside the River Slaney should not be missed. In about an hour and a half, a guide takes you through 9,000 years of Irish history—from the first evidence of humans on this island, at around 7000 BC, to the Norman settlements of the mid-12th century. Full-scale replicas of typical dwelling places illustrate the changes in beliefs and lifestyles. Highlights of the tour include a prehistoric homestead, a *crannóg* (lake dwelling), an early Christian *rath* (fortified farmstead), a Christian monastery, a horizontal water mill, a Viking longhouse, and a Norman castle. There are also examples of pre-Christian burial sites and a stone circle. Most of the exhibits are "inhabited" by students in appropriate dress who will answer questions. The riverside site includes several nature trails. ⊠ *Ferrycarrig, 5 km (3 mi) north of Wexford Town on N11, Co. Wexford,* ☎ *053/20733,* ⓦⒺⒷ *www.inhp.com.* ▣ *€7.* ☉ *Daily 9:30–6:30.*

OFF THE BEATEN PATH	**CURRACLOE BEACH** – This was the location used for the Normandy landing in Stephen Spielberg's film *Saving Private Ryan*. It's a popular swimming place in summer and is home to many migratory birds in the winter. It is 9 km (5½ mi) long, with a 1-km (½-mi) nature trail in the seashore sand dunes. ⊠ *11 km (7 mi) northeast of Wexford Town, Co. Wexford.*

Dining and Lodging

$$ ✕ **La Riva.** Lots of people opt for two or three starters at this charming first-floor bistro, in order to try as many of owner-chef Warren Gillen's unusual combos as possible. The menu is extensive, and a wide selection of fresh seafood is available. The bistro, with a modern Mediterranean interior design and friendly staff, is right in the center of town, near the TIO. ⊠ *Henrietta St., Co. Wexford,* ☎ *053/24330. MC, V. Closed Jan.*

$–$$ ✕ **Heavens Above.** Chef Liam Ford cooks up a storm in this delightful evening restaurant and the pub—called the Sky and the Ground—below it. Main courses include wild venison noisettes panfried in a juniper berry and cognac sauce, and roast suckling pig glazed with honey and served with a lemon sauce. You can listen to traditional music in the pub Monday through Wednesday. ⊠ *S. Main St., Co. Wexford,* ☎ *053/ 21273. MC, V. Closed Sun.*

$–$$ ✕ **Oak Tavern.** The pub-restaurant in this family-run old-world inn on the River Slaney is a good place to stop for a bite on your way into Wexford Town. In cold weather, you can warm yourself beside the log fires that blaze in the lounge; in fair weather, you can relax on the riverside terrace. The menu includes steaks, local salmon, and plainly cooked seafood. The tavern is about 2 km/1 mi from town, and not far from the gates of the Irish National Heritage Park on the N11 Dublin road. ⊠ *Enniscorthy Rd., Co. Wexford,* ☎ *053/20922. AE, MC, V.*

$$$ ✕ **Ferrycarrig.** Regular visitors to Wexford Town love this hotel, which overlooks the Slaney Estuary 3 km (2 mi) from town on N11.

One of Ireland's not-so-numerous millionaires takes over the entire hotel for three weeks each year. Even with its very modern architecture, the hotel blends well into its peaceful, riverside location—for example, trees have been placed just offshore to encourage birds to perch there. Choose between dining in the casual Boathouse Bistro or the more formal Tides Restaurant, which serves modern French cuisine. All the bedrooms have wonderful views of the river and some also have balconies. ✉ *Ferrycarrig Bridge, Co. Wexford,* ☎ *053/20999,* FAX *053/20982,* WEB *www.griffingroup.ie. 103 rooms with bath. 2 restaurants, indoor pool, health club, fishing, bar. AE, DC, MC, V.*

$–$$ ☷ **White's Hotel.** If you're looking for a friendly, convivial place in the heart of town, try this redbrick hotel, established in 1779 and fronted by a modern conservatory. The guest rooms are a hodgepodge of different styles, though each has an old-fashioned, comfortable charm. Forty additional executive bedrooms have been added in the reclaimed Abbey Street wing. There's live music in the Shelmalier Bar every Friday and Saturday. ✉ *George's St., Co. Wexford,* ☎ *053/22311,* FAX *053/45000. 82 rooms with bath. Restaurant, health club, 2 bars. AE, DC, MC, V.*

$ ☷ **McMenamin's Town House.** Early breakfast by arrangement and exceptional comfort—for the price range—make this four-story Victorian villa an ideal stopover en route to or from the Rosslare ferries. Book months rather than weeks in advance if you want a room here during the Opera Festival. The bedrooms are spacious, warm, and immaculate, with large pieces of highly polished Victorian furniture and antique beds, including a mahogany half-tester. There are about eight choices at breakfast, including fresh fish of the day or porridge. Make sure you taste Kay and Seamus McMenamin's homemade whiskey marmalade. ✉ *3 Auburn Terr., Redmond Rd., Co. Wexford,* ☎ FAX *053/ 46442,* WEB *www.wexford-bedandbreakfast.com. 5 rooms with bath. MC, V. Closed last 2 wks of Dec.*

Nightlife and the Arts

Touring companies and local productions can be seen in Wexford at the **Theatre Royal** (✉ High St., Co. Wexford, ☎ 053/22400). The **Wexford Opera Festival** (☎ 053/22144 box office), held during the last two weeks of October and the beginning of November, is the town's leading cultural event. The festival has been on for half a century; seldom-performed operas with top talent from all over the world are featured. Along with an ever-expanding fringe element, the festival supplies a feast of concerts and recitals that start at 11 AM and continue until midnight.

Outdoor Activities and Sports

BICYCLING

If you'd like to explore the long, sandy coast of this area at a leisurely pace, rent bicycles at **Hayes Cycles** (✉ 108 Main St., Co. Wexford, ☎ 053/22462).

HORSEBACK RIDING

Curracloe House Equestrian Centre (✉ Curracloe, Co. Wexford, ☎ 053/ 37582) will take you cantering on the spectacular Curracloe Beach (although local authority regulations are presently trying to ban beach riding) or trekking through the Wexford Sloblands. Facilities include a 25-jump cross-country course. **Horetown Equestrian Centre** (✉ Horetown House, Foulksmills, Co. Wexford, ☎ 051/565–786) specializes in residential riding holidays—cross-country riding across farmland—and will teach you how to play polo-crosse. **Shelmalier Riding Stables** (✉ Trinity, Forth Mountain, Taghmon, Co. Wexford, ☎ 053/39251) has cross-country riding across 3,000 acres of forest and mountainous terrain.

SPECTATOR SPORTS

Gaelic football and hurling can be seen at the **Wexford Park GAA** (✉ Clonard Rd., Co. Wexford), or Gaelic Athletic Association. Horse races are held regularly (every few months) at the **Wexford Racecourse** (✉ Bettyville, Co. Wexford, ☎ 053/42307) on the N25 at the outskirts of Wexford Town.

Shopping
At **Barker's** (✉ 36–40 S. Main St., Co. Wexford, ☎ 053/23159) you can find Waterford crystal at factory prices; you can also find local pottery and other crafts.

En Route You'll find the signpost for **Johnstown Castle Gardens** by following N25 for 5 km (3 mi) toward Rosslare. The castle itself, a massive, Victorian-Gothic building in gray stone, is now an agricultural college, but the attractive and well-maintained grounds, with ornamental lakes and more than 200 different trees and shrubs, are open to the public. The main attraction is the **National Museum of Agriculture and Rural Life**, housed in the quadrangular stable yards, which shows what life was once like in rural Ireland. It also contains a 5,000-square-ft exhibition on the potato and the Great Famine (1845–49). ☎ *053/42888.* ⌨ *Gardens €2, May–Sept.; museum €4.* ◷ *Gardens daily 9:30–5:30. Museum Apr.–May and Sept.–Nov., weekdays 9–12:30 and 1:30–5, weekends 2–5; June–Aug., weekdays 9–5, weekends 11–5; Dec.–Mar., weekdays 9–12:30 and 1:30–5.*

ALONG THE COAST TO WATERFORD

This journey takes you along mainly minor roads through the prettiest parts of the coast in Counties Wexford and Waterford, pausing midway to explore Waterford City on foot.

Rosslare

❷❹ *16 km (10 mi) southeast of Wexford Town on R470.*

Sometimes called Ireland's sunniest spot, the village of Rosslare is a seaside resort with an attractive beach. Rosslare Harbour, 8 km (5 mi) south of the village, is one of Ireland's busiest ports, and the terminus for car ferries from Fishguard and Pembroke in Wales and for Cherbourg and Roscoff in France. Vacationers generally head here to hike, golf, sun, and swim.

Dining and Lodging

$$$$ ✕⊡ **Kelly's.** Owned and run by the Kelly family since 1895, this tra-
★ ditional seaside resort hotel is only available for seven-day breaks. Its extensive recreational facilities are the draw. Guest rooms are decorated with comfortable, rustic furnishings; rooms facing the front have lovely sea views. Waterford glass chandeliers hang in the Ivy Room, where the menu includes fresh local produce served in classic French style. You can also dine in La Marine, a casual, bistro-style restaurant, which does a fine job of cooking up Mediterranean-style Irish produce. ✉ *Co. Wexford,* ☎ *053/32114,* ⊠ *053/32222,* ⓦⓔⓑ *www.kellys.ie. 106 rooms with bath. 2 restaurants, 18-hole golf course, 4 tennis courts, hair salon, bicycles, croquet, squash. AE, MC, V. Closed Dec.–Feb.*

$ ⊡ **Tuskar House Hotel.** For an ideal spot to unwind, book a room at this small, family-run hotel, in a quiet area near the ferry port. The bright and comfortable rooms are decorated with functional, modern furniture. For the best views of the sea, try to get a room at the rear of the hotel, and, if possible, one with a balcony. Public rooms have lots of polished pine, glass, and greenery. Seafood is a specialty at the restaurant. ✉ *St. Martin's Rd., Rosslare Harbour, Co. Wexford,*

☎ *053/33363,* FAX *053/33033,* WEB *www.tuskarhousehotel.com. 30 rooms with bath. Restaurant, bar. AE, DC, MC, V.*

Nightlife and the Arts

Portholes bar at the Hotel Rosslare (⊠ Rosslare Harbour, Co. Wexford, ☎ 053/33110) is a popular spot for lively, traditional Irish music twice a week during the summer.

Outdoor Activities and Sports

Rosslare Golf Club (⊠ Rosslare Strand, Co. Wexford, ☎ 053/32203) is a 27-hole, par-72 championship links. A mixture of links and parkland can be found at the 18-hole, par-72 **St. Helen's Bay** (⊠ Kilrane, Co. Wexford, ☎ 053/33234).

Kilmore Quay

㉕ *22 km (14 mi) south of Rosslare on R739.*

A quiet, old-fashioned seaside village of thatched and whitewashed cottages noted for its fishing industry, Kilmore Quay is also popular with recreational anglers and bird-watchers. From the harbor there is a pleasant view to the east over the flat coast that stretches for miles. **Kehoe's Pub** is the hub of village activity; its collection of maritime artifacts is as interesting as that of many museums. During two weeks in July (generally mid-July), the village hosts a lively **seafood festival** (☎ 053/29922) with a parade, seafood barbecues, and other events.

☾ The **Saltee Islands,** Ireland's largest bird sanctuary, are a popular offshore day trip from Kilmore Quay. (From mid-May to mid-September, look for boats at the village waterfront or on the marina to take you to the islands, weather permitting.) In late spring and early summer, several million seabirds nest among the dunes and on the rocky scarp on the south of the islands. Even if you are not an ornithologist, it's worth making the trip at these times to observe the sheer numbers of gulls, kittiwakes, puffins, guillemots, cormorants, and petrels.

The **Kilmore Quay Maritime Museum** is on board the lightship *Guillemot.* The boat, built in 1923, is the last Irish lightship to be preserved complete with cabins and engine room, and it contains models and artifacts relating to the maritime history of the area. ☎ *053/21572.* ◻ *€2.55.* ☾ *May–Sept., daily noon–6; Apr. and Oct., weekends noon–6.*

Dining and Lodging

$$ ✕ **Silver Fox.** Simplicity and freshness define the food at this busy family-run seafood restaurant. Chef and co-owner Nicky Cullen offers up to a dozen seafood options, including a very popular grilled lemon sole, topped with a creamy sauce of fresh prawns, scallops, mushrooms, and onions—plus a sprinkling of cheese. He also cooks a few non-seafood options: stuffed garlic mushrooms and deep-fried St. Killian (local Camembert-like) cheese. ⊠ *Kilmore Quay, Co. Wexford,* ☎ *053/29888. Reservations essential. AE, MC, V. Closed Mid-Jan.–mid-Feb. No lunch Mon–Sat.*

$ ▦ **Quay House.** From this whitewashed guest house—originally the village post office—it's only a 3-min walk to the pier. The solid old house has been carefully refurbished with Douglas fir pine floors throughout and country pine bedroom furniture. Guests—generally outdoor types—are encouraged to socialize in the lounge and the dining room. A room for drying and storing diving equipment is available. ⊠ *Kilmore Quay, Co. Wexford,* ☎ *053/29988,* FAX *053/29808,* WEB *www. quayhouseguesthouse.com. 10 rooms with bath. Restaurant, fishing. MC, V.*

Shopping

Country Crafts (✉ Kilmore Quay, Co. Wexford, ☎ 053/29885), which overlooks the harbor of Kilmore Quay, has Irish-made crafts, antique pine furniture, and paintings by local artists.

En Route On leaving Kilmore Quay, make your way north to R736, and then head west through Duncormick and on to Wellington Bridge. Past the bridge, head toward Fethard-on-Sea on the **Ring of Hook** drive. This is a strange and atypical part of Ireland, where the land is exceptionally flat and the narrow roads are straight.

The Ring of Hook leads out to Hook Lighthouse and north again to **Duncannon,** a small resort with a sandy beach and a delightful atmosphere, on the north side of Waterford Harbour. Its history is marked by the visits of two kings: James II beat a hasty retreat out of Ireland through Duncannon port after his defeat at the Battle of the Boyne in 1690, and his successor, William III, also spent some days here before leaving for England. The imposing, star-shape stone **Duncannon Fort** was built in the 16th century on the site of an Iron Age fortification; it was placed on the water's edge as a defense against a feared attack by the Spanish Armada. ✉ *Duncannon, Co. Wexford,* ☎ *051/389–454.* ⌁ *€4.* ☉ *June–Sept., daily 10–5:30.*

Ballyhack

★ ㉖ *34 km (21 mi) west of Kilmore Quay.*

On the upper reaches of Waterford Harbour, the pretty village of Ballyhack, with its square castle keep, wooden buildings, thatched cottages, and green, hilly background, is admired by painters and photographers. A small car ferry makes the five-minute crossing to Passage East and Waterford. The gray-stone keep of **Ballyhack Castle** dates from the 16th century. It was once owned by the Knights Templars of St. John of Jerusalem, who held the ferry rights by royal charter; traditionally, they were required to keep a boat at Ballyhack to transport injured knights to the King's Leper Hospital at Waterford. The first two floors have been renovated and house a number of local history exhibits. The last admission is 45 minutes before closing. ☎ *051/389–468,* WEB *www.heritageireland.ie.* ⌁ *€1.25.* ☉ *Mid-June–mid-Sept., daily 9:30–6:30.*

Dining and Lodging

$$$ ✕⚏ **Dunbrody Country House.** The seventh Marquess of Donegall, Dermot Chichester, used to live at this stylish and pleasantly informal country retreat. Kevin and Catherine Dundon now own and run the sprawling two-story Georgian manor house. Kevin is a master chef with international experience, and Catherine oversees the restoration program. The spacious rooms, which are individually decorated, and furnished with Georgian antiques, have peaceful country views. In the oak-floor dining room, which overlooks a small sunken garden that's floodlit at night, you'll get excellent contemporary Continental cuisine. ✉ *Arthurstown, New Ross, Co. Wexford,* ☎ *051/389–600,* FAX *051/389–601,* WEB *www.dunbrodyhouse.com. 13 rooms with bath, 6 suites. Restaurant, horseback riding, bar. AE, DC, MC, V.*

Waterford City

10 km (6 mi) west of Ballyhack by ferry and road (R683), 62 km (39 mi) southwest of Wexford Town, 158 km (98 mi) southwest of Dublin.

The largest town in the Southeast and Ireland's oldest city, Waterford was founded by the Vikings in the 9th century and was taken over by

Strongbow, the Norman invader, with much bloodshed in 1170. The city resisted Cromwell's 1649 attacks—his phrase "by Hook or by Crooke" refers to his two siege routes, one via Hook Head, the other via Crooke Village on the estuary—but fell the following year and did not prosper again until 1783, when George and William Penrose set out to create "plain and cut flint glass, useful and ornamental," and thereby set in motion a glass-manufacturing industry without equal. The best Waterford glass was produced from the late 1780s to the early 19th century. This early work, examples of which can be found in museums and public buildings all over the country, is characterized by a unique, slightly opaque cast that is absent from the modern product.

Waterford has better-preserved city walls than anywhere else in Ireland but Derry. Initially, the slightly run-down commercial center doesn't look too promising. You'll need to park your car and proceed on foot to discover the heritage that the city has made admirable efforts over the past decade to preserve. The compact town center can be visited in a couple of hours. Allow at least another hour if you intend to take the Waterford Crystal factory tour.

The **city quays**—at the corner of Custom House Parade and Peter Street—are a good place to begin a tour of Waterford City. (The TIO is also down there, at the Granary on Merchant's Quay.) The city quays stretch for nearly 2 km (1 mi) along the River Suir and were described in the 18th century as the best in Europe.

㉗ **Reginald's Tower,** a waterside circular tower on the east end of Waterford's quays, marks the apex of a triangle containing the old walled city of Waterford. Built by the Vikings for the city's defense in 1003, it has 80-ft-high, 10-ft-thick walls; an interior stairway leads to the top. The tower served in turn as the residence for a succession of Anglo-Norman kings (including Henry II, John, and Richard II), a mint for silver coins, a prison, and an arsenal. It is said that Strongbow's marriage to Eva, the daughter of Dermot MacMurrough, took place here in the late 12th century, thus uniting the Norman invaders with the native Irish. It has been restored to its original medieval appearance and furnished with appropriate 11th- to 15th-century artifacts. ⊠ *The Quay,* ☎ *051/304–220.* ⊡ *€2.* ☉ *Easter–May and Oct., daily 10–5; June–Sept., daily 9:30–6:30.*

㉘ One of Waterford's finer Georgian buildings, **City Hall,** on the Mall, dates from 1783 and was designed by John Roberts, a native of the city. On the way you'll pass some good examples of domestic Georgian architecture—tall, well-proportioned houses with typically Irish semicircular fanlights above the doors. The arms of Waterford hang over City Hall's own entrance, which leads into a spacious foyer that originally was a town meeting place and merchants' exchange. The building contains two lovely theaters, an old Waterford dinner service, and an enormous 1802 Waterford glass chandelier, which hangs in the Council Chamber (a copy of the chandelier hangs in Independence Hall in Philadelphia). The Victorian horseshoe-shape **Theatre Royal** is the setting for the annual Festival of Light Opera in September. ⊠ *The Mall,* ☎ *051/309–900.* ⊡ *Free.* ☉ *Weekdays 10–5.*

㉙ The **Bishop's Palace** is among the most imposing of the remaining Georgian town houses. Only the foyer is open to the public. ⊠ *Alongside City Hall on the Mall.* ⊡ *Free.* ☉ *Weekdays 9–5.*

Off of Colbeck Street along Spring Garden Alley, you'll see one of the remaining portions of the **old city wall**; there are sections all around the town center.

Waterford City

PEOPLE'S PARK

220 yards

200 meters

Bishop's Palace **29**

Blackfriars Abbey........ **33**

Christ Church Cathedral **30**

City Hall **28**

French Church **31**

Holy Trinity Cathedral **34**

Reginald's Tower **27**

St. Olaf's Church **32**

Victorian Clock Tower **35**

Waterford Glass Factory **37**

Waterford Treasures/Tourist Information Office **36**

③⓪ The Church of Ireland **Christ Church Cathedral** is the only neoclassical Georgian Cathedral in Ireland. The story of Waterford City from
the Norman invasion to the present day is told in an audiovisual presentation. ✉ *Henrietta St.,* ☎ *051/858–958.* 🎫 *€2.55.* ⊙ *Audiovisual show Apr.–May and Sept.–Oct., weekdays 11:30, 2:30, and 4; June–
Aug., Mon.–Sat. 9:30, 11:30, 2:30, and 4, Sun. 2:30 and 4; cathedral
daily.*

③① Roofless ruins are all that's left of **French Church** (✉ Greyfriar's St.),
a 13th-century Franciscan abbey. The church, also known as Greyfri-
ars, was given to a group of Huguenot refugees (hence the "French")
in 1695. A splendid east window remains amid the ruins. The key is
available at Reginald's Tower.

③② **St. Olaf's Church** (✉ St. Olaf's St.) was built, as the name implies, by
the Vikings in the mid-11th century. All that remains of the old church
is its original door, which has been incorporated into the wall of the
existing building (a meeting hall).

③③ The ruined tower of **Blackfriars Abbey** (✉ High St.) belonged to a Dominican abbey founded in 1226 and returned to the crown in 1541
after the dissolution of the monasteries. It was used as a courthouse
until Cromwellian forces destroyed it in the 17th century.

③④ The Roman Catholic **Holy Trinity Cathedral** (✉ Barronstrand St. between High St. and the clock tower on the quays) has a simple facade
and a richly (some would say garishly) decorated interior with high,
vaulted ceilings and ornate Corinthian pillars. It was designed in neoclassical style by John Roberts (who also designed Christ Church
Cathedral and City Hall). Surprisingly, it was built in the late 18th century—when Catholicism was barely tolerated—on land granted by the
Protestant city fathers.

③⑤ The **Victorian Clock Tower** (✉ Merchant's Quay) was built in 1864 with
public donations. Although it has no great architectural merit, it serves
as a reminder of the days when Waterford was a thriving, bustling port.

③⑥ **Waterford Treasures,** above the southeast's main TIO, uses interactive
audiovisual technology to guide you through 1,000 years in the history of Waterford. Entertaining and educational, the exhibition displays
Waterford's rich inheritance of rare and beautiful artifacts, from the
Charter Roll 1372, a list of all charters granted to Waterford up to that
time, written in Latin on vellum, to the sword of King Edward IV to
18th-century crystal. A restaurant and a shop are also on the premises.
✉ *The Granary, Merchant's Quay,* ☎ *051/304–500.* 🎫 *€6.* ⊙ *Sept.–
May, daily 10–5; June–Aug., daily 9:30–9.*

If the weather is favorable, consider taking a **cruise** along Waterford's
harbor and the wide, picturesque estuary of the River Suir. A luxury
river cruiser departs from the quay beside Reginald's Tower. You can
purchase tickets at the TIO. ✉ *Galley Cruises,* ☎ *051/421–723.* ⊙
Tours June–Aug., daily at 3, weather permitting.

③⑦ The city's most popular attraction is the **Waterford Glass Factory,**
about 2 km (1 mi) from the TIO. (Take the N25 Waterford–Cork road
south from the quay, or ask at the tourist office about the regular bus
service.) When the factory opened in 1783, it provided English royalty with a supply of ornate handcrafted flatware, chandeliers, and decorative pieces. Over the years, its clientele and product line diversified,
and today the United States is the biggest market. The tour of the factory takes you through the specialized crafts of blowing, cutting, and
polishing glass—all carried out against a noisy background of glow-
ing furnaces and ceaseless bustle. An extensive selection of crystal is

on view (and for sale) in the showroom. To reserve a place in a 60-minute tour, which includes an optional 18-minute audiovisual show, call the factory or the tourist office. ✉ *Cork Rd., Kilbarry,* ☎ *051/332–500.* 🎫 *€6.* ⏲ *Nov.–Mar., weekday tours 9:30–3:15; Apr.–Oct., daily tours 8:30–4.*

Dining and Lodging

$$–$$$ ✕ **Wine Vault.** Yes, in the cellar of this Elizabethan town house, there really is a wine vault—and what a vault it is, with more than 350 labels. The ground floor houses a busy, informal bistro, with polished wooden tables. Head chef Fergal Phelan uses traditional Irish ingredients to produce intriguing dishes. Monkfish is a favorite. ✉ *High St., Co. Waterford,* ☎ *051/853–444. AE, MC, V. Closed Sun.*

$$ ✕ **Dwyers of Mary Street.** Walls painted in shades of gray and wine,
★ and beech dressers displaying both antique and modern glass soften and warm the interior of the old Royal Irish Constabulary barracks, which is where you'll find this French-influenced restaurant. The menu changes every four weeks; a typical meal might consist of a tartlet of Jerusalem artichokes and roast scallops, followed by a venison loin roast, carved on a bed of celeriac, and served with a port-and-orange sauce. ✉ *8 Mary St., Co. Waterford,* ☎ *051/877–478,* 🌐 *www.dwyersrest.com. Reservations essential. AE, DC, MC, V. No lunch. No dinner Sun.*

$$$$ ✕🏨 **Waterford Castle.** A magnificent 17th-century stone castle (with 19th-century additions) occupies its own 310-acre island in the River Suir. You can only reach the island, 3 km (2 mi) outside Waterford City, by car ferry. The Great Hall and the drawing room have fine oak paneling, ornate antique furniture, and tapestries. Guest rooms are luxuriously decorated and have four-poster beds. At the Munster Room restaurant, adorned with oak furniture and deep-burgundy Donegal carpet, the food tends to country-style dishes: poached salmon, asparagus served in puff pastry, and bread-and-butter pudding. ✉ *The Island, Ballinakill, Co. Waterford,* ☎ *051/878–203,* 📠 *051/879–316,* 🌐 *www.waterfordcastle.com. 14 rooms with bath, 5 suites. Restaurant, 18-hole golf course, 2 tennis courts, fishing, croquet. AE, DC, MC, V.*

$$$ 🏨 **Granville Hotel.** In the heart of Waterford you'll find a floodlit landmark overlooking the River Suir. It's one of Ireland's oldest hotels, with many historical connections. The patriot Thomas Francis Meagher was a previous owner, and Charles Stuart Parnell addressed mass meetings from its balcony when campaigning for Home Rule. The public rooms have an old-world Georgian character; bedrooms are decorated in 18th-century style. Ask for a room at the back if traffic disturbs you. ✉ *Meagher Quay, Co. Waterford,* ☎ *051/305–555,* 📠 *051/305–502,* 🌐 *www.granville-hotel.com. 99 rooms with bath. Restaurant, bar. AE, DC, MC, V.*

$ 🏨 **Foxmount Farm & Country House.** For a pleasant change of pace, you can stay on a working dairy farm in the peaceful countryside. This elegant 17th-century creeper-clad farmhouse on its own extensive grounds has an informal style, with welcoming log fires and intriguing antiques. It's about 5 km (3 mi) outside town on the road to the Passage East ferry. Your host, Margaret Kent, is renowned for her evening meals (residents only). She uses the farm's produce, and fruit and herbs from her own garden. You're invited to bring your own wine and enjoy a glass or two around the hearth after dinner. ✉ *Passage East Rd., Co. Waterford,* ☎ *051/874–308,* 📠 *051/854–906. 5 rooms with bath. Dining room, tennis court. No credit cards. Closed Nov.–mid-Mar.*

Nightlife and the Arts

You can see a wide selection of work by contemporary artists at the **Dyehouse Gallery and Waterford Pottery** (✉ Dyehouse La.,, ☎ 051/

844–770). Culture buffs: don't miss the **Garter Lane Arts Centre** (✉ 22A O'Connell St., ☎ 051/855–038). Call ahead for a schedule of upcoming concerts, exhibits, and theater productions at the center. **T&H Doolan's Bar** (✉ 32 George's St., ☎ 051/872–764) hosts traditional Irish music most summer nights and on Monday and Tuesday year-round. **Waterford International Festival of Light Opera** (☎ 051/874–402), the only competitive event of its kind, is a great draw for amateur musical societies from Ireland and Great Britain. The festival runs for 17 nights every September at the **Theatre Royal** (✉ City Hall, The Mall, ☎ 051/874–402). The **Waterford Show** tells the story of Waterford's culture and heritage through music, song, and dance. Book at Waterford Crystal or the Tourist Information Office (☎ 051/875–788). The show takes place at City Hall, 9 PM Thursday, Saturday, and Sunday, May–September. The admission cost of €10.15 includes a preshow drink and a glass of wine during the show.

Outdoor Activities and Sports

GOLF

Faithlegg Golf Club (✉ Faithlegg House, Checkpoint, ☎ 051/382–241) is an 18-hole, par-72 course set in mature landscape on the banks of the River Suir. **Waterford Castle Golf Club** (✉ The Island, Ballinakill, ☎ 051/871–633) is an 18-hole, par-72 course that claims to be Ireland's only true island course.

HORSEBACK RIDING

Horses are available by the hour at **Kilotteran Equitation Centre** (✉ Kilotteran, ☎ 051/384–158).

SPECTATOR SPORTS

Gaelic football and hurling can be seen at the **Waterford GAA Grounds** (✉ Walsh Park).

Shopping

You'll find the best selection of crystal in Waterford City on show at **Joseph Knox** (✉ 3 Barronstrand St., ☎ 051/875–307). The **Waterford Design Centre** (✉ 44 The Quay, ☎ 051/856–666) has two floors devoted to Irish crafts, gifts, and fashion.

While in Waterford, definitely pay a visit to the world-famous **Waterford Glass Factory** (✉ Cork Rd., Kilbarry, ☎ 051/332–500). The showroom displays an extensive selection of Waterford crystal and Wedgwood china.

Dunmore East

⬤ 16 km (10 mi) southeast of Waterford City via R683 and R684.

Dunmore East is a quaint, one-street fishing village of thatched cottages and an attractive lighthouse at the head of Waterford Harbour. You'll find many colorful but noisy kittiwakes who nest in the steep cliffs overlooking the harbor. Plenty of small beaches and cliff walks are nearby, and you get a wonderful view of the estuary from the hill behind the village.

Dining

$$ ✕ **Ship Restaurant.** Chef Billy Fitzpatrick emphasizes fresh, local seafood at this simply furnished restaurant—on the ground floor of a 19th-century house overlooking the bay. The cuisine mixes French and Irish influences. Start with an arrangement of seafood with ratatouille enhanced by gazpacho sauce. Entrées include grilled or panfried black sole and roulade of Dover sole filled with saffron mousse. ☎ 051/383–141, FAX 051/383–144. AE, DC, MC, V.

Tramore

㊴ *11 km (7 mi) south of Waterford City on R675, 4 km (2½ mi) west of Dunmore East.*

☾ Tramore's 5-km-long (3-mi-long) **beach** is a popular escape for families from Waterford and other parts of the Southeast, as the many vacation homes and camper parks indicate. It is Ireland's biggest seaside resort and a dream-come-true for young children, but it is not to everybody's taste. A 50-acre amusement park, a miniature railway, and vacation home developments overshadow part of the seafront. (The upper half of town is more quiet and reserved.) At the western end of the beach, the sand gives way to rocky cliffs guarded by the Metal Man, a giant cast-iron figure who stands atop a great pillar. It's said that if a young woman hops on one foot around the base of the pillar three times, she will be married within a year. This custom, which is still observed in a lighthearted way, can be traced back to a stone that stood on the spot centuries ago and was used in ancient Celtic fertility rites.

Dining and Lodging

$$ ✕ **Esquire.** Originally built in 1932 as a gentlemen's bar, the upstairs restaurant here retains the air of a gentleman's club. Patron and chef Paul Horan applies his skills to fresh local produce. A full à la carte menu with such dishes as smoked salmon, Irish peppered steak with brandy, and vegetarian specials is served; a simpler—and faster—barfood menu is also available. ⊠ *Cross Market St., Co. Waterford,* ☎ *051/381–324. AE, MC, V.*

$ ✕⛺ **Annestown House.** Romantically perched above the sea, this large, white Victorian house has its own private path down to Annestown Cove, one of many secluded coves along this breathtakingly beautiful stretch of coast between Tramore and Dungarvan. The house has been in the family of John Galloway since 1820. John and his wife, Pippa, welcome guests into a home full of nooks and crannies, lots of books, and a large billiard table. Bedrooms are generally large and full of character, with wonderful sea views at the front of the house. Dinner is served at 7:45 PM; book by noon. ⊠ *Annestown, Co. Waterford,* ☎ *051/396–160,* ℻ *051/396–474,* ⓦ *www.annestown.com. 5 rooms with bath. Tennis court, billiards, croquet. AE, MC, V. Closed Nov.–mid-Mar.*

Outdoor Activities and Sports

GOLF

The Comeragh Mountains overlook the **Tramore Golf Club** (⊠ Newtown Hill, ☎ 051/386–170), an 18-hole championship parkland course.

SPECTATOR SPORTS

Horse races are held regularly at **Tramore Racecourse** (⊠ signposted on R675 from Waterford, ☎ 051/381–425).

En Route West of Tramore on R675 you'll find **Annestown,** a small, quiet resort town with a good, sandy beach. The former copper-mining center of **Bunmahon,** now a fishing village popular with vacationers, is 8 km (5 mi) from here. A scenic footpath, signposted from Bunmahon, follows the Mahon River as it tumbles down from the Comeragh Mountains. This pleasant coastal drive offers views of unusual rock formations in the cliffs interspersed with sand dunes, as well as various rare flowers and birds. Attractive, easily accessible beaches are at **Stradbally** and **Clonea.**

Dungarvan

40 *42 km (26 mi) southwest of Tramore on R675.*

With their covering of soft grasses, the lowlands of Wexford and eastern Waterford gradually give way to heath and moorland; the wetter climate of the hillier western Waterford countryside creates and maintains the bog. The mountains responsible for this change in climate rise up behind Dungarvan, the largest coastal town in County Waterford. This bustling fishing and resort spot is situated at the mouth of River Colligan, which empties into Dungarvan Bay here. It's a popular base for climbers and hikers.

OFF THE
BEATEN PATH
RING (AN RINNE) – In this Gaeltacht area on Dungarvan Bay, the Irish language is still in daily use—this is unusual in the south and east of the country. In Colaiste na Rinne, a language college, courses have been provided in Irish since 1909. ⊠ *7 km (4¼ mi) southeast of Dungarvan, off N674F.*

Dining and Lodging

$$ ✕ **The Tannery.** Mediterranean and Asian spices occasionally surface in the cooking of chef-owner Paul Flynn. The secret, he says, is knowing when to meddle in what is otherwise classic French and Italian cuisine. Quiet mainstream jazz provides sophisticated background music in the high-ceiling room with tall windows in an old waterside tannery. ⊠ *10 Quay St., Co. Waterford,* ☎ *058/45420. AE, DC, MC, V. Closed Mon. No dinner Sun., Sept.–June, and 2 wks in Jan.*

$ ▦ **The Gold Coast Golf Hotel.** With great views of Dungarvan Bay, the hotel is one of the newest parts of a family-run and family-friendly property, including 16 self-catering holiday cottages (built around the 37-bedroom hotel), and 10 golf villas on the edge of its woodland course on a links setting. Rooms are bright, comfortable, and spacious. Guests can use the facilities of the Gold Coast's sister hotel, the Clonea Strand, just 2½ km (1½ mi) away; they include a games room, leisure complex, and Clonea's 3-km (2-mi) sandy beach. ⊠ *Co. Waterford,* ☎ *058/42249 or 058/42416,* ⬛ *058/43378,* ⬛ *www.clonea.com. 37 rooms with bath. Restaurant, 18-hole golf course, tennis court, indoor pool, gym, fishing, bar, playground. AE, DC, MC, V.*

Nightlife and the Arts

A *ceilí* (Irish dance) is held nightly during the summer at **Colaiste na Rinne** (⊠ Ring, ☎ 058/46104).

Outdoor Activities and Sports

BICYCLING

If you are tempted to explore the coast of the Dungarvan area and the nearby Nire Valley on two wheels, bicycles can be rented at **Tony O'Mahony** (⊠ 14 Sexton St., Abbeyside, ☎ 058/43346).

GOLF

West Waterford Golf Club (⊠ Coolcormack, ☎ 058/43216) is an 18-hole, par-72 parkland course open year-round.

SPECTATOR SPORTS

Hurling and football are played at **Fraher Field GAA.**

THE NIRE VALLEY, THE BLACKWATER VALLEY, AND COUNTY TIPPERARY

"It's a long way to Tipperary . . .": so run the words of that famed song sung all over the world since World War I. Actually, Tipperary is *not* so far to go, considering that, as Ireland's biggest inland county, it's within easy striking distance of Waterford and Cork. Moving in from the coastline, you can travel through some of Ireland's most lush pasturelands and to some of its most romantic sites, such as Lismore Castle. The Nire Valley, in the mountains between Dungarvan and Clonmel, is a popular area for hiking and pursuing other outdoor pleasures. The Blackwater Valley is renowned for its beauty, peacefulness, and excellent fishing. Some of the finest racehorses in the world are raised in the fields of Tipperary, which is also the county where you'll find the Rock of Cashel—the greatest group of monastic ruins in all Ireland.

The Nire Valley

41 *29 km (18 mi) northwest of Dungarvan on R672.*

A visit to the Nire Valley is worthwhile only if you have time to take a walk in this remote but enchanting spot. The valley of the River Nire starts in the village of **Ballymacarbry** and runs along the base of the Comeragh Mountains. Both forest and mountain walks pass through quiet country where sheep far outnumber people. **Knocknagriffin,** the highest peak in the Comeraghs, at 2,476 ft, with views back to Waterford on the coast and inland to Tipperary Town, is easily accessible to a moderately fit walker.

Dining and Lodging

$-$$ ✕🖬 **Hanora's Cottage.** It's one of Ireland's premier B&Bs, built in the
★ heart of the Nire Valley in the late 19th century. The sizable guest rooms (large by cottage standards) are decorated with pretty chintz curtains and spreads; six have hot tubs and three have double hot tubs. This is especially nice if you take part in the main activities here—golf (nearby), riding, and walking. The less energetic simply unwind in front of the open fire and wait to be fed dishes like fillet of salmon in prawn and Chablis sauce or medallions of filet steak with onions, mushrooms, and mustard. ✉ *Ballymacarbry, Co. Waterford,* ☎ *052/36134,* 𝔽𝔸𝕏 *052/ 36540. 11 rooms with bath. Dining room, hot tub. MC, V.*

Outdoor Activities and Sports

Explore the Nire Valley on horseback by joining a guided hack from **Melody's Riding Stables** (✉ Ballymacarbry, ☎ 052/36147).

Ardmore

42 *24 km (15 mi) south of Dungarvan on N25.*

Ardmore is a delightful village, with ancient roots, on its own peninsula at the base of a tall cliff. In the 5th century, St. Declan is reputed to have disembarked here from Wales and founded a monastery, 30 years before St. Patrick arrived in Ireland. Ardmore's monastic remains are found on the top of the cliff. The ruined, 12th-century **Cathedral of St. Declan** has some ogham stones inside and weathered but interesting biblical scenes carved on its west front. The saint is said to be buried in **St. Declan's Oratory,** a small early Christian church that has
★ been partially reconstructed. The 97-ft-high **round tower,** one of 70 round towers remaining in Ireland, is in exceptionally good condition. Round towers were built by the early Christian monks as watchtowers and belfries but came to be used as places of refuge for the monks

and their valuables during Viking raids. This is the reason the doorway is 15 ft above ground level—once inside, the monks could pull the ladder into the tower with them.

Lismore

43 *40 km (25 mi) northwest of Ardmore on N72 and R671.*

The enchanting little town of Lismore is built on the banks of the Blackwater, a river famous for its trout and salmon. Popular with both anglers and romantics, from the 7th to the 12th century it was an important monastic center, founded by St. Carthac (or Carthage), and it had one of the most renowned universities of its time. The village has two cathedrals, a Roman Catholic one from the late 19th century and the Church of Ireland St. Carthage's, which dates from 1633 and incorporates fragments of an earlier church.

★ As you cross the bridge entering Lismore, you will be struck by a dramatic view of the magnificent **Lismore Castle,** a vast, turreted gray-stone building atop a rock that overhangs River Blackwater. There has been a castle here since the 12th century, but the present structure, built by the sixth Duke of Devonshire, dates from the mid-19th century. The house is not open to the public, unlike the upper and lower gardens, which consist of woodland walks, including an unusual yew walk said to be more than 800 years old, and an impressive display of magnolias, camellias, and shrubs. ☎ *058/54424.* ⌸ *€4.* ☾ *Apr.–Oct., daily 1:45–4:45.*

En Route Leaving Lismore, heading east on N72 for 6½ km (4 mi) toward Cappoquin, a well-known coarse-angling center, you can pick up R669 north into the **Knockmealdown Mountains.** Your route is signposted as the Vee Gap road, the Vee Gap being its summit, from where you'll have superb views of the Tipperary plain, the Galtee Mountains in the northwest, and a peak called Slievenamon in the northeast. If the day is clear, you should be able to see the Rock of Cashel, ancient seat of the kings of Munster, some 32 km (20 mi) away. Just before you enter the Vee Gap, look for a 6-ft-high mound of stones on the left side of the road. It marks the grave of Colonel Grubb, a local landowner who liked the view so much that he arranged to be buried here standing up so that he could look out over the scene for all eternity.

You might like to break your journey and visit **Mount Melleray Abbey.** This was the first post-Reformation monastery, founded in 1832 by the Cistercian Order in what was then a barren mountainside wilderness. Over the years the order has transformed the site into more than 600 acres of fertile farmland. The monks maintain strict vows of silence, but visitors are welcome to join in services throughout the day and are permitted into most areas of the abbey. It is also possible to stay in the guest lodge by prior arrangement. ✉ *Cappoquin, south of the Vee Gap, signposted off R669, 13 km (8 mi) from Lismore, Co. Waterford,* ☎ *058/54404,* FAX *058/52140.* ⌸ *Free.* ☾ *Daily 7:45 AM–8 PM.*

Dining and Lodging

$$–$$$ ✕⊞ **Richmond House.** Deep in the countryside, just outside Cappoquin, you'll find a handsome three-story Georgian country house with an informal, unpretentious, and very relaxing environment—under the personal supervision of owners Claire and Paul Deevy. The public rooms, with log fires and traditional rust-and-cream decor, are reminiscent of the old-world country hotel. Paul, a talented chef, uses local produce whenever possible to create dishes like cassoulet of local seafood (scallops, monkfish, salmon, Dover sole, and prawns) with saf-

fron cream sauce. ⊠ *Cappoquin, Co. Waterford,* ☎ *058/54278,* FAX *058/54988,* WEB *www.richmondhouse.net. 9 rooms with bath. Restaurant, fishing, horseback riding, bar. AE, DC, MC, V. Closed last wk of Dec.–mid-Jan.*

Cahir

④ *37 km (23 mi) north of Lismore, at crossroads of R668, N24, and N8.*

Cahir Castle, on a rocky island on the River Suir, in the middle of the town, is one of Ireland's largest and best-preserved castles, retaining its dramatic keep, tower, and much of its original defensive structure. An audiovisual show and guided tour are available upon request. ☎ *052/41011.* 🎟 €2.55. ☉ *Mid-Mar.–mid-June and mid-Sept.–mid-Oct., daily 9:30–5:30; mid-June–mid-Sept., daily 9–7:30; mid-Oct.–mid-Mar., daily 9:30–4:30; last admission 45 mins before closing.*

Dining and Lodging

$ ✕🖭 **Bansha Castle.** Venture into the heart of quiet, wooded country backed by the Glen of Aherlow, about 8 km (5 mi) from Cahir on the N24 Tipperary road, to this 18th-century stone house with a Norman-style round tower. Large rooms, all with great views, are simply furnished with plain carpets and mahogany reproduction pieces, but walls are decorated in strong, vibrant colors. John's wife, Teresa, uses locally grown organic produce in her good home cooking. Outdoor activities, such as walking, golfing, salmon and trout fishing, and horseback riding, are nearby. ⊠ *Bansha, Co. Tipperary,* ☎ *062/54187,* FAX *062/54294. 6 rooms, 5 with bath. Dining room. No credit cards.*

Outdoor Activities and Sports

Explore the Galtee mountains and the Glen of Aherlow on horseback with **Bansha House Stables** (⊠ Bansha, ☎ 062/54194).

En Route To your left as you drive from Cahir to Tipperary Town on N24 is the **Glen of Aherlow,** a lovely 16-km-long (10-mi-long) wooded stretch skirting the River Aherlow and its tributaries between the Galtee Mountains to the south and the Slievenamuck Hills to the north. The highest summit in the Galtees is the 3,018-ft Galtymore Mountain.

Tipperary Town

④⑤ *22 km (14 mi) northwest of Cahir on N24.*

Tipperary Town, a dairy-farming center at the head of a fertile plain known as the Golden Vale, is a good starting point for climbing and walking in the hills around the Glen of Aherlow, but the small country town, on the River Ara, is worth visiting in its own right, too. In **New Tipperary,** a neighborhood built by local tenants during Ireland's Land War (1890–91), old buildings, like Dalton's Heritage House, have been restored; you can visit the Heritage House by calling the offices of Clann na hEireann. You can also visit the old **Butter Market** on Dillon Street; the **Churchwell** at the junction of Church, Emmet, and Dillon streets; and the grave of the grandfather of Robert Emmett—one of the most famous Irish patriots—in the graveyard at St. Mary's Church. A statue of Charles Kickham, whose novel *The Homes of Tipperary* chronicled the devastation of this county through forced emigration, has a place of honor in the center of town. Adjacent to **St. Michael's Church,** with its stained-glass window of a soldier killed during World War I, is Bridewell Jail. The **headquarters of Clann na hEireann** (⊠ 45 Main St., ☎ 062/33188) researches the origins and history of surnames throughout Ireland and promotes clan gatherings.

Nightlife and the Arts

Tipperary is famous for its traditional music and dancing, which happen when the mood strikes. Ask locals to recommend a good pub for a session.

Outdoor Activities and Sports

Tipperary Racecourse (✉ Limerick Junction, ☎ 062/51357) is 5 km (3 mi) northwest of town.

Cashel

46 *17 km (11 mi) northeast of Tipperary Town on N74.*

Cashel is a market town on the busy Cork–Dublin road, with a lengthy history as a center of royal and religious power. From roughly AD 370 until 1101, it was the seat of the kings of Munster, and it was probably at one time a center of Druidic worship. Here, according to legend, St. Patrick arrived in about AD 432 and baptized King Aengus, who became Ireland's first Christian ruler. One of the many legends associated with this event is that St. Patrick plucked a shamrock to explain the mystery of the Trinity, thus giving a new emblem to Christian Ireland.

★ The awe-inspiring, oft-mist-shrouded **Rock of Cashel** is one of Ireland's most visited sites. The rock itself, a short walk to the north of the town, rises as a giant, circular mound 200 ft above the surrounding plain; it's crowned by a tall cluster of gray monastic remains. Legend has it that St. Patrick baptized King Aengus here and that the devil, flying over Ireland in a hurry, took a bite out of the Slieve Bloom Mountains to clear his path (the gap, known as the Devil's Bit, can be seen to the north of the rock) and spat it out in the Golden Vale.

The best approach to the rock is along the **Bishop's Walk,** a 10-minute hike that begins outside the drawing room of the Cashel Palace hotel on Main Street.

The **museum** across from the entrance to the Rock provides a 15-minute audiovisual display, as well as enthusiastic young guides who will ensure that you don't miss the many interesting features of the buildings on top of the Rock of Cashel.

The shell of **St. Patrick's Cathedral** is the largest building on the summit. The 13th-century cathedral was originally built in a flamboyant variation on Romanesque style, but it was destroyed by fire in 1495. The restored building was desecrated during the 16th century in an ugly incident in which hundreds of townspeople who had sought sanctuary in the cathedral were burned to death when Cromwell's forces surrounded the building with turf and set it afire. A series of sculptures in the north transept represent the apostles, other saints, and the Beasts of the Apocalypse. Look for the octagonal staircase turret that ascends beside the **Central Tower** to a series of defensive passages built into the thick walls. From the top of the Central Tower, you'll have a wonderful view of the surrounding plains and mountains. Another passage gives access to the **round tower,** a well-preserved, 92-ft-high building.

The entrance to **Cormac's Chapel,** the best-preserved building on top of the Rock, is behind the south transept of the cathedral. The chapel was built in 1127 by Cormac Macarthy, king of Desmond and bishop of Cashel (combination bishop-kings were not unusual in the early Irish church). Note the high corbeled roof, modeled on the traditional covering of early saints' cells (as at Glendalough and Dingle); the typically Romanesque, twisted columns around the altar; and the unique carvings around the south entrance. ✉ *Rock of Cashel,* ☎ 062/61437, ⓦⒺⒷ *www.heritageireland.ie.* ▣ €4.40. ⏱ *Mid-Mar.–mid-June, daily 9:30–5:30; mid-June–mid-Sept., daily 9–7:30; mid-Sept.–mid-Mar., daily 9:30–4:30.*

In the same building as the TIO, the **Cashel of the Kings Heritage Center** explains the historic relationship between the town and the Rock and includes a scale model of Cashel as it looked during the 1600s. ✉ *City Hall,* ☎ 062/62511. ⏱ *Daily 9:30–5:50.*

The **G. P. A. Bolton Library,** on the grounds of the St. John the Baptist Church of Ireland Cathedral, has a particularly fine collection of rare books, manuscripts, and maps, some of which date from the beginning of the age of printing in Europe. ✉ *John St.,* ☎ 062/61944. ▣ €2. ⏱ *Mon.–Sat. 9:30–5:30, Sun. noon–5:30.*

Dining and Lodging

$$ ✕ **Chez Hans.** It oozes old-world charm. This small, converted Victo-
★ rian church at the foot of the Rock of Cashel is furnished with dark wood and tapestries, which provide a wonderfully elegant background for the white-linen tables. The chef serves contemporary cuisine with a hint of nouvelle and does wonders with fresh Irish ingredients—especially seafood. You can get salmon, hake, or mussels, served in a light chive velouté. Another specialty is roast rack of Tipperary spring lamb with a fresh herb crust. ✉ *Rockside, Co. Tipperary,* ☎ 062/61177. *Reservations essential. MC, V. Closed Sun.–Mon. and 1st 3 wks in Jan. No lunch.*

$$$$ ✕▦ **Cashel Palace.** Antiques and spacious bathrooms characterize
★ the luxurious guest rooms on the first floor of the main house. Rooms on the second floor—formerly the servants' quarters (called the Mews)—are cozier, though not small. The Bishop's Buttery restaurant relies on game in season, local lamb and beef, and fresh fish creatively prepared, and also serves simple, light meals all day. Don't miss the lovely gardens at the rear of the house, where you can see the descendants of the original hop plants used by Richard Guinis to brew the first "Wine of Ireland." Guinis went on, with his son, Arthur, to found the famous Guinness Brewery in Dublin. ✉ *Main St., Co. Tipperary,* ☎ 062/62707, ⒻⒶⓍ 062/61521, ⓦⒺⒷ *www.cashel-palace.ie. 23 rooms with bath. 2 restaurants, fishing, bar. AE, DC, MC, V.*

$$ ▦ **Dundrum House Hotel.** Nestled beside the River Multeen, 12 km (7½ mi) outside busy Cashel, you'll find this magnificent, four-story Georgian house. Sixteen high-ceilinged bedrooms take up the main house; the rest are in a three-story wing built during the house's previous incarnation as a convent. All the older rooms have large pieces of early Victorian furniture and lovely views of the surrounding parkland. The old convent chapel, stained-glass windows intact, is now a cocktail bar. Elaborate plaster ceilings, attractive period furniture, and open fires make the spacious dining room and lounge inviting. ✉ *Dundrum, Co. Tipperary,* ☎ 062/71116, ⒻⒶⓍ 062/71366, ⓦⒺⒷ *www.dundrumhousehotel. com. 85 rooms with bath. 2 restaurants, 18-hole golf course, pool, sauna, steam room, fishing, 2 bars. AE, DC, MC, V.*

Nightlife and the Arts

You can enjoy folksinging, storytelling, and dancing evenings from June through September, Tuesday through Saturday, at the **Bru Boru Heritage Center** (☎ 062/61122) at the foot of the Rock of Cashel. Entertainment usually begins at 9 PM and costs €13, €35 with dinner.

Outdoor Activities and Sports

GOLF

The natural features of the mature Georgian estate at Dundrum House Hotel have been incorporated into an 18-hole, par-72 course for the

County Tipperary Golf and Country Club (✉ Dundrum House Hotel, Dundrum, ☎ 062/71717).

About 20 km (12 mi) north of Cashel, **Semple GAA Stadium** (✉ Thurles, ☎ 0504/22702) is where major hurling and football championships in the Southeast take place, as well as many exciting minor contests.

Clonmel

47 *24 km (15 mi) southeast of Cashel on R688.*

As the county seat of Tipperary, Clonmel is set on the prettiest part of the River Suir, with wooded islands and riverside walks. It is one of Ireland's largest and most prosperous inland towns. There has been a settlement here since Viking days; in the 14th century the town was walled and fortified as a stronghold of the Butler family. At one end of town is the **West Gate,** built in 1831 on the site of the medieval one. Among other notable buildings are the **Main Guard,** built in 1695 to house the courts of the Palatinate, a separate jurisdiction ruled by the Butlers, and the **Franciscan friary** and **St. Mary's Church of Ireland,** both of which incorporate remains of earlier churches and some interesting tombs and monuments.

Dining and Lodging

$$–$$$ ✕ **Mulcahy's of Clonmel.** In this superb series of interconnecting bars and restaurant areas you'll find a wide selection of food, from the East Lane Cafe's à la carte to the daily carvery lunch to the Kitchen Grill menu of good pub grub, like deep-fried scampi. Mulcahy's has 10 modern bedrooms over the pub. ✉ *47 Gladstone St., Co. Tipperary,* ☎ *052/ 22825. AE, DC, MC, V.*

$$–$$$ ✕🏠 **Hotel Minella.** This granite-faced Georgian manor hotel is in a quiet neighborhood on the bank of the River Suir. The bedrooms, particularly those in the front and in the east wing, have fine views of the river. Three of the eight suites have four-poster beds and private steam rooms; the remaining five have hot tubs. The Victorian furnishings in the main house are comfortable; walls are decorated with hunting prints. The oak-paneled dining room has a good reputation for well prepared traditional Irish cuisine. ✉ *Coleville Rd., Co. Tipperary,* ☎ *052/22388,* FAX *052/24381,* WEB *www.hotelminella.ie. 62 rooms with bath, 8 suites. Restaurant, health club, fishing, bar. AE, DC, MC, V.*

Outdoor Activities and Sports

Clonmel Golf Club (✉ Lyreanearla, ☎ 052/24050) is an 18-hole course on the slopes of the Comeragh Mountains, 5 km (3 mi) from Clonmel.

Hurling and Gaelic football are played at the **Clonmel GAA Grounds** (✉ Western Rd., ☎ 052/23873). Horse races are held at **Clonmel Racecourse** (✉ Powerstown Park, ☎ 052/25719).

Carrick-on-Suir

48 *20 km (12 mi) east of Clonmel on N24.*

Carrick-on-Suir lies partly in County Tipperary and partly in County Waterford. The beautifully restored **Ormonde Castle** is the town's main attraction. The castle, dating from 1450, is fronted by the 16th-century Ormonde Manor House, an interesting and well-preserved Tudor mansion. The town is one of several claiming to be the birthplace of Anne Boleyn, and the house is said to have been built in order to entertain her daughter, Queen Elizabeth I, who never visited here. The castle contains some good early stuccowork, especially in the 100-ft Long Room, and many arms and busts of the English queen. ☎ *051/640–787.* ✍ *€2.55.* ☉ *Mid-June–Sept., daily 9:30–6:30.*

Shopping
The **Tipperary Crystal Factory Shop** (✉ Ballynoran, ☎ 051/641–188), a factory outlet that offers free tours of the glass-cutting facility weekdays between 10 and 3:30, has a showroom in a replica thatched cottage, open daily.

THE SOUTHEAST A TO Z

To research prices, get advice from other travelers, and book travel arrangements, visit www.fodors.com.

AIR TRAVEL

AIRPORTS
Waterford Regional Airport is on the Waterford–Ballymacaw road in Killowen. Waterford City is 9½ km (6 mi) from the airport. A hackney cab from the airport into Waterford City costs approximately €15.

➤ AIRPORT INFORMATION: **Waterford Regional Airport** (☎ 051/875–589).

BOAT AND FERRY TRAVEL
The region's primary ferry terminal is found just south of Wexford Town at Rosslare. Stena Sealink sails directly between Rosslare Ferryport and Fishguard, Wales. Pembroke, Wales, and France's Cherbourg and Roscoff can be reached on Irish Ferries.

➤ BOAT AND FERRY INFORMATION: **Irish Ferries** (☎ 053/33158). **Stena Sealink** (☎ 053/33115).

BUS TRAVEL
Bus Éireann makes the Waterford–Dublin journey six times daily for about €8.85 one-way. There are five buses daily between Waterford City and Limerick and four between Waterford City and Rosslare. The Cork–Waterford journey is made twelve times daily. In Waterford City, the terminal is Waterford Bus Station.

➤ BUS INFORMATION: **Bus Éireann** (☎ 01/836–6111 in Dublin; 051/879–000 in Waterford).

CAR RENTAL
The major car-rental companies have offices at Rosslare Ferryport, and in most large towns rental information can be found through the local tourism office. Typical car-rental prices start at about €55 per day (€32 per day for 7 days) with unlimited mileage, and they usually include insurance and all taxes. Budget has offices in Rosslare Harbour and at Waterford Airport. Hertz has offices in Rosslare Harbour and Waterford City.

➤ LOCAL AGENCIES: **Budget** (✉ The Ferryport, Rosslare Harbour, ☎ 053/33318; ✉ Waterford Airport, ☎ 051/421–670). **Hertz** (✉ Rosslare Harbour, ☎ 053/33238; ✉ Waterford City, ☎ 051/878–737).

CAR TRAVEL
Waterford City, the regional capital, is easily accessible from all parts of Ireland. From Dublin, take N7 southwest, change to N9 in Naas, and continue along this highway through Carlow Town and Thomastown until it terminates in Waterford. N25 travels east–west through Waterford City, connecting it with Cork in the west and Wexford

Town in the east. From Limerick and Tipperary Town, N24 stretches southeast until it, too, ends in Waterford City.

ROAD CONDITIONS
For the most part, the main roads in the Southeast are of good quality and are free of congestion. Side roads are generally narrow and twisting, and drivers should keep an eye out for farm machinery and animals on country roads.

EMERGENCIES
➤ CONTACTS: **Police, fire, ambulance** (☎ 112 or 999). **Waterford Regional Hospital** (✉ Ardkeen, ☎ 051/848–000).

LODGING
BED-AND-BREAKFASTS
For a small fee, Bord Fáilte will book accommodations anywhere in Ireland through its central reservations system. B&Bs can be booked at local visitor information offices as well when they are open.
➤ CONTACT INFORMATION: **Bord Fáilte** (☎ 800/223–6470 in the U.S. and Canada; 800/039–7000 in the U.K.; 02/9299–6177 in Australia; 09/379–8720 in New Zealand, WEB www.irelandvacations.com).

OUTDOOR ACTIVITIES AND SPORTS
FISHING
For further information on angling activities in the region, contact the Southern Regional Fisheries Board.
➤ CONTACTS: **Southern Regional Fisheries Board** (✉ Anglesea St., Clonmel, Co. Tipperary, ☎ 052/80055).

SPECTATOR SPORTS
Tickets to major Gaelic football and hurling matches are usually taken up by members, but for smaller venues, or for some of the less fiercely contested matches, inquire at local TIOs.

TOURS
BUS TOURS
Irish City Tours in Kilkenny operates open-top coach tours from the castle gate Easter through September, daily 10:30–5.
➤ FEES AND SCHEDULES: **Irish City Tours** (☎ 01/458–0054).

WALKING TOURS
Walking tours of Kilkenny are arranged by Tynan Tours, and operate daily April to October, and November to March, Tuesday to Saturday, from the Kilkenny TIO. Burtchaell Tours in Waterford City leads a Waterford walk at noon and 2 PM daily from March through September. It leaves from the Granville Hotel. Walking tours of historic Wexford Town can be prebooked for groups by contacting Seamus P. Molloy.
➤ FEES AND SCHEDULES: **Burtchaell Tours** (☎ 051/873–711). **Seamus P. Molloy (Wexford Town Walking Tours)** (☎ 053/22663). **Tynan Tours** (☎ 87/265–1745).

TRAIN TRAVEL
Waterford City is linked by Irish Rail service to Dublin. Trains run from Plunkett Station in Waterford City to Dublin four times daily, making stops at Thomastown, Kilkenny, Bagenalstown, and Carlow Town. The daily train between Waterford City and Limerick makes stops at Carrick-on-Suir, Clonmel, Cahir, and Tipperary Town. The train between Rosslare and Waterford City runs twice daily.
➤ TRAIN INFORMATION: **Irish Rail** (☎ 01/836–6222 in Dublin; 051/873–401 in Waterford).

VISITOR INFORMATION
Ten Tourist Information Offices (TIOs) in the Southeast are open all
year (not all have fax numbers). They are Carlow Town, Carrick-on-
Suir, Clonmel, Dungarvan, Enniscorthy, Gorey, Kilkenny, Lismore,
Waterford City, and Wexford Town. Another seven TIOs are open sea-
sonally: Ardmore (June–mid-September); Cahir (May–September);
Cashel (April–September); New Ross (May–September); Rosslare
(April–September); Tipperary Town (May–October); Tramore (June–
August).

➤ TOURIST INFORMATION: **Ardmore** (✉ Ardmore, Co. Waterford, ☎
024/94444). **Cahir** (✉ Castle Car Park, Co. Tipperary, ☎ 052/41453).
Carlow Town (✉ Bridewell La., Co. Carlow, ☎ 0503/31554, FAX 0503/
30065). **Carrick-on-Suir** (✉ Heritage Centre, Main St., Co. Tipperary,
☎ 051/640–200). **Cashel** (✉ Cashel Heritage Centre, Co. Tipperary,
☎ 062/62511, FAX 062/61789). **Clonmel** (✉ Community Office, 8
Sarsfield St., Co. Tipperary, ☎ 052/22960, FAX 052/26378). **Dungarvan** (✉ The Courthouse, Co. Waterford, ☎ 058/41741, FAX 058/
45020). **Enniscorthy** (✉ Wexford Museum, The Castle, Co. Wexford,
☎ 054/34699). **Gorey** (✉ Markethouse, Main St., Co. Wexford, ☎
055/21248, FAX 055/22521). **Kilkenny** (✉ Shee Alms House, Rose Inn
St., ☎ 056/51500, FAX 056/63955). **Lismore** (✉ Heritage Centre, Co.
Waterford, ☎ 058/54975, FAX 058/53009). **New Ross** (✉ Harbour Centre, The Quay, Co. Wexford, ☎ 051/421–857). **Rosslare** (✉ Rosslare
Ferry Terminal, Kilrane, Rosslare Harbour, Co. Wexford, ☎ 053/
33232, FAX 053/33421). **Tipperary Town** (✉ 3 James St., Co. Tipperary, ☎ 062/51457). **Tramore** (✉ Town Centre, Co. Waterford, ☎ 051/
281–572). **Waterford City** (✉ 41 The Quay, Co. Waterford, ☎ 051/
875–823, FAX 051/876–720). **Wexford Town** (✉ Crescent Quay, Co.
Wexford, ☎ 053/23111, FAX 053/41743).

6 THE SOUTHWEST

IN AND AROUND CORK AND KILLARNEY, THE RING OF KERRY, THE DINGLE PENINSULA, AND SHANNONSIDE

Five-star scenery: the varied, pastoral landscape—from Kinsale along the coast west to Mizen Head in the far southwest corner to the glorious mountains and lakes of Killarney—dazzles. And the food! Thanks to its accomplished chefs and the bounty of farms, fields, lakes, and coast, County Cork has become a little paradise of fresh, rustic Irish cuisine. You'll also find a mild climate, the nation's second- and third-largest cities, and extensive Irish-speaking areas.

Updated by
Alannah
Hopkin

CORK, KERRY, LIMERICK, AND CLARE—the sound of these South-west Ireland county names has an undeniably evocative Irish lilt. A varied coastline, spectacular scenery (especially around the famous lakes of Killarney), and a mild climate have long attracted visitors to this region. Although the Southwest contains Cork and Limerick—Ireland's second- and third-largest cities—its most notable attractions are rural: miles and miles of pretty country lanes meandering through rich but sparsely populated farmland. Even in the two main cities the pace of life is perceptibly slower than in Dublin. To be in a hurry in this region is to be ill-mannered. It was probably a Kerryman who first remarked that when God made time, he made plenty of it.

As you look over thick, fuchsia hedges at thriving dairy farms or stop off at a wayside restaurant to sample the region's seafood or locally raised meat, it's difficult to imagine that some 150 years ago this area was decimated by famine. Thousands perished in the fields and the work-houses, and thousands more took "coffin ships" from Cobh in Cork Harbour to the New World. Between 1845 and 1849 the population of Ireland decreased by more than a million, or roughly 30% (according to the 1841 census, the Irish population was 8,175,124). Many small villages in the Southwest were wiped out. The region was battered again in the War for Independence and the Civil War that was fought with intensity in and around "Rebel Cork" between 1919 and 1921. Economic recovery didn't pick up until the late 1960s, and tourist developments were low-key until the mid-1990s.

The Irish economic boom coincided with a marketing push to increase visitor numbers. The result has been a mixed blessing. For example, the main roads in the Southwest are no longer traffic-free, but the roads themselves have been upgraded. There is a bigger choice of accommodations, with better facilities, but many of the newer hotels and bed-and-breakfasts are bland. Even the traditional warm Irish welcome is less ubiquitous than it was in the past, given the increased pace of everyday life. Furthermore, the natural environment has come under pressure with the commercial and industrial development of the region. There is now a greater awareness, however, that economic development is threatening the existence of the very factors that attracted visitors in the first place: uncrowded roads, pollution-free beaches and rivers, easy access to golf and fishing, and unspoiled scenery where wildflowers, untamed animals, and rare birds could thrive. Thus the Southwest is consciously trying to preserve and improve its natural amenities while catering to greater visitor numbers.

South of the city of Cork, the main business and shopping town of the region, the resort town of Kinsale is the gateway to an attractive coastline, mainly rocky and indented, containing Roaring Water Bay, with its main islands, and the magnificent natural harbor, Bantry Bay. The southwest coast of the region is formed by three peninsulas: the Beara, the Iveragh, and the Dingle; the road known as the Ring of Kerry makes a complete circuit of the Iveragh Peninsula. Killarney's sparkling blue lakes and magnificent sandstone mountains, inland from the peninsulas, have a unique and romantic splendor, immortalized in the 19th century by the writings of William Thackeray and Sir Walter Scott. Around the Shannon estuary you enter "castle country," an area littered with ruined castles and abbeys as a result of Elizabeth I's attempt to subdue the old Irish province of Munster in the 16th century. Limerick City, too, bears the scars of history from a different confrontation with the English—the Siege of Limerick, which took place in 1691. Today, it is Limerick's other "scars"—described so memorably in Frank Mc-

Court's best-seller *Angela's Ashes*—that now lure travelers to discover (or rediscover) the city.

Although the Southwest has several sumptuous country-house hotels, it's basically an easygoing, unpretentious region, where informality and simplicity prevail. As in the rest of Ireland, social life revolves around the pub, and a visit to your "local" is the best way to find out what's going on.

Pleasures and Pastimes

Dining

The Southwest—especially County Cork—rivals Dublin as Ireland's food-culture epicenter. Cork has astonishing resources: sparkling waters full of a wide array of fish, acre after acre of potato fields, cows galore, wild mushrooms and berries, and much more. Cork's dedicated, inventive chefs turn this bounty into a feast in food markets (Cork City's English Market, most notably), bakeries, cafés, restaurants, B&Bs, and country houses. In tiny Shanagarry, Darina and Tim Allen train hundreds of chefs every year at their Ballymaloe Cookery School. Outstanding restaurants and the International Gourmet Festival in October draw crowds to Kinsale, the "Gourmet Capital of Ireland." Whether trained at home or abroad, area chefs put a premium on fresh, local (often organically grown) produce. Restaurants outside main cities tend to be seasonal, and choice will be limited between November and mid-March. To sample the region's best cuisine, consult our five-day gastronomic tour, below.

CATEGORY	THE REPUBLIC*
$$$$	over €29
$$$	€22–€29
$$	€13–€21
$	under €13

Per person for a main course at dinner

Lodging

You'll find some of the most sumptuous country-house hotels in Ireland in the Southwest. Though some country houses appear grand, their main aim is to provide a relaxed stay in beautiful surroundings. There are more modest establishments as well—many in spectacular seaside locations. A good pair of walking boots and a sensible raincoat are more useful here than a fancy wardrobe. If you want to dress for dinner, as some people do, feel free. By and large, however, informality rules. Keep in mind that facilities may be minimal—only expensive hotels have fitness centers, for instance. Most hotels can, however, organize golf, deep-sea fishing, freshwater angling, and horseback riding. Most B&Bs have introduced private bathrooms and, in the larger towns, televisions and direct-dial phones in rooms. Accommodations in West Cork, Killarney, and Dingle are seasonal; between November and March, many places close down, but outside these months—especially from July to mid-October—hotels are busy, so book well in advance. If your first choice for a hotel is full, ask for a recommendation to similar lodgings nearby.

CATEGORY	THE REPUBLIC*
$$$$	over €230
$$$	€178–€230
$$	€127–€178
$	under €127

All prices are for two people in a double room, VAT included.

Nightlife and the Arts

Mid-June through September, you'll find musical entertainment in pubs on most nights; in other seasons, Thursday through Sunday are the busiest times. Dingle is the best place for traditional Irish music; elsewhere, pubs and clubs offer a mix of traditional, country, rock, and jazz. Spontaneous music sessions are common, especially on the Dingle Peninsula; elsewhere, performances usually begin around 9. Nightclubs are usually attached to hotels or bars; they are open from about 10:30 PM until 2 AM. Expect to pay a €6.35–€12.70 cover fee.

Outdoor Activities and Sports

BICYCLING

You'll find some of the most spectacular scenery in the country around Glengarriff, Killarney, and Dingle. The length of the hills—rather than their steepness—is the challenge here, but without the hills there wouldn't be such great views. A less-strenuous option, equally scenic but on a smaller scale, is the coast of West Cork between Kinsale and Glengarriff. The Beara Peninsula proves very popular with cyclists, who enjoy its varied coastal scenery and relative lack of vehicles. Traffic can be a problem in July and August on the Ring of Kerry, where there is a lack of alternative routes to the one main circuit. Because of the various mountain ranges in the area, rain is never far off, except on the hottest summer days, so always carry a light, waterproof jacket. For bicycle rentals, expect to pay about €9 per day, or €40 for seven days, with a €50 refundable deposit. Book well in advance between May and September, as demand is high and availability is limited.

FISHING

Besides having an abundance of facilities for sea angling and a wealth of salmon and trout rivers, the Southwest enjoys the bonus of scenic surroundings—be it the black-slate cliffs of the coast or the lush vegetation of Killarney and the Ring of Kerry. Shore fishing is available all along the coast, from Cobh in the east to Foynes in the west. The whole region offers excellent opportunities for lake and river fishing, although most anglers head for Waterville or Killarney. Coarse anglers will find pike at Macroom and coarse-angling facilities at Mallow and Fermoy. The deep-sea fishing season runs from April to October. Boat rentals cost about €50.80 per person per day. Boats can be rented at Ballycotton, Cork Harbour in Cobh, Midleton, Passage West, Crosshaven, Kinsale, Courtmacsherry, Clonakilty, Castletownshend, Valentia Island, Fenit, and Dingle.

GOLF

Many of the Southwest's 18-hole courses are world-famous, championship clubs set amid wonderful scenery. The leading courses in the region—Cork Golf Club, the Old Head Golf Links, Waterville Golf Links, Killarney Golf and Fishing Club, and Tralee Golf Club—are all covered in depth in Chapter 10.

HIKING

The far Southwest around Killarney and Dingle is classic hiking country, with spectacular scenery and a feeling of wilderness—even though you're never more than 3 or 4 km (2 or 3 mi) from civilization. On higher ground, fog can come down very quickly, so follow local advice on weather conditions and adjust your schedule accordingly. Two signposted, long-distance walking trails wind through the region: the 214-km (134-mi) Kerry Way begins in Killarney and loops around the Ring of Kerry, and the 153-km (95-mi) Dingle Way loops from Tralee around the Dingle Peninsula. Both routes consist of paths and "green (unsurfaced) roads," with some stretches linked by surfaced roads. In general, these routes, although rough underfoot, are suitable for families, particularly in summer. The 209-km (130-mi) Beara Way mainly is an off-road walk around the rugged Beara Peninsula in West Cork.

The Blackwater Way is a 168-km (104-mi) trail that follows the lower slopes of the Knockmealdown Mountains to the rich farms and woodlands of the Blackwater Valley. The Sheep's Head Way encircles the Sheep's Head Peninsula and has glorious views of Bantry Bay along its 88-km (55-mi) route. Additional walks can be found in Killarney National Park; Gougane Barra, northeast of Ballylickey off R584 in County Cork; Farran, off N22 about 16 km (10 mi) west of Cork City in County Cork; the Ballyhoura Mountains on the Cork-Limerick border, off N20 at Ballyhea about 16 km (10 mi) north of Buttevant; and Currachase Forest Park, east of Askeaton off N69 in County Limerick.

Exploring the Southwest

Our coverage of the Southwest is organized into seven sections: Cork City (which includes a side trip to the ever-popular Blarney Castle, home of the Blarney Stone); East Cork and the Blackwater Valley (covering Youghal and Ballymaloe); Kinsale to Glengarriff via Bantry Bay (Mizen Head, Cape Clear, and other points in the far Southwest); the Ring of Kerry; In and Around Killarney; the Dingle Peninsula; and North Kerry and Shannonside. We begin in Cork (under the assumption that you'll approach from points east) and make a clockwise sweep of the area. We end on the northern fringe, crossing over the border from County Kerry into County Limerick and then briefly dipping into the very southeastern reaches of County Clare in the area immediately around Shannon Airport. If you fly into Shannon, you can easily travel the entire sequence in reverse, or pick and choose from those places that interest you.

Among the most notable attractions in the Southwest are the Lakes of Killarney, which require a day or more; you simply must explore these wonders partly on foot to enjoy them fully. Killarney also makes a good base for discovering the Ring of Kerry and the Dingle Peninsula. The main cities in the area—Cork, Tralee, and Limerick—have quiet charm, but they cannot compete with the magnificent scenery farther west. Kinsale is a favorite starting point for a leisurely drive through the coast west to Bantry, which can take one day or three, depending on your appetite for unscheduled stops and impromptu exploration. Two national parks, Glengarriff near the sea and Gougane Barra in the mountains, are also worth visiting.

Numbers in the text correspond to numbers in the margin and on the Southwest, Cork City, and Killarney and Environs maps.

Great Itineraries

IF YOU HAVE 3 DAYS

Base yourself in ☒ **Killarney** ㊷ for both nights, and reserve one day for a leisurely exploration of Killarney's famous lakes and mountains. Visit the **Gap of Dunloe** ㊾ on an organized tour and walk or ride horseback through the gap itself, crossing the lake beyond by rowboat. The next day head for the Ring of Kerry via **Killorglin** ㊶ and enjoy the mix of subtropical vegetation caused by the nearby Gulf Stream and rugged cliffs. On the third day, follow the granite-walled Pass of Keimaneigh to **Bantry** ㉜. A cliff-top road runs between Bantry and Glengarriff, with wonderful sea views along the 24-km (15-mi) Bantry Bay inlet. The stretch of road between **Glengarriff** ㉝ and Killarney, known as the tunnel road, is one of Ireland's most famous scenic routes. It comes into Killarney past the **Ladies' View** ㊿, little changed since it impressed Queen Victoria's ladies-in-waiting almost 150 years ago.

Apart from the innovative chefs working in the kitchens of some of Dublin's finest restaurants, Cork is indisputably Ireland's leading food region—with lovely country-house hotels serving food prepared from the freshest local ingredients; the country's leading cooking school; and its self-proclaimed "Gourmet Capital." If you're a dedicated foodie or you've already done a wider sweep through the country and you want to focus on one region, our five-day itinerary, taking in the Southwest's best food, may be for you. Begin in ⊡ **Cork City** ①–⑱ and stop in at the not-to-be-missed **English Market** ⑬. Stay overnight and sample the classic French cuisine at ⊡ **Fleming's,** an elegant Georgian house on its own grounds. On the next day head out to ⊡ **Ballymaloe House** in **Shanagarry** ㉔, for 50 years the Allen family farm and today run by three generations of the family. The decor is simple but elegant country-style, and the emphasis is on fresh local produce and fish from nearby Ballycotton. If you plan carefully, you may be able to fit in a one-day cooking class at the **Ballymaloe Cookery School and Gardens,** 2 km (1 mi) away, also run by the Allen family. At the least, the gardens, with their wide variety of herbs and edible plants, are a pleasant way to see food before it hits the table. Next drive northwest to ⊡ **Mallow** ㉖ in the Blackwater Valley to ⊡ **Longueville House,** another family-run operation, albeit on a grander scale. Proprietor William O'Callaghan's President's Restaurant earns raves as one of the finest in Ireland; he also runs one of Ireland's only vineyards. From here, head to ⊡ **Kenmare** ㉞, where the luxurious ⊡ **Park Hotel** has terraced lawns sweeping down to Kenmare Bay; stroll in the gardens before sampling the renowned modern Irish cuisine of its outstanding restaurant. The following day drive back toward the pretty waterfront village of ⊡ **Kinsale** ㉘, where spots like **The Vintage** restaurant and the ⊡ **Blue Haven Hotel** have helped earn the town the title, "Gourmet Capital of Ireland." Return to Cork City the next day.

Start at **Bunratty Castle** ㉓, the nearest attraction to Shannon Airport and a must-see for first-time visitors. Continue on to ⊡ **Limerick City** ㉒ and take a look at either the restored **King John's Castle** or the Celtic and medieval treasures at the **Hunt Museum.** Spend the night in Limerick; the following day, head south for Blarney, where you can kiss the Blarney Stone at **Blarney Castle** ⑲ and browse through Ireland's largest selection of crafts shops. Then proceed to ⊡ **Cork City** ①–⑱, where you can make an overnight stop. Take a walk around the city center and enjoy the city's lively nightlife—its pubs, restaurants, and theater performances. The next day head east to Cork Harbour to visit **Cobh** ㉑, where the Queenstown Heritage Centre documents the history of Irish emigration. Cross the harbor by ferry and visit ⊡ **Kinsale** ㉘, a historic little port built on hilly slopes, with a star-shape fort dating from 1620 on its large, natural harbor. The town is a fashionable resort with gourmet restaurants, crafts shops, and art galleries. The following day, drive through scenic West Cork around Bantry Bay and into **Glengarriff** ㉝, where you can take a boat to the subtropical gardens of Ilnacullin (also known as Garnish Island), a few minutes offshore. Continue on to ⊡ **Kenmare** ㉞, a pretty village on a river estuary, and then go on to ⊡ **Killarney** ㊷ via a scenic road known as the Windy Gap. Spend the night here and make an early start the next day, either taking a half-day tour of the **Gap of Dunloe** ㊾ or viewing the splendid scenery in the park around **Muckross House** ㊺. In the afternoon, leave for the Ring of Kerry, driving past ⊡ **Sneem** ㉟ through subtropical vegetation to ⊡ **Waterville** ㊱ or ⊡ **Caragh Lake** on the west side of the Ring. From Cahirciveen you can see the Dingle Peninsula

ATLANTIC OCEAN

CLARE

Kilkee
Kilrush
Killimer
Tarbert
60 Glin
N69
N67
N6
N69

*Mouth of
the Shannon*
Ballybunion

Listowel **59**
R523
Abbeyfeale

Ardfert
Tralee **58**
N21
Castleisland
N21
R57

**Kilmakedar Church
Gallarus Oratory**
*Brandon
Bay*
*Tralee
Bay*
Kilcummin
Blennerville
N70
R559

Mt. Brandon
Ballydavid
Connor
Pass
DINGLE PENINSULA
Castlemaine

Ballyferriter **56**
Dunquin **55** **53**
Slea Head **54**
52 **Dingle
Town** **51**
Ventry
Dunbeg
R561
Inch
Annascaul

41 **Killorglin**
Rossbeigh
Glenbeigh **40**
*Caragh
Lake*
R562
**Killarney
Area** **42** **50**
N72

*Blasket
Islands*
Dingle Bay
Kerry
Ring
of
N70
*Lake
Leane*
Muckross

IVERAGH PENINSULA
KERRY
*Upper
Lake*
*KILLARNEY
NATIONAL
PARK*
N

Cahirciveen **39**
R568
N70
R569

**Valentia
Island** **37**
*Staigue
Fort*
Sneem **35**
Tahilla
34 **Kenmare**
R584

Ballinskelligs
Ballinskelligs *Bay* **36**
Ring
of
Kerry
Parknasilla
R571
N71
Gougane Ba
National Par

Waterville
N70
Kenmare River
33 **Glengarriff**
Ballylickey

**Skellig
Islands** **38**
Eyenes
BEARA PENINSULA
Garnish
Island
R586

Allihies
Castletownbere
R572
32 **Bantry**
N71

*Dursey
Island*
Bere Island
Bantry Bay
Durrus
Ballydehob
Skibbereen

Schull
R592
N71
30 R596
Castletowns

**Mizen
Vision**
Goleen
Roaring Water Bay
R595
31 **Baltimore**

Crookhaven
*Cape Clear
Island*
*Sherkin
Island*

Tuamgraney

Ennis

Quin

**Craggaunowen
65 Project**

Killaloe

Nenagh

**64 Knappogue
Castle**

Shannon

**Bunratty Castle
63 and Folk Park**

**Limerick 62
City**

■ Plassey

TIPPERARY

Thurles

N75

River Shannon

Foynes

Askeaton

N20

LIMERICK

N24

Cashel

N8

R518

61 Adare

Rathkeale

Croom

Holycross

N74

Newcastle
West

Ballingarry

Tipperary

N21

N20

Milford

Kilmallock

Kilfinnane

Cahir

N24

R576   R579

Clogheen

Mitchelstown

N8

WATERFORD

Kanturk 27

Castletownroche

N72

N72

26

25

Lismore

Dungarvan

N72

Mallow

Fermoy

River Blackwater

N72

CORK

Rathcormac

N20

N8

**Blarney
Castle 19**

Cork City

Youghal

Blarney

1 **18**

**Fota
Island**

Midleton

N25

22

Macroom

R579

R617

20

24

R629

N22

N71

N27

N28

21

Cloyne

23 Shanagarry

Cobh

Ballycotton

R600

*Cork
Harbour*

Dunmanway

N71

Bandon

Kilbrittain

R600

28 Kinsale

Timoleague 29

■ **Charles Fort**

N

R597

Clonakilty

Courtmacsherry

Rosscarbery

Glandore
ion Hall
d

Celtic Sea

KEY	
——	Rail Lines
🚢	Ferry

0   20 miles

0   30 km

across the water and the stretch of road that you will take to reach ⊞ **Dingle Town** ㉒, the next overnight stop and the best base for exploring the peninsula. A short drive outside town, you'll find the spectacular cliffs and early Christian remains beyond **Slea Head** ㉔. On the final day, drive across the Connor Pass and up to ⊞ **Tralee** ㉘, which has a lively museum devoted to County Kerry's past and a steam railway running from nearby **Blennerville** ㉗. From Tralee, return to Limerick City and Shannon Airport on the Adare road (N21) or take N69 to Tarbert and the ferry into County Clare to reach Galway and the west of Ireland.

When to Tour the Southwest

The weather is most likely to be warm and sunny in July and August, but there is no guarantee against rain. July and August are the busiest months, with Irish, British, and Continental tourists heading for the area in large numbers. Visiting in high season means the bars and restaurants of the area will be lively but also crowded. The best time to visit the Southwest is in the "shoulder seasons"—May through June and September through October, when the weather will still be mild; most if not quite all accommodations and attractions will be open, and crowds can be avoided. It may be wet, but it seldom gets cold in this part of the world.

CORK CITY

254 km (158 mi) south of Dublin, 105 km (65 mi) south of Limerick City.

The major metropolis of the south, Cork is Ireland's second-largest city (population 175,000), but put this in perspective—roughly half of Ireland's 3.6 million people live in and around Dublin, a city 10 times the size. Though small relative to the capital, Cork is a spirited, lively place, with a formidable pub scene, a lively traditional music scene, a respected and progressive university, attractive art galleries, and offbeat cafés. Preparations are already under way for 2005, when Cork will be designated European City of Culture.

The city received its first charter in 1185 from Prince John of Norman England, and it takes its name from the Irish word *corcaigh,* meaning "marshy place." The original 6th-century settlement was spread over 13 small islands in the River Lee. Major development occurred during the 17th and 18th centuries with the expansion of the butter trade, and many attractive Georgian-design buildings with wide bowfront windows were constructed during this time. As late as 1770, Cork's present main streets—Grand Parade, Patrick Street, and the South Mall—were submerged under the Lee. Around 1800, when the Lee was partially dammed, the river divided into two streams that now flow through the city, leaving the main business and commercial center on an island, not unlike Paris's Ile de la Cité. As a result, the city features a number of bridges and quays, which, although initially confusing, add greatly to the port's unique character.

"Rebel Cork" emerged as a center of the Nationalist Fenian movement in the 19th century. The city suffered great damage during the War of Independence in 1919–21, when much of its center was burned. Cork is now regaining some of its former glory as a result of sensitive commercial development and an ongoing program of inner-city renewal. In late summer and early autumn, the city hosts some of Ireland's premier festivals, including October's huge **Cork Jazz Festival,** which draws about 50,000 visitors from around the world; the **Cork Film Festival,** also in October; and a number of others.

Exploring Cork City

"Cork is the loveliest city in the world. Anyone who does not agree with me either was not born there or is prejudiced." Whether or not Cork merits this accolade of native poet and writer Robert Gibbings, the city does have plenty to recommend it, including several noteworthy historic sites. These, though spread out, are still best visited on foot. Patrick Street is the center city's main thoroughfare.

A Good Walk

Start your walk on Grand Parade, the geographical center of the city—where you find the **Tourist Information Office** ①. **Bishop Lucey Park** ②, a green space opposite the TIO, leads to the **Triskel Arts Centre** ③, where you can see arts exhibitions and films and find out about arts events around town. From here, take Washington Street to the corner of Grattan Street, where you'll find the restored 19th-century **Court House** ④. Backtrack to North Main Street and take it to the **Cork Vision Centre** ⑤, housed in a once derelict 18th-century church, where a helpful scale model of the city can be seen. Continue down North Main Street to the River Lee. If churches appeal to you, cross Shandon Bridge and climb the hill (a serious hike) to St. Mary's Pro-Cathedral. Halfway up the hill on the right is Shandon, a maze of tiny terraced houses, in the midst of which is **St. Anne's Church** ⑥, and Cork's old butter market, the Firkin Crane. Leaving the Firkin Crane at your back, return to the river by Upper Street. Cross the river on the modern Christy Ring Bridge, which leads to **Cork Opera House** ⑦, where touring productions and variety acts perform, and **Crawford Municipal Art Gallery** ⑧. Beside the gallery is **Paul Street** ⑨, Cork's liveliest shopping area, containing boutiques, bookstores, and cafés. Take one of the narrow left-hand lanes to reach **Patrick Street** ⑩, Cork's main, pedestrianized shopping street. Following it to your left, you'll come upon **Patrick's Bridge** ⑪, from where you'll have a view of the steep north side of the city. Take Winthrop Street, off Patrick Street, to Oliver Plunkett Street, and admire the neoclassic **General Post Office** ⑫; browse, if you wish, at the shops nearby. Return, via Oliver Plunkett Street, to the Grande Parade, with the **English Market** ⑬, a covered food market, on your right. A left will take you to a pedestrian footbridge across the river; go right, following the quays westward, until you reach Bishop Street and the 19th-century Gothic **St. Finbarre's Cathedral** ⑭.

To extend your walk by about 3 km (2 mi), turn left upon leaving the cathedral and take the small road downhill on the right. Go left where it meets the river and cross the bridge to Lancaster Quay. Follow the street, which turns into Western Road, and make a left—you'll reach the architecturally noteworthy campus of **University College, Cork** ⑮. Across Western Road is the **Mardyke** ⑯, a riverside walk that leads to the well-tended **Fitzgerald's Park** ⑰ and the **Cork Public Museum,** where you can soak up interesting tidbits about Cork's history. Turn left out of the museum and take Daly Bridge, which will lead you to Sunday's Well, a hilly residential area with the castlelike **Cork City Gaol** ⑱. Return to the city center along Sunday's Well Road and North Mall, where you can enjoy the sight of several carefully restored Georgian houses.

TIMING

You could easily complete the first part of this walk, from the TIO to St. Finbarre's Cathedral, in a morning or an afternoon, depending on how seriously you intend to take advantage of shopping opportunities along the way. However, if you plan to visit everything, then allow a full day, with a break for lunch at the Farmgate Café in the English Market. Also note that the Crawford Gallery and the English Market are closed on Sunday.

Sights to See

② **Bishop Lucey Park.** This tiny green park in the heart of the city was opened in 1985 in celebration of the 800th anniversary of Cork's Norman charter. During its excavation, workers unearthed portions of the city's original fortified walls, now preserved just inside the arched entranceway. Sculptures by contemporary Cork artists are scattered throughout the park. ⊠ *Grand Parade, Washington Village.* ☞ *Free.*

⑱ **Cork City Gaol.** This castlelike building contains an austere, 19th-century prison. Life-size figures occupy the cells, and sound effects illustrate the appalling conditions that prevailed in the gaol from the early 19th century through the founding of the Free State after the 1916 Uprising. A **Radio Museum** in the Governor's House tells the history of broadcasting in Cork. ⊠ *Sunday's Well Rd., Sunday's Well,* ☎ *021/ 430–5022,* WEB *www.cork-guide.ie/citygaol.htm.* ☞ *€5.* ☉ *Oct.–Easter, daily 10–4; Easter–Sept., daily 9:30–5.*

⑦ **Cork Opera House.** This unattractive concrete hulk went up in 1965 to replace the much-loved, ornate old opera house that was ruined in a fire. Attempts to integrate the Opera House with its neighbor, the Crawford Municipal Art Gallery, have softened its grim facade. The piazza outside the opera house has pavement cafés and street performers. ⊠ *Lavitt's Quay, City Center South,* ☎ *021/427–0022,* WEB *www.corkoperahouse.ie.*

⑤ **Cork Vision Centre.** In an area that was once the bustling heart of medieval Cork, the center provides an excellent introduction to the city's geography and history. The centerpiece is a detailed 1:500 scale model of Cork, showing how it has grown and changed over the ages. ⊠ *N. Main St., Washington Village,* ☎ *021/427–9925,* WEB *www.corkvisioncentre.com.* ☞ *By donation. Guided tours of city model on request €1.50.* ☉ *Tues.–Sat. 10–5.*

④ **Court House.** A landmark in the very center of Cork, this magnificent classical building has an imposing Corinthian portico and is still in use as the district's main court house. The exterior has been cleaned and fully restored and looks every bit as good as when it was built in 1835. ⊠ *Washington St., Washington Village,* ☎ *021/427–2706.* ☉ *Weekdays 9–5.*

★ ⑧ **Crawford Municipal Art Gallery.** The large redbrick building, built in 1724 as the Custom House, is now Ireland's leading provincial art gallery. An imaginative expansion added an extra 10,000 square ft of gallery space—for visiting exhibitions and adventurous shows of modern Irish artists, mounted by the gallery itself. The permanent collection includes landscape paintings depicting Cork in the 18th and 19th centuries. Take special note of works by Irish painters William Leech (1881–1968), Daniel Maclise (1806–70), James Barry (1741–1806), and Nathaniel Grogan (1740–1807). The café, run by the Allen family of Ballymaloe, is a good place for a light lunch or a homemade sweet. ⊠ *Emmet Pl., City Center South,* ☎ *021/427–3377,* WEB *www.synergy.ie/crawford.* ☞ *Free.* ☉ *Weekdays 9–5, Sat. 9–1.*

★ ⑬ **English Market.** Food lovers: head for one of the misleadingly small entrances to this large covered market, housed in an elaborate, red-and-brown-brick and cast-iron Victorian building. (Its official name is the Princes Street Market, and it's also known locally as the Covered Market.) A turn-of-the-20th-century predecessor to today's urban farmers' markets, this is a great place to get a sense of Cork's thriving food scene. Among the 140 stalls, keep an eye out for the **Alternative Bread Co.,** which produces more than 40 varieties of handmade bread every day. **Iago,** Sean Calder-Potts's deli, has fresh pasta, lots of cheeses, and charcuterie. You'll find olive oil, olive-oil soap, and olives from

Greece, Spain, France, and Italy at the **Olive Stall. Kay O'Connell's Fish Stall,** in the market's legendary fresh-fish alley, sells local smoked salmon. **O'Reilly's Tripe and Drisheen** is the last existing retailer of a Cork specialty, tripe (cow's stomach), and *drisheen* (blood sausage). Upstairs is the Farmgate, an excellent café. ⊠ *Entrances on Grand Parade and Princes St., City Center South.* ☉ *Mon.–Sat. 9–5:30.*

⑰ **Fitzgerald's Park.** Beside the north channel of the River Lee in the west of the city, this small, well-tended park contains the **Cork Public Museum,** a Georgian mansion that houses a well-planned exhibit of Cork's history from ancient times to the present, with a strong emphasis on the city's Republican history. ⊠ *Western Road,* ☎ *021/427–0679.* ⊡ *Free.* ☉ *Weekdays 11–1 and 2:15–5, Sun. 3–5.*

⑫ **General Post Office.** This neoclassical building with an elegant colonnaded facade was once Cork's Opera House. It dominates a street otherwise occupied by fashion boutiques, jewelry stores, and antiques shops. ⊠ *Oliver Plunkett St., City Center South,* ☎ *021/427–2000.* ☉ *Weekdays 9–5:30, Sat. 9–5.*

NEED A BREAK? The friendly, old **Long Valley** (⊠ Winthrop St., City Center South, ☎ 021/427–2144), popular with artists, writers, students, and eccentrics, serves tea, coffee, pints, and oversize sandwiches.

---

⑯ **Mardyke.** This is a popular riverside walk—it links the city center with Fitzgerald's Park, beside a pitch where cricket, very much a minority sport in Ireland, is played on summer weekends. ⊠ *Western Road.*

⑩ **Patrick Street.** Extending from Grand Parade in the south to Patrick's Bridge in the north, Panna (as it's known locally)—Cork's main shopping thoroughfare, a pedestrian priority area with wide sidewalks—contains a mainstream mix of department stores, clothes shops, pharmacies, and bookshops. Most stores are open Monday through Thursday and Saturday 9–5:30, Friday 9–7, and some open Sunday 2–5. If you look above some of the standardized plate-glass and plastic shop facades here, you'll see examples of the bowfront Georgian windows that are emblematic of old Cork. The street saw some of the city's worst fighting in the years 1919–21, during the War of Independence. ⊠ *City Center South.*

⑪ **Patrick's Bridge.** From this vantage point on the River Lee you can look back past the statue of Father Mathew (1790–1861), Cork's temperance apostle, down the curve of Patrick Street, and north across the river to St. Patrick's Hill, at the tall Georgian houses there. The hill is so steep that steps are cut into the pavement. Tall ships that once served the butter trade used to load up beside the bridge at Merchant's Quay before heading downstream to the open sea. The design of the large, redbrick shopping center on the site today evokes the warehouses of old. ⊠ *Patrick St., City Center South.* ☉ *Freely accessible.*

⑨ **Paul Street.** A narrow street between the River Lee and Patrick Street and parallel to both, Paul Street is the backbone of the trendy shopping area that now occupies Cork's old French Quarter. The area was first settled by Huguenots fleeing religious persecution in France. The Paul Street Piazza is a popular place for street theater and entertainment. The shops here offer the best in modern Irish design—from locally made fashion items to handblown glass—and, in an alley north of the piazza, a good selection of antiques. ⊠ *City Center South.*

⑥ **St. Anne's Church.** The church's pepper-pot Shandon Steeple, which has a four-sided clock and is topped with a golden, salmon-shape weather vane, is visible from most vantage points in the city and is the

Cork City

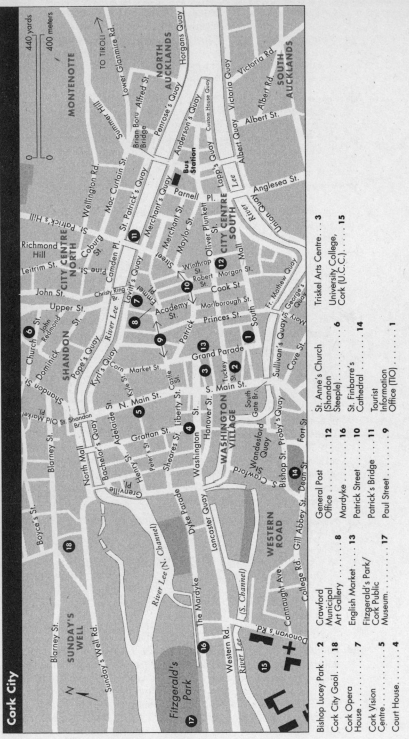

440 yards
400 meters

TO TIROLI →

MONTENOTTE

NORTH AUCKLANDS

SOUTH AUCKLANDS

Lower Glanmire Rd.
Summer Hill
Brian Boru Alfred St.
Bridge
Penrose's Quay
Anderson's Quay
Custom House Quay
Horgans Quay
Victoria Rd.
Victoria Quay
Albert Rd.
Albert St.

Bus Station

Lapp's Quay
Albert Quay
Lee
Anglesea St.

Parnell Pl.

Wellington Rd.
Mac Curtain St.
St. Patrick's Quay
Merchant's Quay
Merchant St.
Maylor St.
Winthrop
Oliver Plunkett
Robert Morgan St.
St.
Cook St.
Marlborough St.
Princes St.

CITY CENTRE NORTH
CITY CENTRE SOUTH

Richmond Hill
St. Patrick's Hill
Coburg St.
Camden Pl.
Pine St.
Christy Ring Br.
Lavitt's Quay
Emmet Pl.
Academy St.

Leitrim St.
John St.
Upper St.
John Redmond
Church St.
Dominick St.
Shandon St.

SHANDON

Pope's Quay
River Lee
Kyrl's Quay
Corn Market St.
Patrick St.
Grand Parade
Tuckey St.

Union Quay
River Lee
South Mall

Mary St.
Fr. Mathew Quay
George's Quay
Sullivan's Quay
Cove St.

S. Main St.
South Gate Br.

N. Main St.
Adelade St.
Liberty St.
Castle St.
Hanover St.
Washington St.

WASHINGTON VILLAGE

St. Old Market Pl.
Shandon Br.
Blarney St.
Bachelor's Quay
North Mall
Henry St.
Peter's St.
Sheares St.
Grattan St.
Proby's Quay
Wandesford Quay
Crawford St.
Bishop St.
Dean St.
Fort St.

Boyce's St.
Blarney St.

SUNDAY'S WELL
Sunday's Well Rd.

N

Grenville Pl.
Dyke Parade
Bishop Lucey Park
Lancaster Quay
Western Rd.
College Rd.
Gill Abbey St.
Connaught Ave.
Donovan's Rd.
Western Road

WESTERN ROAD

The Mardyke
River Lee (N. Channel)
River Lee (S. Channel)

Fitzgerald's Park

Bishop Lucey Park ... 2
Cork City Gaol ... 18
Cork Opera House ... 7
Cork Vision Centre ... 5
Court House ... 4

Crawford Municipal Art Gallery ... 8
English Market ... 13
Fitzgerald's Park/ Cork Public Museum ... 17

General Post Office ... 12
Mardyke ... 16
Patrick Street ... 10
Patrick's Bridge ... 11
Paul Street ... 9

St. Anne's Church (Shandon Steeple) ... 6
St. Finbarre's Cathedral ... 14
Tourist Information Office (TIO) ... 1

Triskel Arts Centre ... 3
University College, Cork (U.C.C.) ... 15

chief reason why St. Anne's is so frequently visited. The Bells of Shandon were immortalized in an atrocious but popular 19th-century ballad of that name. Your reward for climbing the 120-ft tower is the chance to ring the bells, with the assistance of sheet tune cards, out over Cork. Beside the church, Firkin Crane, Cork's former 18th-century butter market, houses two small performing spaces. Adjacent is the Shandon Craft Market. ⊠ *Church St., Shandon.* ☞ *€1.50, €2 including bell tower.* ☉ *May–Oct., Mon.–Sat. 9:30–5; Nov.–Apr., Mon.–Sat. 10–3:30.*

OFF THE BEATEN PATH
ST. MARY'S PRO-CATHEDRAL – Dating from 1808, it is architecturally undistinguished and chiefly worth the uphill hike only if you are interested in tracing your Cork ancestors—its presbytery has records of births and marriages dating from 1784. ⊠ *Cathedral Walk, Shandon,* WEB *www.corkcathedral.com.* ☞ *Free.* ☉ *Daily 9–6.*

⑭ **St. Finbarre's Cathedral.** This was once the entrance to medieval Cork. According to tradition, St. Finbarre established a monastery on this site around AD 650 and is credited as the founder of Cork. The present, compact, three-spire Gothic cathedral, which was completed in 1879, belongs to the Church of Ireland and houses a 3,000-pipe organ. ⊠ *Bishop St., Washington Village,* ☎ *021/496–3387,* WEB *www.cathedral. cork.anglican.org.* ☞ *Free.* ☉ *Daily 9–6.*

❶ **Tourist Information Office (TIO).** This is the place to make reservations and find out about happenings in and around the Cork-Kerry region. ⊠ *Grand Parade, City Center South,* ☎ *021/427–3251,* WEB *www. southwestireland.travel.ie.* ☉ *Weekdays 9–6, Sat. 9–1.*

❸ **Triskel Arts Centre.** In a converted pair of town houses, the centre displays exhibitions of contemporary arts and crafts. It also has a coffee shop, a small auditorium that shows films, and live theater. It's a good place to get the pulse of artsy goings-on about town. ⊠ *Tobin St., Washington Village,* ☎ *021/427–2022.* ☞ *Free.* ☉ *Weekdays 11–6, Sat. 11–5, and during advertised performances.*

★ ⑮ **University College, Cork.** The Doric porticoed gates of U.C.C. stand about 2 km (1 mi) from the center of the city. The college has a campus population of about 10,000, and is a constituent of the National University of Ireland. The main quadrangle is a fine example of 19th-century university architecture in the Tudor-Gothic style, reminiscent of many Oxford and Cambridge colleges. Several ancient ogham stones are on display, as are occasional exhibitions of archival material from the old library. The **Honan Collegiate Chapel,** to the east of the quadrangle, was built in 1916 and modeled on the 12th-century, Hiberno-Romanesque style, which is best exemplified by the remains of **Cormac's Chapel** at Cashel. Most noteworthy about the chapel is its collection of arts and crafts, altar furnishings, and textiles in the Celtic Revival style, and its stained-glass windows. Three large modern buildings have been successfully integrated with the old, including the **Boole Library,** named for mathematician George Boole (1815–64), a past alumnus, whose Boolean algebra laid the foundation for modern computing. Both indoors and out the campus is enhanced by works from its collection of contemporary Irish art, one of the best in the country. Take a stroll through the pleasant landscaped grounds. ⊠ *Western Road,* ☎ *021/ 490–3000,* WEB *www.ucc.ie.* ☞ *Free.* ☉ *Weekdays 9–5, but call to confirm Easter wk, July–Aug., and mid-Dec.–mid-Jan.*

Dining and Lodging

$$–$$$$ ✕ **Ivory Tower.** Seamus O'Connell, the adventurous young owner-chef of this small town-center restaurant, describes his approach as "trans-

ethnic fusion." He has cooked in Mexico and Japan, and has devised a brilliantly eclectic menu: wild duck with vanilla, sherry, and jalapeños; pheasant tamale; and blackened shark with banana ketchup are typical of the surprising—and accomplished—combinations offered here. There are bare wooden floors and stick-back chairs in the first-floor Georgian dining room, and original artwork on display. ⊠ *35 Princes St., Washington Village,* ☎ *021/427–4665. MC, V. Closed Sun.–Mon.*

$$–$$$ ✕ **Café Paradiso.** This simple, café-style restaurant serves such tasty Mediterranean-style food that even dedicated meat eaters forget that it's (egads) vegetarian. Chef Denis Cotter garners raves for his risottos with seasonal vegetables (such as pumpkin and radicchio), his gougère-choux pastry rings with savory fillings, and his excellent homemade desserts. The room is basic, with assorted tables and spindly chairs; the daily special is chalked up on a board, and the food is served on enormous platters. The restaurant is near the university and across from Jurys Hotel. ⊠ *16 Lancaster Quay, Western Road,* ☎ *021/427–7939. DC, MC, V. Closed Sun.–Mon. and last 2 wks in Aug.*

$$–$$$ ✕ **Lovett's.** The Lovett family has been setting high standards on the Cork gastronomic scene since 1977. You'll find Lovett's in the family's Georgian house, surrounded by leafy grounds in a prosperous suburb, and the formal dining room is lined with portraits of 18th-century Cork society. The wine list is extensive—it emphasizes vineyards whose owners have Irish roots, having left Ireland for the Bordeaux and other wine-making regions during the 18th-century. As for food, start with hot black-and-white pudding terrine with onion and raisin confit, followed perhaps by black sole on the bone with citrus butter. The brasserie ($) is more informal. ⊠ *Churchyard La., off Well Rd., Douglas,* ☎ *021/429–4909. AE, DC, MC, V. Closed Sun.–Mon., first wk in Aug., and 1 wk at Christmas. No lunch.*

$$ ✕ **Jacobs on the Mall.** Mercy Fenton's imaginative cooking is one attraction here; the other is the location—an erstwhile Victorian-style Turkish bath. The high-ceilinged room has an enormous skylight, cast-iron pillars, and modern art on the walls; a tall banquette divides the room. Starters include duck liver parfait with plum chutney, and oysters with ginger and lime relish. For a main course, try steamed brill with crisp vegetable parcels, or roast rump of lamb with mash (mashed potatoes), vegetables, and a thyme jus. For dessert you must get the date and butterscotch pudding with bourbon cream. ⊠ *30A South Mall, City Center South,* ☎ *021/425–1530. AE, DC, MC, V. Closed Sun.*

$–$$ ✕ **The Coalquay Café.** The style is minimalist and portions generous and tempting, with imaginative combinations of the freshest ingredients. The café is a smaller, more intimate annex of the fashionable Bodega Bar, a stylish bar—in a converted wine warehouse—that serves the same menu. Share a selection of freshly baked breads with olive oil while you choose from the contemporary, Irish-accented menu. Start with smoked haddock and leek chowder, and deep-fried chili peppers with a blue cheese dip. There are vegetarian and seafood options (seared scallop salad with tangy hazelnut dressing, steamed mussels with lemongrass, coriander, and lime), and meat dishes from the grill. ⊠ *Cornmarket St., City Center South,* ☎ *021/427–2880. AE, MC, V. Closed Mon.–Tues. No lunch.*

$–$$ ✕ **Isaac's.** This popular brasserie-style restaurant is north of the river (cross at Patrick's Bridge and turn right) in a converted warehouse. High ceilings, well-spaced tables covered in oilcloth, modern art, and jazz music create an eclectic, energetic atmosphere. The East-meets-Mediterranean menu includes many tempting dishes—warm salads with Clonakilty black pudding, and king prawns in spicy tomato sauce. ⊠ *MacCurtain St., City Center North,* ☎ *021/450–3805. AE, MC, V. No lunch Sun.*

$–$$ ✕ **Proby's Bistro.** The menu at this riverside bistro is mainly rustic Italian—bruschetta, polenta, risotto, mixed-leaf salads with flavored oils—with occasional Eastern and Tex-Mex influences. It's in a striking and stylish modern building, with patio tables and sun umbrellas optimistically placed on the terrace. The spacious ground-floor restaurant has an open fire, oilcloth-covered tables, and bold Mediterranean furnishings that suit the light, flavorsome food. It's also convenient—near St. Finbarre's Cathedral and a short walk from the main shopping area. ✉ *Proby's Quay, Crosses Green, Washington Village,* ☎ *021/431–6531. MC, V. Closed Sun.*

$ ✕ **Farmgate Café.** On a terrace above the fountain at the Princes Street ★ entrance to Cork's English Market, this is one of the best lunch spots in town. One side of the terrace is open to the market and operates as self-service; the other side is glassed in and served by waiters (reservations advised). Tripe and drisheen are always on the menu; daily specials include less challenging but no less traditional dishes, such as corned beef with *colcannon* (potatoes and cabbage mashed with butter and seasonings) and loin of smoked bacon with *champ* (potato mashed with scallions or leeks). ✉ *English Market, City Center South,* ☎ *021/427–8134. MC, V. Closed Sun. No dinner. Last food orders 4 PM.*

$$$$ ✕▦ **Jurys Cork Hotel.** Beside the River Lee, a five-minute walk from the city center, you'll find a modern, variously two- and three-story structure made of smoked glass and steel. Bedrooms, plain but spacious, have quilted spreads, small sofas, and floor-to-ceiling picture windows. The most desirable rooms overlook the interior patio garden and pool. Cork's Bar is popular among locals at lunch and in the early evening. The Glandore Restaurant serves an à la carte international menu with an emphasis on fresh local produce. ✉ *Western Rd., Western Road Co. Cork,* ☎ *021/427–6622,* ℻ *021/427–4477,* ⦿ *www. jurysdoyle.com. 188 rooms with bath. Restaurant, 2 tennis courts, indoor-outdoor pool, health club, squash, cable TV, 2 bars, meeting rooms. AE, DC, MC, V.*

$$–$$$ ✕▦ **Clarion Hotel & Suites.** This urban riverside hotel, a two-minute walk from Patrick Street, has spacious, modern, one- and two-bedroom suites with kitchens. Rooms are furnished with handcrafted light-oak furniture. Regular rooms are large, and half of them have river views. Polished marble floors and warm terra-cotta–color walls enhance the stylish Med of the Mall bar and restaurant, overlooking the river. The restaurant serves Mediterranean cuisine, with a wide range of pasta dishes, and entrées ranging from panfried fillet of red mullet to char-grilled steaks. Four penthouses have terrace views of the city and the river. ✉ *Morrison's Quay, City Center South Co. Cork,* ☎ *021/427–5858,* ℻ *021/427–5833,* ⦿ *www.choicehotels.com. 30 rooms with bath, 26 suites. Restaurant, kitchenettes (some), cable TV, bar. AE, DC, MC, V.*

$–$$ ✕▦ **Hotel Isaac's.** A stylish renovation has turned this city-center hotel from an old warehouse into a busy restaurant and accommodation complex. Rooms are bright and cheerful, with polished wood floors and rustic pine furniture. The restaurant and some of the rooms overlook a tiny courtyard garden with a waterfall cascading down one side. The dining room also operates as Greene's Restaurant, where they serve seafood—king prawns with chili sauce, oysters poached in Guinness, brill, swordfish, and hake—as well as other intriguing concoctions using fresh produce. Think veal with apricot stuffing, Asian vegetables, and ginger soufflé. ✉ *48 MacCurtain St., City Center North Co. Cork,* ☎ *021/450–0011,* ℻ *021/450–6355,* ⦿ *www.isaacs.ie. 36 rooms with bath. Restaurant, cafeteria, cable TV, Ping-Pong. AE, MC, V.*

$ ✕▦ **Flemings.** This elegant Georgian house has a large dining room ($$$) with plush Louis XV–style chairs, gilt-framed portraits, and crystal chandeliers. Owner-chef Michael Fleming applies French technique to local meat and seafood, which is served with seasonal vegetables, some of which come from the garden. Starters may include *foie gras de canard* or hot oysters, while typical main courses are pot roast of guinea fowl and "symphony of seafood" in a champagne sauce. The quiet, spacious rooms have brocade bedspreads and curtains. Ask about the special-value "dine and stay" package. ⊠ *Silver Grange House, Tivoli Co. Cork,* ☎ *021/482–1621,* FAX *021/482–1178. 4 rooms with bath. Restaurant, cable TV, bar. AE, DC, MC, V.*

$$$$ ⊞ **Hayfield Manor.** Built in a surprisingly successful pastiche of the coun-
★   try-house style, the Manor sits beside the university campus, five minutes' drive from the city center. A splendid, carved-wood double staircase dominates marble-floor lobby, and a wood-paneled library overlooks the walled patio and garden. Rooms are spacious and furnished in a vaguely Louis XV style. The Victorian-style bar serves lunch, and then bar food until 7 PM, when the Manor Room restaurant opens for dinner. ⊠ *College Rd., Western Road Co. Cork,* ☎ *021/431–5600,* FAX *021/431–6839,* WEB *www.hayfieldmanor.ie. 53 rooms with bath. Restaurant, cable TV, indoor pool, health club, bar, meeting rooms. AE, DC, MC, V.*

$$$ ⊞ **Kingsley Hotel.** Think great location, beside the river and close to open countryside, and still just a 10-min walk from the city center. This is half the the reason why you'll like one of Cork's newer hotels. The other: stylish but comfortable furnishings, and a friendly staff. The rear of the hotel overlooks a pretty section of the River Lee, complete with weir and boating (rowing) club. The lobby and lounge are decked out in dark wood with upright velvet arm chairs, like an old-style gentleman's club. The Guest Library has leather chesterfield sofas and leads on to a pretty riverside terrace. Otters Brasserie has a reputation for imaginative food, including game in season and local seafood. Rooms are equipped with spacious bathrooms, super-king-size beds, mahogany furniture, work stations, and CD and music players. The health center boasts a 200-meter pool and outdoor hot tub. ⊠ *Victoria Cross, Western Road,* ☎ *021/480–0500,* FAX *021/480–0527,* WEB *www.kingsleyhotel.com. 69 rooms with bath. Restaurant, cable TV, indoor pool, health club, bar. AE, DC, MC, V.*

$–$$ ⊞ **Rochestown Park.** Set in 7 lovely acres of mature gardens in the fashionable suburb of Douglas, 5 km (3 mi) south of the city, this stylish, friendly hotel has an excellent location if you want to make a fast getaway the next morning. It's also a popular meeting place for locals (you'll get good lunch food at the bar) and a favored base among regular travellers. It was built around a Victorian manor house once used as a convent. Good access to the city's four-lane ring road includes a view of same from some rooms, which is compensated for by the river estuary beyond. Rooms are decorated in a modern style, with cotton spreads, wool carpets, and light-oak fixtures. The large health center specializes in thalassotherapy—seaweed wraps and baths. ⊠ *Rochestown Rd., Douglas, Co. Cork,* ☎ *021/489–2233,* FAX *021/489–2178,* WEB *www.rochestownpark.com. 162 rooms with bath. Restaurant, cable TV, indoor pool, health club, bar, meeting rooms. AE, DC, MC, V.*

$ ⊞ **Jurys Cork Inn.** This modern budget hotel pursues the same policy as its Dublin and Galway counterparts, charging per room, each of which sleeps three adults or two adults and two children. Beside a busy bridge over the River Lee, the inn is a short walk from the city center and bus and rail stations. Rooms are well appointed for the price range: bright and airy with light-wood trim and matching drapes and spreads. ⊠ *Anderson's Quay, City Center South Co. Cork,* ☎ *021/427–6444,* FAX *021/427–6144,* WEB *www.jurysdoyle.com. 133 rooms with bath. Restaurant, cable TV, bar. AE, DC, MC, V.*

$ 🏠 **Seven North Mall.** Angela Hegarty's home, a substantial, 250-year-old tall, terraced house on a tree-lined mall, overlooking the River Lee, is a favorite among many discerning visitors to Cork. The period-style furnishings have a quiet elegance. From here it's only a short walk to theaters, art galleries, the shopping district, and some excellent restaurants. A limited amount of off-road parking is available. Rooms are spacious and stylishly decorated with modest antiques. ✉ *7 North Mall, Sunday's Well Co. Cork,* ☎ *021/439–7191,* FAX *021/430–0811,* WEB *www.karenbrown.com/ireland/seven.html. 5 rooms with bath. Cable TV. MC, V. Closed 2 wks at Christmas.*

$ 🏠 **Victoria Lodge.** This unusual B&B was built in the early 20th century as a Capuchin monastery. Breakfast is served in the spacious old refectory with its oak benches and paneled walls; the common room doubles as a television lounge. The bedrooms are similar to hotel rooms, with custom-made mahogany veneer furniture, matching drapes and spreads, and muted dark green and dark red color schemes. There is no bar or restaurant, but the swanky Kingsley Hotel is just a step around the corner. Victoria Lodge is a five-minute drive from the town center, with plenty of parking, and is also accessible by several bus routes. ✉ *Victoria Cross, Western Road Co. Cork,* ☎ *021/454–2233,* FAX *021/454–2572. 30 rooms with bath. Cable TV. AE, MC, V.*

Nightlife and the Arts

See the *Examiner* or the *Evening Echo* for details about movies theater, and live music performances.

Festivals and Seasonal Events

Ireland's oldest film festival, the **Cork Film Festival** (☎ 021/427–1711), established in 1956, has evolved into one of the country's most important cinema events. New feature-length films and documentaries from Ireland and abroad share the bill with short films—the festival's specialty. The festival usually takes place during the second week of October. In late October, the **Cork Jazz Festival** (☎ 021/427–0463) brings major national and international performers to venues throughout the city.

Galleries

The **Fenton Gallery** (✉ Wandesford Quay, Washington Village, ☎ 021/431–5294, WEB www.artireland.net) shows work by important Irish artists. The **Lavit Gallery** (✉ 5 Father Mathew St., off South Mall, City Center South, ☎ 021/427–7749, WEB www.the lavitgallery.com) sells work by members of the Cork Arts Society and other Irish artists. Offbeat exhibits can be found at the **Triskel Arts Centre** (✉ Tobin St., off S. Main St., Washington Village, ☎ 021/427–2022). The **Vangard Gallery** (✉ Carey's La., Paul St., City Center South, ☎ 021/427–8718) exhibits leading contemporary Irish artists.

Music and Theater

Cork Opera House (✉ Lavitt's Quay, City Center South, ☎ 021/427–0022) is Cork's major hall for touring productions and variety acts. Smaller theatrical productions are staged at the **Everyman Palace** (✉ MacCurtain St., City Center North, ☎ 021/450–1673), with an ornate Victorian interior.

Pubs and Nightclubs

Traditional musicians occasionally gather at **An Spailpin Fanach** (✉ 28 S. Main St., Washington Village, ☎ 021/427–7949). Night owls will appreciate the late-night music club at the Cork Opera House, the **Half Moon** (✉ Half Moon St., City Center South, ☎ 021/427–0022), which showcases live jazz and blues from up-and-coming local bands most weekends from 11 PM. **La Bodega** (✉ Cornmarket St., City Center South,

☎ 021/427–2878), a converted wine warehouse, is the hip meeting spot for Cork's thirtysomethings. The bar at the **Metropole Hotel** (✉ Mac-Curtain St., City Center North, ☎ 021/450–8122) is one of the best places in Cork for jazz. **Pavilion** (✉ Carey's La., City Center South, ☎ 021/427–6228) has late-night disco every night except Tuesdays.

Outdoor Activities and Sports

Bicycles

Rent a bike to explore the city and its environs at **Rothar Cycle Tours** (✉ 2 Bandon Rd., at Barrack St., Shandon, ☎ 021/431–3133).

Fishing

Get your fishing tackle, bait, and licenses, and friendly advice on local fishing resources, at **T. W. Murray** (✉ 87 Patrick St., City Center South, ☎ 021/427–1089).

Golf

Redesigned by Dr. Alister MacKenzie in 1927, **Cork Golf Club** (✉ Little Island, , ☎ 021/435–3451) is one of the finest and most challenging inland courses in Ireland. **Douglas Golf Club** (✉ Douglas, ☎ 021/489–1086) is a tree-lined, parkland, 18-hole course in the southern suburbs of the city. **Lee Valley Golf Club** (✉ Clashanure, Ovens, ☎ 021/733–1721), a par-72, 18-hole, championship course, is 15 minutes west of the city. **Monkstown Golf Club** (✉ Parkgarriffe, Monkstown, ☎ 021/484–1376) is an 18-hole, par-70, strategically bunkered parkland course 11 km (7 mi) southeast of the city.

Horseback Riding

Hitchmough Riding School (✉ Highland Lodge, Monkstown, ☎ 021/437–1267) has an indoor arena for all-weather riding. **Pinegrove Riding School** (✉ White's Cross, ☎ 021/430–3857) has one- and two-hour hacks in the countryside north of the city.

Shopping

Antiques

Irene's (✉ 22 Marlboro St., City Center South, ☎ 021/427–0642) sells antique jewelry. **Mills Antiques** (✉ 3 Paul's La., City Center South, ☎ 021/427–3528) carries Irish, English, and European paintings, printings, silver, porcelain, and small furniture. **Pinnacle** (✉ 44A MacCurtain St., City Center North, ☎ 021/450–1319) stocks antique pine, glass, porcelain, paintings, and prints. **Victoria's** (✉ 2 Oliver Plunkett St., City Center South, ☎ 021/427–2752) carries interesting jewelry, Victoriana, and period clothes.

Books

Mercier Bookshop (✉ 18 Academy St., City Center South, ☎ 021/427–5040), off Patrick Street, sells new books and publishes its own list of Irish and local-interest titles.

Clothing

Fashion lovers will find a choice of internationally famous designer labels at the tiny but elegant boutique called the **Dressing Room** (✉ 8 Emmet Pl., City Center South, ☎ 021/427–0117), opposite the entrance to the Cork Opera House. **Monica John** (✉ French Church St., City Center South, ☎ 021/427–1399) sells locally designed high-fashion ladies' wear, as well as some imported lines. **Quills** (✉ 107 Patrick St., City Center South, ☎ 021/427–1717) has a good selection of Irish-made fashion and casual wear for both women and men. For casual weatherproof clothing, try the **Tack Room** (✉ Unit 3, Academy St., City Center South, ☎ 021/427–2704).

Department Store

Brown Thomas (✉ 18 Patrick St., City Center South, ☎ 021/427–6771) is Cork's leading department store. The fashion floor is well worth a visit to check out items by Irish and international designers. Refuel at the coffee shop, where healthful open sandwiches and homemade soup are available. The ground floor has an excellent cosmetics hall and a good selection of Irish crystal and designer menswear.

Music

Fans of Irish music should visit the **Living Tradition** store (✉ 40 Mac-Curtain St., City Center North, ☎ 021/450–2040).

Shopping Center

The **Merchant's Quay Shopping Centre** (✉ Merchant's Quay, City Center South, ☎ 021/427–5466) is the largest indoor mall in downtown Cork.

Sporting Goods

The **Golf Addict** (✉ 6 Emmet Pl., City Center South, ☎ 021/427–3393) stocks everything the serious golfer could need, as well as a fun selection of nonessential golf paraphernalia and gifts. **Great Outdoors** (✉ 23 Paul St., City Center South, ☎ 021/427–6382) caters to most outdoor sports needs. **Matthews** (✉ Academy St., City Center South, ☎ 021/427–7633) has a wide selection of sporting gear. For inexpensive rainwear, go to **Penney's** (✉ 27 Patrick St., City Center South, ☎ 021/ 427–1935).

Side Trips From Cork City

Blarney, 10 km (6 mi) northwest of Cork City on R617, and Cork Harbour, 16 km (10 mi) east of the city, make perfect day trips. Blarney's main attractions are Blarney Castle and the famous Blarney Stone, while Cork Harbour's draws include Fota Island, with an arboretum, a wildlife park, and Fota House—a renovated hunting lodge and estate— and the lovely fishing port of Cobh.

Blarney

"On Galway sands they kiss your hands, they kiss your lips at Carney, but by the Lee they drink strong tea, and kiss the stone at Blarney." This famous rhyme celebrates one of Ireland's most noted icons—the Blarney Stone, which is the main reason most people journey to Blarney, a small community built around a village green. In the center of Blarney is **Blarney Castle,** or what remains of it: the ruined central keep is all that's left of this mid-15th-century stronghold. The castle contains the famed **Blarney Stone,** set in a wall below the castle's battlements; kissing the stone, it is said, endows the kisser with the fabled "gift of gab." It's 127 steep steps to the battlements. To kiss the stone, you must lie down on the battlements, hold on to a guardrail, and lean your head way back. It's good fun and not at all dangerous. Expect a line from mid-June to September 1; while you wait, you can admire the views of the thickly wooded River Lee valley below and chuckle over how the word "blarney" came to mean what it does. As the story goes, Queen Elizabeth I wanted Cormac MacCarthy, Lord of Blarney, to will his castle to the crown, but he consistently refused her request with eloquent excuses and soothing compliments. Exhausted by his comments, the queen reportedly exclaimed, "This is all Blarney. What he says he rarely means."

Visitors can also take pleasant walks around the castle grounds; **Rock Close** contains oddly shaped limestone rocks landscaped in the 18th century and a grove of ancient yew trees that is said to have been the center of Druid worship. ☎ *021/438–5252,* WEB *www.blarneycastle.ie.*

✉ €5.50. ⊙ *May and Sept., Mon.–Sat. 9–6:30, Sun. 9–5:30; June–Aug., Mon.–Sat. 9–7, Sun. 9–5:30; Oct.–Apr., Mon.–Sat. 9–sundown, Sun. 9–5:30.*

Two hundred yards from the castle, **Blarney Castle House** was built in 1784 in the style of a Scottish baronial mansion. The three-story, gray-stone building has picture-book turrets and fancy, stepped gables. The interior features Elizabethan and Victorian antiques, a fine stairwell, and numerous family portraits. ☎ *021/438–5252,* WEB *www.blarneycastle.ie.* ✉ €5. ⊙ *June–mid-Sept., Mon.–Sat. noon–5.*

DINING AND LODGING

$–$$ ✕ **Blair's Inn.** This traditional country inn, just a 5-min drive from Blarney on R578, in the village of Cloghroe, is a perfect haven from the tour-bus culture that prevails in the village. It has a wooded riverside location and is famed for its exuberant window-box displays. In summer, enjoy the beer garden; in winter warm wood fires flicker in the cozy interior. Freshly prepared local produce is served in generous portions: favorites include Irish stew with lamb, carrots, and potatoes, as well as corned beef. Live entertainment is booked every Sunday from 9 PM, plus Monday from May to October. ✉ *Cloghroe,* ☎ *021/438–1470. MC, V.*

$ ⌂ **Maranatha Country House.** This substantial Victorian manor house, surrounded by 27 acres of woodlands, is in the village of Tower, less than a 15-min drive from the city. It's a handy base if you plan on taking trips to Killarney and West Cork. Drive through Blarney village on the R617 for 2 mi and you will see the sign on the right. Hosts Douglas and Olwen Venn live here with their family. All rooms are spacious with romantic views, and are individually decorated with antiques. The Regal Suite has a sunken bath with a hot tub and a four-poster bed. Breakfast is served in the conservatory, which looks over rolling lawns and majestic trees; the modern world seems miles away. ✉ *Tower,* ☎ *021/438–5102. 6 rooms with bath. No smoking. MC, V. Closed Dec.–mid Mar.*

OUTDOOR ACTIVITIES AND SPORTS

Muskerry Golf Club (✉ Carrigrohane, near Blarney, ☎ 021/438–5297) is an 18-hole, par-71 parkland course.

SHOPPING

Blarney has more crafts shops than anyplace else in Ireland. Most of these stores are concentrated south and west of the village green, a 2-min walk from the castle. A shopping visit here can be profitably used for price comparison and bargain hunting; in spite of appearances, these shops, in general, will not rip you off. **Blarney Woolen Mills** (☎ 021/438–5280, WEB www.blarney.ie) has the largest stock and the highest turnover of all of Blarney's crafts shops. They sell everything from Irish-made high fashion to Aran hand-knit items to leprechaun key rings.

Cork Harbour

To explore Cork Harbour, follow the signposts for Waterford on N25 along the northern banks of the River Lee. Alternatively, a suburban rail service from **Kent Station** (☎ 021/450–6766 for timetable) has stops at Fota Island and Cobh (pronounced cove), and it offers better harbor views than the road.

☞ ② On **Fota Island** you'll find a 70-acre **Wildlife Park** (WEB www.fotawildlife.ie) that's an important breeding center for cheetahs and wallabies. (It also has monkeys, zebras, giraffes, ostriches, flamingos, emus, and kangaroos.) Next door to the Wildlife Park is **Fota House** (☎ 021/481–5543, WEB www.fotahouse.com), a renovated 18th-century hunting lodge with a magnificent garden and arboretum. The lodge was built in the mid-18th century for the powerful Smith Barry family, which owned vast tracts of land in South Cork, including the whole of Fota Island. The next generation of Smith Barrys employed the renowned architects Richard and William Vitruvius Morrison to convert the lodge into an impressive, Classical Regency-style house—one of few examples in Ireland—that has been painstakingly restored to its original splendor. This is the feather in Fota House's hat. The beautiful, symmetrical facade is relatively unadorned, in contrast to the elaborate gilded plasterwork of the formal reception rooms. The servant's quarters, which survived the years intact, are almost as big as the house proper. There's a tea room, where you can relax and have some cake and scones, and a crafts shop at the house. ⊠ *12 km east of Cork; take N25 to R624 to get to Fota Island, then take the main Cobh road,* ☎ *Wildlife Park 021/481–2678; Fota House 021/481–5543.* ⊠ *Wildlife Park €7; Fota House €5, parking €2, gardens and arboretum free.* ☉ *Wildlife Park mid-Mar.–Oct., Mon.–Sat. 10–6, Sun. 11–6; Nov.–St. Patrick's Day, Sat. 10–3, Sun. 11–3; Fota House, gardens, and arboretum daily Mon.– Sat., 10–6; Sun. 11–6.*

★ ㉑ Many generations who departed the port of Cork on immigrant ships for the New World left from **Cobh,** a pretty fishing port and seaside resort with a considerable 19th-century presence and maritime history. The **Queenstown Story,** in the old Cobh railway station, re-creates the experience of the million emigrants who left the town between 1750 and the mid-20th century. It also tells the stories of the great transatlantic liners, including the *Titanic,* whose last port of call was Cobh, and the *Lusitania,* which was sunk by a German submarine off this coast on May 7, 1915, with the loss of 1,198 lives. Many of the *Lusitania's* victims are buried in Cobh, which has a memorial to them on the local quay. ⊠ *Great Island, 24 km (15 mi) from Cork City on R624,* ☎ *021/481–3591,* WEB *www.cobhheritage.com.* ⊠ *€5.* ☉ *Feb.–Nov., daily 10–6.*

The best view of Cobh is from **St. Colman's Cathedral,** an exuberant neo-Gothic granite church designed by Pugin in 1868. Inside, granite niches portray scenes of the Roman Catholic Church's history in Ireland, beginning with the arrival of St. Patrick. ⊠ *Cobh,* ☎ *021/481– 3222,* WEB *www.cloyne.irl.com.* ⊠ *Free.*

Cork Harbour opens to the sea some 8 km (5 mi) from Cobh at **Roches Point.** One-hour harbor tours from Marine Transport are a splendid way to take in Cobh's glorious watery environs. ⊠ *Kennedy Pier,* ☎ *021/481–1485.* ⊠ *€4.45.* ☉ *Tours May–Sept., daily at 10, 11, noon, 1:30, and 2:30.*

OUTDOOR ACTIVITIES AND SPORTS

Fota Island Golf Club (⊠ Carrigtwohill, ☎ 021/488–3700) is a par-72, 18-hole course.

Explore Cork Harbour from the water by renting a sailing dinghy from **International Sailing Center** (⊠ 5 E. Beach, Cobh, ☎ 021/481–1237).

EAST CORK AND THE BLACKWATER VALLEY

Although most visitors to Cork head west out of the city for the scenic coastal areas between Cork and Glengarriff, the east and the north of the county are also worth exploring. East Cork, Youghal in particular, is popular with Irish tourists—who love the long, sandy beaches here. The main attraction in North Cork is the Blackwater River, which crosses the county from east to west. It's famous for its trout

and salmon fishing and its scenery. This section starts in the far corner of the county at Youghal and works its way west toward the Kerry
border.

Youghal

㉒ *48 km (30 mi) east of Cork City on N25, 74 km (46 mi) south of Waterford.*

Youghal (pronounced yawl), an ancient walled seaport with a fine natural harbor, has a long, sandy beach, making it a popular summer day-
trip destination for Corkonians. The town is right on the mouth of the
Blackwater River, on the border between Counties Cork and Waterford. It was included in a 40,000-acre land grant given to Sir Walter
Raleigh by Elizabeth I in the late 16th century—according to local legend, Sir Walter Raleigh planted the first potatoes in Ireland here, a claim
disputed by several other locations (and by all accounts he spent little
time here). The town is in the throes of some major investment, aimed
at updating its appeal.

The **clock tower** (⊠ Main St.), Youghal's main landmark (from 1776)
was originally built as a jail. A set of steps beside the clock tower leads
up to a well-preserved stretch of the old town walls. From here there
is a magnificent panorama of the town and the estuary. The **Youghal
Heritage Centre** relates the town's history through an audiovisual presentation. If this whets your appetite, trained guides are available to
show you the town; a walking tour takes about an hour and a half. ⊠
Market Sq., ☎ *024/20170,* ᵂᴱᴮ *www.youghal.ie.* ▱ *€1.50, tour €3.50.*
☉ *June–mid-Sept., daily 9:30–7; mid-Sept.–May, weekdays 9:30–5:30.*

At the Youghal **quays,** you may see today's catch being unloaded from
one of the small, brightly painted trawlers that fish these waters. The
Moby Dick Lounge Bar (⊠ Market Sq., ☎ 024/92756) contains memorabilia of the filming here of John Huston's version of Melville's
Moby-Dick, in which Youghal masqueraded as New Bedford, Massa-
chusetts. **St. Mary's Collegiate Church** (on top of the town walls) dates
from the 13th century and contains many interesting monuments, including the tomb of Richard Boyle (1566–1643), who succeeded Sir
Walter Raleigh as Mayor of Youghal and became the first earl of Cork.
The brightly painted monument commemorates his three wives and
16 children and is similar to the monument in St. Patrick's' Cathedral
in Dublin, which Sir Richard ordered because he was not sure whether
he would die in Dublin or Youghal. ⊠ *Emmet Pl.,* ☎ *024/92350.* ▱
Free. ☉ *Key available from adjacent lodge.*

Dining and Lodging

$$–$$$ ✕▥ **Aherne's.** In the Fitzgibbon family since 1923, Aherne's has a highly
★ regarded seafood restaurant and bar with a magnetic appeal—it even
draws food lovers from Cork City (it's less than an hour's drive). Popular main courses include hot buttered lobster, grilled salmon with fresh
fennel, and more elaborate creations, such as plaice (flounder) stuffed
with oysters in a red-wine sauce. The inexpensive bar food includes
seafood pie topped with mashed potatoes. The 12 bedrooms, which
occupy their own modern wing, are furnished with Victorian and
Georgian antiques. ⊠ *163 N. Main St., Co. Cork,* ☎ *024/92424,* ꜰᴬˣ
024/93633, ᵂᴱᴮ *www.ahernes.com. 12 rooms with bath. Restaurant,
cable TV, bar, fishing. AE, DC, MC, V.*

$ ▥ **Ballymakeigh House.** Consider this the Irish farmhouse of your
★ dreams. From the conservatory behind the creeper-clad house you can
breakfast on one of Margaret Browne's fresh strawberry muffins while
watching the cows amble home. The cozy rooms are impeccably kept.

This is the kind of place where most people end up staying much longer than just one night. Dinner is no longer served on the premises, but transport is provided, if necessary, to the family-owned Browne's Restaurant, two miles away. The lodging has a wine license, so you can buy wine by the glass or by the bottle here. The house is signposted off N25, 9½ km (6 mi) west of Youghal. ⊠ *Killeagh, Co. Cork,* ☎ *024/ 95184,* ℻ *024/95370. 6 rooms with bath. Cable TV, tennis court, bicycles, Ping-Pong. MC, V. House closed Nov.–Mar.*

Outdoor Activities and Sports

Youghal Golf Club (⊠ Knockavery, Co. Cork, ☎ 024/92787) is a scenic, 18-hole, par-70 course that overlooks the bay.

Shanagarry

㉓ *27 km (17 mi) southwest of Youghal via N25 and R632.*

There are two reasons to come to Shanagarry: Ballymaloe House, one of Ireland's first country-house hotels, and Ballymaloe Cookery School and Gardens, Ireland's top destination for chefs-in-training. Ballymaloe House, on the eastern edge of the village, and has brought a stream of visitors to the area. The cooking school is Ireland's finest. In other respects, Shanagarry, well off the beaten track, is not especially notable—it was once a quiet farming village, chiefly known for its Quaker connections. The most famous Shanagarry Quaker was William Penn (1644–1718), the founder of the Pennsylvania colony, who grew up in **Shanagarry House,** still a private residence in the center of the village. The entry gates are across from **Shanagarry Castle,** now owned and being restored by the potter and entrepreneur Stephen Pearce. The house's most famous tenant since William Penn was Marlon Brando, who stayed here in the summer of 1995 while filming *Divine Rapture* in nearby Ballycotton.

On the other side of the village from Ballymaloe House, **Ballymaloe Cookery School and Gardens,** run by Darina and Tim Allen (daughter-in-law and son of Ballymaloe House original founders Myrtle and the late Ivan Allen), attracts budding chefs from all over Ireland and, increasingly, from points beyond. It has a wealth of cooking classes and programs that range from one day to 12 weeks. (You'll find graduates in the kitchens of many Irish restaurants—that often promote the connection.) Darina Allen, one of Ireland's best-known chefs, tends formal herb, fruit, and vegetable gardens, as well as a Celtic maze (about knee-high). A meal or a snack at the Garden Café, serving the famous Ballymaloe-style fresh food as well as pizzas from a wood-burning oven, will add greatly to your visit. ⊠ *Kinoith House,* ☎ *021/464–6785,* WEB *www.cookingisfun.ie.* 🎫 *Gardens €5.* ⊙ *May–Sept., daily 9–6.*

OFF THE
BEATEN PATH

BALLYCOTTON – Five kilometers (3 miles) beyond Shanagarry on R629, this pretty fishing village is built on the top of a cliff overlooking an island where large colonies of seabirds breed. There are pleasant cliff walks and a beach nearby.

Dining and Lodging

$$$–$$$$ ✕🏠 **Ballymaloe House.** Originally a farmhouse and family home, albeit on a grand scale, Ballymaloe is one of Ireland's best known country houses. It still functions partly as a working farm, and is surrounded by pleasant, fertile countryside. Each guest room is elegantly, if simply, decorated. Myrtle Allen, the doyenne of Irish cooking, presides over the dining room, which houses the family's notable Irish art collection. Chef Rory O'Connell presents a six-course, haute Irish menu that relies on fresh fish from nearby Ballycotton, local lamb and beef, and

homegrown herbs and vegetables—testament to Myrtle's practice of supporting small, local food purveyors. ✉ *Co. Cork*, ☎ *021/465–2531*, FAX *021/465–2021*, WEB *www.ballymaloe.ie. 32 rooms with bath. Restaurant, bar, tennis court, pool, some pets allowed; no TV in most rooms. AE, DC, MC, V.*

$ ✕🔟 **Barnabrow House.** Although only 500 yards from the gates of Ballymaloe, this is no pale imitation. Owners John and Geraldine O'Brien stylishly combined the old and the new when they renovated the interior of this rambling 17th-century house. Specially made modern wood furniture sits beside Victorian antiques, against intensely colored walls. It's romantic, relaxed, and practical. Rooms in the main house have high ceilings and canopied beds; those in the courtyard are cozier, with low-beamed ceilings. The Trinity Rooms Restaurant, with a high-beamed ceiling and dark red walls, emphasizes fresh local produce—imaginatively prepared. ✉ *Cloyne*, ☎ FAX *021/465–2534*, WEB *www.barnabrowhouse.com. 21 rooms with bath. Restaurant, bar; some pets allowed; no room TVs, no smoking. MC, V.*

Shopping

The ceramicist Stephen Pearce makes tableware and bowls in four signature styles that are available in many Irish crafts shops. He sells a wide selection at his own **Stephen Pearce Emporium** (✉ near Cloyne, ☎ *021/464–6262*), where he also stocks an interesting range of Irish-made crafts.

Midleton

㉔ *12 km (8 mi) east of Cork City on N25, 15 km (9 mi) northwest of Shanagarry on R629.*

Midleton is famous for its school, Midleton College, founded in 1696, and its distillery, founded in 1825 and modernized in 1975, which manufactures spirits—including Irish whiskey—for distribution worldwide. It's also a pleasant market town at the head of the Owenacurra estuary, near the northeast corner of Cork Harbour. Its gray-stone buildings date mainly from the early 19th century.

The **Jameson Heritage Centre** has tours of the Old Midleton Distillery, to show you how Irish whiskey—*uisce beatha,* "the water of life"—was made in the old days. The old stone buildings are excellent examples of 19th-century industrial architecture, and an impressively large old waterwheel is still in operation. The biggest pot still in the world, a copper dome capable of holding 32,000 imperial gallons of whiskey, is also found here. Early in the tour, requests are made for a volunteer "whiskey taster"—so be alert if this option appeals. The tours end with a complimentary glass of Jameson's Irish whiskey (or a soft drink). A crafts center and café are also on the premises. ✉ ☎ *021/461–3594*, WEB *www.irishwhiskeytrail.com.* 🎟 *€5.75.* ☾ *Mar.–Oct., daily 9–4:30; Nov.–Feb., tours only, weekdays at 12:30 and 3, weekends at 2 and 4.*

Fermoy

㉕ *35 km (22 mi) north of Cork City on N8, 43 km (27 mi) west of Youghal on R634 (Tallow Rd.), which adjoins N72.*

An army town dating mainly from the mid-19th century—and now popular with fishers—Fermoy is a major crossroads on the Dublin–Cork road (N8); the east–west road that passes through town (N72) is an attractive 98-km (61-mi) alternative route to Killarney. Its bridge spanning the Blackwater is flanked by two weirs dating from 1689.

Dining and Lodging

$–$$ ✕🔟 **Ballyvolane House.** An informal country-house atmosphere characterizes this imposing 1728 stone mansion surrounded by extensive gardens—beyond which you'll find a 100-acre dairy farm. Dinner is served at a large table in the elegant dining room; family silver is set on white linens. The rooms are exceptionally large, sitting areas are generous, and furnishings consist of a rich assortment of antiques and family heirlooms. Both dinner and accommodation must be booked at least 24 hours in advance. The village of Castlelyons is signposted off N8 in Rathcormac, just south of Fermoy. ⊠ *Castlelyons, Co. Cork,* ☎ *025/36349,* FAX *025/36781,* WEB *www.ballyvolanehouse.ie. 6 rooms with bath. Dining room, fishing; no room phones, no room TVs, no smoking. AE, MC, V.*

Outdoor Activities and Sports

For local information on salmon and trout angling contact the **Salmon Angler's Association** (Liam McGarry, ⊠ Moorepark,Co. Cork, ☎ 025/31422).

Mallow

㉖ *30 km (18 mi) west of Fermoy on N72.*

Mallow, an angling center and market town, was, in the 18th century, a popular spa—often mentioned in the same breath as Bath. Mallow lies at the intersection of the Cork–Limerick and Waterford–Killarney roads, within an hour's drive of all four towns. At the bottom of Mallow's Main Street, you'll find the **Clock House,** a half-timber building dating from 1855. It shares the site with the Rakes of Mallow Club, the headquarters of the notorious 18th-century gamblers, drinkers, and fortune hunters remembered in the song "The Rakes of Mallow." Not much remains today of Mallow's glory, but the old **Spa Well** can still be seen in the town center, and there are several interesting facades with overhanging bay windows on Main Street, dating from the 18th and early 19th centuries. The English novelist Anthony Trollope lived at No. 139 for a time, and he rode with the Duhallow Hunt, enhancing the fame of the local pack. The ruins of the late 16th century **Mallow Castle** are at the bottom of the main street behind (freely accessible) ornamental gates. The castle was burned by the Jacobites in 1689, and its stables were later converted into a house, which is still in use as a private home. From here you can view the white fallow deer that are unique to Mallow and were originally presented by Elizabeth I.

OFF THE BEATEN PATH
ANNE'S GROVE GARDENS – These gardens were inspired by the ideas of William Robinson, a 19th-century gardener who favored naturalistic planting. Exotic foliage borders paths winding down to the Blackwater; magnificent spring magnolias and primulas and summer hydrangeas are among the plants on view in the rolling countryside. ⊠ *Castletownroche, 12 km (7 mi) east of Mallow,* ☎ *022/26145.* 🎫 *€4.* 🕙 *Mid-Mar.–Sept., Mon.–Sat. 10–5, Sun. 1–6.*

Dining and Lodging

$$$–$$$$ ★ ✕🏠 **Longueville House.** It's the cream of the crop among the region's superlative country-house hotels, on a tranquil 500-acre estate that rolls down to the river. Limestone quoins frame the facade of the imposing Georgian mansion. Interestingly, you'll find an unusual extension to the house on the eastern end—a Victorian-era glass-and-iron conservatory. Bedrooms are comfortable, and are decorated with fine antiques. At the Presidents' Restaurant, chef William O'Callaghan, son of founding proprietors Michael and Jane O'Callaghan, serves an outstanding and elegant Irish-French–style menu prepared largely using produce from the houses's own farm, garden, and river. ⊠ *Co. Cork,* ☎ *022/47156,* FAX *022/47459,* WEB *www.longuevillehouse.ie. 20 rooms with*

bath. Restaurant, cable TV, fishing, bar, meeting rooms. AE, DC, MC, V. Closed late Dec.–Mar.

Outdoor Activities and Sports

Mallow Golf Club (✉ Ballyellis, Co. Cork, ☎ 022/21145) is an 18-hole, par-72 parkland course with excellent views of the Blackwater Valley.

Kanturk

㉗ *15 km (9 mi) west of Mallow on N72 and R579.*

Kanturk lies at the confluence of two rivers, the Allow and the Dalua. It is more of a village than a town, but its interesting Victorian shopfronts bear witness to its past importance as a market town. The freely accessible **Kanturk Castle** (✉ 2 km/1 mi outside town on the R579 Banteer Rd.) was built by a local MacCarthy chieftain in 1601, but its completion was prevented by English neighbors who complained that it was too large for an Irishman. Ornate stone fireplaces and mullioned windows in the five-story shell give some idea of the scope of MacCarthy's ambitions.

Dining and Lodging

$$–$$$$ ✕🏠 **Assolas Country House.** This ivy-covered 17th-century manor
★ possesses the air of a dignified family home, and hosts Joe and Hazel Bourke have perfected the picture by furnishing the house and its bedrooms with period antiques. Dinner begins in front of the blazing log fire in the drawing room, where guests peruse the night's menu over aperitifs. Old Bourke family silver is on the tables in the red Queen Anne dining room. Hazel's refined culinary skills, as well as the well-manicured gardens, are renowned. ✉ *Co. Cork,* ☎ *029/50015,* 🅵🅰🅇 *029/ 50795,* 🆆🅴🅱 *www.assolas.com. 9 rooms with bath. Restaurant, tennis court, boating, fishing; no room TVs. MC, V. Closed Nov.–mid-Mar.*

KINSALE TO GLENGARRIFF VIA BANTRY BAY

This section takes you on a scenic drive of about 136 km (85 mi) around the unspoiled coast of West County Cork. We begin at the historic old port—and now booming seaside town—of Kinsale and meander through a variety of seascapes to the lush vegetation of Glengarriff. The drive from Kinsale to Glengarriff takes less than two hours non-stop, but the whole point of making this journey is to linger in places that tickle your fancy.

Kinsale

★ **㉘** *29 km (18 mi) southwest of Cork City on R600.*

Eager foodies flock to Kinsale—long considered, among those in the know, to be Ireland's culinary capital—for its annual Gourmet Festival each fall. The town center, at the tip of the wide, fjordlike harbor opening out from the River Bandon, consists of small streets lined by upscale shops and eateries with colorful, pastel facades. Its steep, narrow streets climb up the slopes of Compass Hill. Tall, slate-roof and unusual slate-front houses have an unmistakable Spanish influence, which can be traced back to the Battle of Kinsale in 1601, when the Irish and Spanish joined forces to fight the English—and lost. The loss was a serious one for the Irish aristocracy, and they soon took off for Europe, leaving behind their lands to English settlers. Kinsale went on to become an important fishing port as well as a British army and naval base.

Especially during the first week in October, when Kinsale hosts its annual **Gourmet Festival,** its many fine restaurants live up to their impressive billing. But foodies alone can't claim Kinsale; yacht owners and deep-sea anglers are also a big presence here. Kinsale has two yacht marinas, and numerous skippers with deep-sea angling boats offer day charters. Kinsale Yacht Club hosts racing and cruising events during the sailing season, which runs from March to October for hardy souls and from June to August for those who prefer warmer weather. Kinsale is also where you'll find Ireland's only bareboat charter company (see Sail Ireland Charters, below).

Desmond Castle and the International Museum of Wine. This 15th-century fortified town house—originally built as a custom house—has a charmingly dark history. It was used as a prison for French and American seamen in the 1700s, and was subsequently a jail and then a workhouse. Now it houses the International Museum of Wine, which tells the story of Ireland's long involvement with the wine trade. Many Irish emigrants became involved in the wine trade in France, and later generations of emigrants started wine making in California, Australia, and New Zealand. ✉ *Cork Street,* ☎ *021/477–4855,* WEB *www.heritageireland.ie.* 🖾 € *6.34.* ☉ *Mid–Apr. to mid–June, Tues.–Sun. 10–6; mid-June–mid-Oct., daily 10–6; closed mid-Oct.–mid-Apr.*

Cuttings and memorabilia from the wreck of the *Lusitania* are among the best artifacts in Kinsale's local **museum,** housed in the town's 17th-century, Dutch-style courthouse. The 1915 inquest into the *Lusitania*'s sinking took place in the **courtroom,** briefly making it the focus of the world's attention; it has been preserved as a memorial. ✉ *Old Courthouse, Market Pl.,* ☎ *021/477–2044.* 🖾 € *2.50.* ☉ *Mon.–Sat. 11–5, Sun. 3–5.*

On the harbor shore on the east side of the Bandon's estuary, the British built **Charles Fort** in the late 17th century, in the wake of their defeat of the Spanish and Irish forces. One of the best-preserved "star forts" in Europe, it encloses some 12 acres on a cliff top (it's similar to Fort Ticonderoga in New York State). If the sun is shining, take the footpath signposted **Scilly Walk;** it winds along the edge of the harbor under tall, overhanging trees and then through the village of Summer Cove. ✉ *3 km (2 mi) east of town,* ☎ *021/477–2684,* WEB *www.heritageireland.ie.* 🖾 € *3.10.* ☉ *Mid-Mar.–Oct., daily 10–6; Nov.–mid-Mar., weekends 10–5.*

The **Spaniard Inn** (✉ Scilly, ☎ 021/477–2436) looks over the town and harbor from a hairpin bend on the road to Charles Fort. Inside, sawdust-covered floors and a big open fire make this onetime fishermen's bar a cozy spot in the winter. In the summer, you can take a pint to the sunny veranda and watch the world go by on land and sea.

Dining and Lodging

$$$–$$$$ ✕ **The Vintage.** It's informal, but it's also one of Ireland's original front-parlor, cottage-style restaurants, and the place to come for a special occasion. The cozy, low-beamed interior is enhanced by Swiss owner Raoul de Gendre's art collection. Tables are beautifully set, with specially designed glassware and white linen tablecloths. Chef Federic Pastorino toils over an ambitious à la carte European menu with Irish influences, such as Lobster Dublin Lawyer (whole lobster with mustard-whiskey sauce). Appetizers include caviar and fresh duck foie gras. The wine list has more than 150 primarily European wines. ✉ *50 Main St.,* ☎ *021/477–2502,* WEB *www.vintagerestaurant.ie. AE, DC, MC, V. Closed Jan.–mid-Feb. No lunch.*

$$–$$$ ✕ **The Cottage Loft.** The hand-painted purple and yellow traditional wooden shopfront sets the tone for this cozy town-center eatery, which manages to be consistently different from everyone else on the block.

Owner-chef Michael Buckley's menu is selective—but intriguing. Possible starters include breast of pigeon marinated in red wine and served with a dark-chocolate sauce; a main course might include a kebab of local seafood with lightly curried fruit sauce. Steak, with optional pepper or Irish whiskey sauce, is a strong seller. ⊠ *6 Main St.,* ☎ *021/ 477–2803. AE, MC, V. No lunch.*

$$–$$$ ✕ **Man Friday.** The name refers to Kinsale's alleged connection with the original Robinson Crusoe, Alexander Selkirk (Kinsale was reputedly his last port of call before shipwreck). Man Friday occupies a series of interconnecting rooms and has a terrace for drinks in fine weather. Steaks and seafood, prepared in an unpretentious Continental style, are the main business here. The generous portions, along with the bustling atmosphere, make it the sort of place that locals and visitors alike return to again and again. On a hilltop overlooking Kinsale Harbour, it's about 1 km (½ mi) outside town. ⊠ *Scilly,* ☎ *021/477– 2260. AE, DC, MC, V.*

$$–$$$ ✕ **Restaurant Antibes.** The smallish dining room has a plaster-decorated ceiling, Art Deco posters of its namesake, elegant blue-and-white napery, and a good buzz. Antibes is known for its traditional seafood dishes—sole on the bone and Dublin Bay prawns with herb butter. It also serves rack of lamb and generously sized steaks with optional brandy and pepper sauce, as well as some vegetarian dishes. Desserts are substantial affairs: profiteroles come with chocolate and butterscotch sauces, and homemade ice creams are served in a brandy snap basket. ⊠ *Pearse St. and the Glen,* ☎ *021/477–2125. AE, DC, MC, V. Closed Nov.–mid-Mar. No lunch.*

$$ ✕ **The Bulman.** Kinsale has other pub-restaurants, but none can boast the idyllic waterside location of this ever-popular bar. At lunchtime simple pub grub—mussels steamed in white wine, perhaps, or a meaty burger and chips—is served at the bar. In the evening the first-floor restaurant has tables with splendid views of the sun setting over the harbor. The menu includes freshly made pasta, Thai chicken curry, local salmon with lemon-herb butter sauce, and steaks. ⊠ *Summercove,* ☎ *021/477– 2131. MC, V. No lunch Sun.*

$$ ✕ **Max's Wine Bar.** The enthusiastic French owner-chef Olivier Queva and his partner, Anne Marie Galvin, run this intimate, informal restaurant in a charmingly converted old town house. The low-beamed ceilings and polished antique tables of different shapes and sizes positively ooze old-world charm. The wine list is long, and includes a good selection of French and New World wines, ranging in price from €15.25 to €76, with most priced around €30. This is the place to come for a light lunch, especially if you're keen on salads. At dinner, Olivier's classical French background is evident in his treatment of the daily catch and in his clever ways with unusual cuts, like oxtail and pig's trotters. ⊠ *Main St.,* ☎ *021/477–2443. MC, V. Closed Nov.–mid-Mar.*

$ ✕ **Crackpots.** At Carole Norman's "ceramic café" you can sample from
★   the eclectic menu without going bankrupt. Choices range from Moroccan meatballs with cous cous to Thai-style prawns with fragrant rice, and always include a local steak option with garlic butter or Irish whiskey sauce. This grocery shop has been transformed into a simple but elegant eatery, with warm yellow walls and two cozy dining areas, one of which has a small open fire. Behind the restaurant is Carole's pottery workshop; if you like your dinner plate, you can buy it. ⊠ *3 Cork St.,* ☎ *021/477–2847, MC, V. Closed Mon.–Wed. Nov.–Mar.*

$$$–$$$$ ✕🏢 **Blue Haven.** A seafood restaurant and a small hotel occupy this attractive, yellow-stucco, blue-trim town house. Rooms are in the main house and the adjacent house. New rooms have custom-designed dark-oak furniture, canopied antique beds, and spacious baths; those in the main house, though generally smaller, are cheerfully decorated

with paintings by local artists. Inexpensive bar food is served until 9:30 PM in the lounge bar, the patio, and the conservatory, which all have swagged curtains and nautical brass. The quiet, pastel-color restaurant overlooks a floodlit garden with a fountain adorned by cherubs. ⊠ *3 Pearse St., Co. Cork,* ☎ *021/477–2209,* FAX *021/477–4268. 17 rooms with bath. Restaurant, cable TV, fishing, bar. AE, DC, MC, V.*

$–$$ ✕🖭 **The White House.** It's one of the oldest inns in Kinsale, and, remarkably, it manages to maintain its traditional warm Irish welcome—despite the hustle-bustle due to its popularity. You can get food in the bar and in Chelsea's Bistro. The best options are traditional Irish dishes, such boiled bacon and cabbage—served with enormous boiled potatoes. The fish of the day is often a sophisticated combination, such as plaice fillets stuffed with crab meat mousse, due to the fact that the pub shares a kitchen with Restaurant Antibes. Bedrooms vary in size, but all have fully tiled, good-size bathrooms and pastel color schemes; you'll find the quietest rooms on the upper floors. Ask about the 2- and 3-day dinner-and-lodging specials. ⊠ *Pearse St. and the Glen, Co. Cork,* ☎ *021/477–2125,* FAX *021/477–2045,* WEB *www.whitehouse-kinsale.ie. 12 rooms with bath. Restaurant, cable TV, bar. AE, DC, MC, V.*

$$$$ 🖭 **Old Bank House.** Owned and managed with sophisticated flair by a
★ Swiss-Irish couple, Michael and Marie Riese, the tall, narrow Georgian town house has large, high-ceilinged rooms with tall windows, double-glazed against traffic noise. Pretty touches—dried flower arrangements and modern prints—add to the hotel's elegance. The higher the room the better the view, so regulars will be glad to hear that an elevator has been installed. Michael was previously chef-owner of Vintage restaurant, and his breakfasts are memorable. ⊠ *Pearse St., Co. Cork,* ☎ *021/477–4075,* FAX *021/477–4296,* WEB *www.oldbankhousekinsale.com. 17 rooms with bath. Cable TV. AE, MC, V.*

$$$ 🖭 **Perryville House.** By far the most luxurious accommodation in town,
★ this pink, double-fronted 19th-century house with an attractive wrought-iron balcony overlooks the inner harbor. The public rooms are beautifully decorated, giving the impression of a private home. Front bedrooms have sea views, but ones at the rear are quieter (key in July and August, when the town gets busy and traffic increases). All rooms, imaginatively furnished with Victorian antiques, have extra-large beds, fresh flowers, robes, and all the extras you would expect at a top-grade hotel. The lodging has a wine license, so you can buy wine by the glass or by the bottle here. ⊠ *Long Quay, Co. Cork,* ☎ *021/477–2731,* FAX *021/477–2298,* WEB *www.perryvillehouse.com. 28 rooms with bath. Cable TV; no kids under 13, no smoking. AE, DC, MC, V. Closed Nov.–Mar.*

$$–$$$ 🖭 **Sovereign House.** If you're looking for history in this heritage town, here's the real thing. Built in 1708 as the home of the Sovereign (Lord Mayor) of Kinsale, this imposing Queen Anne town house has a symmetrical stone facade and a quiet, central location. The interior is furnished in the baronial style with heavy family heirlooms, stone-flagged floors, and original fireplaces. Rooms are large and luxurious, with many original features, including some massive exposed beams and Victorian-style bathrooms. James McKeown provides a warm welcome, and can advise you on local golf, fishing, and dining. The lodging has a wine license, so you can buy wine by the glass or by the bottle here. ⊠ *Newman's Mall, Co. Cork,* ☎ *021/477–2850,* FAX *021/477–4723. 4 rooms with bath. Billiards, cable TV; no smoking. MC, V. Closed Nov.–Feb.*

$$ 🖭 **Innishannon House.** Considered one of the most romantic small hotels in Ireland, Innishannon House was built in 1720 in the Petit Château style on the banks of the river Bandon. Its wooded rural location, about 6 km (4 mi) from Kinsale, and its peaceful riverside gardens, make it an ideal country retreat. Rooms in the rambling old house vary greatly in shape and size, but all are full of character and furnished with genuine antique pieces, and overlook the gardens and river. The hotel is just off the main N71, making it a good base for touring. ⊠ *Innishannon, Co. Cork,* ☎ *021/477–5121,* FAX *021/477–5609,* WEB *www.innishannon-hotel.ie. 13 rooms with bath. Restaurant, bar, boating, fishing, cable TV, meeting rooms AE, DC, MC, V.*

$ ⚏ **Kilcaw House.** Value for the money and off-road parking make this guest house a good choice. On busy weekends, when the town buzz continues into the small hours, Kilcaw's location—2 km (1 mi) outside town on the Cork side of the R600—guarantees peace and quiet. An open fire in the lobby, polished pine floors, and striking colors add character to the farmhouse-style building. Rooms are well equipped, spacious, and uncluttered, with country pine furniture and throw rugs on the wooden floors. ⊠ *Pewter Hole Cross, Co. Cork,* ☎ *021/477–4155,* FAX *021/477–4755,* WEB *www.kilcawhouse.com. 7 rooms with bath. Cable TV. AE, MC, V.*

Nightlife and the Arts

The **Boom Boom Room** (⊠ Guardwell, ☎ 021/477–2382) has late-night dancing for the over-25s. The **Shanakee** (⊠ Market St., ☎ 021/477–4472) is renowned for live music—both rock and Irish traditional. Check out the **Spaniard Inn** (⊠ Scilly, ☎ 021/477–2436) for live rock and folk groups.

Outdoor Activities and Sports

BICYCLES

Rent a bike from **D&C Cycles** (⊠ 18 Main St., Co. Cork, ☎ 021/477–4884) to explore the picturesque hinterland of Kinsale.

FISHING

For deep-sea angling contact William Van Dyk (☎ 021/477–8944) or Arthur Long (☎ 021/477–8969), both of whom operate out of **Castlepark Marina** (⊠ Castlepark, Co. Cork). For bare-boat charters, call **Sail Ireland Charters** (⊠ Tirdent Hotel, Kinsale, Co. Cork, ☎ 021/477–2927, FAX 021/477–4170, WEB www.sailireland.com).

WATER SPORTS

The **Oysterhaven Holiday and Activity Center** (⊠ Oysterhaven, ☎ 021/477–0738) rents sailboarding equipment, including wet suits.

Shopping

Boland's (⊠ Pearse St., ☎ 021/477–2161) sells some unusual items, including sweaters, designer rainwear, and linen shirts exclusive to this shop only. **Giles Norman Photography Gallery** (⊠ 44 Main St., ☎ 021/477–4373) sells unique black-and-white photographs of Irish scenes. The **Keane on Ceramics** (⊠ Pier Rd., ☎ 021/477–2085) gallery represents the best of Ireland's ceramics artists. **Kinsale Crystal** (⊠ Market St., ☎ 021/477–4463) is a master cutter's studio that sells 100% Irish, handblown, hand-cut crystal. **Victoria Murphy** (⊠ Market Quay, ☎ 021/477–4317) sells a selection of small antiques and antique jewelry.

En Route   Leave Kinsale through its center, and follow the quays, driving west along the Bandon River toward the bridge on R600. This takes you through **Garretstown Woods** (signposts for Clonakilty on R600), carpeted with wild bluebells in April. You'll then travel past the edge of Courtmacsherry Bay, alongside a wide, saltwater inlet that teems with curlew, plover, and other waders.

Timoleague

㉙   *19 km (12 mi) west of Kinsale on R600.*

The romantic silhouette of its ruined abbey dominates the view when you're approaching the small town of Timoleague on the Argideen River estuary. The tiny village of multi-colored houses marks the eastern end of the Seven Heads Peninsula, which stretches around to Clonakilty. A mid-13th-century **Franciscan abbey** at the water's edge is Timoleague's most striking monument. (Walk around the back to find the entrance gate.) The abbey was sacked by the English in 1642 but, like many other ruins of its kind, was used as a burial place until the late-20th century. A tower and walls with Gothic-arched windows still stand, and you can trace the ground plan of the old friary—chapel, refectory, cloisters, and wine cellar (at one time the friars were well-known wine importers).

Timoleague Castle Gardens are right in the village. Although the castle is now a picturesque ruin adjoining a modest early 20th-century house in gray stone, the original gardens have survived. Palm trees and other frost-tender plants flourish in the mature shrubbery. There are two large, old-fashioned walled gardens, one for flowers and one for fruits and vegetables. ☎ 023/46116. ⌧ €3. ☉ *Easter weekend and June–Aug., daily noon–6.*

Courtmacsherry, the pretty village of multicolor cottages glimpsed across the water, has sandy beaches that make it a popular holiday resort. It can be reached by following the signposts from Timoleague.

OFF THE BEATEN PATH

CLONAKILTY – Many storefronts in this small market town, 9½ km (6 mi) from Timoleague on R600/N71, have charmingly traditional, hand-painted signs and wooden facades. **Inchydoney,** 3 km (2 mi) outside of town, is one of the area's finest sandy beaches. **De Barra's** is the best of several traditional music pubs in town. (⌧ 55 Pearse St., ☎ 023/33381).

OFF THE BEATEN PATH

BIRTHPLACE OF MICHAEL COLLINS – The birthplace of Michael Collins (1890–1922) is signposted 9 km (6 mi) west of Timoleague off N71 (past the village of Lissavaird). You can see the ground plan of the simple homestead where the controversial founder of the modern Irish Army was born. There's also a bronze memorial (freely accessible), and another memorial in the nearest village, **Woodfield,** opposite the pub where Collins is said to have had his last drink on the day he was shot in an ambush.

Dining

$$–$$$ × **Casino House.** Stop midway between Kinsale and Timoleague, on
★ the coastal R600, for a meal at this traditional farmhouse, which has been converted to a distinctively stylish informal restaurant. The two small dining rooms—one blue and one green—have private sitting rooms for pre-dinner drinks next to an open fire. Menu highlights from the talented Croatian owner-chef Michael Relja include starters of garlic prawn salad and lobster risotto; mains include roast loin of lamb served with Roman gnocchi. Summer fruits with sabayon are one of the fine seasonal desserts. ⌧ *Coolmaine, Kilbrittain,* ☎ *023/49944. MC, V. Closed Wed. mid-Jan.–mid-Mar.; Easter–Oct.; and Mon.– Thurs. Nov.–early Jan.*

Skibbereen

③⓪ *85 km (53 mi) west of Kinsale, 35 km (22 mi) west of Timoleague.*

Skibbereen is the main market town in this neck of southwest Cork, and a good base for nearby sights. The weekly cattle market on Wednesdays and country market on Fridays—and the plethora of pubs punctuated by bustling shops and coffeehouses—keep the place jumping year-round.

The **Mizen Vision Visitor Centre,** which occupies a lighthouse at the tip of the Mizen head (follow the R591 through Goleen to the end of the road), is the most southerly point of the Irish mainland. The lighthouse itself is perched on a rock at the tip of the headland; to reach it, you must cross a dramatic 99-step suspension footbridge. The lighthouse was completed in 1910; the Engine Room and Keepers' House have been restored by the local community. The exhilaration of massive Atlantic seas swirling 164 ft below the footbridge, and the great coastal views, guarantee a memorable outing. ⊠ *Harbour Rd., Goleen,* ☎ *028/ 35115,* WEB *www.westcorkweb.ie/mizenvision.* ☎ *€4.50.* ⊗ *Mid-Mar.– May and Oct., daily 10:30–5; June–Sept., daily 10–6; Nov.–mid-Mar., weekends 11–4.*

Dining and Lodging

$$$ ✕ **Island Cottage.** This unlikely venture has become a pilgrimage spot
★ for food lovers, who praise the high standard of cooking and the island location. Hosts John Desmond and Ellmary Fenton prepare a set five-course menu utilizing local produce, some of it picked in the wild, on the island. Expect good, honest food, freshly sourced, and unfussily prepared. Cape Clear turbot with sea spinach is typical; for dessert, try the terrine of vanilla ice cream with meringue in blackberry sauce. Cookery courses and demonstrations can be arranged, as can off-season visits for groups. Advance booking is necessary; call for details about the 4-minute nightly ferry ride to the island. ⊠ *Heir Island,* ☎ *028/ 38102,* WEB *www.islandcottage.com. No credit cards. Closed mid-Sept.–mid-May, and Mon.–Tues. June–Sept. No lunch.*

$–$$ ✕🏠 **West Cork Hotel.** Designed in an attractive old-colonial style, this family-run hotel in a large Victorian building on the River Ilen is an excellent value. Rooms are comfortable, and a good value for the price range. The restaurant, famous for its steaks, serves fashionable dishes like Louisiana crab cakes as well as traditional favorites. ⊠ *Bridge St., Co. Cork,* ☎ *028/21277,* FAX *028/22333,* WEB *www.westcorkhotel.com. 36 rooms with bath. Restaurant, bar, fishing, cable TV. AE, DC, MC, V.*

$ ✕🏠 **Heron's Cove.** Expect to see herons outside your window at Sue Hill's idyllic harborside retreat. The modern house, built on the edge of a secluded sea inlet, is only a few minutes by foot from Goleen's appealing village center. The exceptionally well equipped rooms, furnished in part with antiques, have excellent views from every window. During summer, fresh local seafood stars on the menu, which also includes lamb, duck, and steak. Fresh herb sauces and homemade mayonnaise make subtle accompaniments, and there's a terrific wine list. Off-season (November–March), evening meals are prepared for guests only. ⊠ *The Harbour, Goleen, Co. Cork,* ☎ *028/35225,* FAX *028/ 35422,* WEB *www.heronscove.com. 5 rooms with bath. Restaurant, fishing, cable TV; no room phones, no smoking. AE, DC, MC, V.*

Nightlife and the Arts

The **West Cork Arts Center** (⊠ North St., ☎ 028/22090) has regular exhibits of work by local artists, and the on-site crafts shop sells items made by area artisans.

Outdoor Activities and Sports

Bicycles to explore West Cork's coast and country can be rented from **N. W. Roycroft** (⊠ Ilen St., ☎ 028/21235).

Baltimore

③ *13 km (8 mi) southwest of Skibbereen on R595.*

The beautiful, crescent-shape fishing village of Baltimore is a popular sailing center and attracts its share of vacationing families from Ire-

BACK OF THE BEYOND

RUSTIC, SEAFARING CHARM and cheerful fishing villages abound in a tiny, remote corner of the world just west of Timoleague. From Timoleague, take the N71 road, which briefly joins the sea at **Rosscarbery,** and turn left at the signpost for lovely Glandore at the end of the causeway. Glandore and Union Hall are twin fishing villages on either side of the landlocked Glandore Harbour. With its steep hill, pretty church, and emerald harbor, **Glandore** is a popular destination for people coming from the U.K. and Germany. The influx of affluent visitors and expensive yachts is less obvious in **Union Hall,** where fishing trawlers still tie up at the quay. You know you're in a remote spot when you're driving along tiny roads without route numbers.

Castletownshend, clearly signposted from Union Hall via Rineen, has an unusual number of graciously designed, large stone houses, mostly dating from the mid-18th century, when it was an important trading center. The main street runs steeply down a hill to the 17th century castle (built by the Townshends) and the sea. The sleepy town awakens in July and August, when its sheltered harbor bustles. Sparkling views await from the cliff-top perch of St. Barrahane's Church, which has a medieval oak altarpiece and three stained-glass windows by the early 20th-century Irish artist Harry Clarke. The low-beamed interior of **Mary Ann's** (☎ 028/36146), one of the oldest bars in the country, is frequented by a very friendly mix of visitors and locals and is a good place for a pint and serves outstandingly good bar food. Writer Edna O'Brien claims it's her favorite pub in the whole world.

land and abroad, especially during the peak summer months. The village was sacked in 1631 by a band of Algerian sailors; as a result, watchtowers were installed at the harbor mouth to protect the town.

Sherkin Island, one of Baltimore's two famous attractions, is 1 km (½ mi) off the coast, only a 10-minute ferry ride away. Seven ferries are scheduled daily (☎ 028/20125 for times). On the island, you'll find the ruins of **Dún Na Long Castle** and **Sherkin Abbey,** both built around 1470 by the O'Driscolls, a seafaring clan known as the "scourge of the Irish seas." The island's population today is 90, and there are several safe, sandy beaches and abundant wildlife.

The rugged, dramatic **Cape Clear Island** (WEB www.oilean-chleire.ie) is part of the West Cork Gaeltacht, or Irish-speaking area. The ferry to the 2- by 5-km (1- by 3-mi) island, which is 6 km (4 mi) offshore, takes about an hour from Baltimore (€12.70 round-trip; ☎ 028/39119 for sailing times). It's exciting to watch the skipper thread his way through the many rocks and tiny islands of Roaring Water Bay. You'll get excellent views of the **Fastnet Rock Lighthouse,** which is the focus of a biennial yachting race. Sparsely populated (about 150 residents), the island has little road traffic, a few bars, a youth hostel, and a few simple B&Bs. It's otherwise unspoiled, and a place where you can take some terrific walks. Bird-watchers will relish their time here—Cape Clear is the southernmost point of Irish territory, and its observatory, the oldest in the Republic, has racked up all kinds of sightings of rare songbird migrants. Whales, dolphins, and large flocks of oceangoing birds

☺ can be seen offshore in the summer. In late August, the **International Story-telling Festival** (☎ 028/39157), a long weekend of simple entertainment for kids, takes place (beware, it gets packed).

Outdoor Activities and Sports

Sailing dinghies and sailboards can be rented by the hour or the day from **Baltimore Sailing School** (⊠ The Pier, ☎ 028/20141).

Bantry

32 *25 km (16 mi) northwest of Skibbereen on N71.*

Beautiful Bantry House is the sole reason to come to this rather unprepossessing town with a large market square at the head of Bantry Bay. Bantry's long plaza attracts artisans, craftspeople, and musicians in summer. As you enter Bantry, on the right-hand side of the road you'll
★ see the porticoed entrance to **Bantry House.** One of Ireland's most magnificent houses, it was built in the early 1700s, then subsequently altered and expanded later that century. The house as it looks today is largely the vision of Richard White, the second earl of Bantry, who also created the Italianate gardens that surround it. On his European grand tours, Richard gobbled up fine art, furniture, and other antiques, including Aubusson tapestries said to have been ordered by Louis XV for the marriage of Marie-Antoinette to the Dauphin. Some of the rooms are now a little shabby, but the beauty of the location compensates for the lack of polish. The long climb to the top of the rear garden pays off with what has been called "one of the great views in Ireland"—overlooking the sea. Next to the house is the **Bantry 1796 French Armada Exhibition Center,** a small but worthwhile museum illustrating the abortive attempt by Irish Nationalist Wolfe Tone and his French ally General Hoche to land 14,000 troops in Bantry Bay to effect an uprising. ☎ 027/50047, WEB *www.cork-guide.ie/bnry_hse.htm.* ✉ *House, museum, and gardens €9.50; gardens only, €4.* ☉ *Mar.–Oct., daily 9–6.*

Dining and Lodging

$$$ ✕🏠 **Sea View House.** Among private, wooded grounds overlooking
★ Bantry Bay, you'll find a large, three-story, 19th-century country-house hotel that's an excellent value for the money. Owner-manager Kathleen O'Sullivan keeps an eagle eye on what was, until 1980, her private home. Inlaid antique furniture, polished brass, and ornate curtains speak of luxury and elegance. Bedrooms with sea views have small sofas in the bay windows; others have views of the wooded gardens. Polished tables in the elegant dining room are set with crocheted mats and linen napkins; service is friendly and informal. ⊠ *Ballylickey, Co. Cork,* ☎ *027/50073,* FAX *027/51555. 16 rooms with bath. Restaurant, fishing, bar, cable TV. AE, DC, MC, V. Closed mid-Nov.–mid-Mar.*

$$–$$$ ✕🏠 **Blair's Cove House.** In the converted stables of a Georgian mansion overlooking Dunmanus Bay, gleaming silverware, pink tablecloths, and a large crystal chandelier are set off, jewel-in-the-rough style, against stone walls and exposed beams. A covered, heated terrace overlooks the rose-filled courtyard and fountain and is used in summer. The cuisine is French-Irish (the owners are French), using fresh local produce. The old stone outbuildings were converted into the elegant, well-equipped rooms, furnished with country antiques. The morning views of Dunmanus Bay are breathtaking. ⊠ *Blair's Cove, Durrus,* ☎ *027/61041. 3 rooms with bath. Cable TV, some pets allowed. DC, MC, V. Restaurant closed Sun., July–Aug., and Sun.–Mon. Sept.–June.*

Nightlife and the Arts

During the world-class **West Cork Chamber Music Festival,** roughly 20 concerts are held from the last weekend in June through the first in July in the library at exquisite Bantry House. For information on themes and international guest artists for this year's event, or for news of other chamber music concerts held at Bantry House throughout the year, contact the West Cork music office (✉ 1 Bridge St., ☎ 027/52788, WEB www.westcorkmusic.com).

Outdoor Activities and Sports

Bantry Park Golf Club (✉ Donemark, Co. Cork, ☎ 027/50579) is an 18-hole, par-71 course that overlooks Bantry Bay.

Shopping

One of the Southwest's larger independents, **Bantry Bookstore** (✉ New St., ☎ 027/50064) has six rooms full of new, antiquarian, and secondhand books. **Manning's Emporium** (✉ Ballylickey, ☎ 027/51049) is a showcase for locally made farmhouse cheeses, pâtés, and salamis—an excellent place to put together a picnic or just to browse.

En Route   Check out the glorious sweep of **Bantry Bay,** on your left as you climb out of Bantry past Ballylickey on N71.

Glengarriff and the Beara Peninsula

③ One of the jewels of Bantry Bay is **Glengarriff,** the "rugged glen" much loved by Thackeray and Sir Walter Scott. It lies 14 km (8 mi) northwest of Bantry on N71, 21 km (13 mi) south of Kenmare. The descent into wooded, sheltered Glengarriff reveals yet another variety of landscape: thanks to the Gulf Stream, it's mild enough down here for subtropical plants to thrive. Trails along the shore are covered with rhododendrons, and offer beautiful views of the nearby inlets, loughs, and lounging seals. You are very much on the beaten path, however, with crafts shops, tour buses, and boatmen soliciting your business by the roadside.

On **Ilnacullin** (also known as Garnish Island), about 10 minutes offshore, you'll find beautiful, formal Italian gardens; shrubberies with rare subtropical plants; and excellent views from the Grecian temple. From the island's Martello tower, built at the end of the 18th century, the British watched for attempted landings by Napoleonic forces, including Hoche's ill-fated one. (The price for the boat ride is fixed at €6.35 round-trip.) ☎ *027/63040,* WEB *www.heritageireland.ie.* ▨ *€3.10.* ☉ *July–Aug., Mon.–Sat. 9:30–6:30, Sun. 11–7; Apr.–June and Sept., Mon.–Sat. 10–6:30, Sun. 1–7; Mar. and Oct., Mon.–Sat. 10–4:30, Sun. 1–5; last landing 1 hr before closing.*

Glengarriff is the gateway to the far quieter and more peaceful **Ring of Beara,** a 137-km (85-mi) scenic drive that encircles the Beara Peninsula on R572. The least famous of the southwest's three peninsulas is also the least frequented—and, some would say, the most ruggedly beautiful. One of the main attractions is the Beara Way, a 196-km (120-mi) way-marked walking route, which visits many of the peninsula's prehistoric archaeological remains. Just beyond the busy fishing port of Castletownbere lie the ruins of Dunboy Castle and House (freely accessible). **Dursey Island,** at the tip of the peninsula, is a bird-watcher's paradise accessible only by cable car. From Dursey Island, head for tiny **Allihies,** the former site of a huge copper mine, which now houses some of Ireland's leading artists; their studios can be visited from May to September. This is also great hiking country—known for some of the most scenic stretches of the Beara Way. Continue along a breathtaking coastal road to Eyeries—a brightly painted village overlooking

Coulagh Bay—and then up the south side of the Kenmare River to Kenmare. If you have time left over after exploring the Ring of Beara, you might want to backtrack to R584 and visit **Gougane Barra National Park** (WEB www.coillte.ie/tourism_and_recreation/guagan.htm), where the hermit St. Finbarr had his mountain retreat. It's the source of the River Lee, and has nature trails.

Lodging

$ ⊞ **The Old Presbytery.** This solid waterside house, amid 4 acres of gardens, used to be the home of the parish priest. It's about 1 km (½ mi) from the busy fishing port of Castletownbere, on a narrow peninsula. Try the Bishop's Room for maximum grandeur, but all the rooms are comfortable and individually furnished, with pleasant sea views. Breakfast is served in the conservatory, which overlooks the house's private cove. This is an excellent base for touring Beara. Hosts David and Mary Wrigley will arrange dinner at one of the restaurants nearby, most of which specialize in local seafood. ⊠ *Brandy Hall, Castletownbere,* ☎ *027/70424,* FAX *027/70420. 5 rooms with bath, cable TV. MC, V. Closed Oct.–Mar.*

THE RING OF KERRY

Running along the perimeter of the Iveragh Peninsula, the dramatic Ring of Kerry is probably the single most popular tourist route in Ireland. Stunning mountain and coastal views are around almost every turn of the road. The only drawback: on a sunny day, it seems like half the tourists in Ireland are there, packed into buses, on bikes, or backpacking along the same two-lane road. Because tour buses ply the Ring counterclockwise, we recommend that independent travelers take it clockwise, starting at Kenmare. If you don't want to risk meeting tour buses on a narrow road, however, follow the tour in reverse order, starting at Killorglin. Either way, bear in mind that the majority of tour buses will be leaving Killarney between 9 and 10 AM. The trip covers 176 km (110 mi) on N70 (and briefly R562) if you start and finish in Killarney; the journey will be 40 km (25 mi) shorter if you only venture between Kenmare and Killorglin. Allow at least one full day to circumnavigate the Ring. And because rain blocks views across the water to the Beara Peninsula in the east and the Dingle Peninsula in the west, hope for sunshine. It makes all the difference.

Kenmare

③④ *21 km (13 mi) north of Glengarriff, 34 km (21 mi) south of Killarney on N71.*

A lively touring base with an unusually wide selection of restaurants and accommodations for such a small place, Kenmare is a small market town at the head of the sheltered Kenmare River estuary. The town was founded in 1670 by Sir William Petty (Cromwell's surveyor general, a multitasking entrepreneur), and most of its buildings date from the 19th century, when it was part of the enormous Lansdowne Estate—itself assembled by Petty. The **Kenmare Heritage Centre** explains the history of the town and supplies a walking route pointing out places of interest. *The Square,* ☎ *064/41233.* ⊡ *Free.* ☉ *Easter–Sept., Mon.– Sat. 9:30–5:30.*

Dining and Lodging

$$ ✕ **An Leath Phingin.** The name means "The Half Penny." It's a stylish little place with exposed stone walls and modern pine tables, and it specializes, oddly enough, in northern Italian cuisine. The explanation lies in owner-chef Con Guerin's links with Bologna, where he learned

the art of making fresh pasta. The combination of Irish and Italian dishes are reflected in a starter of baked aubergine with olive oil, tomato, local goat's cheese, and basil, or a 12-inch Quattro Formaggi pizza with four Irish cheeses—Milleens, Cashel Blue, local goat's, and Gubeen. ⊠ *35 Main St.,* ☎ *064/41559. MC, V. Closed mid-Nov.–mid-Dec.*

$$ ✕ **The Lime Tree** In an old stone-built schoolhouse just outside the walls of the Park Hotel, this was one of the first of a wave of stylish restaurants to hit Kenmare 20 years ago. An open fire, exposed stone walls and a minstrel's gallery (on a large balcony above the main room) contribute greatly to the buzz here. Try one of the absolutely delicious and imaginative vegetarian options—millefeuille of goat's cheese with spicy crumble—or go for local free-range duck, or Kerry lamb oven roasted with sweet mint pesto. Leave room for a warm dessert, such as blackberry and pear fruit crumble. ⊠ *Shelburne St.,* ☎ *064/41839. MC, V. Closed Nov.–Apr.*

$–$$ ✕ **Packies.** Owner-chef Maura O'Connell Foley established Kenmare's original first-class restaurant, the Lime Tree, but has since opted for a quieter life at Packies. The small room has a flagstone floor, an exposed-stone fireplace, and paintings by local artists. The delicious Mediterranean-cum-Irish menu includes wild smoked salmon with red onion and caper salsa, and rack of lamb with rosemary and garlic sauce. ⊠ *Henry St.,* ☎ *064/41508. MC, V. Closed Sun. and Nov.–mid-Mar.*

$$$$ ✕🏨 **Park Hotel.** It's no surprise that this magnificent 1897 stone ★ château is one of Ireland's premier country-house hotels. Spectacular views of the Caha Mountains from the 11-acre property, and the terraced lawns sweeping down to the bay are unmistakably fine. Owner-manager Francis Brennan has successfully recaptured the hotel's heyday—a marble fireplace and a tall grandfather clock preside over the thickly carpeted lobby, the spacious bedrooms are individually designed with late-Victorian furniture, and walnut or mahogany bedroom suites have matching wardrobes, chests of drawers, and headboards. Be sure to eat at the restaurant here, which serves a justly famed version of modern Irish cuisine. ⊠ *Co. Kerry,* ☎ *064/41200,* FAX *064/41402,* WEB *www.parkkenmare.com. 40 rooms with bath, 9 suites. Restaurant, 18-hole golf course, tennis court, fishing, bicycles, croquet, Ping-Pong, library, bar, cable TV, some pets allowed. AE, DC, MC, V. Closed Jan. 2–mid-Apr.*

$$$$ ✕🏨 **Sheen Falls Lodge.** The magnificent setting—300 secluded acres of lawns, semitropical gardens, and forest between Kenmare Bay and the falls of the River Sheen—is easily matched by this rambling, bright-yellow, slate-roof manor house, built by the descendants of Sir William Petty, and the former seat of the earls of Kerry. The public rooms, decorated in warm orange tones, include a mahogany-paneled library with more than 1,000 books, mainly of Irish interest, and a billiards room adjacent to the bar. The bedrooms offer stunning bay or river views. The restaurant, La Cascade—it overlooks the falls—serves modern Irish cuisine. ⊠ *Co. Kerry,* ☎ *064/41600,* FAX *064/41386,* WEB *www.sheenfallslodge.ie. 45 rooms with bath, 8 suites, 8 superior-deluxe rooms. Restaurant, tennis court, indoor pool, health club, fishing, billiards, croquet, horseback riding, library, bicycles, bar, cable TV, meeting rooms. AE, DC, MC, V. Closed Jan.*

$ 🏨 **Muxnaw Lodge.** A romantic black-and-white house with steep gables, the lodge was built in 1801 and has a magical view over Kenmare Bay. It is surrounded by mature gardens and trees and is only a short walk from town. Rooms are spacious and cozy, individually decorated with interesting antique furniture. They also have such conveniences as tea- and coffee-making facilities. In general, the lodge is genteel and old-world. Dinner, with local produce and plain home cooking, must be booked by noon. Bring your own wine. ⊠ *Castletown-*

bere Rd., Co. Kerry, ☎ 064/41252. 5 rooms with bath. Tennis court, fishing, cable TV, some pets allowed; no smoking. MC, V.

$ ☐ **Sallyport House.** Across the bridge on the way into Kenmare, this substantial 1932 family home has been enlarged to serve as a comfortable B&B. The spotless rooms, all with harbor or mountain views, are furnished with a variety of Victorian and Edwardian antiques. Janey Arthur has placed family heirlooms in all rooms; if you are interested in old Irish furniture, ask for a tour. ⊠ *Glengarriff Rd., Co. Kerry, ☎ 064/42066, FAX 064/42067, WEB www.sallyporthouse.com. 5 rooms with bath, cable TV. No credit cards. Closed Nov.–Mar.*

Nightlife
Try **O Donnabhain** (⊠ Henry St., ☎ 064/41361) for traditional music.

Outdoor Activities and Sports
Seafari (⊠ Kenmare Pier, ☎ 064/83171, WEB www.seafariireland.com) has two-hour, eco-nature and seal-watching cruises and also runs the Marine Activities Centre (May–October, weather permitting), which offers sea fishing, sailboat day trips, sailboarding, canoeing, waterskiing, and tube rides.

Shopping
Avoca Handweavers (⊠ Moll's Gap, ☎ 064/34720) sells wool clothing and mohair rugs and throws in a wide range of colors and weaves. **Black Abbey Crafts** (⊠ 28 Main St., ☎ 064/42115) specializes in fine Irish-made crafts. **Cleo's** (⊠ 2 Shelbourne St., ☎ 064/41410) stocks Irish-made wool and linen, and Irish hand knits, which have striking designs, often drawn from Ireland's past.

Sneem

③⑤ *27 km (17 mi) southwest of Kenmare on N70.*

This is one of the prettiest villages in Ireland—and, it can seem, one of the most popular. Sneem (from the Irish for "knot") is settled around an English-style green on the estuary of the Ardsheelaun River, its streets filled with houses washed in different colors. Also, look for "the pyramids" (as they are known locally) beside the parish church. These 12-ft-tall, traditional stone structures with stained-glass insets look as though they have been here forever. In fact, the sculpture park was completed in 1990 to the design of the Kerry-born artist James Scanlon, who has won international awards for his work in stained glass.

Staigue Fort, signposted 4 km (2½ mi) inland at Castlecove, is one of the finest examples of an Iron Age stone fort in Ireland. Approximately 2,500 years old, this structure, made from local stone, is almost circular and about 75 ft in diameter, with only one entrance—on the south side. From the Iron Age (from 500 BC to the 5th century AD) and early Christian times (6th century AD), such "forts" were, in fact, the fortified homesteads for several families of one clan (and also where their cattle lived). The walls at Staigue Fort are almost 13 ft wide at the base and 7 ft wide at the top; they still stand at 18 ft on the north and west sides. Within the walls stairs lead to narrow platforms on which the lookouts stood. (Private land must be crossed to reach the fort, and a nominal "compensation for trespass" of €1 is often requested by the landowner.)

Lodging
$$$$ ☐ **Parknasilla Great Southern.** A porter in a frock coat and striped gray pants typifies the elegant and slightly stuffy early 20th-century sensibility of this grand old hotel. General de Gaulle, Princess Grace, and George Bernard Shaw all stayed here (and this is where Shaw wrote

much of *Saint Joan*). Some rooms are a bit plain, but are still taste-fully decorated—in soft pinks and blues. Continental cuisine is served in the Pygmalion Restaurant. The sheltered coastal location—3 km (2 mi) south of Sneem—and excellent sporting facilities make it an ideal retreat. ⊠ *Parknasilla, Co. Kerry,* ☎ *064/45122,* FAX *064/45323,* WEB *www.greatsouthernhotels.com. 84 rooms with bath, 1 suite. Restaurant, cable TV, 9-hole golf course, tennis court, indoor pool, sauna, windsurfing, boating, fishing, horseback riding, bar, meeting rooms, some pets allowed. AE, DC, MC, V.*

$ 🏠 **Tahilla Cove Country House.** An idyllic location—with its own stone jetty in a sheltered private cove—gives this place its particular charm. The house itself is modern and much-added-to over the years. No doubt it won't be difficult to enjoy the plump chintz armchairs and open log fire in the large sitting room, or to laze on the terrace overlooking 14 acres of subtropical gardens and the cove. Rooms vary in size, and are comfortably furnished, and all but two have sea views. ⊠ *Tahilla Cove, Co. Kerry,* ☎ *064/45204,* FAX *064/45104,* WEB *www.sneem.com. 9 rooms with bath. Restaurant, cable TV, fishing, bar, some pets al-lowed. AE, DC, MC, V. Closed mid-Oct.–Mar.*

En Route **Derrynane House** was once the home of Daniel O'Connell (1775–1847), "The Liberator," who campaigned for Catholic Emancipation (the granting of full rights of citizenship for Catholics), which became a re-ality in 1828. The house with its lovely garden and 320-acre estate now forms **Derrynane National Park.** The south and east wings of the house (which O'Connell himself remodeled) are open to visitors and contain much of the original furniture and other items associated with O'Connell. ⊠ *Near Caherdaniel, 30 km (18 mi) west of Sneem off N70,* ☎ *066/947–5113.* 🖼 *House €2.50, parking free.* ☉ *Jan.–Mar. and Nov.–Dec., weekends 1–5; Apr. and Oct., Tues.–Sun. 1–5; May–Sept., Mon.–Sat. 9–6, Sun. 11–7.*

Waterville, Valentia Island, and the Skelligs

Waterville: 35 km (22 mi) west of Sneem, 5 km (3 mi) north of Ca-herdaniel on N70; Valentia Island: 21 km (13 mi) northwest of Wa-terville; Skellig Islands: 40 km (25 mi) west of Waterville.

③⑥ **Waterville** is famous for game-fishing opportunities, its 18-hole cham-pionship golf course (adopted as a warming-up spot for the British Open by Tiger Woods, who was a big hit with the local community), and for the fact that Charlie Chaplin and Charles de Gaulle once spent their summers here. Besides all that, the village, like many others on the Ring of Kerry, has a few restaurants and pubs, but little else. There is ex-cellent salmon and trout fishing at nearby Lough Currane.

OFF THE BEATEN PATH | **BALLINSKELLIGS –** Outside Waterville, a scenic detour is signposted from the main Ring to this small, Irish-speaking fishing village with an old monastery, a pub, and a fine sandy beach.

SHOP AT CILL RIALAIG – This imaginatively designed gallery and crafts shop 1 km (½ mi) before Ballinskelligs village on the R566 is the retail outpost of an artists' retreat, Cill Rialaig. A cluster of derelict old stone cottages in a deserted village have been renovated as artists' studios, at-tracting both Irish and international artists for residencies. Their work is exhibited in the gallery space at the shop, which sells an excellent selec-tion of Irish-made crafts, and work by visiting visual artists, past and present. You can visit ceramics, metal work, and jewelry making crafts workshops here. There's also a coffee shop. ⊠ *Cill Rialaig,* ☎ *066/ 947–9277.* 🖼 *Free.* ☉ *Daily 11–5.*

③⑦ In the far northwestern corner of the Ring, **Valentia Island** lies across Portmagee Channel. Some of the romance of visiting an island has been lost since Valentia was connected to the mainland by a road bridge in 1971. The island still gives its name to weather reports, but the station that monitors the Atlantic weather systems has now moved onto the nearby mainland.

★ ③⑧ The **Skelligs**—Little Skellig, Great Skellig, and the Washerwoman's Rock—are distinctive conical-shape rock islands visible from Valentia Island on a clear day. The largest rock, the Great Skellig, or **Skellig Michael**, rises 700 ft out of the Atlantic. It has the remains of a settlement of early Christian monks, reached by climbing 600 increasingly precipitous steps. In spite of 1,000 years of battering by Atlantic storms, the church, oratory, and beehive-shape living cells are surprisingly well preserved.

The **Skellig Experience**, where the road bridge joins Valentia Island, contains exhibits on local bird life, the history of the lighthouse and keepers, and the life and work of the early Christian monks. There is also a 15-minute audiovisual show that allows you to "tour" the monastery on Skellig Michael without leaving dry land. If, however, you'd like to see the Skelligs up close (landing is prohibited without a special permit), you can take a 1½-hour guided cruise. Little Skellig is the breeding ground of more than 22,000 pairs of gannets, while **Puffin Island** to the north has a large population of shearwaters, storm petrel, and puffins. Photographers will love the boat trip, but take note that the waters are choppy at the best of times. ⊠ *Valentia,* ☎ *066/947–6306.* ⛫ *Center €5.10, cruise €20.30 (includes admission to center).* ☉ *Apr.–June and Sept., daily 9:30–5; July–Aug., daily 9:30–7; call to confirm weather-dependent cruise times.*

Dining and Lodging

$–$$ ✕⛫ **Smuggler's Inn.** Lucille and Harry Hunt's small, family-run cliff-top pub is on a 2-km-long (1-mi-long) sandy beach, and has an immensely popular—among locals and travellers—restaurant with fine, fresh seafood. It's an ideal spot for a leisurely dinner ($$$) or a quick pint and sandwich. Bedrooms are individually decorated with chintz spreads and curtains; in seven of them expect great sea views. ⊠ *Cliff Rd., Waterville, Co. Kerry,* ☎ *066/947–4330,* FAX *066/947–4422,* WEB *www.welcome.to/the smugglersinn. 10 rooms with bath. Fishing, cable TV. AE, DC, MC, V. Closed Nov.–Feb.*

$$–$$$ ⛫ **Butler Arms.** Charlie Chaplin loved it here. The building—with white, castellated corner towers—is a familiar landmark on the Ring. It has been in the same family for three generations, and the regular clientele—predominantly male—return year after year for the excellent fishing and golf facilities nearby. The accommodations are neither smart nor chic, but the rambling old lounges with open turf fires are comfortable places to relax and converse. ⊠ *Waterville, Co. Kerry,* ☎ *066/947–4144,* FAX *066/947–4520,* WEB *www.butlerarms.com. 30 rooms with bath. Restaurant, cable TV, tennis court, fishing, horseback riding, cable TV. AE, DC, MC, V. Closed Nov.–Mar.*

Nightlife
Head to the **Inny Tavern** (⊠ Inny Bridge, Waterville, ☎ 066/947–4512) for live Irish music.

Outdoor Activities and Sports
Waterville Golf Links (⊠ Co. Kerry, ☎ 066/947–4102), an 18-hole, par-72 course, is one of the toughest and most scenic in Ireland or Britain.

Cahirciveen

39 *18 km (11 mi) north of Waterville on N70, 27½ km (17 mi) southwest of Glenbeigh.*

Cahirciveen (pronounced cah-her-sigh-*veen*) is the gateway to the western side of the Ring of Kerry, and the main market town and shopping center for South Kerry, at the foot of Bentee Mountain. The **O'Connell Memorial Church** (⌂ Main Rd.), a large and elaborate neo-Gothic church that dominates the main street, was built in 1888 of Newry granite and local black limestone to honor the local hero, Daniel O'Connell—it's the only church in Ireland named after a layman. Following the tradition in this part of the world, the town's modest, terraced houses are painted in different colors—the brighter the better. The **Cahirciveen Heritage Centre** is housed in the converted former barracks of the Royal Irish Constabulary, an imposing, castlelike structure built after the Fenian Rising of 1867 to suppress any further revolts. The community-funded center has well-designed displays depicting scenes from times of famine in the locality, the life of Daniel O'Connell, and the restoration of this fine building from a blackened ruin. ⌂ *Barracks,* ☏ *066/947-2777,* ⓌⒺⒷ *www.kerry-insight.com.* ⌕ *€3.20.* ☽ *June–Sept., Mon.–Sat. 10–6, Sun. 2–6; Mar.–May and Oct., weekdays 9:30–5:30.*

En Route The road from Cahirciveen to Glenbeigh is one of the Ring's highlights. To the north is Dingle Bay and the jagged peaks of the Dingle Peninsula, which will, in all probability, be shrouded in mist. If they are not, the gods have indeed blessed your journey. The road runs close to the water here, and beyond the small village of Kells, it climbs high above the bay, hugging the steep side of Drung Hill before descending to Glenbeigh. Note how different the stark character of this stretch of the Ring is from the gentle, woody Kenmare Bay side.

Glenbeigh

40 *27 km (17 mi) northeast of Cahirciveen on N70, 11½ km (7 mi) west of Killorglin.*

On a boggy plateau by the sea, the block-long town of Glenbeigh is a popular holiday base, with excellent hiking in the **Glenbeigh Horseshoe,** as the surrounding mountains are known, and exceptionally good trout fishing on Lough Coomasaharn.

Worth a quick look, the **Kerry Bog Village Museum** is a cluster of reconstructed, fully furnished cottages, which gives a vivid portrayal of the daily life of the region's working class in the early 1800s. ⌂ *Beside Red Fox Bar,* ☏ *066/976-9184.* ⌕ *€3.50.* ☽ *Mar.–Nov., daily 8:30–7; Jan.–Feb. by request.*

A signpost to the right outside Glenbeigh points to **Caragh Lake,** a tempting excursion to a beautiful expanse of water set among gorse- and heather-covered hills and majestic mountains. The road encircles the lake, hugging the shoreline much of the way.

OFF THE BEATEN PATH **ROSSBEIGH –** North of Glenbeigh, this beach consists of about 3 km (2 mi) of soft, sandy coastline backed by high dunes. It faces Inch Strand, a similar formation across the water on the Dingle Peninsula.

Dining and Lodging

$$–$$$ ✕⌂ **Caragh Lodge.** Seven acres of spectacular gardens filled with azaleas, camellias, and magnolias surround this mid-19th century fishing lodge—now a charming old house by Caragh Lake. Two large rooms in the main house are furnished with Victorian and Georgian antiques, rooms in the courtyard and the garden annex are smaller, and another block has six larger rooms and one suite. Comfortable sitting rooms overlook the lake, as does the dining room. Owner Mary Gaunt supervises the four-course, set dinner menu (nonguests should book in advance). The food is Irish, with produce from gardens, homemade bread, and local meats and seafood. ⊠ *Caragh Lake, Killorglin, Co. Kerry,* ☎ *066/976–9115,* FAX *066/976–9316,* WEB *www.caraghlodge.com. 14 rooms with bath, 1 suite. Restaurant, tennis court, sauna, boating, fishing; no rooms TVs. AE, DC, MC, V. Closed mid-Oct.–mid-Apr. No lunch.*

\$\$\$ 🔟 **Ard na Sidhe.** Sidhe (pronounced sheen) means "Hill of the Fairies,"
★ and this secluded, gabled Edwardian mansion certainly looks like it belongs in a fairy tale. The house is built of ivy-covered stone walls, and is punctuated by casement windows set in stone mullions. Attractive, large rooms have coordinated carpets and spreads, and lovely floral drapes on bay windows; rooms in the main building are the nicest. Antiques and fireplaces populate the traditionally furnished lobby and lounges. The hotel also has delightful lakeside gardens. ⊠ *Caragh Lake, near Killorglin, Co. Kerry,* ☎ *066/976–9105,* FAX *066/976–9282. 20 rooms with bath. Restaurant, boating, fishing, bar. AE, DC, MC, V. Closed Oct.–3rd wk in Apr.*

Outdoor Activities and Sports
Dooks Golf Club (☎ 066/976–8205) is a challenging traditional links on the shore of Dingle Bay.

Killorglin

 14 km (9 mi) east of Glenbeigh, 22 km (14 mi) west of Killarney.

The last stop on the Ring before Killarney (or the first, if you're going counterclockwise), the hilltop town of Killorglin is the scene of the **Puck Fair,** three days of merrymaking during the second weekend in August. A large billy goat with beribboned horns, installed on a high pedestal, presides over the fair. The origins of the tradition of King Puck are lost in time. Though some horse, sheep, and cattle dealing still occurs at the fair, the main attractions these days are free outdoor concerts and extended drinking hours. The crowd is predominantly young and invariably noisy, so avoid Killorglin at fair time if you've come for peace and quiet. On the other hand, if you intend to join in the festivities, be sure to book accommodations well in advance.

Dining
\$\$–\$\$\$ ✕ **Nick's Seafood and Steak.** Owner-chef Nick Foley comes from the family that established Killarney's famous eatery, Foley's, and has made a name for himself as a talented chef serving generous, simply prepared portions of the best local produce. The old, stone town house has a bar–cum–dining room at street level and a quieter dining room on the floor above. Foley is known for offering a wide choice of local seafood, and for his steaks. In winter, sample the haunch of Kerry venison in red-wine and juniper sauce. ⊠ *Main St.,* ☎ *066/976–1219. AE, DC, MC, V. Closed Nov. and Mon.–Tues. Dec.–Easter.*

IN AND AROUND KILLARNEY

One of southwest Ireland's most attractive locales, Killarney is also the most heavily visited city in the region (its proximity to the Ring of Kerry and to Shannon Airport helps to ensure this). Light rain is typical of the area around Killarney, but because of the region's topography, it seldom lasts long. Indeed, the clouds' approach over the lakes, and the subsequent showers, can actually add to the spectacle of the ever-changing scenery. The rain is often followed within minutes by brilliant sunshine and, yes, even a rainbow.

Exploring Killarney and Environs

Killarney: 87 km (54 mi) west of Cork City on N22, 19 km (12 mi) southeast of Killorglin, 24 km (15 mi) north of Glengarriff.

If writers like Sir Walter Scott and William Thackeray had to struggle finding the superlatives to describe the lakes and mountains of Killarney, it is not surprising that they remain among the most celebrated—and indisputably the most commercialized—attractions in Ireland. Killarney's heather-clad mountains, lush subtropical vegetation, and deep-blue lakes dotted with wooded isles have left a lasting impression on a long stream of visitors, beginning in the 18th century with the English travelers Arthur Young and Bishop Berkeley. Visitors in search of the natural beauty so beloved by the Romantic movement began to flock to the Southwest. By the mid-19th century, Killarney's stunning scenery was considered as exhilarating and awe-inspiring as anything in Switzerland or England's Lake District. The influx of affluent visitors that followed the 1854 arrival of the railway transformed the lives of Kerry's impoverished natives and set in motion a snowball of commercialization that continues today.

But the beauty of the surrounding area—an unbeatable combination of wild mountain scenery and lush foliage—persists. The air smells of damp woods and heather moors. Amazingly, the vegetation is splendid at any time of year. The red fruits of the Mediterranean strawberry tree (*Arbutus unedo*) are at their height in October and November. Also at that time, the bracken turns rust, contrasting with the many evergreens. In late April and early May, the purple flowers of the rhododendron *ponticum* put on a spectacular display. (This Turkish import has adapted so well to the climate that its vigorous growth threatens native oak woods, and many of the purple plants are being dug up by volunteers in an effort to control their spread.)

Killarney National Park—more than 24,700 acres of lake and mountain scenery, a good portion of it wilderness—encompasses much of the Killarney environs. The park is famous for its native natural habitats and species, including oak holly woods, yew woods, and red deer. Signposted self-guiding trails within the park introduce these habitats. At the heart of the national park is Muckross Demesne; the entrance is 4 km (2½ mi) from Killarney on N71. The National Park Visitor Center is at Muckross House. Cars are not allowed in Muckross Demesne; you can either walk, hire a bicycle, or take the traditional Killarney option and use a jaunting car, a pony, and trap (*See* Tours, *in* the A to Z section).

42 You may want to limit time spent in **Killarney** itself if discos, Irish cabarets, and singing pubs—the last a local specialty with a strong Irish-American flavor—aren't your thing. Killarney's nightlife is at its liveliest from May to September; the Irish and Europeans pack the town in July and August. Peak season for Americans follows in September and October. At other times of the year, particularly from November to mid-March, when many of the hotels are closed, the town is quiet to the point of being eerie. Given the choice, go to Killarney in April, May, or early October.

★ **43** **Aghadoe** (⊠ 5 km [3 mi] west of Killarney on the R562 Beaufort–Killorglin road) is an outstanding place to get a feel for what Killarney is all about: lake and mountain scenery. Stand beside Aghadoe's 12th-century ruined church and round tower, and watch the shadows creep gloriously across the Lower Lake, with Innisfallen Island in the distance and the Gap of Dunloe to the west.

44 **Torc Waterfall** (⊠ Killarney National Park, N71 [Muckross Rd.], 8 km [5 mi] south of Killarney) is reached by a footpath that begins in the parking lot outside the gates of the Muckross Demesne. After your first view of the roaring cascade, which will appear after about 10 minutes' walk, it's worth the climb up a long flight of stone steps to the second, less-frequented clearing. WEB *www.heritageireland.ie.*

45 **Muckross House,** a 19th-century, Elizabethan-style manor, now houses the **Kerry Folklife Centre,** where bookbinders, potters, and weavers demonstrate their crafts. The elegantly furnished rooms portray the lifestyle of the landed gentry in the 1800s, while downstairs in the basement you can experience the conditions of servants employed in the house. Inside you'll also find the **Killarney National Park Visitor Centre.** The informal grounds are noted for their rhododendrons and azaleas, the water garden, and the outstanding limestone rock garden. In the park beside the house, the **Muckross Traditional Farms** comprise reconstructed farm buildings and outhouses, a blacksmith's forge, a carpenter's workshop, and a selection of farm animals, including poultry and cattle. It's a reminder of the way things were done on the farm before the electricity and the mechanization of farming. Meet and chat with the farmers and their wives as they go about their work. ⊠ *Killarney National Park, Muckross Demesne, Muckross Rd. (N71), 6½ km (4 mi) south of Killarney,* ☎ *064/31440,* WEB *www.muckross-house.ie/.* ☜ *Visitor center free, farms or house €5, farms and house €8.* ☉ *House Sept.–June, daily 9– 5:30. Visitor center Nov.–mid-Mar., on request; mid-Mar.–June and Sept.–Oct., daily 9–6; July–Aug., daily 9–7. Farms mid-Mar.–Apr., weekends 2–6; May, daily 1–6; June–Sept., daily 10–7; Oct., daily 2–6.*

46 The 15th-century Franciscan **Muckross Friary** is amazingly complete, although roofless. The monks were driven out by Oliver Cromwell's army in 1652. An ancient yew tree rises above the cloisters and breaks out over the abbey walls. Three flights of stone steps allow access to the upper floors and living quarters, where you can visit the cloisters and what was once the dormitory, kitchen, and refectory. ⊠ *Killarney National Park, Muckross Demesne, Muckross Rd. (N71), 4 km (2½ mi) south of Killarney.* ☜ *Free.* ☉ *Mid–June–early Sept., daily 10–5.*

47 **Ross Castle,** a fully restored 14th-century stronghold, was the last place in the province of Munster to fall to Oliver Cromwell's forces in 1652. A later dwelling has 16th- and 17th-century furniture. ⊠ *Knockreer Estate, off Muckross Rd. (N71), 2 km (1 mi) south of Killarney,* ☎ *064/35851.* ☜ *€3.80.* ☉ *Apr. and Oct., daily 10–5; May and Sept., daily 9–6; June–Aug., daily 9–6:30.*

48 The romantic ruins on **Innisfallen Island** date from the 6th or 7th century. Between 950 and 1350 the *Annals of Innisfallen* were compiled here by monks. (The book survives in the Bodleian Library in Oxford.) To get to the island, which is on Lough Leane, you can rent a rowboat at Ross Castle (€3.80 per hour), or you can join a cruise (€7.60) in a covered, heated launch.

★ **49** Massive, glacial rocks form the side of the **Gap of Dunloe,** one of Killarney's primary sights. The gap is a narrow mountain pass that stretches for 6½ km (4 mi) between MacGillicuddy's Reeks, Ireland's highest mountains to the west, and the Purple Mountains. Five small lakes are strung out beside the road. (The rocks create strange echoes: give a shout to test it out.) Cars are banned from the gap, but in summer the first 3 km (2 mi) are busy with horse and foot traffic, much of which turns back at the halfway point.

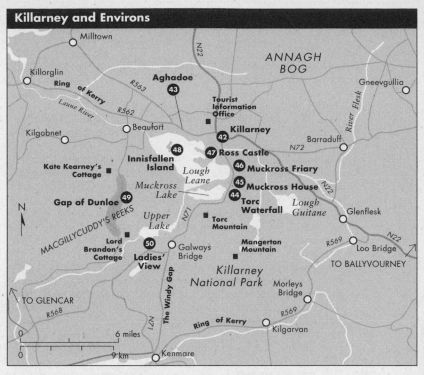

Killarney and Environs

At the entrance to the Gap of Dunloe, **Kate Kearney's Cottage** (✉ 19 km [12 mi] west of Killarney, ☎ 064/44116) is a good place to rent a jaunting car or pony. Kate was a famous beauty who sold illegal *poteen* (moonshine) to visitors from her home, contributing greatly, one suspects, to their enthusiasm for the scenery. Appropriately enough, it's now a pub and a good place to pause for a glass of Irish coffee.

The southern end of the gap is marked by **Lord Brandon's Cottage**, a tea shop serving soup and sandwiches. From here, a path leads to the edge of the Upper Lake, where you can journey onward by rowboat. It is an old tradition for the boatman to carry a bugle and illustrate the echoes. The boat passes under Brickeen Bridge and into the Middle Lake, where 30 islands are steeped in legends, many of which your boatman is likely to recount. Look out for caves on the left-hand side on this narrow stretch of water. ✉ *7 km (4½ mi) west of Killarney.* ⏰ *Easter–Sept., 10 AM–dusk.*

★ ㊿ If the weather is fine, head southwest 19 km (12 mi) out of Killarney on N71 to **Ladies' View,** a panorama of the three lakes and the surrounding mountains. The name goes back to 1905, when Queen Victoria was a guest at Muckross House. Upon seeing the view, her ladies-in-waiting were said to have been dumbfounded by its beauty.

Dining and Lodging

$$$–$$$$
★ ✕ **Fredrick's.** Breathtaking views of Killarney's lakes from the rooftop restaurant of the Aghadoe Heights hotel make this the ultimate romantic venue. The food, too, is outstanding. You'll dine in style—silver candelabra, white linen, and fully upholstered (seat and back) chairs. Ask for a front table when you book. Chef Robin Suter prepares a French menu, and varies dishes according to what's in season. Main courses include both classics—black sole grilled or meunière—and more un-

usual dishes, such as medallions of veal with crab soufflé. This is one of the more expensive restaurants in Ireland, but the experience is unforgettable. ⊠ *Aghadoe Heights,* ☎ *064/31766. Jacket and tie. AE, DC, MC, V.*

$$$ ✕ **Gaby's Seafood.** Expect the best seafood in Killarney. Gaby's small
★   dining room has tiled floors, pine booths, and red-gingham cloths with matching lamp shades. Try the seafood mosaic (seven or eight kinds of fresh fish in a cream-and-wine sauce) or lobster Gaby (shelled, simmered in a cream-and-cognac sauce, and served back in the shell). ⊠ *17 High St.,* ☎ *064/32519. AE, DC, MC, V. Closed Sun. and mid-Feb.–mid-Mar. No lunch.*

$$ ✕ **Dingles.** If you want to feel more like a local than a visitor, then Gerry and Marie Cunningham's relaxed Killarney town-center restaurant is the place to go. Open fires, old church pews, and interesting bric-a-brac make the place chock full of character, and Gerry supplies the warm welcome that keeps the locals coming back. Marie uses the best local ingredients in simple, unshowy dishes, such as roast rack of Kerry lamb, or baked crab and prawns au gratin. ⊠ *40 New St.,* ☎ *064/31079. AE, DC, MC, V. Closed Nov.–Mar. No lunch.*

$–$$ ✕ **Sheila's.** Simply furnished with stripped-pine tables and red paper place mats, Sheila's has fed the people of Killarney and its visitors for more than 30 years. The unpretentious menu includes Irish specials—such as corned beef with cabbage and Irish stew (Kerry lamb stewed with barley, carrots, onion, and potatoes). In a town bedeviled by tourist traps, this friendly spot is an excellent value. The restaurant is licensed to serve wine only. ⊠ *75 High St.,* ☎ *064/31270. AE, DC, MC, V.*

$$$$ ✕🖭 **Aghadoe Heights.** Between the unforgettable lake views from the bluff it's perched on, and the eight acres of grounds that ensure absolute peace and quiet, Aghadoe Heights doesn't disappoint. Neither does the luxurious interior—a pleasant combination of antique and modern styles. Most bedrooms have lake views, and all are relatively large, with good-size bathrooms, matching floral drapes and spreads, lace-covered cushions, and fitted natural wood furniture. Fredericks Restaurant serves French food, and specializes in local seafood and meats. The hotel is 4 km (2½ mi) outside Killarney (on the Tralee side, signposted off N22). ⊠ *Aghadoe Heights, Co. Kerry,* ☎ *064/31766,* ℻ *064/31345,* 🕸 *www.aghadoeheights.com. 72 rooms with bath, 3 suites. Restaurant, cable TV, tennis court, indoor pool, sauna, fishing, bar, meeting rooms. AE, DC, MC, V.*

$$$–$$$$ ✕🖭 **Killarney Park.** A family-run hotel near the town center, this is for you if you like understated, luxurious surroundings. Although the building is modern, the lobby is in a Victorian country-house style—with a sweeping staircase. Sofas and armchairs are invitingly grouped around open fires. Rooms are spacious, with soothing color schemes and well-chosen antiques. There's also a fine library to lounge in. The staff's warmth and commitment are an important part of the experience here. The formal restaurant—in a large, opulent room with heavy drapes—exemplifies the grand style of hotel dining rooms, and serves classic continental cuisine with Irish influences. Simpler meals are served in the Garden Bar. ⊠ *Kenmare Pl., Co. Kerry,* ☎ *064/35555,* ℻ *064/35266,* 🕸 *www.killarneyparkhotel.ie. 3 suites, 20 junior suites, 30 rooms with bath. Restaurant, cable TV, indoor pool, health club, hot tub, outdoor hot tub, bicycles, billiards, bar, library, in-room safes, meeting rooms. AE, DC, MC, V. Closed Dec. 9–26.*

$ ✕🖭 **Foley's.** Rooms in this 19th-century former coaching inn are decorated with Victorian antiques and old country furniture, including sofas and chaises lounges. Windows are double-glazed, so the rooms are quieter than you would expect for a hotel right in the center of Killarney.

Chef-owner Carol Hartnett makes use of local ingredients, including superior Irish cream and butter. Roulade of trout stuffed with prawn mousse and grilled T-bone steak with garlic butter are typical. The wine list includes more than 200 selections, and a pianist entertains in summer. ⊠ *23 High St., Co. Kerry,* ☎ *064/31217,* FAX *064/34683. 32 rooms with bath. Restaurant, cable TV. AE, DC, MC, V. Closed Nov.–mid-Mar.*

$ ✕⊡ **The Mills Inn.** If you wince at tour-bus crowds, consider staying a 15-min drive away from town—in this old coaching inn. Ballyvourney is a small village on the main Cork–Killarney road, beside the rapid-flowing River Sullane. On the property you'll find an old castle ruin, as well as a stable yard and pretty gardens. The bar, established in 1755, is popular with Irish-speaking locals, and has music sessions on Wednesday and Sunday nights. In the rooms, well insulated from bar and traffic noise, you'll find cozy cottage-style furnishings. The restaurant serves generous portions of local beef and seafood from Kenmare; at the bar you'll get simple, hearty fare, such as Irish stew. ⊠ *Ballyvourney, Macroom, Co. Cork,* ☎ *026/45237,* FAX *026/45454,* WEB *www. millsinn.ie. 12 rooms with bath. Restaurant, cable TV, 2 bars. MC, V.*

$$$–$$$$ ⊡ **Europe.** A secluded lakeside location (a 5-min drive from Killarney) and a luxurious but unfussy style give this modern, five-story hotel the edge over its competitors. Most bedrooms have solid-pine trim, a lake view, and a private balcony. The spacious lounges and lobbies, although a bit impersonal, have picture windows overlooking the lake and mountains, an imaginative display of old carved timber, and antiques. The sports facilities, including an Olympic-size pool, are among the best and most up-to-date in the area. ⊠ *Killorglin Rd., Fossa, Co. Kerry,* ☎ *064/31900,* FAX *064/32118,* WEB *www.iol.ie/khl. 205 rooms with bath. 2 restaurants, cable TV, tennis court, indoor pool, sauna, fishing, bicycles, horseback riding, 2 bars,. AE, DC, MC, V. Closed Nov.–mid-Mar.*

$$$ ⊡ **Beaufort House.** You'll find this secluded Georgian house, amidst 40 acres of woodland, proves convenient to both Killarney and the Ring of Kerry. Donald and Rachel Cameron warn their guests that while they offer peace and privacy; two children and a dog also live here. The hall, library, and drawing room all have open fires. The large, uncluttered rooms are furnished with a variety of antiques. A superb stretch of private salmon and trout fishing is available nearby on the River Laune. The house is 9 km (5½ mi) outside Killarney, on the Killorglin road. ⊠ *Beaufort, Co. Kerry,* ☎ *064/44764,* FAX *064/44764,* WEB *www. beaufortireland.com. 4 rooms with bath, 4 cottages. Fishing. MC, V. Closed Nov.–Easter, except by arrangement.*

$–$$ ⊡ **Arbutus.** Run by the friendly Buckley family since it was built more than 60 years ago, Arbutus is a good budget choice in Killarney's town center—a short step from the bus and train stations and a 3-min walk from the main shopping and dining areas. There's an open fire in the lobby, and a quiet, oak-paneled bar that's popular with locals. Ask for one of the spacious rooms—with updated furnishings—in the second-story section. ⊠ *College St., Co. Kerry,* ☎ *064/31037,* FAX *064/ 34033,* WEB *www.arbutuskillarney.com. 36 rooms with bath. Restaurant, bar. AE, DC, MC, V.*

$–$$ ⊡ **Glencar House.** Hikers, anglers, and wilderness lovers will enjoy both the Kerry Highlands and this rambling two-story house—an old hunting lodge built in 1670 by the Earl of Lansdowne. Today it's a small, unpretentious country house, with huge elk antlers over the fireplace and stuffed birds and animals at every turn. Rooms are relatively large, with country pine furniture and breathtaking views of Killarney's famous mountains, the MacGillicuddy's Reeks. The house is a 20-min drive from Killarney and a 10-min drive from Killorglin. (From Killarney, turn off the N72 Killorglin road for Beaufort, and turn right at the first T-junction.) ✉ *Glencar, Co. Kerry,* ☎ *066/976–0102,* FAX *066/976–0167,* WEB *www.glencarhouse.com. 18 rooms with bath. Restaurant, fishing, bar, pets by arrangement. MC, V.*

$ 🖾 **Earls Court House.** In a quiet suburb within walking distance of Killarney's center, this comfortable guest house is furnished with interesting antiques collected by Emer Moynihan, who likes to greet her guests with tea or coffee and scones. Bedrooms are spacious, with large bathrooms and an elegant mix of antique and reproduction Victorian furniture. Breakfast is served at mahogany tables in a large, sunny, wooden-floored room; menu choices include pancakes and kippers. The house has a wine license. ✉ *Woodlawn Junction, Muckross Rd. (N71), Co. Kerry,* ☎ *064/34009,* FAX *064/34366,* WEB *www.killarney-earlscourt.ie. 11 rooms with bath. MC, V.*

$ 🖾 **Lime Court.** This budget accommodation, one of many springing up along the Muckross Road between Killarney and the national park, is only a 5-min walk from the town center. The modern building has two large bay windows in front; rooms are in an extension behind it, away from the road. Antiques and large potted plants decorate the reception area; a baby grand piano anchors the spacious lounge. The relatively large guest rooms overlook green fields and are light, airy, and plainly but comfortably furnished, with small sitting areas. Lime Court has a wine license. ✉ *Muckross Rd. (N71), Co. Kerry,* ☎ *064/34547,* FAX *064/34121,* WEB *www.lime-court.com. 16 rooms with bath. Cable TV. AE, MC, V.*

Medieval Banquets

At the **Killarney Manor Banquet** you'll get a five-course meal hosted by "Lord and Lady Killarney" in their castellated 1860 manor house. Waitresses in 19th-century costume serve the food—you can choose between poached salmon or roast Kerry lamb for the main course. The entertainment is excellent by any standards: a team of professional singers and dancers perform favorite Irish tunes. ✉ *Loreto Rd.,* ☎ *064/31551.* 🖾 *Entertainment plus 5-course meal and mulled-wine reception €40, entertainment only €17.75.* ☉ *Apr.–Oct., meal daily at 8 PM; entertainment 8:45–10:45.*

Nightlife and the Arts

Singing bars—where a professional leads the songs and encourages audience participation and solos—are popular in Killarney. Try the **Laurels** (✉ Main St., ☎ 064/31149). **Buckley's Bar** (✉ College St., ☎ 064/31037) in the Arbutus Hotel has traditional entertainment nightly from June to September. The **Crypt Nightclub** (✉ College Sq., ☎ 064/31038) is a spook-theme late-night venue for the over-23s. **Gleneagles** (✉ Muckross Rd., ☎ 064/31870) is the place for big-name cabaret—from Sharon Shannon to the Wolfe Tones—and also has a late-night disco.

Outdoor Activities and Sports

FISHING

Salmon and brown trout populate Killarney's lakes and rivers. To improve your technique contact **Angler's Paradise** (✉ Loreto Rd., Muckross, ☎ 064/33818), where the Michael O'Brien International Fishing School organizes game, coarse, and deep-sea fishing trips by day or by night. **O'Neill's** (✉ Plunkett St., ☎ 064/31970) provides fishing tackle, bait, and licenses.

GOLF

Beaufort Golf Course (✉ Churchtown, Beaufort, ☎ 064/44440) has an 18-hole, par-71 course surrounded by magnificent scenery, and unlike most other Irish golf clubs, it has buggy-, trolley-, and club-rental facilities. For many, the two courses at the legendary **Killarney Golf and**

Fishing Club (✉ Mahony's Point, ☎ 064/31034) are the chief reason for coming to Killarney.

The **Kerry Way,** a long-distance walking route, passes through the **Killarney National Park** on its way to Glenbeigh (detailed leaflet from the TIO). For the less adventurous, four safe and well-signposted nature trails of varying lengths are at hand in the national park. Try the 4-km (2½-mi) Arthur Young's Walk, which passes through old yew and oak woods frequented by Sika deer. You can reach the **Mangerton walking trail,** a small tarred road leading to a scenic walking trail that encircles Mangerton Lake, by turning left off N71 midway between Muckross Friary and Muckross House (follow signposts). The summit of **Mangerton Mountain** (2,756 ft) can be reached on foot in about two hours—less should you choose to rent a pony. It's perfect if you want a fine, long hike with good views of woodland scenery. **Torc Mountain** (1,764 ft) can be reached off Route N71; it is a satisfying 1½-hour climb, with lake views. Do not attempt mountain climbing in the area in misty weather, because visibility can quickly drop to zero.

Killarney Riding Stables Ltd. (✉ Ballydowney, ☎ 064/31686) organizes four- and seven-day treks in Killarney National Park, with accommodation. Riding by the hour or half day is also available.

Shopping

Shopping in Killarney means crafts and souvenirs, and the most reliable crafts stores are on Main Street and High Street; they all carry a standard range of crystal, hand knits, T-shirts, sweatshirts, and tweed hats. **Blarney Woolen Mills** (✉ 10–11 Main St., ☎ 064/33222) has a large selection of crafts, clothing, and souvenirs. **Bricín Craft Shop** (✉ 26 High St., ☎ 064/34902) has an interesting collection of handmade crafts, including candles, ceramics, and handwoven wool. Visit the **Frank Lewis Gallery** (✉ 6 Bridewell La., beside General Post Office, ☎ 064/ 34843) for original paintings and sculptures. **MacBee's** (✉ New St., ☎ 064/33622) is a stylish modern boutique stocking the best of Irish high fashion. The **Sweater Company** (✉ 3 New St., ☎ 064/35406) carries classic and designer knitwear.

THE DINGLE PENINSULA

The Dingle Peninsula stretches for some 48 km (30 mi) between Tralee (pronounced tra-*lee*) in the east and Slea Head in the west. Small in size yet topographically diverse and brazenly scenic, Dingle's peninsula is composed of rugged mountains and cliffs, interspersed with softly molded glacial valleys and lakes. Along its coast unravel long, sandy beaches and rocky cliffs pounded by the Atlantic Ocean. On the coastal plains, drystone walls enclose small, irregular fields, while exceptional prehistoric and early Christian remains are scattered throughout the peninsula. Dingle is notorious for its heavy rainfall and an impenetrable sea mist, which can strike at any time of year. (If it does, sit it out in Dingle Town or the village of Dunquin and enjoy the friendly bars, cafés, and crafts shops.) At its far western end, west of Dingle Town, the peninsula, like parts of County Kerry, is Gaeltacht: Irish is still spoken on a daily basis, although like most other Gaeltacht communities, it is bilingual nowadays, with English as the second language.

The peninsula can be covered in a long day trip of about 160 km (99 mi). If mist or continuous rain is forecast, postpone your trip until visibility improves. From Killarney, Killorglin, or Tralee, head for Castlemaine, and take the coast road (R561 and R559) to the town of

Dingle. You'll pass through the sheltered seaside resort of Inch, 19 km (12 mi) west of Castlemaine and 45 km (28 mi) northwest of Killarney, where the head of Dingle Bay is cut off by two sand spits that enclose Castlemaine Harbour. Inch has a 6½-km (4-mi) sandy beach backed by dunes that are home to a large colony of natterjack toads.

Annascaul

51 *7 km (4½ mi) west of Inch.*

Near the junction of the Castlemaine and Tralee roads, Annascaul was an important livestock center until the 1930s. This explains why such a small village has such a wide road—cattle trading was carried out in the streets—and also why it boasts so many pubs for so few residents. Photographers will be tempted to snap **Dan Foley's** (☎ 066/915–7252) flamboyantly painted pub. Wander in for a pint; the legendary Dan Foley, who was a magician, a farmer, and an expert on local history, is no longer with us, but tales about him are still told in Annascaul.

Dingle Town

52 *18 km (11 mi) west of Annascaul, 67 km (42 mi) west of Killarney, 45 km (28 mi) west of Killorglin on R561.*

Backed by mountains and facing a sheltered harbor, Dingle, the chief town of its eponymous peninsula, has a year-round population of 1,400 that more than doubles in the summer months. Although many expect Dingle to be a quaint and undeveloped Gaeltacht village, Dingle in fact has lots of crafts shops, seafood restaurants, and pubs. Still, its main streets—the Mall, Main and Strand streets, and the Wood—can be explored in less than an hour. Celebrity hawks, take note: off-season Dingle is favored as a hideaway by several celebrities, including Julia Roberts, Paul Simon, and Dolly Parton. These and others have their visits commemorated on Green Street's "path of stars."

Dingle's pubs are well known for their music, but among them **O'Flaherty's** (✉ Bridge St., at the entrance to town, ☎ 066/915–1983), a simple, stone-floored bar, is something special and a hotspot for traditional musicians. Spontaneous sessions occur most nights in July and August, less frequently at other times. Even without music, this pub provides a good place to compare notes with fellow travelers.

Since 1985 Dingle's central attraction, apart from its music scene, has been a winsome bottle-nosed dolphin who has taken up residence in the harbor. The Dingle dolphin, or **Fungie,** as he has been named, will play for hours with swimmers (a wet suit is essential) and scuba divers, and he follows local boats in and out of the harbor. It is impossible to predict whether he will stay, but boatmen have become so confident of a sighting that they offer trippers their money back if Fungie does not appear. Boat trips (€7.50) leave the pier hourly in July and August between 11 and 6, weather permitting. At other times, call Jimmy Flannery Sr. (☎ 066/915–1163).

Dining and Lodging

$$–$$$ ✕ **Beginish.** It's true Dingle is an oasis in a culinary desert, but this
★   restaurant is outstanding regardless. Muted classical music floats through the small rooms, carpeted in pale green, with fresh flowers on the blue-linen tablecloths. The chef imaginatively interprets French nouvelle cuisine: specialties include Glenbeigh oysters, Dingle Bay lobster Thermidor, and honey glazed duck breast with apple and Calvados sauce. The wine list, with about 100 choices, includes a good selection of half-

bottles. ✉ *Green St.,* ☎ *066/915–1588. AE, DC, MC, V. Closed Mon. and mid-Dec.–mid-Feb. No lunch.*

$$ ✗ **The Chart House.** This square, sparsely furnished room on the eastern edge of town has nautical artifacts, including an antique ship's compass, that complement its name. Owner-chef Jim McCarthy and his team give fresh local produce a light and imaginative Asian-influenced treatment. Black pudding from Annascaul may be paired with ginger-spiced apples, wrapped in phyllo pastry, and served with a bacon jus as a starter, or you may get smoked salmon, served with a wasabi-like spiced horseradish cream. Filet of beef is a perennial favorite, seared and served on a bed of bubble and squeak (fried cabbage and potato) with a peppercorn sauce. ✉ *The Mall,* ☎ *066/915–2255. MC, V. Closed Tues. and Jan.–mid-Feb.*

$$ ✗ **Fenton's.** Step beyond the yellow door of this town house to find a cozy, cottage-style restaurant with quarry-tile floors and local art for sale on the walls. The candlelit tables are covered in oilcloth, but the napkins are linen. The bistro-style menu is straightforward and unfussy, allowing for a quick turnover during Dingle's hectic high season. Some dishes, like the cassoulet of mussels in a garlic cream sauce, are available in starter or main-course portions. Sirloin steak is served with caramelized onions and a red-wine sauce. ✉ *Green St.,* ☎ *066/915–1209. AE, DC, MC, V. Closed mid-Nov.–mid-Mar.*

$$$–$$$$ ✗🏠 **Dingle Skellig.** A 5-min walk from the town center will bring you to this imaginatively designed piece of contemporary architecture, with a beehive-like shape intended to echo local *clocháns* (prehistoric beehive huts). The light-wood-framed, octagonal reception area has specially commissioned stained-glass doors, and original paintings hang in the corridors. Spacious rooms are decorated with modern, pale-wood furniture, and drapes and spreads with bold prints; more than half have sea views (if you want one, say so when reserving). Floor-to-ceiling windows in the Coastguard Restaurant look out over Dingle Bay; this is the town's only eatery right on the water's edge, and, as you'd expect, the specialty is seafood. ✉ *Co. Kerry,* ☎ *066/915–0200,* 📠 *066/915–1501,* 🌐 *www.dingleskellig.com. 110 rooms with bath. Restaurant, cable TV, indoor pool, gym, hot tub, steam room, bar, meeting rooms. AE, DC, MC, V.*

$ 🏠 **Alpine House.** The landmark Alpine is neither spanking new nor old-world. In fact, this plain, family-run, three-story establishment is one of the original guest houses in Dingle, dating from 1963. The location, at the entrance to the town with views over Dingle Bay, is superb. It is quiet, yet Dingle's harbor, pubs, and restaurants are only a 2-min walk away. Private parking is also available. Rooms are bright and cheerful, with pine furnishings, and are well equipped for the price. Alpine House has many fans, so book well in advance, year-round. ✉ *Mail Rd., Co. Kerry,* ☎ *066/915–1250,* 📠 *066/915–1966,* 🌐 *www. alpineguesthouse.com. 10 rooms with bath, cable TV. AE, MC, V.*

$ 🏠 **Greenmount House.** Wonderful views of the town and harbor await at this modern B&B, a short walk uphill from the town center (turn right at the traffic circle at the entrance to Dingle and right again when you come to the first T-junction). A modern bungalow connects to an extension, where six suites each have a sitting room and balcony. Rooms in the original house, though smaller, are impeccable and comfortably decorated with pine beds and floral drapes and spreads. An outstanding breakfast is served in the conservatory, which connects the two buildings. ✉ *Gortonora, Co. Kerry,* ☎ *066/915–1414,* 📠 *066/ 915–1974,* 🌐 *www.greenmounthouse.com. 7 rooms with bath. Lobby lounge, cable TV. MC, V. Closed Dec. 10–27.*

$ 🏠 **Pax House.** Stand on the balcony and watch the fishing boats return with their catch while the sun sets slowly in the west—this modern bungalow has a splendid view of Dingle Harbour from its pretty outdoor terrace. Rooms are simple but well equipped. Breakfast is a generous affair, with fresh seafood on the menu and a selection of Irish cheeses on the buffet. Pax House is 1 km (½ mi) from the town center. ⊠ *Upper John St., Co. Kerry,* ☎ *066/915–1518,* FAX *066/915–2461,* WEB *www.pax-house.com. 12 rooms with bath. Lobby lounge, cable TV. MC, V. Closed Jan.*

Nightlife

Nearly every bar on the Dingle Peninsula, particularly in the town of Dingle, offers music nightly in July and August. **O'Flaherty's** (⊠ Bridge St., at the entrance to town, ☎ 066/915–1983) is a gathering place for traditional musicians—you can hear impromptu music sessions most nights in July and August. For sing-along and dance, try **An Reált— The Star Bar** (⊠ The Pier, ☎ no phone).

Outdoor Activities and Sports

BICYCLES

You're likely to remember a bike ride around Slea Head for a long time to come. Bicycles may be rented at **Dingle Bicycle Hire** (⊠ The Tracks, ☎ 066/915–2166).

Shopping

Don't miss Dingle's café-bookshop, which locals insist is one of the first in the world (it's been there since the 70s). Visit **An Cafe Liteartha** (☎ 066/915–1388) for new and secondhand books of local interest, and for friendly conversation. At **Leác a Ré** (⊠ Strand St., ☎ 066/915–1138) you can get handmade Irish crafts. Lisbeth Mulcahy at the **Weaver's Shop** (⊠ Green St., ☎ 066/915–1688) sells outstanding handwoven, vegetable-dyed woolen wraps, mufflers, and fabric for making skirts.

Ventry

53 *8 km (5 mi) west of Dingle Town on R561.*

The next town after Dingle along the coast, Ventry has a small outcrop of pubs and small grocery stores (useful, since west of Dingle Town you'll find few shops of any kind), and a long, sandy beach with safe bathing and ponies for rent. Between Ventry and Dunquin, you'll find several interesting archaeological sites on the spectacular cliff-top road along Slea Head.

En Route   **Dunbeg,** an Iron Age promontory fort, can be seen on the left below the road, after you pass between two tall hedges of fuchsia bushes about 6 km (4 mi) west of Ventry (follow the signposts across fields). A fortified stone wall cuts off the promontory, and the landward side is protected by an elaborate system of earthworks and trenches. Within the enclosure is a ruined circular building. This was not a homestead but probably a refuge in times of danger.

Continuing west along the coast road beyond Dunbeg, you'll see signs for "Prehistoric Beehive Huts"—*clocháns* in Irish. Built of unmortared stone on the southern slopes of Mt. Eagle, these cells were used by hermit monks in the early Christian period; some 414 exist between Slea Head and Dunquin. Some local farmers, on whose land these monuments stand, charge a "trespass fee" of €.65 to €1.27 from visitors.

Slea Head

★ **54** *16 km (10 mi) west of Dingle Town on R561, 8 km (5 mi) west of Ventry.*

From the top of the towering cliffs of Slea Head at the southwest extremity of the Dingle peninsula the view of the Blasket Islands and the Atlantic Ocean is unforgettable—guaranteed to stop you in your tracks. Alas, Slea Head has become so popular that tour buses, barely able to negotiate the narrow road, are causing traffic jams, particularly in July and August. **Coumenole**, the long, sandy strand below, looks beautiful and sheltered, but swimming here is dangerous. This treacherous stretch of coast has claimed many lives in shipwrecks—most recently in 1982, when a large cargo boat, the *Ranga*, foundered on the rocks and sank. In 1588, four ships of the Spanish Armada were driven through the Blasket Sound; two made it to shelter, and two sank. One of these, the *Santa Maria de la Rosa* is currently being excavated by divers during the summer months.

The largest of the **Blasket Islands** visible from Slea Head, the **Great Blasket** was inhabited until 1953. The Blasket islanders were great storytellers and were encouraged by Irish linguists to write their memoirs. *The Islandman*, by Tomás O Crohán, gives a vivid picture of a hard way of life. "Their likes will not be seen again," O Crohán poignantly observed. The **Blasket Centre** explains the heritage of these islanders and celebrates their use of the Irish language with videos and exhibitions. ⊠ *Dunquin*, ☎ *066/915–6371*, ⬚ *www.heritageireland.ie.* ⬚ *€3.10.* ☉ *Easter–June and Sept., daily 10–6; July–Aug., daily 10–7.*

Dunquin

⑤ *13 km (8 mi) west of Ventry on R559, 5 km (3 mi) north of Slea Head.*

Once the mainland harbor for the Blasket islanders, Dunquin is at the center of the Gaeltacht, and attracts many students of Irish language and folklore. David Lean shot *Ryan's Daughter* hereabouts in 1969. The movie gave the area its first major boost in tourism, though it was lambasted by critics—"Gush made respectable by millions of dollars tastefully wasted," lamented Pauline Kael—sending Lean into a dry spell he didn't come out of until 1984's *A Passage to India*. **Kruger's Pub** (☎ 066/915–6127), Dunquin's main social center, has long been frequented by artists and writers—including Brendan Behan—and it still is; it's also the only eatery for miles and a good place to stop for a bite.

Dunquin's **pier** (signposted from the main road) is surrounded by cliffs of colored Silurian rock, more than 400 million years old and rich in fossils. Down at the pier you'll see *curraghs* (open fishing boats traditionally made of animal hide stretched over wooden laths and tarred) stored upside down, usually covered in canvas. Three or four men walk the curraghs out to the sea, holding them aloft over their heads. Similar boats are used in the Aran Islands, and, when properly handled, they prove extraordinarily seaworthy. If you're interested in going out to the Blaskets, inquire at the pier in June, July, and August for boats heading to Great Blasket during the day, depending on the weather. (There's no scheduled ferry service, and no phone.)

En Route **Clogher Strand,** a dramatic, windswept stretch of rocks and sand, is not a safe spot to swim, but a good place to watch the ocean dramatically pound the rocks when a storm is approaching or a gale is blowing. Overlooking the beach is **Louis Mulcahy's pottery studio.** One of Ireland's leading ceramic artists, Mulcahy produces large pots and urns that are both decorative and functional. You can watch the work in progress and and buy items at workshop prices. ⊠ *Clogher Strand*, ☎ *066/915–6229.* ☉ *Daily 9:30–6.*

Ballyferriter

56 *5 km (3 mi) northeast of Dunquin, 14 km (9 mi) west of Dingle on R559.*

Like the other towns at this end of the Dingle peninsula, Ballyferriter is a Gaeltacht village and mainly a holiday spot for vacationers with RVs, many of them German or Dutch. The area around here is great for walking.

One of the best-preserved, early Christian churches in all of Ireland, **Gallarus Oratory** dates from the 7th or 8th century and ingeniously makes use of corbeling—successive levels of stone projecting inward from both side walls until they meet at the top to form an unmortared roof. The structure is still watertight after more than 1,000 years. ⊠ *8 km (5 mi) northeast of Ballyferriter on R559.* ☒ *Free.*

Kilmakedar Church is one of the finest surviving examples of Romanesque (early Irish) architecture. Although the Christian settlement dates from the 7th century, the present structure was built in the 12th century. Native builders integrated foreign influences with their own local traditions, keeping the blank arcades and round-headed windows but using stone roofs, sloping doorway jambs, and weirdly sculpted heads. Ogham stones and other interestingly carved, possibly pre-Christian stones are on display in the churchyard. ⊠ *8 km (5 mi) northeast of Ballyferriter on R559.* ☒ *Free.*

OFF THE BEATEN PATH

THE CONNOR PASS – This mountain route, which passes from south to north over the center of the peninsula, offers magnificent views of Brandon Bay, Tralee Bay, and the beaches of North Kerry, leaving Dingle Bay in the south. The road is narrow, and the drops on the hairpin bends are precipitous; be sure to nominate a confident driver who is not scared of heights, especially in misty weather. It was from Brandon Bay that Brendan the Navigator (AD 487–577) is believed to have set off on his famous voyages in a specially constructed curragh. On his third trip it is possible that he reached Newfoundland or Labrador, then Florida. Brendan was the inspiration for many voyagers, including Christopher Columbus.

The summit of **Mt. Brandon** (3,127 ft) is on the left as you cross the Connor Pass (from south to north). It's accessible only to hikers. Do not attempt the climb in misty weather. The easiest way to make the climb is to follow the old pilgrims' path, Saint's Road; it starts at Kilmakedar Church and rises to the summit from Ballybrack, which is the end of the road for cars. At the summit, you'll reach the ruins of an early Christian settlement. You can also approach the top from a path that starts just beyond Cloghane (signposted left on descending the Connor Pass); the latter climb is longer and more strenuous.

Blennerville

57 *60 km (37 mi) east of Ballyferriter, 5 km (3 mi) west of Tralee on R560.*

The five-story **windmill** with black and white sails is the main attraction in Blennerville, a village on the western edge of Tralee. The surrounding buildings have been turned into a visitor center, with crafts workshops and an exhibition recalling Blennerville's past as County Kerry's main point of emigration during the Great Famine (1845–49). ☎ *066/712-7777.* ☒ *€3.80.* ☉ *Apr.–Oct., daily 10–5.*

The **Jeanie Johnston Visitor Shipyard** has a recently built replica of a famous 19th-century emigrant vessel, a tall ship named the *Jeanie*

Johnston (1847–58). The three-masted barque is 47 meters long and has an 8-meter beam. In April 2002 she was undergoing sea trials, after which an inaugural voyage to North America is planned. Eventually she will return to Blennerville, where she'll be the centerpiece of a visitor experience that includes audiovisual displays on ship building and Ireland's marine heritage, and a computerized index of Irish emigrants to North America from the 1800s to the present day. ☎ 066/712–9999, WEB *www.jeaniejohnston.com.* ✉ €5. ☉ *Daily 9:30–5:30.*

A very popular **steam railway** shuttles back and forth along the 3 km (1½ mi) of tracks between Blennerville and Tralee, with departures from each terminus every half hour from May through September. ☎ 066/712–7444. ✉ €4.

Tralee

58 *5 km (3 mi) northeast of Blennerville, 50 km (31 mi) northeast of Dingle on R559.*

County Kerry's capital and its largest town, Tralee (population 21,000) has long been associated with the popular Irish song "The Rose of Tralee," the inspiration for the annual **Rose of Tralee International Festival.** The last week of August, Irish communities worldwide send young women to join native Irish competitors; one of them is chosen as the "Rose of Tralee." Visitors, musicians, and entertainers pack the town then. A two-day horse race meeting—with seven races a day— runs at the same time, which contributes to the crowds. Tralee is also the home of **Siamsa Tíre**—the National Folk Theatre of Ireland, which stages dances and plays based on Irish folklore.

Kerry the Kingdom, Tralee's major cultural attraction, traces the history of Kerry's people from 5000 BC to the present, using dioramas and an entertaining audiovisual show. There's also a streetcar ride through a life-size reconstruction of Tralee in the Middle Ages. ✉ *Ashe Memorial Hall, Denny St.,* ☎ *066/712–7777,* WEB *www.kerrycountymuseum.com.* ✉ €7. ☉ *Sept.–July, Mon.–Sat. 10–6; Aug., Mon.–Sat. 10–8.*

☺ Ireland's biggest water complex, **AquaDome,** includes sky-high water slides, a wave pool, raging rapids, water cannons, and other thrills. Adults can seek refuge in the Sauna Dome. ✉ *Dingle Rd.,* ☎ *066/712–8899,* WEB *www.discoverkerry.com/aquadome.* ✉ €7. ☉ *Mid-May–Aug., daily 10–10; Sept.–mid-May, weekdays 2–10, weekends 11–8.*

Lodging

$$$–$$$$ 🏨 **Ballyseede Castle.** Golfers, take note: the former Fitzgerald Castle
★ is within easy reach of five of the best courses in the region. Victorian additions complement this 15th-century, three-story building. Individually decorated rooms are generously furnished with antiques, and two magnificent drawing rooms with ornamental plasterwork and marble fireplaces complete the picture. Try the Yeats room; it's one of the fanciest. Ballyseede is 3 km (2 mi) east of Tralee on the main Limerick road (N21). ✉ *Co. Kerry,* ☎ *066/712–5799,* FAX *066/712–5287. 12 rooms with bath. Restaurant, cable TV, fishing, horseback riding, bar. MC, V.*

$$$ 🏨 **Brandon.** Although it's not especially exciting, Brandon—a modern five-story hotel in the center of town—is the only place in Tralee with a pool and fitness center. The decent-size rooms are furnished plainly with chunky pine furniture and have uninspiring urban views. The restaurant is reputable. Rates shoot up during the Rose of Tralee Festival (late August) and the Listowel races (third week in September). ✉ *Princes St., Co. Kerry,* ☎ *066/712–3333,* FAX *066/712–5019,* WEB *www.*

brandonhotel.ie. 182 rooms with bath. Restaurant, cable TV, indoor pool, health club, fishing, horseback riding, 2 bars, meeting rooms. AE, DC, MC, V.

$$ ⌂ **Abbeygate.** Built on the site of Tralee's old marketplace, Abbeygate is an attractive modern hotel. It's essentially in the town center, but it occupies a quiet spot behind the main—contemporary—shopping street. It has nicely sized rooms with country-style wood furniture and large, tiled bathrooms. The Old Market Place Pub, a rambling, imaginatively designed bar, seats 500 people and is built in the traditional style, with wood floors, open fireplaces, and a cozy atmosphere. There is bar food at lunchtime, and music and dancing nightly from June to September— and at least three nights a week at other times. ⊠ *Maine St., Co. Kerry,* ☎ *066/712–9888,* ⒻⒶⓍ *066/712–9821,* ⓌⒺⒷ *www.abbeygate-hotel.com. 100 rooms with bath. Restaurant, cable TV, 2 bars, meeting rooms. AE, DC, MC, V.*

Nightlife and the Arts

Ballad sessions are more popular here than traditional Irish music. **Horan's Hotel** (⊠ Clash St., ☎ 066/712–1933) has dance music and cabaret acts nightly during July and August, and on weekends only during the off-season.

Try to catch the **National Folk Theater of Ireland** (Siamsa Tíre). Language is no barrier to this colorful entertainment, which re-creates traditional rural life through music, mime, and dance. ⊠ *Godfrey Pl.,* ☎ *066/712–3055.* ▣ *€15.25.* ☉ *Shows July–Aug., Mon.–Sat. at 8:30 PM; May–June and Sept., Tues. and Thurs. at 8:30 PM.*

Outdoor Activities and Sports

BICYCLES

You can rent bicycles from **Tralee Bicycle Supplies** (⊠ Strand St., ☎ 066/712–2018).

GOLF

Tralee is the heart of great golfing country. The **Ballybunion Golf Club (Old Course)** (⊠ Ballybunion, ☎ 068/27146) is universally regarded as one of golf's holiest grounds. The **Tralee Golf Club** (⊠ West Barrow, Ardfert, ☎ 066/713–6379) is a seaside links with cliffs, craters, and dunes.

HORSEBACK RIDING

El Rancho Farmhouse and Riding Stables (⊠ Ballyard, ☎ 066/712–1840) specializes in residential trekking holidays on the Dingle trail between Tralee and the Dingle Peninsula.

OFF THE
BEATEN PATH

BALLYBUNION – A detour 41 km (25 mi) northwest of Tralee on N69 and R553 will take you to this seaside resort, famous for its long, sandy beach and championship golf course. A large bronze statue of former president Clinton commemorates a round he played in 1998.

NORTH KERRY AND SHANNONSIDE

Until several decades ago, Shannon meant little more to most people— if it meant anything at all, that is—than the name of the longest river in the British Isles, running for 273 km (170 mi) from County Cavan to Limerick City in County Clare. But mention Shannon nowadays and people think immediately of the major airport, which has become the principal gateway to western Ireland. In turn, what also comes to mind are many of the glorious sights of North Kerry and Shannonside: a slew of historic castles, including Bunratty, Glin, and Knappogue (several sponsor wonderful medieval banquets); Adare, sometimes called "Ireland's Prettiest Village," and the neighboring Adare Manor, one of Ireland's grandest country-house hotels; and Limerick City, which attracts visitors tracing the memories so movingly captured in Frank McCourt's international best-seller *Angela's Ashes*. Picking up where the Dingle Peninsula route left off, this section begins in Listowel, in the northwest of County Kerry, and then jumps across the Kerry-Limerick border, where the first stop is Glin, on the south side of the Shannon estuary. Limerick City, the Republic's third largest, and those parts of County Clare on the north side of the Shannon round it out. A hint to travelers arriving at Shannon Airport: if you plan to focus on the Southwest, follow the trips outlined in this chapter from back to front.

Listowel

59   *27 km (16 mi) northeast of Tralee on N69.*

The small, sleepy market town of Listowel comes alive for its annual horse race during the third week of September. You reach the town from the west, by driving along a plain at the base of Stack's Mountain.

Dining and Lodging

$ ✕🏨 **Allo's Bar and Bistro.** Just off Listowel's main square, this traditional-style rustic bar, which dates from 1859, serves the best local foods, freshly prepared. Chef Armel Whyte and his partner, Helen Mullane, prepare local beef and lamb, and local seafood, including lobsters, scallops, and oysters, and are best known for their imaginative combinations of traditional and contemporary Irish cooking. The bedrooms are spacious, and are furnished with stylish antiques and four-poster beds, and have large, Connemara marble bathrooms. ⊠ *41 Church St.,* ☎ FAX *068/22880. 3 rooms with bath. Restaurant, bar. AE, MC, V. Bar, bistro closed Sun.*

En Route   From Listowel, head north on N69 18 km (11 mi) to **Tarbert,** the terminus for the **ferry to Killimer** in West Clare, a convenient 20-minute shortcut if you're heading for the west of Ireland. The **Shannon,** with a length of 273 km (170 mi), is the longest river in Ireland or Britain. The magnificent estuary stretches westward for another 96 km (60 mi) before reaching the sea.

Glin

60   *6½ km (4 mi) east of Tarbert on N69, 51 km (32 mi) north of Tralee on N69.*

The Fitzgerald family has held the title of Knight of Glin since the 14th century. While the family has built numerous structures in the area, ★ the present **Glin Castle,** situated on the banks of the Shannon, dates only from 1785. Between 1820 and 1836 the 25th knight added crenellations and Gothic details to make the house look more like an ancestral home. A delicate plasterwork ceiling, painted in the original red and green, graces the neoclassic hall, which opens onto a splendid "flying" staircase: two risers that join to a single central tongue. The present Knight of Glin (the 29th), Desmond Fitzgerald, a Harvard-educated art historian, is an expert on Irish decorative arts (and an outspoken arts advocate), so it's fitting that the house has an exceptional collection of Irish 18th-century mahogany and walnut furniture. ☎ *068/34173,* WEB *www.glincastle.com.* ⊠ *€5.50.* ☯ *May–June, daily 10–noon and 2–4; other times by appointment.*

··

OFF THE   **FLYING BOAT MUSEUM** – Nine kilometers (5½ mi) east of Glin on N69,
BEATEN PATH   Foynes was the landing place for transatlantic air traffic in the 1930s

and 1940s. This museum in the terminal of the original Shannon Airport celebrates Foynes's aviation history; it's a must for flying buffs. ☎ 069/ 65416. 🖾 €3.80. ⊙ Apr.–Oct., daily 10–5.

Dining and Lodging

$$$$ ✕🏨 **Glin Castle.** Experience Irish castle living at the Fitzgerald family home, one of the world's outstanding private houses—with 500 acres of formal gardens, parkland, and a dairy farm. Ballybunion is the nearest golf course. The large elegant rooms showcase Glin's famous collection of Irish furniture, yet remain comfortable and user-friendly. Country-house cuisine is served in the dining room, beneath portraits of Fitzgerald ancestors. On the menu you'll find locally produced meat and poultry and freshly caught fish, as well as produce from the walled garden. Nonresidents are welcome for dinner but must reserve in advance. ⊠ Co. Limerick, ☎ 068/34112, 🆁🅰🆇 068/34364, 🆆🅴🅱 www.glincastle.com. 15 rooms with bath. Tennis court, boating, fishing, croquet, horseback riding, cable TV, pets by arrangement, meeting rooms, kids over 10 only. AE, DC, MC, V.

En Route   **Castle Matrix** in Rathkeale, east of Glin on R518—dates from 1440, when it was in possession of the earls of Desmond. Confiscated by Elizabeth I, the castle was as a meeting place for the poets Edmund Spenser and Walter Raleigh in 1589. Raleigh subsequently brought the first potato tubers from North Carolina to Castle Matrix, from where they were distributed throughout south Munster (the old provincial name for the region). In 1962, the late colonel Sean O'Driscoll, an American architect, bought Castle Matrix and restored it. The library has an important collection of documents relating to the "Wild Geese," Irish mercenaries who served in European armies in the 17th and 18th centuries. ⊠ Rathkeale, ☎ 069/64284. 🖾 €4. ⊙ Mid-May–mid-Sept., Sat.–Tues. 11–5.

Adare

★ ⑥₁   19 km (12 mi) southwest of Limerick City on N21, 82 km (51 mi) northeast of Tralee on N21, 40 km (25 mi) east of Glin.

A picture-book village with several thatched cottages amid wooded surroundings on the banks of the River Maigue, Adare is rich in ruins; on foot, you can locate the remains of two 13th-century abbeys, a 15th-century friary, and the keep of a 13th-century Desmond castle. Providing that once-upon-a-time allure that has helped make this famous as one of Ireland's prettiest villages, the many stone-built cottages, often adorned with colorful, flower-filled window boxes, have a centuries-old look; they were, in fact, built in the mid-19th century by the third Earl of Dunraven, a popular landlord, for the tenants on his estate. Nowadays they house various boutiques selling traditional Irish crafts and antiques and also a gourmet restaurant called Wild Geese. Adare Manor, an imposing Tudor–Gothic Revival mansion, which was once the grand house of the Dunraven peerage, is now a celebrated luxury hotel.

Dining and Lodging

$$$–$$$$ ✕ **Wild Geese.** In a series of small dining rooms in this low-ceiling thatched cottage, co-owner and chef David Foley uses the best local produce to create seriously good food in imaginative combinations. Try roast rack of lamb with tempura vegetables and beetroot jus or roast breast of duck on creamed leeks with deep-fried mushroom won tons. Lobster is a popular summer option, thermidor (in brandy and cream sauce) or cooked in garlic butter, served with hollandaise sauce. The "Wild Geese" dessert platter for two lets you sample all desserts, including the fantastic homemade ice cream. The restaurant is opposite the Dunraven Arms. ✉ *Rose Cottage,* ☎ *061/396451. AE, DC, MC, V. Closed Sun.–Mon. and 3 wks in Jan. No lunch.*

$$$-$$$$ ✕🏨 **Dunraven Arms.** Adare's landmark inn, established in 1792, oozes old-world charm. It makes a popular first port of call if you're arriving at Shannon Airport, 40 km (25 mi) northwest. Interestingly, Charles Lindbergh stayed in Room 6 while he advised on the airport's design. Paintings and prints of horseback riders decorate the dark walls of the cozy bar and lounges. The comfortable bedrooms are tastefully furnished with antiques. Junior suites in the newer wing have antique four-poster beds. The elegant Maigue Restaurant specializes in modern Irish cuisine; informal dining is offered in the pretty bar area. ✉ *Main St., Co. Limerick,* ☎ *061/396633,* ℻ *061/396541. 76 rooms with bath, 6 executive suites, 14 junior suites. Restaurant, cable TV, indoor pool, health club, fishing, horseback riding, bar, meeting rooms. AE, DC, MC, V.*

$$ ✕🏨 **Mustard Seed at Echo Lodge.** Dan Mullane's spacious Victorian
★ country-house hotel and restaurant has themed guest rooms—black-and-white, carnival, Chinese, and so on—and looks out over the countryside. Chef Tony Schwartz uses only the best local produce, plus herbs and vegetables from his organic garden. Shark is an unusual seafood option in summer; more typical is the honey-glazed lamb shank with a cassoulet of beans and homegrown baby vegetables. Fruits from the garden are used in such desserts as hot crunchy apple-and-black-currant crumble with Calvados, cream, and caramel sauce. The hotel is 13 km (8 mi) southwest of Adare in Ballingarry. ✉ *Ballingarry, Co. Limerick,* ☎ *069/68508,* ℻ *069/68511. 17 rooms with bath, 3 suites. Restaurant, bar, library; no kids. AE, MC, V.*

$-$$ ✕🏨 **Fitzgeralds Woodlands House Hotel.** In the energetic and capable hands of the Fitzgerald family, this small-scale B&B has evolved into a thriving modern hotel. It's set in 44 acres of pretty, landscaped grounds, on the Limerick side of the village. Rooms are relatively spacious, individually decorated in various modern styles, and well maintained. Expect to see locals in Timmy Mac's bar, a popular meeting place. The Brennan Rooms serves a traditional Irish table d'hôte menu: local lamb, pork, and beef. More adventurous cooking takes place in the bistro-style coffee shop in Timmy Mac's, which serves locally grown organic food. ✉ *Knockanes, Co. Limerick,* ☎ *061/605100,* ℻ *061/396073,* 🌐 *www.woodlands-hotel.ie. 84 rooms with bath, 8 suites. 2 restaurants, cable TV, indoor pool, health club, fishing, horseback riding, bar, meeting rooms. AE, DC, MC, V.*

$$$$ 🏨 **Adare Manor.** Play king or queen for a day at this strikingly grand (and, interestingly, American-owned) Victorian Gothic mansion—once the abode of the earls of Dunraven. There are vast stone arches, heavy wood carvings, and a decorated ceiling in the baronial central hall—but the glorious 36-ft-high, 100-ft-long gallery, wainscoted in oak, is the architectural highlight. The eight "staterooms" in the original house are the most sumptuous, with huge marble bathrooms, and stone-mullioned windows. Most rooms have super-king-size beds; all have heavy drapes and thick carpets and overlook the 840 acres of grounds. Adare's golf course, designed by Robert Trent Jones, is considered one of Ireland's best. ✉ *Co. Limerick,* ☎ *061/396566,* ℻ *061/396124,* 🌐 *www.adaremanor.ie. 63 rooms with bath. Restaurant, cable TV, 18-hole golf course, indoor pool, sauna, fishing, horseback riding, 2 bars, meeting rooms. AE, DC, MC, V.*

Outdoor Activities and Sports

GOLF

Adare Manor Golf Course (☎ 061/396204) is an 18-hole, par-69 parkland course.

The **Clonshire Equestrian Center** (☎ 061/396770) has all-weather riding facilities and will also organize trail riding and residential holidays.

Shopping

Adare Gallery (✉ Main St., ☎ 061/396898) sells Irish-made jewelry, porcelain, and woodwork, as well as original paintings. **Carol's Antiques** (✉ Main St., ☎ 061/396977) sells antique furniture, silver, china, and objects of art from one of Adare's tiny cottages. At **George Stacpoole** (✉ Main St., ☎ 061/396409) you'll find antiques and books.

Limerick City

62 *19 km (12 mi) northeast of Adare, 198 km (123 mi) southwest of Dublin.*

Before you ask, there's *no* direct connection between Limerick City and the facetious five-line verse form known as a limerick, which was first popularized by the English writer Edward Lear in his 1846 *Book of Nonsense*. The city, at the head of the Shannon estuary and at the intersection of a number of major crossroads, is an industrial port and the fourth-largest city in the Republic (population 75,000). If you fly into or out of Shannon Airport, and have a few hours to spare, do take a look around, as the city, after undergoing significant economic revitalization, has been spiffed up—it's no longer an unattractive place marked by high unemployment and a higher crime rate than elsewhere in the Republic. Frank McCourt's childhood memoir, *Angela's Ashes*—set in Limerick, where McCourt grew up desperately poor—has also helped to pique interest in the city's fortunes today. The area around the cathedral and the castle is the old part of the city, dominated by mid-18th-century buildings with fine Georgian proportions.

Like most other Irish coastal towns, Limerick was originally a 9th-century Danish settlement; Richard I granted the city's charter in 1197. In 1691, after the Battle of the Boyne, the Irish retreated to the walled city, where they were besieged by William of Orange, who made three unsuccessful attempts to storm the city but then raised the siege and marched away. A year later, another of William's armies overtook the city for two months, and the Irish opened negotiations. The resulting Treaty of Limerick—which guaranteed religious tolerance—was never ratified, and 11,000 men of the Limerick garrison joined the French Army rather than fight in a Protestant "Irish" army.

★ In the Old Customs House on the banks of the Shannon in the city center, the **Hunt Museum** has the finest collection of Celtic and medieval treasures outside the National Museum in Dublin. Ancient Irish metalwork, European objets d'art, and a selection of 20th-century European and Irish paintings—including works by Jack B. Yeats—are on view. A café overlooks the river. ✉ *Rutland St.,* ☎ *061/312833,* WEB *www.ul.ie.* 🎟 *€5.* 🕙 *Oct.–Apr., Tues.–Sat. 10–5, Sun. 2–5; May–Sept., Mon.–Sat. 10–5, Sun. 2–5.*

Limerick is a predominantly Catholic city, but the Protestant **St. Mary's Cathedral** is the city's oldest religious building. Once a 12th-century palace—pilasters and a rounded Romanesque entrance were part of the original structure—it dates mostly from the 15th century (the black-oak carvings on misericords in the choir stalls are from this period). ✉ *Bridge St.,* ☎ *061/416238.* 🕙 *Daily 9–6.*

The office of the **Limerick Regional Archives** (✉ Michael St., ☎ 061/415125, WEB www.mayo-ireland.ie) is in the Granary, built in 1774 for grain storage. For a small fee, the Archives provides a genealogical research service.

RISEN FROM THE ASHES: FRANK McCOURT'S LIMERICK

THE ALCOHOLIC PA. The starving, shivering brood of children. The sheep's head for Christmas. The rags for diapers. The little white coffin. And the long-suffering, abused ma. These are some of the elements that rivet the reader of *Angela's Ashes* (1996, Scribners), Frank McCourt's memoir of his impoverished childhood in Limerick—a rags-to-riches story, with the riches always being more spiritual than material. Called by *Newsweek* "the publishing event of the decade," and compared by some to the *Grapes of Wrath* in its power, pain, and joy, *Angela's Ashes* has sold a few million hardcover copies, won the Pulitzer, and gone Hollywood. The book seems to speak to the Irish in everyone's soul if best-seller lists, from Japan to Germany, are any indication. Not surprisingly, the city of Limerick—the rain-sodden setting of this 1930–40s hard-luck saga—has become a new pilgrimage place for readers eager to partake of the tearfulness of it all. Busloads of McCarthys and O'Dwyers now clamber over the sites described in the book, ending up at South's pub to raise a pint in Frank's honor and to count their blessings.

In the memoir narrated from a child's perspective, Limerick looms as "a gray place with a river that kills." Many children, including McCourt's twin brothers, succumb to tuberculosis, with the rest to run an obstacle course—in shoes with flapping soles—of flea-ridden bedcovers, cane-wielding teachers, doomsday-spouting priests, and fathers who drink their paycheck, beat their wives, and tell their sons to search the skies for the Angel of the Seventh Step, bringer of new babies. Yes, Limerick has its historic sights—King John's Castle, St. Mary's Cathedral, and other landmarks of the town's medieval district—but now the down-and-out addresses of McCourt's childhood draw as much attention from visitors.

As it turns out, the slums described so unflinchingly in the book have long been torn down; in fact, Limerick today is flush with new money, renovated 19th-century Georgian row houses, prosperous shopping malls, and restaurants with fancy names like Quenelles. Even the dread River Shannon has undergone a makeover—swans, not refuse, now navigate its flowing stream. Nevertheless, plenty of *Angela's Ashes* sites remain: Leamy's National School on Hartstonge Street, where "Hoppy" O'Halloran and other schoolmasters used to beat any charges who couldn't add 19 to 47; the St. Vincent de Paul Society, where Angela once went begging for furniture and other assistance; People's Park, where Frank once took his younger brothers to make them forget their empty stomachs; plus many other emotional landmarks.

Like the Irish *shanachie*—storyteller—still spouting tales at many a local pub, Frank McCourt has dug deep into the communal wellspring of Irish memory. The fact that his story has nothing to do with leprechauns and Celtic queens and everything to do with a family history that most families would wish to hide, let alone hang out in the sun to dry, says a good deal about the new Ireland and its people's wish for closure. McCourt's childhood experiences may not have been the happiest, but they are surely worth reading about, remembering, and revisiting, as so many travelers are now making a point of doing.

First built by the Normans in the early 1200s, **King John's Castle** still bears traces on its north side of the 1691 bombardment. If you climb the drum towers (the oldest section), you'll have a good view of the town and the Shannon. Inside, a 22-minute audiovisual show illustrates the history of Limerick and Ireland; an archaeology center has three excavated, pre-Norman houses; and two exhibition centers display models of Limerick's history from its founding in AD 922. ⊠ *Castle St.,* ☎ *061/411201,* WEB *www.shannonheritage.com/KingJohnsCastle/.* ⊠ *€5.50.* ☉ *Apr.–Sept., daily 9:30–5; Oct.–Mar., weekends 9:30–5.*

On **O'Connell Street,** you'll find the main shopping area, which mainly consists of modest chain stores. However, the street lies one block inland from (east of) the Arthur's Quay Shopping Centre, a shopping mall, which, along with the futuristic Tourist Information Center, is one of the first fruits of a civic campaign to develop Limerick's Shannonside quays. **Cruises Street,** a pedestrian thoroughfare, has Limerick's most chic shops (even though they are chiefly high-street multiples, meaning same formula, different location) and an inviting atmosphere (with occasional street entertainers); it is on the opposite side of O'Connell Street from the Arthur's Quay Shopping Centre.

Plassey, 5–10 minutes from Limerick on the ring road (signposted Dublin N7), is the setting for the University of Limerick, which has a small, but very attractive, campus on rolling lawns, and notable for having several striking architectural features.

Dining and Lodging

$$ ✕ **Freddy's Bistro.** Tucked away into a quiet lane between busy O'-Connell and Henry streets, this informal two-story restaurant fills a charming 18th-century coach house. Old brick walls are complemented by the warm color scheme, which glows in candlelight. Pasta with smoked chicken and seafood tagliatelle are popular; for dessert try the hot, sticky toffee pudding. ⊠ *Theatre La., off Lower Glentworth St.,* ☎ *061/418749. MC, V. Closed Sun.–Mon. No lunch.*

$$ ✕ **Green Onion Café.** The Irish-French chef team of Marie Munnelly and Geoff Gloux produces a witty, stylish menu at this hip young eatery across the road from the Hunt Museum. The large room, which used to be the town hall, is divided into intimate spaces through a judicious use of booths and two floors. Typical dishes include smoked Irish cheese (Gubbeen) and spinach tartlet, pork fillet coated in pistachio nuts with herb butter, jerk chicken with jalapeño salsa, and salmon with basil beurre blanc. For dessert, try the prune and toffee pudding with roasted nutty butterscotch. ⊠ *Old Town Hall Building, Rutland St.,* ☎ *061/400710. AE, DC, MC, V. Closed Sun.*

$–$$ ✕ **Jasmine Palace.** Limerick City abounds in Chinese restaurants, and many would claim this one, which has been here the longest, is the best. Irish steak is served on a sizzling platter with black bean sauce; the duck and prawn pot is an individual stew pot with pieces of duck and whole king prawns in a rich, spicy sauce. This second-floor eatery is in the town center, on the main street (opposite the Royal George Hotel). ⊠ *37 O'-Connell St.,* ☎ *061/412484. AE, DC, MC, V. No lunch Mon.–Sat.*

$ ✕ **Mortell's.** If you've never tried fish-and-chips, *this* is the place to start. Only the freshest local seafood is served at this simple café. You can also get full Irish breakfasts and baked goods. Mortell's has been in the family for more than 40 years, and everything, from the doughnuts to the brown bread to the mayo, is made on the premises. It's in the main shopping area. ⊠ *49 Roches St.,* ☎ *061/415457. AE, DC, MC, V. Closed Sun. No dinner.*

$$–$$$ ✕🖽 **Castletroy Park.** This large, redbrick-and-stone hotel, which
★   grandly crowns a hill on the outskirts of town, has splendid views of

the university campus and the surrounding countryside. The lobby, with its polished wood and Oriental rugs, leads to a conservatory–cum–coffee shop overlooking an Italian-style courtyard. The guest rooms, scented with potpourri, are decorated with solid wood furniture, muted floral drapes and spreads, and rag-rolled walls. The fitness center is one of the best around. You can mix with the locals in the Merry Pedlar Pub and Bistro or enjoy a formal meal in MacLaughlin's restaurant. ⊠ *Dublin Rd., Co. Limerick,* ☎ *061/335566,* FAX *061/331117,* WEB *www.castletroy-park.ie. 78 rooms with bath, 7 suites, 22 executive rooms. 2 restaurants, cable TV, in-room data ports, indoor pool, health club, bar, meeting rooms. AE, DC, MC, V.*

$–$$ 🏨 **Greenhills.** This friendly, family-run hotel is a modern low-rise in a quiet, suburban area, where N18 meets the city-center route. Twenty minutes from Shannon and five minutes from the city center, it makes an excellent touring base. The best and newest rooms are in a quiet wing above the fitness center and are big enough to have a small couch, tables, and chairs. All the rooms are color-coordinated in various styles, with dark-wood furniture and tiled bathrooms. Children will love the pool, and in high season can take part in the hotel's children's club. ⊠ *Ennis Rd., Co. Limerick,* ☎ *061/453033,* FAX *061/453307,* WEB *www.greenhillsgroup.com. 55 rooms with bath. 3 restaurants, cable TV, coffee shop, tennis court, indoor pool, sauna, steam room, bar, children's programs (ages 4–12), bar, meeting rooms. AE, DC, MC, V.*

$ 🏨 **Jurys Inn.** Clean, airy, and in good shape, unlike some of Limerick's other budget spots, this hotel is part of the Jurys chain, which rents per room rather than per person. (The "inn," though, is something of a misnomer, as the hotel is large and relatively anonymous.) Rooms are a good size for the price bracket and have light-wood furnishings. It overlooks an urban stretch of the Shannon being converted from industrial to leisure use and is a short step from the main shopping and business district. ⊠ *Lower Mallow St., Mount Kennett Pl., Co. Limerick,* ☎ *061/207000,* FAX *061/400966,* WEB *www.jurysdoyle.com. 151 rooms with bath. Restaurant, cable TV, bar. AE, DC, MC, V.*

Nightlife and the Arts

ART GALLERIES

The **Belltable Arts Center** (⊠ 69 O'Connell St., ☎ 061/319866) has a small auditorium for touring productions and exhibition space. The **Dolmen Gallery** (⊠ Honan's Quay, ☎ 061/417929) shows work by contemporary artists and has an excellent café. The **Limerick City Gallery** (⊠ Pery Sq., ☎ 061/310633) has a small, permanent collection of Irish art and mounts exhibits of contemporary art.

PUBS, CABARET, AND DISCOS

The Officer's Club upstairs at the **Castle Lane Tavern** (⊠ Nicholas St., King's Island, ☎ 061/318044) has live dinner entertainment Tuesday through Saturday in the form of an Irish cabaret, culminating in a "hooley" with audience participation. Sessions often take place in the downstairs bar. **Hogan's** (⊠ 20–24 Old Clare St., ☎ 061/411279) has a traditional music session every Tuesday and Friday year-round. The **Locke Bar** (⊠ 3 George's Quay, ☎ 061/413733), a riverside pub, is one of Limerick's oldest bars, dating from 1724, and has traditional music Sunday, Monday, and Tuesday nights. Traditional music is featured at **Nancy Blake's Pub** (⊠ 19 Denmark St., ☎ 061/416443) year-round Sunday–Wednesday from 9 PM. **William G. South's Pub** (⊠ The Crescent, ☎ 061/318850) is an old-fashioned Limerick pub that's typical of the age of Frank McCourt's *Angela's Ashes*. There's no music, but do drop by for bar food (1:30 to 3, Mon.–Sat.) or a drink, and soak up the atmosphere.

Outdoor Activities and Sports

BICYCLES

Bicycles can be rented from the **Bike Shop** (⊠ O'Connell Ave., ☎ 061/
315900).

FISHING

You can get fishing tackle, bait, and licenses at **Steve's Fishing Tackle**
(⊠ 19 Catherine St., ☎ 061/413484).

GOLF

Castletroy Golf Club (⊠ Golf Links Rd., Castletroy, ☎ 061/335753)
is a challenging 18-hole, par-71 parkland course in the city suburbs.

Limerick Golf and Country Club (⊠ Ballyneety, ☎ 061/351881) is an
18-hole, par-72 parkland course.

HORSEBACK RIDING

Clarina Riding Center (⊠ Clarina, near Limerick City, ☎ 061/353087)
has riding by the hour.

Shopping

The **Arthur's Quay Shopping Centre** (⊠ Arthur's Quay, ☎ 061/419888)
near the TIO is Limerick's biggest indoor mall. **Celtic Bookshop** (⊠ 2
Rutland St., ☎ 061/401155) specializes in books of Irish interest.
Lane Antiques (⊠ 45 Catherine St., ☎ 061/339307) is an old-world
gallery that sells antiques, prints, paintings, collectibles, and antiquarian books.

Bunratty Castle and Folk Park

★ ☾ ⑥ *18 km (10 mi) west of Limerick City on N18 (the road to Shannon
Airport).*

Bunratty Castle and Folk Park are two of those rare attractions that
appeal to all age groups and which manage to be both educational and
fun. The castle, built in 1460, has been fully restored and decorated with
15th- to 17th-century furniture and furnishings. It gives a wonderful
insight into the life of those times. As you pass under the walls of Bunratty, look for the three "murder holes," which allowed defenders to
pour boiling oil on attackers below. On the castle grounds, and every
bit as quaint as some first-time visitors expect all of modern Ireland to
be, **Bunratty Folk Park** re-creates a 19th-century village street and has
examples of the traditional rural housing of the region. Exhibits include
a working blacksmith's forge; demonstrations of flour milling, bread
making, candle making, thatching, and other traditional skills; and a
variety of farm animals in reconstructed small holdings. An adjacent
museum of agricultural machinery cannot compete with the furry and
feathered live exhibits. Medieval banquets are held at the castle twice
nightly for those who want to dine on Roast Beast and quaff mead made
from fermented honey, apple juice, clover, and heather. ☎ *061/361511,*
WEB *www.shannonheritage.com.* ☒ *€9.50.* ☉ *Sept.–May, daily 9:30–
5:30 (last entry 4:15); June–Aug., daily 9:30–7 (last entry 6).*

A *ceili* at Bunratty Folk Park is the next-best thing if you can't get a
reservation for a banquet; this program features traditional Irish dance
and song and a meal of Irish stew, soda bread, and apple pie. ☎ *061/
360788,* WEB *www.shannonheritage.com.* ☒ *€38, including wine.* ☉
May–Sept., daily at 5:45 and 9.

No visit to Bunratty is complete without a drink in **Durty Nelly's** (☎
061/364072), an old-world (but touristy) pub beside the Folk Park entrance. Its fanciful decor that has inspired imitations around the world.

Knappogue Castle and Craggaunowen Project

21 km (13 mi) and 27 km (17 mi) north of Bunratty, respectively.

64 A 15th-century MacNamara stronghold, **Knappogue Castle** has been extensively restored and furnished in 15th-century style. Its name means the "hill of the kiss," and, like Bunratty, it's a venue for medieval-style banquets. The castle looks spectacular at night when flood-lit. ⊠ *5 km (3 mi) southeast of Quin on R649,* ☎ *061/368103,* WEB *www.shannonheritage.com.* 🎟 *€6.50.* 🕙 *May–Sept., daily 9:30–4:30.*

65 The **Craggaunowen Project** includes Craggaunowen Castle, a 16th-century tower house restored with furnishings from the period. Particularly worth seeing are the two replicas of early Celtic-style dwellings that have been constructed on the castle grounds. On an island in the lake, reached by a narrow footbridge, is a clay-and-wattle *crannóg,* a fortified lake dwelling; it resembles what might have been built in the 6th or 7th century when Celtic influence still predominated in Ireland. The reconstruction of a small ring fort shows how an ordinary farmer would have lived in the 5th or 6th century, at the time Christianity was being established. Characters from the past explain their Iron Age (500 BC–AD 450) lifestyle; show you around their small holding, stocked with animals; and demonstrate crafts skills from bygone ages. It is a strange experience to walk across the little wooden bridge above reeds rippling in the lake into Ireland's Celtic past as a jumbo jet passes overhead on its way into Shannon Airport—1,500 years of history compressed into an instant. ⊠ *Kilmurry, Sixmilebridge, signposted off the road to Sixmilebridge about 10 km (6 mi) east of Quin,* ☎ *061/ 367178,* WEB *www.shannonheritage.com.* 🎟 *€6.50.* 🕙 *Apr.–mid-Oct., daily 9–6.*

Medieval Banquets

If you're a first-time visitor, don't miss the **medieval banquets** held at the Bunratty and Knappogue castles. Do note, though, that both events cater largely to overseas visitors, many of them on organized tours, and they're likely to have little appeal for independent travelers in search of "the real Ireland." But if you're up for it, take the warmhearted evening of Irish hospitality in the lighthearted spirit in which it is offered. Medieval banqueting may not be authentic, but it's fun. At Bunratty, you'll be welcomed by Irish colleens in 15th-century dress, who bear the traditional bread of friendship, then led off to a honey-and-mead reception. Before sitting down at the long tables in the candlelit great hall, you don a bib. You'll need it, because you'll be eating the four-course meal medieval-style—with your fingers. Serving "wenches" take time out to sing a few ballads or pluck the strings of a harp. Because the banquets are so popular, book as far in advance as possible. *Bunratty and Knappogue:* ☎ *061/360788.* 🎟 *4-course meal, wine, mead, and entertainment €45.50.* 🕙 *Daily, subject to demand, at 5:45 and 8:45.*

THE SOUTHWEST A TO Z

To research prices, get advice from other travelers, and book travel arrangements, visit www.fodors.com.

AIRPORTS AND TRANSFERS

The Southwest has two international airports: Cork on the Southwest coast, and Shannon in the West. Cork Airport, 5 km (3 mi) south of Cork City on the Kinsale road, is used primarily for flights to and from the United Kingdom. Regular 30-minute internal flights are scheduled between Shannon and Dublin, Shannon and Cork, and Cork and

Dublin. Shannon Airport, 26 km (16 mi) west of Limerick City, is the point of arrival for all transatlantic flights; it also serves some flights from the United Kingdom and Europe. Kerry County Airport at Farranfore, 16 km (10 mi) from Killarney, mainly services small planes, but it is gradually increasing its commercial traffic with at least one daily flight from London.

➤ AIRPORT INFORMATION: **Cork Airport** (☎ 021/431–3131). **Kerry County Airport** (☎ 066/976–4644). **Shannon Airport** (☎ 061/471444).

TRANSFERS

Bus service runs between Cork Airport and the Cork City Bus Terminal every 30 minutes, on the hour and the half hour. The ride takes about 10 minutes and costs about €2.55. Bus Éireann runs a regular bus service from Shannon Airport to Limerick City between 8 AM and midnight. The ride takes about 40 minutes and costs €4.45.

You'll find taxis outside the main terminal building at Shannon and Cork airports. The ride from Shannon Airport to Limerick City costs about €25.40; from Cork Airport to Cork City costs about €7.60.

➤ SHUTTLES AND TAXIS: **Bus Éireann** (☎ 061/474311). **Cork City Bus Terminal** (✉ Parnell Pl., ☎ 021/450–6066).

BOAT AND FERRY TRAVEL

From the United Kingdom, the Southwest has two ports of entry: Rosslare (in County Wexford) and Cork City. Stena Sealink sails directly between Rosslare Ferryport and Fishguard, Wales. Pembroke, Wales, and France's Cherbourg and Roscoff can be reached on Irish Ferries. Swansea–Cork Ferries, which can also be accessed from the United Kingdom, operates a 10-hour crossing between the two ports on a comfortable, well-equipped boat. Supabus will get you to the Swansea ferry from anywhere in the United Kingdom.

➤ BOAT AND FERRY INFORMATION: **Irish Ferries** (☎ 053/33158). **Stena Sealink** (☎ 053/33115). **Swansea–Cork Ferries** (☎ 1792/456116).

BUS TRAVEL

Bus Éireann operates Expressway services from Dublin to Limerick City, Cork City, and Tralee. Add approximately one hour to the journey time by train. Most towns in the region are served by the provincial Bus Éireann network. The main bus terminals in the region are at Cork, Limerick, and Tralee.

Train connections between Rosslare Harbour and Cork City, Limerick City, and Tralee all involve changing at Limerick Junction, so the journey time is usually longer than by car or bus. It is quicker and cheaper, if less comfortable, to use the long-distance buses that service the ferries. Euroline leaves London's Victoria Coach Station daily and travels overnight via Bristol to Fishguard, then on to Cork, Killarney, and Tralee. Timetables can be obtained by calling Euroline in Luton, England. An Irish company, Slattery's, runs a bus service from London to Cork and Tralee. The journey to Cork via Rosslare is by bus and ferry, and, at about 14 hours, arduous.

FARES AND SCHEDULES

The provincial bus service, cheaper and more flexible than the train, covers all the region's main centers. Express services are available between Cork City and Limerick City (twice a day); Cork and Tralee (once a day, high season only); and Killarney, Tralee, Limerick, and Shannon (once a day, twice in peak season).

If you plan to travel extensively by bus, a copy of the Bus Éireann timetable (€1.30 from bus terminals) is essential. As a general rule, the smaller the town, and the more remote, the less frequent its bus service. For example, Kinsale, a well-developed resort 29 km (18 mi) from Cork, is served by at least five buses a day, both arriving and departing; Castlegregory, a small village on the remote Dingle Peninsula, has bus service only on Friday.

➤ Bus Information: **Bus Éireann** (☎ 01/836–6111 in Dublin; 061/313333 in Limerick; 021/450–8188 in Cork; 066/712–3566 in Tralee). **Cork Station** (✉ Parnell Pl., ☎ 021/450–8188). **Euroline** (✉ Luton, England, ☎ 1582/404511 add the prefix 00–44 if dialing from Ireland). **Limerick Station** (✉ Colbert Station, ☎ 061/313333). **Slattery's** (✉ London, ☎ 020/7482–1604 add the prefix 00–44 if dialing from Ireland). **Tralee Station** (✉ Casement Station, ☎ 066/712–3566).

CAR RENTAL

All the major car-rental companies have desks at Shannon and Cork airports.

➤ Major Agencies: **Alamo** (✉ Cork Airport, ☎ 021/431–8638). **Avis** (✉ Cork Airport, ☎ 021/428–1111; ✉ Killarney, ☎ 064/36655; ✉ Shannon Airport, ☎ 061/471094). **Budget** (✉ Cork Airport, ☎ 021/431–4000; ✉ Killarney, ☎ 064/34341; ✉ Shannon Airport, ☎ 061/471361). **Dan Dooley** (✉ Shannon Airport, ☎ 061/471098). **Enterprise** (✉ Cork Airport, ☎ 021/434–7388). **Hertz** (✉ Cork Airport, ☎ 021/496–5849; ✉ Shannon Airport, ☎ 061/471369). **Murray's Europcar** (✉ Cork Airport, ☎ 021/491–7300; ✉ Killarney, ☎ 064/31237; ✉ Shannon Airport, ☎ 061/701200). **Payless Bunratty** (✉ Shannon Airport, ☎ 061/328328). **Randles** (✉ Killarney, ☎ 064/31237).

CAR TRAVEL

The main driving access route from Dublin is N7, which goes 192 km (120 mi) directly to Limerick City; from Dublin, pick up N8 in Portlaoise and drive 257 km (160 mi) to Cork City. The journey time between Dublin and Limerick runs just under 3 hours; between Dublin and Cork it takes about 3½ hours. From Rosslare Harbour by car, take N25 208 km (129 mi) to Cork; allow 3½ hours for the journey. You can pick up N24 in Waterford for the 211-km (131-mi) drive to Limerick City, which also takes about 3½ hours.

A car is the ideal way to explore this region, packed as it is with scenic routes, attractive but remote towns, and a host of out-of-the-way restaurants and hotels that deserve a detour. Getting around the Southwest is every bit as enjoyable as arriving, provided you set out in the right frame of mind—a relaxed one. There is no point in imposing a rigid timetable on your journey when you are visiting one of the last places in Western Europe where you are as likely to be held up by a donkey cart, a herd of cows, or a flock of sheep as by road construction or heavy trucks.

ROAD CONDITIONS

Roads are generally small, with two lanes (one in each direction). You will find a few miles of two-lane highway on the outskirts of Cork City, Limerick City, and Killarney, but much of your time will be spent on roads so narrow and twisty that it is not advisable to exceed 64 kph (40 mph).

EMERGENCIES

➤ Contacts: **Ambulance, police, fire** (☎ 999). **Southern Health Board** (✉ Dennehy's Cross, Cork, ☎ 021/454–5011).

➤ Pharmacies: **Phelan's** (✉ 9 Patrick St., Cork, ☎ 021/427–2511). **P. O'Donoghue** (✉ Main St., Killarney, ☎ 064/31813). **Roberts** (✉ 105 O'Connell St., Limerick, ☎ 061/414414).

LODGING
BED-AND-BREAKFASTS

For a small fee, Bord Fáilte (the Irish Tourist Board) will book accommodations anywhere in Ireland through its central reservations system. B&Bs can be booked at local visitor information offices when they are open; however, even these reservations will go through the central reservations system.

➤ RESERVATION SERVICES: **Bord Fáilte** (WEB www.ireland.travel.ie).

OUTDOOR ACTIVITIES AND SPORTS
FISHING

Your hotel or the local TIO (Tourist Information Office) can suggest places that rent boats. The latter will also recommend locations for coarse and game fishing, or contact the South Western Regional Fisheries Board.

➤ CONTACTS: **South Western Regional Fisheries Board** (⊠ 1 Nevilles Terr., Macroom, Co. Cork, ☎ 026/41221).

HIKING

Details about the Southwest's eight long-distance hiking trails, related maps, and guides are contained in the Irish Tourist Board publication *Walking Ireland,* available from Tourist Information Offices.

WATER SPORTS

Because of the demands of Irish insurance laws, boat charter is still in its infancy here, with only one company in business for bareboat charter. For the same reason, dinghy rentals are not widespread, and you will need to demonstrate your competence. Sailboards, on the other hand, are relatively easy to rent. Wet suits (also rentable) are essential for sailboarding except on the hottest days in July and August. Rental of sailboarding equipment, including wet suits, starts at about €13 an hour. Sailing dinghies, as well as sailboards, can be rented by the hour (from about €8) or by the day (from about €26). Dinghy- and sailboard-rental contacts are listed under the towns that provide them.

The average cost of a six-berth yacht between 28 and 35 ft ranges from €152 per person per week (low season) to €254 (high season). For details of residential dinghy sailing courses in the Southwest, contact Glenans Irish Sailing Club. Contact Sail Ireland Charters for bareboat charters.

➤ CONTACTS: **Glenans Irish Sailing Club** (⊠ 28 Merrion Sq., Dublin 2, ☎ 01/661–1481, WEB www.glenans-ireland.com). **Sail Ireland Charters** (⊠ Trident Hotel, Kinsale, Co. Cork, ☎ 021/477–2927, FAX 021/477–4170).

TOURS
BUS TOURS

Bus Éireann, part of the state-run public-transport network, offers a range of day and half-day guided tours from June to September. They can be booked at the bus stations in Cork or Limerick or at any TIO. A full-day tour costs €15.25, half-day €9.50, both exclusive of meals and refreshments. Bus Éireann also offers open-top bus tours of Cork City on Tuesday and Saturday in July and August for €5.10.

Dero's Tours, Corcoran's Tours, and Killarney & Kerry Tours will organize full-day and half-day trips by coach or taxi around Killarney and the Ring of Kerry.

➤ FEES AND SCHEDULES: **Corcoran's Tours** (⊠ 10 College St., Killarney, Co. Kerry, ☎ 064/36666). **Dero's Tours** (⊠ 22 Main St., Killarney, Co. Kerry, ☎ 064/31251). **Killarney & Kerry Tours** (⊠ Innisfallen, 15 Main St., Killarney, Co. Kerry, ☎ 064/33880).

Gerry Coughlan of Arrangements-Unlimited can prearrange special-interest group tours of the region. Half-day and full-day tours are individually planned for groups of 10 or more to satisfy each visitor's needs. Country House Tours organizes self-driven or chauffeur-driven group tours with accommodations in private country houses and castles. It also conducts special-interest tours, including gardens, architecture, ghosts, and golf. Into the Wilderness organizes guided walking, climbing, and cycling tours in the Kerry Highlands and Killarney National Park.

Shannon Castle Tours will escort you to an "Irish Night" in Bunratty Folk Park or take you to a medieval banquet at Bunratty or Knappogue Castle; although the banquets aren't authentic, they are boisterous occasions and full of goodwill.

Destination Killarney is the foremost Killarney tour operator. Besides offering full-day and half-day tours of Killarney and Kerry by coach or taxi, the group will prearrange your visit, lining up accommodations, entertainment, special-interest tours, and sporting activities in one package. A full-day (10:30–5) tour costs from €13 to €18 per person, excluding lunch and refreshments. The Killarney Local Circuit tour is an excellent half-day 10:30–12:30 orientation. The memorable Gap of Dunloe tour at €18 includes a coach and boat trip. Add €15 for a horseback ride through the gap. More conventional day trips can also be made to the Ring of Kerry, the Loo Valley, and Glengarriff; the city of Cork and Blarney Castle; Dingle and Slea Head; and Caragh Lake and Rossbeigh.

Jaunting cars (pony and trap) that carry up to four people can be rented at a stand outside Killarney TIOs. They can also be found at the entrance to Muckross Estate and at the Gap of Dunloe. A ride costs between €15.25 and €30.48, negotiable with the driver, depending on duration (one to two hours) and route. Tangney Tours is the leading jaunting-car company and will also organize tours by coach or water bus, as well as entertainment.

➤ FEES AND SCHEDULES: **Arrangements Unlimited** (⊠ 1 Woolhara Park, Douglas, Cork City, Co. Cork, ☎ 021/429–3873, FAX 021/429–2488, WEB www.arrangements.ie). **Country House Tours** (⊠ 71 Waterloo Rd., Dublin 4, ☎ 01/668–6463, FAX 01/668–6578, WEB www.tourismresources.ie). **Destination Killarney** (⊠ Scott's Gardens, Killarney, Co. Kerry, ☎ FAX 064/32638, WEB www.gleneagle-hotel.com). **Into the Wilderness** (⊠ Climber's Inn, Glencar, Killarney, Co. Kerry, ☎ 066/976–0101, WEB www.climbersinn.com). **Shannon Castle Tours** (⊠ Bunratty Folk Park, Bunratty, Co. Clare, ☎ 061/360788, WEB www.shannonheritage.ie). **Tangney Tours** (⊠ Kinvara House, Muckross Rd., Killarney, Co. Kerry, ☎ 064/33358).

Limerick City Tours provides inexpensive walking tours of Limerick from June to September (and by arrangement other months). St. Mary's Action Centre has a walking tour of Limerick's historic centers and of locations highlighted in Frank McCourt's *Angela's Ashes*.

➤ FEES AND SCHEDULES: **Limerick City Tours** (⊠ Noel Curtin, Rhebogue, Co. Limerick, ☎ 061/311935). **St. Mary's Action Centre** (⊠ 44 Nicholas St., Limerick, Co. Limerick, ☎ 061/318106, WEB www.iol.ie/~smidp/).

TRAIN TRAVEL

From Dublin Heuston Station, the region is served by three direct rail links to Limerick City, Tralee, and Cork City. Journey time from Dublin to Limerick is 2½ hours; to Cork, 2¾; to Tralee, 3¾.

The rail network, which covers only the inner ring of the region, is mainly useful for moving from one touring base to another. Except during the peak season of July and August, only four trains a day run between Cork (or Limerick) and Tralee. More frequent service is offered between Cork City and Limerick City, but the ride involves changing at Limerick Junction—as does the journey from Limerick to Tralee—to wait for a connecting train. Be sure to ascertain the delay involved in the connection. The journey from Cork to Tralee takes about 2 hours; from Cork to Limerick, about 1¼ hours; from Limerick to Tralee, about 3 hours.

➤ TRAIN INFORMATION: **Dublin Heuston Station** (☎ 01/836–6222). **Inquiries** (☎ 061/315555 in Limerick; 021/450–6766 in Cork; 066/712–3522 in Tralee).

VISITOR INFORMATION

Bord Fáilte provides a free information service; its TIOs also sell a selection of tourist literature. For a small fee it will book accommodations anywhere in Ireland.

Seasonal TIOs in Bantry, Cahirciveen, and Clonakilty are open from May to October; offices in Dingle and Kinsale are open from March to November; the TIO in Kenmare is open April to October, and the one in Youghal is open May to mid-September. All of the seasonal TIOs are generally open Monday–Saturday 9–6; in July and August they are also open Sunday 9–6. Year-round TIOs can be found in Adare, Blarney, Cork City, Killarney, Limerick, Shannon, Skibbereen, and Tralee and are open Monday–Saturday 9–6; in July and August they are also open Sunday 9–6.

➤ TOURIST INFORMATION: **Adare** (⊠ Heritage Centre, ☎ 061–396255, WEB www.shannon-dev.ie). **Bantry** (⊠ Co. Cork, ☎ 027/50229, WEB www.southwestireland.travel.ie). **Blarney** (⊠ Co. Cork, ☎ 021/438–1624, WEB www.southwestireland.travel.ie). **Cahirciveen** (⊠ The Old Barracks, Co. Kerry, ☎ 066/947–2589, WEB www.southwestireland.travel.ie). **Clonakilty** (⊠ Co. Cork, ☎ 023/33226, WEB www.southwestireland.travel.ie). **Cork City** (⊠ Grand Parade, Co. Cork, ☎ 021/427–3251, FAX 021/427–3504, WEB www.southwestireland.travel.ie). **Dingle** (⊠ Co. Kerry, ☎ 066/915–1188). **Kenmare** (⊠ Co. Kerry, ☎ 064/41233). **Killarney** (⊠ Aras Fáilte, Beech Rd., Co. Kerry, ☎ 064/31633, FAX 064/34506, WEB www.southwestireland.travel.ie). **Kinsale** (⊠ Pier Rd., Co. Cork, ☎ 021/477–2234; 021/477–4417 off-season, FAX 021/477–4438). **Limerick** (⊠ Arthur's Quay, Co. Limerick, ☎ 061/317522, FAX 061/317939, WEB www.shannon-dev.ie). **Shannon Airport** (⊠ Co. Clare, ☎ 061/471664, FAX 061/471661, WEB www.shannon-dev.ie). **Skibbereen** (⊠ North St., Co. Cork, ☎ 028/21766, FAX 028/21353). **Tralee** (⊠ Ashe Memorial Hall, Denny St., Co. Kerry, ☎ 066/712–1288, FAX 066/712–1700, WEB www.shannon-dev.ie). **Youghal** (⊠ Co. Cork, ☎ 024/92390).

7 THE WEST

CLIFFS OF MOHER, THE BURREN,
GALWAY CITY, THE ARAN ISLANDS,
CONNEMARA, COUNTY MAYO

With the most westerly seaboard in Europe, the West remains a place apart—the most Irish part of Ireland. Nature's magnificence awaits: the majestic Cliffs of Moher, the eerie expanse of the Burren, the "hidden kingdom" of Connemara, and the Aran Islands, which do constant battle with the stormy Atlantic. But there are also grand baronial houses to visit—Ashford Castle and Kylemore Abbey—and Galway, the city that loves to celebrate. As one of Europe's fastest-growing metropolises, it has much to be happy about.

Updated by
Elizabeth A.
Whisler

WHILE MOST OF IRELAND CHARGES HEADFIRST into the 21st century, the West retains an unspoiled and rugged way of life. Compared to the East, which claims Dublin and its environs, residents of the major cities and towns in the West have embraced their cultural history by supporting the arts and traditional music while slowly but steadily moving into modern times. Without a doubt, the West is distinctively different from the rest of Ireland. Within Ireland, the West refers to the region that lies west of the River Shannon; most of this area falls within the old Irish province of Connaught. The coast of this region lies at the far western extremity of Europe, facing its nearest neighbors in North America across 3,200 km (2,000 mi) of Atlantic ocean. While the East, the Southwest, and the North were influenced by either Norman, Scots, or English settlers, the West escaped systematic resettlement and, with the exception of the walled town of Galway, remained purely Irish in language, social organization, and general outlook far longer than the rest of the country. The land in the West, predominantly mountains and bogs, did not immediately tempt the conquering barons. Oliver Cromwell was among those who found the place thoroughly unattractive, and he gave the Irish chieftains who would not conform to English rule the choice of going "to Hell or Connaught."

It wasn't until the late 18th century, when better transport improved communications, that the West started to experience the so-called foreign influences that had already Europeanized the rest of the country. The West was, in effect, propelled from the 16th century into the 19th. Virtually every significant building in the region dates either from before the 17th century or from the late 18th century onward. As in the Southwest, the population of the West was decimated by the Great Famine (1845–49) and by the waves of mass emigration that persisted until the 1950s. Towns were unknown in pre-Christian Irish society, and even today, more than 150 years after the famine, many residents still live on small farms rather than in towns and villages. Especially during the wet, wintry months, you can still walk out of your country house, hotel, or B&B in the morning and smell the nearby turf fires.

Today, the West is, for many, the most typically Irish part of the country. Particularly in western County Galway, you'll find the highest concentration of Gaeltacht (Irish-speaking communities) in all of Ireland, with roughly 40,000 native Irish speakers making their homes here. The country's first Irish-language TV station broadcasts from the tiny village of Spiddle, on the north shore of Galway Bay in the heart of the Gaeltacht. Throughout this area, you'll see plenty of signs that are in Irish only. Who would suspect that Gaillimh is the Irish for Galway? But wherever you go in the West, you'll not only see, but more importantly *hear*, the most vital way in which traditional Irish culture survives here—musicians play in pubs all over the West, and they are recognized as being the best in the Republic.

A major factor in the region's recovery from economic depression has been the lure of its spectacular scenery to visitors. So far, the development that has come with the cultivation of tourism in the West has been mercifully low-key. Yes, residents of the West have encouraged the revival of such cottage industries as knitting, weaving, and woodworking. But they have become strong environmentalists as well, lobbying on behalf of land preservation. This is perhaps the result of having witnessed much of the bogland in Connemara and County Mayo being overfarmed for its peat, leaving behind bereft swaths of land. The 5,000-acre Connemara National Park is the result of a successful lobby for peatland protection, and is among the few protected places in one of Ireland's most important bogland areas. With increasing investment in the West, time will tell how long this part of the country will remain undeveloped. Residents are already being faced with the difficult task of striking a balance between conservation and economic prosperity.

There may be no better example of the way the West is balancing change with tradition than its thatched cottages, which have become popular as holiday homes. Some of the traditional whitewashed cottages are truly old, while others have been built to resemble the old. Of course, it's nothing new that the West's greatest virtue for visitors—apart from its glorious scenery and high-flying capital city—is its people. No matter how many times you get out of the car for a photo-op (and we guarantee that you'll *fly* through rolls of film here), the stories that you're going to tell when you show your friends and family those pictures are going to be about the *seisún*, or session (informal performance of traditional music), you stumbled upon in a small pub; the tiny, far-from-the-madding-crowds lake near Connemara that you made your own; and the great *craic* ("crack," or good conversation and fun) you're likely to discover wherever you go.

Pleasures and Pastimes

The Arts, Festivals, and Seasonal Events

The Irish in the West love their festivals, and they certainly know how to put on a full celebration. The Cúirt Literary Festival and the Galway Oyster Festival are but two of many annual events hosted by Galwegians; however, the highlight of the annual festival calendar is the Galway Arts Festival, which celebrated its 25th anniversary in 2002. During the second two weeks in July, the town—already ordinarily abuzz—welcomes more than 170,000 visitors each year and hosts theater, film, rock, jazz, traditional music, poetry readings, comedy acts, and visual arts exhibitions, plus a joyous parade by the street theater company Macnas, one of several local troupes that, thanks to the festival, has gained international recognition. Throughout the year, Galway's renovated Town Hall Theater lights up its stage for performances by, among many other groups, the 28-year-old Druid Theatre, whose adventurous productions regularly travel to Dublin and London. North of Galway, two smaller but very lively festivals take place. In Connemara, the Clifden Community Arts Week is held in mid-September, while the Westport Arts Festival in Co. Mayo takes place in the last week of September.

Dining

Because the West has a brief high season—from mid-June to early September—and a quiet off-season, it doesn't have as broad a choice of small, owner-operated restaurants as do other parts of Ireland. Often the best place to eat is a local hotel—Sheedy's Restaurant and Country Inn in Lisdoonvarna, for example, which has one of the few excellent chefs in County Clare, or Rosleague Manor in Letterfrack. The dominant style of cuisine in the West might be called "country-house cooking"—classic, dinner-party fare, such as homemade pâté, a seafood cocktail, tournedos or salmon hollandaise, and chocolate mousse. A handful of restaurants in Galway and Clifden, including Kirwan's Lane Creative Cuisine and K. C. Blake's in Galway, and Destry's and Erriseask House in Clifden, showcase adventurous contemporary Irish cooking.

CATEGORY	THE REPUBLIC*
$$$$	over €29
$$$	€22–€29
$$	€13–€21
$	under €13

Per person for a main course at dinner

Lodging

Some of Ireland's finest country-house and castle hotels, distinguished old hotels, and inexpensive B&Bs are in the West. Ashford and Dromoland castles shine as the stars of the region, but less over-the-top places, such as Ballynahinch Castle and Cashel House Hotel—both in Connemara—offer similar comfort on a smaller, more intimate scale. One of the great attractions of staying in the West, however much you pay for the night, is the restful atmosphere of many of these hotels and guest houses, which are often situated in the middle of a large private estate beside a lake or river, overlooking the sea or distant mountains. A majority of the moderately priced hotels are relatively new, and thus more modern than charming, but these newer hotels often have facilities—tennis courts and indoor pools—that are scarce at B&Bs and older hotels. Accommodations are busy in July and August, and the best places are also filled in May, June, and September, particularly on weekends, so reserve well in advance.

CATEGORY	THE REPUBLIC*
$$$$	over €230
$$$	€178–€230
$$	€127–€178
$	under €127

All prices are for two people in a double room, including VAT and a service charge (often applied in larger hotels).

Outdoor Activities and Sports

FISHING

You'll find some of the best angling in Europe on the West's rivers, lakes, and seas. Game fishing for wild Atlantic salmon, wild brown trout, and sea trout is one of the main attractions of the West. The salmon and brown trout season runs from March through September, closing earlier in some waters. Fishing (particularly fly-fishing) is generally at its best between mid-May and mid-June. The sea trout season starts in late May and runs through September; shore fishing is available all along the coast. From April to October, you can hire a boat for deep-sea fishing (about €65 per person per day) from the following ports: Doonbeg, Liscannor, and Ballyvaughan in County Clare; Roundstone, Spiddle, Clifden, Cleggan, and Inishbofin Island in County Galway; and Westport, Ballina, Belmullet, and Killala in County Mayo.

HIKING AND WALKING

If you like challenging hills and relatively rough terrain, the West is excellent hiking country. The unusual, almost lunar landscape of the Burren in County Clare is less demanding than the terrain in Connemara. Here, and in the area to the north of Connemara in South County Mayo, the countryside is sparsely populated and subject to sudden changes in weather—usually a portent of rain. There are four signposted trails in the area. The Burren Way runs from Lahinch Promenade to Ballyvaughan on the shores of Galway Bay, a distance of 35 km (22 mi). The trail runs through the heart of the Burren's limestone landscape, with ever-changing views of the Aran Islands and Galway Bay. The Western Way's County Galway section extends from Oughterard on Lough Corrib through the mountains of Connemara to Leenane on Killary

Harbour, a distance of 50 km (30 mi). Its 177-km (110-mi) County Mayo section known as the Western Way (Mayo) and the Foxford Way continues past Killary Harbour to Westport on Clew Bay, inland to Newport and across the boglands of north County Mayo to the Ox Mountains east of Ballina; this trail includes some of the finest mountain and coastal scenery in Ireland. The Newport Bangor Trail runs for 48 km (30 mi) through the Nephin Mountain range in northwest Mayo, connecting the two towns, Newport and Bangor. A 387-km (240-mi) hiking route through Irish-speaking Connemara stretches along the shores of Galway Bay from Spiddle to Carraroe, Carna, Letterfrack, and Clonbur, on the northern shore of Lough Corrib.

SPECTATOR SPORTS: SAILING AND HORSE RACING

Galway hookers—solid, heavy, broad-beamed sailing boats with distinctive, gaff-rigged, brownish-red sails—can still be seen on the waters of Galway Bay. Enthusiasts maintain a small fleet and hold frequent races on the bay in July and August. Many small horse races are held throughout the year in the West, including trotting races, pony races, beach derbies, and the like. Local Tourist Information Offices (TIOs) can provide details. The main event is the Galway Races, beginning immediately following the end of the Galway Arts Festival, at the end of July and beginning of August. This boisterous, full-scale festival attracts a massive crowd and all manner of sideshows, with cardsharps, fortune-tellers, rifle ranges, and open-air concerts.

Pubs and Live Traditional Music

No matter how you choose to spend your time in the West, be sure to visit at least one pub. For whether you drink a pint of Guinness or any other alcohol, pubs here are more than just bars—they are vital social centers, places to connect with natives and other travelers, to pick up leads about current and local activities, and, above all, to hear Irish traditional music played live.

Shopping

Galway City and Ennis are the West's major shopping areas. Their most interesting shops carry crafts, Irish-made clothing, jewelry, books, and antiques. Connemara has a large concentration of crafts shops; it is the best place in Ireland to buy an Aran sweater—either the traditional, off-white designs or the plain, linen and cotton Aran-style knits in jewel-tone red, green, or blue. The area is also well known for its Connemara marble—light green stone, commonly used in jewelry. Galway City is the place to buy a Claddagh ring. On the Aran Islands, sally rods are woven into attractive baskets (once used for potatoes or turf), and colorful woven belts, known as *críoses,* are hand-plaited from strands of wool. Handwoven woolen or mohair shawls or rugs provide an affordable touch of luxury. Musical instruments, traditionally made furniture, modern lead crystal, batik, handmade beeswax candles, and dried flower arrangements are among the West's many other goods—in addition to tweeds and sweaters, of course.

Exploring the West

This chapter is organized into five parts, covering the territory from south to north. The first section, the Burren and Beyond—West Clare to South Galway, picks up minutes from Shannon Airport and is not far from Ennis, the gateway to coastal County Clare. The second section shows you the very best of buzzing, bustling Galway City, and the third takes you out to the three Aran Islands, standing guard at the mouth of Galway Bay. The fourth section, through Connemara and County Mayo, brings you north of Galway Bay and west of Galway City into the fabled "hidden kingdom" of Connemara and beyond to the highlights of County Mayo: monumental Croagh Patrick, the pretty town of Westport, and the breathtaking Achill Island. The fifth section gives a brief overview of some of the highlights along the North Mayo Coast. Allow at least four days for exploring the region, seven days if you aim to visit the Aran Islands and Achill Island. Although distances between sites are not great, you may want to take scenic— and slower—national secondary routes. Covering 80 km–112 km (50 mi–70 mi) per day on these roads is a comfortable target.

Numbers in the text correspond to numbers in the margin and on the West and Galway City maps.

Great Itineraries

IF YOU HAVE 4 DAYS

Assuming you're arriving in the West via Shannon Airport or by crossing into County Clare via the Killimer–Tarbert ferry, you'll first pass through **Newmarket-on-Fergus** ① or **Ennis** ② if you're heading north, or **Kilrush** ③ if you're going southwest. If the weather's good, head all the way west for the beach town of **Kilkee** ④ or Milltown Malbay. If not, head right for the **Cliffs of Moher** ⑥. Next stop should be the heart of the **Burren** ⑨, though you might want to stop at the **Burren Display Centre** in Kilfenora first to pick up more information about Ireland's strangest landscape. Both **Doolin** ⑦ and ⊞ **Lisdoonvarna** ⑧ are within the Burren and famous for their traditional music. Spend the night in Lisdoonvarna, or in ⊞ **Kinvara** ⑭ or ⊞ **Ballyvaughan** ⑩, both on Galway Bay.

On your second day, head right for ⊞ **Galway City** ⑮–㉘. Spend the morning exploring Galway on foot, poking around its shops, and finding out whether any theater or other performing arts events are on that night. In the afternoon, take a cruise up the River Corrib or drive out along the north shore of Galway Bay to **Salthill** ㉘ and beyond into the Gaeltacht. Eat an early dinner right in Galway before taking in some theater, or drive to one of the restaurants outside town for a leisurely dinner. Whether or not you go to the theater, try to get to a pub in town for some traditional live music and good craic before heading off to bed.

On your third day, you can kick around Galway—easily the liveliest city in Ireland after Dublin and the only large city in the West, so be sure you've had your fill of its buzz before you depart. There are plenty of special events to keep you busy, particularly if you're here during a festival. You also might want either to take the ferry out to the **Aran Islands** ㉙–㉛ for the day or make the quick trip south to **Coole Park** ⑫ and **Thoor Ballylee** ⑬, the two southernmost sites in the west of Ireland important to W. B. Yeats (most of the rest are in County Sligo). Either way, again spend the night in Galway or at one of the country houses outside town (or perhaps even in a B&B on the Aran Islands, if you make it out there). Alternatively, if you're ready for scenery and a smaller town, head out through the moorlands of Connemara through **Oughterard** ㉜ to **Ballynahinch** ㉟ or Roundstone for lunch. Then go on to the Alpine-like coastal village of ⊞ **Clifden** ㊱, where you'll find gorgeous scenery and a surprisingly good selection of pubs and restaurants. Spend the night here or in a country house, hotel, or B&B in or around ⊞ **Cashel** ㉞ or ⊞ **Letterfrack** ㊲.

If you've spent your third night in Galway, or if you have stayed the night in or near Clifden, follow the alternative day-three itinerary above, but don't linger too long in Clifden. Push on, first to Connemara National Park, just outside **Letterfrack** ㊲, then just beyond to Kylemore Abbey in the **Kylemore Valley** ㊳, which has a breathtaking lake-

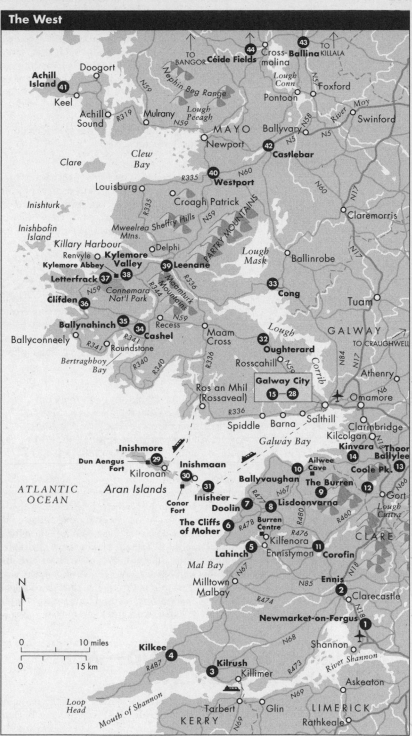

The West

side location and a better-than-average crafts shop. Continue through **Leenane** ㊴ to 🔝 **Westport** ㊵, the prettiest village in County Mayo and a good place to spend the night. On the way, you won't be able to miss the distinctive conical shape of Croagh Patrick, the penitential mountain that was a refuge of St. Patrick during his years spent converting Ireland to Christianity. Try to be in Westport on Thursday, when its old-fashioned farmers' market is held. On your fourth day, make the walk up Croagh Patrick or stroll around Clew Bay and see how many islands you can count. If the weather cooperates, you might want to venture out to **Achill Island** ㊶. At the end of the day, continue north to Sligo or head for a Midlands destination.

IF YOU HAVE 7 DAYS

The four-day itinerary can easily be expanded into a seven-day trip, with the following modifications: spend a full two days exploring western County Clare, staying one night in the seaside town of **Lahinch** ⑤ (especially if you're a golfer or are traveling with one) and another in any of the towns noted above. Depending on how much time you want to spend in Galway, you might want to make it to **Coole Park** ⑫ and **Thoor Ballylee** ⑬ on one of your first two days in the West, rather than taking a bite out of the time you have for Galway and the Aran Islands. Begin your third (rather than your second) day by heading to 🔝 **Galway City** ⑮–㉘. Plan on spending three full days based either right in or just outside Galway. Spend two of these days in Galway itself and one on a day trip out to the **Aran Islands** ㉙–㉛. On your sixth day, follow our alternative day-three itinerary above, ending up either in 🔝 **Cashel** ㉞, 🔝 **Clifden** ㊱, or 🔝 **Letterfrack** ㊲ for the night. Then follow our day-four itinerary above for your seventh day.

When to Tour the West

"Soft weather," as the Irish call on-again, off-again rainy days, is almost always a possibility in the West, but the months of May and October are likelier to be drier than the rest of the year. The Burren is at its best in May, when the wildflowers are in season. April, May, and October are good times for an off-peak visit. In July and August, expect to rub elbows with Irish families taking their holidays here; these are also the best months to hear traditional music. It doesn't take many visitors to overwhelm Galway City's narrow streets, so if you don't love crowds, steer clear in late July, when the Arts Festival and Galway Race take place back-to-back. Many restaurants and accommodations in Connemara and the Burren are seasonal and close from October to Easter, although thanks to a steady rise in demand, the season is definitely extending slightly each year. If you do choose to visit the West between November and March, your choice of places to stay and to eat will be limited, but you do get to feel as though you have the place to yourself. A word of warning, though: during the winter, the weather in the West can be harsh, with gales and rain sweeping in day after day from the Atlantic.

THE BURREN AND BEYOND—WEST CLARE TO SOUTH GALWAY

County Clare claims two of Ireland's unique natural sites: the awesome Cliffs of Moher and the stark, mournful landscape of the Burren, which hugs the coast from Black Head in the north to Doolin and the Cliffs of Moher in the south. Yet western County Clare is widely beloved among native Irish for a natural phenomenon significantly less unique than these: its beaches. Though just another Irish beach town to some, Kilkee, to name just one, is a favorite summer getaway. So whether you're looking for inimitable scenery or just a lovely beach to plunk down on for a few hours and relax in the sun (if you're lucky!), this section will introduce you to the natural wonders of the West.

This journey begins at Newmarket-on-Fergus, within minutes of Shannon Airport, and it makes a good jumping-off point for a trip through the West if you've just arrived in Ireland and are planning to head for Galway. It also follows directly from the end of Chapter 5, which concludes 10 km (6 mi) down the road, at Bunratty Castle and Folk Park (and the Knappogue Castle and Craggaunowen Prolect, also nearby), so be sure to take a moment to glance at those sights to decide whether to include them as you get under way. This area is also the connecting link between County Limerick (and other points in the Southwest) and Galway City. If you're approaching it from the Southwest and you're not going into Limerick City itself, it's easy to begin exploring the region from Killimer, reached via the ferry from Tarbert.

Newmarket-on-Fergus

❶ *13 km (8 mi) north of Shannon Airport on N18.*

A small town in County Clare, Newmarket-on-Fergus is chiefly remarkable nowadays as the town nearest to Dromoland Castle, formerly the home of Lord Inchiquin, chief of the O'Brien clan.

Dining and Lodging

$$$$ ✕🏨 **Dromoland Castle.** This massive, turreted, neo-Gothic castle—
★ the ancestral home of the O'Briens, the descendants of Brian Boru, High King of Ireland—looks the part. It stands beside a lake, surrounded by formal gardens and a golf course. Dating from the 19th century (it replaced its 16th-century predecessor), the castle has grand, plushly carpeted rooms with ancestral portraits, crystal chandeliers, and oak paneling. Bedrooms furnished in Regency style overlook the old Queen Anne stable yard. The vast suites have ruched drapes on the tall windows and Irish-Georgian antiques. Expect outstanding Continental cuisine in the formal, oak-wainscoted Earl of Thomond Restaurant; the Fig Tree restaurant is casual. ✉ *Co. Clare,* ☎ *061/368–144,* ℻ *061/363–355,* ⟨WEB⟩ *www.dromoland.ie. 100 rooms with bath. Restaurant, 18-hole golf course, 2 tennis courts, spa, fishing, bicycles, bar. AE, DC, MC, V.*

$ ✕🏨 **Hunter's Lodge.** A comfortable, unpretentious village pub, the lodge makes an ideal first or last stop for visitors to the West who are traveling via Shannon Airport, 12 km (8 mi) down the road. The pub has an old-world style, with an open fire and a quiet local trade. Well-equipped rooms have timber floors with scatter rugs and are attractively decorated with select pieces of old oak furniture. The restaurant, known for its cheerful service and simply prepared surf and turf, is a good value. ✉ *The Square, Co. Clare,* ☎ *061/368–577,* ℻ *061/368–057. 6 rooms with bath. Restaurant, bar, free parking. AE, DC, MC, V.*

Outdoor Activities and Sports

Dromoland Golf Course (☎ 061/368–144) is one of the most scenic in the country, set in a 700-acre estate of rich woodland on the grounds of Dromoland Castle. The 18-hole, par-71 course has a natural lake that leaves little room for error on a number of holes.

Ennis

❷ *9½ km (6 mi) north of Newmarket-on-Fergus on N18, 37 km (23 mi) northwest of Limerick, 142 km (88 mi) north of Tralee.*

A major crossroads and a convenient stop between the West and the Southwest, Ennis is the main town of County Clare, a pleasant market town with an attractively renovated, pedestrianized center. Ennis has always fostered traditional arts, especially fiddle playing and step-dancing (a kind of square dance). The **Fleadh Nua** (pronounced fla-*nooa*) festival at the end of May attracts both performers and students of Irish music and serves as the venue for the National Dancing Championships. Two statues in Ennis bear witness to the role its citizens have played in Irish democracy. On a tall limestone column above a massive pediment in the town center stands a **statue of Daniel O'Connell** (1775–1847), "The Liberator," who was a member of Parliament for County Clare between 1828 and 1831 and instrumental in bringing about Catholic Emancipation. Outside the courthouse (in the town park, beside the River Fergus, on the west side of Ennis) stands a larger-than-life bronze **statue of Eamon De Valera** (1882–1975), who successfully contested the election here in 1917, thus launching a long political career. Although De Valera was born in the United States, his maternal forebears were from County Clare. He was the dominant figure in Irish politics during the 20th century, serving as prime minister for most of the years from 1937 until 1959, when he resigned as leader of Fianna Fáil, the party he founded, and went on to serve as president of Ireland until 1973.

Dining and Lodging

$$–$$$ ✕ **The Cloister.** The restaurant is built into the walls and garden of Ennis's 13th-century abbey beside the river in the heart of town. Stone walls and floors and open fires give a robust character to the main rooms; there's also a conservatory for lighter, brighter dining. On the bar-food menu you'll find old reliables: Irish stew (lamb, potato, onion, and carrots) and fish pie with mashed potato topping. Classic Continental cuisine is offered on the restaurant menu. Local, traditional musicians, who are among the best in the country, hold sessions almost every night at the bar. ⊠ *Club Bridge, Abbey St., Co. Clare,* ☎ *065/682–9521. MC, V. No lunch Sun.*

$–$$ ✕🖫 **West County.** Catering successfully to both leisure and business travelers is this popular stopping point on the Limerick–Galway road (N18), a lively modern hostelry affiliated with Best Western. It's also just a 5-min walk from Ennis's town center. Rooms are ample; most overlook the car park but at least are quiet. Service is helpful and friendly despite the hotel's relatively large size. In July and August there's nightly Irish cabaret-style entertainment at the bar. Boru's Porterhouse serves traditional Irish fare, including local steak and seafood. ⊠ *Co. Clare,* ☎ *065/682–3000,* 🖳 *065/682–3759,* 🆆🅴🅱 *www.lynchotels.com. 152 rooms with bath. Restaurant, 3 indoor pools, health club, fishing. AE, DC, MC, V.*

$$$ 🖫 **Carnelly House.** For an elegant, convenient base for exploring the West, try this 250-year-old, Queen Anne–style redbrick house, 5 km (3 mi) from Ennis and 16 km (10 mi) from Shannon Airport. The perfectly proportioned drawing room has elaborate plasterwork decorations. The large, comfortable bedrooms have canopied or four-poster beds and bucolic views over the 100-acre estate. Hosts Dermot and Rosemarie Gleeson will fill you in on the beguiling house's colorful history. ⊠ *Clarecastle, Co. Clare,* ☎ *065/682–8442,* 🖳 *065/682–9222,* 🆆🅴🅱 *www.carnellyhouse.com. 5 rooms with bath. Fishing, horseback riding. MC, V. Closed Dec.–Feb.*

Nightlife

Although Ennis is not as fashionable as, say, Galway, it is one of the West's traditional music hot spots. You're likeliest to hear sessions at the following pubs, but keep in mind that sessions don't necessarily take place every night and that the scene is constantly changing. Phone ahead to check whether a session is happening.

Cruise's (⊠ Abbey St., ☎ 065/684–1800). **Fawl's** (⊠ The Railway Bar, 69 O'Connell St., ☎ 065/682–4463). **Kerins'** (⊠ Lifford, ☎ 065/682–0582). **Knox's** (⊠ Abbey St., ☎ 065/682–9264). **O'Halloran's Bar** (⊠ 8 High St., ☎ 065/682–3090). **Preachers** (⊠ The Temple Gate Hotel, The Square, ☎ 065/682–3300).

Outdoor Activities and Sports

BICYCLING

Cycle into the Burren on a bike rented from **M. F. Tierney Cycles & Fishing** (⊠ 17 Abbey St., ☎ 065/682–9433).

GOLF

Ennis Golf Club (⊠ Drumbiggle Rd., ☎ 065/682–4074) is an 18-hole, par-70 parkland course that overlooks the town.

HORSEBACK RIDING

Ballyshannon Riding Establishment (⊠ Ballyshannon House, Quin, ☎ 065/682–5645) offers woodland trail riding and beginners' lessons, and provides riding equipment.

Shopping

Stop in at the **Antique Loft** (⊠ Clarecastle, ☎ 065/684–1969) for collectibles and pine and mahogany antiques. The **Belleek Shop** (⊠ 36 Abbey St., ☎ 065/682–9607) carries Belleek china, Waterford crystal, and Donegal Parian china, as well as Lladró, Hummel, and other collectible china. **Carraig Donn** (⊠ 29 O'Connell St., ☎ 065/682–8188) stocks Waterford glass and other Irish crystal, Belleek and other fine china, and its own array of knitwear. At **Clare Business Center** (⊠ Francis St., ☎ 065/682–0166) you'll find a variety of crafts workshops that sell to the public. **Clare Craft and Design** (⊠ 20 Parnell St., ☎ 065/684–4723) exhibits and sells art, pottery, and crafts produced by local artists. **Shannon Crystal** (⊠ Sandfield Center, Galway Rd., ☎ 065/682–1250) is a factory outlet that has craftsmen displaying the art of hand-cutting lead crystal.

Kilrush

❸ *43 km (27 mi) southwest of Ennis on N68.*

Like most other mid-19th-century towns in West Clare, Kilrush was laid out as a large central square radiating out into the town's main streets. The widest of these leads to the harbor and the docks. This plan makes the small market town (population 3,000) seem bigger than it actually is. The Kilrush Heritage Centre has an exhibition entitled **"Kilrush in Landlord Times"** explaining the history of the town from its beginnings; it's also the starting point for a heritage walk through the town's streets that takes you back to the 19th century. ⊠ *Town Sq., Co. Clare,* ☎ *065/905–1577.* ⛶ *€1.25.* ⊙ *May–Sept., Mon.–Sat. 9:30–5:30, Sun. noon–4.*

Lodging

$ 🏠 **Bruach Na Coille** Michael and Mary Clarke's two-story Georgian-style house, a family run B&B, is across from the Kilrush woods, five minutes from the Killimer-Tarbert Car Ferry. Upon arrival, you are greeted with coffee, tea, and fresh-baked cakes. Bedrooms in the back of the house overlook Loop head and the Shannon estuary; rooms in the front have panoramic views of the countryside. The Kilrush woods are perfect for an after dinner stroll. Guest rooms are decorated in pastels with floral bedspreads and drapes and built-in cabinets and wardrobes. The full Irish breakfast is very plentiful—after sampling eggs, puddings, and soda bread, you may want to skip lunch. ⊠ *Killimer Rd., Co. Clare,* ☎ *065/905–2250,* ⅁ *065/905–2250,* Ⓦ *www.*

clarkekilrush.com. 4 rooms with bath. Hiking, horseback riding. No credit cards. Closed Christmas.

Outdoor Activities and Sports

Kilrush Golf & Sports Club (⊠ Parknamoney, Ennis Rd., ☎ 065/905–1138) is an 18-hole, par-70 course that overlooks the Shannon estuary.

Scattery Island Ferries (⊠ Kilrush Marina, ☎ 065/905–1327) run a 20-min boat trip to Scattery Island, a picturesque destination that has a ruined 6th-century monastic settlement complete with round tower. From May to early September, two-hour dolphin-watching trips (€12.70) run out to the Shannon Estuary, where a school of 40 or so bottle-nosed dolphins regularly plays. Trips are weather permitting and subject to demand; phone ahead to confirm.

Kilkee

4 *12 km (8 mi) west of Kilrush on N68.*

Kilkee is one of the most beloved west-coast beach resorts among native Irish people, many of whom have summered here for generations. Its major draw is its safe bathing—both in the waters along its magnificent long, sandy beach and in deep rock pools known as Pollock holes, which remain full at low tide (they attract scuba divers as well as swimmers). From Kilkee, you can take an excursion to **Loop Head Lighthouse** on R487, about a 38-km (24-mi) round-trip. Loop Head is the westernmost point of County Clare—at the northern tip of the mouth of the Shannon, the very end of its long estuary.

Lodging

$ ⊞ **Thomond Guesthouse and Thalassotherapy Centre.** These facilities by the sea in Kilkee town center offer a rejuvenating break to those interested in sampling Irish spa treatments. "Thalasso" means "water" in Irish, and that is exactly the type of therapy in which the center specializes. This unique getaway spot offers natural seaweed baths, algae body wraps, and facials using products made of marine extracts. The guest rooms are small but comfortable. Most guests book into the guest house for a spa weekend, but rooms are also available for those not partaking in thalassotherapy. You may, of course, feel tempted to get a massage or use the sauna. ⊠ *Grattan St., Kilkee, Co. Clare,* ☎ *065/905–6742,* FAX *065/905–6762,* WEB *www.kilkeethalasso.com. 5 rooms with bath. Hair salon, sauna, spa. MC, V. Closed Feb.*

Outdoor Activities and Sports

Kilkee Golf and Country Club (⊠ East End, ☎ 065/905–6048) overlooks the sea and has spectacular cliff-edge holes. Founded in 1896, it is an 18-hole, par-72 course.

En Route The main route heads north up the coast on N67. Sandy beaches and more Pollock holes can be found by taking a left off the main road at any sign that indicates STRAND and traveling for about 2½ km (1½ mi). One of the seaside towns worth visiting along this route is **Milltown Malbay.**

Lahinch

5 *47 km (30 mi) north of Kilkee on N67, 30 km (18 mi) west of Ennis on N85.*

Lahinch is a busy resort village beside a long, sandy beach backed by dunes, best known for its links golf courses and—believe it or not—its surfing. In 1972, the European Surfing Finals were held here, putting Lahinch on the world surfing map. (The 1995 championships were held in Easky, County Sligo.) Tom and Rosemary Buckley's **Lahinch Surf Shop** (✉ The Promenade, ☎ 065/708–1543) is ground zero for County Clare surfers.

Dining and Lodging

$ ✕🏠 **Armada Hotel.** Spanish Point, just south of Lahinch, is where the Spanish Armada was defeated in the 17th century. Storytellers and lovers of folklore use this event to explain the dark features present in so many inhabitants of the West. There is no better place to contemplate these tales than the Armada Hotel, which majestically crowns the seaside cliffs. The large guest rooms are decorated with bright modern furnishings, and most have a double or two twin beds. The Cape Restaurant, which serves fresh fish, is only 20 ft from land's end. The Flagship bar becomes the venue for a week of ceilí dances and traditional music in July. ✉ *Spanish Point, Milltown Malbay, Co. Clare,* ☎ *065/708–4110,* FAX *065/708–4632,* WEB *www.burkesarmadahotel.com. 61 rooms with bath. Restaurant, bar. MC, V.*

$ 🏠 **The Greenbrier Inn.** Location is everything. The Greenbrier Inn is 250 yards from the beach, town center, and championship golf course. Guest rooms are decorated with simple white linens and antique-style pine furnishings. The rooms and the communal living room have views of Liscanoor Bay and the Atlantic Ocean. Golf enthusiasts will be happy to know that the property is only a 30-min drive to the Doonbeg golf course just south of Lahinch, which was designed by Greg Norman and which opened in 2002. ✉ *Ennistymon Rd., Co. Clare,* ☎ *065/708–1242,* FAX *065/708–1247,* WEB *www.greenbrierinn.com. 14 rooms with bath. Fishing, horseback riding. MC, V.*

Nightlife

For traditional music try the **19th** (☎ 065/708–1440). **O'Looney's** (☎ 065/708–1414) is known as Lahinch's surfers' pub; there's music every night in summer and Saturday nights in the winter.

Outdoor Activities and Sports

The 6,613-yard, 18-hole, par-72 championship course at **Lahinch Golf Club** (☎ 065/708–1003), which opened in 1892, has challenging links, which follow the natural contours of the dunes. The **Castle Course** (☎ 065/708–1003), the newer 18-hole, par-72 Lahinch course, offers a more carefree round of seaside golf, with shorter holes than the championship course at Lahinch Golf Club.

Shopping

The **Design Lodge** (☎ 065/708–1744) is a small shop that carries Irish-made goods, including sweaters, linen, tweed, and other gift items.

The Cliffs of Moher

★ ➏ *10 km (6 mi) northwest of Lahinch on R478.*

One of Ireland's most breathtaking natural sites, the majestic Cliffs of Moher rise vertically out of the sea in a wall that stretches over a long, 8-km (5-mi) swath and as high as 710 ft. You can see stratified deposits of five different rock layers in the cliff face. Numerous seabirds, including a large colony of puffins, make their home in the shelves of rock on the cliffs. On a clear day you can see the Aran Islands and the mountains of Connemara to the north, as well as the lighthouse on Loop Head and the mountains of Kerry to the south. **O'Brien's Tower** is a defiant, broody sentinel built at the cliffs' highest point. The parking area is a favorite spot of performers; in the high season, there's likely to be free entertainment—step dancers, fiddle players, or even a one-man band. The **Visitor Centre**, a good refuge from passing rain squalls, has a gift

shop and tearoom. ☎ 065/708–1565, WEB *www.shannonheritage.com.*
✍ *Free, 2.50 euros park.* ☉ *Cliffs and O'Brien's Tower freely accessible; Visitor Centre open daily 9:30–5:30; O'Brien's Tower open daily Mar.–Oct. 9:30–5:30 weather permitting.*

Doolin

❼ *6 km (4 mi) north of the Cliffs of Moher on R479.*

A tiny village consisting almost entirely of B&Bs, hostels, pubs, and restaurants, Doolin is widely said to have three of the best pubs in Ireland for traditional music. But with the worldwide surge of interest in Irish music during the last decade, the village is more of a magnet for European musicians than it is for young, or even established, Irish artists. On **Doolin Pier,** about 1½ km (1 mi) outside the village, local fishermen sell their catch fresh off the boat—lobster, crayfish, salmon, and mackerel. From spring until early fall (weather permitting), a regular ferry service takes visitors for a 30-minute ride to Inisheer, the smallest of the Aran Islands.

Dining and Lodging

$$$ ✕ **Bruach na Haille.** The name means "the bank of the river Aille," and the river can be seen from the side windows of this charming cottage restaurant, owned by John and Helen Browne for 20 years. The low-beamed, cozy rooms have flagstone floors, old dressers laden with colorful delft china, and open turf fires. Deep-fried Kilshanny cheese is usually on the menu, as well as lobster from the Doolin Pier and the ever-popular sirloin steak with Irish whiskey sauce. ⊠ *Roadford, Co. Clare,* ☎ *065/707–4120,* FAX *065/707–4230. AE, DC, MC, V. Closed Nov.–mid-Mar. No lunch.*

$ ✕🏠 **Aran View House.** Expect nothing less than magnificent views of the Aran Islands in the west, Doolin Pier and the Cliffs of Moher in the south, and the gray limestone rocks of the Burren to the north. The 1736-era house on 100 acres of farmland has been redecorated with lovely antique touches, such as four-poster beds and Georgian reproduction furniture. You can savor the view from the restaurant's bay windows while enjoying the Regency chairs and dusky pink napery. It's located on the coast road in the Fanore direction, about a 10-min walk from Doolin village. ⊠ *Coast Rd., Co. Clare,* ☎ *065/707–4061,* FAX *065/707–4540,* WEB *www.aranview.com. 19 rooms with bath. Restaurant, fishing, bar. AE, DC, MC, V. Closed Nov.–Mar.*

Nightlife

Doolin's three pubs are famous for their traditional music sessions. **Gus O'Connor's** (☎ 065/707–4168) serves excellent bar food. **McDermott's** (☎ 065/707–4700) is popular with locals, and **McGann's** (☎ 065/707–4133) has been run by the same family for 70 years.

Outdoor Activities and Sports

Cycle along the coast on a bike rented from **Patrick Moloney, Doolin Hostel** (☎ 065/707–4006).

Shopping

Doolin Crafts Gallery (☎ 065/707–4309), beside the cemetery and the church, carries only Irish-made goods: sweaters, modern lead crystal, linen, lace, and tweed. A jeweler's workshop and a resident batik maker are also on the premises. Don't miss the 1-acre garden, which has more than 600 plants from all over the world. The garden and the Flagship Restaurant are open daily Easter–September.

Lisdoonvarna

8 *5 km (3 mi) east of Doolin on R478.*

One of only two spa towns in Ireland (the other is Enniscrone, in western County Sligo), Lisdoonvarna has several sulfurous and iron-bearing springs with radioactive properties, all containing iodine. The town grew, in the late 19th century, to accommodate visitors who wanted to "take the waters." The buildings reflect a mishmash of mock-architectural styles: Scottish baronial, Swiss chalet, Spanish hacienda, and American motel. Depending on your taste, it's either lovably kitschy or just plain tacky. If you're curious about health cures, the **Lisdoonvarna Spa and Bath House** is worth a visit. Iron and magnesia elements make the drinking water taste terrible (as does most spa water). In comparison, the bathing water is pleasant, if enervating. Electric sulfur baths, massage, wax baths, a sauna, and a solarium are available at the spa complex, which is on the edge of town in an attractive parkland setting. ☎ 065/707–4023. ⌂ *Complex free, sulfur baths €6.35 (book in advance).* ⊙ *Early June–early Oct., daily 10–6.*

In July and August, Lisdoonvarna is a favorite getaway for Irish under-30s. It's also the traditional vacationing spot for the West's bachelor farmers, who used to congregate here at harvest time in late September with the vague intention of finding wives. (Irish farmers are notoriously shy with women and reluctant to marry, often postponing the event until their mid- or late-fifties, if ever.) This tradition is now formalized in the **Matchmaking Festival** (☎ 065/707–4005), held during late September. Middle-aged singles dance to the strains of country-and-western bands, and a talent contest is held to name the most eligible bachelor.

Dining and Lodging

$–$$ ✕🏨 **Ballinalacken Castle.** One-hundred acres of wildflower meadows surround this sprawling Victorian lodge beside the 16th-century ruins of an O'Brien stronghold, on a hill 4 km (2½ mi) outside Lisdoonvarna. Through the bay windows you'll get fine panoramic views of the Atlantic, the Aran Islands, and the Connemara hills. Some guest rooms have marble fireplaces and high ceilings. The public rooms are a mix of hand-me-downs, modern items, and lovely old Irish oak. Local chef Frank Sheedy, formerly of Sheedy's Inn, who has cooked in some of Ireland's best restaurants, serves an imaginative and sophisticated menu using local seafood, lamb, and beef. ⌂ *Lisdoonvarna, Co. Clare,* ☎ *065/707–4025,* 🅵🅰🆇 *065/707–4025,* 🆆🅴🅱 *www.ballinalackencastle.com. 12 rooms with bath. Restaurant, bar. AE, DC, MC, V. Closed early Oct.–mid-Apr.*

$ ✕🏨 **Carrigann.** Hikers, who come for the guided walks and independent exploration, love this small, friendly hotel, ensconced in trim, pretty gardens, and just a two minutes' walk from the village center. Hosts Mary and Gerard Howard keep a library of special-interest books on the Burren beside the turf fire in the sitting room; their maps and notes are also available. Rooms are modestly furnished but well-equipped for the price range. Gerard also runs his own butcher shop, guaranteeing top-quality meat on the hotel's menu. Meals are supplemented by herbs from the garden and fresh local fish. ⌂ *Lisdoonvarna, Co. Clare,* ☎ *065/707–4036,* 🅵🅰🆇 *065/707–4567,* 🆆🅴🅱 *www.gateway-to-the-burren.com. 20 rooms with bath. Fishing. MC, V. Closed Nov.–Feb.*

$ ✕🏨 **Sheedy's Restaurant and Country Inn.** Originally a 17th-century ★ farmhouse, this small, friendly hotel is only a short walk from the town center and the spa wells. It's been in the hands of the Sheedy family since 1855. Proprietor John Sheedy, who was chef de cuisine at Ash-

ford Castle until moving back home, makes creative use of local produce in contemporary French-Irish style fare. The informal Seafood Bar
in the foyer serves simple dishes: crab claws in garlic butter, local
smoked salmon, and seafood platters. ✉ *Lisdoonvarna, Co. Clare,* ☎
065/707–4026, FAX *065/707–4555,* WEB *www.sheedyscountryhouse.com.
11 rooms with bath. Restaurant, tennis court, bar. AE, MC, V. Closed
Oct.–Mar.*

Nightlife
Country music and ballad singing are popular in the bars of Lisdoonvarna. For traditional music try the **Roadside Tavern** (☎ 065/707–4084).

Shopping
To see an audiovisual presentation on smoking Atlantic salmon, plus
live demonstrations of the oak-smoking process, visit the **Burren Smoke-
house Ltd.** (☎ 065/707–4432). You can also buy neatly packaged
whole sides of salmon to take home.

The Burren

★ ❾ *Extending throughout western County Clare from the Cliffs of Moher
in the south to Black Head in the north, as far southeast as Corofin.*

As you travel north toward Ballyvaughan, the landscape becomes
rockier and stranger. Instead of the seemingly ubiquitous Irish green,
gray becomes the prevailing color. You're now in the heart of the Burren, a 300-square-km (116-square-mi) expanse that is one of Ireland's
fiercest landscapes. The Burren is aptly named: it's an Anglicization
of the Irish word *bhoireann* (a rocky place). Stretching off in all directions, as far as the eye can see, are vast, irregular slabs of fissured
limestone (known as karst) with deep cracks between them. From a
distance, it looks like a lunar landscape, so dry that nothing could possibly grow on it. In the spring (especially from mid-May to mid-June),
the Burren becomes a wild rock garden, as an astonishing variety of
wildflowers bloom between the cracks in the rocks, among them at least
23 native species of orchid. The Burren also supports an incredible variety of wildlife, including frogs, newts, lizards, badgers, stoats, spar-
row hawks, kestrels, and dozens of other birds and animals. The
wildflowers and other plants are given life from the spectacular caves,
streams, and potholes that lie beneath the rough, scarred pavements.
With the advent of spring, *turloughs* (seasonal lakes that disappear in
dry weather) appear on the plateau's surface. Botanists are particularly
intrigued by the cohabitation of Arctic and Mediterranean plants,
many so tiny (and rare, so please do not pick any) you can't see them
from your car window; make a point of exploring some of this rocky
terrain on foot. Numerous signposted walks run through both coastal
and inland areas. For a private guided tour, contact Mary Angela
Keane (☎ 065/707–4003; €31.70 per hour) or Shane Connolly (☎
065/707–7168; €12.70 per person). May and June are peak months
for flora, but a tour is worthwhile at any time of year.

The tiny **Burren Centre** has a modest audiovisual display and other exhibits that explain the Burren's geology, flora, and archaeology. ✉ *Kilfenora, 8 km (5 mi) southeast of Lisdoonvarna on R476, Co. Clare,*
☎ *065/708–8030.* ᠁ *€3.15.* ☉ *June–Aug., daily 9:30–6; mid-Mar.–
May and Sept.–Oct., daily 10–5.*

Beside the Burren Centre in Kilfenora, the ruins of a small 12th-cen-
tury church, once the **Cathedral of St. Fachan,** have been partially restored as a parish church. There are some interesting carvings in the

roofless choir, including an unusual, life-size human skeleton. In a field about 165 ft west of the ruins is an elaborately sculpted **high cross** that is worth examining, even though parts of it are badly weathered.

Nightlife
Vaughan's Pub (☎ 065/708–8004) in Kilfenora is known for its traditional music sessions.

Ballyvaughan

⑩ *16 km (10 mi) north of Lisdoonvarna on N67.*

A pretty little waterside village and a good base for exploring the Burren, Ballyvaughan attracts walkers and artists who enjoy the views of Galway Bay and access to the Burren. Outside Ballyvaughan, you'll see a signpost to the right for **Ailwee Cave,** the only such chamber in the region accessible to those who aren't spelunkers. This vast, 2-million-year-old cave is illuminated for about 3,300 ft and contains an underground river and waterfall. ☎ 065/707–7036. ⌂ €6. ☼ *Early Mar.–June and Sept.–early Nov., daily 10–6 (last tour at 5:30); July–Aug., daily 10–7 (last tour at 6:30).*

Dining and Lodging

$$ ✕⚏ **Gregan's Castle Hotel.** The Haden family runs this quiet, meticulous, large Victorian country house, at the base of the aptly named
★ Corkscrew Hill (on N67, midway between Ballyvaughan and Lisdoonvarna). The house is surrounded by gardens and overlooks Galway Bay and the gray mountains of the Burren. All bedrooms are individually furnished with Georgian and Victorian antiques and William Morris wallpaper. The spacious rooms on the ground floor have private patio gardens but lack the splendid views of the rooms upstairs. The restaurant (jacket and tie are required) serves updated French cuisine. ✉ *Base of Corkscrew Hill, Ballyvaughan, Co. Clare,* ☎ 065/707–7005, ℻ 065/707–7111, ⓦⒺⒷ *www.gregans.ie. 18 rooms with bath, 4 suites. Restaurant, bar, fishing, bicycles, croquet. AE, MC, V. Closed Nov.–Mar.*

$ ✕⚏ **Admiral's Rest.** You can guess from the nautical bric-a-brac on view that this place belongs to a retired naval man—John Macnamara, who is an expert on the Burren's wildlife. In a modernized cottage on the coast road between Lisdoonvarna and Ballyvaughan, the restaurant is across the road from the sea, which is visible through the large windows. Varnished stone floors, stone-topped tables, *súgán* (rope-seated) chairs, and an open wood-and-turf fire make up the rugged furnishings. Seafood is the mainstay here, though everything is tasty. Nine inexpensive B&B rooms with shared baths are in the bungalow next door. ✉ *Fanore, Co. Clare,* ☎ 065/707–6105, ℻ 065/707–6161, ⓦⒺⒷ *www.admiralsrest.com. 9 rooms. AE, MC, V. Closed Nov.–Easter.*

$ ✕⚏ **Hyland's Hotel.** A turf fire greets you in the lobby of the hotel, which is considered somewhat of an artist's haven. This family-run, yellow-and-red coaching inn, right in the heart of the Burren, dates back to the early 18th century. Rooms vary in size and shape, but all have pine furniture and fresh-looking color-coordinated drapes and spreads. If you like mountain views, ask for a room with a skylight looking out over the Burren. The restaurant, cheerfully decorated in country pine with red tablecloths, specializes in simply prepared local produce. There is live music in the bar most nights from June to mid-September and Irish storytelling once a week. ✉ *Ballyvaughan, Co. Clare,* ☎ 065/707–7037, ℻ 065/707–7131. *30 rooms with bath. Restaurant, bar. AE, DC, MC, V. Closed 2nd wk of Jan.–Feb.*

Nightlife

The friendly **Monk's Pub** (☎ 065/707–7059), near the waterfront, has great music sessions.

En Route   From Ballyvaughan, it's a 48-km (30-mi) trip circumnavigating Galway Bay to Galway City. If you're eager to get there, skip the next two towns and head there directly, first passing through Kinvara. If you're on a more leisurely pace, head back south through the Burren on R480 and R476 to Corofin.

Corofin

⑪   *23 km (14½ mi) south of Ballyvaughan, 16 km (10 mi) east of Kilfenora on the R476.*

If you're searching for your Irish roots, Corofin's **Clare Heritage Center** has a genealogical service and advice for do-it-yourselfers. Its displays on the history of the West of Ireland in the 19th century cover culture, traditions, emigration, and famine; it also exposes some grim statistics. In 1841, for example, the population of County Clare was 286,394. Fifty years later, famine and emigration had reduced this number to 112,334, and the population continued to decline, reaching an all-time low of 73,597 in 1956. (It is now heading back to the 90,000 mark.) ☎ 065/683–7955. ☞ €2.55. ⊗ *Apr.–Oct., daily 10–6; Nov.–Mar. (genealogy service only), weekdays 9–5; Heritage Center by appointment.*

In a 15th-century castle on the edge of Corofin, the **Dysert O'Dea Castle Archaeology Centre** has an exhibition on the antiquities of the Burren. Twenty-five monuments stand within a 1½-km (1-mi) radius of the castle; these date from the Bronze Age to the 19th century, and all are described at the center. ☎ 065/683–7722. ☞ €3.15. ⊗ *May–Sept., daily 10–6.*

Coole Park and Thoor Ballylee

Coole Park: 24 km (15 mi) northeast of Corofin on N18; Thoor Ballylee: 5 km (3 mi) north of Coole Park, signposted from N66.

⑫   On the left side north of the little town of Gort is **Coole Park,** once home to Lady Augusta Gregory (1859–1932), W. B. Yeats's patron and his cofounder of Dublin's Abbey Theatre. Yeats visited here often, as did almost all the other writers who contributed to the Irish literary revival in the first half of the 20th century, including George Bernard Shaw and Sean O'Casey. Douglas Hyde, the first president of Ireland, was also a visitor. The house fell derelict after Lady Gregory's death and was demolished in 1941; the grounds are now a national forest and wildlife park. The only reminder of its literary past is the **Autograph Tree,** a copper beech on which many of Lady Gregory's famous guests carved their initials. Picnic tables make this a lovely alfresco lunch spot. ☎ 091/631–804. ☞ *Visitor center €2.55, park free.* ⊗ *Visitor center mid-Apr.–mid-June, Tues.–Sun. 10–5; mid-June–Aug., daily 9:30–6:30; Sept., daily 10–5; park daily 10–dusk.*

⑬   **Thoor Ballylee** is a sight Yeats fans won't want to miss. (It's one of the only major sites in the West that's not in County Sligo.) In his fifties and newly married, Yeats bought this 14th-century Norman tower as a ruin in 1916 for £35/€44. The tower sits beside a whitewashed, thatched-roof cottage, with a tranquil stream running alongside it. Its proximity to Lady Gregory's house at Coole Park made it a desirable location, though it required significant work on Yeats's part to make it livable. He stayed here intermittently until 1929 and penned some of his more mystical works here, including *The Tower* and *The Winding Stair*. It's now fully restored with his original decor and furniture. The audiovisual display is a useful introduction to the poet and his times. ✉ *N66 3 mi outside of Gort, Co. Galway,* ☎ *091/631–436.* 🖭 *€4.* ☉ *Easter–Sept., daily 10–6.*

Kinvara

⑭ *13½ km (8½ mi) east of Ballyvaughan, 15 km (9 mi) northwest of Gort on N67, 25 km (15½ mi) south of Galway City.*

Whether you're coming from Ballyvaughan or from Gort, Kinvara is worth a visit. The picture-perfect village is a growing holiday base, thanks to its gorgeous bay-side locale, great walking and sea angling, and numerous pubs. Kinvara is best known for its long-standing early August sailing event, **Cruinniú na mBád** (Festival of the Gathering of the Boats), in which traditional brown-sailed Galway hookers laden with turf race across the bay. (Hookers were used until the early part of this century to carry turf, provisions, and cattle across Galway Bay and out to the Aran Islands. A sculpture in Galway's Eyre Square honors their local significance.)

On a rock to the north of Kinvara Bay, the 16th-century **Dunguaire Castle** commands all the approaches from Galway Bay. It is said to be on the site of a 7th-century castle built by the King of Connacht. One of its previous owners, Oliver St. John Gogarty, was a surgeon, man of letters, and model for James Joyce's Buck Mulligan, a character in *Ulysses*. Today Dunguaire is used for a medieval banquet that honors local writers and others with ties to the West, including Lady Gregory, W. B. Yeats, Sean O'Casey, and Pádraic Ó'Conaire. ☎ *091/637–108.* 🖭 *Castle €3.10, banquet €40.60.* ☉ *May–Sept., daily 9:30–5; banquet at 5:30 and 8:30.*

Dining and Lodging

$$ ✕ **Moran's Oyster Cottage.** Signposted off the main road on the south side of Clarinbridge, this waterside thatched cottage, the home of the Moran family since 1760, houses a simply furnished restaurant at the back that serves only seafood. It's *the* place to stop to sample the local oysters, grown on a bed in front of the restaurant. ✉ *The Weir, Kilcolgan, Co. Galway,* ☎ *091/796–113,* ℻ *091/796–503. AE, MC, V.*

$ ✕🖬 **Merriman Inn.** Don't let its traditional looks deceive you: this whitewashed, thatched inn on the shores of Galway Bay is in fact a mid-size hotel, decorated with locally made, well-designed furniture, and original crafts, paintings, and sculpture. The bar and lounge both have open fires and a relaxed, friendly atmosphere. Guest rooms are quiet and well equipped. The Quilty Room is a large, airy restaurant. Local seafood—such as tournedos of salmon pan-seared with a confit of fennel and a sharp, spicy jus—is featured on the French-influenced menu, but you can also try succulent local lamb. ✉ *Main St., Kinvara, Co. Galway,* ☎ *091/638–222,* ℻ *091/637–686,* 🕸 *www.merrimanhotel.com. 32 rooms with bath. Restaurant, bar, meeting room. AE, DC, MC, V. Closed Jan.–mid-Mar.*

$ 🖬 **Burren View Farm.** A million-dollar view awaits you at this yellow, two-story B&B on the edge of Galway Bay, 5 km (3 mi) west of Kinvara. It's relatively isolated, as it's on a working sheep and cattle farm. Around the B&B you'll find stone-walled fields dotted with sheep. The breakfast room, sun lounge, and front bedrooms look out across a wide sea inlet to the gray expanse of the Burren. Rooms are plain and homey but clean and well maintained. Wholesome evening meals, Irish or Continental style, are cooked on request, while food is also available in the local pub, a 5-min walk away. ✉ *Doorus, Kinvara,*

Co. Galway, ☎ *091/637–142,* ℻ *091/638–131. 5 rooms, 2 with bath. Dining room, tennis court, fishing. AE, DC, MC, V. Closed Nov.–Mar.*

Nightlife and the Arts

The first weekend in May, Kinvara hosts the annual **Cuckoo Fleadh** (☎ 091/637–145). You can hear traditional music most nights at the **Winkles Hotel** bar (⊠ The Square, ☎ 91/637–137) where Sharon Shannon got her start in the music business.

GALWAY CITY

27 km (12½ mi) north of Kinvara, 219 km (136 mi) west of Dublin, 105 km (65 mi) north of Limerick.

Galway is often said to be a state of mind as much as it is a specific place. The largest city in the West today (population 60,000) and the ancient capital of the province of Connaught, Galway is also one of the fastest-growing cities in Europe. It's an astonishing fact, and you have to wonder where this city can possibly grow. For even though Galway is the largest city in the West, its heart is *tiny*—a warren of streets so compact that if you spend more than a few hours here, you'll soon be strolling along with the sort of easy familiarity you'd feel in your hometown.

For many Irish people, Galway is a favorite weekend getaway, the liveliest place in the Republic, and the city of festivals. It's also a university town: University College Galway (or UCG as it's locally known) is a center for Gaelic culture (Galway marks the eastern gateway to the West's large Gaeltacht). A fair share of UCG's 9,000 students pursue their studies in the Irish language. Galway is, in fact, permeated by youth culture. On festival weekends, you'll see as many pierced and tattooed teenagers and twentysomethings here as you'd find at a rock concert.

But its students aren't its only avant-garde, as Galway has long attracted writers, artists, and musicians. The last keep the traditional music pubs lively year-round. Its two small but internationally acclaimed theater companies draw a steady stream of theater people.

Although you're not conscious of it when you're in the center of town, Galway is spectacularly situated, on the north shore of Galway Bay, where the River Corrib flows from Lough Corrib out into the sea. The seaside suburb of Salthill, on the south-facing shore of Galway Bay, has spectacular vistas across the vividly blue bay to Black Head on the opposite shore.

Galway's founders were Anglo-Normans who arrived in the mid-13th century and fortified their settlement against "the native Irish," as local chieftains were called. Galway became known as "the City of the Tribes" because of the dominant role in public and commercial life of the 14 families who founded it. Their names are still common in Galway and elsewhere in Ireland: Athy, Blake, Bodkin, Browne, D'Arcy, Dean, Font, French, Kirwan, Joyce, Lynch, Morris, Martin, and Skerret. The city's medieval heritage, a fusion of Gaelic and Norman influences, is apparent in the intimate two- and three-story stucco buildings, the winding streets, the narrow passageways, and the cobblestones underfoot.

Galway's growth and popularity mean that at its busiest moments, pedestrians jam-pack its narrow, one-way streets, while cars are gridlocked. If there's a city that doesn't sleep in Ireland, this is it. In fact, if you want to be guaranteed a quiet night's sleep, either ask for a room in the back of your center-city hotel or simply stay outside of town.

Exploring Galway City

Most of the city's sights, aside from the cathedral and the university campus, can be found in a narrow sector of the medieval town center that runs from Eyre Square in a southwesterly direction to the River Corrib. Eyre Square is easily recognizable, as it is the only green space in central Galway. It only takes five minutes to walk straight down Galway's main shopping street, the continuation of the north side of Eyre Square, to the River Corrib, where it ends. Not only is the city center compact, it is also largely pedestrianized, so there is really only one way to see it: on foot. Even the farthest point, the university campus, is less than a 15-minute walk from Eyre Square. A walk to Galway's seaside suburb, Salthill, 3 km (2 mi) west of Galway, and its long seaside promenade, is a favorite local occupation, traditionally undertaken on a Sunday afternoon; for this excursion you may prefer to take the car.

A Good Walk

Orient yourself at **Eyre Square** ⑮, part of which is occupied by **Kennedy Park**. Before you really get going, you may want to stop in at the **Tourist Information Office** ⑯ off the southeast corner of the square. At the top (north side) of Eyre Square, turn left down Williamsgate Street. This is the spine of old Galway. Its name changes four times before it reaches the River Corrib, successively called **William Street, Shop Street, High Street,** and **Quay Street.** If you have any postcards to mail, you may want to stop at the General Post Office, on the left side of Eglinton Street, the first right off Williamsgate Street. At the corner of William and Shop streets, **Lynch's Castle** ⑰ is one of Galway's oldest buildings. Continue down Shop Street to the pedestrian way just beyond Abbeygate Street; here **Lynch Memorial Window** ⑱ and **Collegiate Church of St. Nicholas** ⑲ are adjacent to one another. James Joyce fans might want to make the 30-second detour across Lombard and Market streets to Bowling Green, site of the **Nora Barnacle House** ⑳.

It's a minute's walk from the church to **Tiġ Neaċtain** ㉑ (Naughton's in English, pronounced *knock*-tons), a pub (popular with locals) at the corner of Cross Street and Quay/High Street. This corner is the very heart of old Galway's main historic and commercial district: nearly all the city's best restaurants, bars, boutiques, art galleries, and crafts, antiques, and bookstores line the narrow, winding streets and alleys in this vicinity. Nothing is more than a five-minute walk from anything else. If this area is bursting at the seams, one block to the east of Shop/High Street, between Abbeygate and Cross streets, the quieter Middle Street has a number of worthwhile stores and restaurants, as well as the national Irish-language theater.

The **Spanish Arch** ㉒ and the **Galway City Museum** ㉓ are adjacent, right on the river's east bank, across from the Jurys Galway Inn parking lot. Just beyond Jurys but before crossing the Wolfe Tone Bridge, turn right onto the pedestrian path that parallels the river. Follow it past the William O'Brien Bridge to the **Salmon Weir Bridge** ㉔ (you'll need to jog off the path onto Abbeygate Street just short of the bridge to gain access to it). As you cross the bridge, look ahead to the **Cathedral of Our Lady Assumed into Heaven and St. Nicholas** ㉕ (known locally simply as "the cathedral"). A five-minute walk down University Road brings you to **University College Galway** ㉖. For a pretty stroll back to the center of town, turn right onto Canal Road and follow it back to the intersection of Dominick Street, Fairhill, and Raven Terrace. From here it's a brief jog to Claddagh Quay, which will take you out to the **Claddagh** ㉗. If you're out this far, you may want to continue on to **Salthill** ㉘; otherwise, head back to the center of town.

You could easily take this walk in a morning or afternoon (minus the walk out to Salthill), although if you browse in stores, chat with locals, or stop off for a pint or a cup of tea, you could stretch it out into a *very* leisurely all-day excursion. You may want to plan your day so you hit only what most interests you, leaving time to explore along the bay, get out to Salthill, or take a bay cruise.

Sights to See

25 **Cathedral of Our Lady Assumed into Heaven and St. Nicholas.** On an island forming the west bank of the River Corrib beside the Salmon Weir Bridge, Galway's largest Catholic church was dedicated by Cardinal Cushing of Boston in 1965. The cathedral was built on the site of the old Galway jail; a white cross embedded into the pavement of the adjacent parking lot marks the site of the cemetery that stood beside the prison. ✍ *Free.* ☉ *Freely accessible.*

27 **Claddagh.** On the west bank of the Corrib estuary, this district was once an Irish-speaking fishing village outside the walls of the old town. The name is an Anglicization of the Irish *cladach,* which means "marshy ground." It retained a strong, separate identity until the 1930s, when its traditional thatched cottages were replaced by a conventional housing plan and its unique character and traditions were largely lost. One thing has survived: the Claddagh ring, composed of two hands clasped around a heart with a crown above it (symbolizing love, friendship, and loyalty), is still used by many Irish people as a wedding ring. Traditionally, the ring is worn with the heart facing into you if you're married or otherwise unavailable and with the heart facing outward (indicating your heart is open) if you're still looking for Mr. or Ms. Right. Reproductions in gold or silver are favorite souvenirs of Galway.

19 **Collegiate Church of St. Nicholas.** Built by the Anglo-Normans in 1320 and enlarged in 1486 and again in the 16th century, the church contains many fine carvings and gargoyles dating from the late Middle Ages, and it is one of the best-preserved medieval churches in Ireland. Legend has it that Columbus prayed here on his last stop before setting off on his voyage to the New World. On Saturday mornings, a **street market,** held in the pedestrian way beside the church, attracts two dozen or so vendors and hundreds of shoppers. ⌂ *Lombard St., Center.* ✍ *Free.* ☉ *Daily 8–dusk.*

15 **Eyre Square.** The largest open space in central Galway on the east side of the Corrib, Eyre Square encompasses a hodgepodge of monuments and concrete and grassy areas. In the center is **Kennedy Park,** a patch of lawn named in honor of John F. Kennedy, who spoke from here when he visited the city in June 1963. At the north end of the park, a 20-ft-high steel **sculpture** standing in the pool of a fountain represents the brown sails seen on Galway hookers, the area's traditional sailing boats. Seated beside this sculpture is the genial stone **figure of Pádraic Ó'Conaire,** a pioneer of the Irish-language revival at the turn of the last century who was born in Galway (his birthplace fronting on the docks is marked with a plaque). When he died in a Dublin hospital in 1928, his only possessions were his pipe (a replica of which he holds here), his tobacco, and an apple. Now the entrance to Kennedy Park, the **Browne Doorway** was taken in 1905 from the Browne family's town house on Upper Abbeygate Street; it has the 17th-century coats of arms of both the Browne and Lynch families, called a "marriage stone," because when the families were joined in marriage their coats of arms were, too. Keep an eye out for similar if less elaborate versions of the entranceway as you walk around the old part of town. The **bronze**

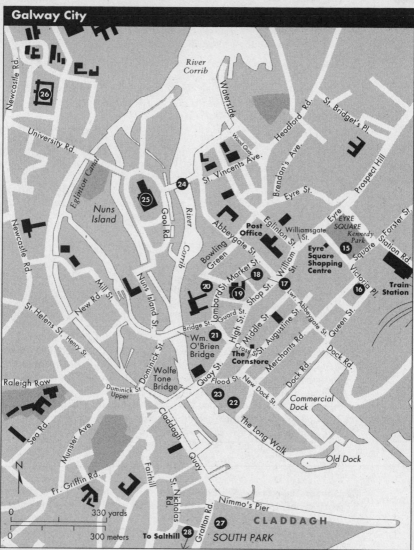

River Corrib

Newcastle Rd.

University Rd.

Eglinton Canal

Newcastle Rd.

Nuns Island

Mill St.

New Rd.

St. Helens St.

Henry St.

Nuns Island St.

Gaol Rd.

River Corrib

Waterside

Wood Quay

Headford Rd.

Brendan's Ave.

St. Bridger's Pl.

Prospect Hill

St. Vincents Ave.

Eyre St.

Forster St.

Station Rd.

Abbeygate St.

Bowling Green

Lombard St.

Market St.

Post Office

Eglinton St.

Williamsgate St.

William St.

Eyre Square Shopping Centre

EYRE SQUARE

Kennedy Park

Victoria Pl.

Train Station

Shop St.

High St.

Guard St.

Cross St.

Bridge St.

St. Augustine St.

Lwr. Abbeygate St.

Queen St.

Merchants Rd.

Dock Rd.

Dock Rd.

Wm. O'Brien Bridge

Dominick St.

The Cornstore

Raleigh Row

Dominick St. Upper

Wolfe Tone Bridge

Sea Rd.

Munster Ave.

Fr. Griffin Rd.

Fairhill

Claddagh Quay

Quay St.

Flood St.

New Dock St.

Middle St.

Commercial Dock

The Long Walk

Old Dock

N

0   330 yards
0   300 meters

To Salthill

Grattan Rd.

St. Nicholas Rd.

Nimmo's Pier

CLADDAGH

SOUTH PARK

Cathedral of Our Lady Assumed into Heaven and St. Nicholas **25**

Claddagh **27**

Collegiate Church of St. Nicholas **19**

Eyre Square **15**

Galway City Museum **23**

Lynch Memorial Window **18**

Lynch's Castle **17**

Nora Barnacle House **20**

Salmon Weir Bridge **24**

Salthill **28**

Spanish Arch **22**

Tig Neáchtain **21**

Tourist Information Office (TIO) **16**

University College Galway (UCG) **26**

cannons were presented at the end of the Crimean War to the Connaught Rangers, a legendary regiment of the British Army made up of Irish men recruited from the West of Ireland.

㉓ Galway City Museum. Next door to the Spanish Arch, the city's civic museum contains an array of materials relating to local history: old photographs, antiquities (the oldest is a stone axe head carbon-dated to 3500 BC), and other historical gewgaws. ⊠ *Spanish Arch,* ☎ *091/ 567–641.* ⊡ *€1.30.* ⊙ *Daily 10–1 and 2:15–5:15.*

⑱ Lynch Memorial Window. Embedded in a stone wall above a built-up Gothic doorway off Market Street, the window marks the spot where, according to legend, James Lynch FitzStephen, mayor of Galway in the early 16th century, condemned his son to death after he confessed to murdering a Spanish sailor who had stolen his girlfriend. When no one could be found to carry out the execution, Judge Lynch hanged his son himself, ensuring that justice prevailed, before retiring into seclusion. ⊠ *Market St., Center.*

⑰ Lynch's Castle. Now a branch of the Allied Irish Banks, this is the finest remaining example in Galway of a 16th-century fortified house—fortified because neighboring Irish tribes persistently raided the village, whose commercial life excluded them. Decorative details on its stone lintels are usually found only in southern Spain. Like the Spanish Arch, it serves as a reminder of the close trading links that once existed between Galway and Spain. ⊠ *Shop St., Center.*

⑳ Nora Barnacle House. On June 16, 1904, James Joyce (1882–1941) had his first date with Nora Barnacle, who would later become his wife. He subsequently chose to set *Ulysses* on this day, now known universally as Bloomsday—"a recognition of the determining effect upon his life of his attachment to her," as Joyce's biographer Richard Ellman has said. Nora was born here, the daughter of a poor baker; today it has a modest collection of photographs, letters, and memorabilia, and a small gift shop. ⊠ *4 Bowling Green, Center,* ☎ *091/564–743.* ⊡ *€1.30.* ⊙ *Mid-May–mid-Sept., Mon.–Sat. 10–5; off-season by appointment.*

㉔ Salmon Weir Bridge. The bridge itself is nothing special, but in season—from mid-April to early July—shoals of salmon are visible from its deck as they lie in the clear river water before making their way upstream to the spawning grounds of Lough Corrib. ⊠ *At the West end of St. Vincent's Ave., Center.*

㉘ Salthill. Three km (2 mi) west of Galway, Salthill is a lively, hugely popular seaside resort with its own fun palace. Its promenade is the traditional place "to sit and watch the moon rise over Claddagh, and see the sun go down on Galway Bay"—as Bing Crosby used to croon in the city's most famous song.

㉒ Spanish Arch. Built in 1584 to protect the quays where Spanish ships unloaded cargoes of wines and brandies, the arch now stands in the parking lot opposite Jurys Galway Inn. It's easily (and often) mistaken for a pile of weathered stones, yet it's another reminder of Galway's—and Ireland's—past links with Spain. ⊠ *The Long Walk, Spanish Arch.*

㉑ Tíg Neáchtain (Naughton's Pub). You can hear traditional music every night at this popular pub, which stands at a busy little crossroads in the heart of the old town. Grab a spot at one of its old-fashioned partitioned snugs at lunchtime for an inexpensive selection of imaginative bar food. It's a good place to mingle with local actors, writers, artists, musicians, and students, although it can get sardine-can crowded. ⊠ *17 Cross St., Spanish Arch,* ☎ *091/566–172.*

When you pack your MCI Calling Card, it's like packing your loved ones along too.

Your MCI Calling Card is the easy way to stay in touch when you travel. Use it to call to and from over 125 countries. Plus, every time you call, you can earn frequent flier miles. So wherever your travels take you, call home with your MCI Calling Card. It's even easy to get one. Just visit **www.mci.com/worldphone** or **www.mci.com/partners**.

EASY TO CALL WORLDWIDE

1. Just enter the WorldPhone® access number of the country you're calling from.
2. Enter or give the operator your MCI Calling Card number.
3. Enter or give the number you're calling.

Austria ◆	0800-200-235
Belgium ◆	0800-10012
Czech Republic ◆	00-42-000112
Denmark ◆	8001-0022
Estonia ★	0800-1122
Finland ◆	08001-102-80
France ◆	0-800-99-0019
Germany	0800-888-8000
Greece ◆	00-800-1211

Hungary ◆	06▼800-01411
Ireland	1-800-55-1001
Italy ◆	800-17-2401
Luxembourg	8002-0112
Netherlands ◆	0800-022-91-22
Norway ◆	800-19912
Poland ∻	00-800-111-21-22
Portugal ∻	800-800-123
Romania ∻	01-800-1800
Russia ◆ ∻	747-3322
Spain	900 99 0014
Sweden ◆	020-795-922
Switzerland ◆	0800-89-0222
Ukraine ∻	8▼10-013
United Kingdom	0800-89-0222
Vatican City	172-1022

◆ Public phones may require deposit of coin or phone card for dial tone. ★ Not available from public pay phones. ▼ Wait for second dial tone. ∻ Limited availability.

EARN FREQUENT FLIER MILES

Find America *with a Compass*

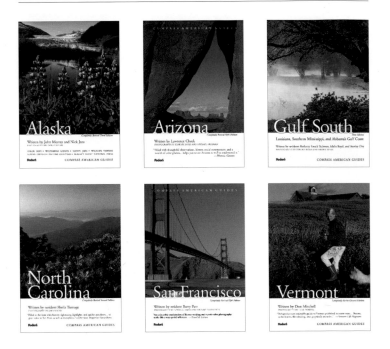

Written by local authors and illustrated throughout
with spectacular color images, Compass American
Guides reveal the character and culture of more than
40 of America's most fascinating destinations. Perfect
for residents who want to explore their own backyards
and for visitors who want an insider's perspective
on the history, heritage, and all there is to see and do.

Fodor's COMPASS AMERICAN GUIDES

At bookstores everywhere.

⑯ **Tourist Information Office.** Just off Eyre Square, around the corner from the bus and train station and the Great Southern Hotel, this is the place to make reservations and find out about the latest happenings around town. ⊠ *1 Victoria Pl., Center,* ☎ *091/56–3081.* ⊙ *Weekdays 9–6, Sat. 9–1.*

㉖ **University College Galway (UCG).** Across the River Corrib, in the northwestern corner of the city, UCG was opened in 1846 to promote the development of local industry and agriculture, but today it's a center for Irish-language and Celtic studies. The Tudor-Gothic–style quadrangle, completed in 1848, is worth a visit, though much of the rest of the campus is architecturally undistinguished. Its library has an important archive of Celtic-language materials, and in July and August, it also hosts courses in Irish studies for overseas students. ⊠ *Newcastle Rd., University.*

Dining and Lodging

$$–$$$ ✕ **Kirwan's Lane Creative Cuisine.** Look for Mike O'Grady's stylish modern restaurant in a revamped alley at the river end of Quay Street. Blue-stained wooden tables, narrow floor-to-ceiling windows, and a quarry-tile floor set the stage for a sophisticated menu. Fresh prawn cocktail is served with sauce Marie-Rose and a passion-fruit mayo; confit of duck leg comes with braised red cabbage, star anise, and balsamic oil. Main courses have similarly unpredictable twists—rack of lamb comes with sweet potato mash, basil oil, and apricots, and on monkfish tails are a simple lemon and coriander dressing. ⊠ *Kirwan's La., Spanish Arch, Co. Galway,* ☎ *091/562–353. AE, DC, MC, V. Closed Sun.*

$$–$$$ ✕ **Nimmo's.** Swiss chef Stephan Zeltner, who established himself on the Galway scene with a small restaurant above Naughton's Pub, now cooks at this riverside location, in an old stone building, with a separately run wine bar downstairs. The long, spacious second-floor room has original paintings on the walls and well-spaced tables set with white linen. Zeltner prepares robust food, exemplified by panfried chicken breast with duck foie gras or noisettes of venison with apple and Calvados. ⊠ *The Long Walk, Spanish Arch, Co. Galway,* ☎ *091/563–565. AE, DC, MC, V. Closed Sun. No lunch.*

$$ ✕ **Malt House.** Hidden away in an alley off High Street in the center of old Galway, Barry and Therese Cunningham's bustling pub-restaurant has long been popular with both locals and visitors for good food served in informal surroundings. You can either eat in the bar itself or in the fancier main room (beamed ceilings; white, rough-cast walls; and chintz curtains) just off the bar. Fresh prawns panfried in garlic butter is popular; and the sirloin steak with green peppercorn sauce and the rack of lamb with a parsley crust should please landlubbers. ⊠ *Old Malte Arcade, High St., Center, Co. Galway,* ☎ *091/563–993. AE, DC, MC, V. Closed Sun. Oct.–Apr.*

$–$$ ✕ **McDonagh's Seafood Bar.** The McDonaghs are one of Galway's most entrepreneurial families, in charge of several hotels and this spot, a longtime town landmark. It underwent a major renovation, and is now partly a fish-and-chips bar and partly a "real" fish restaurant. If you haven't yet tried fish-and-chips, this is the place to start: cod, whiting, mackerel, haddock, or hake is deep-fried in a light batter while you watch. The fish is served with a heap of freshly cooked chips (french fries). Or try Galway oysters au naturel, or a bowl of mussels steamed in wine and garlic. ⊠ *22 Quay St., Spanish Arch, Co. Galway,* ☎ *091/565–001. DC, MC, V. No lunch Sun. Oct.–Apr.*

$ ✕ **Bridge Mills.** Renovations have altered this 400-year-old former grain mill beside the River Corrib into a restaurant and minimall. You can even sit outdoors beside a bubbling stream and watch local fishermen pulling salmon out of the river. Lunch fare includes fresh salads, sandwiches, and hot specials. The dinner menu is more substantial, with large steaks and vegetarian choices, such as spinach and ricotta cannelloni. ✉ *O'Brien's Bridge, Center, Co. Galway,* ☎ *091/566–231. AE, MC, V. No dinner Oct.–mid-May.*

$ ✕ **K. C. Blake's.** K. C. stands for Casey, as in owner-chef John Casey, who turned a medieval stone town house once associated with the Blake family—one of the families who founded Galway—into a dark, ultramodern eatery. Dishes range from traditional Irish beef-and-Guinness stew to funky combinations like black pudding croquettes with pear and cranberry sauce. ✉ *10 Quay St., Spanish Arch, Co. Galway,* ☎ *091/561–826. AE, MC, V.*

$$$–$$$$ ✕🖩 **Glenlo Abbey.** Despite the name, it wasn't a monastery at all, but was in fact a private home, built in 1740. The lobby resembles a gentlemen's club, with parquet floors, chesterfield sofas, and leatherbound books. The spacious bedrooms are in a newer wing and have Georgian-style furniture and king-size beds. The bathrooms have marble walls; some have whirlpool baths. The Pullman Restaurant, two *Orient Express* carriages installed in the grounds, offers a novel dining experience. Informal bar food is served in the Oak Cellar Bar. The hotel is surrounded by its own golf course, and is only five minutes outside the city on N59 Clifden road. ✉ *Bushy Park, Co. Galway,* ☎ *091/526–666,* 🖷 *091/527–800,* 🌐 *www.glenlo.com. 38 rooms with bath, 6 suites. 2 restaurants, 9-hole golf course, tennis court, sauna, fishing, bar. AE, DC, MC, V.*

$$$–$$$$ ✕🖩 **St. Cleran's.** A gorgeous Georgian mansion (35 km/21 mi east of Galway on the N6 Dublin road), and the home of director John Huston in the 1960s, St. Cleran's has been rather dramatically restored by its present owner, entertainer Merv Griffin. Subtlety is not Merv's strong point, and some visitors are overwhelmed by the deep-pile carpets and ubiquitous crystal chandeliers, while others find the furnishings, and the hedonistic luxury they evoke, highly enjoyable. Rooms are decorated with top-quality antiques. You can expect superb views of the rolling countryside, and excellent opportunities for country sports. The elegant, formal restaurant (reservations essential for nonresidents), offers such specialties as sea scallops and noisette of venison. ✉ *Craughwell, Co. Galway,* ☎ *091/846–555,* 🖷 *091/846–600,* 🌐 *www.merv.com/stclerans. 12 rooms with bath. Restaurant, miniature golf, fishing, horseback riding, bar. AE, MC, V.*

$ ✕🖩 **Cregg Castle.** On a 165-acre wildlife preserve about 15 km (9 mi) north of Galway on N17 (turn left for Corrandulla just beyond Claregalway), this 17th-century castle is pleasantly informal, despite its grand interior. This is due to the warm and laid-back greeting you receive from your hosts. The Brodericks, the owners, all play instruments; traditional sessions often take place around the huge log-and-turf fire in the Great Hall. Bedrooms, which vary in shape and size, are decorated mainly with sturdy Victorian bygones. Breakfast is served until noon around an antique dining table that seats 18 people. The restaurant is licensed to serve wine only; reservations for dinner should be made by 12 noon. ✉ *Tuam Rd., Corrandulla, Co. Galway,* ☎ 🖷 *091/ 791–434,* 🌐 *www.indigo.ie/~creggcas. 8 rooms, 7 with bath. Restaurant. AE, MC, V. Closed Nov.–Feb.*

$$$ 🖩 **Ardilaun House.** You'll adore this lovely 19th-century house at the ★ end of a tree-lined avenue in a quiet suburb, midway between the city center and the Salthill promenade. Open fires, fresh flower arrangements, and Regency-style furniture characterize the quiet public rooms overlooking the gardens. The individually designed bedrooms are dec-

orated with a pastel scheme and Irish-made mahogany furniture with brass trim. For views of the bay, book an even-numbered room on the top floor. Other rooms, which are just as pleasant, overlook the flower garden and a fountain. ⊠ *Taylor's Hill, Salthill, Co. Galway,* ☎ *091/ 521–433,* FAX *091/521–546,* WEB *www.ardilaunhousehotel.ie. 81 rooms with bath, 7 suites. Restaurant, indoor pool, health club, 2 bars. AE, DC, MC, V.*

$$$ ☒ **Galway Bay.** It's big and modern, but it's also restful and comfortable, with a panoramic view of Galway Bay. The facade of this giant at the quiet end of Salthill is divided into small-scale sections with peaked gables. The beach and the 1-km (½-mi) promenade, popular with joggers, are right across the road. About 70% of the rooms have a sea view; the rest overlook a quiet residential area. The color-coordinated rooms are sizeable, and have large windows and all-modern facilities, from minibars to in-room data ports. Advantages of staying 3 km (2 mi) outside town include hassle-free parking and quiet nights. ⊠ *The Promenade, Salthill, Co. Galway,* ☎ *091/520–520,* FAX *091/520–530,* WEB *www.galwaybayhotel.net. 148 rooms with bath, 2 suites. Restaurant, coffee shop, indoor pool, health club, sauna, steam room, fishing, bar. AE, DC, MC, V.*

$$–$$$$ ☒ **Galway Great Southern.** Built in 1845 to coincide with the arrival of the railway, and right on Eyre Square, this is still the best address in town. A pianist plays in the large lobby, which, like the two bars, is a popular gathering spot. All the guest rooms are decorated in tastefully muted, color-coordinated schemes, with Georgian-style tables and chairs. The deluxe rooms in the original building have tall ceilings and windows, and are particularly elegant, though those at the front directly above the bar can be noisy late into the night. Rooms in the back, on the fifth floor, have views of Galway Bay. French-Irish cuisine is served at the formal Oyster Room. ⊠ *Eyre Square, Co. Galway,* ☎ *091/564– 041,* FAX *091/566–704,* WEB *www.gsh.ie. 112 rooms with bath, 3 suites. Restaurant, indoor pool, sauna, 2 bars. AE, DC, MC, V.*

$ ☒ **Jurys Galway Inn.** Expect good-quality budget accommodation at this four-story hotel. Each room is big enough for three adults, or two adults and two children, and the fixed-price policy applies to all of them. The light, airy rooms have modern pine fittings, plain carpets and walls, double-glazed windows, and fully equipped bathrooms. Those overlooking the river are quieter than those in front. The atmosphere unavoidably tends toward anonymous-international, but the inn is central—at the foot of Galway's busy Quay Street, right on the banks of the Corrib—and the level of comfort is high for the price range. ⊠ *Quay St., Spanish Arch, Co. Galway,* ☎ *091/566–444,* FAX *091/568– 415,* WEB *www.jurys.com. 128 rooms with bath. Restaurant, bar, parking (fee). AE, DC, MC, V.*

$ ☒ **Norman Villa.** Dee and Mark Keogh's Victorian town house is
★ away from the bustle but within easy walking distance of both the city center and the seaside promenade of Salthill. Brightly painted walls, Victorian brass beds with Irish linen sheets, varnished floorboards, wooden shutters, and fun, offbeat paintings and artifacts characterize this lively, pleasant bed-and-breakfast. ⊠ *86 Lower Salthill, Salthill, Co. Galway,* ☎ FAX *091/521–131. 5 rooms with bath. Free parking. MC, V. Closed last 2 wks in Jan.*

Nightlife and the Arts

Because of its small size and concentration of pubs and restaurants, Galway can seem even livelier at 11 PM than it is at 11 AM. On weekends, when there are a lot of students and other revelers in town, Eyre Square and environs can be rowdy late at night after pub-closing time.

A YEAR-ROUND FLEADH

DUBLIN MAY BE THE POLITICAL capital of Ireland, but Galway is the center of its traditional-music universe, a place where you can hear this music all through the year, whether or not there's a *fleadh*, or traditional music festival, going on. **Galway City** and its environs have given birth to some of the most durable names in Irish music: De Danann, Arcady, singers Dolores and Seán Keane, and the mercurial accordion genius Mairtín O'Connor. Seán Ryan, acknowledged master of the tin whistle, has been playing every Sunday at **Crane's** for nearly 20 years. The hottest sessions these days take place at the **Cottage Bar** in Lower Salthill, where up-and-coming young musicians are drawn by the cozy atmosphere and the fine acoustics. In the city itself, there's still plenty of music to be found at old reliables such as **Tig Neaćhtain's, Taaffe's,** and **Aras na Gael.**

South of Galway the fishing village of **Kinvara** hosts the annual **Cuckoo Fleadh,** a small but growing festival that will turn 10 years old in 2003. Resident musicians like De Danann alumni Jackie Daly and Charlie Piggott play regularly at **Winkles Hotel,** where, in 1989, a very young and relatively unknown accordion player got together with a few friends for a casual recording session. The resulting album, *Sharon Shannon,* went platinum virtually overnight, becoming the most successful traditional-music recording ever released. Today, Shannon, who grew up on a farm outside Corofin, County Clare, and played her first accordion when she was 11, is one of Ireland's leading traditional Irish musicians.

Down the road, the lively market town of **Ennis** (where Shannon took lessons from local maestro Frank Custy) has come into its own, attracting a growing cadre of musicians: the Custys, Siobhán and Tommy Peoples, Josephine Marsh, P. J. King, flute player Kevin Crawford, and accordion whiz kid Murt Ryan, from Tipperary. Sessions take place at an ever-changing roster of pubs: **O'Halloran's Bar, Knox's** and, most notably, **Cruise's** are all hot venues. This last pub boasts an adjacent concert venue where a few years ago a group of local musicians recorded a lovely live album, *The Sanctuary Sessions.* Still available through stores specializing in traditional music, the album is an excellent introduction to Irish music, with the featured artists including most of the above-mentioned musicians as well as banjo player Mary Shannon and the wonderful Galway singer Seán Tyrrell. In May, Ennis is home to the **Fleadh Nua** festival—with concerts, competitions, workshops, and *ceilís* (Irish dancing and song).

On the plus side, if you've been staying out in the countryside and you're ready for a little nightlife, you're certain to find plenty of it here.

Festivals and Seasonal Events

Mid-April's **Cuirt Literary Festival** (☎ 091/565–886) brings in leading Irish and international writers for a week of readings and other events. The **Galway Arts Festival** (☎ 091/583–800), the city's premier annual event, spans the last two weeks in July, and includes drama, film, music, children's events, and a huge parade. At the end of September, the **Galway International Oyster Festival** (☎ 091/527–282) indulges visitors with the "food of the gods." The **Galway Races** at Ballybrit Race Course (to the north of town off N17) start the day after the Galway Arts Festival ends for a week of mad revelry.

Information on most festivals and events can be obtained from Galway's **Department of Arts, Heritage, Gaeltacht, and the Islands** (☎ 091/592–555, WEB www.ealga.ie).

Pubs and Other Nightspots

The best area for traditional music is the area between Eyre Square and the Spanish Arch. There's a big post-nightclub (open till 1 or 2) scene here—there are some clubs in town, but most everyone heads to Salthill, a small suburban community 3 km (2 mi) west of Galway. The main road, Upper Salthill, is lined with clubs. You will usually find a session after about 9 PM at **King's Head** (✉ 15 High St., Center, ☎ 091/566–630). **Paddy's** (✉ Prospect Hill, Eyre Square, ☎ 091/567–843) is a good place for a pint near the bus and train station. **Taaffe's** (✉ 19 Shop St., Center, ☎ 091/564–066) is in the midst of the shopping district and very busy on afternoons, and **Tig Neaćhtain's** (✉ 17 Cross St., Center, ☎ 091/568–820) is *the* place for music in Galway City and each visit will be an experience. **Aras na Gael** (✉ 45 Lower Dominick St., Spanish Arch, ☎ 091/526–509) is one of the few Irish-speaking pubs in the city center. **McSwiggan's** (✉ Eyre Square, ☎ 091/568–917) is a huge place with everything from church pews to ancient carriage lamps contributing to its eclectic character. **Roisin Dubh** (✉ Dominick St., Spanish Arch, ☎ 091/586–540) is a serious venue for emerging rock and traditional bands; it often showcases big, if still-struggling, talents.

For late-night sounds heard from the comfort of your own table, try **Sevn'th Heav'n Restaurant** (✉ Courthouse La., Quay St., Spanish Arch, ☎ 091/563–838), where blues and folk sounds pour forth from 11:30 PM onward. **Cuba** (✉ Eyre Square, ☎ 091/565–991), on three floors, draws diners and salsa lovers for Cuban cocktails and cigars to the beat of Latin music from DJs and live bands.

Galway's post-nightclub scene is formidable. In the center of town is **Central Park Disco** (✉ 36 Upperabbeygate St., Center, ☎ 091/565–974), popular with the twentysomething crowd. The cover hovers around €3.81–€6.35. The **GPO** (✉ Eglinton St., ☎ 091/563–073) is perhaps the most popular disco in Galway City; it's busy with students from the University. Try **Liquid** (☎ 091/722–715) in Salthill for nightly independent and techno music. **Warwick** (☎ 091/521–244) in Salthill plays '70s, '80s, and independent music, except for Sunday, when the dance-hall days return. Admission is €3.80–€9.50.

Theater

An Taibhdhearc (✉ Middle St., Center, ☎ 091/562–024), pronounced awn *tie*-vark, was founded in 1928 by Hilton Edwards and Micháel Macliammóir as the national Irish-language theater. It continues to produce first-class shows, mainly of Irish works in both the English and the Irish languages.

Close-Up

PUB ETIQUETTE

EVEN FOR VETERAN PUB-GOERS, there are still some aspects of Irish public house behavior that can perplex the most seasoned drinker. Most of these complexities come down to language and the way locals use it. Swear words that are little heard in other developed countries find liberal employ here. The Irish have always been experts at giving a sentence even greater poetry with the inclusion of one of these epithets—they have no intention of giving offense; it's simply another tool used to spin a good yarn.

Another source of amusement to outsiders is the rush to the counter when the owner flicks the lights to signify last call. Maybe their pubs close too early, maybe that final pint sipped amidst the publican's plaintive cry, "Have ye no homes to go to?," is the sweetest of them all. The round system is also, unfortunately, a mystery to many visitors. If you get into conversation with them, locals will automatically include you in the round—it's good manners as far as they're concerned, and the strongest means they have of saying "Good to meet you."

And finally, a word to the ladies: please remember that most Irishmen under the age of 85 are driven by an all-consuming desire to flirt outrageously with strangers. You'll hear poetry (Yeats continues to be the best-known aphrodisiac on the island) and sonnets; you might even see a man of 70 doing his version of a Gene Kelly tap dance on a rain-drenched street for a group of astonished women. You may want to play along with it, consider the whole thing another form of theater, and take it as good fun. After all, that's what Irish women have been doing for generations.

The **Druid Theatre** company (✉ Chapel La., Center, ☎ 091/568–617) is esteemed for its adventurous and accomplished productions, mainly of 20th-century Irish and European plays. The players perform at the Royal Court's small stage in London. When they're home, they usually appear at the Town Hall, and they host many productions during the Galway Arts Festival.

Macnas (✉ Fisheries Field, Salmon Weir Bridge, Center, ☎ 091/561–462) is an internationally renowned, Galway-based troupe of performance artists who have raised street theater to new levels. Their participation in the Galway Arts Festival's annual parade is always much anticipated.

Visual Arts and Galleries
Art Euro Gallery (✉ The Bridge Mills, O'Brien's Bridge, Spanish Arch, ☎ 091/562–884) has a collection of free-blown glass and unusual handmade ceramics by Irish and other European artists. High-quality work by local artists can be found at **Kenny's Bookshop & Art Galleries** (✉ High St., ☎ 091/562–739). The art gallery at **University College Galway** (☎ 091/524–411) has a number of exhibits each year.

Outdoor Activities and Sports

Bicycling
Set off to explore the Galway area, especially its coast, by renting a bike from **Mountain Trail Bike Shop** (✉ The Cornstore, Middle St., Center, ☎ 091/569–888).

Kart Racing

Take a short drive from the Galway city center and try **Galway Kart Racing** (⊠ Tuam Rd., ☎ 091/756–844). It's open seven days a week; you can pre-book.

Fishing

You can get fishing licenses, tackle, and bait and arrange to hire a traditional fly-fishing guide or book a sea-angling trip at **Freeny's Sports** (⊠ 19–23 High St., Center, ☎ 091/562–609). **Murt's** (⊠ 7 Daly's Pl., Woodquay, ☎ 091/561–018) can also handle your fishing needs.

Golf

Galway Bay Golf and Country Club (⊠ Renville, Oranmore, ☎ 091/790–500) is an 18-hole, par-72 parkland course, designed by Christy O'Connor Jr., on the shores of Galway Bay. The **Galway Golf Club** (⊠ Blackrock, Salthill, ☎ 091/522–033) is an 18-hole, par-71 course with excellent views of Galway Bay, the Burren, and the Aran Islands. Some of the fairways run close to the ocean.

River Cruising

A **Corrib Cruise** from Wood Quay (behind the Town Hall Theatre at the Rowing Club) is a lovely way to spend a fine afternoon; it lasts 1½ hours and travels 8 km (5 mi) up the River Corrib and about 6 km (4 mi) around Lough Corrib. You can also rent the boat for an evening. ☎ 091/592–447. ⊡ €7.60. ☉ May–Sept., daily at 2:30 and 4:30; July–Aug., daily at 12:30.

Tennis

There are nine courts at the **Galway Lawn Tennis Club** (⊠ Threadneedle St., Salthill, ☎ 091/522–353), available to nonmembers at €5.10 per hour.

Water Sports

Bow Waves (⊠ 11 Ashleigh Grove, Knockacarra, ☎ 091/591–481) schedules individually tailored trips around Galway Bay on high-performance inflatables. Life jackets and wet gear are included in the price. Ride the waves for thrills, or take it easy on a seal and dolphin watch. **Galway Bay Sailing Club** (⊠ Renville, Oranmore, ☎ 091/794–527) offers dinghy sailing and board sailing on Lough Corrib or on coastal waters. Instruction is also available.

Shopping

Bookstores

Charlie Byrne's Bookshop (⊠ The Cornstore, Middle St., Center, ☎ 091/561–766) sells a large, varied selection of used books and remainders. **Kenny's Bookshop & Art Galleries** (⊠ High St., Center, ☎ 091/562–739) has five floors of books on Irish topics, mainly secondhand and antiquarian, as well as prints, maps, and a small art gallery.

Clothing, Crafts, and Gifts

Don't miss **Design Concourse Ireland** (⊠ Kirwan's La., Center, ☎ 091/566–016), a spectacular one-stop shop for the best in Irish handcrafted design. **Design Ireland Plus** (⊠ The Cornstore, Middle St., Center, ☎ 091/567–716; ⊠ The Grainstore, Lower Abbeygate St., Center, ☎ 091/566–620) has an excellent range of contemporary Irish-made crafts and clothing. **Faller's Sweater Shop** (⊠ 25 High St., Center, ☎ 091/564–833; ⊠ 35 Eyre Sq., ☎ 091/561–255) has the choicest selection of Irish-made sweaters, competitively priced. **Meadows & Byrne** (⊠ Castle St., Center, ☎ 091/567–776) sells the best in modern household items. **O'Máille's** (⊠ 16 High St., Center, ☎ 091/562–696) carries Aran sweaters, handwoven tweeds, and classically tailored clothing.

Browse in **Treasure Chest** (✉ William St., Center, ☎ 091/563–862) for china, crystal, gifts, and classic clothing.

Jewelry

The **Claddagh Jewellers** (✉ Eyre Square, ☎ 091/562–310) has a wide selection of traditional Claddagh rings and other jewelry.

Malls

Slightly off the beaten path, the **Cornstore** (✉ Middle St., Center) has some stylish shops selling contemporary goods; the shops tend to be less crowded than their competitors on the main streets. On the southwest side of Eyre Square and imaginatively designed to incorporate parts of the old town walls, the **Eyre Square Shopping Centre** (✉ Eyre Square) offers a wide range of moderately priced clothing and household goods.

Music

Back2Music (✉ 30 Upper Abbeygate St., Center, ☎ 091/565–272) specializes in traditional Irish musical instruments, including the hand-held drum, the *bodhrán* (pronounced bau-rawn). **Mulligan** (✉ 5 Middle St. Court, Center, ☎ 091/564–961) carries more than 6,000 CDs, records, and cassettes, with a large collection of traditional Irish music.

Vintage Goods

Twice as Nice (✉ 5 Quay St., Spanish Arch, ☎ 091/566–332) sells a mix of new and vintage men's and women's clothing, linens, lace, and jewelry at reasonable prices.

THE ARAN ISLANDS

The Aran Islands—Inishmore, Inishmaan, and Inisheer—are remote western outposts of the ancient province of Connaught (though they are not the country's westernmost points; that honor belongs to the Blasket Islands). These three islands were once as barren as the limestone pavements of the Burren, of which they are a continuation. Today, the land is parceled into small, man-made fields surrounded by stone walls. The views from here are spectacular. Witness the uninterrupted expanse of the Atlantic on the western horizon; to the northeast, the Connemara coast and its Twelve Bens; and, to the southeast, County Clare's Burren and the Cliffs of Moher.

The islands have been populated for thousands of years. Nowadays the Irish-speaking inhabitants enjoy a daily air service to Galway (subsidized by the government), motorized curraghs, multichannel TVs, and all the usual modern home conveniences. Yet they have retained a distinctness from mainlanders, preferring simple home decor, very plain food, and tightly knit communities, like the hardy fisher and farming folk from whom they are descended. Crime is virtually unknown in these parts; at your B&B, you'll find no locks on the guest-room doors, and the front-door latch will be left open.

Many islanders have sampled life in Dublin or cities abroad but have returned to raise families, keeping the population stable at around 1,500. Through the years, the islands have also attracted writers and artists, including J. M. Synge (1871–1909), who learned Irish on Inishmaan and wrote about its people in his play *Riders to the Sea*. The film *Man of Aran*, made on Inishmore in 1932 by the American director Robert Flaherty, is a classic documentary recording the islanders' dramatic battles with sea and storm. (The film is shown in the Community Hall in Kilronan, Inishmore, every afternoon during July, August, and early September.)

The only hotel on the islands is on Inis Oírr, but there's no shortage of B&Bs, mostly in simple family homes. The best way to book is through the **Galway City TIO.** Each island has at least one wine-licensed restaurant serving plain home cooking. Most B&Bs will provide a packed lunch and an evening meal (called high tea) on request.

The best time to visit the islands is May and early June while the unusual, Burren-like flora is at its best and before the bulk of the approximately 200,000 annual visitors arrive.

Inis Mór (Inishmore)

29 *24 km (15 mi) south of Ros an Mhíl (Rossaveal), 48 km (30 mi) west of Galway Docks.*

With a population of 900, Inishmore is the largest of the islands and the closest to the Connemara coast. It's also the most commercialized, its appeal slightly diminished by road traffic. In the summer, ferries arriving at **Kilronan,** Inishmore's main village and port, are met by minibuses and pony and cart drivers, all eager to show visitors "the sights." More than 8 km (5 mi) long and about 3 km (2 mi) wide at most points, with an area of 7,640 acres, the island is just a little too large to explore comfortably on foot in a day. The best way to see it is really by bicycle; bring your own or rent one from one of the three vendors right near the quay. The **Aran Heritage Centre** explains the history and culture of the islanders, who for many years lived in virtual isolation from the mainland. ☎ *099/61355.* ▣ *€2.55.* ☼ *Apr.–Oct., daily 10–7.*

★ The main attraction on Inishmore is **Dún Aengus,** one of the finest prehistoric monuments in Europe, dating from about 2000 BC. Spectacularly set on the edge of a 300-ft cliff overlooking a sheer drop, the fort has defenses consisting of three rows of concentric circles. Who the builders were defending themselves against is a matter of conjecture. From the innermost rampart there's a great view of the island and the Connemara coast. In order to protect this fragile monument from erosion, visitors are asked to approach it only through the **visitor center,** which gives access to a 1-km (½-mi) uphill walk over uneven terrain, so wear sturdy footwear. ⊠ *Kilmurvey, 7 km (4 mi) west of Kilronan, Co. Galway,* ☎ *099/61010,* WEB *www.heritageireland.ie.* ▣ *€1.25.* ☼ *Mar.–Oct., daily 10–6; Nov.–Feb., daily 11:30–3:30.*

Lodging

$ 🏠 **Ard Einne Guesthouse.** Almost every window at this B&B on Inishmore looks out to the sea, making it the perfect place to de-stress. Because it's close to the beach and small town, it's a perfect base for exploring the Aran Islands. It's also considered a refuge for writers and artists—the public rooms and guest rooms are relaxed, with light-colored linens and walls paneled with blonde wood. Evening meals are available; they have a wine license. ⊠ *Kilronan, Co. Galway,* ☎ *099/61126,* FAX *099/61388,* WEB *www.dragnet-systems.ie/dira/ardeinne/. 14 rooms with bath. Beach, fishing, horseback riding. MC, V. Closed mid-Dec.–Feb.*

$ 🏠 **Kilmurvey House.** At the foot of Dún Aengus fort, about 6½ km (4 mi) from the quay and the airport (accessible by minibus), this rambling 200-year-old stone farmhouse is the first choice of many visitors to the island—about 60% of them American. ⊠ *Kilronan, Co. Galway,* ☎ *099/61218,* FAX *099/61397. 12 rooms with bath. Dining room. MC, V. Closed Nov.–Mar.*

Nightlife

The place to go for traditional music is the **American Bar** (⊠ Kilronan, ☎ 099/61130). **Joe Watty's** (⊠ Main Rd., ☎ 099/61155) is a good bet for traditional music virtually every night in summer. **Joe Mac's** (☎ 099/61248), right off the pier, is a good place for a pint while waiting for the ferry home.

Outdoor Activities and Sports

Bicycles can be rented from May through October from **Aran Bicycle Hire** (☎ 099/61132), **Burke and Mullin** (☎ 099/61402), and **Costello's** (☎ 099/61241). All three shops are located right off the ferry pier.

Inis Meáin (Inishmaan)

㉚ *3 km (2 mi) east of Inishmore.*

The middle island in both size and location, Inishmaan has a population of about 300 and can be comfortably explored on foot. In fact, you have no alternative if you want to reach the island's major antiquities: Conor Fort, a smaller version of Dún Aengus; the ruins of two early Christian churches; and a chamber tomb known as the Bed of Diarmuid and Grainne, dating from about 2000 BC. You can also take wonderful cliff walks above secluded coves. It's on Inishmaan that the traditional Aran lifestyle is most evident. Until the mid-1930s or so, Aran women dressed in thick, red-woolen skirts to keep out the Atlantic gales, while the men wore collarless jackets, baggy trousers made of homespun tweed with *pampooties* (hide shoes without heels, suitable for walking on rocks), and a wide, hand-plaited belt called a *crios* (pronounced krish). Most islanders still don hand-knitted Aran sweaters, though nowadays they wear them with jeans and sneakers.

Inis Oirr (Inisheer)

㉛ *4 km (2½ mi) east of Inishmaan, 8 km (5 mi) northwest of Doolin.*

The smallest and flattest of the islands, Inisheer can be explored on foot in an afternoon, though if the weather is fine you may be tempted to linger on the long, sandy beach between the quay and the airfield. In the summer, Inisheer's population of 300 is augmented by high school students from all over Ireland attending the Gaeltacht, or Irish-language, school. Only one stretch of road, about 500 yards long, links the airfield and the village.

It's worth making a circuit of the island to get a sense of its utter tranquility. A maze of footpaths runs between the high stone walls that divide the fields, which are so small that they can support only one cow each, or two to three sheep. Those that are not cultivated or grazed turn into natural wildflower meadows between June and August, overrun with harebells, scabious, red clover, oxeye daisies, saxifrage, and tall grasses. It seems almost a crime to walk here—but how can you resist taking a rest in the corner of a sweet-smelling meadow on a sunny afternoon, sheltered by high stone walls with no sound but the larks above and the wind as it sifts through the stones? "The back of the island," as Inisheer's uninhabited side facing the Atlantic is called, has no beaches, but people still swim off the rocks.

The **Church of Kevin,** signposted to the southeast of the quay, is a small, early Christian church that gets buried in sand by storms every winter. Every year the islanders dig it out of the sand for the celebration of St. Kevin's Day on June 14. A pleasant walk through the village takes you up to **O'Brien's Castle,** a ruined 15th-century tower on top of a rocky hill—the only hill on the island.

Lodging

$ ▦ **Hotel Inisheer.** A pleasant, modern low-rise in the middle of the island's only village, a few minutes' walk from the quay and the airstrip, this simple, whitewashed building with a slate roof and half-slated walls has bright, plainly furnished rooms. The five newer rooms are slightly larger than the other 10. The restaurant (open to nonguests) is the best bet on the island, although much of the food is imported frozen. ⊠ *Lurgan Village, Co. Galway,* ☎ *099/75020,* 𝗙𝗔𝗫 *099/75099. 15 rooms, 12 with bath. Restaurant, bicycles, bar. AE, DC, MC, V. Closed Oct.–Mar.*

THROUGH CONNEMARA AND COUNTY MAYO

Bordered by the long expanse of Lough Corrib on the east and the jagged coast of the Atlantic on the west is the rugged, desolate region of western County Galway, known as Connemara. Like the American West, it's an area of spectacular, almost myth-making geography—of glacial lakes; gorgeous, silent mountains; lonely roads; and hushed, uninhabited boglands. The Twelve Bens, "the central glory of Connemara," as author Brendan Lehane has called them, together with the Maamturk Mountains to their north, lord proudly over the area's sepia boglands. More surprisingly, stands of Scotch pine, Norwegian spruce, Douglas fir, and Japanese Sitka grow in Connemara's valleys and up hillsides—the result of a concerted national project that has so far reforested 9% of Ireland. In the midst of this wilderness, you'll find few people, for Connemara's population is sparse even by Irish standards. Especially in the off-season, you're far more likely to come across sheep strolling its roads than another car.

Two main routes—one inland, the other coastal—lead through Connemara. To take the inland route described below, leave Galway City on the well-signposted outer-ring road and follow signs for N59—Moycullen, Oughterard, and Clifden. If you choose to go the coastal route, you'll travel due west from Galway City to Rossaveal on R336 through Salthill, Barna, and Spiddle—all in the heart of the West's strong Gaeltacht, home to roughly 40,000 Irish speakers. Although this is one of the most impressive and unspoiled coastal roads in Ireland, it has been scarred by modern one-story concrete homes—a sort of faux-Spanish hacienda style favored by locals. (Most of the traditional thatched houses in the West are now used as vacation homes.) You can continue north on R336 from Rossaveal to Maam Cross and then head for coastal points west, or pick up R340 and putter along the coast.

Oughterard

🟢 *27 km (17 mi) northwest of Galway City on N59.*

Small and pretty Oughterard (pronounced *ook*-ter-ard) is the main village on the western shores of **Lough Corrib** and one of Ireland's leading angling resorts. The lough is signposted to the right in the village center, less than 1½ km (1 mi) up the road. From mid-June to early September, local boatmen offer trips on the lough, which has several islands. It is also possible to take a boat trip to Cong, at the north shore of the lough. Midway between Oughterard and Cong, **Inchagoill Island** (the Island of the Stranger), a popular destination for a half-day trip, has several early Christian church remains. The cost of boat rides is negotiable; expect to pay about €7.60 per person.

Lodging

$–$$ ⚏ **Connemara Gateway.** This modern low-rise with traditional, gray-slate roofs above whitewashed walls combines the best of the old and the new. With a nod to the classic Irish cottage, the lobby and bar are decorated with wooden and cast-iron artifacts and chintz sofas. Guest rooms have modern furniture and floral wall panels with matching drapes. All have sitting areas beside the large teak-framed windows, which overlook the gardens and the distant hills. There's a strong tour-bus trade, but it doesn't spoil the charming atmosphere. The hotel is about 1 km (½ mi) outside the village on the Galway side of N59. ⌧ *Co. Galway,* ☎ *091/552–328,* ℻ *091/552–332,* ⣿ *www.iol. ie/bizpark/s/sinnott. 62 rooms with bath. Restaurant, tennis court, indoor pool, sauna, fishing, bar. AE, DC, MC, V. Closed Dec.–mid-Feb.*

$–$$ ⚏ **Ross Lake House.** The enthusiastic Henry and Elaine Reid manage this low-key country hideaway—well off the beaten track—near a stream and surrounded by five acres of colorful gardens. The Georgian house has a comfortably furnished interior—Victorian antiques and welcoming open fires. Guest rooms in the converted stables are simpler and a little smaller than those in the house, but all have peaceful garden views. A table d'hôte dinner menu offers good-quality, plain country-house cooking. The house is 5 km (3 mi) from Oughterard. ⌧ *Rosscahill, Co. Galway,* ☎ ℻ *091/550–109,* ⣿ *www.iol.ie/green-book-of-ireland. 13 rooms with bath. Restaurant, tennis court, fishing, horseback riding, bar. AE, DC, MC, V. Closed Nov.–mid-Mar.*

Nightlife

For good music try **Faherty's** (☎ 091/552–194).

Outdoor Activities and Sports

Oughterard Golf Club (☎ 091/552–131) has an 18-hole, par-70 parkland course suitable for novices and others who wish to improve their game.

En Route As you continue northwest from Oughterard on N59, you'll soon pass a string of small lakes on your left; their shining blue waters reflecting the blue sky are a typical Connemara sight on a sunny day. Sixteen kilometers (10 mi) northwest of Oughterard, the continuation of the coast road (R336) meets N59 at **Maam Cross** in the shadow of Leckavrea Mountain. Once an important meeting place for the people of north and south Connemara, it's still the location of a large monthly cattle fair. Walkers will find wonderful views of Connemara by heading for any of the local peaks visible from the road. Beyond Maam Cross, some of the best scenery in Connemara awaits on the road to **Recess,** 16 km (10 mi) west of Maam Cross on N59. At many points on this drive, a short walk away from either side of the main road will lead you to the shores of one of the area's many small loughs. Stop and linger if the sun is out—even intermittently—for the light filtering through the clouds gives splendor to the distant, dark-gray mountains and creates patterns on the brown-green moorland below. In June and July, it stays light until 11 PM or so, and it is worth taking a late-evening stroll to see the sun's reluctance to set. In Recess, **Joyce's** (☎ 095/34604) carries a good selection of contemporary ceramics, handwoven shawls, books of Irish interest, original paintings, and small sculptures.

Cong

❸❸ *23 km (14 mi) northeast of Maam Cross on N59.*

On a narrow isthmus between Lough Corrib and Lough Mask on the County Mayo border, the pretty, old-world village of Cong, near Maam Cross, is dotted with ivy-covered thatched cottages and dilapidated farmhouses. Cong is surrounded by many stone circles and burial mounds, but its most notable ruins are those of the **Augustine Abbey** (✉ Abbey St., ☎ no phone), dating from the early 13th century and still exhibiting some finely carved details. It can be seen overlooking a river near fabulous Ashford Castle.

Cong's 15 minutes of fame came in 1952, when John Ford filmed *The Quiet Man*, one of his most popular films, here; John Wayne plays a prizefighter who goes home to Ireland to court the fiery Maureen O'Hara. (Pauline Kael called the film "fearfully Irish and green and hearty.") The **Quiet Man Heritage Cottage,** in the village center, is an exact replica of the cottage used in the film, with reproductions of the furniture and costumes, a few original artifacts, and pictures of Barry Fitzgerald and Maureen O'Hara on location. ☎ 092/46089. ▦ €3.17. ☻ *Mar.–Nov., daily 10–6.*

Lodging

$$$–$$$$ ⊡ **Ashford Castle.** Built in 1870 for the Guinness family in a mock-
★ Gothic baronial style, this massive, flamboyantly turreted and crenellated castle incorporates an earlier 1228 structure built by the De Burgos family. Now American owned, Ashford is one of Ireland's most luxurious castle-hotels. Large paintings in gilt frames hang from the castle's carved stone walls above polished-wood paneling, illuminated by crystal chandeliers. Deluxe rooms have generous sitting areas, heavily carved antique furniture, and extra-large bathrooms. The suites are vast, furnished with Georgian antiques, and blissfully comfortable. ✉ Co. Mayo, ☎ 092/46003, FAX 092/46260, WEB *www.ashford.ie. 72 rooms with bath, 11 suites. 2 restaurants, 9-hole golf course, 2 tennis courts, health club, boating, fishing, bicycles, horseback riding, 2 bars. AE, DC, MC, V.*

Cashel

❸ *8 km (5 mi) south of Recess on R340, 49½ km (31 mi) west of Cong.*

Cashel is a quiet, extremely sheltered angling center at the head of Bertraghboy Bay. General de Gaulle is among the many people who have sought seclusion here. A word of caution in this area: stray sheep, bolting Connemara ponies, cyclists, and reckless local drivers are all regular hazards on the narrow mountain roads hereabouts.

Dining and Lodging

$$–$$$ ✕⊡ **Cashel House.** Secluded on 40 acres of woodlands at the head of
★ Cashel Bay—with exotic shrubs flowering and Connemara ponies grazing out back—this luxurious country house has possibly more antiques and curios than any other hotel in Ireland. Intricately carved tables, Biedermeier bureaus, gilt mirrors, Georgian bookcases, and ormolu clocks are scattered around the public rooms; more antiques turn up in the bedrooms, which have king-size beds (canopied in the 13 minisuites). Front rooms have views of the sea. The table d'hôte menu in the dining room has more choices than most country houses and is strong on fresh local seafood. ✉ Co. Galway, ☎ 095/31001, FAX 095/31077, WEB *www.cashel-house-hotel.com. 19 rooms with bath, 13 suites. Restaurant, tennis court, beach, boating, fishing, bicycles, horseback riding. AE, DC, MC, V. Closed mid-Jan.–mid-Feb.*

$ ⊡ **Zetland Country House.** Built for the Earl of Zetland on a hill overlooking secluded Cashel Bay, John and Mona Prendergast's mid-Victorian hunting lodge offers an unforgettable experience. Large old trees, wooded grounds, and flowering shrubs set the scene. A dining room with massive antique sideboards adorned with family silver overlooks the bay, as does the large and blissfully serene sitting room. Bedrooms are large and many have sea views, but those with garden views are also attractive. The comfortable quarters are elegantly furnished with Georgian and Victorian antiques of polished mahogany. ⊠ *Co. Galway,* ☎ *095/31111,* FAX *095/31117,* WEB *www.connemara.net/zetland/. 19 rooms with bath. Restaurant, tennis court, fishing, bar. AE, DC, MC, V. Closed Nov.–mid-Apr.*

Outdoor Activities and Sports

Cashel Equestrian Center (⊠ Cashel House, ☎ 095/31001) offers scenic treks and the chance to ride a Connemara pony on its home ground.

Ballynahinch

③⑤ *10 km (6 mi) west of Cashel on R341.*

Along the shores of Ballynahinch Lake you'll see more forested country. Woodland in this part of Ireland indicates the proximity of a "big house" whose owner can afford to plant trees for pleasure and prevent their being cut down for fuel.

Lodging

$$–$$$$ 🏰 **Ballynahinch Castle.** It was built in the late 18th century on the
★ Owenmore River amid 40 walkable wooded acres, and was once the home of Richard Martin (1754–1834), known as "Humanity Dick," and the founder of the Royal Society for the Prevention of Cruelty to Animals. The tiled lobby with Persian rugs has two inviting leather chesterfields in front of an open fire. The biggest bedrooms, in the ground-floor wing, have four-poster beds, and floor-to-ceiling windows overlooking the river. Rooms in the old house are equally comfortable and quiet. The castle is signposted off N59 between Recess and Clifden. ⊠ *Recess, Co. Galway,* ☎ *095/31006,* FAX *095/31085,* WEB *www. commerce.ie/ballynahinch/. 20 rooms with bath, 10 suites. Restaurant, tennis court, fishing, croquet, horseback riding, bar. AE, DC, MC, V. Closed last wk of Dec. and Feb.*

OFF THE
BEATEN PATH
From Ballynahinch, take the N59 to the small seaside town of Roundstone, where you'll find the delightful **Roundstone Musical Instruments.** Owner Malachy Kearns has been handcrafting *bodhráns* (Irish drums) at this music shop and museum for 24 years. The workshop is an old Franciscan monastery with a beautiful bell tower. Besides the bodhráns, you can buy traditional CDs, books, and coffee—and you can also expect a good chat. As Ireland's only bodhrán maker, Malachy, who has even been on an Irish stamp commemorating Irish music, has been commissioned to make drums for Christy Moore, the Chieftains, and the Riverdance Ensemble. If you wish, you can have your drum hand-painted with your family crest, a Celtic design, or your initials while you wait. ⊠ *I.D.A. Craftcenter, Roundstone, Co. Galway,* ☎ *095/35808,* FAX *095/ 35980,* WEB *www.bodhran.com.* ☉ *May–June and Sept.–Oct. daily 9:30–6; July–Aug. daily 9–7; Nov.–April 9:30–6 Mon.–Sat..*

Clifden

★ ③⑥ *23 km (14 mi) west of Recess, 79 km (49 mi) northwest of Galway City on N59.*

With roughly 1,100 residents, Clifden would be called a village by most, but in these parts it's looked on as something of a metropolis. It is far and away the prettiest town in Connemara, as well as its unrivaled "capital." Clifden's first attraction is its location—perched high above Clifden Bay on a forested plateau, its back to the spectacular Twelve Ben Mountains. The tapering spires of the town's two churches add to its alpine feel. A selection of small restaurants, lively bars with music most nights in the summer, pleasant accommodations, and excellent walks make the town a popular base. It's quiet out of season, but in July and August crowds flock here, especially for August's world-famous **Connemara Pony Show.** Horse breeders come from around the world to check out Ireland's finest yearlings and stallions. Clifden's popularity, which has led to a chaotic one-way traffic system and loud techno music blasting out of certain bars, means that if you're over 25 and value your peace and quiet, you'd best choose a base outside town.

A 2-km (1-mi) walk along the beach road through the grounds of the ruined **Clifden Castle** is the best way to explore the seashore. The castle was built in 1815 by John D'Arcy, the town's founder, who laid out the town's wide main street on a long ridge with a parallel street below it. D'Arcy was High Sheriff of Galway, and his greatest wish was to establish a center of law and order in what he saw as the lawless wilderness of Connemara. Before the founding of Clifden, the interior of Connemara was largely uninhabited, with most of its population clinging to the seashore. Take the aptly named **Sky Road** to really appreciate Clifden's breathtakingly scenic setting. Signposted at the west end of town, this high, narrow circuit of about 5 km (3 mi) heads west to Kingstown, skirting Clifden Bay's precipitous shores.

Dining and Lodging

$$ ✕ **Destry's.** Owned by Paddy and Julia Foyle of Quay House, this upbeat town-center eatery on two floors is named for the Marlene Dietrich film *Destry Rides Again*. It's decorated with film memorabilia and local bric-a-brac—look for the skull that sits on top of a Georgian fanlight. The menu is similarly unpredictable, eclectic with a strong Mediterranean influence. There are plenty of pasta dishes, but most diners choose from pork and lamb dishes and chicken dishes which change nightly, making use of unique spices. The signature dessert is "Lethal Chocolate Pud," made from a carefully guarded secret recipe. ✉ *The Square, Co. Galway,* ☎ *095/21722. MC, V. Closed Mon. and Nov.–mid-Mar.*

$$ ✕ **O'Grady's Seafood.** A Clifden institution, this intimate, town-center restaurant serves fresh local produce, primarily seafood, in a style that's more modish than you might expect in the wilds of Connemara. Once a shop, the small main room is decorated in dark pinks and reds with wrought-iron dividers between the tables. Typical main courses might include a duo of monkfish and blackened scallops on a cilantro duxelles with two sauces, or crisp breast of duckling with sweet caramelized onions. ✉ *Market St., Co. Galway,* ☎ *095/21450. MC, V. Closed Sun. and Nov.–Apr.*

$ ✕🛏 **Erriseask House.** The rambling, two-story modern house has its
★ own private beach along the rocky shore of Mannin Bay. Warm wooden floors, well-crafted furniture, and an admirable lack of clutter create a restful and very comfortable interior. Chef David Ryan has won many awards for his fine cooking, which is planned daily. Freshly turf-smoked filet of beef is a house specialty. ✉ *Ballyconneely, Co. Galway,* ☎ *095/ 23553,* 🖷 *095/23639,* 🌐 *www.erriseask.connemara-ireland.com. 12 rooms with bath. Restaurant. AE, DC, MC, V. Closed Oct.–May.*

$ ✕🛏 **Rock Glen Manor House.** Cross the bridge at the west end of
★ town and walk ⅘ km (½ mi) down the R341 Roundstone road to get to John and Evangeline Roche's beautifully converted shooting lodge, built in 1815. Riding boots and tennis rackets in the hall make this feel more like a private home than a top-class hotel. A turf fire warms the large, sunny drawing room, with plump white armchairs, magazines, books, and board games. Guest rooms are nicely furnished with fluffy mohair or chintz bedspreads. In the Victorian-style restaurant,

you can expect such dishes as roasted rack of lamb with an herb crust and mushroom duxelles. ✉ *Co. Galway,* ☎ *095/21035,* FAX *095/21737,* WEB *www.connemara.net/rockglen-hotel. 29 rooms with bath. Restaurant, tennis court, fishing, horseback riding, bar. AE, DC, MC, V. Closed mid-Dec.–mid-Feb. No lunch.*

$ ⊞ **Abbeyglen Castle Hotel.** Amid gardens with waterfalls and streams, the hotel is at the foot of the Twelve Bens. Abbeyglen was built in 1832 by John D'Arcy, who also built Clifden Castle. Each guest room is uniquely decorated with heavy, ornate, dark wood furniture and rich colors befitting a castle. Although it's in a very quiet and seemingly remote location, the hotel becomes busy during afternoon tea, which is complimentary. On the weekends, the Abbeyglen is the best place in town for traditional music. ✉ *Sky Rd., Clifden, Co. Galway,* ☎ *095/ 21201,* FAX *095/21797,* WEB *www.abbeyglen.ie. 29 rooms with bath. Restaurant, tennis court, pool, sauna, fishing, horseback riding, bar. AE, MC, V. Closed mid-Jan.–Mar.*

$ ⊞ **Quay House.** A roaring turf fire in the sitting room greets you at this three-story Georgian house, Clifden's oldest building (1820). It's a short walk from the busy town center, and an oasis of calm beside the harbor quay. Rooms are unusually spacious, and those in the main house are imaginatively decorated with deep-color walls and witty bygones; all but one have sea views. There are also seven studio rooms with balconies overlooking the harbor. Proprietors Julia and Patrick Foyle tucked in homey touches, such as books and model boats. ✉ *Connemara, Co. Galway,* ☎ *095/21369,* FAX *095/21608,* WEB *www.thequayhouse.com. 14 rooms with bath. Some kitchenettes, fishing. MC, V. Closed Nov.–mid-Mar., except by arrangement.*

Nightlife

Abbeyglen Castle (✉ Sky Rd., ☎ 095/21201) has sessions in the bar most nights from June to September and occasional visits by big-name acts.

Outdoor Activities and Sports

BICYCLING

Explore Connemara by renting a bike from **John Mannion & Son** (✉ Railway View, ☎ 095/21160).

GOLF

On a dramatic stretch of Atlantic coastline, the 18-hole, par-72 course at the **Connemara Golf Club** (✉ Ballyconneely, south of Clifden, ☎ 095/ 23502) measures 7,174 yards.

HORSEBACK RIDING

Errislannan Manor Connemara Pony Stud and Riding Center (☎ 095/ 21134) provides mountain treks, instruction, and courses for children.

Shopping

Millar's Connemara Tweeds (✉ Main St., ☎ 095/21038) is a general art-and-crafts gallery with a good selection of traditional tweeds and hand knits. The **Station House Courtyard** (✉ Old Railway Station, ☎ 095/21699) is a newly restored cobbled courtyard with crafts studios and top designer-wear outlets.

En Route   Continue toward Letterfrack through the **Inagh Valley,** which is flanked by two impressive mountain ranges with distinctive, conical-shape peaks, rising almost directly—without any foothills—to over 1,968 ft.

Letterfrack

③⑦ *14 km (9 mi) north of Clifden on the N59.*

The 5,000-acre **Connemara National Park** lies southeast of the village of Letterfrack. Its **visitor center** covers the area's history and ecology, particularly the origins and growth of peat—and presents the depressing statistic that more than 80% of Ireland's peat, 5,000 years in the making, has been destroyed in the last 90 years. You can also get details on the many excellent walks and beaches in the area. ☎ *095/ 41054. ⊠ Park free, visitor center €2.55. ⊗ Park freely accessible; visitor center Apr.–May and Sept.–mid-Oct., daily 10–5:30; June, daily 10–6:30; July–Aug., daily 9:30–6:30.*

Dining and Lodging

$–$$ ✕☵ **Renvyle House.** A lake at its front door, the Atlantic Ocean at its back door, and the mountains of Connemara as a backdrop make for an enthralling setting for this hotel 8 km (5 mi) north of Letterfrack. Once the retreat of the man of letters Oliver St. John Gogarty of Dublin, Renvyle's is rustic and informal; it has exposed beams and brickwork, and numerous open turf fires. All the comfortable guest rooms, elegantly decorated in a floral style, have breathtaking views. The softly lit restaurant's table d'hôte menu is based on traditional Irish fare. ⊠ *Renvyle, Co. Galway,* ☎ *095/43511,* ☏ *095/43515,* 🕸 *www.renvyle.com. 65 rooms with bath. Restaurant, 9-hole golf course, 2 tennis courts, pool, fishing, horseback riding, bar. AE, DC, MC, V. Closed Jan.–Feb.*

$ ✕☵ **Rosleague Manor.** Anne and Patrick Foyle's pink, creeper-clad,
★ two-story Georgian house occupies 30 lovely acres overlooking Ballinakill Bay and the mountains of Connemara. Inside, the clutter of walking and shooting sticks beneath the grandfather clock in the hall sets the informal tone. The solidly comfortable bedrooms are furnished with well-used antiques, four-poster or large brass bedsteads, and drapes that match the William Morris wallpaper. The best rooms are at the front on the first floor, overlooking the bay. At dinner in the superb restaurant, baked monkfish with crispy capers and balsamic vinegar is a typical entrée. ⊠ *Co. Galway,* ☎ *095/41101,* ☏ *095/41168,* 🕸 *www.rosleague.com. 16 rooms with bath. Restaurant, tennis court, sauna, horseback riding, bar. AE, MC, V. Closed Nov.–Mar.*

Nightlife

For traditional music, try the **Bards' Den** (⊠ Main St., Letterfrack, ☎ 095/41042).

Outdoor Activities and Sports

Little Killary Adventure Center (⊠ Salruck, Renvyle, Co. Galway, ☎ 095/43411) provides sailing and windsurfing instruction on sheltered, coastal waters.

Shopping

Connemara Handcrafts (☎ 095/41058), on the N59, carries an extensive selection of crafts and women's fashions made by the stellar Avoca Handweavers; there's also a quaint coffee shop.

Kylemore Valley

③⑧ *6½ km (4 mi) between Letterfrack and the intersection of N59 and R344.*

One of the more conventionally beautiful stretches of road in Connemara passes through Kylemore Valley, which is between the Twelve Bens to the south and the naturally forested Dorruagh Mountains to the north. Kylemore (the name is derived from Coill Mór, Irish for "big wood") looks "as though some colossal giant had slashed it out with a couple of strokes from his mammoth sword," as John FitzMaurice Mills has

★   written. **Kylemore Abbey,** one of the most photographed castles in all of Ireland, is visible across a reedy lake with a backdrop of wooded hillside. The vast Gothic Revival, turreted, gray-stone castle was built as a private home between 1861 and 1868 by Mitchell Henry, a member of Parliament for County Galway, and his wife, Margaret, who had fallen in love with the spot during a carriage ride while on their honeymoon. The Henrys spared no expense—the final bill for their house is said to have come to £1.5 million—and employed mostly local laborers, thereby abetting the famine relief effort (this area was among the worst hit in all of Ireland). In 1920, nuns from the Irish Abbey of the Nuns of St. Benedict, fleeing their abbey in Belgium during World War I, eventually sought refuge in Kylemore, which had been through a number of owners and decades of decline after the Henrys. Still in residence today, the Benedictine nuns now run a girls' boarding school here. Three reception rooms and the main hall are open to the public, as are a crafts center and simple cafeteria. An exhibition and video explaining the history of the house can be viewed year-round at the abbey, and the grounds, which include a 6-acre walled Victorian garden, are freely accessible most of the year. Ask at the crafts shop for directions to the **Gothic Chapel** (a five-minute walk from the abbey), a tiny replica of Norwich Cathedral built by the Henrys. (Norwich was built by the English Benedictines, in a felicitous anticipation of Kylemore's fate.) ⊠ *About ¾ km (½ mi) back from the Kylemore Valley road, Co. Galway,* ☎ *095/41146,* WEB *www.kylemoreabbey.com.* ✉ *Chapel free, exhibition €3.80, garden €3.80.* ☉ *Crafts shop Mar. 17–Nov., daily 10–6; cafeteria Easter–Nov., daily 9:30–6; grounds Easter–Nov., daily 9–dusk; exhibition and garden Easter–Nov., daily 9–5:30.*

En Route   Beyond Kylemore, N59 travels for some miles alongside **Killary Harbour,** a narrow fjord (the only one in Ireland) that runs for 16 km (10 mi) between County Mayo's Mweelrea Mountains to the north and County Galway's Dorruagh Mountains to the south. The harbor has an extremely safe anchorage, 13 fathoms (78 ft) deep for almost its entire length and sheltered from storms by mountain walls. The rafts floating in Killary Harbour belong to fish-farming consortia who artificially raise salmon and trout in cages beneath the water. This is a matter of some controversy all over the West. Although some people welcome the employment opportunities, others bemoan the visual blight of the rafts. **Sea Cruise Connemara** (⊠ Nancy's Point, 2 km [1 mi] west of Leenane on the N59 Clifden road, Co. Galway, ☎ 091/566–736) runs 1½-hour trips around Killary Harbour in an enclosed launch with seating for 120 passengers, plus a bar and restaurant, from mid-April through mid-October.

Leenane

🟢 *18 km (12 mi) east of Letterfrack on N59.*

Nestled idyllically at the foot of the Maamturk Mountains and overlooking the tranquil waters of Killary Harbour, Leenane is a tiny village noted for its role as the setting for the film *The Field,* which starred Richard Harris. Its name appears in Martin McDonagh's *Leenane Trilogy,* an unflattering view of rural Irish life featuring a cast of tragi-comic grotesques. However, although it was an international hit for Galway's Druid Theatre Company, it brought a renown that the people of Leenane presumably could have done without. Leenane's **Cultural Centre** in the center of the small town, illustrates the traditional industry of North Connemara and West Mayo. More than 20 breeds of sheep graze around the house, and there are live demonstrations of carding, spinning, weaving, and the dyeing of wool with natural plant dyes. ☎ 095/42323. ⌨ €3.15. ⊙ Apr.–June and Oct., daily 9:30–7; July–Aug., daily 9–7.

Lodging

$$
★ 🏠 **Delphi Lodge.** In the heart of what is arguably Mayo's most spectacular mountain and lake scenery, 3 miles East of Leenane off N59, this attractive Georgian sporting lodge with a lovely lakeside setting is heavily stocked with fishing paraphernalia. Owners Peter and Jane Mantle are gracious hosts and valuable storehouses of information and stories. The bright, spacious bedrooms, some with lake views, have pine furniture, floral curtains, and wonderfully comfortable beds. Guests dine together; there is an excellent wine list and a self-service bar. ✉ Leenane, Co. Mayo, ☎ 095/42222, FAX 095/42296, WEB www.delphilodge.ie. 12 rooms with bath, 5 seasonal cottages (3-day minimum). Dining room, lounge, fishing, billiards, library. AE, MC, V. Closed mid-Dec.–mid-Jan.

En Route You have two options for traveling onward to Westport. The first is to take the direct route on N59. The second is to detour through the **Doolough Valley** between the Mweelrea Mountains (to the west) and the Sheeffry Hills (to the east) and on to Westport via Louisburgh (on the southern shore of Clew Bay). This latter route adds about 24 km (15 mi) to the trip, but devotees of this part of the West claim that it will take you through the region's most impressive, unspoiled stretch of scenery. If you opt for the longer route, turn left onto R335 1½ km (1 mi) beyond Leenane. Just after this turn, you'll hear the powerful rush of the Aasleagh Falls. You can park over the bridge, stroll along the river's shore, and soak in the splendor of the surrounding mountains.

Look out as you travel north for the great bulk of 2,500-ft **Croagh Patrick**; its size and conical shape make it one of the West's most distinctive landmarks. On clear days a small white building is visible at its summit (it stands on a ½-acre plateau), as is the wide path that ascends to it. The latter is the **Pilgrim's Path,** which about 25,000 people, many of them barefoot, follow each year to pray to St. Patrick in the oratory on its peak. St. Patrick spent the 40 days and nights of Lent here during the period he was converting Ireland to Christianity. The traditional date for the pilgrimage is the last Sunday in July; in the past, the walk was made at night, with pilgrims carrying burning torches, but that practice has been discontinued. The climb can be made in about three hours (round-trip) on any fine day and is well worth it for the magnificent views of the islands of Clew Bay, the Sheeffry Hills to the south (with the Bens visible behind them), and the peaks of Mayo to the north. The climb starts at Murrisk, a village about 8 km (5 mi) before Westport on the R335 Louisburgh road.

Westport

★ ❹⓿ 32 km (20 mi) north of Leenane on R335.

By far the most attractive town in County Mayo, Westport is on an inlet of Clew Bay, a wide expanse of sea dotted with islands and framed by mountain ranges. The architect James Wyatt planned the town in the late 18th century when he was employed to finish nearby Westport House. Westport's streets radiate from its central **Octagon,** where an old-fashioned farmers' market is held on Thursday mornings; look for work clothes, harnesses, tools, and children's toys for sale. Traditional shops—ironmongers, drapers, and the like—dot the streets that lead to the Octagon, while a riverside mall is lined with tall lime trees. The town is a popular fishing center and has several good beaches close by.

At Westport's Quay, about 2 km (1 mi) outside town, a large warehouse has been attractively restored as holiday apartments, and there are some good bars and decent restaurants; its central attraction, however, is **Westport House,** a stately home built on the site of an earlier castle. The house was begun in 1730 to the designs of Richard Castle, added to in 1778, and completed in 1788 by architect James Wyatt for the marquess of Sligo. The rectangular, three-story house is furnished with late-Georgian and Victorian pieces. Family portraits by Opie and Reynolds, old Irish silver, and a collection of old Waterford glass are all on display. The home is superbly situated beside a lake with a small formal garden; additional gardens are undergoing restoration. A word of caution: Westport isn't your usual staid country house. The old dungeons, which belonged to the earlier castle (believed to have been the home of the 16th-century warrior queen, Grace O'Malley), now house video games, and the grounds have given way to a small amusement park for children and a children's zoo. If these elements don't sound like a draw, arrive early when it's less likely to be busy. ⊠ *Off N59 south of Westport turn-off, clearly signposted from the Octagon, Co. Mayo,* ☎ *098/25430.* ☞ *House €8.25, family day ticket for all attractions €38.* ☉ *House May and Sept., weekends 2–5; grounds and house June and Aug. 22–31, daily 2–6; July–Aug. 21, Mon.–Sat. 11:30–6, Sun. 2–6.*

Dining and Lodging

$$–$$$ ✕ **Quay Cottage.** Fishing nets, glass floats, lobster pots, and greenery
★ hang from the high-pitched, exposed-beam roof of this tiny waterside cottage at the entrance to Westport House. It is both an informal wine bar and a shellfish restaurant. Rush-seated chairs, polished-oak tables, and an open fire in the evenings add to the comfortable, none-too-formal atmosphere. Try the chowder special (a thick vegetable and mussel soup), garlic-butter crab claws, or a half-pound steak fillet, and be sure to sample the homemade brown bread and ice cream. The restaurant serves wine only. ⊠ *The Quay, Co. Mayo,* ☎ *098/26412. AE, MC, V. Closed Jan.*

$ ✕🛏 **Newport House.** This handsome, creeper-covered Georgian house beside the Newport River dominates the village of Newport, 12 km (7 mi) north of Westport on N59. Kieran and Thelma Thompson's grand and elegant private home has spacious public rooms furnished with gilt-framed family portraits, Regency mirrors and chairs, handwoven Donegal carpeting, and crystal chandeliers. The sweeping staircase leads to an airy gallery and the bedrooms. These are decorated with pretty chintz drapes and a mix of Victorian antiques and old furniture. Most bedrooms have sitting areas and good views of the river and gardens. Oysters, smoked salmon, and roast breast of duck are served in the dining room, along with homemade ice creams. ⊠ *Newport, Co. Mayo,* ☎ *098/41222,* 𝖥𝖠𝖷 *098/41613,* 𝖶𝖤𝖡 *www.newporthouse.ie. 19 rooms with bath. Restaurant, fishing, bar. AE, DC, MC, V. Closed Oct.– mid-Mar.*

$ ✕🛏 **Olde Railway Hotel.** By far the best bet in Westport's town center, this Victorian railway hotel offers both character and comfort. Fishing trophies, Victorian plates, framed prints, and watercolors brighten up the lobby and lounge. A mix of Victorian and older pieces decorate the sunny bedrooms, which have double-glazed Georgian sash windows. Two top picks: Room 209 has a heavy Victorian bed and a river view; and Room 114 has a Victorian chaise lounge and a large Georgian wardrobe. Overlooking the landscaped gardens, the Conservatory Restaurant serves fresh local produce and game specialties. ⊠ *The Mall, Co. Mayo,* ☎ *098/25166,* 𝖥𝖠𝖷 *098/25090,* 𝖶𝖤𝖡 *www.anu.ie/railwayhotel. 25 rooms with bath. Restaurant, fishing, 2 bars. AE, MC, V.*

$$ 🏨 **Atlantic Coast Hotel.** Converted from an old warehouse, the hotel's original stone exterior maintains an old-fashioned atmosphere—yet the interior is entirely modern. Most guest rooms have two beds and are sparsely decorated in contemporary light-wood furniture and, strangely, orange-and-black print curtains and bedspreads. Rooms have a water view (the hotel is in the quayside area of Westport) and all the conveniences of a 21st-century hotel. There is a nice fireplace in the lobby, and breakfast is served in the rooftop restaurant, which has beautiful views of the bay. ⊠ *The Quay, Co. Mayo, Co. Mayo,* ☎ *098/29000,* FAX *098/29111. 85 rooms with bath. Restaurant, golf course, indoor pool, gym, fishing, bar. AE, MC, V.*

Nightlife

A good spot to try for traditional music and good pub grub is the **Towers Pub and Restaurant** (⊠ The Quay, ☎ 098/26534). In summer months, there are outdoor tables set up here beside the bay. In Westport's town center try **Matt Molloy's** (⊠ Bridge St., ☎ 098/26655); Matt Malloy is not only the owner but a member of the Chieftains. This is a pub where traditional music is of course the main attraction.

Outdoor Activities and Sports

BICYCLING

Enjoy the spectacular scenery of Clew Bay at a leisurely pace on a rented bike from **J. P. Breheny & Sons** (⊠ Castlebar St., ☎ 098/25020).

FISHING

Fishing tackle, bait, and licenses can be obtained at **Patrick Kelly** (⊠ Bridge St., ☎ 098/25982).

GOLF

Westport Golf Club (⊠ Carrowholly, ☎ 098/28262), beneath Croagh Patrick, overlooks Clew Bay. Designed by Fred Hawtree in the early 1970s, the 18-hole, par-73 course has twice been the venue for the Irish Amateur Championship.

HORSEBACK RIDING

Drummindoo Stud and Equitation Center (⊠ Castlebar Rd., ☎ 098/25616) will take you on the Clew Bay Trail, a three-day trek riding on the superb beaches around Clew Bay and staying in farmhouses along the route. Alternatively, you can rent a horse by the hour.

Shopping

Carraig Donn (⊠ Bridge St., ☎ 098/26287) has its own range of knitwear and a good selection of crystal, jewelry, and ceramics. **McCormack's** (⊠ Bridge St., ☎ 098/25619) has a traditional butcher shop downstairs, but upstairs it's an attractive gallery and café with work by local artists for sale. **Satch Kiely** (⊠ Westport Quay, ☎ 098/25775) carries fine antique furniture and decorative pieces. **Westport Crystal** (⊠ The Quay, ☎ 098/27780) is a factory outlet with a range of exclusive stemware and giftware.

Achill Island

★ ㊶ *16 km (10 mi) west of Mulrany, 58 km (36 mi) northwest of West-port.*

Heaven on earth in good weather, when its splendid scenery can be fully appreciated, Achill Island is a destination you'll probably want to head for—but only if you're able to *see* its cliff walks and sandy beaches. At 147 square km (57 square mi) and only 20 ft away from the mainland, this mass of bogs and wild heather is the largest island off Ireland's coast. A short causeway leads from the mainland to **Achill Sound,** the first village on the island. The main road runs through rhododendron plantations to **Keel**, which has a 3-km (2-mi) beach with spectacular cathedral-like rock formations in the cliffs at its east end. There's a longer scenic route signposted ATLANTIC DRIVE. **Dugoort**, on the north shore of the island, is a small village with a beautiful golden strand. Nearby is the cottage used by Heinrich Böll, the German writer and Nobel Prize winner, whose *Irish Diary*, written in the 1950s, has introduced many visitors to this part of Ireland. The cottage today is part of a center for German-Irish cultural exchanges. On Achill's north coast above Dugoort, 2,204-ft **Slievemore** is the island's highest summit. Until just a few years ago, the people of Achill made a very poor living. Tourism has improved things, as has the establishment of cottage industries (mainly knitting) and shark fishing, which is popular from April to July. Alas, Achill's popularity has led to a rash of new, not always appropriate, development, most noticeably clusters (or "villages") of bleak concrete vacation cottages that stand empty for 10 months out of 12.

Lodging

$ 🏨 **Ostan Gob A'Choire.** In the first village you approach arriving from the mainland, this small, waterside, two-story town house (its name means "Achill Sound Hotel") has a brick-and-plate-glass bedroom extension. All bedrooms have sea views, but the nicer ones, with tweed curtains and reproductions of Georgian furniture, are in the old building. The smaller rooms are already a little worn, but they are spotlessly clean and have pleasant views of the Sound. ⊠ *Achill Sound, Co. Mayo,* ☎ *098/45245,* FAX *098/45621,* WEB *www.geocities.com/achillsoundhotel. 36 rooms with bath. Restaurant, bicycles, bar. MC, V. Closed Oct.–Mar.*

Outdoor Activities and Sports

Tour the cliffs of Achill on a bike from the **Ostan Gob A'Choire** (⊠ on the Achill Sound, ☎ 098/45245). Bikes can also be rented from **O'Malley's Island Sports** (⊠ Keel P.O., ☎ 098/43125).

En Route   The shortest route to Ballina (N59 via Bangor and Crossmolina) runs for about 24 km (15 mi) across desolate, almost uninhabited bog, some of which has had its turf cut down to rock level by successive generations searching for fuel. If you intend to visit the Mullet peninsula, take this route. If you are heading directly for Ballina, take the longer but more interesting route by backtracking to Newport and continuing through Castlebar, Pontoon, and Foxford.

Castlebar

42 *40 km (26 mi) east of Achill Island, 18 km (11 mi) east of Westport on N5.*

The administrative capital of Mayo, Castlebar is a tidy little town with an attractive, tree-bordered green. Hatred of landlords ran high in the area, due to the ruthless, battering-ram evictions ordered by the Earl of Lucan. The disappearance in the 1960s of his high-living successor, the seventh earl, after the violent death in London of his children's nanny, is said to have given today's tenants a perfect pretext for withholding their rents. In 1879 Michael Davitt founded the Land League here, in the **Imperial Hotel** (⊠ The Green, ☎ 094/21961); it's worth a visit to check out the Gothic-style dining room, where you'll find simply prepared country food. At the **Linen Hall Arts Centre** (⊠ Linenhall St., ☎ 094/23733), exhibitions and performances are often scheduled.

En Route   As you travel from Castlebar northeast to Ballina, there is a choice of two routes. The longer and more scenic is via the tiny, wooded village of Pontoon, skirting the western shore of Lough Conn and passing through the rough bogland of the Glen of Nephin, beneath the dramatic heather-clad slopes of Nephin Mountain (2,653 ft). The shorter route follows N5 and N58 to Foxford, a pretty village with several crafts and antiques shops. A good place for a break is the **Foxford Woollen Mills Visitor Center,** where you can explore the crafts shop and grab a bite at the restaurant. The "Foxford Experience" tells the story of the wool mill (famous for its tweeds and blankets) from the time of the famine—when it was founded by the Sisters of Charity to combat poverty—to the present day. ⊠ *Foxford, Co. Mayo,* ☎ *094/56756.* ▧ *€3.81.* ☉ *Sept.–June, Mon.–Sat. 10–6, Sun. 2–6; July–Aug., Sun. noon–6; tour every 20 mins.*

Ballina

43 *40 km (25 mi) northeast of Castlebar.*

Ballina's chief attraction is fishing for salmon and trout in the River Moy and nearby Lough Conn. Although it is the largest town in County Mayo (population 7,500), to some eyes, Ballina's town center may appear run-down; however, its unspoiled, old-fashioned shops and pubs contain many treasures. Try the bar food at **Gaughan's** (⊠ O'Rahilly St., ☎ 096/21151), where the classic wooden interior dates back to the mid-19th century. **McGrath's Foodland Delicatessen** (⊠ O'Rahilly St., ☎ 096/21198) is an old-fashioned grocery handy for picnic materials.

Dining and Lodging

$–$$ ✕🏠 **Mount Falcon Castle.** Owner-manager Constance Aldridge's rambling Victorian-Gothic country house 5 km (3 mi) outside Ballina is within easy reach of several beautiful, small beaches. Aldridge is renowned for putting guests at ease; she makes children feel especially welcome. You can salmon fish on the River Moy right on the hotel's extensive grounds; horseback riding, sea fishing, and golf are nearby. Rooms, which overlook the wooded grounds, are furnished comfortably, with a mix of antiques and heirlooms. In the dining room, the country-style home cooking, which takes advantage of local produce, has a fine reputation. ⊠ *Ballina, Co. Mayo,* ☎ *096/70811,* ℻ *096/71517,* 🕸 *www.irelands-blue-book.ie. 10 rooms with bath. Restaurant, tennis court, fishing. AE, DC, MC, V. Closed Feb.–Mar.*

$ ✕🏠 **Enniscoe House.** Colorful corridors, fishing motifs, and quirky, slightly crooked stairways make this pink, Georgian mansion on the shores of Lough Conn a wonderfully appealing spot. Especially delightful are the 150 acres crisscrossed with pleasant walks and 3¼ km (2 mi) of peaceful lakeshore. Owner Susan Kellett, who inherited the house, converted many of the farm buildings into offices, which now house a number of independent organizations, including a Mayo genealogy center and the Cloonamoyne Fishery. The hotel is 4½ km (3 mi) south of Crossmolina and 20 km (13 mi) west of Ballina. Meals include fruits grown in the organic garden. ⊠ *Castlehill, Ballina, Co. Mayo,* ☎ *096/31112,* ℻ *096/31773,* 🕸 *www.enniscoe.com. 6 rooms with bath. Restaurant, fishing, convention center. AE, MC, V. Closed mid-Oct.–Mar.*

$–$$ 🏠 **Downhill Hotel.** Anglers and outdoor types flock to this hotel on 40 wooded acres beside a gushing tributary of the River Moy (just off the N59 Sligo road). The late-Victorian main house feels a little gloomy downstairs, but it's comfortable. Rooms in the newer wing tend to be smaller than those in the main house, but the former have good views of the river across the garden. Rooms in the main house are decorated with Georgian-style furniture and tastefully coordinated quilts and drapes. There's music in the bar on weekends and midweek in July and August.

⊠ *Co. Mayo,* ☎ *096/21033,* FAX *096/21338,* WEB *www.downhillhotel.ie.*
50 rooms with bath. Restaurant, 3 tennis courts, indoor pool, gym, hot
tub, sauna, steam room, fishing, squash, 2 bars, convention center. AE,
DC, MC, V.

Outdoor Activities and Sports

BICYCLING

Head for the coast north of Ballina on a bike from **Gerry's Cycle Cen-**
ter (⊠ 6 Lord Edward St., ☎ 096/70455).

FISHING

Fishing bait, tackle, and licenses can be obtained from **John Walkin**
(⊠ Tone St., ☎ 096/22442).

GOLF

The **Carne Golf Links** at Belmullet Golf Club (⊠ Belmullet, ☎ 097/
82292), 72 km (45 mi) west of Ballina, is one of Ireland's renowned
links courses. **Enniscrone Golf Club** (⊠ Enniscrone, ☎ 096/36297), 13
km (8 mi) north of Ballina, is an 18-hole, par-72 course.

THE NORTH MAYO COAST

Killala, 12 km (7½) mi north of Ballina, is a pleasant little seaside town
overlooking Killala Bay. This was the scene of the unsuccessful French
invasion of Ireland, led by Wolfe Tone in 1798. The history of this tiny
bishopric goes back much further, though, as evidenced by its round,
12th-century tower.

Killala is the gateway to the north Mayo coast, a dramatic, windswept
stretch of cliffs continuing to Erris Head on the Mullet peninsula in
the far west of the county. The sparsely inhabited landscape beneath
an ever-changing sky consists of small farms and open moorland. The
small roads and stunning views are attractive to cyclists, but be
warned: the wind howls in across the Atlantic directly from Iceland,
the nearest land mass. Although there are no signposted trails on this
coast, there are plenty of cliff footpaths and small roads for walkers
to explore. Don't miss the blowholes on Downpatrick Head, great
gaps in the rocks through which plumes of water spew in rough
weather.

★ ④④ Nowadays, the chief reason for visiting this coast is the **Céide Fields.**
Widely recognized as one of Europe's most significant megalithic sites,
the fields consist of rows and patterns of stones that have been preserved under a 5,000-year-old bog. These stones are the remnants of
dwelling places and stone-walled fields built by a peaceful, well-orga-
nized farming community. A striking glass-and-steel pyramid houses
the visitor center, where displays and an audiovisual show bring this
strange landscape to life. Admission includes an optional guided walk
through an excavated section of the stones; wet-weather gear is provided when necessary. ⊠ *R314, 5 km (3 mi) west of Ballycastle, Co.*
Mayo, ☎ *096/43325,* WEB *www.heritageireland.ie.* ⊡ *€3.15.* ◷ *Mid-*
Mar.–May and Oct., daily 10–5; June–Sept., daily 9:30–6:30; Nov., daily
10–4:30; Dec.–mid-Mar. advance bookings only.

Shopping

Hackett & Turpin (⊠ Carrowteige, Ballina, ☎ 097/88925) is a factory
outlet for Irish sweaters. From R314 beyond the Céide Fields, follow
signs for Benwee Head.

THE WEST A TO Z

To research prices, get advice from other travelers, and book travel arrangements, visit www.fodors.com.

AIR TRAVEL

CARRIERS

Aer Lingus has daily flights from London's Heathrow Airport to Galway and Knock via Dublin; the trip takes about two hours. Ryanair flies to Knock daily from London's Luton Airport; flying time is 80 minutes. Loganair flies to Knock from Birmingham, Manchester, and Glasgow.

Aer Arann has four flights daily on weekdays and two flights on weekends to the Aran Islands. During July and August planes leave every half hour. The flights call at all three of the Aran Islands and leave from Connemara Airport. The journey takes about six minutes and costs about €46 round-trip, or about €56 including one night's bed-and-breakfast. For about €32 you can fly one-way and travel one-way by boat from Rossaveal. Ask about other special offers at the time of booking.

➤ AIRLINES AND CONTACTS: **Aer Arann** (☎ 091/593–034).

AIRPORTS AND TRANSFERS

The West's most convenient international airport is Shannon, 25 km (16 mi) east of Ennis in the Southwest. Galway Airport, near Galway City, is used mainly for internal flights, with steadily increasing U.K. traffic. Knock International Airport, at Charlestown—near Knock, in County Mayo—is also used for internal flights and has direct daily services to London's Stansted, Manchester, and Birmingham. A small airport for internal traffic only is also located at Knockrowen, Castlebar, in County Mayo. Flying time from Dublin is 25–30 minutes to all airports. No scheduled flights run from the United States to Galway or Knock; use Shannon Airport. Connemara Airport at Inver, which services the Aran Islands and is 29 km (18 mi) west of Galway, is accessible by shuttle bus.

➤ AIRPORT INFORMATION: **Connemara Airport** (☎ 091/593–034). **Galway Airport** (☎ 091/752–874). **Knock International Airport** (☎ 094/67222). **Knockrowen Airport** (☎ 094/22853). **Shannon Airport** (☎ 061/471–444).

TRANSFERS

Galway Airport is 6½ km (4 mi) from Galway City. No regular bus service is available from the airport to Galway, but most flight arrivals are taken to Galway Rail Station in the city center by an airline courtesy coach. Inquire when you book. A taxi from the airport to the city center costs about €8.90.

If you're flying to Knock International Airport, you can pick up your rental car at the airport. Otherwise, inquire at the time of booking about transport to your final destination. No regular bus service is available from the airport.

BOAT AND FERRY TRAVEL

A ferry leaves Tarbert for Killimer every hour on the half hour and takes 20 minutes, avoiding a 104-km (65-mi) detour through Limerick City. The ferry runs every day of the year except Christmas Day and costs €10.15 one-way, €15.25 round-trip. (Ferries return from Killimer every hour on the hour.)

There are a variety of options for traveling to the Aran Islands. Aran Ferries runs a boat to the Aran Islands from Rossaveal, 32 km (20 mi) west of Galway City, which makes the crossing in 20 minutes and costs about €24 round-trip, including the shuttle bus from Galway. Island Ferries, which has a booking office on Victoria Place opposite the TIO in Galway City, has a one-hour crossing from Rossaveal for €23 round-trip, with up to five sailings a day in summer, weather permitting. Bicycles are transported free off-season, but there may be a charge in July and August: inquire when booking. Discounts are available for families, students, and groups of four or more. If you stay a night or two on the islands, ask about accommodations when booking your ferry, as there are some very competitive deals. Between June and September, O'Brien Ferries has sailings from Galway Docks, a five-minute walk from Eyre Square. The ferries run three times a week in June and September (usually Tuesday, Thursday, and Saturday), daily in July and August. The crossing takes 90 minutes and costs €17.75 round-trip.

If you are heading for Inisheer, the smallest island, the shortest crossing is from Doolin in County Clare. A ferry, operated by Aran Ferries, leaves from Doolin Pier, with up to 12 sailings daily, from June through the end of September. The crossing takes about 20 minutes and costs €20 round-trip.

For travel between the Aran Islands, frequent inter-island ferries are available in summer months, but tickets are nontransferable, so ask the captain of your ferry about his inter-island schedule if you plan to visit more than one island; otherwise, your trip can become expensive.
➤ BOAT AND FERRY INFORMATION: **Aran Ferries** (⊠ TIO, Victoria Pl., Eyre Sq., ☎ 091/568–903 or 091/592–447). **Island Ferries** (☎ 091/565–352). **O'Brien Ferries** (⊠ New Docks, ☎ 091/567–676). **Tarbert–Killimer Ferry** (☎ 065/905–3124).

BUS TRAVEL
Bus Éireann operates a variety of expressway services into the region from Dublin, Cork City, and Limerick City to Ennis, Galway City, Westport, and Ballina, the principal depots in the region. Expect bus rides to last about one hour longer than the time by car.

In July and August, the provincial bus service is augmented by daily services to most resort towns. Outside these months, many coastal towns receive only one or two buses per week. Bus routes are often slow and circuitous, and service can be erratic. A copy of the Bus Éireann timetable (€.95 from any station) is essential. The main bus stations are located at Ennis, Galway City, Westport, and Ballina.
➤ BUS INFORMATION: **Ballina Station** (☎ 096/71800). **Bus Éireann** (☎ 01/836–6111 in Dublin; 061/313–333 in Limerick; 021/508–188 in Cork). **Ennis Station** (☎ 065/682–4177). **Galway City Station** (⊠ Ceannt Station, ☎ 091/562–000). **Westport Station** (☎ 098/25711).

CAR RENTAL
If you haven't already picked up a rental car at Shannon Airport, try the following rental agencies.
➤ LOCAL AGENCIES: **Avis** (⊠ Galway City, ☎ 091/568–886). **Budget** (⊠ Galway City, ☎ 091/566–376). **Casey's Auto Rentals** (⊠ Knock International Airport, Charlestown, Co. Mayo, ☎ 094/24618). **Diplomat Rent A Car** (⊠ Knock International Airport, Charlestown, Co. Mayo, ☎ 094/67252). **Enterprise** (⊠ Galway City, ☎ 091/771–200). **Euro Mobil** (⊠ Galway City, ☎ 091/753–037). **Hertz Rent A Car** (⊠ Galway City, ☎ 091/752–502). **Johnson & Perrot** (⊠ Galway City, ☎ 091/568–886). **National** (⊠ Galway City, ☎ 091/771–929).

CAR TRAVEL

The 219-km (136-mi) Dublin–Galway trip takes about three hours. From Cork City take N20 through Mallow and N21 to Limerick City, picking up the N18 Ennis–Galway road in Limerick. The 209-km (130-mi) drive from Cork to Galway takes about three hours. From Killarney the shortest and most pleasant route to cover the 193 km (120 mi) to Galway (three hours) is N22 to Tralee, then N69 through Listowel to Tarbert and the ferry across the Shannon Estuary to Killimer in County Clare, joining N68 in Kilrush, and then picking up N18 in Ennis.

A car is essential in the West, especially from September through June. Although the main cities of the area are easily reached from the rest of Ireland by rail or bus, transport within the region is sparse and badly coordinated. If a rental car is out of the question, your best option is to make Galway your base and take day tours (available mid-June through September) west to Connemara and south to the Burren, and a day or overnight trip to the Aran Islands. It *is* possible to explore the region by local and intercity bus services, but you will need plenty of time.

ROAD CONDITIONS

The West has good, wide main roads (National Primary Routes) and better-than-average local roads (National Secondary Routes), both known as "N" routes. If you stray off the beaten track on the smaller Regional ("R") or unnumbered routes, particularly in Connemara and County Mayo, you may encounter some hazardous mountain roads. Narrow, steep, and twisty, they are also frequented by untended sheep, cows, and ponies grazing "the long acre" (as the strip of grass beside the road is called) or simply straying in search of greener pastures. If you find a sheep in your path, just sound the horn, and it should scramble away. A good maxim for these roads is: "You never know what's around the next corner." Bear this in mind, and adjust your speed accordingly. Hikers and cyclists constitute an additional hazard on narrow roads in the summer.

ROAD MAPS

A good map, available through newsagents and TIOs, gives Irish and English names where needed.

RULES OF THE ROAD

Within the Connemara Irish-speaking area, signs are in Irish only. The main signs to recognize are Gaillimh (Galway), Ros an Mhil (Rossaveal), An Teach Doite (Maam Cross), and Sraith Salach (Recess).

EMERGENCIES

For a doctor or dentist in County Clare, contact the Mid-Western Health Board; in Counties Galway and Mayo, contact the Western Health Board. Matt O'Flaherty and O'Donnell's are pharmacies in Galway and Westport, respectively.

➤ CONTACTS: **Matt O'Flaherty** (⊠ 39 Eyre Sq., Galway, ☎ 091/562–927). **Mid-Western Health Board** (⊠ Catherine St., Limerick, Co. Limerick, ☎ 061/316–655). **O'Donnell's** (⊠ Bridge St., Westport, ☎ 098/25163). **Police, fire, and ambulance** (☎ 999). **Western Health Board** (⊠ Merlin Park, Galway City, ☎ 091/751–131).

LODGING

BED-AND-BREAKFASTS

For a small fee, Bord Fáilte will book accommodations anywhere in Ireland through its central reservations system. B&Bs can be booked at local TIOs when they are open; however, even these reservations will go through the central reservations system.

➤ CONTACT INFORMATION: **Bord Fáilte** (☎ 800/223–6470 in the U.S. and Canada; 800/039–7000 in the U.K.; 02/9299–6177 in Australia; 09/379–8720 in New Zealand, WEB www.irelandvacations.com).

OUTDOOR ACTIVITIES AND SPORTS

BOARD AND DINGHY SAILING

One- and two-week courses in sailing and board-sailing are available at the Glénans Center, based on an otherwise uninhabited island in Clew Bay near Westport. Contact the center's head office for details.
➤ CONTACTS: **Glénans Center** (✉ 28 Merrion Sq., Dublin, ☎ 01/661–1481).

FISHING

Details of the numerous fisheries in the area are available from the local TIOs, or consult the Irish Tourist Board leaflet "Angling Ireland" (€2.55). Similar leaflets are available on coarse-angling (angling for freshwater fish) and sea-angling.

HIKING

For backcountry walking, consult "Irish Walk Guides—The West," a pamphlet available at local TIOs, and take local advice on weather conditions.

TOURS

Galway City's TIO has details of walking tours of Galway, which are organized by request. All TIOs in the West provide lists of suggested cycle tours.

BUS TOURS

The only full- and half-day guided bus tours in the region start from Galway. Bus Éireann coordinates two full-day tours, one covering Connemara and the other the Burren (each €15.25). Tours run from early June to mid-October only, with the widest choice available between mid-July and mid-August. Book in advance at the Galway City TIO or at Ceannt Railway Station or the Salthill TIO, which also serve as departure points.

Lally Tours runs a day tour through Connemara and County Mayo and another to the Burren. It also operates a vintage double-decker bus, departing from Eyre Square, which runs hourly city tours from 10:30 AM until 4:30 PM.

O'Neachtain Day Tours operates full-day tours of Connemara and the Burren. Tickets, €16.50 each, can be purchased from the Galway City TIO; tours depart across the street.
➤ FEES AND SCHEDULES: **Bus Éireann** (☎ 091/562–000). **Ceannt Railway Station** (☎ 091/562–000). **Lally Tours** (☎ 091/562–905). **O'Neachtain Day Tours** (☎ 091/553–188). **Salthill TIO** (☎ 091/520–500).

TRAIN TRAVEL

Galway City, Westport, and Ballina are the main rail stations in the region. For County Clare, travel from Cork City, Killarney, or Dublin's Heuston Station to Limerick City and continue the journey by bus. Trains for Galway, Westport, and Ballina leave from Dublin's Heuston Station. The journey time to Galway is 3 hours; to Ballina, 3¾ hours; and to Westport, 3½ hours. Train passengers can call for information in Galway, Ballina, and Westport. Rail transportation is not good within the West, however. The major destinations of Galway City and Westport/Ballina are on different branch lines. Connections can only be made between Galway and the other two cities by traveling inland for about an hour to Athlone.

➤ TRAIN INFORMATION: **Ballina Station** (☎ 096/71818). **Galway Station** (☎ 091/564–222). **Heuston Station** (☎ 01/836–6222). **Limerick City Station** (☎ 061/315–555). **Westport Station** (☎ 098/25253).

VISITOR INFORMATION

Bord Fáilte provides free information service, tourist literature, and an accommodations booking service at its TIOs. The following offices are open all year, generally weekdays 9–6, daily during high season: Aran Islands (Inishmore), Ennis, Galway City, Oughterard, and Westport.

Other tourist information offices, which are open seasonally, generally weekdays 9–6 and Saturday 9–1, are as follows: Achill (June–August); Ballina (April–October); Castlebar (May–mid-September); Clifden (March–October); Cliffs of Moher (April–October); Kilkee (May–August); Kilrush (June–August); Salthill (May–September); Thoor Ballylee (April–mid-October).

➤ TOURIST INFORMATION: **Aran Islands (Inishmore)** (✉ Co. Galway, ☎ 099/61263, FAX 099/61420). **Achill** (✉ Co. Mayo, ☎ 098/45384). **Ballina** (✉ Co. Mayo, ☎ 096/70848). **Castlebar** (✉ Co. Mayo, ☎ 094/21207). **Clifden** (✉ Co. Galway, ☎ 095/21163). **Cliffs of Moher** (✉ Co. Clare, ☎ 065/708–1171). **Ennis** (✉ Arthur's Row, Town Center, Co. Clare, ☎ 065/682–8366). **Galway City** (✉ 1 Victoria Pl., Eyre Sq., Co. Galway, ☎ 091/563–081, FAX 091/565–201). **Kilkee** (✉ Co. Clare, ☎ 065/905–6112). **Kilrush** (✉ Co. Clare, ☎ 065/905–1047). **Oughterard** (✉ Main St., Co. Galway, ☎ 091/552–808, FAX 091/552–811). **Salthill** (✉ Salthill, Co. Galway, ☎ 091/520–500). **Thoor Ballylee** (✉ Near Gort, Co. Clare, ☎ 091/631–436). **Westport** (✉ The Mall, Co. Mayo, ☎ 098/25711, FAX 098/26709).

8 THE NORTHWEST

YEATS COUNTRY, DONEGAL BAY,
THE NORTHERN PENINSULAS

On an island where there's no shortage of majestic scenery, the Northwest claims at least its fair share. Cool, clean waters from the roaring Atlantic Ocean shape the terrain into long peninsulas—a raw, sensual landscape that makes it seem as if Earth is still under construction. Clouds and rain linger over mountains, glens, cliffs, beaches, and bogs, to be chased minutes later by sunshine and rainbows. The writer William Butler Yeats and his brother, the painter Jack, immortalized this land in their work. Walk in their footsteps and you too will be struck by the splendidly lush and rugged countryside.

Glance at a map of Ireland that has scenic roads marked in green, and chances are your eye will quickly be drawn to the far-flung peninsulas of the Northwest. At virtually every bend in the roads of Counties Donegal, Leitrim, and Sligo there's something to justify all those green ribbons. But what that something is *now* may not be what it is an hour from now. As Bob Hope once said, if you don't like the weather, just wait five minutes. The air, the light, and the colors of the countryside change as though with a turn of a kaleidoscope. Look once, and see scattered, snow-white clouds flying above tawny slopes. Look again, and suddenly the sun has brilliantly illuminated magnificent reds and purples in the undergrowth. The fickle skies brighten and darken at will, tempting a spectrum of subtle shades from the unkempt gorse and heather, then washing the grassy meadows greener than any green you've ever seen.

Updated by Geoff Hill and Cate Cox

The Northwest covers the most northerly part of Ireland's Atlantic coastline, running from Sligo in the south along Donegal's remote, windswept peninsulas to Malin Head in the far north. These maritime landscapes are said to have given their colors to the most famous local product, handwoven tweed, which reflects the browns of the peaty heathland and the purples of the heather. Donegal, a sparsely populated rural county of small farms and fishing boats, shares its inland border with Northern Ireland; the border is partly formed by the River Foyle. Inland from Sligo is Leitrim, a county best known for its numerous lakes and loughs, some of which join up with the River Shannon, on the easterly border of this region.

County Donegal was part of the near-indomitable ancient kingdom of Ulster, which was not conquered by the English until the 17th century. By the time the English withdrew in the 1920s, they had still not eradicated rural Donegal's Celtic inheritance. It thus shouldn't come as a surprise that County Donegal contains Ireland's largest Gaeltacht (Irish-speaking) area. Driving in this part of the country, you'll either be frustrated or amused whenever you come to a crossroads. Signposts show only the Irish place-names, often so unlike the English versions as to be completely unrecognizable. All is not lost, however, as maps generally give both the Irish and the English names, and locals are usually more than happy to help out with directions (in English)—usually with a yarn thrown in. So if you're in a hurry, first of all you're in the wrong country, and second, you should have started earlier.

Tucked into the folds of the Northwest's hills, modest little market towns and unpretentious villages with muddy streets go about their business quietly. In the squelchy peat bogs, cutters working with long shovels pause to watch and wave as you drive past. Remember to drive slowly along the country lanes, for around any corner you may find a whitewashed thatched cottage with children playing outside its scarlet door, a shepherd leading his flock, a wayward sheep or two looking philosophical about having strayed from their field, or a farmer wobbling along in the middle of the road on his old faithful sit-up-and-beg bicycle.

A raw and sensual landscape, the Northwest is overwhelmingly rural and underpopulated. That's not to say there isn't a bit of hurly-burly here. The Northwest's boomtown, Sligo Town, has gone through a major renaissance—on a typical weekday, its little winding streets are as busy as those of Galway, and it seems to be giving Dublin's Temple Bar a run for its money when it comes to stylish restaurants and trendy people—an amazing feat for a town of only 19,000 souls. Sligo Town pulses not only in the present but with the charge of history, for it was the childhood home of W. B. and Jack Yeats, the place that, more than any other, gave rise to their particular geniuses—or, as Jack put it: "Sligo was my school and the sky above it." More bright lights are found in Letterkenny, which has to its credit the longest main street of any town in Ireland. Glenveagh National Park exemplifies the surprising alliance between nature and culture you'll find in the Northwest. Here, perched on the edge of a glorious lake in the midst of 24,000 acres of some of Ireland's most thrilling wilderness, sits a fairy-tale castle. The castle reflects the life and times of the man who owned it for 50 years: Henry McIlhenny, the millionaire American philanthropist and art collector whose Impressionist paintings now hang in the Philadelphia Museum of Art.

Keep in mind, though, that the whole region—and County Donegal in particular—attracts droves of tourists during July and August; this is a favorite weekend vacation area for people who live in neighboring Northern Ireland. A few places, frankly, are quite spoiled by popularity with tourists, careless development, and uninspired architecture—particularly the ugly bungalows that have replaced thatched cottages and Georgian farmhouses as typical Irish rural homes. The Rosses Peninsula on Donegal's west coast, still sometimes described as beautiful, is marred by too much building. Bundoran, on the coast between Sligo Town and Donegal Town, a cheap and cheerful family beach resort full of so-called "Irish gift shops" and "amusement arcades," is another place to pass through rather than visit. On the whole, though, the Northwest is big enough, untamed enough, and grand enough to be able to absorb all of its summer (and weekend) tourists without too much harm.

Pleasures and Pastimes

Dining

Although the Northwest has not been considered a great gastronomic center, in the last few years Sligo Town has established itself as a sort of last stop for food lovers, with a number of food-related shops worth visiting. On the dining front, here and there, newcomers are serving up well-above-average food in memorable settings, though overall, the majority of restaurants offer plain and simple fare such as traditional Irish lamb stew or bacon and cabbage served with generous helpings of potatoes (often prepared in at least two ways on the same plate), washed down with creamy, lip-smacking pints of Guinness. You're likely to find the finest food at the higher-quality country houses, where chefs elegantly prepare local meat, fish, and produce in a hybrid Irish-French haute cuisine. Another trend: several of the area's more successful restaurants have added accommodations, making them good overnight destinations.

CATEGORY	THE REPUBLIC*
$$$$	over €29
$$$	€22–€29
$$	€13–€21
$	under €13

*Per person for a main course at dinner

Lodging

True, it's the farthest-flung corner of Ireland, but the Northwest has a steady stream of arrivals—especially in July and August. Thanks to the popularity of the Northwest as a weekend getaway for residents of Northern Ireland, good bed-and-breakfasts and small hotels are prevalent. In the two major towns—Sligo Town and Donegal Town—and the small coastal resorts in between, traditional provincial hotels have been modernized (albeit not always elegantly). Yet they retain some of the charm that comes with older buildings and personalized service. Away from these areas, your options are more restricted, and your best overnight choice, with some exceptions, is usually a modest guest house offering bed, breakfast, and an evening meal. Because of its large Gaeltacht population, you should consider staying in an Irish-speaking home; the local Tourist Information Office (TIO) can be helpful in making a booking with an Irish-speaking family. In the Northwest you'll also find a number of first-class country-house hotels where you can expect the gracious professionalism you'll find in comparable properties elsewhere in Ireland.

CATEGORY	THE REPUBLIC*
$$$$	over €230
$$$	€178–€230
$$	€127–€178
$	under €127

*All prices are for two people in a double room, including VAT.

Nightlife

As in other regions in Ireland where there are few large towns, the pub in the Northwest is the center of nightlife. Always ask locally or at your hotel if there's a nearby pub with a weekly session, or informal performance of traditional folk music. Many hotels or large pubs, particularly at resort towns in season, put on some form of entertainment—a disco or live music—most nights of the week. Discos (often called "dances") are usually full of local and visiting teenagers and twentysomethings. These discos are far from sophisticated but are often a lot of fun (and great for meeting people). When there isn't a disco, you will find some kind of live music, usually a local traveling band that plays rock-and-roll standards and country-and-western music. These appeal to an older crowd, often the parents of the kids who danced the night away in the same place the night before.

Outdoor Activities and Sports

BICYCLING

Steep hills, winding and poorly kept roads, occasionally strong winds, and the frequent possibility of cold weather and rain make the Northwest one of Ireland's most challenging areas for cyclists. Now the good news: plenty of low-cost accommodations, astonishing scenery, empty roads, and a chance to stop and chat with the locals can make either serious touring throughout the region or gentle meandering around a small area an immensely rewarding experience.

FISHING

The angling in Ireland's Northwest is of the highest class, attracting enthusiasts and connoisseurs from the world over. Yet there's so much space and so much water that it can feel as if you have the whole place to yourself. There are a dozen sea-fishing festivals during the season, open to visiting anglers. Anglers will find that the best area for brown trout is around Bundoran, including Lough Melvin. In western County Donegal, you'll have good opportunities for catching sea trout. Plenty of salmon and brown trout live in the rivers of southern County Donegal and northern County Sligo. More brown trout can be found in the loughs near Dunfanaghy in northern County Donegal, near Bundoran on the border of Donegal and Sligo counties, and in the border area of Sligo and Leitrim counties. Pike and coarse anglers can cast their lines in the abundant County Leitrim lakes.

GOLF

The Northwest has a large number of 9- and 18-hole courses, most in seaside locations, and several of them are world-class. The Northwest's best 18-hole courses all welcome visitors. Expect to pay greens fees of around €31.75–€50.80 a day.

HIKING AND WALKING

Trails in the Northwest offer the experienced walker plenty of challenges. It helps to be able to read a map, and on high ground you'd be wise not to take any chances with the weather, which can turn wet and misty quite suddenly. In the mountain districts (such as the Blue Stacks, near Donegal Town) you can get in some satisfyingly rough walks with dramatic views. Long-distance footpaths are scattered across County Donegal, in County Leitrim, and around Lough Gill in County Sligo. Good shorter trails are also accessible within Glenveagh National Park.

SURFING

Expect great surfing along the Atlantic shores of Counties Donegal and Sligo. Head to Strandhill, Rossnowlagh, and Bundoran on the Sligo and south County Donegal coasts or to Marble Strand and Rosapenna in north County Donegal. These areas have excellent conditions for world-class surfing, although even at the height of summer only the most brave will venture in without a wet suit. Take note that in Ireland a surf shop can only rent surfing equipment to individuals taking lessons. Establishments recommended by the European Surf Federation and Irish Surfing Association have approved, qualified instructors, and are insured to give surfing instruction.

Sweaters, Tweeds, and China

Most of the Aran sweaters you'll see throughout Ireland are made in County Donegal, the area most associated with high-quality, handwoven tweeds and hand-knit items. Made of plain, undyed wool and knit with distinctive crisscross patterns, Aran sweaters are durable, soft, and often weatherproof and can be astonishingly warm. Not so long ago, these pullovers were worn by every County Donegal fisherman, usually made to a design belonging exclusively to his own family. Today there's a greater variety in patterns, but most of the sweaters still have that unmistakable Aran look. High-quality machine-made tweeds, especially tweed jackets, also have a long history in the area and are widely available. Locally made Parian china is a thin, fine, and pale product of very high quality and workmanship. Elaborate flower motifs and a basket-weave design are two distinctive features of this china, which has been a specialty of Belleek, on the Donegal-Fermanagh border, for more than 100 years.

Exploring the Northwest

This chapter outlines three autonomous routes through the Northwest. These routes can easily be linked if you want to poke around the area over five or so days. The first journey begins in Sligo Town and covers its immediate environs—all the major sights within a roughly 24-km (15-mi) radius, many of which have strong associations with Yeats. The second trip skirts the entirety of Donegal Bay, from Mullaghmore in the south to Glencolumbkille to the far north and west, before heading inland as far as Ardara. The last route begins at the other end of Donegal, in Letterkenny, and covers the far northwest corner of County Donegal before swinging you back around to the Inishowen Peninsula, the tip-top of Ireland, delicately balanced between the Republic and Northern Ireland. If you decide to explore this chapter from back to front (this makes sense if you're arriving in the Northwest from

Northern Ireland), begin with the last itinerary, in Letterkenny; skip the trip to the Inishowen Peninsula; and pick up the middle tour from either Gratan Lough or Burtonport.

Numbers in the text correspond to numbers in the margin and on the Yeats Country and Around Donegal Bay, Sligo Town, and the Northern Peninsulas maps.

Great Itineraries

IF YOU HAVE 2 DAYS

Start your tour in **Sligo Town** ①–⑧, the cozy heart of County Sligo. The settlement is dominated by the stark outline of the hill that rears up to the north of the town—Yeats's "bare Ben Bulben," in whose shadow he asked to be buried. To whet your appetite for the works of one of the world's most famous poets, have a look at the memorabilia in the **Model Arts Centre and Niland Gallery** ②, where there are also some of the starkly atmospheric oils painted by W. B. Yeats's brother, Jack. Take along a volume of Yeats's poetry (or at the least his poem "The Lake Isle of Innisfree") as you follow the signposted Yeats Trail around woody, gorgeously scenic **Lough Gill** ⑩, where you'll begin to understand why this land inspired some of Yeats's finest poems. After the road north passes Yeats's simple grave in **Drumcliff** ⑭ churchyard, take a detour to **Lissadell House** ⑮, the home of the beautiful, aristocratic Gore-Booth sisters, where Yeats was a frequent visitor, and then head on to **Creevykeel** ⑰, an important court tomb dating from 3000 BC. Drive through **Ballyshannon** ⑲, where the River Erne empties into Donegal Bay, and continue on to the large village of ⊞ **Donegal Town** ⑳, a good place to stay the night, for this is where the roads of the area meet and then go their own ways to the north and west.

On the next day take the road to the thriving fishing port of **Killybegs** ㉒, beyond which point the views of Donegal Bay improve as the road twists and turns before descending into Kilcar, a village (like others hereabouts) known for its tweed making. The road then crosses a stretch of barren moorland and reaches **Glencolumbkille** ㉓, a scenic hamlet spread out around the rocky harbor of Glen Bay; it has associations with the reclusive and controversial early Christian missionary St. Columba. On the far side of the Glengesh Pass, the small village of **Ardara** ㉔ is the center of the region's tweed heritage and also a good spot to hear traditional music. Return from here southward to Donegal Town and either to Dublin via Ballyshannon or to Galway via Sligo.

IF YOU HAVE 5 DAYS

For your first two days, follow the first day of the two-day itinerary above, but take *two* whole days to do it. You may want to push on at the end of your second day to ⊞ **Ardara** ㉔ and visit the tweed heritage center there rather than stop at ⊞ **Donegal Town** ⑳, though both have a range of accommodations and some nightlife. On your third day, follow the coast road from Ardara up to Dungloe. Your rate of progress from here on will depend much on the weather and your pace, as the heathery headlands offer innumerable side excursions. North of Dungloe is a large Irish-speaking parish known as **The Rosses** ㉞, which has a wild Atlantic coast off which is the island of **Aranmore**, accessible from Burtonport. Working northward around this peninsula brings you to Bun Beag (Benbeg). From here another optional circuit can be made of the **Gweedore Headland** ㉝, with its bleak dramatic terrain (somewhat marred by modern bungalow development), which will bring you to Bloody Foreland Head, named for the vivid reds that appear on the rock face during the long western sunsets. Meenlaragh, east along the same headland, is the departure point for **Tory Island** ㉜, a rocky, inaccessible place that has nevertheless been inhabited since

Yeats Country and Around Donegal Bay

prehistoric times. Some of the Tory Island fishermen have developed a sideline producing native art.

Dun Fionnachaid ㉛ (Dunfanaghy in English) is a pleasant village built in the Plantation era on the shores of Sheephaven Bay, within easy reach of **Ards Forest Park** ㉚, which has trails leading to prehistoric sites. Near **Creeslough** ㉙, you'll find **Doe Castle,** romantic and dramatically perched on the edge of the southern end of Sheephaven Bay. **Carraig Airt** ㉘, a small village with some enjoyable old-fashioned pubs, gives access to a signposted Atlantic Drive around the Rosguill Peninsula. From here either head south through attractively sleepy Milford to **Ramelton** ㉖, a hilly little town on the edge of Lough Swilly, one of the loveliest of Donegal's big fjordlike inlets, and on to **Letterkenny** ㉕, a convenient base for exploring the rest of the county; or head north to **Rathmullan** ㉗, where a number of hotels are right on the shores of Lough Swilly. If you enjoy modern and contemporary art, on your next day head for the **Glebe House and Gallery,** on the northwest shore of **Gartan Lough** ㊲, which exhibits works by major Impressionists, Picasso, Jack Yeats, and the art of the Tory Islanders. If the outdoors beckons, head northwest for **Glenveagh National Park** ㊱, which also has a delightful Victorian-castle country house; if archaeology is your passion, head east to the dramatic hill fort of **Grianan Ailigh** ㊳, which provides a spectacular panorama of Donegal, Derry, and the Inishowen Peninsula. From Letterkenny head northeast across the border into Northern Ireland and the city of Derry or south for Sligo Town and Galway.

When to Tour the Northwest

In July and August, the Northwest gets busy with families from Northern Ireland, Dublin, and Great Britain. Musicians play most nights at village pubs, and the weather may be warm enough for hardy folk to swim in the sea, but accommodations may be hard to come by. Between November and February, in contrast, the area is empty of tourists, and with good reason—gales bring cold, lashing rain in from the Atlantic, shrouding the wild, lonely scenery that is the Northwest's greatest asset. What's more, because so many of the area's hotels are seasonal, you'll have a limited choice. The best months to visit here are April, May, June, September, and October.

YEATS COUNTRY—SLIGO TOWN AND ENVIRONS

Just as James Joyce made Dublin his own through his novels and stories, Sligo and environs are bound to the work of William Butler Yeats (1865–1939), Ireland's first of four Nobel laureates, and, no less, his brother, Jack B. (1871–1957), one of Ireland's most important 20th-century painters, whose expressionistic landscapes and portraits are as emotionally fraught as his brother's poems are lyrical and plangent. The brothers Yeats intimately knew and eloquently celebrated in their art not only Sligo Town itself but the surrounding countryside with its lakes, farms, woodland, and dramatic mountains that rise up not far from the center of town. Often on this route, you'll have glimpses of Ben Bulben Mountain, which looms over the western end of the Dartry range. The areas covered here are the most accessible parts of the Northwest, easily reached from Galway.

Sligo Town

★ *60 km (37 mi) northeast of Ballina, 138 km (86 mi) northeast of Galway, 217 km (135 mi) northwest of Dublin.*

Sligo (population 19,000), the only sizable town in the whole of the Northwest, is the best place to begin a tour of Yeats Country. It retains all the charm of smaller, sleepier villages, all the while in the throes of an economic boom. Europe's largest videotape factory is just outside of town, it's the center of Ireland's plastics industry, and for the past three years the streets have been ringing with the bite of buzz saws and the tang of resin as apartments, shopping malls, and cinema complexes have been tastefully erected behind traditional facades. By day Sligo is as lively and crowded as Galway, its considerably larger neighbor to the southwest. Locals, students from the town's college, and visitors bustle past its historic buildings and along its narrow sidewalks and winding streets and crowd its one-of-a-kind shops, eateries, and traditional pubs. More than any other town in the Northwest, Sligo has a buzz and energy that come as a surprise to anyone who hasn't visited in the last few years.

Squeezed onto a patch of land between Sligo Bay and Lough Gill, Sligo is clustered on the south shore between two bridges that span the River Garavogue, just east of where the river opens into the bay. The pedestrian zone along the south shore of the river between the two bridges means that you can now enjoy vistas of the river right in the center of town.

Sligo was often a battleground in its earlier days. It was attacked by Viking invaders in 807 and, later, by a succession of rival Irish and Anglo-Norman conquerors. In 1642, the British soldiers of Sir Frederick Hamilton fell upon Sligo, killing every visible inhabitant, burning the town, and destroying the interior of the beautiful medieval abbey. Then, between 1845 and 1849, more than a million inhabitants died in the potato famine or fled to escape it—an event poignantly captured in the words of a letter from local father Owen Larkin to his son in America in 1850, inscribed on a brass plaque down by the river: "I am now I may say alone in the world all my brothers and sisters are dead and children but yourself. We are all ejected out of Lord Ardilaun's ground, the times was so bad and all Ireland in such a state of poverty that no person could pay rent. My only hope now rests with you, as I am without one shilling and I must either beg or go to the poorhouse." Stand there a moment by the river, then turn again to the bustling heart of Sligo today, and marvel at humanity's capacity to reinvent itself.

❶ At the **Yeats Memorial Building** the annual Yeats International Summer School is conducted every August. The **Sligo Art Gallery** shows rotating exhibits of contemporary art; call ahead to see if there will be an exhibition during your visit. Across the street is Rohan Gillespie's innovative **sculpture of the poet,** draped in a flowing coat overlaid with excerpts from his work. It was unveiled in 1989 by Michael Yeats, W. B.'s son, in commemoration of the 50th anniversary of his father's death. ⊠ *Hyde Bridge,* ☏ *071/45847,* FAX *071/47426,* WEB *www.sligoartgallery.com.* 🎫 *Free.* ☉ *Mon.–Sat. 10–5:30.*

❷ The **Model Arts Centre and Niland Gallery,** beautifully housed in a 19th-century school, the **Niland Collection,** is one of Ireland's largest collections of works by contemporary artists from Ireland and abroad. It includes works by Jack B. Yeats, who once said, "I never did a painting without putting a thought of Sligo in it." (Beckett once wrote that Yeats painted "desperately immediate images.") Previously housed in the town library building, it also includes paintings by John Yeats (father of Jack and W. B.), who had a considerable reputation as a portraitist, as well as Sean Keating, Paul Henry, and other leading Irish artists of the 20th century. Some Yeats memorabilia are on display in

Courthouse . . . **4**

Hargadon's . . **7**

Model Arts
Centre and
Niland
Gallery **2**

St. John's
Cathedral . . . **6**

Sligo
Abbey **3**

Sligo County
Museum. **8**

TIO (Tourist
Information
Office). **5**

Yeats
Memorial
Building **1**

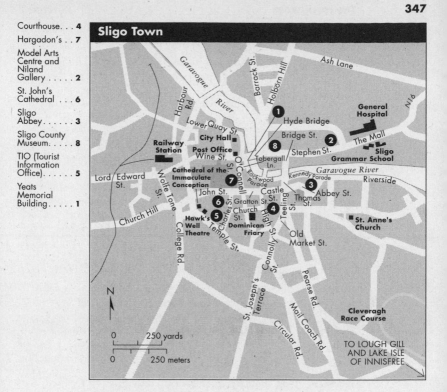

the **Sligo County Museum.** The center has performance and workshop spaces and hosts various literature, music, and film programs. There's also The Atrium café. ⊠ *The Mall,* ☎ *071/41405.* 🔳 *Free.* ⊗ *Tues.–Sat. 10–5:30 and during performances.*

❸ The **Sligo Abbey,** the town's only existing relic of the Middle Ages, was built for the Dominicans by Maurice FitzGerald in 1253. After a fire in 1414, it was extensively rebuilt, only to be destroyed again by Cromwell's Puritans under the command of Sir Frederick Hamilton in 1642. Today the abbey consists of a ruined nave, aisle, transept, and tower. Some fine stonework remains, especially in the 15th-century cloisters. The new visitors center is the base for guided tours, which are included in the admission price. It's accessible to the disabled, including toilets; even the site is accessible, where the ground allows (some parts are quite rocky). A parking lot for cars and buses is nearby. ⊠ *Abbey St.,* ☎ *071/46406,* WEB *www.heritageireland.ie.* 🔳 *€1.90.* ⊗ *Mid-Mar.–Oct., daily 9–6, Nov.–Jan., Fri.–Sun. 9:30–4:30.*

❹ The **Courthouse** (⊠ Teeling St.), built in 1878 in the Victorian Gothic style, has a flamboyant, turreted sandstone exterior. Unfortunately it's not open to casual visitors. After it was built, the structure became a symbol for English power. The Courthouse takes its inspiration from the much larger Law Courts in London. Just north of the Courthouse on the east side of Teeling Street, look for the window designating the law firm **Argue and Phibbs,** one of Sligo's most popular photo-ops.

You'll find the **Dominican Friary,** still a functioning church, on High Street. Notice that along this street and Church and Charles Streets, Sligo has churches of all denominations. Presbyterians, Methodists, and even Plymouth Brethren are represented, as well as Anglicans (Church of Ireland) and, of course, Roman Catholics. According to the Irish writer Sean O'Faolain, "The best Protestant stock in all Ireland is in Sligo." The Yeats family was part of that stock.

⑤ County Sligo's **TIO** (Tourist Information Office) is useful for the whole of the Northwest. It's in the same building as the **Hawk's Well Theatre.** The TIO sells an excellent "Tourist Trail" walking map of Sligo and information about bus tours of Yeats Country. It will also give you details of boat tours of Lough Gill, complete with recitals of Yeats's poetry—an excellent way to see the lough. ⊠ *Temple and Charles Sts.,* ☎ *071/61201.* ⌑ *Free.* ☉ *Sept.–mid-Mar., weekdays 9–1 and 2–5; mid-Mar.–mid-June, weekdays 9–6, Sat. 10–2; mid-June–Aug., Mon.–Sat. 9–8, Sun. 10–6.*

⑥ Designed in 1730 by Richard Castle, who designed Powerscourt and Russborough houses in County Wicklow, little **St. John's Cathedral** (Church of Ireland) has a handsome square tower and fortifications. In the north transept you'll find a memorial to Susan Mary Yeats, mother of W. B. and Jack. Next door is the larger and newer Roman Catholic **Cathedral of the Immaculate Conception** (with an entrance on Temple Street), consecrated in 1874. ⊠ *John St.* ⌑ *Free.* ☉ *Freely accessible.*

⑦ Sligo's most famous pub is **Hargadon's** (⊠ 4 O'Connell St., ☎ 071/ 70933), a dark, old-style public house with cozy, private, wood-paneled snugs (cubicles); stone and wood floors; rust-red interior walls; and a handsome golden-oak and green-painted facade. It's a good place for a bowl of stew and a creamy pint of Guinness. Around the corner from Hargadon's on Wine Street are the offices of the local weekly newspaper, the *Sligo Champion,* whose editor grandly declared, in its first issue in 1836, "Let no one think the *Champion* will be a vehicle of slander—we are determined never to sully our pages with personalities."

⑧ The **Sligo County Museum** has small sections on local society, history, and archaeology, but the main items of interest are first editions by W. B. Yeats and such intriguing memorabilia as the author's personal letters and the Irish tricolor (flag) that draped his coffin when he was buried at nearby **Drumcliff.** The church adjoining the museum has some works by Jack Yeats. Internet service is free on request. ⊠ *Stephen St.,* ☎ *071/42212.* ⌑ *Free.* ☉ *Tues.–Sat. 10–5.*

Dining and Lodging

$–$$ ✕ **Bistro Bianconi.** With all-white furnishings—blond wood and white-tile floors—the Bistro Bianconi lives up to its name. But the minimalism ends there. The menu (Italian) is full of fireworks; there's a page-long list of fancy pizzas baked in the wood-burning oven. Baked cannelloni and ravioli are also popular. ⊠ *44 O'Connell St.,* ☎ *071/ 41744. AE, MC, V. Closed Sun.*

$$$ ✕🏠 **Markree Castle.** From the front, this fortresslike 1640 castle looks slightly forbidding and cold, but seen from the garden in the back, it is spare and elegant. The ancestral home of Charles Cooper, who now owns and manages it with his wife, Mary, Markree is Sligo's oldest inhabited castle. Public rooms include an oak-paneled entry hall with a large stained-glass window at the top of the grand staircase, a skylit gallery that doubles as the bar, and a formal dining room with ornate Louis XIV plasterwork. Bedrooms (somewhat haphazardly furnished) occupy various floors and wings; bathrooms are modernized. The kitchen offers up an excellent three-course table d'hôte menu for €31.75; on Sunday a traditional lunch attracts a sizable, family-oriented crowd. The castle sits on a 1,000-acre estate 11 km (7 mi) south of Sligo Town just off N4. ⊠ *Collooney, Co. Sligo,* ☎ *071/67800,*

FAX *071/67840. 30 rooms with bath. Restaurant, horseback riding, bar. AE, DC, MC, V.*

$$–$$$ ✕⊡ **Coopershill.** Seven generations of the O'Hara family have lived
★ in this three-story Georgian farmhouse since it was built in 1774. Beyond the elegant, symmetrical stone facade, with its central Palladian window, the large public rooms are furnished with an appealing mix of antique and modern furniture. The spacious, beautifully furnished bedrooms have pretty floral wallpaper, and most have four-poster or canopy beds. In the tranquil dining room overlooking the woods, meals made with fresh Irish ingredients and a wide choice of wines are served by candlelight from a grand sideboard set with family silver and crystal. Coopershill is signposted from Drumfin crossroads, 17 km (11 mi) southeast of Sligo off N4. ⊠ *Riverstown, Co. Sligo,* ☎ *071/65108,* FAX *071/65466,* WEB *www.coopershill.com. 8 rooms with bath. Dining room, tennis court, boating, fishing, billiards; no room TVs. AE, DC, MC, V. Closed Nov.–Mar.*

$–$$ ✕⊡ **Cromleach Lodge.** Comfort is a no brainer at this small country
★ hotel on a hillside, with fantastic views out over Lough Arrow and a pleasant, country-style interior. Bedrooms are spacious, decorated in pastel shades, and look out over the lough. The restaurant (reservations required) is notable; all the tables have panoramic views. Two typical—and delicious—entrées include fillet of turbot on a julienne of fennel with Pernod cream, and a warm salad of marinaded lamb fillet with organic lentils. The staff can guide you to beautiful walks in the area—walks ranging from 20 minutes to two hours. The hotel is off N4 at Castlebaldwin, 27 km (17 mi) east of Sligo and 8 km (5 mi) east of Ballymote. ⊠ *Lough Arrow, Castlebaldwin, Co. Sligo,* ☎ *071/65155,* FAX *071/65455,* WEB *www.cromleach.com. 10 rooms with bath. Restaurant, golf privileges, hiking, bar, Internet at reception, meeting room. AE, DC, MC, V. Closed Nov.–Jan.*

$–$$ ✕⊡ **Temple House.** This vast Georgian mansion on more than 1,000 acres, with a working farm and organic garden, has been in owners Sandy and Deb Perceval's family since 1665. Rooms are furnished with Georgian and Victorian furniture, including mahogany tables and sideboards and the original rugs. Outside are formal terraced gardens and a pike fishing lake with waterside footpaths. Deb prepares the evening meal (book by noon), using farm-fresh produce, accompanied by fine wines. Typical entrées include herbed leg of lamb with roast potatoes, tomato fondue and glazed carrots, and poached wild salmon with hollandaise and cucumber sauce. Children can sleep in an annex to your room, and high tea is served for younger visitors at 6:30 PM daily—since they're not allowed in the dining room in the evenings. Sandy has allergies, so avoid using perfumes, deodorants, and aerosols. The house is about 19 km (12 mi) south of Sligo, signposted off N17. ⊠ *Ballymote, Co. Sligo,* ☎ *071/83329,* FAX *071/83808,* WEB *www.templehouse.ie. 6 rooms with bath. Dining room, boating, fishing; no room phones or TVs. AE, MC, V. Closed Dec.–Mar.*

$ ✕⊡ **Glebe House.** In this roomy and elegant Georgian house, beautifully restored by Franco-Irish couple Marc and Brid Torrades, expect a relaxed place with simple but pleasantly furnished rooms and a restaurant with a splendid reputation for using fresh local ingredients with a fancy edge. Typical entrées include wild salmon from the river on the property, flavored with sorrel from the house's herb garden and served in puff pastry. Or indulge in other stars of the menu: chicken pie, hot buttered oysters, filet steak with whiskey, and duck with olives. To get here take the N4 from Sligo toward Dublin and follow the sign for Coolaney at the second roundabout. ⊠ *Coolaney Rd., Collooney, Co. Sligo,* ☎ *071/67787,* FAX *071/30438,* WEB *www.glebehouse-restaurant. com. 6 rooms: 3 with bath, 3 with shower. Restaurant, 18-hole golf course,* *fishing, hiking, meeting rooms; no room TVs. AE, DC, MC, V. Closed mid-Nov.–mid-Mar..*

$$ ▥ **Sligo Park Hotel.** Why do predictable, reliable comforts appeal only to business travelers? Here you can expect a first-rate fitness center, dancing and piano entertainment on some evenings, and a modern, well-designed, and extremely comfortable establishment—not to mention the friendly staff and excellent restaurant (with a well-chosen wine list). It's 2 km (1 mi) out of Sligo Town on N4, and is a reasonable base if you're coming to Yeats Country. ⊠ *Pearse Rd., Co. Sligo,* ☎ *071/60291,* FAX *071/69556,* WEB *www.leehotels.ie. 110 rooms with bath. Restaurant, tennis court, indoor pool, health club, bar. AE, DC, MC, V.*

$ ▥ **Silver Swan Hotel.** In the center of Sligo Town on the Hyde Bridge you'll find a comfortable and inexpensive hotel with a wonderful view of the Garavogue River rushing beneath the bridge. The 1960s-style exterior may disturb style purists, but the interior has been redecorated and the bedrooms refurbished with dark-wood modern furnishings. Noise can be a problem when the hotel is hosting live music sessions on Saturday, so ask for a room away from the louder public rooms below. ⊠ *Hyde Bridge, Co. Sligo,* ☎ *071/43231,* FAX *071/42232. 29 rooms with bath. Restaurant, bar. AE, DC, MC, V.*

Nightlife and the Arts

PUBS AND CLUBS

A few miles south of town, a popular spot with the locals, the **Thatch** pub (⊠ Thatch, Ballysadare, ☎ 071/67288), has traditional music sessions from Thursday to Sunday. Open later than most other pubs, **Toffs** (⊠ Kennedy Parade, ☎ 071/61250) has a sizable dance floor that teems with Sligo's younger set bopping to a mix of contemporary dance music and older favorites.

FESTIVALS AND SEASONAL EVENTS

Established in 1959, the **Yeats International Summer School** takes place during the first two weeks of August. Scholarly lectures, poetry readings, and various side events are open to the public. For details contact the Yeats Society (⊠ Yeats Memorial Building, Hyde Bridge, ☎ 071/42693, WEB www.yeats-sligo.com).

Dozens of high-profile and local performers take part in the **Sligo Arts Festival** (☎ 071/69802), held during late May and early June.

THEATER

Sligo Town's **Hawk's Well Theatre** hosts amateur and professional companies from all over Ireland (and occasionally from Britain) in an eclectic mix of shows. ⊠ *Temple St.,* ☎ *071/61526.* ▧ *€5.08–€20.32.* ☾ *Box office Mon.–Sat. 10–6; call for show times.*

Outdoor Activities and Sports

BICYCLING

Explore Lough Gill, Rosses Point, and other areas of scenic beauty by renting a bicycle from **Gary's Cycles** (⊠ Quay St., ☎ 071/45418); fees are €8.89 per day, €50.79 per week.

GOLF

County Sligo Golf Club (⊠ Rosses Point, ☎ 071/77186), also known as Rosses Point, is one of Ireland's great championship links.

HORSEBACK RIDING

For riding in the countryside around Sligo, contact the **Sligo Riding Centre** (⊠ Carramore, ☎ 071/61353).

Shopping

Sligo Town has the Northwest's most thriving shopping scene, with lots of food-related, crafts, and hand-knits shops. In addition to stylish sweaters, **Carraig Donn** (✉ 41 O'Connell St., ☎ 071/44158, WEB www.carraigdonn.com) carries pottery, glassware, linens, and children's Aran knits. The **Cat & the Moon** (✉ 4 Castle St., ☎ 071/43686, WEB www.thecatandthemoon.com) specializes in eclectic and stylish Irish-made crafts, jewelry, pottery, ironwork, and scarves. The upscale deli **Cosgrove and Son** (✉ 32 Market St., ☎ 071/42809) sells everything from Parma ham to Carageen moss boiled in milk (a local cure for stomach upsets). Stock up here for a picnic. **Cross Sections** (✉ 2 Grattan St., ☎ 071/42265) sells lovely tableware, glassware, and kitchenware. **Tir na nóg** (✉ Grattan St., ☎ 071/62752), Irish for "Land of the Ever-young," sells organic foods, including local cheeses and honeys, and other health-oriented items; a sister store across the street sells cards and posters.

Knocknarea

❾ *8 km (5 mi) southwest of Sligo Town on R292 Strandhill Rd.*

Knocknarea—the "cairn-heaped grassy hill," as Yeats called it—rises 1,083 ft to the southwest of Sligo Town on a promontory that juts into Sligo Bay. The mountain is also memorably depicted in W. B.'s brother Jack's painting *Knocknarea and the Flowing Tide.* A car park on R292 gives pedestrian access (a 45-minute walk) to the summit, where there's a tremendous view of the mountains of Counties Donegal and Sligo. At its summit, and visible from a distance, sits a huge cairn—a heaped-stone monument made with 40,000 tons of rock. The cairn is traditionally associated with "passionate Maeve," as Yeats called her, the 1st-century AD Celtic queen of Connaught who went to war with the men of Ulster in a bid to win the mighty Bull of Cuailgne, and who was subsequently killed while bathing in a lake. The story is told in the *Táin,* the greatest of all the Irish heroic legends. Romantics like to think that Maeve is buried in this massive cairn, although archaeologists suspect that it more likely covers a 3,000-year-old passage grave. Either way, it's a pleasant climb on a summer day, and nature has installed a handy stream for washing your boots as you take the lane back down.

Strandhill, a seaside resort with a touch of charm, is 3 km (2 mi) northwest of Knocknarea, off R292. It has a fine, sandy beach and rolling waves favored by surfers. The **Perfect Day Surf Club** (✉ Strandhill, ☎ 071/68464) offers 1½ hrs of instruction plus equipment for €20. It caters to surfing novices and aficionados alike and is approved by the European Surf Federation and Irish Surfing Association. **Celtic Seaweed Baths** (✉ Strandhill, ☎ 071/68686) offers a one-hour steam and seaweed bath treatment for €19.05.

En Route **Carrowmore,** the largest group of megalithic tombs in all of the British Isles, is a short drive southeast of Knocknarea (on the minor road back to Sligo Town). The oldest of the 60 tombs, dolmens, and other ruins here predate those at Newgrange by roughly 700 years; most are communal tombs dating from 4800 BC, though unfortunately more than 100 have been badly damaged, leaving around 40. A restored cottage houses a small exhibition about the tombs. ✉ *Carrowmore,* ☎ *071/ 61534.* ▢ *€1.90.* ☉ *May–Oct., daily 9:30–6:30.*

Lough Gill

★ **❿** *1½ km (1 mi) east of Sligo Town on R286, 17½ km (11 mi) east of Knocknarea.*

Beautiful, gentle Lough Gill means simply "Lake Beauty" in Irish. When the soldiers of Sir Frederick Hamilton sacked Sligo in 1642, legend has it that they flung the silver bell of the abbey into the depths of Lough Gill, where today it is said that only the "pure" can hear it ring. In fine weather the lough and its surroundings are serenity itself: sunlight on the meadows all around, loughside cottages, the gentle sound of water, salmon leaping, a yacht sailing by. To get to the Lough from Sligo Town, take Stephen Street, which turns into N16 (signposted to Manorhamilton and Enniskillen). Turn right almost at once onto R286. Within minutes you will find gorgeous views of the lake so adored by the young Yeats.

On the eastern shore of Lough Gill, **Parke's Castle** is a sturdy, fortified house built in the 17th century by an English planter (a colonist settling on Irish lands confiscated from Catholic owners) who needed the strong fortifications to defend himself against a hostile populace. His relations with the people were made worse by the fact that he obtained his building materials mainly by dismantling a historic fortress on the site, formerly belonging to the clan leaders of the O'Rourkes of Breffni (once the name of the district). The entrance fee includes a short video show on the castle and local history. There's also a snack bar. In the summer, boat tours of the lough leave from here. Times vary, but the Sligo TIO has up-to-date information. ⊠ *Fivemile Bourne, on R288,* ☎ *071/64149.* ⌑ *€2.55.* ☉ *Mar. 13–17, daily 10–5; Apr.–May, Tues.–Sun. 10–5; June–Sept., daily 9:30–6:30; Oct., daily 10–5.*

A few minutes' walk along a footpath south of Parke's Castle lie the handsome ruins of **Creevelea Abbey.** In fact not an abbey but a friary, Creevelea was founded for the Franciscans in 1508 by a later generation of O'Rourkes. It was the last Franciscan community to be founded before the suppression of the monasteries by England's King Henry VIII. Like many other decrepit abbeys, the place still holds religious significance for locals—who revere it. One curiosity here is the especially large south transept; notice, too, its endearing little cloisters, with well-executed carvings on the pillars of St. Francis of Assisi. ⊠ *Signposted at Dromahair on R288.* ⌑ *Free.* ☉ *Freely accessible.*

Dining and Lodging

$ ✕⌑ **Stanford Village Inn.** This stone-fronted inn is one of the only stops where you can gain sustenance near Lough Gill. It has six newly refurbished, country-style rooms. A hearty meal of traditional home-cooked food, an open fire, and, if your timing is good, an impromptu session of traditional Irish music await you. The inn is off of R288, 19 km (12 mi) outside of Sligo Town. ⊠ *Dromahair, Co. Leitrim,* ☎ *071/64140,* ⓕⓐⓧ *071/64770. 6 rooms with bath. Restaurant, bar. MC, V.*

Lake Isle of Innisfree

⓫ *15 km (9 mi) south of Sligo Town via Dromahair on N4 and R287.*

In 1890 William Butler Yeats was walking through the West End of London when, seeing in a shop window a ball dancing on a jet of water, he was suddenly overcome with nostalgia for the lakes of his Sligo home. It was the moment, and the feeling, that shaped itself into his most famous poem, "The Lake Isle of Innisfree":

I will arise and go now, and go to Innisfree,
And a small cabin build there, of clay and wattles made:
Nine bean-rows will I have there, a hive for the honey-bee,
And live alone in the bee-loud glade.

Though there is nothing visually exceptional about Innisfree (pronounced *innish*-free), the "Lake Isle" is a must-see if you're a Yeats fan. To reach Innisfree from Dromahair, take R287, the minor road that heads back along the south side of Lough Gill, toward Sligo

Town. Turn right at a small crossroads, after 4 or 5 km (2 or 3 mi), where signposts point to Innisfree. A little road leads another couple of miles down to the lakeside, where you can see the island just offshore.

OFF THE
BEATEN PATH
DOONEY ROCK – On the southwestern end of Lough Gill, a little beyond the Innisfree turnoff, a tranquil nature walk takes you to this rock, from the top of which is a picturesque panorama of the lake and of Cottage Island; this is where Yeats daydreamed, contemplated the lake's islands, and imagined a fiddler on the rock who made "folk dance like a wave of the sea." A brochure from the wooden box in the parking lot gives the particulars of the area's diverse flora, as well as a few interesting historical tidbits.

Manorhamilton

⑫ *25 km (15 mi) east of Sligo Town.*

The small rural town of Manorhamilton was built in the 17th century for the Scottish planter Sir Frederick Hamilton, who had been given the local manor house by Charles I of England (hence the town's name). The manor itself is now an ivy-covered ruin, and there's not much to see here. The surrounding scenery, however, is spectacular.

En Route   On your way to Rosses Point, stop at **Glencar Lough,** where you'll find several waterfalls; a footpath veering off from a parking lot leads to one of the highest. The lake is fed by the River Drumcliff and streams at the foot of the Dartry Mountains: "Where the wandering water gushes/From the hills above Glencar/In pools among the rushes/That scarce could bathe a star," as Yeats put it in his poem "The Stolen Child." ✉ *16 km (10 mi) west of Manorhamilton on N16; right at waterfall signpost.*

Rosses Point

⑬ *8 km (5 mi) northwest of Sligo Town on R291, 38½ km (24 mi) west of Manorhamilton.*

It's obvious why Yeats and his brother Jack often stayed at Rosses Point during their summer vacations: glorious pink and gold summer sunsets over a seemingly endless stretch of sandy beach. **Coney Island** lies just off Rosses Point. Local lore has it that the captain of the ship *Arathusa* christened Brooklyn's Coney Island after this island, but there's probably more legend than truth to this, as it's widely agreed that New York's Coney Island was named after the *konijn* ("wild rabbits" in Dutch) that abounded there during the 17th century. If you're a golfer, definitely check out the popular **County Sligo Golf Club** (Rosses Point, ☎ 071/77186). It's one of Ireland's grand old venues, as it's more than a century old, and has hosted hosted most of the country's major championships. It has magnificent views of the sea and Ben Bulben. The **Sligo Yacht Club** (Rosses Point, ☎ 071/77168), with a fleet of some 25 boats, has sailing and social programs, and regularly hosts races.

Drumcliff

⑭ *7 km (4½ mi) north of Sligo Town on N15, 15 km (9½ mi) northeast of Rosses Point.*

W. B. Yeats lies buried with his wife, Georgie, in an unpretentious grave in the cemetery of Drumcliff's simple Protestant church, where his grandfather was rector for many years. Yeats actually died on the French

Riviera in 1939, but it took almost a full decade for his body to be brought back here—to the place that more than any other might be called his soul-land. In the poem "Under Ben Bulben," he spelled out not only where he was to be buried but also what should be written on the tombstone: "Cast a cold eye/On life, on death./Horseman, pass by!" It is easy to see why the majestic Ben Bulben (1,730 ft), with its sawed-off peak (not unlike Yosemite's Half-Dome), made such an impression on the poet: the mountain gazes calmly down upon the small church, as it does on all of the surrounding landscape—and at the same time stands as a sentinel facing the mighty Atlantic.

In addition to its significance as a Yeats site, Drumcliff is where St. Columba, a recluse and missionary who established Christian churches and religious communities in Northwest Ireland, is thought to have founded a monastic settlement around AD 575. The monastery that he founded before sailing off to the Scottish isle of Iona flourished for many centuries, but all that is left of it now is the base of a **round tower** and a carved **high cross** (both across N15 from the church) dating from around AD 1000, with scenes from the Old and New Testaments, including Adam and Eve with the serpent and Cain slaying Abel.

The **Drumcliff Visitors' Centre** (⊠ next to the Protestant church, ☎ 071/ 44956) is a good place to stop for a snack and to pick up some local crafts, Yeats poetry, and books about him; it's open from March through October.

Lissadell House

🅖 *14½ km (9 mi) northwest of Sligo Town, 3½ km (2 mi) west of Drumcliff, signposted from N15.*

Beside the Atlantic waters of Drumcliff Bay, on the peninsula that juts out between Donegal and Sligo bays, Lissadell—"That old Georgian mansion," as Yeats called it—is an austere but classic residence built in 1834 by Sir Robert Gore-Booth. An enlightened landlord, he mortgaged the house to help his poverty-stricken tenants during the famine years. His descendants still own Lissadell, which is filled with all manner of artifacts brought back from every corner of the globe by the family, who were great travelers. Aficionados of all things Yeatsian will appreciate the house, for the family became good friends of William Butler Yeats, who recalled seeing the house often as a child from his grandmother's carriage. On a visit to the house in 1894, he met the two Gore-Booth daughters, Eva and Constance, and subsequently recalled their meeting in verse: "The light of evening, Lissadell,/Great windows open to the south,/Two girls in silk kimonos." Eva became a poet, while sister Constance Markievicz led a dramatic political life as a fiery Irish nationalist, taking a leading role in the 1916 Easter Uprising against the British. She survived the uprising, going on to become the first woman member of the Dáil (Irish Parliament).

Lissadell was designed by the London architect Francis Goodwin. Its two most notable features are a dramatic 33-ft-high gallery, with 24-ft-tall Doric columns, clerestory windows, and skylights; and the dining room, where Constance's husband, Count Markievicz, painted portraits of members of the family and household employees on the pilasters. A copy of Yeats's poem, "In Memory of Eva Gore-Booth and Con Markievicz," is displayed in the house. The woods of the Lissadell estate have become a forestry and wildlife reserve; they house Ireland's largest colony of barnacle geese, along with several other species of wildfowl, and are a fine place for bird-watchers. ☎ *071/63150.* ⊠ €3.81. ☉ *June–mid-Sept., Mon.–Sat. 10:30–12:30 and 2–4:15.*

AROUND DONEGAL BAY

As you drive north from Sligo Town to Donegal Town, the glens of the Dartry Mountains (home of Ben Bulben) gloriously roll by to the east, while coastal fields offer startling views across the waters of Donegal Bay to the west. In the distant horizon the Donegal hills beckon. This stretch, dotted with numerous prehistoric sites, has become the Northwest's most popular vacation area. You'll pass a few small and unremarkable seashore resorts, and in some places you may find that haphazard and fairly tasteless construction detracts from the scenery. In between these minor resort developments, you'll find wide-open spaces free of traffic. The most intriguing part of this area lies on the north side of the bay—all that rocky indented coastline due west of Donegal Town. Here you enter the heart of away-from-it-all: County Donegal.

Mullaghmore

⑯ *20 km (13 mi) northeast of Lissadell House, 37 km (24 mi) north of Sligo Town.*

In high season, the picturesque, sleepy fishing village of Mullaghmore gets congested with tourists. Its main attractions: a 3¼-km-long (2-mi-long) sandy beach; the turreted, fairy-tale Classie Bawn, the late Lord Louis Mountbatten's home (he, his grandson, and a local boy were killed when the IRA blew up his boat in the bay in 1979); and Ben Bulben rising up in the distance. A short drive along the headland is punctuated by unobstructed views beyond the rocky coastline out over Donegal Bay. When the weather is fair, you can see all the way across to St. John's Point and Drumanoo Head in Donegal.

Dining and Lodging

$ ✕⊞ Beach Hotel. If there's a chill in the air, you can warm up at the roaring fires in the restaurant and residents' lounge of this large harborside Victorian hotel. The dramatic brick red building is decorated in a nautical theme to commemorate the loss of three galleons of the Spanish Armada in the bay in September 1588. Enjoy wonderful views of the pier and the bay from the hotel bars, or tuck into the de'Cuellar Restaurant's acclaimed seafood menu. Try the favorites: hot crab claws, lobster, and the house seafood platter. Save room for the homemade apple and rhubarb crumble. A four-course set meal costs €29. ⊠ *Co. Sligo,* ☎ *071/66103,* ℻ *071/66448,* ⌨ *www.beachhotelmullaghmore.com. 28 rooms with bath. Restaurant, indoor pool, hot tub, sauna, steam room, gymnasium, horseback riding, 2 bars. AE, MC, V.*

Creevykeel

⑰ *3 km (2 mi) southeast of Mullaghmore, 16 km (10 mi) north of Drumcliff signposted from N15.*

Creevykeel is one of Ireland's best megalithic court-tombs. The site (signposted) lies off the road, just beyond the edge of the village of Cliffony. You'll see a burial area and an enclosed open-air "court" where rituals were performed around 3000 BC. Bronze artifacts found here are now in the National Museum in Dublin.

Bundoran

⑱ *12 km (8 mi) northeast of Creevykeel on N15.*

Resting on the south coast of County Donegal, Bundoran is one of Ireland's most popular seaside resorts, a favorite haunt of the Irish from both the North and the South. If souvenir shops and amusement arcades aren't your thing, north of the town center is a handsome beach at **Tullan Strand,** washed by good surfing waves. Between the main beach and Tullan, the Atlantic has sculpted cliff-side rock formations that the locals have christened with whimsical names such as the Fairy Bridges, the Wishing Chair, and the Puffing Hole (this last one blows wind and water from the waves pounding below).

Outdoor Activities and Sports

FISHING

Good fishing is 6½ km (4 mi) away from Bundoran at **Lough Melvin.** Ask locally for **Pat Barrett's Tackle Shop** (⊠ Main St., ☏ 072/41504) for bait, tackle, and local information.

GOLF

Bundoran Golf Club (☏ 072/41302, WEB www.bundorangolfclub.com) is an 18-hole, par-70 course on the cliffs above Bundoran beach.

Ballyshannon

🔟 *6½ km (4 mi) north of Bundoran on N15.*

The former garrison town of Ballyshannon rises gently from the banks of the River Erne and has good views of Donegal Bay and the surrounding mountains. Come in early August, when this quiet village springs to life with a grand festival of folk and traditional music. The town is a hodgepodge of shops, arcades, and hotels; its triangular central area has several bars and places to grab a snack. The town was also the birthplace of the prolific Irish poet William Allingham. The biggest and most popular pub is **Seán Óg's** (⊠ Market St., ☏ 072/58964), which has live traditional music on Wednesday and contemporary music on weekends.

You'll find exquisite chinaware and porcelain at the **Donegal Irish Parian China Factory,** the Republic's largest manufacturer of Parian china (so named because it resembles the clear white marble from the Greek island of Paros). There's a free 15-minute tour, a 10-minute video, and a showroom, shop, and tearoom.

OFF THE BEATEN PATH

LOUGH DERG – From Whitsunday to the Feast of the Assumption (June to mid-August), tens of thousands beat a path to this lake, ringed by heather-clad slopes. In the center of the lough, Station Island—known as St. Patrick's Purgatory—is one of Ireland's most popular pilgrimage sites. It's also the most rigorous and austere of such sites in the country. Pilgrims stay on the island for three days without sleeping, and eat only black tea and dry toast. They walk barefoot around the island, on its flinty stones, to pray at a succession of shrines. The pilgrimage has been followed since time immemorial; during the Middle Ages, devotees from foreign lands flocked here. To reach the shores of Lough Derg, turn off the main N15 Sligo–Donegal road in the village of Laghy onto the minor R232 Pettigo road, which hauls itself over the Black Gap and descends sharply into the border village of Pettigo, about 21 km (13 mi) from N15. From here, take the Lough Derg access road for 8 km (5 mi). Note: nonpilgrims may not visit the island from June to mid-August. To find out more or to become a pilgrim, write to the Reverend Prior. ⊠ *Lough Derg, Pettigo, Co. Donegal.*

Dining and Lodging

$$ ✕🏠 **Sand House Hotel.** Behind the mock manor-house exterior of this 19th-century former fishing lodge lies a large, modern hotel. Right on Donegal Bay, about 8 km (5 mi) northwest of Ballyshannon and 16

km (10 mi) south of Donegal Town, this makes a peaceful, well-positioned base for sightseeing along the coastline; the hotel has access to 3 km (2 mi) of beach. Renovated, well-kept bedrooms are beautifully decorated with antiques and overlook either the sea or the Donegal hills. The restaurant caters to the plain, hearty appetites of Irish vacationers looking for something a bit special. Fresh seafood, including Donegal Bay oysters and mussels, is the daily specialty. ⊠ *Rossnowlagh, Co. Donegal,* ☎ *072/51777,* FAX *072/52100,* WEB *www.sandhouse-hotel.ie. 60 rooms with bath. Restaurant, golf privileges, tennis court, horseback riding, Ping-Pong, fishing, bar, Internet, meeting rooms. AE, DC, MC, V. Closed Nov.–Jan.*

Nightlife and the Arts

In early June, during the **Ballyshannon Drama Festival** (☎ 072/52109), the town hosts different drama companies for a program of mainly Irish plays. Held on the bank holiday weekend at the beginning of August, the **Ballyshannon Music Festival** (☎ 072/51088, WEB www.ballyshannonfolkfestival.com) is one of Ireland's largest, longest-running, and best folk-music events. You can hear both well-known and unknown folk and traditional musicians, while impromptu sessions pop up at pubs. Street entertainment includes activities for children. A party atmosphere prevails, attracting up to 12,000 visitors annually.

Shopping

The goods of the best-known producer of Belleek chinaware, **Belleek Pottery Ltd.** (⊠ 6½ km [4 mi] away, on the border between the Republic and the North, ☎ 028/6865–8501 in Northern Ireland, WEB www.belleek.ie), can be found in the shops of Donegal and Sligo.

About 1½ km (1 mi) west of Belleek, before the border to Northern Ireland, you'll find **Celtic Weave China** (⊠ R230, Cloghore, ☎ 072/51844, WEB www.celticweavechina.ie). This small family business specializes in the basket-weave design and in elaborate floral decoration, and they can make a single piece of china to your specifications. Prices range from €7 upward, but most pieces cost less than €125.

Donegal Irish Parian China Factory (⊠ on N15 south of Ballyshannon, ☎ 072/51826, WEB www.donegalchina.ie) makes delicate, cream-color pottery by traditional methods, to a large degree by hand. The factory sells its wares at lower prices than you'll see in retail stores. The least expensive items (spoons or thimbles) cost around €7.50. A full tea set starts at about €315.

Donegal Town

20 *21 km (13 mi) north of Ballyshannon, 66 km (41 mi) northeast of Sligo Town.*

With a population of about 3,000, Donegal is Northwest Ireland's largest small village—marking the entry into the back-of-the-beyond of the wilds of County Donegal. The town is centered on the triangular Diamond, where three roads converge (N56 to the west, N15 to the south and the northeast) and the mouth of the River Eske pours gently into Donegal Bay. You should have your bearings in five minutes, and seeing the historical sights takes less than an hour; if you stick around any longer, it'll probably be to do some shopping—arguably Donegal's top attraction.

Donegal was previously known in Irish as Dun na nGall, "Fort of the Foreigners." The foreigners were Vikings, who set up camp here in the 9th century to facilitate their pillaging and looting. They were driven out by the powerful O'Donnell clan (originally Cinel Conail), who made it the capital of Tyrconail, their extensive Ulster territories. Donegal was rebuilt in the early 17th century, during the Plantation period, when Protestant colonists were planted on Irish property confiscated from their Catholic owners. The **Diamond,** like that of many other Irish villages, dates from this period. Once a marketplace, it has a 20-ft obelisk monument to the Four Masters.

Donegal Castle was built by clan leader Hugh O'Donnell in the 1470s. More than a century later, this structure was the home of his descendant Hugh Roe O'Donnell, who faced the might of the invading English and was the last clan chief of Tyrconail. In 1602 he died on a trip to Spain while trying to rally reinforcements from his allies. In 1610, its new English owner, Sir Basil Brooke, reconstructed the little castle, adding the fine Jacobean fortified mansion with towers and turrets that can still be seen today (he was responsible for the Diamond, as well). The small enclosed grounds are pleasant; inside, there are only a few rooms to see, including the garderobe (the rest room) and a great hall with an exceptional vaulted wood-beam roof. ⊠ *Tirchonaill St., near north corner of the Diamond,* ☎ *073/22405.* ⊡ *€3.80.* ☉ *Easter–Oct., daily 9:30–6:30.*

The ruins of the **Franciscan abbey,** founded in 1474 by Hugh O'Donnell, are a five-minute walk south of town at a spectacular site perched above the Eske, where it begins to open up into Donegal Bay. The complex was burned to the ground in 1593, razed by the English in 1601, and ransacked again in 1607; the ruins include the choir, south transept, and two sides of the cloisters, between which lie hundreds of graves dating back to the 18th century. The abbey was probably where the *Annals of the Four Masters* was written from 1632 to 1636. The *Annals* chronicles the whole of Celtic history and mythology of Ireland from earliest times up to the year 1618. The **Four Masters** were four monks who believed (correctly, as it turned out) that Celtic culture was doomed after the English conquest, and they wanted to preserve as much of it as they could. At the National Library in Dublin, you can see facsimile pages of the monks' work; the original is kept under lock and key. ⊠ *Off N15, behind Hyland Central Hotel.* ⊡ *Free.* ☉ *Freely accessible.*

Dining and Lodging

$ ✕ **Blueberry Tea Room.** At this pleasant ground-floor restaurant and café, across the street from Donegal Castle, proprietors Brian and Ruperta Gallagher serve breakfast, lunch, afternoon tea, and a light evening meal—always using home-grown herbs. Daily specials—Irish lamb stew, pasta dishes, and quiche—are served from 8 AM to 8 PM. Soups, sandwiches, salads, and fruit are on the regular menu, along with homemade desserts, breads, scones, and jams. Upstairs is an Internet café. ⊠ *Castle St.,* ☎ *073/22933. V. Closed Sun.*

$$$$ ✕⊡ **St. Ernan's House.** On its own wooded tidal island in Donegal Bay,
★ a five-minute drive from town, St. Ernan's is one of the most spectacularly situated country houses in Ireland. The two-story house was built by a nephew of the Duke of Wellington in 1826. Brian and Carmel O'Dowd, the meticulous owner-managers, have created a relaxed, serene environment. Guest rooms are simple but elegant, with antiques and views of the bay. Dinner, from a light meal ($$) to a leisurely five-course meal ($$$$), is served in the intimate, elegant dining room (open to nonguests). On the menu, which changes nightly, you'll find dishes based on fresh local produce, prepared in Irish country-house style. Pigeon and quail with oyster mushrooms is a typical starter; lamb in a rich red wine sauce or wild salmon might follow. A stroll around the island is a perfect way to finish off the evening. ⊠ *St. Ernan's, Co.*

Donegal, ☎ *073/21065,* FAX *073/22098,* WEB *www.sainternans.com. 8 rooms with bath, 2 suites. Restaurant. MC, V. Closed Nov.–Easter.*

$$ ✕⌷ **Harvey's Point.** At the foot of the Blue Stack Mountains, nestled beside Lough Eske, this Swiss-owned hotel has spacious, well-equipped bedrooms, where you'll find complimentary decanters of brandy and sherry. The dining room, which has spirit-lifting lake views, sets the scene for a meal of wild Irish smoked salmon (in generous helpings), monkfish, duck, and other fresh Irish fare served with a French twist. ✉ *Lough Eske, Co. Donegal,* ☎ *073/22208,* FAX *073/22352,* WEB *www.harveyspoint.com. 20 rooms with bath. Restaurant, tennis court, boating, bicycles, bar. AE, DC, MC, V.*

$$$ ⌷ **Hyland Central.** Right on Donegal's central square, this family-run hotel is affiliated with Best Western. Huge picture windows in the back reveal lovely views of Donegal Bay. The efficient staff serves good, filling food in the large dining room. ✉ *The Diamond, Co. Donegal,* ☎ *073/21027,* FAX *073/22295. 112 rooms with bath. Dining room, indoor pool, health club. AE, DC, MC, V.*

Nightlife and the Arts

The **Abbey Hotel** (✉ The Diamond, ☎ 073/21014, WEB www. whites-hotelsireland.com) has music every night in July and August and a disco every Saturday and Sunday night throughout the year. During the summer, people pack **McGroarty's Bar** (✉ north side of the Diamond, ☎ 073/21049) for traditional music Thursday nights, contemporary on Saturdays and Sundays; it's also a good place to stop for a casual bite.

Outdoor Activities and Sports

About 8 km (5 mi) from Donegal Town is **Donegal Golf Club** (✉ Murvagh, Laghy, Co. Donegal, ☎ 073/34054, WEB www.donegalgolfclub.ie), with one of Ireland's great championship courses.

Shopping

Browse a While (✉ Main St., ☎ 074/22783) is a good place to stop off if you're in the mood for some light reading. The shop is stocked with tons of magazines and a small selection of pulp fiction. Long the principal marketplace for the region's wool products, Donegal Town has several smaller shops with local hand weaving, knits, and crafts. The main store in town, **Magee's** (✉ The Diamond, ☎ 073/22660, WEB www.mageeshop.com), carries renowned private-label tweeds for both men and women (jackets, hats, scarves, suits, and more), as well as pottery, linen, and crystal. **Simple Simon's** (✉ The Diamond, ☎ 073/22687), the only fresh food shop in town, sells organic vegetables, essential oils, and other whole-earth items, as well as breads and cakes from the kitchen on the premises. They also sell a lot of local Irish cheeses. About 1½ km (1 mi) south of town, beside the main N15, you'll find the **Donegal Craft Village,** a complex of workshops where you can buy pottery, handwoven goods, and ceramics from local young craftspeople. You can even watch the items being made.

En Route As you travel west on N56, which runs slightly inland from a magnificent shoreline of rocky inlets with great sea views, it's worthwhile turning off the road from time to time to catch a better view of the coast. About 6½ km (4 mi) out of Donegal Town, N56 skirts **Mountcharles,** a bleak hillside village that looks back across the bay.

Bruckless

㉑ *19 km (12 mi) west of Donegal Town on N56.*

Don't be fooled by the round tower in the churchyard at Bruckless— it's 19th-century, not medieval. Soon after Bruckless, N56 turns inland across the bogs toward Ardara. The road now becomes R263, which runs through attractive heathland and wooded hills down to Killybegs.

Dining and Lodging

$ ✕⌂⊞ **Castle Murray House Hotel.** Panoramas of distant mountains, the sapphire-blue waters of MacSwyne's Bay, and the long, narrow peninsula, punctuated at its tip by a lighthouse, await you at this hotel 1½ km (1 mi) out on the 9½-km-long (6-mi-long) St. John's Point Peninsula. The original house has been extended and modernized; rooms are basic but comfortable. Natives trek here for the restaurant ($$), where Thierry Delcros, the French-born owner-chef, prepares superb French cuisine. Selections might include filo-wrapped parcel of duck or the specialty of the house, prawns and monkfish in garlic butter. The hotel is 21 km (13 mi) west of Donegal Town. ⊠ *St. John's Point, Dunkineely, Co. Donegal,* ☎ *073/37022,* ₣₳ₓ *073/37330,* ₩Ɛ฿ *www.castlemurray. com. 10 rooms with bath. Restaurant, bar. MC, V. Closed mid-Jan.– mid-Feb. and Mon.–Tues. mid-Feb.–Easter and Oct.–mid-Jan.*

$ ⊞ **Bruckless House.** A two-story 18th-century farmhouse on the north side of Donegal Bay, 8 km (5 mi) outside Killybegs and within an easy drive of Glencolumbkille, Ardara, and Donegal Town, this unusual bed-and-breakfast occupies 19 acres, including woods, gardens, and a meadow where Irish draft horses and Connemara ponies roam. Public rooms in the main building have a fine view of Bruckless Bay; the rooms have an Asian flavor reflecting years spent in Hong Kong by the owners, Clive and Joan Evans. Upstairs, the bedrooms are conventional but comfortable. A separate two-bedroom self-catering gate lodge, the former servants quarters, is at the entrance to the estate. Wholesome breakfasts are prepared with fruit from the Evanses' prizewinning garden and freshly laid eggs from their hens. ⊠ *Co. Donegal,* ☎ *073/37071,* ₣₳ₓ *073/37070,* ₩Ɛ฿ *www.iol.ie/~bruc/bruckless.html. 4 rooms, 2 with bath; 1 2-bedroom gate lodge. Dining room, Internet on request; no room phones, no room TVs. AE, MC, V. Closed Oct.– Mar.*

Killybegs

㉒   *6½ km (4 mi) west of Bruckless, 28 km (17 mi) west of Donegal Town on R263.*

Trawlers from Spain and France are moored in the harbor at Killybegs, one of Ireland's busiest fishing ports. Though it's one of the most industrialized places along this coast, it's not without some charm, thanks to its waterfront location. Killybegs once served as a center for the manufacture of Donegal hand-tufted carpets, which can be found in the White House and the Vatican. The **Harbour Store** (⊠ Main St., ☎ 073/32122, ₩Ɛ฿ www.killybegs.ie), right on the wharf, has plenty to make both fishermen and landlubbers happy, including boots and rain gear, competitively priced sweaters, and unusual bright yellow or orange fiberglass-covered gloves (made in Taiwan).

Dining and Lodging

$ ✕⌂⊞ **Bay View Hotel.** Directly across from Killybegs's harbor, the Bay View is the town's most bustling spot. The hotel is spare and modish, nicely paneled in light wood, and the modern, functional bedrooms are pleasantly decorated in pale colors. The Irish table d'hôte menu changes daily, with Bruckless mussels in a white wine and garlic sauce and braised young duckling served with market vegetables and an orange and cherry coulis. The hotel is well placed for seeing the glorious north shore of Donegal Bay. Special rates include greens fees for Portnoo (outside Ardara) and Murvagh (outside Donegal) for golfers. ⊠ *Main St., Co. Donegal,* ☎ *073/31950,* ₣₳ₓ *073/31856,*

WEB *www.bayviewhotel.ie. 40 rooms with bath. Restaurant, indoor pool, health club, bar, Internet. AE, MC, V.*

En Route The narrows, climbs, and twists of R263 afford terrific views of Donegal Bay before descending into pretty **Kilcar,** a traditional center of tweed making. The next village, signposted by its Irish name, An Charraig (Carrick), clings to the foot of the **Slieve League Mountains,** whose dramatic, color-streaked ocean cliffs are, at 2,000 ft, the highest in Ireland and among the most spectacular. To see the cliffs, take the little road to the Irish-speaking village of Teelin, 1½ km (1 mi) south from Carrick. Then take the narrow lane (signposted to Bunglass) that climbs steeply to the top of the cliffs. For an even more thrilling perspective—presuming you're hardy—walk on the difficult coastal path from Teelin.

Glencolumbkille (Gleann Cholm Cille)

❷❸ *8 km (5 mi) west of Carrick, 27 km (17 mi) west of Killybegs on R263.*

At the far end of a stretch of barren moorland, the tiny hamlet of Glencolumbkille (pronounced glen-colm-*kill*) clings dramatically to the rockbound harbor of Glen Bay. Because it is at the heart of County Donegal's shrinking Gaeltacht, or Irish-speaking region, it has a strong, rural Irish flavor, as do its pubs and brightly painted row houses. Its name means St. Columba's Glen (or, alternatively, Columba's Glen Church); the legend goes that St. Columba, the Christian missionary, lived here during the 6th century with a group of followers. Some 40 prehistoric cairns, scattered around the village, have become connected locally with the St. Columba myths. The **House of St. Columba,** on the cliff top rising north of the village, is a small oratory said to have been used by the saint himself. Inside, stone constructions are thought to have been his bed and chair. Every year on June 9, starting at midnight, local people make a 3-km (2-mi) barefoot procession called "An Turas" (the journey) around 15 medieval crosses and ancient cairns, collectively called the stations of the cross.

Near the beach in Glencolumbkille is the **Folk Village,** an imaginative museum of rural life. Three small cottages, with bare-earth floors, represent the very basic living conditions of the 1720s, 1820s, and 1920s. The complex, which was built after local priest Father McDyer started a cooperative to help combat rural depopulation, includes an interpretive center, 1881 schoolhouse, nature walk, tea shop, and crafts shop selling local handmade products, including, intriguingly, wines made from fuchsias and bluebells. ☎ *073/30017.* ✆ *€2.55.* ☉ *Easter–Sept., Mon.–Sat. 10–6, Sun. noon–6.*

Ardara

★ ❷❹ *28 km (17 mi) northeast of Glencolumbkille, 40 km (25 mi) northwest of Donegal Town.*

At the head of a lovely ocean inlet, the unpretentious, old-fashioned hamlet of Ardara—for centuries an important wool-trading center and now a great place to buy a chunky Aran sweater—is built around the L-shape intersection of its two main streets. (If you come from Glencolumbkille, expect a scenic drive full of hairpin curves and steep hills as you cross over Glengesh Pass.) Great cloth fairs were once held on the first of every month, and cottage workers in the surrounding countryside still provide Ardara (and County Donegal) with high-quality, handwoven cloths and hand knits. Ardara, which bills itself as "Ireland's capital of handwoven tweeds and knitwear," has several stores to choose from. You can hear traditional music year-round at a num-

ber of pubs in Ardara. The long-established **Nesbitt Arms** (⌧ Main St.,
☎ 075/41103) is a good place for a reasonably priced drink and snack.
It can get very crowded during high season.

Dining and Lodging

\$–\$\$ ✕ **L'Atlantique Restaurant.** French couple Laure and Cyrille Troesch
cook up excellent seafood in this relaxed little restaurant. Lobster, their
specialty, drives the top price of main courses up, but the four-course
fixed-price menu at €16.38 is an excellent value. ⌧ *Main St.,* ☎ *075/
41707. MC, V. No dinner Sun.*

\$ ✕🖾 **Woodhill House.** John and Nancy Yates's spacious home stands
★   on 4 acres of wooded grounds only ½ km (¼ mi) from Ardara. The cream-
color exterior is Victorian, but parts of the interior and the coach house
date from the 17th century and the home contains a small agricultural
museum. High ceilings and marble fireplaces are in the fine public rooms;
the hall has a lovely round table and stained-glass window. Bedrooms
are less grand but large, with superb views of the Donegal highlands.
Visitors and locals alike enjoy frequent Irish folk music sessions in the
bar. The 40-seat restaurant uses fresh, local ingredients on its Cordon
Bleu à la carte and table d'hôte menus, with meals prepared in a
French-Irish style. Entrées might include duck in port wine sauce, wild
local salmon with garlic and spinach sauce, or rack of lamb with herbs
picked from the 18th-century walled garden. The elaborate desserts
are all homemade. ⌧ *Donegal Rd., Co. Donegal,* ☎ *075/41112,* 🅵🅰🅇
075/41516, 🆆🅴🅱 *www.woodhillhouse.com. 9 rooms with bath. Restaurant, horseback riding, fishing, bar. AE, DC, MC, V. Closed Christmas wk.*

\$ 🖾 **Green Gate.** For an alternative to country houses and village ho-
tels, try Frenchman Paul Chatenoud's remote cottage overlooking Ardara, the Atlantic, and spectacular Donegal scenery—it's one of Ireland's
most beautiful little guest houses. The four spare rooms are in a converted stone outbuilding with a thatched roof. Chatenoud, as charming as his hideaway, will eagerly direct you to Donegal's best-kept secrets.
To reach the hotel from Ardara, follow the sign for Donegal and turn
right after 200 yards. ⌧ *Ardvally, Co. Donegal,* ☎ *075/41546. 4
rooms with bath. No credit cards.*

\$ 🖾 **Greenhaven House.** Only a few minutes from the village, Eileen Mol-
loy's modern, one-story home has its own gardens and marvelous
views of the nearby mountains and bay. You'll be warmed by a peat
fire in the lounge and wake up to a hearty breakfast (included). Eileen
can also advise you on shopping for hand knits and other items. ⌧
Portnoo Rd., Co. Donegal, ☎ 🅵🅰🅇 *075/41129. 6 rooms with bath. Dining room, lounge; no room phones. No credit cards. Closed Dec.*

Nightlife and the Arts

For a small, old-fashioned village, Ardara has a surprising number of
pubs, many of which have traditional music in the evenings. The **Central Bar** (⌧ Main St., ☎ 075/41311) has music almost every night during the summer and on weekends the rest of the year. One of the
smallest bars in the Republic, **Nancy's Pub** (⌧ Front St., ☎ 075/
41187) has some corners that make you wonder if you've wandered
into the owner's sitting room; it finds space for a folk group several
nights a week in the high season.

Outdoor Activities and Sports

Rent a bike (€12.50 per day, €50 per week, group discounts) from
Donal Byrne (⌧ West End, ☎ 075/41156).

Shopping

Many handwoven and locally made knitwear items are on sale in Ardara; some stores commission goods directly from knitters, and prices

are about as low as you'll find anywhere. Handsome, chunky Aran hand-knit sweaters (€76–€127), cardigans (similar prices), and scarves (€20.32) are all widely available. Stores like **Campbells Tweed Shop** (⊠ Front St., ☎ 075/41128) carry ready-to-wear tweeds—sports jackets for women run up to about €152; for men, up to about €190. **C. Bonner & Son** (⊠ Front St., ☎ 075/41303) stocks factory knitwear from €29 to €100, as well as pottery, tweeds, jewelry, and gifts. **E. Doherty (Ardara) Ltd.** (⊠ Front St., ☎ 075/41304) sells handwoven tweeds from scarves for €25 to capes for €170, as well as traditional Irish products, such as glassware and linen, from Ardara and other parts of the country.

NORTHERN DONEGAL

Traveling on northern County Donegal's country roads, you'll feel as if you've escaped at last from the world's hurry and hassle. There's almost nothing up here but scenery, and plenty of it: broad, island-studded loughs of deep, dark tranquility; unkempt, windswept, sheep-grazed grasses on mountain slopes; ribbons of luminous greenery following sparkling streams; and the mellow hues of wide bog lands, all under shifting and changing cloudscapes. This trip—apart from Inishowen Peninsula, which is included as a separate excursion at the end—could take anywhere from one day to a week, depending on how low a gear you slip into after a few breaths of Donegal air. It begins in Letterkenny, the largest town in the county (population 6,500), but if you want to pick up the journey from Ardara, then follow the itinerary in reverse. If you choose to abbreviate the trip, try at least to catch the rewarding Fanad and Rosguill peninsulas and the drive around Sheephaven Bay. Just one word of warning—don't be a bit surprised if you find a sheep standing in the middle of a mountain road looking as though you, rather than it, are in the wrong place.

Letterkenny

㉕ *55 km (34 mi) northeast of Ardara, 51 km (32 mi) northeast of Donegal Town, 35 km (21 mi) west of Derry.*

One of the fastest-growing towns in all of Ireland, Letterkenny, like Donegal to the south, is at the gateway to the far Northwest; you're likely to come through here if you're driving west out of Northern Ireland. Letterkenny's claim to fame has been that it has the longest main street in the whole country. Also distinctive is its towering neo-Gothic Victorian **St. Eunan's Cathedral.** None of Letterkenny's shops or pubs are particularly special, but lots of locals bustling around make it an interesting place to get a feel for what it's like to live in a modest-size Irish town. If you're here in mid-August, check out the **Letterkenny Folk Festival,** which attracts musicians from all over Europe. The main County Donegal **TIO,** loaded with maps, literature, and advice, is 1½ km (1 mi) south on the Derry road, N13. ☎ 074/21160. ☉ *Sept.– May, weekdays 9–5; June, Mon.–Sat. 9–6; July–Aug., Mon.–Sat. 9–8, Sun. 10–2.*

Dining and Lodging

$$ ✕▥ **Mount Errigal Hotel.** One of County Donegal's smartest and most modern hotels, although not at all posh, this property appeals to both business and family-vacation visitors. Service is friendly and professional. The clean and comfortable bedrooms are efficiently arranged with light-colored wood furnishings. The Glengesh, the hotel's popular and softly lit restaurant, decorated in the Roman style, serves contemporary Irish food. The bar buzzes with locals seeking a relaxed night

The Northern Peninsulas

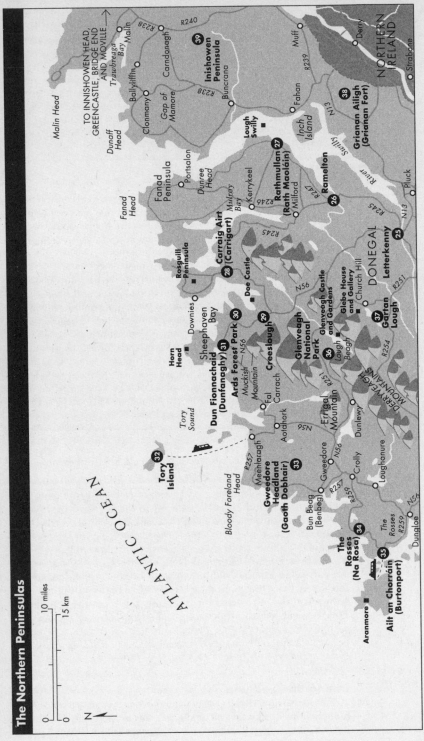

NORTHERN IRELAND

Derry

Strabone

Muff

R229

Fahan

N13

Pluck

N13

R245

DONEGAL

Letterkenny

R251

Grianan Ailigh
(Grianan Fort)

38

25

26

Ramelton

R247

Milford

R246

Grianan Ailigh

Church Hill

Gartan
Lough

37

Glebe House
and Gallery

Glenveagh Castle
and Gardens

Lough
Beagh

Glenveagh
National
Park

36

R254

DERRYVEAGH
MOUNTAINS

R251

N56

Creeslough

29

R253

N56

Errigal
Mountain

Dunlewy

Loughanure

N56

Crolly

R259

Gweedore

R257

Bun Beag
(Benbeg)

The
Rosses

R259

N56

Dungloe

34

The
Rosses
(Na Rosa)

35

Ailt an Chorráin
(Burtonport)

Aranmore

Gweedore
Headland
(Gaoth Dobhair)

33

Meenlaragh

R257

Bloody Foreland
Head

Tory
Sound

32

Tory
Island

Dun Fionnachaidh
(Dunfanaghy)

31

Ards Forest Park

30

Sheephaven
Bay

Horn
Head

Downies

Doe Castle

28

Carraig Airt
(Carrigart)

Rosguill
Peninsula

Fanad
Head

Fanad
Peninsula

Dunree
Head

Portsalon

Kerrykeel

Midroy
Bay

Lough
Swilly

27

Rathmullan
(Rath Maoláin)

Inch
Island

River Swilly

Inishowen
Peninsula

39

Buncrana

R238

Gap of
Mamore

Clonmany

Ballyliffin

Carndonagh

R238

R240

Malin

Trawbreaga
Bay

Dunaff
Head

Malin Head

TO INNISHOWEN HEAD,
GREENCASTLE, BRIDGE END
AND MOVILLE

ATLANTIC OCEAN

N

0   10 miles
0   15 km

Muckish
Mountain

Fal
Carrach

Aoidhork

Fanad

Loughanure

out, and folk music, jazz, or dancing is frequently scheduled on weekends. ⊠ *Ballyraine, Co. Donegal,* ☎ *074/22700,* FAX *074/25085,* WEB *www.mounterrigal.com. 105 rooms with bath, 2 suites. Restaurant, indoor pool, gymnasium, health club, 2 bars, Internet, meeting rooms. AE, DC, MC, V.*

Ramelton

㉖ *13 km (8 mi) northeast of Letterkenny on R245.*

A small, handsome former Plantation town built by the prosperous Stewart family, Ramelton (or Rathmelton, though the pronunciation is the same) climbs uphill from a river harbor close to **Lough Swilly,** one of the loveliest of Donegal's big, fjordlike ocean inlets. The village was the birthplace of Francis Makemie (1658–1708), who preached here before emigrating and founding the American Presbyterian church. In the 18th century it was an important port that exported salmon, butter, grain, linen, and iodine (made from the local seaweed). Houses of wealthy merchants of the time lined the Mall, but the coming of the railway to nearby Letterkenny heralded the end of Ramelton's prosperity. However, Lough Swilly continued to play its part in history, sheltering vast fleets of British ships during the First World War, when Ireland was still part of the Empire. The **Bridge Bar** (⊠ Bridge End, ☎ 074/ 51119), consistently named among the top 100 pubs in Ireland, has long been favored by locals and summertime visitors as a place to meet for a drink. Enjoy a good, hearty meal (dinners are served upstairs, away from the bar), and take in the bands that regularly pack the place at night.

Rathmullan (Rath Maoláin)

㉗ *11 km (7 mi) northeast of Ramelton on R247.*

An ancient harbor village set among green fields, Rathmullan (its Irish name means "ring fort of Maoláin") looks across the broad expanse of Lough Swilly to the Inishowen hills on the eastern shore. In the last five years or so, holiday homes have sprung up near Lough Swilly's sandy shores, bringing with them vacationers who swell the town's ordinarily tiny population and make for a livelier summer scene. If you'd like to take an hour or two and familiarize yourself with this little town's main sights, history, and flora and fauna, pick up "Rathmullan: A Walking Tour," a 28-page, handwritten guide penned by resident Margaret Carton and published by the National Trust for Ireland. It's available at the County Donegal TIO, Letterkenny bookshops, or Rathmullan House. There's nothing quite comparable for any other town in Ireland, so if this sounds like your cup of tea, don't pass it up.

Rathmullan's modest harbor was where English naval officers, posing as ordinary merchant seamen, captured Red Hugh O'Donnell in 1587. They invited him aboard to taste some of their "cargo of foreign wines," and the sociable clan leader fell for it. Once on board, he was shipped to imprisonment in Dublin Castle. After six years he escaped and returned to Donegal with added determination to defend his homeland—but to no avail. In 1607, Rathmullan's harbor was the scene of the Flight of the Earls, the great exodus of Ulster nobility, which brought to an end the 13-year war with the English. The **Flight of the Earls Heritage Centre** commemorates this momentous event and the period that immediately followed, when the million-acre Ulster territories became part of the English domain. Two years later the Plantation era began: English and Scots colonists were "planted" here, and with them were sown the seeds of the Troubles that still dominate the

affairs of Northern Ireland across the border. ☎ *No phone.* ▱ *€2.55.*
⊙ *Easter–Sept., Mon.–Sat. 10–6, Sun. noon–6:30.*

Dining and Lodging

$$$ ✕▣ **Rathmullan House.** Behind the signature facade of this two-story
★ mansion awaits one of the country's most appealing country houses—
a rambling place that's graceful *and* relaxed, and well situated for vis-
iting all of Donegal. The public rooms, including the charmingly
bright-yellow drawing room, are decorated with fine antiques and oil
paintings. Bedrooms vary from old-fashioned basic to grand, but all
have antiques, well-appointed bathrooms, elegant wallpaper, and lovely
fabrics. Rooms in the front overlook Lough Swilly and its long, sandy,
deserted beach, steps from the front door. In a pavilion with a tented
ceiling and floor-to-ceiling windows, the dining room has views of the
gardens and lake, and a delicious menu that changes every few days.
Breakfast (included) is a feast. There's also a speedboat available for
a spin, and deep-sea angling. ⊠ *Rathmullan, Co. Donegal,* ☎ *074/*
58188, ℻ *074/58200,* ⊞ *www.rathmullanhouse.com. 24 rooms with*
bath. Dining room, lounge, tennis courts, indoor pool, massage, steam
room, beach, croquet, boating, fishing, bar, library, Internet, meeting
rooms. AE, DC, MC, V. Closed Jan.–mid-Feb.

$$ ▣ **Fort Royal Hotel.** On 18 acres of verdant grounds beside Lough Swilly,
Tim Fletcher's spacious, comfortable hotel, once an aristocratic pri-
vate home, is a decent alternative to the Rathmullan House. It attracts
a regular clientele, who enjoy its relaxed professionalism and marvelous
location. Children under 10 dine at 6. ⊠ *Rathmullan, Co. Donegal,*
☎ *074/58100,* ℻ *074/58103,* ⊞ *www.fortroyalhotel.com. 15 rooms*
with bath. Restaurant, 9-hole golf course, tennis court, beach, squash,
bar. AE, DC, MC, V. Closed Nov.–Mar.

En Route Extending north from here is the barren and rock-strewn **Fanad Peninsula.** The signposted Fanad Scenic Drive takes you 27 km (17 mi) up
along the west shore of Lough Swilly to low-lying Fanad Head at its
northern tip, then down again through the tiny resort village of Kerrykeel, with views of long, narrow Mulroy Bay twisting and turning
to your right. If you want to cut the journey short, you can take the
back road directly from Rathmullan to Kerrykeel for 9½ km (6 mi).

Carraig Airt (Carrigart)

㉘ *14 km (9 mi) north of Ramelton on R245, 35 km (22 mi) northwest*
of Rathmullan.

A small village with a lot of charm and many old-fashioned pubs, Carraig Airt (Carrigart) is at the base of a slender isthmus. This is the neck
of the extremely beautiful **Rosguill Peninsula,** which has a rocky heart
and a fringe of sand dunes and beaches and is encircled by the signposted 15-km (9-mi) **Atlantic Drive.** It's not as far off the beaten track
as you might think; you'll see several caravan sites and housekeeping
cottages, popular with people from Northern Ireland. The little resort
town of **Downings** (Na Dúnaibh), near Carrigart, has a long, sandy
beach and good fishing; tweeds can be bought from **John McNutt Homespun Tweeds Factory** (☎ 074/55158) and linens from **McNutts of Donegal Ltd.** (☎ 074/55643).

Outdoor Activities and Sports

Horses for hacking or trekking on the Rosguill Peninsula can be rented
at **Carrigart Riding School** (⊠ Co. Donegal, ☎ 074/53583).

Creeslough

㉙ *16 km (10 mi) southwest of Carraig Airt on N56.*

To the southwest of the Rosguill Peninsula and across Sheephaven Bay lies this small town at the foot of Muckish Mountain. Nearby, on the southern end of Sheephaven Bay, stands **Doe Castle,** protected on three sides by the sea and by a moat on its fourth side. The tall, weather-beaten tower is at the center of a complex structure enclosed within sturdy defenses. Described by attacking English forces in 1587 as "the strongest fortress in all the province," the impressive edifice dates from at least 1440, when it became the home of MacSweeney Doe, one of the "gallowglasses" (from the Irish *gall o glach*)—foreign mercenaries employed by the O'Donnell clan. Despite the castle's present poor condition, it was still occupied by his descendants until 1890. MacSweeney Doe's curiously carved tombstone is fixed to the southwest tower of the outer wall. ⊠ *5½ km (3½ mi) off N56, signposted south of Creeslough.* 🎫 *Free.* ☉ *Usually open; if locked, inquire at caretaker's cottage on approach path.*

Ards Forest Park

㉚ *9½ km (5 mi) north of Creeslough on N56.*

Clinging to Sheephaven Bay's southwest shore, the 1,188-acre Ards Forest Park (reached by passing through adjacent Creeslough [pronounced *creesh*-la]) is the former wooded estate of a Capuchin friary; the friary itself is still occupied by the Capuchins. Four prehistoric, fortified sites and one dolmen lie within the grounds, which offer some of the most varied landscape of any of Ireland's national forest parks, including rivers, loughs, salt marshes, valleys, and, of course, the bay. If the weather is fine, the park's forest trails and picnic sites are great places to enjoy the scrubbed sea air. ☎ *074/21139.* 🎫 *Free; parking €2.55 weekends Easter–June and July–Sept.* ☉ *Daily 8 AM–9 PM.*

Dun Fionnachaid (Dunfanaghy)

㉛ *8 km (5 mi) northwest of Ards Forest Park.*

On the edge of Sheephaven Bay, Dun Fionnachaid (Dunfanaghy) is a tidy, former Plantation village. If you're ready for a short break, the hotel noted below serves decent, unpretentious local grub for about €10 for lunch. **The Workhouse** illustrates fascinating, but harsh, workhouse life by following the story of 'Wee Hannah' from her farmhouse upbringing to an eventual peaceful old age. The center has a café, and an Irish handicrafts shop. ⊠ *Dunfanaghy,* ☎ *074/36540,* ⟨WEB⟩ *www. theirishfamine.com.* ☉ *Apr.–Sept., Mon.–Sat. 10–5, Sun. noon–5; Mar. and Oct. by prior arrangement.*

When the tide goes out, the vast sand flats of **Killyhoey Beach** are uncovered and the sea recedes into the far distance, but as it rises again, the sands are submerged in double-quick time. On the west side of Dunfanaghy, the signpost to **McSwyne's Gun** (McSwyne is the old spelling of MacSweeney) leads to a huge, natural blowhole that gives out a deafening bang when the tide rushes in during rough weather.

★ A little back road runs from Dunfanaghy up to **Horn Head,** the most spectacular of County Donegal's Atlantic headlands. From its sheer 600-ft cliffs, the views along the coast to the other headlands ranged one behind the other are inimitable. Bird-watchers should note that the cliffs are packed with hundreds of seabirds, including puffins and guillemots.

Dining and Lodging

$$ ✕🔲 **Arnold's Hotel.** Right at the entrance to the village, this friendly hotel has been run by three generations of the Arnold family and is a favorite with Irish vacationers. Rooms are unassuming and relaxed; the best overlook the landscaped garden. You can eat generous, traditional Irish meals in the dining room or in the more casual Garden Bistro. Special-interest classes, such as photography, writing, bridge, painting and wine-tasting, are available on the weekends. ⊠ *Main St., Dunfanaghy, Co. Donegal,* ☎ *074/36208,* FAX *074/36352,* WEB *www. arnoldshotel.com. 30 rooms with bath. Dining room, bar, tennis court, horseback riding, baby-sitting. AE, DC, MC, V. Closed Dec.–mid-Mar. and weekdays in Nov.*

En Route   West of Dunfanaghy the terrain is rougher, wilder, and rockier; you're also likely to hear the Irish language being spoken. The N56 reaches round 11 km (7 mi) to **Fal Carrach** (Falcarragh), the site of an Irish-language college. Another 13 km (8 mi) around the rugged seashore, in good weather, you can catch a ferry from **Meenlaragh** (near Gortahork) to Tory Island.

Tory Island

㉜ *14½ km (9 mi) offshore.*

Harsh weather and difficult currents make Tory Island fairly inaccessible. (The boat trip lasts more than an hour on seas that are rough even on the best days; be prepared to get soaked, too.) Despite being rocky, ocean-battered, and barren (not even a single tree), the island has been inhabited since prehistoric times. Islanders speak their own dialect and refer to the mainland as "Ireland." Prehistoric and medieval relics are scattered about the landscape. Poised on the cliffs is the partly ruined, pink-granite **round tower** with its conical cap still intact. At Tory Island's eastern end, the prehistoric ruin, **Balor's Fort,** was purportedly the residence of Balor, the terrifying, one-eyed Celtic god of night and darkness. At the northeastern tip, the **Wishing Stone** has the power, it is said, to destroy enemies. Still talked about is the time (1884) when the stone's powers were invoked against the British gunboat *Wasp,* whose passengers (mainly policemen) had come to collect taxes—something the islanders were unaccustomed to paying. The ship sank, and all but six of the crew were lost.

Most of the islanders live the simple life of fisherfolk, though quite a few have unexpected sidelines as artists. In 1968, the well-known Irish painter Derek Hill met islander James Dixon, who felt that he could do a better job of painting than Hill. Many other Tory Island residents thought they could, too, and today the Tory Island artists, depicting their own life and landscape in a naive style using nothing more than standard house paints, are widely acclaimed and have exhibited elsewhere in Ireland, including Glebe House and Gallery in Gartan Lough and abroad. **Dixon's Gallery** sells the work of the Tory islanders; prices range from €63 to €254.

Dining and Lodging

$ ✕🔲 **Tory Island Hotel (Ostan Thoraig).** After living and working in England for 10 years, native islander Pat Doohan returned with his wife, Berney, to build and run the Tory Island Hotel. (He also watches over the nearby Dixon's Gallery.) The comfortable guest rooms are large, sunny, and nicely decorated in a peach, blue, and green palette, with matching curtains and bedspreads. A fireplace warms the bar, which is a popular local hangout. Traditional music sessions and *ceilí* dancing regularly liven things up. The restaurant overlooks the sea. ⊠ *Co.*

Donegal, ☎ *074/35920,* ℻ *074/35613,* ⓦⓔⓑ *www.toryhotel.com. 14 rooms with bath. Restaurant, bar. MC, V. Closed Nov.–Mar.*

Gweedore Headland (Gaoth Dobhair)

㉝ *27 km (17 mi) east of Meenlaragh on R257.*

When you return from Tory Island to Meenlaragh, you're on the edge of the Gweedore Headland, which can be circumnavigated on the coast road (R257). Gweedore is rocky, sparsely covered with heather and gorse, and low-lying until you reach its northernmost point, **Bloody Foreland Head.** This dramatic name for once does not recall the slaughter of some historic battle, describing instead the vivid red hues of the gaunt rock face when illuminated at sunset.

The Rosses (Na Rosa)

㉞ *13 km (8 mi) south of Bloody Foreland Head on R259.*

The next distinctive headland south of Gweedore (on the road south after you pass through Bun Beag [Benbeg] and Croithli [Crolly]) is the Rosses (Na Rosa in Irish, meaning "the headlands")—even more beautiful than Gweedore. The bleak but dramatic terrain here, as at Gweedore, has not benefited from a liberal sprinkling of modern bungalows. The coast road (R259) struggles over the inhospitable, stony landscape, crisscrossed with water channels and strewn with more than 100 lakes. Yet quite a number of people manage to survive here, many of them Irish speakers (this is the heart of the Donegal Gaeltacht). The decline of population and living standards was reversed by Patrick Gallagher (1873–1964), who became known as Paddy the Cope. Son of a poor local family, he left school at 10, went to Scotland as a farmhand, and saved enough money to return home in the 1950s and buy a small holding of his own. Gallagher, affectionately remembered throughout the area, persuaded the citizens around the Rosses to set up cooperatives to bring in new farming methods and machinery, as well as cooperatively owned stores to keep prices down.

Ailt an Chorráin (Burtonport)

㉟ *16 km (10 mi) southwest of Crolly on R259.*

The village of Ailt an Chorráin (Burtonport), which claims to land more salmon and lobster than any other fishing port in Ireland, is the departure point for a trip over to **Aranmore,** 6½ km (4 mi) offshore. Aranmore means "big island," and it is indeed the largest and most populous of County Donegal's rocky offshore fragments. The ride out takes 25 minutes, but although it's fairly accessible, the island still feels remote and ungoverned. It has been inhabited for thousands of years (about 1,000 people live on it today), and it offers good fishing as well as striking cliff scenery and views back onto the Rosses; there's a prehistoric fort on its south side. 🚢 *Ferry €3.17.* ☉ *7 crossings daily.*

Back on the mainland, if you follow the coast another 6½ km (4 mi) southeast, R259 rejoins N56 at **An Clochan Liath** (Dungloe), a pleasant little fishing town regarded as the capital of the Rosses, though there's little to do or see here.

En Route Traveling on N56 north from Dungloe, go a couple of miles beyond Gaoth Dobhair (Gweedore) village, on the little River Clady, and take R251 to skirt the south side of **Errigal Mountain** to the village of Dunlewy, 26 km (16 mi) east of Dungloe. This whole drive passes through some of the best scenery in all of County Donegal. Serene Errigal looks especially grand from Dunlewy. On the edge of Dunlewy Lough, the

Dunlewy Centre is an interesting place to pause for a look at a reconstructed 19th-century weaver's home. Here you can watch a demonstration of old-style weaving and an audiovisual show, then have a guided tour of the cottage. Half-hour boat trips on the lake include storytelling and a history of the area. A café and crafts shop are also on the premises. ⊠ *Dunlewy,* ☎ *075/31699.* ▣ *Weaving demonstration, show, and tour €4.50; boat trip €4.50.* ☉ *Easter–Oct., Mon.–Sat. 10:30–6, Sun. 11–7.*

Glenveagh National Park

★ ❸❻ *45 km (28 mi) east of Ailt an Chorráin (Burtonport) on R251, 27 km (17 mi) northwest of Letterkenny.*

Bordered by the Derryveagh Mountains (Derryveagh means "forest of oak and birch"), Glenveagh National Park encompasses 24,000 acres of wilderness—mountain, moorland, lakes, and woods—that has been called "the largest and most dramatic tract in the wildest part of Donegal." Within its borders, a thick carpet of russet-color heath and dense woodland rolls down the Derryveagh slopes into the broad, open valley of the River Veagh (or Owenbeagh), which opens out into Glenveagh's spine: long and narrow, dark and clear **Lough Beagh.**

The Glenveagh lands have long been recognized as a remote and beautiful region. Between 1857 and 1859, John George Adair, a ruthless gentleman farmer, assembled the estate that now makes up the park. In 1861, he evicted the estate's hundreds of poor tenants without compensation and destroyed their cottages. Nine years later, Adair began to build **Glenveagh Castle** on the eastern shore of Lough Veagh, but he soon departed for Texas. He died in 1885 without returning to Ireland, but his widow, Cornelia, moved back to make Glenveagh her home. She created the four different **gardens** covering 27 acres, planted the luxuriant rhododendrons here, and began the job of making this flamboyantly turreted and battlemented 19th-century folly livable.

The gardens and castle as they appear today are almost entirely an American invention—the product of the loving attentions of Glenveagh's last owner. U.S. millionaire Henry P. McIlhenny bought the estate in 1937 and, beginning in 1947, lived here for part of every year for almost 40 years. An avid art collector and philanthropist, McIlhenny decorated every inch of the house himself and entertained lavishly. The house has been maintained just as it was on his last occupancy in 1983; later that year, he made a gift of the house to the nation. He had sold the government the surrounding land in 1975, which it opened to the public in 1984 as Ireland's third national park.

Beyond the castle, footpaths lead into more remote sections of the park, including the **Derrylahan Nature Trail,** a 1½-km (1-mi) signposted trail where you may suddenly catch sight of a soaring falcon or chance upon a shy red deer. The park is the home of one of Ireland's two largest herds; the other is at Killarney. Guided walks are held May through October. The visitor center at the park's entrance has a permanent exhibition on the local way of life and on the influence of climate on the park's flora and fauna. Skip the sleep-inducing audiovisual and instead have a bite to eat in the cafeteria. ⊠ *Church Hill,* ☎ *074/37090.* ▣ *Roundtrip bus from visitor center €1, guided tour of castle €2.50.* ☉ *Easter–Oct., daily 10–6:30.*

Gartan Lough

❸❼ *13 km (8 mi) southeast of Glenveagh on R251, 17 km (11 mi) northwest of Letterkenny.*

Gartan Lough and the surrounding mountainous country are astonishingly beautiful. St. Columba was supposedly born here in AD 521, and the legendary event is marked by a huge cross at the beginning of a footpath into the national park. (Close to Church Hill village, Gartan Lough is technically within the national park and is administered partly by the park authorities.) Nearby are other dubious "relics" of the saint, which are popularly believed to possess magical powers: the Natal Stone, where the saint is thought to have first opened his eyes, and the Stone of Loneliness, where he is said to have slept. However, the superstitions do rub off—the soil of Gartan was carried by soldiers from the area to the trenches of the First World War as a protective relic.

On the northwest shore of Gartan Lough, just off R251, you'll find **Glebe House and Gallery,** a fine Regency manor with 25 acres of gardens. For 30 years, Glebe House was the home of the distinguished landscape and portrait artist Derek Hill, who furnished the house in a mix of styles with art from around the world; in 1981 he gave the house and its contents, including his outstanding art collection, to the nation. Highlights include paintings by Renoir and Bonnard, lithographs by Kokoschka, ceramics and etchings by Picasso, and the paintings *Whippet Racing* and *The Ferry, Early Morning* by Jack B. Yeats, as well as Donegal folk art produced by the Tory islanders. The decoration and furnishings of the house, including original William Morris wallpaper, are also worth a look. ⊠ *Church Hill,* ☎ *074/37071.* ⊠ *€2.55.* ⊙ *Easter and mid-May–Sept., Sat.–Thurs. 11–6:30.*

At the **Colmcille Heritage Centre** you can learn more about St. Columba and his times. Return to R251 and turn right almost at once onto R254 in Church Hill; straightaway you'll arrive at the exhibition and interpretation center, which has medieval manuscripts, stained glass, and displays tracing the decline of the Celtic religion and the rise of Irish Christianity. Audiovisual displays and interactive computer presentations enhance the historical journey. There's a little tearoom for snacks, and the staff can show you walks in the area. ⊠ *Gartan, Church Hill,* ☎ *074/37306.* ⊠ *€2.* ⊙ *May–Sept., Mon.–Sat. 10:30–6:30, Sun. 1–6:30; June–Aug., Mon.–Sat. 10–6:30, Sun. noon–6:30.*

Grianan Ailigh (Grianan Fort)

★ ㊳ *29 km (18 mi) northeast of Letterkenny on N13.*

A circular stone Celtic fort, the Grianan Ailigh (Grianan Fort) definitely merits a visit, although it is, like the Inishowen Peninsula, northeast of Letterkenny and thus closer to Northern Ireland than the majority of Donegal sites covered here. The fortress crowns an 810-ft hill; on a fine day, the panorama of the rolling Donegal and Derry landscape is breathtaking. To the north lies the Swilly estuary, flowing around Inch Island into Lough Swilly. On either side rise the hills of the Fanad and Inishowen peninsulas, though they're often partly veiled by mists. As for the fort, what you'll see is a circular stone enclosure with a diameter of about 76 ft, which you can enter through a gate (it's open most of the year). Inside, earth ramparts and concentric defenses punctured by passages surround a sturdy central structure. No one knows when Grianan Fort was built, but it was probably an Iron Age fortress. Its position was accurately recorded in the 2nd century AD by the geographer Ptolemy of Alexandria. In the 5th century it became the seat of Ulster's O'Neill chieftains and remained so until the 12th century, despite serious attempts by their enemies to destroy it, especially in the year 674 and again in 1101. The present-day fortress, however, owes a good deal to overzealous "restoration" in the 1870s by Dr. Walter

Bernard, a Derry historian; before that, it was in ruins. If you're traveling north on N13, look for signs to Buncrana, because the easy-to-miss sign for the fort is opposite. Instead of turning to Buncrana, take the narrow lane that climbs and turns for more than 2 km (1 mi) to the top of the hill. The fort is freely accessible.

Inishowen Peninsula

39 *Peninsula circuit from Fahan to Muff via Malin Head and Inishowen Head: 161 km (100 mi).*

The most northerly point in all of Ireland, the huge Inishowen Peninsula is a grandly green, wild piece of land with a solid, mountainous interior. It's flanked by Lough Swilly on one side and Lough Foyle on the other, and the battering Atlantic thrashes to the north. Despite a string of small and untempting coastal resorts, the peninsula remains unspoiled and less traveled than most other parts of the country. If you decide to make the Inishowen circuit (known as the "Inishowen 100," for its length in miles) plus the 64-km (40-mi) round trip to reach it from Letterkenny, you'll need to allow at least one whole day, though it's possible to make an abbreviated visit in less time.

Just off of R238, as you head toward Buncrana, is **Fahan** (pronounced fawn), which has monastic ruins that include the early Christian **St. Mura cross slab.** A popular, downscale beach resort favored by Derry denizens, **Buncrana** has a 14th-century O'Doherty tower that gradually became part of an 18th-century mansion. Shortly after you pass Buncrana, turn left at the fork in the road away from R238 onto the coast road, which will take you past the 19th-century fort on Dunree Head, up and over the spectacular viewpoint of the **Gap of Mamore,** where the 1,250-ft Croaghcarragh rises up on one side and the 1,361-ft Mamore Hill echoes it on the other. The road heads north toward Dunaff Head, where Lough Swilly opens into the ocean. Rejoin R238 at Clonmany and take it through Ballyliffin, a small resort town with an O'Doherty tower on the beach, and a convenient place for a snack or meal.

By the junction of R238 and R240, you'll see a church with a curious remnant of early Christianity against one wall—the decorated, 7th-century **Donagh Cross,** accompanied by a couple of pillar stones. The strange carvings on the stones clearly date from a pre-Christian period. Around the corner from the Donagh Cross, **Carndonagh,** the area's main market town, has several more medieval monastic remains; Slieve Snaght, Inishowen's highest peak, at 2,019 ft, lies just southwest of town. As Slieve Snaght runs up beside Trawbreaga Bay, R238 turns into R242 shortly before the picturesque village of **Malin;** it's another 16 km (10 mi) up to **Malin Head,** the most northerly point in all of Ireland and an important spot for birds migrating south in autumn. Although it has good views, Malin Head is not as dramatic a spot as some of the other headlands.

From Malin Head, take the signposted route across the peninsula to Moville, a sleepy waterside resort on the Lough Foyle side. From here, it's 8 km (5 mi) to **Inishowen Head,** the peninsula's rocky eastern tip. On the way to the head, at Greencastle, you'll see the fortifications of foreigners who tried to control the nine counties of Ulster: a 14th-century Anglo-Norman fortress and an English fort built five centuries later to defend against French support for the Irish. The drive along the lough shore toward Derry, though attractive, is punctuated by small, uninteresting villages whose modernized pubs cater to visitors from Derry. If you want to turn away from Derry toward Letterkenny before reaching the border, take R239 from Muff to **Bridge End,** where you'll find one of the most attractive of Ireland's many new Catholic churches.

Dining and Lodging

$–$$ ✕ **Corncrake Restaurant.** Five years ago, Bríd McCartney and Noreen Lynch gave up the Dublin rat race to open the most stylish restaurant between Derry and New York. They grow all their own herbs and specialize in seafood and lamb. Standouts include salmon *coubliac* (mélange of fresh salmon, tarragon, and leeks in hollandaise sauce, baked in a buttery pastry envelope) as a main course and fallen chocolate soufflé with prunes and Armagnac for dessert. The two also run excellent weekend cooking courses for €275, which includes all meals, instruction, and accommodation at the nearby Rossaor House. ✉ *Milbrae, Carndonagh,* ☎ *077/74534. No credit cards.*

$$ ✕▦ **St. John's Country House and Restaurant.** A cozy, old-fashioned
★ feeling prevails at this restored lakeside Georgian house. With comfortable, elegant rooms, the hotel is relaxing—and this is enhanced by the exceptional hospitality of host Reggie Ryan. Homemade bread is baked daily—to serve with the fresh garden soups and pâtés. The five-course table d'hôte menu changes monthly. Appetizers may include seafood chowder or a terrine of salmon and monkfish wrapped in spinach. Fillets of brill with herbs and fennel sauce, and Donegal rack of lamb with mascarpone risotto and rosemary are typical main courses. Desserts include homemade ice creams and carrageen moss with fruit coulis. ✉ *Fahan, Co. Donegal,* ☎ *077/60289,* ℻ *077/60612,* ⓦⒺⒷ *http://homepage.tinet.ie/~stjohnscountryhouse/. 4 rooms with bath, 1 suite. AE, DC, MC, V. Closed mid-Feb.–mid-Mar.*

Outdoor Activities and Sports

For hacking and trekking on the Inishowen Peninsula contact **Lenamore Stables** (✉ Muff, ☎ 077/84022), which offers excellent rates for bed-and-breakfast, with riding included.

Shopping

National Knitting Centre and Cranaknits Sweater Shop (✉ St. Oran's Rd, Lisfannon, Buncrana, ☎ 077/62355) sells hand-knit goods and offers residential courses in traditional Irish hand knitting.

THE NORTHWEST A TO Z

To research prices, get advice from other travelers, and book travel arrangements, visit www.fodors.com.

AIR TRAVEL

CARRIERS

Aer Arann has direct, daily flights between Donegal Airport and Dublin, and Sligo Airport and Dublin. British Airways Express flies to Eglinton (Derry) Airport from Manchester and Glasgow. Ryanair has flights to Knock Airport from London Stansted daily.
➤ AIRLINES AND CONTACTS: **Aer Arann** (☎ 1890/462726). **British Airways Express** (☎ 0845/626747). **Ryanair** (☎ 01/609–7800).

AIRPORTS AND TRANSFERS

The principal international air-arrival point to the Northwest is the tiny airport at Charlestown, Knock International Airport, 54½ km (34 mi) south of Sligo Town. City of Derry Airport, a few miles over the border, receives flights from Manchester and Glasgow. City of Derry (also called Eglinton) is a particularly convenient airport for reaching northern County Donegal. Donegal Airport, in Carrickfinn, is not far from Dungloe and typically receives flights from Dublin. Sligo Airport at Strandhill, 8 km (5 mi) west of Sligo Town, is the other area airport.

➤ AIRPORT INFORMATION: **City of Derry Airport** (☎ 028/7181–0784). **Donegal Airport** (☎ 075/48232). **Knock International Airport** (☎ 094/67222). **Sligo Airport** (☎ 071/68280 or 071/68318).

TRANSFERS

If you aren't driving, Knock Airport becomes less attractive, as you'll have no easy public transportation link to your destination, except the once-a-day (in season) local bus to Charlestown, 11 km (7 mi) away. Nor can you rely on catching a bus at the smaller airports, except at Sligo Airport, where buses run from Sligo Town to meet all flights.

Knock Airport has a convenient car-rental desk. You can also pick up rental cars at Sligo and Eglinton (Derry) airports. You can also get taxis—both cars and minibuses—right outside Knock Airport. The average rate is €1.27 per mile. However, if you're not flying into Knock, you may have to phone a taxi company. Phone numbers of taxi companies are available from airport information desks and are also displayed beside pay phones inside the airport terminals.

➤ TAXI COMPANIES: **Castle Cabs** (☎ 087/638–8588). **OK Cabs** (☎ 087/639–6666). **Tom Cronnolly** (☎ 087/244–0597). **S & S Cabs** (☎ 087/850–5045).

BUS TRAVEL

Bus Éireann can get you from Dublin to Sligo Town in four hours for €12.10 one-way, €18.40 round-trip. Four buses a day from Dublin are available. Another bus route, five times a day from Dublin (six on Friday), goes to Letterkenny, in the heart of County Donegal, in 4¼ hours, via a short trip across the Northern Ireland border; it's €12.70 one-way, €18.40 round-trip. Other Bus Éireann services connect Sligo Town to towns all over Ireland. Bus Éireann also operates out of Sligo Town and Letterkenny to destinations all over the region, as well as to other parts of Ireland. From Sligo Town, you can reach almost any point in the region for less than €12.70. McGeehans is one of several local bus companies linking towns and villages in the Northwest.

➤ BUS INFORMATION: **Bus Éireann** (☎ 01/836–6111 in Dublin; 071/60066 in Sligo Town; 074/21309 in Letterkenny). **McGeehans** (☎ 075/46150).

CAR RENTAL

You can rent a car in Sligo Town from Euro Mobil. Murray's Europcar rents cars from Sligo Airport and also has a branch at Knock Airport. A medium-size four-door costs around €65 per day with unlimited mileage (inclusive of insurance and taxes) or around €345 per week. If you're planning to tour mostly northern County Donegal, you may find it more convenient to rent a car in Derry from Ford. If you're planning to drive a rental car across the border to Northern Ireland, inform the company in advance and check the insurance policy.

➤ LOCAL AGENCIES: **Euro Mobil** (☎ 071/67291, WEB www.parksgroup.com). **Ford** (☎ 028/7136–7137, WEB www.desmondsford.com). **Murray's Europcar** (☎ 094/67221 at Knock Airport).

CAR TRAVEL

Sligo, the largest town in the Northwest, is relatively accessible on the main routes. The N4 travels the 224 km (140 mi) directly from Dublin to Sligo, but you need to allow at least four hours for this journey. The N15 continues from Sligo Town to Donegal Town and proceeds from Donegal Town to Derry City, just over the border in the province of Northern Ireland. The fastest approach for anyone driving up from the West and the Southwest is on N17, connecting Sligo to Galway, though the landscape is undistinguished.

ROAD CONDITIONS

Roads are uncongested, but in some places they are in a poor state of repair (French bus drivers refused to take their buses into County Donegal some summers back, as a gesture of protest about the state of the roads). In the Irish-speaking areas, signposts are written only in the Irish (Gaelic) language, which can be confusing. You need to prepare beforehand for this by checking the Irish place-names on your route.

EMERGENCIES

➤ CONTACTS: **Ambulance, police, fire** (☎ 999). **Letterkenny General Hospital** (✉ High Rd., Letterkenny, Co. Donegal, ☎ 074/25888). **Sligo General Hospital** (✉ The Mall, Sligo Town, Co. Sligo, ☎ 071/71111).

FESTIVALS AND SEASONAL EVENTS

Outside Sligo Town, the Northwest has few serious arts activities and events, though there are a number of festivals and seasonal events. The local press, including the *Donegal Democrat,* the *Leitrim Observer,* and *Sligo Champion,* has useful events listings.

LODGING

BED-AND-BREAKFASTS

For a small fee, Bord Fáilte (the Irish Tourist Board) will book accommodations anywhere in Ireland through its central reservations system. B&Bs can be booked at local visitor information offices when they are open; however, even these reservations will go through the central reservations system.

➤ RESERVATION SERVICES: **Bord Fáilte** (WEB www.ireland.travel.ie).

OUTDOOR ACTIVITIES AND SPORTS

BIRD-WATCHING

➤ CONTACTS: **Irish Wild Bird Conservancy** (✉ 8 Longford Pl., Monkstown, Co. Dublin, ☎ 01/280–4322, WEB www.birdwatchireland.ie).

FISHING

A fishing license is not needed for sea fishing or for coarse and pike angling. For game fishing (salmon and sea trout), the license costs €3.80 for 1 day, €12.70 for 21 days, or €31.75 for a full season. The full-season license is valid throughout the country; there's also a local annual license, valid only in the Northwest, for €15.24. Senior citizens are exempt from these costs. You can obtain licenses for County Donegal from the Northern Regional Fisheries Board. Please note that by law, although it is rarely, if ever, checked, you must purchase share certificates if you intend to do coarse fishing or angling for brown trout in County Donegal; the rates are €3.80 for one day, €6.35 for 21 days, or €15.25 for a season. For licenses in Counties Sligo and Leitrim, contact the Northwestern Regional Fisheries Board. Some tackle shops are also permitted to sell licenses.

For complete information on fishing in the Northwest waters, suitable accommodations, details of boat rentals, and so on, ask the Irish Tourist Board (☞ Visitor Information) for the annual *Anglers' Guide.*

Bait, tackle, and local information can be found at the following places: in County Donegal, at John McGill, O'Doherty's, and Pat Barrett; in County Leitrim, at Geraghty's and Aodh Flynn; and in County Sligo, at Barton Smith.

➤ CONTACTS: **Aodh Flynn** (✉ Deerpark, Manorhamilton, ☎ no phone). **Barton Smith** (✉ Hyde Bridge, Sligo Town, ☎ 071/42356). **Geraghty's** (✉ Main St., Carrick-on-Shannon, ☎ 078/21316). **John McGill** (✉ Main St., Ardara, ☎ no phone). **Northern Regional Fisheries Board**

(✉ Ballyshannon, Co. Donegal, ☎ 072/51435). **Northwestern Regional Fisheries Board** (✉ Ballina, Co. Mayo, ☎ 096/22623). **O'Doherty's** (✉ Main St., Donegal Town, ☎ no phone). **Pat Barrett** (✉ Finner Rd., Bundoran, ☎ 072/41504).

GOLF

For a full list of golf courses in the region, contact the Irish Tourist Board or local TIOs (☞ Visitor Information). For details about the Northwest's championship courses, including Donegal Golf Club, County Sligo Golf Club, and Enniscrone Golf Club, see Chapter 10.

HIKING

Contact Field Officer, Long Distance Walking Routes Committee, to learn about Northwest walking routes.
➤ CONTACTS: **Field Officer, Long Distance Walking Routes Committee** (✉ Irish Sports Council, 21 Fitzwilliam Sq., Dublin 2, ☎ 01/676–3837).

HORSEBACK RIDING

Ask the Association of Irish Riding Establishments for information on recognized establishments that offer full riding vacations—including lodging.
➤ CONTACTS: **Association of Irish Riding Establishments** (✉ Mespil Hall, Kill, Co. Kildare, ☎ 045/877208, WEB www.horseireland.com).

SURFING

➤ CONTACTS: **Irish Surfing Association** (✉ Tigh-na-Mara, Rossnowlagh, Co. Donegal, ☎ 096/49020).

TOURS

BUS TOURS

Bus Éireann has budget-priced, guided, one-day bus tours of the Donegal Highlands and to Glenveagh National Park, which start from Bundoran, Sligo Town, Ballyshannon, and Donegal Town. For a friendly, relaxed minibus tour of the area in July and August, call John Houze. He is a knowledgeable guide who leads popular tours to Lough Gill (€12.70, not including admissions to sites) and north of Sligo Town to Drumcliff, Lissadell House, and Glencar lake and waterfall (€8.25). He also does a full-day tour, including a boat trip to the Lake Isle of Innisfree (€25.39).
➤ FEES AND SCHEDULES: **Bus Éireann** (☎ 071/60066 or 074/21309, WEB www.buseireann.ie). **John Houze** (☎ 071/42747 or 086/225–5555).

WALKING TOURS

Walking tours of Sligo Town usually depart twice daily in July and August from the TIO. They are free and last about 1 to 1½ hours. However, the guides are generally students, so a tip of €1.25 or €2.55 is welcome. Check details with the TIO.
➤ FEES AND SCHEDULES: **Walking tours of Sligo Town** (TIO; ☎ 071/61201).

TRAIN TRAVEL

Sligo Town is the northernmost direct rail link to Dublin. From Dublin three trains a day are available, and the journey takes 3 hours and 20 minutes. The fare is €18.40 one-way or day-return, €24.15 round-trip. If you want to get to Sligo Town by rail from other provincial towns, you'll be forced to make some inconvenient connections and take roundabout routes. The rest of the region has no railway services. Contact Irish Rail.
➤ TRAIN INFORMATION: **Irish Rail** (☎ 01/836–6222).

VISITOR INFORMATION

The TIO in Sligo Town (in the extreme south of the region) is the main visitor information center for the whole Northwest. It's open September to mid-March, weekdays 9–1 and 2–5; mid-March to mid-June, weekdays 9–6, Saturday 10–2; and mid-June to August, Monday–Saturday 9–8, Sunday 10–6. If you are traveling in County Donegal in the North, try the TIO at Letterkenny about 1½ km (1 mi) out of town. It is open September to May, weekdays 9–1 and 2–5; June, Monday–Saturday 9–1 and 2–6; July to August, Monday–Saturday 9–8 and Sunday 10–2. The offices at Bundoran, Donegal Town, and Dungloe are open only during the summer months (usually the first week in June to the second week in September). You can also contact the Irish Tourist Board (Bord Fáilte).

➤ TOURIST INFORMATION: **Bord Fáilte** (☎ 01/602–4000, 669/792083, or 1850/230330 [within Ireland]; 800/223–6470 in the U.S. and Canada; 800/039–7000 in the U.K.; 02/9299–6177 in Australia; 09/379–8720 in New Zealand, WEB www.irelandvacations.com). **Bundoran** (✉ Main St., Co. Donegal, ☎ 072/41350). **Donegal Town** (✉ Quay St., Co. Donegal, ☎ 073/21148, FAX 073/22762). **Dungloe** (✉ Village Center, Co. Donegal, ☎ 075/21297). **Letterkenny** (✉ Derry Rd., Co. Donegal, ☎ 074/21160, FAX 074/25180). **Sligo Town** (✉ Temple and Charles Sts., Co. Donegal, ☎ 071/61201, FAX 071/60360).

9 NORTHERN IRELAND

BELFAST, THE ANTRIM COAST, DERRY, LOUGH ERNE, AND THE MOUNTAINS OF MOURNE

With peace—precious peace—abiding, it's a fine time to discover this overlooked corner of Europe. Northern Ireland offers some unique treasures, including Palladian stately houses, the Giant's Causeway, and two rapidly changing cities—Derry and Belfast, both noted for Victorian architecture, fascinating museums, and an energetic nightlife. Outdoor enthusiasts will revel in the rugged mountains of Mourne, largely inaccessible except on foot, and the 896 km/560 mi Ulster Way, which winds around six counties.

Updated by
Geoff Hill

L EGEND HAS IT THAT WELL OVER A MILLENNIUM ago a marauding chieftain caught sight of the shores of Northern Ireland from the deck of his boat and offered this green and fertile land to whichever of his two sons could first lay hand on it. As the two rival sons rowed for the shore in their separate boats, one began to draw ahead—whereupon the other drew his sword, cut off his own hand, and threw it onto the beach—and so, by blood and sacrifice, won this province. To this day the arms of Northern Ireland feature this same severed limb: the celebrated "Red Hand of Ulster."

From this bardic tale to the most recent Troubles of 1969 to 1994, Northern Ireland has had a long and often ferocious history. But come here and you'll find any thoughts of violence vanishing in the face of the country's outstanding natural beauty; its magnificent, stately houses; and the genuine, open hospitality of its inhabitants. The Six Counties, or Ulster (as Northern Ireland is often called), cover less than 14,245 square km (5,500 square mi) in all, but within their boundaries they contain some of the most unspoiled scenery you could hope to find— the granite Mountains of Mourne; the Giant's Causeway, made of extraordinary volcanic rock; more than 320 km (200 mi) of coastline with long, unspoiled beaches and hidden coves; and rivers and leaf-sheltered lakes that provide fabled fishing grounds, among them the largest freshwater lake in Europe, Lough Neagh. Ancient castles and Palladian-perfect 18th-century houses are as numerous here as almost anywhere else in Europe, and each has its own tale of heroic deeds, dastardly treachery, and lovelorn ghosts. Northern Ireland not only houses this great heritage in stone, but has also given the world an even greater legacy—its celebrated descendants. Nearly one in six of the more than 4½ million Irish who made the fateful journey across the Atlantic to seek their fortune in the New World was from Ulster, and of this group (and from their family stock), more than a few left their mark in America: Davy Crockett, President Andrew Jackson, General Ulysses S. Grant, President Woodrow Wilson, General Stonewall Jackson, financier Thomas Mellon, merchant Paul Getty, writers Edgar Allan Poe and Mark Twain, and astronaut Neil Armstrong.

Present-day Northern Ireland, a province under the rule of the United Kingdom, includes six of the old Ulster's nine counties and retains its sense of separation, both in the vernacular of the landscape and (some say) in the character of the people. The hardheaded and industrious Scots-Presbyterians, imported to make Ulster a bulwark against Ireland's Catholicism, have had a profound and ineradicable effect on the place. The North has more factories, neater-looking farms, better roads, and—in its cities—more of the two-story redbrick houses typical of Great Britain than does the Republic. For all that, the border between North and South is of little consequence if you're just here to see the country.

Ireland's ancient history truly began in the North, when settlers came to the banks of the River Bann 9,000 years ago. Five thousand years later Bronze Age settlers built the great stone circles idiomatic in the North to Counties Down and Tyrone, and later the Iron Age brought the Celts. St. Patrick, son of a Roman official and once a slave in County Antrim, returned to spread Christianity in the 5th century. But from the first Norman incursions in the 12th century onward, the English made greater and greater inroads into Ireland, endeavoring to subdue what they believed was a potential enemy. Ulster proved the hardest part to conquer, but in 1607 Ulster's beaten Irish nobility fled their homeland forever, many of them going to France and Spain, in the great exodus known as the Flight of the Earls. Their abandoned lands were distributed by the English to "the Planters"—staunch Protestants from England and Scotland.

After three centuries of smoldering tensions and religious strife, 1916 saw the Easter Uprising and then, in the parliamentary elections of 1918, an overwhelming Nationalist vote across Ireland for Sinn Féin ("Ourselves Alone"), the party that believed in independence for all of Ireland. In the five northeastern counties of Ulster, however, only seven seats went to the Nationalists, and 22 to the Unionists, who wanted to remain an integral part of the United Kingdom. At 2:10 AM on December 6, 1921, in the British prime minister's residence at 10 Downing Street, Michael Collins—the Republican leader and controversial hero—signed the Anglo-Irish Treaty. This designated a six-county North to remain in British hands in exchange for complete independence for Ireland's 26 counties as the Irish Free State.

Fast-forward to 1968, when, in the spirit of the student protesters in Paris and Washington, and after 40 years of living with an apparently permanent and sectarian Unionist majority, students in Belfast's Queen's University launched a civil rights movement, claiming equal rights in jobs, housing, and opportunity. The brutality with which these marches were suppressed in front of the world's press led to worldwide revulsion, riots, and counter-riots. The Irish Republican Army (IRA), which had lain dormant for decades, hijacked what was left of the shattered civil rights movement, which once had a smattering of Protestant students among its ranks. Armed British troops who had at first been welcomed by many in the Catholic ghettos as protectors from Protestant paramilitaries now found themselves welcomed by neither side. Britain imposed Direct Rule. No one was happy, and the decades of guerrilla conflict that ensued between the IRA, the UDA/UVF (Protestant/Loyalist paramilitaries), and the British government continued in a mix of lulls and terrors—apart from the IRA's annual Christmas "truce"—until the summer of 1994, when the "Provos," as they are colloquially known, called an ongoing cease-fire, confirmed in July 1997.

Belfast reveled in its peace. New hotels, shopping malls, and restaurants came off dusty drawing boards. People who had not seen the city's center for a quarter of a century gazed at its bright lights. Today, the IRA and Loyalist cease-fires are still in place, but major divisions remain. The various shades of Unionism are closely identified with the "planted" Protestant population, while Nationalists are inextricably associated with the "native" Irish community, which traces its genetic inheritance back to the Iron Age Celtic invaders and which is almost entirely Catholic. Today, in blue-collar Protestant areas you'll see curbstones and lampposts painted in the British colors of red, white, and blue; entwined British and Red Hand Ulster flags fluttering from tall poles raised in pocket-handkerchief front yards; and countless signs and crests declaring proud devotion to Ulster and the Queen. By contrast, in Nationalist Catholic districts, you'll note the green, white, and gold of the Irish Republic's Tricolor flickering in the breeze.

Don't worry if this all seems impossibly complex. Even locals say wryly, "If you understand Northern Ireland politics, you're missing the point." In any case, the province's turbulent history cannot mask the fact that it is a region incredibly rich in natural beauty and artistic treasures, such as the great Georgian estates and Belfast's Victorian architecture. For overseas travelers, Northern Ireland remains one of the increasingly rare forgotten spots of Europe.

Pleasures and Pastimes

Dining

While it has nowhere near the number of innovative restaurants as Dublin (which is five times more populous), Belfast has witnessed an influx of international influences with restaurants, bistros, wine bars, and—as in Dublin—European-style café-bars where you can get good food *and* linger over a drink.

By and large, though, hearty, unpretentious cooking predominates, with good-quality, fresh local fish and meat simply prepared. You're virtually guaranteed to find certain traditional dishes on menus here, such as Guinness and beef pie; champ (creamy, buttery mashed potatoes with scallions); oysters from Strangford Lough; Ardglass herring; mussels from Dundrum; and smoked salmon from Glenarm. A widespread favorite is the Ulster fry, an inexpensive pub plate of bacon, black pudding, mushrooms, sausages, tomatoes, and eggs, served with potato or soda bread—one of the reasons Northern Ireland has one of the highest rates of heart disease in the world. The delights of ethnic restaurants, including Chinese, Japanese, Indian, Persian, and Thai, are now found in Belfast, and even beyond.

Casual dress is acceptable at most establishments, though jeans are discouraged. As for the cost of a meal here, by the standards of the Republic or the United States, or even the rest of the United Kingdom, restaurant prices are surprisingly moderate. A service charge of 10% may be indicated on the bill; it is customary to pay this, unless the service was bad.

CATEGORY	NORTHERN IRELAND*
$$$$	over U.K.£18
$$$	U.K.£13–U.K.£18
$$	U.K.£7–U.K.£12
$	under U.K.£7

Per person for a main course at dinner

Festivals

Festivals, marches, and other excuses to gather fill the calendar in Ulster—certainly as much as in the South, and possibly more so. Every village in Nationalist areas has its own annual celebration; such *fleadhs* (festivals, pronounced flahs) are especially common in June and July. If you're interested in the Troubles, you may want to see the often-controversial Orangemen's (Unionist) March on July 12 and the Ancient Order of Hibernians' (Nationalist) marches of August 15. The Belfast Folk Festival in September is a weekend of traditional Irish music and dance at downtown locations. The Belfast Festival at Queen's University, which lasts three weeks each November, is the North's cultural high point of the year. Its heady mix of drama, music, dance, and film is centered on the Queen's University campus—the most pleasant area of town.

Lodging

Since the advent of the 1994 cease-fire, major hotel chains both in the Republic and abroad have been investing in the North. In Belfast's environs visitors can choose from the humblest terraced town houses or farm cottages to the grandest country houses. Dining rooms of country-house lodgings frequently reach the standard of top-quality restaurants. All accommodations in the province are inspected and categorized by the Northern Ireland Tourist Board Information Centre, which publishes all names, addresses, and ratings in the handbook *Where to Stay* (U.K.£4.99). The tourist board can also give you information about the hundreds of excellent-value special offers available in the low season from October to March—single nights to weekend deals, the most intimate B&Bs to Belfast's finest hotels.

CATEGORY	NORTHERN IRELAND*
$$$$	over U.K.£120
$$$	U.K.£90–£120
$$	U.K.£60–£90
$	under U.K.£60

All prices are for two people in a double room, including 17.5% local sales tax and a service charge (often applied in larger hotels).

Outdoor Activities and Sports

BICYCLING

Roads are good and fairly traffic-free, so cycling is popular. Once in the countryside you will often have the run of long, winding roads, but be prepared for unpredictable weather. There's no need to have a bike of your own—many towns have places where you can rent them.

BIRD-WATCHING

The province has an unexpectedly wide range of habitats and bird species for such a tiny area. The best time to come is winter, but even in summer visitors can participate in first-class bird-watching, especially on the Antrim uplands, all down the Antrim coast, and on the nearby islands.

FISHING

With a 606-km (466-mi) coastline, part on the Atlantic and part on the Irish Sea, as well as major lakes and an abundance of unpolluted rivers, the North is a great place for anglers. Set your rod for salmon on the Bann, Bush, and Foyle rivers and for brown trout in their tributaries. There are bigger lake trout in Loughs Neagh, Melvin, and Erne, while pike and other coarse (white) fish abound in the Erne. Turbot and plaice are taken off the north coast, where sea bass may be caught from the shore.

HIKING AND WALKING

Northern Ireland is magnificent walking country. Ask at tourist offices for details of their local walking and cycling trails, 14 of which spring off the Ulster Way, an 896-km (560-mi) trek for serious hikers that runs around the six counties and links up with marked trails on the other side of the border. The terrain never demands more than a pair of sturdy walking shoes. Many cities and towns have their own historic and scenic trails, including a multitude of serene walks within striking distance of Belfast.

HORSEBACK RIDING

Sitting on the back of a horse or pony is a great way to travel into places that are out of bounds to motorists. Woodland, beaches, and rough country become accessible on guided rides, some suitable for complete beginners. There are some 35 riding and trekking centers around the province, and several of them offer accommodations.

SPECTATOR SPORTS

As on the rest of the island, people in Ulster take their sport seriously, particularly Saturday's soccer and rugby and Sunday's hurling and Gaelic football events. Dates of local matches are listed in local newspapers. Greyhound racing has roots deep in the Celtic psyche. During the summer, you'll come across the very English sport of cricket being played throughout the province. There are two horse racing tracks—the one at Downpatrick is particularly atmospheric. One oddity is the ancient precursor of bowls, called bullets, which is still played in County Armagh.

It involves throwing bowls (originally they were cannonballs, hence the name) along a narrow, winding country lane; the first to cover 3 km (2 mi) is the winner. The All-Ireland Championship for this sport is held in early August in Armagh. Tourist offices carry details of local and province-wide events. If you fancy something different, Belfast now has its own ice hockey team, the Giants, playing at the Odyssey center.

Shopping

The best of the North's traditional products, many made according to time-honored methods, include the exquisite linen and superior hand-made woolen garments that you might associate only with the Republic of Ireland. Handmade lacework also remains a handicraft from the country-women of some Northern Ireland districts. Keep an eye out for hand-cut crystal from County Tyrone and for the mellow, cream-color Parian china of Belleek. Traditional music CDs and the unadorned blackthorn walking stick are two good choices at the other end of the price scale.

Exploring Northern Ireland

With as fine a setting as you'll find anywhere in Britain, the city of Belfast is Northern Ireland's main gateway. A naturally lively, friendly city, Belfast has plenty of distinguished hotels and restaurants, fascinating muse-ums, Victorian architecture, and strong maritime connections. It is tes-timony to the spirit of Belfast that the long years of sectarian violence have not dimmed its vivacity. Northern Ireland's second city, Derry, is also looking to the future and has an appealing personality all its own—beautiful rows of Georgian houses are being restored, and mu-seums, tourist attractions, and crafts shops have opened in the small city center, which is still enclosed by its medieval walls and one of Eu-rope's best-preserved examples of a fortified town.

Along the shores of the North's coasts and lakes, green, gentle slopes descend majestically into hazy, dark-blue water against a background of more slopes, more water, and huge, cloud-scattered skies. The Antrim Coast is among the most scenic in all of Ireland, while Dun-luce Castle, the Giant's Causeway, and the small towns along the east coast give the traveler a choice of sites along the excellent roads. En-niskillen, in County Fermanagh, is bright and bustling, and the sur-rounding Lough Erne has magnificent lake views, as well as one of Ireland's most impressive round towers, on Devenish Island. On the other side of Enniskillen stand Castle Coole and Florence Court, two graceful mansions of the 18th-century Anglo-Irish nobility.

Numbers in the text correspond to numbers in the margin and on the Northern Ireland and Belfast maps.

Great Itineraries

IF YOU HAVE 2 DAYS

The first day leave the bustling Victorian industrial metropolis of **Belfast** ①–⑯, the starting and ending point of your itinerary, and head north to the remarkable natural formations of the **Giant's Cause-way** ㉔ and the teetering cliff-top remains of **Dunluce Castle** ㉖ via the breathtaking **Glens of Antrim** ㉑, ending the day in the dramatically re-juvenated city of 🏛 **Derry** ㉚–㊳. The next day head south to the tran-quil beauty of **Lough Erne,** and visit to the ancient monastic site of **Devenish Island** ㊺, the historic town of **Enniskillen** ㊻, and the exquisite neoclassic beauty of **Castle Coole** ㊼. Finish your second day back in 🏛 **Belfast.**

IF YOU HAVE 4 DAYS

Leave **Belfast** ①–⑯ and head north to the **Glens of Antrim** ㉑ with a look at the characteristic twin towns of rugged **Cushendall** and pretty

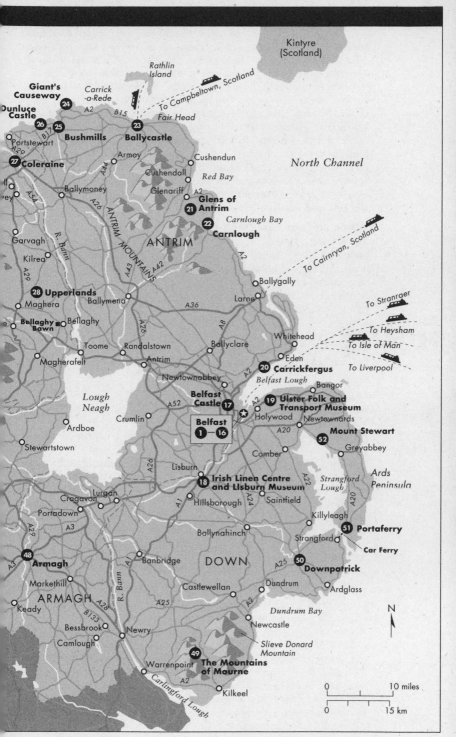

Cushendun before heading for the **Giant's Causeway** ㉔ and **Dunluce Castle** ㉖. Then follow the coast road via Downhill as far as **Derry** ㉚–㊳, where you'll spend the night. The following day head south for **Belleek** ㊷, home of the famous pottery, via the emotive **Ulster-American Folk Park** ㊴ and the reconstructed dwellings of the **Ulster History Park** ㊵; don't miss the holy islands of **White** ㊹ and **Devenish** ㊺. Spend the night in or around the historic town of **Enniskillen** ㊻. The next day follow the road to leafy **Armagh** ㊽, Ireland's ecclesiastical capital, and Navan Centre, on the site of the legendary fort of the Red Branch Knights. Travel southeast to the magnificent **Mountains of Mourne** ㊾ via Bessbrook, a pretty Quaker model village that also happens to be home to the busiest military helicopter base in Europe. Pass through Newry and Kilkeel, finishing the day in **Portaferry** (51). The last day make your way to Belfast along the shores of Strangford Lough to the fairy-tale gardens of **Mount Stewart** (52) and the brilliantly designed **Ulster Folk and Transport Museum** ⑲. Return to Belfast.

When to Tour Northern Ireland

The best time to visit the area is from May to September, when the weather is a little friendlier to travelers, especially in coastal and lake areas. Apart from holiday weekends there should be no trouble getting accommodation anywhere outside Belfast. If heading for Belfast, book in advance. Most of the city's cultural events—except early August's lively West Belfast Festival—take place in the autumn.

BELFAST

167 km (104) mi north of Dublin.

Belfast was a great Victorian success story, an industrial boomtown whose prosperity was built on trade—especially linen and shipbuilding (the *Titanic* was built here, giving Belfast the nickname "Titanic Town"). The key word here, of course, is *was*—linen is no longer a major industry, and shipbuilding has severely suffered. For two decades, news about Belfast was news about the Troubles—until the 1994 cease-fire. Since then, the North's capital city has benefited from major hotel investment, gentrified quaysides, a heralded performing arts center, and heartfelt efforts on the part of the tourist board to claim for the North its share of the visitors pouring into the Euro-buzzing Emerald Isle. Although the 1996 bombing of offices at the Canary Wharf in London disrupted the 1994 peace agreement, cease-fire was officially reestablished on July 20, 1997, and this embattled city began its quest for a newfound identity. This is a fascinating place in the throes of a major historical transition, a city with some of the warmest, wryest people in all of Ireland—all with a palpable will to move forward.

Before English and Scottish settlers arrived in the 1600s, Belfast was a tiny village called Béal Feirste ("sandbank ford") belonging to Ulster's ancient O'Neill clan. With the advent of the Plantation period (when settlers arrived in the 1600s), Sir Arthur Chichester, from Devon in southwest England, received the city, and his son was made Earl of Donegall. Protestant French Huguenots fleeing persecution settled near here, bringing their valuable linen-work skills. In the 18th century, Belfast underwent a phenomenal expansion—its population doubled in size every 10 years, despite an ever-present sectarian divide. Although the Anglican gentry despised the Presbyterian artisans—who, in turn, distrusted native Catholics—Belfast's growth continued at a dizzying speed. Having laid the foundation stone of the city's university in 1845, Queen Victoria returned to Belfast in 1849 (she is recalled in the names of buildings, streets, bars, monuments, and other places around the city), and in the same year, the university opened and took the name Queen's College. Nearly 40 years later, in 1888, Victoria granted Belfast its city charter. Today its population is 300,000—one-quarter of all Northern Ireland's citizens.

Belfast is a fairly compact city, its center made up of roughly three contiguous areas that are easy to navigate on foot; from the south end to the north it's about an hour's leisurely walk.

Golden Mile

This arrowhead-shape area extending from Howard Street in the north to Shaftesbury Square at the southern tip, bordered on the west by Great Victoria Street and on the east by Bedford Street and Dublin Road, is a great area to begin an exploration of Belfast. Although it doesn't quite glow the way the name suggests, bustling Golden Mile and its immediate environs harbor some of Belfast's most noteworthy historic buildings. In addition, the area is filled with hotels, major civic and office buildings, as well as some restaurants, cafés, and stores. Even if you don't end up staying here, you're likely to pass through it often.

A Good Walk

Begin your stroll at the centrally located **Europa Hotel** ① and the **Grand Opera House** ② next door. Even if you're just starting out, at least poke your head in the glorious **Crown Liquor Saloon** ③, a restored Victorian gin palace across the street from the Europa. From the Crown, turn right along Great Victoria Street and then right again onto Howard Street to reach Belfast's Donegall Square, dominated by its columned and domed **City Hall** ④. Walk away from Donegall Square and up May Street, taking an almost immediate right onto Alfred Street. When you come to the junction with Clarence Street, the Tudor-Gothic **St. Malachy's Church** ⑤ will be on your left-hand side. Stop in to gaze awhile at the beautiful fan-vaulted ceiling. From here, walk to the end of Clarence Street, and turn right onto Bedford Street into the Golden Mile proper, where you will come upon **Ulster Hall** ⑥.

TIMING

You'll need about 1½ hours to enjoy the offerings on this route—you can extend this time depending on how long you would like to spend soaking up the atmosphere of places like the Crown Liquor Saloon on your way.

Sights to See

★ ④ **City Hall.** The massive, exuberant Renaissance Revival City Hall dominates Donegall Square. Built between 1898 and 1906 and modeled on St. Paul's Cathedral in London, it was designed by Brumwell Thomas, who was knighted but had to sue to get his fee. Before you enter, take a stroll around Donegall Square, where you'll find statues of Queen Victoria; a monument commemorating the *Titanic* (built in Belfast); and a column honoring the U.S. Expeditionary Force, which landed in the city on January 26, 1942—the first contingent of the U.S. Army to land in Europe. When U.S. president Bill Clinton visited in November 1995, a huge reception was held on the green front lawn; it included a performance by hometown boy Van Morrison, whose "Days Like This" had become an unofficial anthem of the 1994 cease-fire. Head inside under the porte cochere at the front of the building. From the entrance hall (the base of which is a **whispering gallery**), the view up to the heights of the 173-ft **Great Dome** is a feast for the eyes. With its complicated series of arches and openings, stained-glass windows, Italian marble inlays, decorative plasterwork, and paintings, this is Belfast's most ornate public space—homage to the might of the British empire. The guided tour gives access to the Council Chamber, Great Hall, and Reception Room, all upstairs. ⊠ *Donegall Sq.,* ☎ *028/ 9032–0202,* WEB *www.belfastcity.gov.uk.* 🖾 *Free.* ☉ *Mon.–Thurs. 9– 5; Fri 9–4.30; guided tours June–Sept., weekdays at 10:30, 11:30, and 2:30, Sat. at 2:30; Oct.–May, Mon.–Sat. at 2:30.*

★ ❸ **Crown Liquor Saloon.** Opposite the Europa Hotel on Great Victoria Street and now owned by the National Trust (the United Kingdom's official conservation organization), the Crown is one of Belfast's glories: built in 1894, the bar has richly carved woodwork around cozy snugs (cubicles), leather seats, colored tile work, and abundant mirrors. It has been kept immaculate and is still lit by gas—and, most importantly, is perfect for a pint of Guinness and a plate of oysters. When you settle in your snug, note the little gunmetal plates used by the Victorians for lighting their matches. ⊠ *46 Great Victoria St.,* ☎ *028/9027–9901,* WEB *www.belfasttelegraph.co uk/crown.* ☉ *Daily 11:30 AM–midnight.*

❶ **Europa Hotel.** A landmark in Belfast, the Europa is a monument to the resilience of the city in the face of the Troubles. The most bombed hotel in western Europe, it has been targeted 11 times by the IRA since the early 1970s and refurbished every time. Today, owned by affable Ulster millionaire hotel magnate Billy Hastings, it shows no signs of its explosive history. ⊠ *Great Victoria St. at Glengall St.,* ☎ *028/9032– 7000,* WEB *www.hastingshotels.com.*

★ ❷ **Grand Opera House.** Designed in 1894 by the famous theater architect Frank Matcham, the Grand Opera House exemplifies the Victorian age's fascination with the East. Beautifully restored in the 1970s, it's worth a visit—even if you don't go to a show—for a chance to admire the opulent gilt moldings, ornamental plasterwork, and exquisite angel-and-cherub-laden ceiling fresco by contemporary Irish artist Cherith McKinstry. It's also where Van Morrison's 1984 album *Live at the Grand Opera House, Belfast,* was recorded. But by far the best way to see and enjoy the place is to attend a show—musicals, operas, or conventional theater. ⊠ *Great Victoria St.,* ☎ *028/9024–1919,* WEB *www.goh.co.uk/menu.htm.*

❺ **St. Malachy's Church.** Just inside the doors to St. Malachy's Cathedral is a memorial to its chief benefactor, Captain Thomas Griffiths. The church, designed by Thomas Jackson, was built in 1844, and its interior is well worth a viewing. Pay particular attention to its fan-vaulted ceiling. While many of the original fixtures and fitting have succumbed to the ravages of time, this swirling masterpiece of plasterwork survives intact. Inspiration for the design was taken from the chapel of Henry VII at Westminster Abbey in London. Note the 150-year-old church organ. ⊠ *Alfred St.,* ☎ *028/9032–1713.* 🖾 *Free.*

❻ **Ulster Hall.** The home of the Ulster Orchestra, and host to occasional rock concerts (one of the most famous being Led Zeppelin's world stage debut of the song "Stairway to Heaven" in March 1971), Ulster Hall was originally built as a ballroom in 1862. The hall was the venue for the political rallying of Nationalist politicians, such as Charles Stewart Parnell (1846–91) and Patrick Henry Pearse (1879–1916), before the Irish Republic was formed in 1921. It also houses a splendid Mulholland Organ, a Victorian instrument of considerable size. ⊠ *Bedford St.,* ☎ *028/9032–3900,* WEB *www.ulsterhall.co uk.*

Central District

Belfast's Central District, which is immediately north of the Golden Mile, extends from Donegall Square north almost to St. Anne's Cathedral. It's not geographically the center of the city, but it's the old heart

BELFAST'S WALL MURALS

IN NORTHERN IRELAND they say the Protestants make the money and the Catholics make the art, and as with all clichés, there is some truth in it.

It is a truth that will become clear as you look up at the gable walls of blue-collar areas of Belfast on which the two communities have expressed themselves in colorful murals that have given rise to one of the more quirky tours of the city. For while the wildly romantic Catholic murals can often aspire to the levels of Sistine Chapel Lite, those in Protestant areas (like the tough, no-nonsense Shankill and the Newtownards Road) are more workmanlike efforts that sometimes resemble war comics without the humor.

It was not always this way. In Protestant areas, murals were once painted by skilled coachbuilders to mark the 12th of July celebrations of the defeat of the Catholic king James by King William at the Battle of the Boyne. As such, they typically depicted William resplendent in freshly laundered scarlet tunic and plumed cap, sitting on a white stallion that has mastered the art of walking on water. On the banks of the Boyne sits a mildly disheveled James, the expression on his face making him look as if he has just eaten an overdose of anchovies.

Other popular themes in Protestant areas are the Red Hand of Ulster, symbolizing the founding of the province, and, on Carnmore Street, the 13 Protestant apprentice boys shutting the gates of Derry against King James in 1688, leading to the famous siege. More recently, though, Protestant murals have taken on a grimmer air, and typical subjects include wall-eyed paramilitaries perpetually standing firm against increasing liberalism, nationalism, and all the other-isms that Protestants see eroding their stern, Bible-driven way of life.

Nationalist murals, on the other hand, first sprang up in areas like the Falls Road in 1981, when IRA inmates of the Maze prison began a hunger strike in an unsuccess-ful bid to be recognized by the British government as political prisoners rather than common criminals. Ten died, and the face of the most famous, Bobby Sands, looks down now from a gable wall on the Falls Road alongside the words: "Our revenge will be the laughter of our children."

Since then, themes of freedom from oppression and a rising Nationalist confidence have expressed themselves in murals that romantically and surreally mix and match images from the *Book of Kells,* the Celtic Mist mock-heroic posters of Irish artist Jim Fitzpatrick, assorted phoenixes rising from ashes, and revolutionaries clad in splendidly idiosyncratic sombreros and bandannas from other ideological battlegrounds in Mexico and South America. Irish Gaelic words and phrases that you will see springing up regularly include the much-used slogan "Ti-ocfaidh çr Içʺ (pronounced chucky-ar-la and meaning) "Our day will come" and the simple cry "Saoirse" (pronounced seer-she) meaning "Freedom".

Less political are two fascinating community projects. The first, at Springhill Community Park, is the largest art project of its kind in Ireland, made up of traditional Celtic symbols such as birds, dogs, spirals, and knots, mingled with the art of several other mythologies by designer Gerard Kelly, who started it in 1998 with the aid of local children and finally completed it two years later. The other project, in the Upper Springfield area of Ballymurphy, was created by local people who used murals and mosaics to express their particular view of myths, legends, history, and their own family stories.

The murals in both Protestant and Catholic areas are safe to view in daylight and outside the sensitive week of the 12th of July marches by Protestant Orangemen. However, the most sensible way would be to take a guided tour with Citybus or Belfast City Tours.

of Belfast. Shoppers note: it also has the highest concentration of retail outlets in town. It's a frenetic place—the equivalent of Dublin's
Grafton and Henry streets in one—where both locals *and* visitors
shop. Cafés, pubs, offices, and stores of all kinds, from department stores
to the Gap and Waterstone's (there's even a Disney store), occupy the
redbrick and white-Portland-stone buildings and modern architecture
that line its narrow streets. Many of the streets are pedestrianized, so
it's a good place to take a leisurely stroll and browse—and see some
sights to boot.

A Good Walk

Begin at the **Linenhall Library** ⑦, the gray building on Donegall Square's
northwest corner. Walk north up Donegall Place, Belfast's main shopping street, where you'll find the main **Northern Ireland Tourist Board
Information Centre** ⑧. Continue down Donegall Place as it becomes
Royal Avenue, and turn right onto Church Street, at the end of which
is **St. Anne's Cathedral** ⑨. Take Donegall Street to North Street and
go east down **High Street** to busy Victoria Street and the leaning **Albert Memorial Clock Tower** ⑩. From here, walk up Queen's Square to
the river and Donegall Quay. You'll be able to see parts of Belfast's
historic shipyards and two of the world's largest cranes in the Harland and Wolff shipyard, which built the *Titanic*. Veer left at the river
to the **Lagan Lookout Visitor Centre** ⑪. Perched on the river, the center is opposite the back of the **Custom House** ⑫. Walking south down
Oxford Street will bring you to Waterfront Hall on the river at the end
of the street. From here, you can return to the city center via busy Chichester Street. Or instead wander north behind St. Anne's to the Cathedral Quarter, a maze of cobbled streets that the city fathers plan to
transform over the next few years into a funky combination of Temple Bar in Dublin and the Left Bank in Paris.

TIMING
It is easy to get waylaid shopping and investigating sights along the
river when taking this walk, so give yourself at least two hours to cover
the area comfortably.

Sights to See

⑩ **Albert Memorial Clock Tower.** Tilting a little to one side, not unlike Pisa's
more notorious leaning landmark, the clock tower was named for
Queen Victoria's husband, Prince Albert. The dilapidated square on
which it stands underwent a face-lift in 2002. The tower itself is not
open to the public. ⊠ *Victoria Sq.*

⑫ **Custom House.** The 19th-century architect Charles Lanyon designed
the Custom House. This building, along with many others in Belfast,
including the main building of Queen's University and the unusual Sinclair Seaman's Church, bear the hallmarks of his skill. It's not open to
the public, but it's worth circling the house to view the lofty pediment
of Brittania, Mercury, and Neptune on the front, carved by acclaimed
stonemason Thomas Fitzpatrick. ⊠ *Donegall Quay.*

★ **High Street.** Off High Street, especially down to Ann Street (parallel
to the south), run narrow lanes and alleyways called entries. Though
mostly cleaned up and turned into chic shopping lanes, they still hang
on to something of their former raffish character, including distinctive
pubs with little-altered Victorian interiors. Among the most notable
are the **Morning Star** (⊠ Pottinger's Entry off High St.), with its large
windows and fine curving bar; **White's Tavern** (⊠ wine-cellar entry
off High St.), Belfast's oldest pub, founded in 1630, which, although
considerably updated, still has a warm and comfortable ambience, with
plush seats and a big, open fire; **Magennis's Whiskey Café** (⊠ 84 May

St.), in splendid counterpoint to the Waterfront Hall's space-age ambience; and **McHugh's** (✉ Queen's Sq.), in what is reckoned to be the city's oldest extant building, dating from 1710.

🐦 ⓫ **Lagan Lookout Visitor Centre.** Right at the edge of Lagan Weir, the center delves into the history of the River Lagan and the weir by means of interactive exhibits. It is a good way for children to learn about the river's history and surroundings. At night, the exterior of the building is flooded with blue light, adding to the feel that the riverside developments in Belfast have been inspired by the Southbank in London. The shipyard cranes visible beyond—Samson and Goliath—are two of the world's largest. The Lagan Boat Company runs guided one hour tours of the River Lagan. For details see their Web site. ✉ *Lagan Weir, Donegall Quay,* ☎ *028/9031–5444.* 🎫 *Boat trips, U.K.£3.* ☯ *Apr.–Sept., weekdays 11–5, Sat. noon–5, Sun. 2–5; Oct.–Mar., Tues.– Fri. 11–3:30, Sat. 1–4:30, Sun. 2–4:30.* **Lagan Boat Company** ✉ *48 St. John's Close, Laganbank Rd., Belfast BT1 3LX,* ☎ *028/9033–0844, 077/1891–0423, www.laganboatcompany.com,* WEB *www.laganside.com.*

❼ **Linenhall Library.** This gray building on Donegall Square's northwest corner is in fact a comfortable private library, founded in 1788 and designed by Charles Lanyon. The library has an unparalleled collection of 80,000 documents relating to the Troubles; it is also a perfect hideaway for relaxing with a newspaper or soaking up the old-world atmosphere in the library's café. An early librarian, Thomas Russell, was hanged in 1803 for supporting an Irish uprising. On the walls are paintings and prints depicting Belfast views and landmarks. Much of this artwork is for sale and makes excellent and original souvenirs or gifts. ✉ *17 Donegall Sq. N,* ☎ *028/9032–1707,* WEB *www.linenhall.com.* 🎫 *Free.* ☯ *Weekdays 9:30–5:30, Sat. 9:30–4.*

❽ **Northern Ireland Tourist Board Information Centre.** Pick up maps and details for travel in Northern Ireland here. The office incorporates the plush, comprehensive Belfast Welcome Centre—the main tourist office for Belfast city, run by the Belfast Visitor and Convention Bureau. ✉ *47 Donegall Pl.,* ☎ *028/9024–6609,* FAX *028/9031–2424,* WEB *www.discovernorthernireland.com.* ☯ *Sept.–Apr., Mon.–Sat. 9:30– 5:30; June–Aug., Mon.–Sat. 9–7, Sun. noon–5.*

❾ **St. Anne's Cathedral.** A somber heaviness and deep, rounded arches are the hallmarks of the Irish neo-Romanesque style, and both elements dominate this large edifice, which is basilican in plan and was built at the turn of the 20th century. Lord Carson (1854–1935), who was largely responsible for keeping the six counties inside the United Kingdom, is buried here beneath a suitably austere gray slab. New landscaping around the Anglican cathedral provides a place to rest your legs in good weather. The guides on duty will show you around the cathedral for no charge. ✉ *Donegall St.,* ☎ *028/9032–8332,* WEB *www.belfastcathedral.com.* 🎫 *Free.* ☯ *Weekdays 9:15–4:45, Sat. 9:15–4.*

NEED A BREAK?	At the start of Royal Avenue, turn left onto Bank Street to find **Kelly's Cellars** (✉ 30–32 Bank St.), a traditional bar with loads of character. Try the two specialties: Ulster fry or champ and sausages. Two centuries ago, Kelly's Cellars was the regular meeting place of a militant Nationalist group, the Society of United Irishmen, whose leader, Wolfe Tone (who was a Protestant), is remembered as the founder of Irish Republicanism.

392

Albert Memorial
Clock Tower 10

Botanic Gardens ...15

City Hall 4

Crown Liquor
Saloon 3

Custom House 12

Europa Hotel 1

Grand Opera
House 2

Lagan Lookout
Visitor Centre 11

Linenhall Library 7

Northern Ireland
Tourist Board
Information
Centre 8

Queen's
University 14

St. Anne's
Cathedral 9

St. Malachy's
Church 5

Ulster Hall 6

Ulster Museum 16

Union Theological
College 13

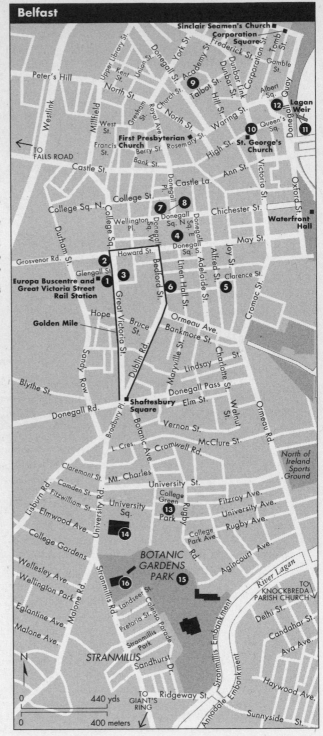

Belfast

☼ **W5: Whowhatwherewhywhen.** Part of the Odyssey complex in Belfast's docklands, this science discovery center takes a high-tech, hands-on approach to interpreting science, engineering, and technology for adults and children. Video displays and flashing lights provide a modernistic feel, and you can do everything from explore the weather to build bridges and robots. ⊠ *2 Queen's Quay,* ☎ *028/9046–7700,* WEB *www.w5online.co.uk.* ⊡ *€6.50.* ☉ *Weekdays 10–6, weekends noon–6; last admission at 5.*

University Area

At Belfast's southern end, this part of the city around Queen's University is by far the most appealing place for a casual stroll. Dotted with parks, botanical gardens, and leafy streets with fine, intact two- and three-story 19th-century buildings, the area evokes an older, more leisurely pace of life. The many pubs and excellent restaurants make this the center of the city's nightlife.

A Good Walk

From the southern tip of Shaftesbury Square, head farther south down **Botanic Avenue** and watch the cityscape of the Golden Mile quickly transform into the more peaceful and residential university area. Take note of the **Lower Crescent**, with its range of bars and restaurants, on your right. Continue, crossing University Street, and you will soon find the **Union Theological College** ⑬ on your left. To your right, you will see the side of **Queen's University** ⑭; walk around the campus via University Square and University Road to the **Stranmillis** area of the city and Stranmillis Road. In to the left are the **Botanic Gardens** ⑮; enclosed in the gardens is the **Ulster Museum** ⑯.

TIMING

Allow a leisurely morning or afternoon to visit the sights, taking your time at the Botanic Gardens and Ulster Museum.

Sights to See

★ ⑮ **Botanic Gardens.** Laid out in 1827 on land that slopes down to the River Lagan, tucked between **Queen's University** and the **Ulster Museum,** these gardens are a glorious haven of grass, trees, flowers, curving walks, and wrought-iron benches where it was not unusual, in their Victorian heyday, to find 10,000 of Belfast's citizens strolling on a Saturday afternoon. Begun in 1839 and completed in 1852, the **Palm House,** constructed of curved iron and glass, is the oldest curvilinear greenhouse in the world—a technical marvel designed by Charles Lanyon in 1839. The **Tropical Ravine House,** though not architecturally distinguished, has an outstanding collection of tropical flora. If you stay in the university area, this is easily the nicest place in Belfast for an early morning stroll or jog—and if it's cold and rainy you can always take shelter in the steamy jungles of the Tropical Ravine. ⊠ *Stranmillis Rd.,* ☎ *028/9032–4902.* ⊡ *Free except during concerts.* ☉ *Gardens daily dawn–dusk. Palm House and Tropical Ravine House Apr.–Sept., weekdays 10–5, weekends 1–5; Oct.–Mar., weekdays 10–4, weekends 2–4.*

⑭ **Queen's University.** Dominating University Road is Queen's University itself. The main university buildings, modeled on Oxford's Magdalen College and designed by the ubiquitous Charles Lanyon, were built in 1849 in a Tudor Revival style. The long, handsome redbrick-and-sandstone facade of the main building has large leaded-glass windows, with three square towers and crenellations galore. **University Square,** really a terrace, is another treasure from the same era. There is a Seamus Heaney library, named after the Ulster-born 1997 Nobel

Prize–winning poet. The Visitors Centre displays university artifacts and hosts exhibitions, and a there's a small shop where you can buy gifts and university souvenirs. ⊠ *University Rd.,* ☎ *028/9033–5252.* ☾ *May–Sept., Mon.–Sat. 10–4; Oct.–Apr., weekdays 10–4.*

Stranmillis. Once its own village, now the off-campus quarter, Stranmillis is one of Belfast's more appealing neighborhoods, filled with tree-lined residential streets on which you'll see pottering academics and find a wide choice of ethnic eateries. You can get here via Stranmillis Road (near the **Ulster Museum**). Here you'll also find "Little Paris," a stretch of shops and cafés that extends down to the riverside towpath along the Lagan. **Malone Road** joins the river farther south, close to the out-of-town **Giant's Ring** (off Ballyleeson Road), a large, Neolithic earthwork focused on an impressive dolmen. To get this far, unless you're a vigorous walker (it's possible to come all the way on the Lagan towpath), you'll be happier driving in a car or taking a bus: Ulsterbus 13 passes close to the site, and on the return journey it will take you back to Donegall Square.

★ ⑯ **Ulster Museum.** In the southwest corner of the **Botanic Gardens,** the museum's three floors are devoted to the history and prehistory of Ireland and, in particular, Northern Ireland, together with a considerable collection of 19th- and 20th-century fine art. (You can get a free guidebook at the reception desk.) An impressive (large) skeleton of the now extinct Irish giant deer is a highlight of the natural history section. Other major holdings are the trove of jewelry and gold ornaments—as well as a cannon and other armaments—recovered from the Spanish Armada vessel *Girona* and two sister galleons sunk off the Antrim coast in 1588. But the most imaginative, user-friendly sections are on the first floor: one exhibit colorfully traces the rise of Belfast's crafts, trade, and industry; another tells the story of the Nationalist movement and explains the separation of the North from the rest of the country. A small café is on level three. ⊠ *Stranmillis Rd.,* ☎ *028/9038–3000,* WEB *www.ulstermuseum.org.uk.* ▣ *Free.* ☾ *Weekdays 10–5, Sat. 1–5, Sun. 2–5.*

⑬ **Union Theological College.** Like **Queen's University,** on the opposite side of the street, the Union Theological College, with its colonnaded, Doric facade, owes the charm of its appearance to architect Charles Lanyon. The building's other claim to fame is that, before the completion of the parliament buildings at Stormont, Northern Ireland's House of Commons was convened in the library, and the college's chapel played host to the Senate. ⊠ *108 Botanic Ave.,* ☎ *028/9020–5080.* ▣ *Free.* ☾ *Tours by appointment.*

Dining

The food scene in Belfast is experiencing the same renaissance as the city itself. The choice of restaurants is more limited than in Dublin, but two or three of Belfast's best kitchens are a match for anything else you'll find in Ireland. The best chefs—Michael Deane, the Rankins, and Robbie Millar—have brought back to Ireland, from their work abroad, a sophisticated, internationalist approach to cooking. Beyond the top-tier places, there are plenty of other restaurants where you'll find fresh local fish and delectable meat dishes prepared simply but with style.

$$$$ ✕ **Shanks.** Like many of Ireland's other best young chefs, Robbie Mil-
★ lar studied under Cayenne's Paul Rankin, and he spares nothing to produce wonderful fish and game dishes. How demanding is he? A scuba diver handpicks large, fresh scallops from the Copeland Islands in the Irish Sea (they're more tender than scallops dredged by a trawler off

CHURCHES AROUND THE CITY

BELFAST HAS SO MANY CHURCHES you could visit a different one nearly every day of the year and still not make it to all of them. The oldest house of worship is the Church of Ireland **Knockbreda Parish Church** (⊠ Church Rd. off A24 on the south side of the city). This dark, sturdy, and atmospheric structure was built in 1737 by Richard Cassels, who designed many of Ireland's finest mansions. It quickly became *the* place to be buried—witness the vast 18th-century tombs in the churchyard. Closer to the city center, the **First Presbyterian Church** (⊠ Rosemary St.) dates from 1783 and has an interesting elliptical interior. It also hosts lunchtime concerts. The Church of Ireland's **St. George's** (⊠ High St.), built in 1816, has a tremendous Georgian portico and pretty box pews. By the riverfront is one of the most appealing churches, Presbyterian **Sinclair Seamen's Church** (⊠ Corporation Sq. off Donegall Quay). It was designed by Charles Lanyon, the architect of **Queen's University**, and has served the seafaring community since 1857. A maritime theme pervades the building: the pulpit is shaped like a ship's prow; the bell is from HMS *Hood*, sunk in 1916; and even the collection plates are shaped like lifeboats.

the sea bottom). Start with grilled tuna with spiced eggplant chutney, and indulge in the standout main course—peppered loin of venison with red cabbage. A three-course set menu is U.K.£38. Shanks is 19 km (12 mi) from Belfast, signposted off the Crawfordsburn Road (turn *right* off the Belfast–Bangor Road, or you can take a train from Belfast to Bangor and then a taxi). The restaurant is on a vast 3,000-acre golf clubhouse-estate. ⊠ *Blackwood Golf Centre, Crawfordsburn Rd., Bangor,* ☎ *028/9185–3313,* WEB *www.shanksrestaurant.com. Reservations essential. AE, MC, V. Closed 3 wks in July and Sun.–Mon. No lunch Sat.*

$$–$$$ ✕ **Aldens.** East Belfast was a gastronomic wilderness until this cool
★ modernist restaurant opened with chef Cath Gradwell at the helm. Now city-center folk regularly make the 10-minute pilgrimage to take advantage of a seafood-rich menu at some of the most reasonable prices in town. The set dinner menus Monday to Thursday are particularly good value—U.K.£15 for three courses. The mood is relaxed, the staff are perpetually friendly, and the wine list is one of the best around. Standout starters include crab risotto with sweet pepper and coriander; top entrées are roast breast of duck with Seville orange jus and potato rosti, and wild boar sausages with rich onion gravy and mashed potato. ⊠ *229 Upper Newtownards Rd., Belfast,* ☎ *028/9065–0079. AE, DC, MC, V. No lunch weekends, no dinner Sun.*

$$–$$$ ✕ **Deane's.** Chef Michael Deane became a celebrity for fantastic food
★ in a tiny open kitchen—in an equally tiny Victorian railroad station—a few miles outside Belfast. In 1995, he moved into a much larger two-story room—a brasserie downstairs and formal restaurant upstairs—in the center of Belfast, close to City Hall. Deane's tastes are eclectic—he has worked in Bangkok, and the influence of Thai cooking is re-

vealed in his especially subtle way with spices. Squab is a Deane specialty, served as a kedgeree with cucumber and quail eggs for a starter. For a main dish try French squab with local rabbit, roast potato and parsnip with Madeira. The ravioli of lobster is excellent. Set-menu options include U.K.£31 for two courses, U.K.£7.50 for dessert, and a 10-course Prestige Menu for U.K.£55. ⊠ *34–40 Howard St.,* ☎ *028/9033–1134 restaurant; 028/9056–0000 brasserie,* WEB *www.deanes-belfast.com. AE, MC, V. Restaurant closed Sun.–Tues., brasserie closed Sun.–Mon.*

$$ ✕ **Cayenne.** Celebrity TV chefs Paul and Jeanne Rankin, innovative cooks who travel widely, run this Golden Mile spot. The Rankins' previous venture here, the renowned Roscoff, spearheaded the transformation of fine dining in Belfast. The less formal Cayenne serves fusion cuisine with an Asian twist—miso-glazed cod, char-grilled rib eye with red onion and mushroom *bruschetta,* and wok-smoked salmon with Bombay potatoes and fresh coriander. Tempting desserts include white chocolate cheesecake tart and lemongrass crème brûlée. Cayenne takes last orders until 11:15, so it's great if you want a meal after an opera or concert in Waterfront Hall. ⊠ *Shaftesbury Sq. at end of Great Victoria St.,* ☎ *028/9033–1532. AE, DC, MC, V. Closed Sun. No lunch Sat.*

$$ ✕ **La Belle Époque.** Relaxed and intimate, this well-established restaurant with an art nouveau interior is charmingly French. On the very reasonably priced menu you'll find a delectable appetizer of smoked salmon stuffed with fish mousse in a horseradish sauce, and a fine fillet of beef with whole grain mustard cream sauce for a main course. Try the freshly made fruit sorbets for dessert. The set-price lunch menu is a particularly good value. ⊠ *61 Dublin Rd.,* ☎ *028/9032–3244. Reservations essential. AE, DC, MC, V. Closed Sun. and Mon. No lunch Sat.*

$$ ✕ **Nick's Warehouse.** Nick Price's cool, cozy wine bar and adjacent restaurant are among Belfast's most relaxing watering holes. At the busy bar you can get warm salads with a range of nut oils, and tasty casseroles. In the slightly more formal restaurant (reservations essential), favorites include duck with red cabbage and apple compote, and halibut with langoustine and sweet peppers. Finish off your meal with a sampling of the cheese selection. The wine and imported beer lists are impressive. Nick's is on a narrow, cobbled street near the increasingly fashionable Laganside area. ⊠ *35 Hill St.,* ☎ *028/9043–9690. AE, MC, V. Closed Sun. No lunch Sat. No dinner Mon.*

$–$$ ✕ **The Morning Star.** You'll find the 19th-century Morning Star halfway down a narrow lane, in the heart of Belfast. It's one of the city's most historic pubs—there's a traditional bar downstairs and a cozy velvet and wood-paneled restaurant upstairs. Head chef Seamus McAlister, far from resting on the pub's laurels, is constantly experimenting, and is known for his quirky takes on local ingredients. Seasonal standards include hearty venison and game in winter, lamb in spring, and in summer tender beef or Lough Neagh silver eels, which Seamus prepares simply, panfried in their own oil and served with buttery champ. However, he's also more than happy to cook ostrich, kangaroo, crocodile, and anything else exotic he can get his hands on. ⊠ *17–19 Pottingers Entry,* ☎ *028/9023–5986. AE, MC, V.*

$–$$ ✕ **The Northern Whig.** The latest addition to Belfast entrepreneur Jas Mooney's stable of designer pubs, The Northern Whig is housed in an elegant former newspaper building, with a spacious and stylish wood and leather interior dominated by three 30-ft-high statues of Soviet heroes that once topped Communist Party headquarters in Prague. In the evenings, one wall slides away so you can watch old black-and-white movies, a jazz band, or a DJ playing laid-back blues, soul, or retro. The food is brasserie-style—good, not astonishing. It's the environment, the thoughtful wine list, and the cocktail bar, which specializes in rare vodkas, that are the draw. ⊠ *2 Bridge St.,* ☎ *028/9050–9888. MC, V.*

$–$$ ✕ **Rajput.** You won't leave this Indian restaurant feeling as if you've been kissing a flame-thrower: in even the Rajput's hottest dishes, nuanced flavors shine through. Top entrée choices include "Raj Supreme Chicken Masala," a hot yet aromatic mingling of spices, nuts, and herbs, and lamb *tikka,* in a sauce so red it will be immediately attracted to any item of light-colored clothing within five yards. (Just red, not red-hot, so don't worry.) For side dishes, favorites include a tasty *saag aloo* of spicy potatoes and spinach. Wash it all down with cold Indian lager. ⊠ *461 Lisburn Rd.,* ☎ *028/9066–2168. AE, MC, V.*

$–$$ ✕ **Sun Kee.** This unpretentious little spot has the mark of all truly good Chinese restaurants—the Chinese people who live in the area eat here. They dig into huge portions while watching the large TV in the corner, then rush upstairs for a quick game of mah-jongg. Ignore the nononsense look of the place—the food is terrific. While you can't go wrong with beef in green pepper sauce and *char sui* (marinated and barbecued) pork, this is a good place to take a risk with dishes such as duck's web or fish-head soups, or such entrées as eel or roasted pork belly. The helpful staff will even choose for you if you tell them your tastes. Sun Kee does not have a liquor license, so bring your own booze. ⊠ *38 Donegall Pass,* ☎ *028/9031–2016. No credit cards. Closed mid-July–mid-Aug. No lunch.*

$ ✕ **Kitchen Bar.** Come at lunch for the Irish stew, Ulster fry, or host Pat Catney's famous "Paddy's Pizza"—made on a base of traditional Irish soda bread. Lunch is what this place is known for; it's a great place to mingle with city-center worker bees, should you want to. Make sure you wash your lunch down with a draft beer—real ale aficionados flock here, thanks to its great selection, for the Kitchen Bar's annual beer festival during the first week of October. If you can't make it for lunch, join the others arriving for traditional music on Friday nights. ⊠ *16 Victoria Sq.,* ☎ *028/9032–4901. MC, V.*

$ ✕ **Long's.** Long's has been serving fish-and-chips in its tiny and completely basic Athol Street premises in the south of the city for the past 80 years. It's a legend among all sorts—garbage collectors, millionaires, and everyone in between flock here for the standard fish-and-chips served with bread, butter, and a mug of tea. Long's continues to pack them in, claiming no more reason than the freshest of ingredients and a secret batter recipe that has been handed down over the decades. Demand is so intense they've opened another shop in Donegall Pass, a 1-min walk from Shaftesbury Square. Slightly larger but not much less basic than the original, it also offers haddock, smoked fish, Dover sole, and skate with your chips. ⊠ *39 Athol St.,* ☎ *028/9032–1848;* ⊠ *15 Donegall Pass,* ☎ *028/9024–1644. No credit cards. Closed Sun.*

$ ✕ **Roscoff Café.** This city-center bakery-café is a good choice if you want to enjoy the culinary delights of chefs Paul and Jeanne Rankin (of Cayenne) without breaking the bank. Roscoff's has a Parisian feel to it, especially if the weather is fine and you're sitting outside. Try the walnut bread, sun-dried tomato bread, focaccia, and the delicious soups and desserts. ⊠ *27–29 Fountain St.,* ☎ *028/9031–5090. No credit cards. Closed Sun.*

Lodging

Airport and Environs

$$$$ 🏨 **Dunadry Hotel and Country Club.** Ten minutes from Belfast International Airport, this spacious, whitewashed former mill on 10 acres of land is a hotel of considerable charm. Renovations made use of large wooden components from the old mill's massive linen beetling (polishing) engines in the stairwell and a gallery over the bar. Bedrooms are large; the best open onto the inner courtyard. The restaurant is a popular spot for local weddings, so you may find yourself in the midst of a real Irish celebration. ⊠ *2 Islandreagh Dr., Dunadry, Co. Antrim BT41 2HA,* ☎ *028/9443–4343,* FAX *028/9443–3389,* WEB *www.mooney-hotelgroup.com. 83 rooms with bath. Restaurant, indoor pool, gym, croquet, bar, meeting rooms. AE, DC, MC, V.*

$$$$ ⊞ **Hilton Templepatrick.** Ensconced in 220 acres of wooded parkland and with its own 18-hole championship golf course, this modern hotel is 10 minutes from Belfast International Airport and 20 minutes from Belfast city center. Rooms are generously equipped, with satellite TV and full bathroom. The location is particularly good if you're planning a brief visit to the province and don't want to stay in the city. The hotel has an exercise room. ⊠ *Castle Upton Estate, Templepatrick, Co. Antrim BT39 0DD,* ☎ *028/9443–5500,* FAX *028/9443–5511,* WEB *www.stakis.co.uk. 129 rooms with bath, 1 suite. Restaurant, 18-hole golf course, 2 tennis courts, indoor pool, gym, sauna, bar, meeting rooms. AE, DC, MC, V.*

Central District

$$$$ ⊞ **Belfast Hilton.** This riverside hotel should be able to cater to your every whim and, with its excellent fitness and leisure facilities, it's a great place to unwind after experiencing the wilds of the countryside. Rooms are well equipped and comfortable, and the restaurant serves contemporary cuisine; along with some of the suites, it has good views of the river and across the city. The hotel is beside Waterfront Hall, in an area undergoing urban renewal. ⊠ *4 Lanyon Pl., BT1 3LP,* ☎ *028/ 9027–7000,* FAX *028/9027–7277,* WEB *www.hilton.com. 182 rooms with bath, 14 suites. Restaurant, cable TV, in-room data ports, indoor pool, beauty salon, sauna, bar, business services, meeting rooms, designated pet rooms, no-smoking floors. AE, DC, MC, V.*

Golden Mile

$$$$ ⊞ **Tensq.** You don't get much more downtown or contemporary than this fashionable boutique hotel right behind City Hall—the neoclassical facade of this former post office hides a serene interior that houses Red, a popular and fashionable urban bar, the cool yet cozy Wine Café, and the Restaurant Porcelain, where chef Niall McKenna struts his stuff cooking Japanese and European classics. Highlights include seared beef on crispy onions, followed by honey and hazelnut tart with thyme ice cream. Main courses are U.K.£10–U.K.£18. Also in the hotel is a deli and a café. The bedrooms are minimalist but welcoming—rooms are simple but beautiful, with big beds, soft armchairs, a hi-fi, and fresh flowers daily. There are ISDN lines for computers in all rooms, and a DVD and CD library at the hotel. ⊠ *10 Donegall Sq. South, BT1 5JD,* ☎ *028/9024–1001,* FAX *028/9024–3210,* WEB *www.ten-sq.com. 23 rooms with bath. Restaurant, in-room data ports, 2 bars, concierge, free parking. AE, MC, V.*

$$$–$$$$ ⊞ **Holiday Inn Belfast.** Expect outstanding facilities at a reasonable price, and a room rate that gets you a double or twin bed and a sofa that can be folded down into a double bed for two children. It also has a superb location—a 10-minute walk from the city center and only 5 minutes from the Golden Mile, heart of the city's nightlife. Furnishings are modernist blond wood and leather, and rooms are best described as Japan-meets-Sweden: strong, simple colors and sliding wooden screens (a lovely touch) instead of curtains. ⊠ *22 Ormeau Ave., BT2 8HS,* ☎ *0870/400–9005,* FAX *028/9062–6546,* WEB *www.holiday-inn.co.uk. 170 rooms with bath. Restaurant, indoor pool, aerobics, gym, hot tub, massage, sauna, steam room, bar. AE, DC, MC, V.*

$$ 🏨 **Benedict's of Belfast.** With a facade that stands out from the drab terraces of Bradbury Place, Benedict's of Belfast is a friendly, lively, and convenient base for exploring the Golden Mile and university area. Rooms on the second floor are bright and colorful, and have wooden floors; rooms on the third floor are darker, with an Asian touch—dark wood and light walls, simple but comfortable. If you don't feel like straying too far from home for some nightlife, Benedict's has a buzzing bar and restaurant serving finely done Continental food. ✉ *7–21 Bradbury Pl., BT7 1RQ,* ☎ *028/9059–1999,* FAX *028/9059–1990,* WEB *www.benedictshotel.co.uk. 32 rooms, 30 with bath. Restaurant, cable TV, in-room data ports, bar, meeting rooms. AE, DC, MC, V.*

$$ 🏨 **Jurys Belfast Inn.** The first Jurys north of the border brings the chain's flat-rate pricing formula—one price for up to three adults or two adults and two children—to the Golden Mile. Once you get past the forbidding warehouselike exterior, a spacious, marble-tiled foyer with warm green and salmon hues awaits. Some rooms overlook College Square, the cricket lawn of the elegant dusky-brick Royal Belfast Academical Institution, built in 1814 by JoanSoane. The Arches restaurant offers well-prepared hotel food. Tartan fabrics and dark wood decorate the Inn Pub, which serves pub-grub all day. ✉ *Fisherwick Pl., BT2 7AP,* ☎ *028/9053–3500,* FAX *028/9053–3511,* WEB *www.jurys-doyle.com. 190 rooms with bath. Restaurant, bar, in-room data ports, meeting rooms, non-smoking floors. AE, DC, MC, V.*

Outside the City Center

$$$$ 🏨 **Culloden Hotel.** One of only two five-star hotels in Northern Ireland—the other is the Belfast Hilton—it's the flagship in a fleet of hotels run by local hotelier Billy Hastings. This 19th-century former Scottish baronial mansion stands amid 12 lovely acres of parkland. Public areas have ornate woodwork, Louis XV chandeliers, decorative plasterwork, and stained glass. Guest rooms, both in the original section and in a newer wing, are decorated with silk-and-velvet fabrics and have fine views. The dining areas include the French Mitre restaurant and the Grill Bar, which serves both snacks and full meals. The hotel is 8 km (5 mi) from the city center on A2, and is close to the Ulster Folk and Transport Museum. ✉ *142 Bangor Rd., Holywood, Co. Down BT18 0EX,* ☎ *028/9042–5223,* FAX *028/9042–6777,* WEB *www.hastingshotels.com. 79 rooms with bath, 10 suites. Restaurant, grill, tennis court, indoor pool, hair salon, massage, sauna, croquet, squash, nightclub, laundry service, Internet on request, meeting rooms, no-smoking rooms. AE, DC, MC, V.*

$$$$ 🏨 **The McCausland Hotel.** Clean and simple lines, a feeling of space and light, and an aura of sumptuous minimalism are the hallmarks of this luxury hotel created from a pair of 1867 grain warehouses, with the original cast-iron pillars and beams retained throughout. The well-equipped bedrooms, with entertainment centers that include TVs, VCRs, and CD players, are tastefully color-coordinated. Dining, under the capable, inspired hands of chef Eamonn O'Cathain, takes place in the Marco Polo bar-bistro or the more formal Merchants Brasserie. On the edge of the blossoming Laganside area, the hotel is a 5-minute walk from the city center, the Waterfront Hall, and the Odyssey complex, and 20 minutes from the start of the Golden Mile. There's an exercise room (free for guests) in a nearby private health club. ✉ *34–38 Victoria St., BT1 3GH,* ☎ *028/9022–0200,* FAX *028/9022–0220,* WEB *www.slh.com. 60 rooms with bath, 6 suites. Restaurant, bar, meeting rooms. AE, DC, MC, V.*

$$–$$$ 🏨 **Rayanne House.** Famous both for its food and for its hospitality, this family-owned country house run by the devoted Anne McClelland is in leafy Holywood, 10 km (6 mi) from Belfast city center. Rooms

are airy, each with individual, traditional furnishings and nice views of the gardens. The Rayanne breakfast includes a traditional Irish grill, along with such specialties as prune soufflé on a purée of green figs and hot Rayanne baked cereal (laced with spices, fresh fruit, whiskey, honey, and cream). These are served in an intimate dining room, among family antiques, paintings, and candelabra. Lunch and dinner are by request 24 hours in advance. ⊠ *60 Demesne Rd., Holywood, Co. Down BT18 9EX,* ☎ ꜰᴀх *028/9042–5859. 9 rooms with bath. Dining room. MC, V.*

University Area

$$$ 🔲 **Ash-Rowan Guest House.** Former restaurateurs Sam and Evelyn Ha-
★   zlett own and run this outstanding B&B in a spacious Victorian home on a tranquil residential avenue. Thomas Andrews, designer of the ill-fated *Titanic*, brought his bride to live here after their wedding, then went off to work 14-hour days at the Harland and Wolff shipyard. Every bedroom has been decorated in a tasteful, individual style, and each has a private bath and TV. Guests have access to the reading lounge and the wide range of books around the house. Breakfasts and dinners, prepared by the owners, are first-rate; the house is no-smoking. ⊠ *12 Windsor Ave., BT9 6EE,* ☎ *028/9066–1758,* ꜰᴀх *028/9066–3227. 5 rooms with bath. Dining room, lounge, no smoking. MC, V. Closed 1 wk at Christmas.*

$$$ 🔲 **Dukes Hotel.** Although this distinguished redbrick Victorian building has only 20 rooms, it has big-hotel amenities, including a spacious lobby, extensive exercise facilities, and a restaurant that serves healthy, local cuisine (traditionalists won't be disappointed, however, as fried food can be had). The hotel's color scheme is a distinguished, executive-style gray, enlivened with plenty of greenery, and a waterfall splashes down parallel to the stairs. While not exceptional, the rooms are modern and comfortable, decorated in neutral shades. The lively bar is popular with staff and students from nearby Queen's University. ⊠ *65–67 University St., BT7 1HL,* ☎ *028/9023–6666,* ꜰᴀх *028/ 9023–7177. 20 rooms with bath. Restaurant, sauna, bar, meeting rooms. AE, DC, MC, V.*

$$$ 🔲 **Wellington Park Hotel.** Formerly a private residence and currently run by the Mooney family, this modernized establishment is among the best in the university area. The quiet, contemporary bedrooms are well designed, with built-in wood furniture; some have sleeping lofts. There's live music Friday and Saturday nights (soul, jazz, and Irish). You'll get traditional European food in both the bar and restaurant—though the menu in the restaurant is slightly more expansive and expensive than in the bar. ⊠ *21 Malone Rd., BT9 6RU,* ☎ *028/9038–1111,* ꜰᴀх *028/ 9066–5410,* ᴡᴇʙ *www.mooneyhotelgroup.com. 75 rooms with bath. Restaurant, bar, laundry service, meeting rooms. AE, DC, MC, V.*

$$ 🔲 **Madison's.** This is one of Belfast's liveliest spots—it's on the lovely, tree-lined Botanic Avenue, with plenty of cafés and shops, and only a few minutes by foot from the university. The hotel is run with gracious aplomb by the Mooney family (proprietors of the Dunadry Hotel and Country Club and Wellington Park Hotel). Its facade and public areas are decorated in a modish Barcelona-inspired take on art nouveau. The bedrooms, in cool yellows and rich blues, are sparely furnished but comfortable. The downstairs bar houses a restaurant that serves tasty contemporary cuisine at reasonable prices. Guests have access to the extensive fitness facilities of Queen's University, including a pool. ⊠ *59 Botanic Ave., BT7 1JL,* ☎ *028/9050–9800,* ꜰᴀх *028/9050–9808,* ᴡᴇʙ *www.mooneyhotelgroup.com. 35 rooms with bath. Restaurant, bar, business services. AE, MC, V.*

$ ⌑ **Old Rectory.** Mary and Jerry Callan's well-appointed house, built in 1896 as a rectory, is decorated in pastels and has good views of the mountains. Complimentary whiskey is served each evening. Rare in Ulster B&Bs, a healthy alternative to the hearty Ulster fry is served at breakfast, including smoked salmon, scrambled eggs, fresh fruit salad, vegetarian sausages, home-made low-sugar jams, wheaten bread, and freshly squeezed blended juices. ✉ *148 Malone Rd., BT9 5LH,* ☎ *028/9066–7882,* ☏ *028/9068–3759. 6 rooms with bath. No credit cards.*

Nightlife and the Arts

Nightlife

Belfast has dozens of pubs packed with relics of the Victorian and Edwardian periods. Although pubs typically close around 11:30 PM, many city-center/Golden Mile nightclubs stay open until 1 AM.

CITY CENTER/DOCKS

The **Apartment** (✉ 2 Donegall Sq. W, ☎ 028/9050–9777), beside City Hall, is the city center's trendiest bar, serving drinks and brasserie-style pub grub to Belfast's cool twentysomethings. **Bittles Bar** (✉ 70 Upper Church La., ☎ 028/9031–1088), on Victoria Square, serves pub grub. **Kelly's Cellars** (✉ 30–32 Bank St.), open since 1720, offers blues on Saturday night. The **Kitchen Bar** (✉ 16 Victoria Sq., ☎ 028/9032–4901) is a real ale bar with traditional music on Friday night. **Madden's Bar** (✉ 74 Smithfield St., ☎ 028/9024–4114) is a popular pub with traditional tunes. **McHugh's** (✉ 29–30 Queen's Sq., ☎ 028/9050—9990, ₩ÐB www.mchughesbar.com), in Belfast's oldest building, dating from 1711, has three floors of bars and restaurants, and has live music on weekends. **Pat's Bar** (✉ 19–22 Prince's Dock St., ☎ 028/9074–4524) has first-rate sessions of traditional music on Wednesday evenings. The **Rotterdam** (✉ 54 Pilot St., ☎ 028/9074–6021), which housed convicts bound for Australia until it became a pub in 1820, is filled with fascinating old junk and has traditional Irish music on Mondays and folk, jazz, and blues from Thursday to Saturday.

GOLDEN MILE AREA

The glorious **Crown Liquor Saloon** is far from being the only impressive old pub in the Golden Mile area—most of Belfast's evening life takes place in bars and restaurants here. There are a number of replicated Victorian bars with more locals and fewer visitors.

The **Beaten Docket** (✉ 48 Great Victoria St., ☎ 028/9024–2986), named after a losing betting slip, is a noisy, modern pub that attracts a young crowd; here you'll find up-to-the-minute music. **Benedict's** (✉ 7–21 Bradbury Pl., ☎ 028/9059–1999) is a bar, music venue, disco, 150-seat restaurant, and hotel. Straying from the Victorian-style public house, the **Limelight** (✉ 17 Ormeau Ave., ☎ 028/9032–5968) is a disco-nightclub with cabaret on Tuesday, Friday, and Saturday, and music on other nights. The **Manhattan** (✉ 23 Bradbury Pl., ☎ 028/9023–3131, ₩ÐB www.belfastpubs-n-clubs.com), a.k.a. the M-Club, is Belfast's hottest place for dedicated clubbers, with TV soap-opera celebrities flown in weekly to mix with the local nighthawks. **Morrisons** (✉ 21 Bedford St., ☎ 028/9024–8458) is a haunt of media types. It has a music lounge upstairs, where there's a mix of jazz, rock, and discussions for film buffs arranged by local directors in conjunction with the Northern Ireland Film Council; Saturday, it's rock; Sunday, Irish music. **Robinson's** (✉ 38 Great Victoria St., ☎ 028/9024–7447), two doors from the Crown, is a popular pub that appeals to a young crowd with folk music in its Fibber Magee's bar on Saturday and funk in the trendy BT1 wine and cocktail bar on weekends.

The stylish and modern **Bar Twelve** (⊠ Crescent Town House, 13 Lower Crescent, ☎ 028/9032–3349, WEB www.crescenttownhouse.com) is an excellent venue for some fashionable wine sipping. The **Botanic Inn** (⊠ 23–27 Malone Rd., ☎ 028/9066–0460), known as "the Bot" to its student clientele, is a big, popular disco-pub. The **Chelsea Wine Bar** (⊠ 346 Lisburn Rd., ☎ 028/9068–7177) is packed with affluent professionals determined to prove that 30 is where life begins. The contemporary cuisine is reasonably priced. **Cutter's Wharf** (⊠ 4 Lockview St., ☎ 028/9066–2501), down by the river south of the university, is at its best on summer evenings and at the Sunday jazz brunch. The **Eglantine Inn** (⊠ 32–40 Malone Rd., ☎ 028/9038–1994), known as "the Egg," faces the Bot across Malone Road. The **Empire Music Hall** (⊠ 42 Botanic Ave., ☎ 028/9032–8110), a deconsecrated church, is the city's leading music venue. Stand-up comedy nights are usually on Tuesday. The **Fly Bar** (⊠ 56 Lower Crescent, ☎ 028/9023–5666), with its over-the-top but impressive interior, playing on the fly theme, is a lively spot for a cocktail in the evening. **Lavery's Gin Palace** (⊠ 12 Bradbury Pl., ☎ 028/9032–7159) mixes old-fashioned beer-drinking downstairs with dancing upstairs. On the increasingly fashionable Lisburn Road south of the Golden Mile, **TaTu** (⊠ 701 Lisburn Rd., ☎ 028/9038–0818) is a spacious emporium to industrial chic filled with the sort of cool young crowd who think 30 is old. It serves good brasserie-style food.

The Arts

The **Northern Ireland Arts Council** (☎ 028/9038–5200) produces the monthly *Artslink* poster-brochure listing happenings throughout Belfast and the North; it's widely available throughout the city. The **Belfast Festival at Queen's University,** which lasts three weeks each November, is the city's major arts festival. For information, contact the Festival Office (⊠ 25 College Gardens, BT9, ☎ 028/9066–6321). The **Belfast Folk Festival** has broad-ranging traditional and contemporary music and dance events on weekends during the summer months. For updates, contact the Northern Ireland Arts Council. Information about the **Promenade Concerts,** themed classical music concerts taking place in June, can be obtained from the Ulster Orchestra ticket office (☎ 028/9066–8798).

Bell Gallery. Nelson Bell's Victorian home in the leafy university suburbs is a gathering place for many of Ireland's more traditional—representational—painters. ⊠ *13 Adelaide Park, Malone Rd.,* ☎ *028/9066–2998.* ☼ *Weekdays 9–5 and by appointment.*

Fenderesky Gallery. Under the same roof as the **Crescent Arts Centre,** Iranian philosopher Jamshid Mirfenderesky's gallery is one of the few in Ireland with a staple of modern Irish artists known throughout Europe. ⊠ *Crescent Arts Centre, 2 University Rd.,* ☎ *028/9023–5245.* ☼ *Tues.–Sat. 11:30–5:30.*

Ormeau Baths Gallery. The white, airy spaces of this former municipal bathhouse now display the work of major contemporary international and Irish artists. ⊠ *18A Ormeau Ave.,* ☎ *028/9032–1402.* ☼ *Tues.–Sat. 9:30–5:30.*

Belfast has several city-center movie theaters that show major British and American box-office favorites. **Queen's Film Theatre** (⊠ University Sq. Mews, off Botanic Ave., ☎ 028/9024–4857), Belfast's main art cinema, shows domestic and foreign movies on its two screens. **UGC Cinemas** (⊠ Dublin Rd., ☎ 0870/155–5176 for 24-hr information and credit card bookings) has 10 screens.

Grand Opera House. This beautifully restored Victorian playhouse has no company of its own but books shows from all over the British Isles and sometimes farther afield. It puts on a constant stream of West End musicals and plays of widely differing kinds, plus occasional operas and ballets. It's worth going to a show if only to enjoy the atmosphere of the opera house itself. ⊠ *2 Great Victoria St.,* ☎ *028/9024–1919 booking; 028/9024–9129 24-hr information,* WEB *www.goh.co.uk.* ⊠ *U.K.£6–U.K.£30.*

The Odyssey. This major millennium project, opened in 2001, includes a 10,000-seat arena, IMAX cinema, interactive science center, bistros, bars, and themed restaurants. In addition to major concerts, it also hosts Belfast's first professional ice hockey team, the Giants. ⊠ *Queen's Quay,* ☎ *028/9045–1055,* WEB *www.theodyssey.co.uk.*

Waterfront Hall. Everyone in Belfast sings the praises of this striking civic structure. From the looks of it, the hall is an odd marriage of *Close Encounters* modern and Castel Sant'Angelo antique. It houses a major 2,235-seat concert hall (for ballet, symphony, rock, and Irish music) and a 500-seat studio space (for modern dance, jazz, and experimental theater). The river-view Terrace Café restaurant and two bars make the hall a convenient place to eat, have a pint, and enjoy the river views before or after your culture fix. ⊠ *Lanyon Pl.,* ☎ *028/9033–4400,* WEB *www.waterfront.co.uk.*

King's Hall. This is the major venue for pop and rock concerts. ⊠ *484 Lisburn Rd.,* ☎ *028/9066–5225.*

Ulster Hall. Home to the Ulster Orchestra, which plays Friday evenings during its winter season, the hall has excellent acoustics and a splendid Victorian organ. ⊠ *Bedford St.,* ☎ *028/9032–3900.*

Belfast Civic Arts Theatre. Near the university area, this venue specializes in comedies and other lightweight productions. ⊠ *41 Botanic Ave.,* ☎ *028/9031–6900.*

Crescent Arts Centre. "The Crescent" to its habitués, this huge, rambling stone building, a former girls' high school off the campus end of Bradbury Place, is a focus for experimental theater and dance, provocative art in its Fenderesky Gallery, and experimental jazz. ⊠ *2–4 University Rd.,* ☎ *028/9024–2338.*

Lyric Theatre. In the south of Belfast, at King's Bridge on the banks of the Lagan, the Lyric stages thoughtful drama inspired by traditional and contemporary Irish culture. ⊠ *Ridgeway St.,* ☎ *028/9038–1081.* ⊠ *U.K.£6–U.K.£12.50; call to confirm prices.*

Old Museum Arts Centre (OMAC). A powerhouse of challenging, avant-garde theater and modern dance, OMAC also has a risk-taking art gallery. ⊠ *7 College Sq. N,* ☎ *028/9023–3332.*

Shopping

Belfast's main shopping streets include Donegall Place, High Street, Royal Avenue, and several of the smaller streets connecting them. The whole area is mostly traffic-free (except for buses and delivery vehicles), so you'll find it pleasant to wander and window-shop. **Castle Court** (⊠ 10 Royal Ave., ☎ 028/9023–4591) is the city's largest, most varied upscale shopping mall. **Clark and Dawe** (⊠ 485 Lisburn Rd., ☎ 028/ 9066–8228) makes and sells men's and women's suits and shirts. **Craftworks** (⊠ Bedford House, 16–22 Bedford St., ☎ 028/9024–4465) stocks crafts by local designers. The long thoroughfare of **Donegall Pass,** running from Shaftesbury Square at the point of the Golden Mile east to Ormeau Road, is a unique mix of biker shops and antiques arcades, and a good place to stroll. **Hoggs** (✉ 10 Donegall Sq. W, ☎ 028/9024–2232) stocks a good selection of linen, Tyrone crystal, Belleek china, and figurines. **Natural Interior** (✉ 51 Dublin Rd., ☎ 028/9024–42656) has Irish linen throws, trimmed in velvet, by the designer Larissa Watson-Regan. It also stocks her vividly colored wall panels and cushions. For something completely different, **Open Window Productions** (✉ Unit 25, Smithfields Market, ☎ 028/9032–9669, WEB www.anto.tv) makes 12-inch-high puppets of Northern Ireland politicians. For U.K.£175, you can have one made to order of a favorite celebrity, or even of yourself. If you've an interest in bric-a-brac, visit the enormous, renovated **St. George's Market,** an indoor flea market on May Street, every Tuesday and Friday morning. **Smyth and Gibson** (✉ Bedford House, Bedford St., ☎ 028/9023–0388) makes and sells beautiful, luxurious linen and cotton shirts and accessories. Opposite Castle Court, **Smyth's Irish Linens** (✉ 65 Royal Ave., ☎ 028/9024–2232) carries a large selection of handkerchiefs, tablecloths, napkins, and other traditional linen goods, which make excellent souvenirs or presents. **Steensons** (✉ Bedford House, Bedford St., ☎ 028/9024–8268) sells superb, locally designed jewelry.

Side Trips

The three sights below are closer to Belfast than others covered in this chapter. However, none of the sites along the Ards Peninsula and the north coast are more than a few hours' drive from Belfast—perfect for day trips.

Belfast Castle

⑰ Situated in Cave Hill Country Park, Belfast Castle was originally built for the Marquis of Donegall in 1865. In 1934 the castle was passed into the hands of Belfast Corporation. While the castle functions primarily as a restaurant, it also houses the **Cave Hill Heritage Centre** with information about the castle's history and natural surroundings. The best reason to visit the castle for a day trip, however, is to take a stroll in the lovely ornamental gardens and then make the ascent to **McArt's Fort.** This promontory, at the top of sheer cliffs 1,200 ft above the city, affords an excellent view across Belfast. To get there, you will need to take the path uphill from the parking lot, take a right at the next intersection of pathways, and then keep left as you journey up the sometimes steep hill to the fort. It's a good idea to drop into the Northern Ireland Tourist Board Information Centre for detailed directions on walks in this scenic area. You could also take in nearby **Belfast Zoo** (✉ Antrim Rd., ☎ 028/9077–6277, 🎟 April–Sept. U.K.£6, Oct.–Mar. U.K.£5, ☉ April–Sept. 10–5, Oct.–Mar. 10–2:30, closed Christmas day), which has underwater views of the resident penguins and sea lions and a children's farm. City buses 45 and 51 will bring you to both the castle and the zoo. ✉ *About 4 km (2½ mi) north of Belfast on Antrim Rd.,* ☎ *028/9077–6925.* 🎟 *Free.* ☉ *Heritage center daily 9–6; tours of castle by appointment.*

Irish Linen Centre and Lisburn Museum

⑱ In the 18th, 19th, and early 20th centuries, linen, a natural fabric woven from the fibers of the flax plant, was the basis of Ulster's most important industry—and thus of much of its folk history and song. A century ago, 240,000 acres were given over to flax, whose pretty blue flowers sparkle for just a week in early July, and 400 acres were designated as "bleach greens," where the woven fabric whitened in the summer sun. Eventually, American cotton and Egyptian flax killed off the mass-production linen trade, which had been centered on Lisburn, in mills powered by the River Lagan. What now survives of the linen industry does so by producing high-quality designer fabrics, plus traditional expensive damask. Today at the Irish Linen Centre and Lisburn Museum, a series of rooms trace this history. Weaving is demonstrated on a turn-of-the-20th-century hand loom (although the attached shop has a disappointing choice of linen goods). ⊠ *12 km (8 mi) southwest of Belfast, Market Sq., Lisburn,* ☎ *028/9266–3377.* ⊠ *Free.* ☉ *Mon.–Sat. 9:30–5.*

Ulster Folk and Transport Museum

⑲ Devoted to the province's social history, the excellent Ulster Folk and Transport Museum vividly brings the North's past to life with a score of reconstructed buildings transported here from around the region; these structures represent different facets of northern life—a traditional weaver's dwelling, terraces of Victorian town houses, an 18th-century country church, a village flax mill, a farmhouse, and a rural school. Inside you'll usually find a cheery fire and an appropriately dressed attendant who will explain what it was like actually to live in them. You start your visit with the **Folk Gallery,** which explains the background of each building. Across the main road (by footbridge) is the beautifully designed **Transport Museum,** where exhibits include locally built airplanes and motorcycles; the iconoclastic car produced by former General Motors whiz kid John De Lorean in his Belfast factory in 1982; and a moving section on the *Titanic,* the Belfast-built luxury liner that sank on her first voyage, in 1912, killing 1,500 of the passengers and crew. A miniature railway runs on Saturday in summer. You'll find the Ulster Folk and Transport Museum 16 km (10 mi) northeast of Belfast, in some 70 acres around Cultra Manor, encircled by a larger park and recreation area. ⊠ *Cultra, near Holywood,* ☎ *028/9042–8428,* WEB *www.nidex.com.* ⊠ *U.K.£4.* ☉ *Mar.–June, weekdays 10–5, Sat. 10–6, Sun. 11–6; July–Sept., Mon.–Sat. 10–6, Sun. 11–6; Oct.–Feb., Mon.–Fri. 10–4, Sat.–Sun. 11–5.*

AROUND COUNTIES ANTRIM AND DERRY

Starting and finishing in Belfast, you can take a circular route through a portion of the North that allows you to pass through some fair-size towns, as well as drive in open country through splendid natural scenery. From medieval towns such as Carrickfergus, you'll travel past the natural wonder of the Giant's Causeway and the man-made brilliance of the castle at Dunluce before arriving in the old walled city of Derry.

Carrickfergus

⑳ *16 km (10 mi) northeast of Belfast, 24 km (15 mi) south of Larne.*

Carrickfergus, on the shore of Belfast Lough, grew up around its ancient castle. When the town was enclosed by ramparts at the start of the 17th century, it was the only English-speaking town in Northern Ireland. Not surprisingly, this was the loyal port where William of Orange chose to land on his way to fight the Catholic forces at the Battle of the Boyne in 1690. However, the English did have one or two small setbacks, including the improbable victory in 1778 of John Paul Jones, the American naval hero, over the British warship HMS *Drake.* (This, by the way, was America's first naval victory during the Revolutionary War.) After the sea battle, the inhabitants of Carrickfergus stood on the waterfront and cheered Jones because they supported the American Revolution.

Carrickfergus Castle, one of the first and one of the largest of Irish castles, is still in good shape. An impressive sight, perched on a rock ledge, it was built in 1180 by John de Courcy, provincial Ulster's first Anglo-Norman invader. Apart from being captured briefly by the French in 1760, the castle stood as a bastion of British rule right up until 1928, at which time it still functioned as an English garrison.

Walk through the castle's 13th-century gatehouse into the Outer Ward. Continue into the Inner Ward, the heart of the fortress, where the five-story keep stands, a massive, sturdy building with walls almost 8 ft thick. Inside the keep, you'll find the **Cavalry Regimental Museum** with historic weapons and an impressive, vaulted Great Hall. These days Carrickfergus Castle hosts entertaining medieval banquets (inquire at Carrickfergus tourist information office, ☎ 028/9336–6455, or the Northern Ireland Tourist Board Information Centre, ☎ 028/9023–1221); if you're here at the beginning of August, you can enjoy the annual Lughnasa festival, a lively medieval-costume entertainment. ☎ 028/ 9335–1273, WEB www.ehsni.gov.uk. ✉ U.K.£2.70. ◷ Apr.–Sept., Mon.–Sat. 10–6, Sun. 2–6; Oct.–Mar., Mon.–Sat. 10–4, Sun. 2–4.

Structures that remain from Carrickfergus's past include **St. Nicholas's Church,** built by John de Courcy in 1205 (remodeled in 1614) and the handsomely restored North Gate in the town's medieval walls. Dobbins Inn on High Street, which has been a hotel for more than three centuries, is a popular watering hole with locals.

The **Andrew Jackson Centre,** in a thatched cottage just outside of town, tells the tale of U.S. president Andrew Jackson, whose parents emigrated from here in 1765. This cottage was not their actual home but a reconstruction of an 18th-century thatched cottage thought to resemble it. ✉ 2 km (1 mi) northeast of Carrickfergus, Boneybefore, Larne Rd., ☎ 028/9336–6455, WEB www.carrickfergus.org. ✉ U.K.£1.20. ◷ Apr.–May, weekdays 10–4, weekends 2–4; June–Sept., weekdays 10–6, weekends 2–6.

Dining and Lodging

$$$ ✕☷ **Galgorm Manor.** The Gillies bar is decidedly Irish, the dining room cosmopolitan, the manor house itself photogenic, and the estate grounds—where you may go riding and practice archery by arrangement—cinematic. Full privileges to Galgorm Castle, an 18-hole, par-72 golf course five minutes from the hotel, are an added treat. The River Maine, a good brown-trout river, flows within sight of many of the large rooms. The restaurant serves hearty portions of traditional Irish food. Galgorm is off A42 3 km (2 mi) west of Ballymena, 32 km (20 mi) inland of Larne, 40 km (25 mi) north of Belfast. ✉ 136 Fenaghy Rd., Ballymena, Co. Antrim BT42 1EA, ☎ 028/2588–1001, FAX 028/ 2588–0080, WEB www.galgorm.com. 24 rooms with bath. Restaurant, golf privileges, fishing, archery, horseback riding, bar, meeting rooms. AE, MC, V.

En Route Signposted on the left, 2½ km (1½ mi) off A2, heading away from Carrickfergus, is **Dalway's Bawn.** Built in 1609, it's the best surviving example of an early *bawn,* or fortified farmhouse, occupied by a Protestant Planter.

Glens of Antrim

★ ㉑ *Nine glens in the 86 km (54 mi) between Larne and Ballycastle.*

Soon after Larne, the coast of County Antrim becomes spectacular—wave upon wave of high, green hills curve down to the hazy sea, dotted with lush and gently curved glens, or valleys, first carved out by glaciers at the end of the last Ice Age. A narrow, winding, two-lane road

(A2, known locally as the Antrim Coast Road) hugs the slim strip of land between the hills and the sea, bringing you to the magnificent Glens of Antrim, nine wooded river valleys running down from the escarpment of the Antrim Plateau to the eastern shore. Until the building of this road in 1834, the glens were home to isolated farming communities—people who adhered to the romantic, mystical Celtic legends and the everyday use of the Irish language. The Glens are worth several days of serious exploration. Even narrower B-roads curl west off A2, up each of the beautiful glens where trails await hikers.

Carnlough

❷ *24 km (15 mi) north of Larne, 22½ km (14 mi) east of Ballymena, 43 km (27 mi) southeast of Ballycastle.*

A little resort made of white limestone, Carnlough overlooks a charming harbor that's surrounded by stone walls. The harbor can be reached by crossing over the limestone bridge from Main Street, built especially for the Marquis of Londonderry. The small harbor, once a port of call for fishermen, now shelters pleasure yachts. Carnlough is surrounded on three sides by hills that rise 1,000 ft from the sea. There's a small tourist office inside the post office here, which you'll find useful if you need information on exploring the scenic Glens of Antrim and the coast road.

Dining and Lodging

$$ ✕☲ **Londonderry Arms Hotel.** This ivy-covered traditional inn right on Carnlough Harbor was built as a coaching inn in 1848. What awaits are lovely seaside gardens, gorgeous antique furnishings, regional paintings and maps, lots of fresh flowers, and Georgian furnishings. In 1921 Sir Winston Churchill inherited it; since 1947 it has been owned and run by the hospitable O'Neill family. Both the original and the newer rooms have lovely Georgian antiques and luxurious fabrics, and are immaculately kept. The restaurant serves substantial, traditional Irish meals that emphasize fresh, local seafood, simply prepared. The hotel is disability-accessible, with a separate elevator. ✉ *20 Harbour Rd., Co. Antrim BT44 0EU,* ☎ *028/2888–5255,* ꄮ *028/2888–5263,* ꄳ *www.glensofantrim.com. 35 rooms with bath. Restaurant, bar, meeting rooms. AE, DC, MC, V.*

$$$ ☲ **Ballygally Castle.** At the Larne end of the North Antrim coast drive, 40 km (25 mi) from Belfast, stands an impressive, turreted castle that faces Ballygally Bay. Built by a Scottish lord in 1625, the castle is a fine place where you can enjoy a good night's sleep and a hearty breakfast, and indulge at its Dungeon Bar (its substantial stone walls justify the name). Modern facilities are integrated with old Scots baronial design, though the extension clashes with the original style. Bedrooms, some in the castle turrets—one complete with milady's ghost—have been individually decorated, with comfortable furnishings. On Saturdays in the dining room, a decent table d'hôte evening meal is served to music; a Sunday high tea is also available. ✉ *274 Coast Rd., Ballygally, Co. Antrim BT40 2QZ,* ☎ *028/2858–3212,* ꄮ *028/2858–3681,* ꄳ *www.hastingshotels.com. 45 rooms with bath. Dining room, fishing, bar, baby-sitting. AE, DC, MC, V.*

En Route   Between Carnlough and Ballycastle you'll find stunning scenery. Glenariff, opening onto Red Bay at the village of Glenariff (also known as Waterfoot), is considered the loveliest of the glens. For a good day trip go to **Glenariff Forest Park,** the largest and most accessible of Antrim's valleys. Inside are picnic facilities and dozens of good hikes, notably the 5½-km (3½-mi) **Waterfall Trail** (follow the blue arrows), which offers outstanding views of Glenariff River and its waterfalls and passes by small but swimmable loughs. Detailed maps are available at the visitor center, which has a small self-serve cafeteria. ⊠ *98 Glenariff Rd.,* ☎ *028/2175–8232.* ☞ *Vehicles U.K.£3, pedestrians U.K.£1.50.* ⊙ *Daily 10 AM–dusk.*

At Cushendall, you'll see Turnley's Tower—a curious, fortified square tower of red stone, built in 1820 as a curfew tower and jail for "idlers and rioters"—standing at a crossroads in the middle of the village. If you want a break from the Antrim coast, stay on A2 direct to Ballycastle. But if you prefer to stay by the sea, turn right at the tower in the direction of **Cushendun,** a tiny jewel of a village designed by Clough Williams-Ellis, who also designed the famous Italianate village of Portmeirion in Wales. From this part of the coast you can see the Mull of Kintyre on the Scottish mainland. If you have firm nerves, take the narrow and precipitous coastal road north past dramatically beautiful **Murlough Bay** to **Fair Head**; others will prefer to rejoin A2 via B92, left, after a few miles and descend—passing on the left the ruins of the Franciscans' 16th-century **Bonamargy Friary**—into Ballycastle.

Ballycastle

❷❸ *19⅓ km (12 mi) east of Giant's Causeway, 37½ km (23 mi) north of Carnlough.*

Ballycastle is the main resort town in the glens, at the northern end of the Glens of Antrim drive. People from the province flock here in the summer. The town is shaped like an hourglass—with its strand and dock on one end, its pubs and chippers on the other, and the 1-km (½-mi) Quay Road in between. Beautifully aged shops and pubs line its Castle, Diamond, and Main streets.

From Ballycastle town you have a view of L-shape **Rathlin Island,** where in 1306 the Scottish king Robert the Bruce took shelter in a cave (under the east lighthouse) and, according to the popular legend, was inspired to continue his armed struggle against the English by watching a spider patiently spinning its web. It was on Rathlin in 1898 that Guglielmo Marconi set up the world's first cross-water radio link, from the island's lighthouse to Ballycastle. Bird-watching and hiking are the island's main activities. Unless the sea is extremely rough, a ferryboat makes regular journeys (twice daily in winter, more frequently in summer). Although the island is only 9½ km (6 mi) away from shore, the trip can take 45 minutes; be mindful of the weather to ensure that you can return the same day.

Every year since 1606, on the last Monday and Tuesday in August, Ballycastle has hosted the **Oul' Lammas Fair,** a modern version of the ancient Celtic harvest festival of Lughnasa (Irish for "August"). Ireland's oldest fair, this is a very popular two-day event at which sheep and wool are still sold alongside the wares of more modern shopping stalls. Treat yourself to the fair's traditional snacks, "dulse" (sun-dried seaweed), and "yellow man" (rock-hard yellow toffee).

Off the coast, 8 km (5 mi) west of Ballycastle, you can see the **Carrick-a-Rede** rope bridge, which spans a 60-ft gap between the mainland and Carrick-a-Rede Island. The island's name means "rock in the road" and refers to how it stands in the path of the salmon who follow the coast as they migrate to their home rivers to spawn. For the past 150 years salmon fishermen have set up the rope bridge in late April, taking it down again after the salmon season ends. The bridge is open to the public and offers some heart-stopping views of the crashing waves below. If you summon up the nerve to cross it once, of course you then have to do it again to get back to the mainland. ⊠ *Signposted on B15.* 🎫 *Free.* ⊙ *Daily Apr.–Sept. 10–6; Daily July–Aug. 10–8.*

Dining

$–$$$
★

✕ **Wysner's.** Head chef Jackie Wysner has won several awards for both this small family restaurant and the eponymous butcher's next door. Menus vary daily, though the cooking emphasizes fresh local ingredients—from the hills and the sea. Specialties of the upstairs restaurant include North Atlantic salmon (caught nearby at Carrick-a-Rede), fillet of halibut with langoustine, and filet of beef with mustard-seed cream sauce. A daytime menu is served downstairs in the informal French-style café. ⊠ *16–18 Ann St., Ballycastle,* 🕾 *028/2076–2372. MC, V. Closed Sun.*

Giant's Causeway

★ ㉔ *19½ km (12 mi) west of Ballycastle, 86 km (54 mi) north of Belfast.*

Imagine this singularly strange natural phenomenon: a mass of 37,000 mostly hexagonal pillars of volcanic basalt, clustered like a giant honeycomb and extending hundreds of yards into the sea. This, the Giant's Causeway, is Northern Ireland's premier tourist attraction. Legend has it the causeway was created 60 million years ago, when boiling lava, erupting from an underground fissure that stretched from Northern Ireland to the Scottish coast, crystallized as it burst into the sea, and formed according to the same natural principle that structures a honeycomb. As all Ulster folk know, though, the scientific truth is that the columns were created as stepping-stones by the giant Finn McCool in a bid to reach a giantess he'd fallen in love with on the Scottish island of Staffa (where the causeway resurfaces). Unfortunately, the giantess's boyfriend found out, and in the ensuing battle Finn pulled out a huge chunk of earth and flung it toward Scotland. The resulting hole became Lough Neagh, and the sod landed to create the Isle of Man.

To reach the causeway, you can either walk 1½ km (1 mi) down a long, scenic hill or take a minibus from the visitor center. West of the causeway, **Port-na-Spania** is the spot where the 16th-century Spanish Armada galleon *Girona* went down on the rocks. The ship was carrying an astonishing cargo of gold and jewelry, some of which was recovered in 1967 and is now on display in the Ulster Museum in Belfast. Beyond this, **Chimney Point** is the name given to one of the causeway structures on which the Spanish fired, thinking that it was Dunluce Castle, which is 8 km (5 mi) west.

Arriving by car at the Giant's Causeway, you'll first reach a cliff-top parking lot beside the **visitor center,** which houses displays about the area and an audiovisual exhibition explaining the formation of the causeway coast. ⊠ *44 Causeway Rd., near Bushmills,* 🕾 *028/2073–1855,* 🌐 *www.nationaltrust.org.uk.* 🎫 *Visitor center: audio visual exhibition U.K.£1, parking U.K.£3.* ⊙ *Causeway freely accessible; visitor center May–Aug., daily 10–4.30; Sept.–Oct., weekdays 10–5:30, weekends 10–6; Nov.–Feb., daily 10–5.*

Bushmills

㉕ *10 km (6 mi) northeast of Coleraine, 14 km (8½ mi) east of Portstewart, 19½ km (12 mi) west of Ballycastle.*

The oldest licensed distillery in the world, Bushmills was first granted a charter by King James I in 1608, though historical records refer to a distillery here as early as 1276. Bushmills produces the most famous of Irish whiskeys—its namesake, Bushmills—and what is widely regarded as the best, the rarer black-label version known to aficionados as Black Bush. One-hour tours begin in the mashing and fermentation room, proceed to the maturing and bottling warehouse, and end with a complimentary shot of *uisce beatha,* the "water of life," in the visitor center–gift shop. ☎ *028/2073–1521,* WEB *www.whiskeytours.ie.* ☑ *U.K.£3.95.* ⊙ *Apr.–Oct., Mon.–Sat. tours continuously 9:30–4, Sun. noon–4; Nov.–Mar., Mon.–Sat. 5 tours 10:30–3:30, Sun. 4 tours noon–3:30.*

Lodging

$$$$ ☒ **Bushmills Inn.** Owner Roy Bolton has overseen the transformation of this cozy old coaching inn, found just off the main square, or diamond, as they're referred to in Ulster. Stripped pine, peat fires, and gas lights warm the public rooms. The livery stables now house the informal restaurant, serving fresh and hearty food, and the bar, always full of good spirits; out front are three tables so that you can dine and drink alfresco. (Parents will appreciate the baby listening service—you leave the tot in the room, with a phone that records any noise, and the staff alerts you if the baby cries.) Some of the bedrooms are quite small, so ask to see before you decide. The distillery is a stroll away, as is the salmon-filled River Bush. ☒ *9 Dunluce Rd., Co. Antrim BT57 8QG,* ☎ *028/2073–2339,* FAX *028/2073–2048,* WEB *www.bushmills-inn.com. 32 rooms with bath. Restaurant, bar, meeting rooms, Internet on request. AE, MC, V.*

Dunluce Castle

★ ㉖ *8 km (5 mi) southwest of Giant's Causeway, 3 km (2 mi) west of Bushmills.*

Halfway between Portrush and the Giant's Causeway, dramatically perched on a cliff at land's end, Dunluce Castle is one of the North's most evocative ruins. Originally a 13th-century Norman fortress, it was captured in the 16th century by the local MacDonnell clan chiefs—the so-called "Lords of the Isles." They enlarged the castle, paying for some of the work with their profits from salvaging the Spanish galleon *Girona,* and made it an important base for ruling northeastern Ulster. Perhaps they expanded the castle a little too much, for in 1639 faulty construction caused the kitchens (with the cooks) to plummet into the sea during a storm. Nearby you'll find the refurbished **Dunluce Centre,** an entertainment complex with three floors of interactive play zones, shops, and a café. ☒ *Port Ballintree,* ☎ *028/7082–4444,* WEB *www.touristnetuk.com/ni.dunluce.* ☑ *U.K.£5 plus rides (U.K.£2.75–U.K.£3.95).* ⊙ *Easter week 10–7; Apr.–June, weekends 12–7; Jun.–Aug., daily 10–8; Sept.–Mar., weekends 12–5.*

Dining

$–$$ ✕ **Ramore Wine Bar and Coast.** On Portrush's picturesque harbor, where
★ a haven of boats are tucked away from the resort's brasher amusements, this spot does double duty. Upstairs, in an inexpensive bistro-style wine bar with panoramic views, the daily offerings are posted on a blackboard. Downstairs, the more expensive draw is chef George McAlpin's Pacific Rim–inflected way with local Atlantic fish and shellfish, which is one of Northern Ireland's top dining experiences. Menus change every three months, but Grand Marnier soufflé, a regular dessert, is always an indulgent way to finish. Coast specializes in homemade pizza, pasta, and char-grills. ☒ *The Harbor,* ☎ *028/7082–4313,* FAX *028/7082–3194. MC, V. Coast closed Mon. and Tues. evenings only; wine bar open daily.*

Outdoor Activities and Sports

The **Royal Portrush Golf Club** (☒ Dunluce Rd., ☎ 048/7082–2311, ☒ Fees: weekdays, U.K.£85 (Dunluce), U.K.£30 (Valley); weekends,

U.K.£95 (Dunluce), U.K.£37.50. (Valley). ⊗ Visitors: weekdays) includes the championship Dunluce course—a sea of sand hills and curving fairways. The Valley course is a less-exposed, tamer track. The Dunluce, in a poll of Irish golf legends, was voted the best in Ireland. **Portstewart Strand,** in Portrush, to the west of town (signposted as "The Strand" at all major junctions in Portrush), has some of Ireland's best surfing.

Coleraine

㉗ *13 km (8 mi) southwest of Dunluce Castle, 48 km (30 mi) east of Derry.*

The 5th century BC town of Coleraine became the home of the University of Ulster in 1968. The River Bann flows through the town, dividing the county of Antrim from that of Derry. As well as being a fishing town, Coleraine has an important linen industry.

Some of Ireland's oldest remaining relics, dating from the very first inhabitants of this island (about 7000 BC), were found on Mountsandel, just south of Coleraine. One of the many dolmens in this region is called Slaghtaverty—after an evil dwarf who used his magical harp to mesmerize women. He was buried alive and upside down by the great Finn McCool (maker of the Giant's Causeway), so the sounds of his harp would not escape from the ground.

Lodging

$$ ⛩ **Greenhill House.** This charming Georgian country house, a peaceful retreat run by Elizabeth and James Hegarty, has pleasantly decorated bedrooms, substantial breakfasts, and excellent dinners of locally caught fish, Ulster beef, and homemade bread and cakes. Dinner must be booked by noon. Greenhill House is about 13 km (8 mi) south of Coleraine. ⊠ *24 Greenhill Rd., Aghadowey, Co. Derry BT51 4EU,* ☎ *028/7086–8241,* FAX *028/7086–8365,* WEB *www.greenhill.house.bt-internet.co.uk. 6 rooms with bath. Dining room, Internet on request. MC, V. Closed Nov.–Feb.*

Upperlands

㉘ *32 km (20 mi) south of Coleraine, 56 km (35 mi) northwest of Belfast.*

Upstream from Coleraine, the River Bann—rich in eels for roasting and smoking and in salmon for poaching—flows out of Lough Neagh. On its left bank are the towns and fortifications of the 17th-century Planters, built by London's Livery Companies, whose descendants developed the linen industry. Today, virtually all of that rural industrial heritage is gone, with the notable exception of the village of Upperlands. Make sure you tour **William Clark and Sons,** a working linen mill where age-old wooden machinery still beetles (polishes) threads for the linen linings of suits for England's Royals. There's also a small linen museum here. ⊠ *Upperlands,* ☎ *028/7954–7200.* ⛩ *Free.* ⊗ *Mon.–Thurs. 10–4 by arrangement only.*

Dining and Lodging

$$$$ ✕⛩ **Ardtara House.** A 19th-century Victorian home built by a de-
★ scendant of the founder of the town's first linen mill, Ardtara is the North's finest country-house hotel. The gorgeously furnished terra-cotta and pink drawing room, with original plaster moldings and a marble fireplace, looks out on the wide front lawn and tennis court. The eight large bedrooms are furnished with antiques; each has a fireplace, as do some of the elegantly appointed marble bathrooms. The hotel's restaurant is in the former snooker room, with dark paneled walls, a wallpapered hunting scene, and a huge skylight. The terrine of duck

appetizer is popular, as is the stellar poached fillet of lamb with buttered Savoy cabbage entrée. You'll feel at home here—owner Mae-Beth Fenton and her staff strive for a calm and relaxed style, and it works splendidly. ⊠ *8 Gorteade Rd., Co. Derry BT46 5SA,* ☎ *028/7964–4490,* ꜰᴀx *028/7964–5080. 8 rooms with bath. Restaurant, tennis court, meeting room. AE, MC, V.*

Limavady

㉙ *21 km (13 mi) west of Coleraine, 34 km (21 mi) northwest of Upperlands, 27 km (17 mi) east of Derry.*

In 1851, at No. 51 on Limavady's Georgian main street, Jane Ross wrote down the tune played by a traveling fiddler and called it "Londonderry Air," better known now as "Danny Boy." While staying at an inn on Ballyclose Street, William Thackeray (1811–63) wrote his rather lustful poem "Peg of Limavaddy" about a barmaid. Among the many Americans descended from Ulster emigrants was President James Monroe, whose relatives came from the Limavady area.

Dining and Lodging

$$$ ✕🅼 **Radisson Roe Park Hotel & Golf Resort.** One of the North's most deluxe resorts, the Radisson rests amid 155 acres of countryside on the banks of the River Roe. Bedrooms have satellite TV and other amenities. Dining options are various: Green's restaurant is formal and international; the Coach House brasserie is a relaxed place where golfers congregate; and O'Cahan's bar takes its name from a local chieftain besieged on a riverside promontory, whose Irish wolfhound leaped an impossible chasm to bring relief—doubtless an inspiration to golfers flagging at the ninth. ⊠ *Roe Park, Co. Derry BT49 9LB,* ☎ *028/7772–2222,* ꜰᴀx *028/7772–2313,* ᴡᴇʙ *www.radissonroepark.com. 64 rooms with bath. 2 restaurants, 18-hole golf course, indoor pool, gym, beauty salon, massage, sauna, steam room, fishing, aerobics, horseback riding, 2 bars, baby-sitting, Internet, meeting rooms. AE, DC, MC, V.*

Derry

109 km (68 mi) north of Belfast, 53 km (33 mi) north of Omagh, 27 km (17 mi) southwest of Limavady.

Derry's name is a shadow of its history. Those in favor of British rule call the city Londonderry, its old Plantation-period name; the "London" part was tacked on in 1613 after the Flight of the Earls, and the city and county were handed over to the Corporation of London, which represented London's merchants. They brought in a large population of English and Scottish Protestant settlers, built new towns for them, and reconstructed Derry within the city walls, which survive almost unchanged to this day. Both before then and after, Derry's sturdy ramparts have withstood many fierce attacks and have never been breached, which explains the city's coy sobriquet, "The Maiden City." The most famous attack was the historic siege of 1688–89, after 13 apprentice boys slammed the city gates in the face of the Catholic king James II. The inhabitants, who held out for 105 days and were reduced to eating dogs, cats, and laundry starch, nevertheless helped to secure the British throne for the Protestant king William III.

Whatever you choose to call it, Derry is one of Northern Ireland's most underrated towns. If Belfast was the Beethoven of Northern Ireland, Derry would be the Mozart—fey, witty, and a touch surreal. Every Halloween, for example, the entire populace turns out decked in wild homemade costumes, and pubs have been known to refuse a drink to anyone who hasn't made the effort to dress up. Despite the derelict factories along the banks of the River Foyle and a reputation marred by Troubles-related violence, the city has worked hard to move forward. Such efforts show in the quaint, bustling town center, encircled by 20-ft-tall 17th-century walls. The city's winding streets slope down to the Foyle, radiating from the Diamond—Derry's historic center where St. Columba founded his first monastery in 546. Fine Georgian and Victorian buildings sit side by side with gaily painted Victorian-fronted shops, cafés, and pubs.

Derry, incidentally, has links to Boston that date as far back as the 17th and 18th centuries, when many Derry residents escaped their hardships at home by emigrating to that U.S. city and beyond. Aviation fans, take note: Derry was where Amelia Earhart touched down, on May 21, 1932, after her historic solo flight across the Atlantic. Local lore has it that the first man to reach her airplane greeted her in typically unfazed Derry fashion: "Aye, and what do you want, then?"

To really experience Derry's history, stroll along the parapet walkway atop the ramparts of the **city walls,** built between 1614 and 1618 and one of the few intact sets of city walls in Europe. Pierced by eight gates (originally four) and as much as 30 ft thick, the gray-stone ramparts are only 1½ km (1 mi) all around; today most of the life of the town actually takes place outside of them. You can walk the walls on your own, following the sites below in a counterclockwise direction; or, from June through September, you can join one of the guided walks from the city's Tourist Information Centre.

The **Tourist Information Centre** is the most strategic place to start your tour of the city, whether by yourself or on one of the guided walks. Tours are run by several companies. All are booked through and leave from the tourist office up to five times a day. Walking tours last just under two hours. If you're tired of walking, the Foyle Civic Bus Tour leaves at 2 PM every Tuesday during July and August. ⊠ *44 Foyle St.,* ☎ *028/7126–7284 or 028/7137–7577,* 🖷 *028/7137–7992,* 🕸 *www.derryvisitor.com.* 🎟 *Center free, walking tour U.K.£4.* ⏱ *Mar. 15–June and Oct. weekdays 9–5, Sat. 10–5; July–Sept. weekdays 9–7, Sat. 10–6, Sun. 10–5.*

Guildhall, at the entrance to the old city, is an ornate Victorian stone and sandstone building dating from 1890. It has impressive stained-glass windows that were actually shattered by two IRA bombs in June 1977 and rebuilt by the Campbell's firm in Belfast, who had installed the original windows in 1890 and still had the plans (now that's a filing system). The Guildhall, where Derry city council meets monthly, is the site of musical recitals and heated political rallies. ⊠ *Guildhall Sq.,* ☎ *028/7137–7335.* 🎟 *Free.* ⏱ *Weekdays 9–5.*

The **Tower Museum,** which chronicles the history of Derry, is inside the reconstructed O'Doherty's Tower, which was originally built in 1615 by the O'Dohertys for their overlords, the O'Donnells, in lieu of tax payments. Highlights include a small section on the eccentric Bishop Frederick Augustus Hervey (1763–1803), who conducted a lifelong affair with the mistress of Frederick William II of Prussia, built the now derelict Downhill Castle above the cliffs outside the city, and allegedly had his curates stage naked sprints along the beach while he horsewhipped them. The winners were awarded with the most lucrative parishes in the district. The vivid "Story of Derry" exhibition covers the city's history, from its origins as a monastic settlement in an oak grove and including the beginnings of the Troubles in 1969, after years of institutionalized discrimination in jobs and public housing (a well-known Derry innuendo is that the skeleton in the city's coat of arms

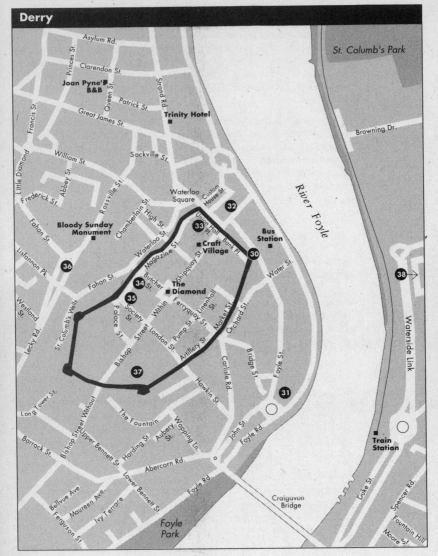

Derry

Apprentice Boys'
Memorial Hall **35**

Calgach Centre . . . **34**

City walls **30**

Free Derry
Corner **36**

Guildhall **32**

St. Columb's
Cathedral **37**

Tourist Information
Centre **31**

Tower Museum **33**

Workhouse **38**

was actually a Catholic waiting for a house). It is, in fact, Walter de Burgo, a forebear of singer Chris de Burgh, who was starved to death in the dungeons of Greencastle after a dispute with his cousin William. There's an excellent virtual museum on-site celebrating the life and legacy of St. Columba. Call ahead if you would like to visit the museum on a Sunday. ☒ *Union Hall Pl.,* ☏ *028/7137–2411.* ☝ *U.K.£4.20.* ☉ *Sept.–June, Tues.–Sat. 10–5; July–Aug., Mon.–Sat. 10–5, Sun. 2–5.*

㉞ At the **Calgach Centre** you'll find the **Fifth Province,** an inspired high-tech celebration of the city's history from its earliest days, as well as its importance in creating the Irish diaspora of 17 million people. You begin by sitting on a Neolithic mound while the voice of veteran actor Richard Harris intones in a ghostly voice the history of Derry, from the sylvan oak grove beloved by the chieftain Calgach right up to the city's finest hour, when local boy Bernardo O'Higgins was made president of Chile. From there it's into a comfortable armchair for a virtual-reality time trip through the coming of the Vikings and the Normans, the flight of the Irish nobility from English persecution in 1601, and the famine of 1845–49, when 1½ million emigrated to the United States and a million more died of starvation. It's moving stuff, grippingly presented. The center also hosts touring exhibitions. ☒ *4–22 Butcher St.,* ☏ *028/7137–3177.* ☝ *U.K.£3.* ☉ *Mon.–Fri. 9–5; shows weekdays at 11:30 and 2:30.*

㉟ The baronial-style **Apprentice Boys' Memorial Hall** is a meeting place for the exclusively Protestant organization set up in 1715 to honor 13 apprentice boys who slammed the city gate in the face of the Catholic King James in 1688 and began the Siege of Derry, which has been a symbol of Protestant stubbornness ever since. Inside, there's an initiation room in which 20,000 have pledged to uphold Protestant values, and a magnificently chaotic museum filled to the brim with furniture, firearms, books, bombs, swords, and sculpture. It's a fascinating glimpse into a hitherto closed world. An upstairs bar and dance hall—now used for meetings, initiations, and social events, organized by the Apprentice Boys—has walls lined with 12 banners representing the lost tribes of Israel. (Some Protestants believe the lost tribes of Israel finally ended up in Northern Ireland and are their forebears.) ☒ *Society St.,* ☏ *028/7126–7284 Derry; 028/7137–7577 for tours.* ☝ *Donations accepted.* ☉ *Tours by arrangement only.*

Walker Memorial, a statue of the governor of Derry during the siege, is a symbol of Derry's divided nature. It was blown up by the IRA in 1973, and the story goes that the statue's head rolled down the hill into the Catholic Bogside, where it was captured by a local youth. He ransomed it back to the Protestants for a small fortune, and today it sits on the shoulders of a replica of the original statue beside the Apprentice Boys' Memorial Hall.

㊱ At **Free Derry Corner** (☒ Fahan and Rossville Sts.) is the white gable wall where Catholics defiantly painted the slogan "You are now entering Free Derry" as a declaration of a zone from which police and the British Army were banned until 1972, when the army broke down the barricades. That same year, 13 civil rights marchers were shot by British soldiers in an event that rankles Catholics to this day. "Bloody Sunday," as it became known, is commemorated by the mural of a civil rights march.

㊲ **St. Columb's Cathedral** was the first Protestant cathedral built in the United Kingdom after the Reformation, and contains the oldest and largest bells in Ireland (dating from the 1620s). It's a treasure house of Derry Protestant emblems, memorials, and relics from the siege of

A POLITICAL ABC

DUP. Right-wing Democratic Unionist Party, founded by firebrand preacher Reverend Ian Paisley in 1971. Now increasingly sidelined.

IRA. Irish Republican Army. Largest group of Republican paramilitaries, responsible for thousands of murders and bombings.

Orange Order. Protestant organization whose annual 12th of July marches celebrate the 1690 victory of Protestant King William of Orange over Catholic King James.

Loyalist. Extreme Unionist.

Nationalist. Anyone supporting a united Ireland.

Northern Ireland Assembly. Regional government, sitting at Stormont.

Police Service of Northern Ireland. Formerly Royal Ulster Constabulary, whose name was changed in 2001 as part of a package of reforms to attract more Catholics.

Republican. Extreme Nationalist.

SDLP. Social, Democratic, and Labour Party. Largest and most moderate Nationalist party.

Sinn Féin. Literally Ourselves Alone, political counterpart of IRA, although now firmly installed in democratic Northern Ireland Assembly.

Troubles. The 1969–97 campaign by Republican and Loyalist terrorists in which 3,636 people were killed.

UDA. Ulster Defence Association. Largest Loyalist paramilitary group, involved in hundreds of murders.

UFF and UVF. Ulster Freedom Fighters and Ulster Volunteer Force, breakaway Loyalist paramilitary groups.

Ulster. Historic name for northern province of Ireland. Now generally used, especially by Protestants, to describe Northern Ireland.

Ulster Unionist Party. Largest and most moderate Unionist party.

Unionist. Anyone supporting continuing union with Great Britain.

1688–89. The church was built in 1633 in simple Planter's Gothic style, and with an intricate, corbeled roof and austere spire. In the vestibule is the 270-pound mortar ball that during the siege was fired over the wall with an invitation to surrender sent by King James. Legend has it that when they read it, every man, woman, and child in the city rushed to the walls and shouted, "No surrender!"—a Protestant battle cry to this day. The **Chapter House Museum** has the oldest surviving map of Derry (from 1600) and the Bible owned by Governor George Walker during the siege. Nearby is the spot where in 1870 Cecilia Alexander wrote the hymn "There Is a Green Hill Far Away." ⊠ *London St., off Bishop St.,* ☎ *028/7126–7313.* 🖃 *U.K.£1.* ⊙ *Apr.–Oct., daily 9–5; Nov.–Mar., daily 9–1 and 2–4.*

㊳ Across the River Foyle from the city walls, the **Workhouse** was built in 1832 to alleviate poverty but became the end of the road for people who had tried in vain to make their lives better. During the famine years (1845–49), the city was the main emigration port for Northern Ireland, and many families came to Derry hoping to get on a boat; instead, unable to afford the trip, they ended up in the Workhouse in utter despair. Inside, families were separated, and this was often the last time children saw their parents alive. From the beginning to the end of the famine, 1½ million people left Ireland and 1 million died.

Many of the descendants of those who left, of course, came back during the Second World War, when thousands of U.S. servicemen arrived in the city in 1942 to turn it into a base for the Battle of the Atlantic. The **Workhouse Museum,** on the top two floors of the Workhouse, chronicles the story of that battle, from the Yanks' arrival in the January rain (which prompted one of them to ask if the city's barrage balloons were actually there to stop the place from sinking) through the end of the war when 64 U-boats lined up in the harbor to surrender, like a convention of retired sharks, to 1946, when the city's biggest export was G.I. brides. The museum also details life in the Workhouse and has some thoughtful exhibits about famine in general. There is a space for traveling exhibitions that change regularly; call for details. ⊠ *23 Glendermott Rd.,* ☎ *028/7131–8328.* 🖃 *Free.* ⊙ *Sept.–June, Mon.–Thurs. 10–4:30, Sat. 10–4:30; July–Aug., Mon.–Sat. 10:30–4:30. Tours by arrangement.*

NEED A BREAK?   Derry is packed with agreeable pubs, but **Badgers** (⊠ 16 Orchard St., ☎ 028/7136–0763) has the best range of wholesome food. It's also the watering hole for local media types, artists, writers, and musicians.

Dining and Lodging

$$ ✕ **Spice.** It's worth the walk up the hill from town to this cozy restaurant with food that draws heavily on Pan-Asian influences. Main course highlights include crab claws and red Thai curry, served with plain or fried rice or noodles. ⊠ *162–164 Spencer Rd.,* ☎ *028/7134–4875.* MC, V.

$$$–$$$$ ✕🏨 **Beech Hill.** Past a fairy-tale gatehouse and set among clumps of beech trees, streams, and a duck pond, Beech Hill is a grand 1729 country home very much attuned to the present—with enough extras to satisfy the most demanding traveler. Chef Adrian Catterall draws many Northwest politicos, with Eurocrats in tow, who appreciate his classical French cooking with the best (often organic and local) ingredients. The vast honeymoon suite, with a four-poster bed, overlooks the gardens. Rooms in the old building are decorated in Georgian style; 10 rooms in a modern extension are larger and contemporary. A small museum celebrates the fact that Beech Hill housed a contingent of U.S. Marines during World War II. The house is 3 km (2 mi) south of the city, left off A6. ⊠ *32 Ardmore Rd., Co. Derry BT47 3QP,* ☎ *028/ 7134–9279,* FAX *028/7134–5366,* WEB *www.beech-hill.com. 27 rooms with bath. Restaurant, gym, hot tub, massage, sauna, bar, meeting rooms, Internet on request. AE, MC, V.*

$ 🖼 **The Merchant's House.** Many of the architectural sights in the city are in the area around Joan Pyne's elegant guest house, from Art Deco to neo-Gothic. No. 16 Queen Street was originally a Victorian merchant's family home built to Georgian proportions, then a rectory and bank before Joan turned it into the city's grandest guest house. Previous guests include the late Hurd Hatfield, star of the movie *The Picture of Dorian Gray.* Joan also owns a similar but smaller house three minutes' walk away, which serves as an annex. ⊠ *16 Queen St., Co. Derry BT48 7EQ,* ☎ *028/7126–4223,* FAX *028/7126–6913,* WEB *www.thesaddlershouse.com. 12 rooms, 8 with bath. MC, V.*

Nightlife and the Arts

ART GALLERIES

The **Context Gallery** (⊠ 5–7 Artillery St., ☎ 028/7137–3538, WEB www.contextgallery.org) shows works by up-and-coming Irish and international artists. The **McGilloway Gallery** (⊠ Shipquay St., ☎ 028/7136–6011) stocks a broad selection of representational modern Irish art. Owner Ken McGilloway serves wine on Friday evenings until 9 PM during selected exhibitions. The **Orchard Gallery** (⊠ Orchard St., ☎ 028/7126–9675) is known across Europe for its political and conceptual art. The **Verbal Arts Centre** (⊠ Mall Wall, ☎ 028/7126–6946, WEB www.verbalartscentre.co.uk) hosts regular exhibitions and storytelling events, re-creating the great old Irish tradition of fireside tales.

PUBS AND CLUBS

The **Gweedore Bar** (⊠ 16 Waterloo St., ☎ 028/7126–3513) is a favorite for hip-hop and house music. You'll find traditional Irish music at **Peadar O'Donnell's** (⊠ 63 Waterloo St., ☎ 028/7137–2318). **Sugar Nightclub** (⊠ 33 Shipquay St., ☎ 028/7126–6017) is the place for disco.

THEATER AND OPERA

The **Playhouse** (⊠ 5–7 Artillery St., ☎ 028/7126–8027) shows traditional and contemporary theater and also holds contemporary music concerts. The newest edition to the theater scene is the catch-all **Millennium Theatre** (⊠ East Wall, ☎ 028/7126–4455), where you'll find everything and anything—from comedians to musicians to plays—on stage.

Shopping

Shopping in town is generally low-key and unpretentious, but some upscale gems of Irish craftsmanship can be found here. Stroll up Shipquay Street to find small arts and crafts stores and an indoor shopping center. **Ogmios** (⊠ 34 Great James St., ☎ 028/7127–9794) is a specialist shop with an extensive range of Irish language books, cards, crafts, and music items, including hand-made instruments. **Bookworm** (⊠ 16 Bishop St., ☎ 028/7128–2727) is "the best bookshop in Ireland," according to writer Nuala O'Faoláin. Off Shipquay Street, the **Trip** (⊠ 29 Ferryquay St., ☎ 028/7137–2382) is a teenage clothing shop that specializes in knitwear. Stop at the gift shop, **Pauline's Patch** (⊠ 32 Shipquay St. ☎ 028/7127–9794), for knickknacks. **Thomas the Goldsmith** (⊠ 7 Pump St., ☎ 028/7137–4549) stocks exquisite work by international jewelry designers. **Occasions** (⊠ 48 Spencer Rd., ☎ 028/7132–9595) sells Irish crafts and gifts. At **Casson's Interiors** (⊠ 16 Carlisle Rd., ☎ 028/7136–0020) you'll find stylish furniture and accessories for the home.

En Route From Derry, head across County Tyrone toward Enniskillen. Take A5 south via **Strabane,** birthplace of the surrealist novelist Brian O'Nolan, alias Flann O'Brien. Here you'll find the well-preserved, 18th-century **Gray's Print Shop** (✉ 49 Main St., ☎ 028/7188–4094). John Dunlap (1746–1812), who apprenticed here as a printer before emigrating to Philadelphia, founded America's first daily newspaper, the *Philadelphia Packet,* in 1771 and was also the man who printed and distributed the American Declaration of Independence. James Wilson, grandfather of President Woodrow Wilson, also emigrated from here.

For a delightfully rustic alternative route, drive along the minor road B48, which skirts the foot of the **Sperrin Mountains** and reaches all the way to Omagh. Or, you may want to head north from Derry to the **Inishowen Peninsula,** the northernmost point of Ireland.

AROUND COUNTIES TYRONE, FERMANAGH, ARMAGH, AND DOWN

During the worst of the Troubles, parts of these four counties that border the Republic were known as bandit country. But now visitors can enjoy a worry-free trip through the calm countryside and stop in at some very "Ulster" towns, distinct from the rest of Ireland. The area includes the great houses of Castle Coole and Florence Court; the ancient, ecclesiastical city of Armagh; and the wild Sperrin Mountains.

Ulster-American Folk Park and Ulster History Park

Folk Park: 51 km (31½ mi) south of Derry; History Park: 6 km (4 mi) northeast of the Folk Park.

39 The excellent **Ulster-American Folk Park and Ulster History Park** recreates a Tyrone village of two centuries ago, a log-built American settlement of the same period, and the docks and ships that the emigrants to America would have used. The centerpiece of the park is an old whitewashed cottage, now a museum, which is the ancestral home of Thomas Mellon (1855–1937), the U.S. millionaire banker and philanthropist. Another thatched cottage is a reconstruction of the boyhood home of Archbishop John Hughes, founder of New York's St. Patrick's Cathedral. Exhibitions trace the contribution of the Northern Irish people to American history. The park also has a crafts shop and café. ✉ *Camphill,* ☎ *028/8224–3292,* WEB *www.folkpark.com.* ✐ *U.K.£4.* ☉ *Apr.–Sept., Mon.–Sat. 10:30–6, Sun. 11–6:30; Oct.–Mar., weekdays 10:30–5; last admission 1½ hrs before closing.*

40 The **Ulster History Park** documents Irish history from the first known settlers to the 17th-century arrival of the Plantation settlers. The open-air displays include lath and rawhide huts, primitive farms and stockades, a round tower, and an oratory. ✉ *Cullion, Lislap, Gortin, off B48,* ☎ *028/8164–8188.* ✐ *U.K.£3.75.* ☉ *Apr.–Sept., Mon.–Sat. 10:30–6, Sun. 11–6:30; Oct.–Mar., weekdays 10:30–5; last admission 1½ hrs before closing.*

En Route It's worth veering off the beaten track to the **Linen Green** (✉ Moygashel, ☎ 028/8775–3761, WEB www.thelinengreen.com), off the M1 Motorway between Belfast and Omagh (leave at Junction 15 near the town of Dungannon). At the **Paul Costelloe Factory Store** you can get Costelloe's internationally acclaimed linen-wear at a discount.

Omagh

❹① *43 km (27 mi) northeast of Enniskillen, 7½ km (4½ mi) south of the Ulster-American Folk Park.*

Omagh, the county town of Tyrone, lies close to the Sperrin Mountains, with the River Strule to the north. Playwright Brian Friel was born here. Sadly, it is more recently known as the scene of the worst atrocity of the Troubles, when an IRA bomb killed 29 people in August 1998. The town has two places of worship—a Church of Ireland church and a Catholic double-spire church.

En Route   North of Omagh the country is pretty and rustic, with small farm villages. Head east on A505 into the pensive landscape of moist heath and bog. Left of the road, **Beaghmore** is a strange Bronze Age ceremonial site preserved for millennia beneath a blanket of peat. It has seven stone circles and 12 cairns. Farther along, A505 reaches **Wellbrook Beetling Mill,** where locally made linen was first "beetled"—pounded with noisy, water-driven hammers to give it a smooth finish. The National Trust keeps the mill in working order. ⊠ *Corkhill,* ☏ *028/8675–1735.* ▧ *U.K.£2.50.* ☉ *Mar.–June and Sept., weekends noon–6; July–Aug., daily noon–6.*

A little beyond Wellbrook you'll come to **Cookstown,** an odd Plantation village with a broad main street. From here, head down the back lanes to **Lough Neagh,** at 396 square km the largest lake in the British Isles, noted for an abundance of eels. On its shore at **Ardboe** stands a remarkable 10th-century high cross more than 18 ft tall and richly carved with biblical scenes.

Belleek

❹② *41½ km (26 mi) southwest of Omagh.*

You'll find the world-famous Belleek Pottery in the old town of Belleek, on the northwestern edge of Lower Lough Erne. On the riverbank stands the visitor center of **Belleek Pottery Ltd.,** producers of Belleek chinaware and porcelain. There's a factory, showroom, exhibition, Belleek pottery museum, and café. On weekdays, tours of the factory run every half-hour. You'll find hardly any noise coming from machinery in the workshops, as everything here is handmade—they use the exact process invented in 1857. The showroom is filled with beautiful but pricey gifts: a cup-and-saucer set costs about U.K.£25–U.K.£30, and a bowl in a basket-weave style (very typical of Belleek) could put you out several hundred pounds. ☏ *028/6865–8501,* ⊞ *www.belleek.ie.* ▧ *U.K.£2.50.* ☉ *Shop and showroom Apr.–June and Sept., weekdays 9–6, Sat. 10–6, Sun. 2–6; July–Aug., weekdays 9–6, Sat. 10–6, Sun. 11–6; Oct.–Mar., weekdays 9–5:30. Tours Mon.–Thurs. 9:15–12:15 and 2:15–4:15, Fri. 9:15–3:15. Call to confirm weekend hrs.*

Lough Erne

❹③ *131 km (82 mi) west of Belfast, 100 km (62 mi) south of Derry, 19 km (12 mi) north of Enniskillen.*

If you're driving in the vicinity of Lough Erne, don't rush—take your time and enjoy the panoramas of green, wooded hills stretching down to the still waters.

Castle Archdale Country Park, on the north side of Lough Erne, on the B82, has a lakeside marina and a museum containing a World War II exhibition on the Battle of the Atlantic. ⊠ *Signposted down a narrow*

road about 6½ km (4 mi) from Kesh, ☎ *028/6862–1588.* ◻ *Free.* ◷
Call for hrs.

Outdoor Activities and Sports

Inland cruising on the Erne waterway—777 square km (300 square mi)
of lakes and rivers—is one of the North's major treats. Upper and
Lower Lough Erne are enclosed by some of Ireland's finest scenery and
are studded with more than 100 little islands. Out on the lakes and the
River Erne, which links them, you'll have all the solitude you want, but
you'll find company at lough-side hostelries. To hire a boat, contact **Erne
Charter Boat Association** (⌧ Belleek Charter Cruising, Erne Gateway
Centre, Corry, Belleek, ☎ 028/6865–8027 WEB www.angelfire.com/
co/belleekcruising). Expect to pay at least U.K.£350 to hire a four-
berth cruiser for two or three nights.

White Island and Devenish Island

*White Island: 16 km (10 mi) north of Enniskillen; Devenish Island: 4
km (2½ mi) north of Enniskillen.*

④ From Castle Archdale, a ferry (☎ 028/6862–1333) runs from June
through September, Tuesday through Sunday (U.K.£3), taking passengers
to see the carved Celtic figures on **White Island.** After you drive 13 km
(8 mi) south from Castle Archdale Park to where the B82 joins the A32,
a small sign shows the way to catch the little boat (☎ 028/6632–3110)

④ that runs daily from April through September over to **Devenish Island.**
The extensive but ruined 12th-century monastery on Devenish is Ireland's best example of a round tower—it is 82 ft tall—and a richly carved
high cross.

Enniskillen

④ *43 km (27 mi) southwest of Omagh, 77 km (48 mi) west of Armagh.*

Enniskillen is the pleasant, smart-looking capital of County Fermanagh
and the only place of any size in the county. The town center is, strikingly, on an island in the River Erne between Upper and Lower Lough
Erne. The principal thoroughfares, Townhall and High Streets, are
crowded with old-style pubs and rows of redbrick Georgian flats. The
tall, dark spires of the 19th-century St. Michael's and St. MacArtin's
cathedrals, both on Church Street, tower over the leafy town center.

The waterfront **Enniskillen Castle** is one of the best-preserved monuments
in the North. Built by the Maguire clan in 1670, this stronghold houses
the local history collection of the **Fermanagh County Museum** and the
polished paraphernalia of the **Royal Inniskilling Fusiliers Regimental Museum.** A **Heritage Centre** also stands within the curtilage of the castle.
⌧ *Castlebarracks,* ☎ *028/6632–5000,* WEB *www.enniskillencastle.co.uk.*
◻ *U.K.£2.* ◷ *Jan.–Apr. and Oct.–late Dec., Mon. 2–5, Tues.–Fri. 10–
5; May–June and Sept., Mon. and Sat. 2–5, Tues.–Fri. 10–5; July–Aug.,
Mon. and weekends 2–5, Tues.–Fri. 10–5.*

At the riverside, the 16th-century **Water Gate,** between two handsome
turrets, protected the town from invading armies.

Beyond the West Bridge you'll find **Portora Royal School,** established
in 1608 by King James I. On its grounds are some ruins of Portora Castle. Among writers educated here are Samuel Beckett and Oscar Wilde,
the pride of the school (until his trial for homosexuality).

Among the several relaxed and welcoming old pubs in Enniskillen's
town center, the one with the most appeal is **Blake's of the Hollow** (⌧
6 Church St., ☎ 028/6632–2143) on the main street, a place hardly

altered since it opened in 1887. Its name derives from the fact that the heart of the town lies in a slight hollow and the pub's landlord is named William Blake (don't ask, he's not related to the English poet, painter, and engraver).

OFF THE
BEATEN PATH
FLORENCE COURT – Legend has it you can hear the "song of the little people" here. It's one of the most impressive of the North's grand Anglo-Irish mansions—and better, it's smack in an enchanting park. Built around 1730 for John Cole, father of the first earl of Enniskillen, the three-story Palladian Florence Court was damaged by fire in the 1950s. But thanks to a fine restoration, you can see abundant rococo plasterwork in the dining room, Venetian room, and, best, the famous staircase—all are ascribed to Robert West, one of Dublin's most famous stuccadores (plaster workers). ⊠ 11 km (7 mi) south of Enniskillen on A4 and A32, ☎ 028/6634–8249, WEB www.nationaltrust.org.uk. ⊡ Grounds U.K.£2.50 (refunded on admission to mansion), mansion U.K.£3. ⊙ Grounds daily Oct.–April. 10–4, daily May–Sept. 10–8. Mansion Mar.–May, weekends and public holidays 12–6; June, daily 1–6; July–Aug., daily 12–6; Sept., weekends 12–6.

Castle Coole

★ ㊼ *3 km (2 mi) southeast of Enniskillen.*

In the 18th century and through most of the 19th, the Loughs of Erne and their environs were remote places—far from Ireland's bustling cities. But it was just this isolated green and watery countryside that attracted the Anglo-Irish gentry. They built grand houses—among them, Castle Coole is widely considered to be the finest. This "uncommonly perfect" mansion (to quote the eminent architectural historian Desmond Guinness) stands in its own landscaped oak woods and parkland at the end of a long, tree-lined driveway. Although the Irish architect Richard Johnston made the original drawings in the 1790s and was responsible for the foundation, the castle was, for all intents and purposes, the work of James Wyatt, commissioned by the first Earl of Belmore. One of the best-known architects of his time, Wyatt, who was based in London, did much work in Ireland, but he only visited the country once, and he never came here. Alexander Stewart was the resident builder-architect who oversaw much of the building's construction. The architect wasn't the only imported element; in fact, much of Castle Coole was transported over from England, including the main facade, which is clad in Portland stone shipped from Dorset to Ballyshannon and then hauled over land by horse and cart. And what a facade it is—in perfect symmetry, white colonnaded wings extend from either side of the mansion's three-story, nine-bay center block, with a pedimented central portico. It is perhaps the apotheosis in Ireland of the 18th century's reverence for the Greeks, and it bears a touch of Palladian sensibility.

Inside, the house is remarkably well preserved; most of the lavish plasterwork and original furnishings are still in place. On its completion in September 1798, the construction had cost U.K.£70,000 and the furnishings another U.K.£22,000, compared to the U.K.£6 million cost of a restoration in 1995–96, during which anything not in keeping with the original design was removed. The saloon is one of the finest rooms in the house, with a vast expanse of oak flooring, gilded Regency furniture, and gray scagliola pilasters with Corinthian capitals. The present earl of Belmore still lives on the estate and uses one wing of the house. ⊠ Dublin Rd. (A4), ☎ 028/6632–2690, WEB www.nationaltrust.org.uk. ⊡ U.K.£3.50 mansion. ⊙ Grounds Oct.–April daily 10–4, May–Sept.

daily 10–8. Mansion Mar.–May, weekends and public holidays 12–6; June Wed.–Mon. 12–6; July–Aug., daily 12–6; Sept., weekends 12–6.

Lodging

$$$ 🏨 **Blessingbourne.** This Victorian Gothic house, with mullioned windows, stables, and carriage museum, sits on a pretty lake. Meals can be eaten with the Lowry family, the proprietors. One of the bedrooms has a four-poster bed. A visit makes the diversion to Fivemiletown— so named because it is 5 mi from anywhere—worthwhile. ⊠ *Fivemiletown, Co. Tyrone BT75 0QS, ☎ 028/8952–1221. 4 rooms without bath. Dining room. No credit cards.*

Outdoor Activities and Sports

If you're over in the Enniskillen–Lough Erne area, guides at the **Ulster Lakeland Equestrian Park** (⊠ Necarne Castle, Irvinestown, ☎ 028/6862–1919) can teach you to ride or take you on a pony trek through the 200 rolling acres of this Gothic-looking castle's parkland. Rates begin at U.K.£8 for 30 minutes. There are rooms to stay in, a bar, and a restaurant.

Armagh

48 *64 km (40 mi) west of Belfast, 77 km (48 mi) east of Enniskillen.*

The small but ancient ecclesiastical city of Armagh, despite the pleasing Georgian terraces around the elegant Mall east of the town center, can seem drab. Having suffered as a trouble spot in the sectarian conflict, though, it is now the scene of some spirited and sympathetic renovation. Here St. Patrick founded a church, and the town has remained a religious center to the present day; in fact, *two* Armagh cathedrals are dedicated to Ireland's patron saint. Despite the 1921 partition of Ireland into two parts, the seat of the Catholic archbishop of Ireland remains here, as does the seat of the archbishop of the Anglican Church of Ireland.

Armagh's main attraction is the **Astronomy Centre and Planetarium,** but as we went to press the center was planning a major 1-to 3-year refurbishment, and was uncertain of the starting date; phone for details. It contains models of spacecraft, video shows of the sky, and hands-on computer displays. The **Earthorium** explores the world from three levels—its interior, surface, and atmosphere. The outdoor 30-acre **AstroPark** has a model solar system. A **16-inch telescope** is open two nights per month, September through April (call for specific dates). **Robinson Dome**, also known as "the 10-inch dome" for the 1875 Grub telescope it houses, is open in spring and summer months. ⊠ *College Hill, ☎ 028/3752–3689. 🎟 AstroPark and Robinson Dome free; Earthorium U.K.£1; special shows and other exhibitions U.K.£3.75. 🕘 Sept.–June, weekdays 10–4:45, Sat. 1:15–4:45; July–Aug., Sun. 1:15–4:15. Call for show times.*

Dedicated to St. Patrick, the pale limestone, Victorian-Gothic **Catholic Cathedral** rises above a hill to dominate the north end of Armagh. Inside, the rather gloomy interior is enlivened by a magnificent organ whose potential is fully realized at services by long-time Belgian resident Baron George Minne.

Near the town center, a squat, battlemented tower identifies the **Protestant cathedral,** in simple, early 19th-century Perpendicular-Gothic style. It stands on the site of much older churches and contains several relics of Armagh's long history, including sculpted, pre-Christian idols. Brian Boru, the great High King (king of all Ireland) who visited Armagh in 1004—and was received with great ceremony—is buried here.

In 1014, at the Battle of Clontarf, he drove the Vikings out of Ireland—but was killed after the battle was won. ⊠ *Abbey St.,* WEB *www.stpatricks-cathedral.org.* ☒ *Free.* ⊙ *April–Oct 10–5, Nov.–Mar. 10–4.*

Past the 13th-century Franciscan friary ruins, in the stables of the former archbishop's demesne, the **Palace Stables Heritage Centre** presents a diorama of everyday life—upstairs and downstairs—in the 18th-century days of the extremely wealthy Baron Rokeby, Church of Ireland archbishop Richard Robinson. He commissioned local architect Francis Johnston, who had designed much of Georgian Dublin, to create a new Armagh out of the slums into which it had degenerated. The archbishop gave the city a clean water supply and a sewer system, then turned the city's racecourse into an elegant mall. He paved and lit the streets; financed improvements to the Bishop's Palace and the Protestant cathedral; and endowed the public library, the observatory, the Royal School, and the county infirmary. ⊠ *Palace Demesne, Friary Rd.,* ☎ *028/3752–9629.* ☒ *U.K.£3.50.* ⊙ *Apr.–Aug., Mon.–Sat. 10–5, Sun. 1–6; Sept.–Mar., Mon.–Sat. 10–5, Sun. 2–5.*

Just outside Armagh, **Navan Fort** is Ulster's Camelot—the region's ancient capital. Excavations date evidence of activity going back to 700 BC. The fort has strong associations with figures of Irish history and legend. Thousands of years ago it is said to have been the site of the palace of Queen Macha; subsequent legends call it the barracks of the legendary Ulster warrior Cuchulainn and his Red Branch Knights. Remains dating from 94 BC are particularly intriguing: a great conical structure, 120 ft in diameter, was formed from five concentric circles made of 275 wooden posts, with a 276th, about 12 yards high, situated in the center. In a ritual whose meaning is not known, it was filled with brushwood and set on fire. The **Navan Centre** rehearses the Red Branch Knights' tales—Ireland's *Iliad* and Ulster's *Camelot* combined. ⊠ *3 km (2 mi) west of Armagh on A28,* ☎ *028/3752–5550.* ☒ *Centre U.K.£3.95, fort free.* ⊙ *Fort freely accessible. Centre Apr.–June and Sept., weekdays 10–6, Sat. 11–6, Sun. noon–6; July–Aug., Mon.–Sat. 10–6, Sun. 11–6; Oct.–Mar., weekdays 10–5, Sat. 11–5, Sun. noon–5.*

Lodging

$$$ 🛏 **Drumsill Hotel.** On 15 acres of mature wooded grounds, this modern hotel is 1½ km (1 mi) northwest of Armagh on A29 road, signposted to Moy. The bedrooms are bright and airy, decorated in shades of cream and yellow. Brown's Bistro serves Continental cuisine. There is occasionally live music at the bar during summer. ⊠ *35 Moy Rd., Co. Armagh BT61 8DL,* ☎ *028/3752–2009,* FAX *028/3752–5624. 10 rooms with bath. Restaurant, bar, meeting rooms. MC, V.*

En Route   Leave Armagh to the southeast on A28, driving toward Newry. Instead of going the entire way on the main road, after about 9½ km (6 mi), you'll have a more enjoyable drive if you take B133, on the right. This will lead you through a rustic, drumlin landscape of vivid green pastures. The appearance of villages changes as you return toward the River Bann; houses and farms begin to resemble those of Britain rather than those in the Republic.

The Mountains of Mourne

49   *51 km (32 mi) south of Belfast, 52½ km (32½ mi) southeast of Armagh.*

In the words of the popular song by Percy French, the Mountains of Mourne "sweep down to the sea"—from 2,000-ft summits. East of the unprepossessing border town of Newry, this area was long considered ungovernable, its hardy inhabitants living from smuggling contraband into the numerous rocky coves on the seashore. Much of the Mourne range is still inaccessible except on foot. The countryside is gorgeous: high, windswept pasture and moorland threaded with bright streams, bound by a tracery of drystone walls, and dotted with sheep and whitewashed farmhouses snuggled in stands of sycamore. It's the perfect landscape for away-from-it-all walkers, cyclists, and serious climbers. Climbers should inform their hotel when and where they're heading before setting off. **Northern Ireland Centre for Outdoor Activities** (⌧ Bryansford, Newcastle, ☎ 028/4372–2158) offers advice on hill-climbing and navigation courses.

Newcastle, a bracing Victorian cold-water bathing station, is the main center for visitors to the hills. Looming above Newcastle is **Slieve Donard,** its panoramic, 2,805-ft summit grandly claiming views into England, Wales, and Scotland "when it's clear enough"—in other words, rarely, say the pessimists. The world's largest **maze,** grown to symbolize the convoluted path to peace, is the latest addition to **Castlewellan Forest Park,** which comprises 1,150 acres of forested hills running between the Mourne Mountains and Slieve Croob. With the maze, lake, secluded arbors, and **arboretum,** the park makes an excellent introduction to the area. ⌧ *Castlewellan,* ☎ *028/4377–8664,* WEB *www.forestserviceni.gov.uk.* ⌧ *Vehicles U.K.£4, pedestrians U.K.£2.* ☉ *Daily dawn–dusk.*

Covering 1,200 acres and entered through picturesque Gothic gateways, **Tollymore Forest Park** extends up the valley of the River Shimna. You'll find many pretty stone bridges over the sparkling waters here. ⌧ *Tullybrannigan Rd., Newcastle,* ☎ *028/4372–2428.* ⌧ *Vehicles U.K.£4, pedestrians U.K.£2.* ☉ *Daily dawn–dusk.*

Farther into the mountains, the road to the **Silent Valley** reservoir parklands leads to more mountain views and excellent photo-ops. Take B27 from Kilkeel; after 6 km (4 mi), turn right. ☎ *028/9074– 6581.* ⌧ *Vehicles U.K.£3, pedestrians U.K.£1.50.* ☉ *Apr.–Sept., daily 10–6:30; Oct.–Mar., daily 10–4.*

Lodging

$$$$ ⌂ **Slieve Donard Hotel.** A lavish redbrick monument to Victoriana, this turreted Victorian hotel stands like a palace on spacious green lawns at one end of Newcastle's 6½-km (4-mi) sandy beach. The heavily traditional furnishings will make you feel as if you're stepping back to the town's turn-of-the-20th-century heyday as an elegant seaside resort (though the rooms have every modern comfort). Ask for a room that overlooks the water. At the entrance to the grounds, the relaxed Percy French gatehouse pub serves adequate seafood dishes; there's music every Friday and Saturday night. The Royal County Down Golf Club is next door. The hotel has two exercise rooms. ⌧ *Downs Rd., Newcastle, Co. Down BT33 0AH,* ☎ *028/4372–3681,* FAX *028/4377–4830,* WEB *www.hastingshotels.com. 126 rooms with bath. Dining room, 2 tennis courts, indoor pool, gym, hair salon, hot tub, steam room, bar. AE, DC, MC, V.*

$$$ ⌂ **Burrendale Hotel & Country Club.** Thanks to owner Sean Small's sense of style, this low-slung, modern building, shaded by clumps of beech, is one of the most relaxing establishments on the North's east coast. Staff members are cheery, and bedrooms are decorated in quiet tones. Chefs at the Cottage Kitchen and Vine restaurants are competent (the former is casual, the latter more formal), and clearly aim to please the locals, who like their plates overflowing. ⌧ *51 Castlewellan Rd., Newcastle, Co. Down BT33 0JY,* ☎ *028/4372–2599,* FAX *028/ 4372–2328,* WEB *www.burrendale.com/home. 68 rooms with bath. 2 restaurants, indoor pool, gym, hot tub, sauna, steam rooms, 2 bars, Internet, meeting rooms. AE, DC, MC, V.*

$$$ **Glassdrumman Lodge.** For those who wish to be pampered as well as immersed in the ancient Kingdom of Mourne, Graeme and Joan Hall's eclectically simple and stylish lodge is the place. The outside of the house is less than spectacular, but those at the impressively busy estate grow their own crops, raise their own farm animals, churn their own butter, and bake their own bread. Rooms are decorated in bright colors and have large windows with glorious views. The Halls have frankly thought of everything—overnight laundry service, complimentary car washing. Horseback riding and trekking can also be arranged. ✉ *Mill Rd., Annalong, Co. Down BT34 4RH,* ☎ *028/4376–8451,* FAX *028/4376–7041. 10 rooms with bath, 2 suites. Restaurant, horseback riding, laundry service, business services, meeting rooms. AE, MC, V.*

Outdoor Activities and Sports

The **Royal County Down** (✉ Newcastle, ☎ 028/4372–3314, WEB www.royalcountydown.org) is considered by many golfers to be one of the finest courses in the world.

Downpatrick

(50) *35 km (22 mi) south of Belfast, 50 km (31 mi) east of Newry.*

Downpatrick used to be called "Plain and Simple Down" but had its name changed by John de Courcy, a Norman knight who moved to the town in 1176. De Courcy set about promoting St. Patrick, the 5th-century Briton who was captured by the Irish and served as a slave in the Down area before he escaped to France, where he learned about Christianity and bravely returned to try to convert the local chiefs. Although it is not true that Patrick brought a new faith to Ireland—there was already a bishop of Ireland before Patrick got here—he must have been a better missionary than most because he did indeed win influential converts. The clan chief of the Down area gave him land at the village of Saul, near Downpatrick, to build a monastery.

Downpatrick's hilltop **cathedral,** which lay ruined from 1538 to 1790 (it reopened in 1818), preserves parts of some of the earlier churches and monasteries that have stood on the site since the 6th century. Even before that time, the cathedral site had long been an important fortified settlement, and Down takes its name from the Celtic word "dun," or fort. In the churchyard, a somber slab inscribed "Patric" is supposedly the saint's tomb, which is a bit of a fraud, since no one knows where Patrick is buried. It might be here, at Saul, or, some scholars argue, more likely at Armagh. *Free.* *Freely accessible.*

For some hard facts concerning the patron saint of Ireland, visit the newly expanded **St. Patrick Centre** next to the cathedral; it's housed, together with the **Down Museum,** inside a former 18th-century jail. ✉ *The Mall,* ☎ *028/4461–9000,* WEB *www.saintpatrickcentre.com.* *U.K.£4.50.* *Oct.–Mar., daily 10–5; Apr.–May and Sept., Mon.–Sat. 9:30–5:30, Sun. 10–5:30; June–Aug., Mon.–Sat. 9:30–7, Sun. 10–6.*

Portaferry

(51) *30 km (18½ mi) south of Newtownards, 13 km (8 mi) east of Downpatrick.*

You'll have to cross Strangford Lough on the 24-vehicle car ferry from Strangford to reach Portaferry (U.K.£4.50 per vehicle, foot passengers U.K.£1), another quiet fishing village with old fortifications to guard this once-strategic channel, which joins the lough to the sea. The ferry crossing takes 10 minutes or less, and boats leave every half hour throughout the day. Departures from Strangford are on the half hour and hour, and from Portaferry on the three-quarter hour and the quarter hour: weekdays 7:30 AM–10:30 PM, Saturday 8 AM–11 PM, and Sunday 9:30 AM–10:30 PM.

Exploris, Portaferry's unusual aquarium, has models of the underwater environment in Strangford Lough and examples of 70 species that call the lough their home. Some of these creatures may not be what you expect: seals, found regularly by the aquarium staff and rescued from death on nearby shores (and, in one mysterious episode, in the middle of an inland field), as well as several large, long-lived species of fish that still inhabit the lake. ⊠ *The Rope Walk,* ☎ *028/4272–8062,* WEB *www.exploris.org.uk.* ⌕ *U.K.£5.40.* ⊘ *Apr.–Aug., Mon.–Fri. 10–6, Sat. 11–6, Sun. 1–6; Sept.–Mar., Mon.–Fri. 10–5, Sat. 11–5, Sun. 1–5.*

Dining and Lodging

$$–$$$ ✕ **Grace Neill's.** Reputed to be the oldest pub in Ireland, Grace Neill's served its first pint in 1611 and has hosted such luminaries as Peter the Great, Franz Liszt, and John Keats. Behind the original pub, more a cupboard under the stairs with bar stools, is the cozy Library Bar and the Bistro Bistro restaurant. Food ranges from a simple peppered beef sandwich with a pint of Guinness in the bar to very good French provincial cooking with a bit of Irish in the restaurant. Highlights include lobster bisque, roast lamb rump with thyme and mint, or pork and leek sausages with traditional champ. Catering to a variety of musical tastes, on Friday nights music from the piano bar filters through as you eat, on Sunday afternoons you get jazz, bluegrass on Wednesday evenings, and Funk on Saturday. ⊠ *33 High St., Donaghadee BT21 0AH,* ☎ *028/9188–1595,* FAX *028/9188–2553,* WEB *www.graceneills. co.uk. AE, MC, V. Closed Mon.*

$$$ ✕▥ **Portaferry Hotel.** Standing on the quayside (or "strand") over-
★ looking the narrow channel that connects Strangford Lough to the sea, this centuries-old, comfortable whitewashed inn has well-kept, simply furnished double rooms. The main action takes place in the popular bar and restaurant, where you can get huge breakfasts, country lunches, and old-fashioned evening meals. Live Strangford oysters, stuffed mussels, Dublin Bay prawns, scallops with bacon and garlic, and grilled turbot are briskly served to the Belfast and Dublin regulars who appreciate the fresh, frill-and-fad-free seafood. Watch the sun set across the water from the bar window, or better still, book one of the sought-after rooms at the front. ⊠ *10 The Strand, Co. Down BT22 1PE,* ☎ *028/4272–8231,* FAX *028/4272–8999,* WEB *www.portaferryhotel.com. 14 rooms with bath. Restaurant, bar, meeting rooms. AE, DC, MC, V.*

$$ ✕▥ **Dufferin Arms Coaching Inn.** Next door to Killyleagh Castle, this lively 1803 inn is presided over by Kitty Stewart and Morris Crawford. The atmosphere of the beautiful Georgian building is that of a rustic pub; the comfortable furnishings include luxurious bedrooms with four-poster beds. Downstairs, the original stables have been converted into the Kitchen Restaurant, a banquet hall with a long bar where medieval feasts and formal dinner parties often take place. They specialize in rustic Irish cooking—poached salmon and roast duck in cherry sauce. One of the bars has snugs, another an open fire; diversions such as pub quizzes and Cajun and jazz music keep things lively. ⊠ *31–35 High St., Killyleagh, Co. Down BT30 9QF,* ☎ *028/4482–8229,* FAX *028/ 4482–8755,* WEB *www.dufferincoachinginn.co.uk. 6 rooms with bath. Restaurant, 3 bars, Internet on request, meeting rooms. AE, MC, V.*

Mount Stewart

52 *21 km (13 mi) north of Portaferry.*

Mount Stewart is the grand 19th-century family home of the Marquesses of Londonderry, who also built one of London's most sumptuous residences on Park Lane. It was constructed in two stages, where an earlier house stood: George Dance designed the west facade (1804–05), and William Vitruvius Morrison designed the neoclassic main part of the building (1845–49). The landscaped gardens are populated with surprising stone carvings of rare and extinct creatures. The house contains one of George Stubbs's most famous portraits, that of the celebrated racehorse Hambletonian, after he won one of the most prominent contests of the 18th century. The octagonal Temple of the Winds is a copy of a similar structure in Athens, and there's a remarkable bathhouse and pool at the end of the wooded peninsula just before the entrance to the grounds. ✉ *Newtownards,* ☎ *028/4278–8387,* WEB *www.nationaltrust.org.uk.* 🖾 *U.K.£3.50.* ⊙ *May–Sept., Wed.–Mon. 1–6; Apr. and Oct., weekends 1–6.*

Lodging

$$ 🖼 **The Old Inn.** On the outside, this 1614 coaching inn, which is reputedly Ireland's oldest, looks the part. It's pure 17th-century old-world England, with a sculpted thatched roof, half doors, and leaded-glass windows. Inside there are roaring open fires in winter. Some of the bedrooms have four-poster beds and sitting rooms. The Churn Bistro's menu is solidly Irish, the staff jovial, and the locals inquisitive. Previous guests have included Peter the Great, the legendary highwayman Dick Turpin, and former president George Bush. Crawfordsburn is 16 km (10 mi) from Belfast. ✉ *15 Main St., Crawfordsburn, Co. Down BT19 1JH,* ☎ *028/ 9185–3255,* FAX *028/9185–2775,* WEB *www.theoldinn.com. 32 rooms with bath. Restaurant, 2 bars, Internet on request. AE, DC, MC, V.*

NORTHERN IRELAND A TO Z

To research prices, get advice from other travelers, and book travel arrangements, visit www.fodors.com.

AIR TRAVEL

CARRIERS

Scheduled services from the United States and Canada are routed through Dublin, Glasgow, London, or Manchester.

Frequent services to Belfast's two airports are scheduled throughout the day from London Heathrow, London Gatwick, and Luton (all of which have fast coordinated subway or rail connections to central London) and from 17 other U.K. airports. Flights take about one hour from London. British Midland Airways flies from Belfast International and Belfast City to London Heathrow. British European Airways flies from Belfast City to Gatwick and London City Airport. EasyJet flies from Belfast International to Luton, Liverpool, and Amsterdam.

➤ AIRLINES AND CONTACTS: **Aer Lingus** (☎ 0845/973–7747; 01/886–8888 Dublin office). **British Airways** (☎ 0845/773–3377). **British European Airways** (☎ 0870/567–6676). **British Midland Airways** (☎ 0870/607–0555). **EasyJet** (☎ 0870/600–0000).

AIRPORTS AND TRANSFERS

Belfast International Airport at Aldergove is the North's principal air arrival point, 30½ km (19 mi) from Belfast. Belfast City Airport is the second airport, 6½ km (4 mi) from the city. It receives flights from U.K. provincial airports, from London Gatwick and Heathrow, and from

Stanstead and Luton (both near London). City of Derry Airport is 8 km (5 mi) from Derry and receives flights from Glasgow and Manchester.
➤ AIRPORT INFORMATION: **Belfast City Airport** (☎ 028/9093–9093, WEB www.belfastcityairport.com). **Belfast International Airport at Aldergove** (☎ 028/9448–4848, WEB www.bial.co.uk). **City of Derry Airport** (☎ 028/7181–0784).

TRANSFERS

Ulsterbus operates a shuttle bus every half hour (one-way U.K.£5, round-trip U.K.£8) between the Belfast International Airport and Belfast city center. From Belfast City Airport, you can travel into Belfast by train from Sydenham Halt to Central Station or catch a taxi from the airport-to your hotel. If you arrive at the City of Derry Airport, you may need to call a taxi to get to your destination.
➤ TAXIS AND SHUTTLES: **Eglinton Taxis** (☎ 028/7181–1231). **Foyle Taxis** (☎ 028/7126–3905). **Ulsterbus** (☎ 028/9033–3000).

BIKE TRAVEL
Bike rentals cost about U.K.£10 a day, U.K.£40 a week; local TIOs can offer suggestions for good cycling routes. In Belfast rent from Mc-Conrey Cycles. Irish Cycle Tours offers tours of Belfast at 6:30 PM weekdays and 10 AM and 2 PM weekends for U.K.£18 singles, U.K.£30 couples. They also organize 3- to 7-day tours of the Mournes, Glens of Antrim, Causeway Coasts, and Fermanagh lakelands.
➤ BIKE TOURING: **Irish Cycle Tours** (☎ 028/9064–2222, WEB www.irishcycletours.com. **McConvey Cycles** (✉ 183 Ormeau Rd., ☎ 028/9033–0322).

BOAT AND FERRY TRAVEL
Norse Merchant Ferries has 11-hour daytime or overnight car ferries that connect Belfast with the English west-coast port of Liverpool every night. P&O European Ferries has a one-hour sailing to Larne from Cairn-ryan, Scotland; infrequent trains take passengers on to Belfast. The Sea-Cat high-speed catamaran sails between Belfast and Troon in Scotland. In high season (late March through September) it also sails between Belfast and Heysham in England, taking four hours, and between the Isle of Man and Belfast. The StenaLine HSS fast catamaran sails between Belfast and Stranraer, Scotland. The catamaran sailing time is 1½ hours.
➤ BOAT AND FERRY INFORMATION: **Norse Merchant Ferries** (✉ Victoria Terminal 2, West Bank Rd., ☎ 028/9077–9090, WEB www.norsemerchant.com). **P&O European Ferries** (☎ 0870/242–4777, WEB www.poirishsea.com). **SeaCat and Steam Packet Company Services** (☎ 0870/552–3523, WEB www.seacat.co.uk). **StenaLine HSS** (☎ 028/9074–7747, WEB www.stenaline.com).

BUS TRAVEL
Northern Ireland's main bus company, Ulsterbus, runs direct service between Dublin and Belfast. Queries about Ulsterbus service, or any other bus service in Northern Ireland, can be dealt with by the central call-center of Translink. The Republic's Bus Éireann runs direct services to Belfast from Dublin. Buses arrive at and depart from Belfast's Europa Buscentre; the ride takes three hours. Buses to Belfast also run from London and from Birmingham, making the Stranraer ferry crossing.

You can take advantage of frequent and inexpensive Ulsterbus links between all Northern Ireland towns. The Europa Buscentre is just behind the Europa Hotel. The Laganside Buscentre is around the corner from the Albert Clock and about 1 km (½ mi) from Central Station. Within Belfast, visitors have access to good city-bus service. All routes start from Donegall Square; you'll find a kiosk there where you can pick up a timetable. Another contact is Citybus.

CUTTING COSTS

If you want to tour the North by bus, a Freedom of Northern Ireland Ticket allows unlimited travel on bus or train (U.K.£10 per day, U.K.£27.50 for three days, and U.K.£40 per week). An Irish Rover ticket from Ulsterbus covers Ireland, north and south, and costs U.K.£42 for three days, U.K.£93 for eight, and U.K.£145 for fifteen. An Emerald Card (bus and rail) costs U.K.£124 for 8 days and U.K.£214 for 15 days. For specific fares and schedules, call Translink.

➤ Bus Information: **Bus Éireann** (☎ 01/836–6111 in Dublin). **Translink** (☎ 028/9066–6630). **Stranraer ferry** (☎ 01776/702262). **Citybus** (☎ 028/9024–6485).

CAR RENTAL

You can choose among several local rental companies, but renting a car won't be cheap. A compact car costs U.K.£150–U.K.£250 per week (including taxes, insurance, and unlimited mileage). If you're planning to take a rental car across the border into the Republic, inform the company and check its insurance procedures. Following are some of the main rental offices. A U.K.£180 security deposit is required at the Ford agency in Derry.

➤ Local Agencies: **Avis** (✉ Belfast International Airport, Belfast, ☎ 0870/606–0100 or 028/9442–2333; ✉ Belfast City Airport, Belfast, ☎ 0870/606–0100 or 028/9045–2017; ✉ Great Victoria St., Belfast, ☎ 028/9024–0404). **Dan Dooley** (✉ Belfast International Airport, Belfast, ☎ 028/9445–2522, WEB www.dandooley.com). **Europcar** (✉ Belfast International Airport, Belfast, ☎ 0800/068–0303 or 028/9442–3444; ✉ Belfast City Airport, Belfast, ☎ 0800/068–0303 or 028/9045–0904, WEB www.europcar.ie). **Ford** (✉ Desmond Motors, City of Derry Airport, Derry, ☎ 028/7136–0420). **Hertz** (✉ Belfast International Airport, Belfast, ☎ 028/9442–2533; ✉ Belfast City Airport, Belfast, ☎ 020/9073–2451).

CAR TRAVEL

Many roads from the Irish Republic into Northern Ireland were once closed for security reasons, but all are now reinstated, leaving you with a choice of legitimate crossing points. Army checkpoints at all approved frontier posts are rare, and few customs formalities are observed. The fast N1/A1 road connects Belfast to Dublin in 160 km (100 mi) with an average driving time of just over two hours.

PARKING

Belfast has many parking garages, as well as street meter-ticket parking. Before parking on the street, check the posted regulations: during rush hours many spots become no-parking.

ROAD CONDITIONS

In general, you'll find roads here are in much better shape and signposted more clearly than in the Irish Republic. Bad rush-hour delays can occur on the West Link in Belfast joining M1 (heading south or west) and M2 (heading east or north). But on the whole, driving is quicker and easier in the North than in areas south of the border.

CONSULATES

➤ Canada: (✉ 378 Stranmillis Rd., Belfast BT9 5EU, ☎ 028/9066–0212).

➤ New Zealand: (✉ New Balance House, 118A Lisburn Rd., Glenavy, Co. Antrim BT29 4NY, ☎ 028/9264–8098).

➤ United States: (✉ Queen's House, 14 Queen St., Belfast BT1 6EQ, ☎ 028/9032–8239).

EMERGENCIES

The general emergency number is 999. Belfast City Hospital is one of two main hospitals in Belfast with an emergency room; the Royal Victoria Hospital is the other. Altnagelvin Hospital in Derry has an emergency room.

➤ CONTACTS: **Altnagelvin Hospital** (✉ Belfast Rd., Derry, ☎ 028/7134–5171). **Ambulance, police, fire, coast guard** (☎ 999). **Belfast City Hospital** (✉ Lisburn Rd., Belfast, ☎ 028/9032–9241). **Belfast's main police station** (✉ 6–10 N. Queen St., ☎ 028/9065–0222). **Royal Victoria Hospital** (✉ Grosvenor Rd., Belfast, ☎ 028/9024–0503).

LODGING

You can book a reservation for all types of accomodations online, through the Northern Ireland Tourist Board's Web site. The fee is €4.

For details on youth hostels in Belfast and elsewhere, contact Hosteling International, Northern Ireland, at the Belfast International Youth Hostel; this modern and comfortable hostel has 128 beds.

➤ CONTACTS: **Northern Ireland Tourist Board** (WEB www.discovernorthernireland.com). **Hosteling International, Northern Ireland** (✉ 22 Donegall Rd., Belfast BT12 5JN, ☎ 028/9032–4733, FAX 028/9043–9699, WEB www.hini.org.uks).

MONEY MATTERS

CURRENCY

The North uses British currency. Euros are rarely accepted. You'll sometimes be given bank notes, drawn on Ulster banks; be sure not to get stuck with a lot of these when you leave, because they are accepted with reluctance, if at all, in the rest of the United Kingdom and will be difficult to change at banks back home.

CURRENCY EXCHANGE

Main banks are open weekdays 9:30–4:30, smaller branches weekdays 10:30–3:30. Changing money outside banking hours is possible at Thomas Cook branches. The branch at Belfast Airport is open daily 6:45 AM–8 PM; the branch at Donegall Place is open from Monday through Wednesday and Friday through Saturday 9–5:30, Thursday 10–5:30. You can also change bills at Travelex Worldwide Money.

➤ EXCHANGE SERVICES: **Thomas Cook** (✉ 11 Donegall Pl, ☎ 028/9455–4455, WEB www.thomascook.com). **Travelex Worldwide Money** (✉ Belfast Airport, ☎ 028/9442–2536, WEB www.travelex.co.uk).

OUTDOOR ACTIVITIES AND SPORTS

BIRD-WATCHING

Murphy's Wildlife Tours leads tours in all seasons, though if you're an advanced birder, you may want to concentrate on wintering wildfowl and waders that have migrated all the way from North America to the shores of Loughs Foyle, Neagh, and Strangford. For information, ideas, and details of field-study groups, contact Northern Ireland TIOs and the Royal Society for the Protection of Birds.

➤ CONTACTS: **Murphy's Wildlife Tours** (✉ 12 Belvoir Close, Belvoir [pronounced beaver] Park, Belfast, ☎ 028/9069–3232). **Royal Society for the Protection of Birds** (✉ Belvoir Park Forest, Belfast, ☎ 028/9049–1547).

FISHING

Northern Ireland's system of pricing and administrating fishing licenses and permits can seem anachronistic, unnecessarily complex, and bewildering. No license is needed for sea fishing. To catch freshwater fish, whether coarse or game, you need a rod license from the Fisheries Conservancy Board. You will need a license from the Foyle Fisheries Commission if you are fishing in the Derry area. Depending on the area, you may need a local permit. The good news is that all fishing licenses and Department of Agriculture and Fisheries permits are available from the Northern Ireland Tourist Board Information Centre. A number of Tourist Information Offices and tackle shops around the province stock fishing licenses and permits.

In the main angling areas, the following are useful contacts: Albert Atkins; Carlton Park Fishing Centre; Hook, Line & Sinker; Joe Mullan; Joseph Braddell; Lakeland Tackle & Guns; Moyle Outdoor Angling; and Tommy McCutcheon.

➤ CONTACTS: **Albert Atkins** (✉ 67 Coleraine Rd., Garvagh, ☎ 028/2955–8555). **Carlton Park Fishing Centre** (✉ Belleek, ☎ 028/6865–8181). **Fisheries Conservancy Board** (✉ 1 Mahon Rd., Portadown, ☎ 028/3833–4666, WEB www.fcbni.org). **The Locks Agency** (✉ 22 Victoria Rd., Derry, ☎ 028/7134–2100, WEB www.locks-agency.com). **Hook, Line & Sinker** (✉ 43 South St., Newtownards, ☎ 028/9181–1671). **Joseph Braddell** (✉ 11 North St., Belfast, ☎ 028/9032–0525). **Lakeland Tackle & Guns** (✉ Sligo Rd., Enniskillen, ☎ 028/6632–3774). **Moyle Outdoor Angling** (✉ 17 Castle St., Ballycastle, ☎ 028/2076–9521). **Tommy McCutcheon** (✉ 114 Sandy Row, Belfast, ☎ 028/9024–9509).

GOLF

All golf courses and clubs are listed in the Northern Ireland Tourist Board's information guide No. 17, "Golf—Where to Play," available from main tourist offices.

HIKING AND WALKING

The Ulster Way is experiencing some difficulties and is being investigated by the Environment and Heritage Service. Instead, try Waymarked Ways Northern Ireland, a network of eight walking routes open for walkers to enjoy—six more are being developed. (The 14 walks add up to about 600 km.) The Countryside Access and Activity Network for Northern Ireland (CAAN) distributes the brochure free; you can also get it from the Northern Ireland Tourist Board Information Centre. Each route has a specific map guide to accompany it, and is available individually at tourist information centers (U.K.£50p). The complete set of eight guides are available from CAAN for U.K.£5.50. Tougher walks in the hills are outlined in the informative handbook in the Irish Walks series, No. 4, *The North East,* by Richard Rogers, published by Gill & Macmillan, which is available in local book and sporting goods stores in Northern Ireland; it gives precise details of 45 hill walks, complete with descriptions of the wildflowers you'll see along the way. For hikes in the Mountains of Mourne, you can obtain maps and details of suggested routes from the Mourne Countryside Centre. Celtic Journeys arranges wildlife and cultural walks.

➤ CONTACTS: **Countryside Access and Activity Network for Northern Ireland (CAAN)** (✉ House of Sport, Upper Malone Rd., Belfast, County Antrim, ☎ 028/9038–3848, www.countrysiderecreation.com, WEB www.waymarkedways.com). **Celtic Journeys** (✉ 111 Whitepark Rd., Ballycastle, ☎ 028/2076–9651). **Gill & Macmillan** (✉ Goldenbridge, Inchicore, Dublin 8, ☎ 01/453–1005). **Mourne Countryside Centre** (✉ 91 Central Promenade, Newcastle, ☎ 028/4372–4059).

HORSEBACK RIDING AND PONY TREKKING

About 3¼ km (2 mi) south of center-city Belfast, the Lagan Valley Equestrian Centre runs pony treks and offers lessons—both group and private. Group lessons and trekking cost U.K.£10 hourly, private lessons are U.K.£17. The center is open weekdays 10–9, Saturdays 10–6:30.

➤ CONTACTS: **Lagan Valley Equestrian Centre** (✉ 170 Upper Malone Rd., Belfast, ☎ 028/9061–4853).

TOURS

BOAT TOURS

On the Lower Lough Erne, Erne Tours operates *Kestrel,* a 63-seat water bus, which leaves Round O pier at Enniskillen during the summer at 10:30, 2:15, 4:15, and 7:15 on Tuesday, Thursday, and Sunday for a two-hour trip on beautiful Lough Erne. On weekdays the boat makes a half-hour stop at Devenish Island. From May to June there are Sunday trips at 2:30, and occasionally tours run at other times of the year.
➤ FEES AND SCHEDULES: Erne Tours (☎ 028/6632–2882).

BUS TOURS

Citybus in Belfast offers two tours. The three-hour Belfast City Tour for U.K.£9 includes the Harland and Wolff shipyard, City Hall, Queen's University, the Ulster Museum, Botanic Gardens, and the Grand Opera House. Tours leave Castle Place Monday and Friday at noon and take three hours. The Belfast Through the Millennium Tour, for U.K.£8, includes Loyalist and Nationalist political wall murals, City Hall, the Odyssey complex, the Waterfront Hall, and the Golden Mile. It leaves Castle Place Tuesday–Thursday and Saturday at noon and 2:30 PM.

MiniCoach operates day tours of Belfast, the Giant's Causeway, the Mountains of Mourne, Mount Stewart Gardens, and the Ulster Folk and Transport Museum. Ulsterbus operates half-day or full-day trips June through September from Belfast to the Glens of Antrim, the Giant's Causeway, the Fermanagh lakes, Lough Neagh, the Mountains of Mourne, and the Ards Peninsula. Ulsterbus has also teamed up with the Old Bushmills Distillery to run the Bushmills Bus, an open-top tour bus running from Coleraine to the Giant's Causeway via the coast resorts; you also visit Bushmills to observe whiskey making. Call Ulsterbus in Coleraine for details.
➤ FEES AND SCHEDULES: Citybus (✉ Milewater Rd., ☎ 028/9024–6485, WEB www.citybus.co.uk). MiniCoach (✉ 22 Donegall Rd., ☎ 028/9032–4733, WEB www.minicoachni.co.uk). Ulsterbus (✉ Milewater Rd., ☎ 028/9033–3000, 028/9033–7004, or 028/7034–3334 in Coleraine [Bushmills Bus]).

DRIVING TOURS

Belfast City Tours does 90-minute tours in a London-style black taxi of both Loyalist and Nationalist areas. The cost is U.K.£8 per person for three or more, or U.K.£20 per taxi if less than three. Individual black taxis also do personalized tours at U.K.£17 per hour for up to four people. The Loyalist tours leave from North Street, the Nationalist tours from King Street.
➤ FEES AND SCHEDULES: Belfast City Tours (☎ 0800/052–3914). Loyalist Tours (☎ 028/9032–8775). Nationalist Tours (☎ 028/9059–0800).

WALKING TOURS

Historical Pub Tours of Belfast offers walking tours of the city's pubs on Thursday at 7 PM and Saturday at 5 PM. The cost is U.K.£5. In Derry, walking tours (U.K.£4) and bus tours (U.K.£3) are organized through the city's Tourist Information Centre.
➤ FEES AND SCHEDULES: Derry Tourist Information Centre (☎ 028/7126–7284). Historical Pub Tours of Belfast(☎ 028/9068–1278).

TRAIN TRAVEL

The Dublin–Belfast Express train, run jointly by Northern Ireland Railways and Iarnród Éireann, travels between the two cities in about two hours. Six trains (check timetables, as some trains are much slower) run daily in both directions (three on Sunday) between Dublin and Belfast's misnamed Central Station. A free shuttle bus service from Belfast Central Station will drop you off at City Hall or Ulsterbus's city-center Europa Buscentre. You can change trains at Central Station for the city-center Great Victoria Street Station, which is adjacent both to the Europa Buscentre and the Europa Hotel.

Northern Ireland Railways runs only four rail routes from Belfast's Central Station—which is not, in fact, that centrally located: northwest to Derry via Coleraine and the Causeway Coast; east to Bangor along the shore of Belfast Lough; northeast to Larne (for the P&O European ferry to Scotland); and south to Dublin. There are frequent connections to Central Station from the city-center Great Victoria Street Station and from Botanic Station in the university area. For more information contact Northern Ireland Railways.

CUTTING COSTS

A Freedom of Northern Ireland Ticket allows unlimited travel on trains (U.K.£10 per day, U.K.£27.50 for three days, and U.K.£40 per week).

➤ TRAIN INFORMATION: **Botanic Station** (✉ Botanic Ave., ☎ 028/9089–9411). **Central Station** (✉ E. Bridge St., ☎ 028/9089–9411). **Europa Buscentre** (☎ 028/9033–3000). **Great Victoria Street Station** (✉ Great Victoria St., ☎ 028/9043–4424). **Iarnród Éireann** (☎ 01/855–4477). **Northern Ireland Railways** (✉ 28 Wellington Pl., Belfast, ☎ 028/9089–9411).

VISITOR INFORMATION

The Northern Ireland Tourist Board Information Centre in Belfast is the main tourist information center for the whole of the North. The office is open September through June, Monday 9:30–5:15, Tuesday–Saturday 9–5:15; and July through August, Monday 9:30–7, Tuesday–Saturday 9–7, Sunday noon–4. Year-round local offices are listed below by town. During June through August, many more towns and villages open TIOs.

➤ TOURIST INFORMATION: **Northern Ireland Tourist Board Information Centre** (✉ 35 Donegall Pl., BT1 5AU, ☎ 028/9023–1221 or 028/9024–6609, FAX 028/9023–9936 or 028/9031–2424, WEB www. discovernorthernireland.com, www.gotobelfast.com). **Armagh** (✉ 40 English St., Co. Armagh BT6 17BA, ☎ 028/3752–1800). **Ballycastle** (✉ 7 Mary St., Co. Antrim BT54 6QH, ☎ 028/2076–2024). **Bangor** (✉ Quay St., Co. Down BT20 5ED, ☎ 028/7037–0069). **Carrickfergus** (✉ Heritage Plaza, Co. Antrim BT38 7DG, ☎ 028/9336–6455). **Coleraine** (✉ Railway Rd., Co. Derry BT52 IPE, ☎ 028/7034–4723). **Derry** (✉ Foyle St., Co. Derry BT48 6AT, ☎ 028/7126–7284 or 028/7137–7577). **Downpatrick** (✉ 74 Market St., Co. Down BT30 6L2, ☎ 028/4461–2233). **Enniskillen** (✉ Lakeland Visitor Centre, Shore Rd., Co. Fermanagh BT74 7EF, ☎ 028/6632–3110). **Giant's Causeway** (✉ Visitor Centre, Co. Antrim BT57 8SU, ☎ 028/2073–1855). **Killymaddy** (✉ Ballygally Rd., Co. Derry BT70 ITF, ☎ 028/8776–7259). **Larne** (✉ Narrow Gauge Rd., Co. Antrim BT40 1XB, ☎ 028/2826–0088). **Limavady** (✉ Connell St., Co. Derry BT49 OHA, ☎ 028/7772–2226). **Lisburn** (✉ Market Sq., Co. Antrim BT28 IAG, ☎ 028/9266–0038). **Newcastle** (✉ Central Promenade, Co. Down BT33 OAA, ☎ 028/4372–2222). **Newtownards** (✉ Regent St., Co. Down BT23 4AD, ☎ 028/9182–6846). **Newry** (✉ Town Hall, Bank Parade, Co. Armagh BT35 6HR, ☎ 028/3026–8877).

WEATHER

Call Weathercall for a Northern Ireland weather forecast, and Marine Call for a maritime forecast.

➤ CONTACTS: **Marine Call** (☎ 0891/505365). **Weathercall** (☎ 0891/500427).

10 IRISH GREENS
GOLFING IN IRELAND

In the last decade, Ireland invested almost $400 million to make the country Europe's premier golf destination—and has succeeded. Many new courses have opened, and Ireland now attracts some of the most sought after tournaments. Thanks to all this, it's no surprise that golf has become the new religion in Ireland.

Updated by
Muriel and
Graham
Bolger

By Jonathan
Abrahams

Ask MOST GOLFERS WHERE TO FIND the golf vacation of a lifetime—breathtaking and diverse courses, lovely settings, history seeping into every shot—and they'll probably say Scotland. Unless, of course, they've been to Ireland.

Ireland doesn't lag far behind in its golfing history. Its oldest course dates back to 1881, and the Golfing Union of Ireland is the oldest golfing union in the world. It started in 1891: all of the nine original clubs were in Ulster. Now the number of affiliated golf clubs is 4002, with over 200,000 members—and there are still more clubs which aren't members.

Despite windy, rainy, and often misty weather, real golfers will not be deterred by the vagaries of the elements or the lack of golf carts on many courses in rougher terrain. Those kinds of golfers will instead be challenged by some of the most beguiling and frustrating courses in the world. You don't have to be a native to join in this passion, which attracts players from around the globe. Tom Watson, winner of five British Opens, lists Ballybunion as his favorite course; so does the legendary writer Herbert Warren Wind—who, from an American viewpoint, put Irish golf on the map when he wrote, "To put it simply, Ballybunion revealed itself to be nothing less than the finest seaside course I have ever seen." And although Ballybunion was generally considered the prize jewel of the Emerald Isle, many others throughout the country now rival it. The list is almost endless—from such classics as Portmarnock and Waterville to newer courses, including Mount Juliet, The K Club, and The Old Head of Kinsale.

You should know, also, that there's more to Irish golf than its great links courses. Druids Glen features prominently alongside the likes of the K Club, Mount Juliet, Carlow, and Fota Island in every debate on the great inland golf courses. And while it's purely a matter of opinion as to which is best (depending, of course, on your last score card), Druids Glen played host to the Irish Open Golf Championship for three years and was voted European Golf Course of the year at the prestigious Hertz International Travel Awards. It is commonly said that every great course produces great champions—that's certainly true of Druids Glen, which produced winners of the caliber of Montgomery and Garcia.

The wonderful, challenging natural terrain is one the things that makes Irish golf so remarkable. Of the estimated 150 top-quality links courses in the world, 39 of them are in Ireland. Most of their leading courses were designed by celebrated golf architects, such as Tom Morris, James Braid, Harry Colt, and Alister MacKenzie, who capitalized on spectacular landscapes: Ireland is one of those remarkable places where mountains and sea meet with nature as her architect. Scraggly coastline and rolling hills of heather dominate the courses here, not the other way around.

- **The Weather Factor.** You see all different kinds of weather in Ireland—driving winds, rain, sleet, and sunshine—and you may see it all in one round. There are no rain checks here. You play unless there's lightning, so pack your sweaters and rain gear, especially if you're planning your trip between fall and spring.

- **The Sunday Bag Factor.** If you don't have a golf bag that's light enough for you to carry for 18 holes, invest in one before your trip. Electric carts are generally available only at the leading venues, so you usually have the option of using a caddy or caddy car (pull cart) or carrying your own bag. Many courses have caddies but will not guarantee their availability because they're not employed by the course directly—so you may have only the option of toting your bag yourself. Be prepared and take a carryall, or Sunday bag.

- **The Private Club Factor.** Unlike those in America, most private golf clubs in Ireland are happy to let visitors play their course and use their facilities. It's important to remember, however, that the course is indeed there for the members first, and the majority of the club's concerns lie with them. For example, Ireland's oldest club, Royal Belfast in Northern Ireland, does not accept playing visitors. For many others, you'll need a letter of introduction from your club in America to secure your playing privilege. Preferred days for visitors are listed below, but it's always a good idea to call in advance and make sure that the club will make time for you.

- **The Northern Ireland Factor.** Some of the best and most beautiful courses are in Northern Ireland, where the leading venues—like Royal County Down and Royal Portrush—are less remote than in the Republic. Remember that this part of the island is under British rule, so all currency is in U.K. pounds, although many clubs and business will accept the euro.

North of Dublin

County Louth Golf Club. Like many other Irish courses, County Louth is better known as its hometown, Baltray, a village sandwiched by the Boyne Estuary to the west and the Irish Sea to the east. Long hitters will love the atypical layout, a par-73 that features five par-5s, but beware the well-protected, undulating greens. ⊠ *Baltray, Drogheda, Co. Louth,* ☎ *041/982–2329. 18 holes. Yardage: 6,783. Par 73.* 🖃 *Fees: weekdays, €80; weekends, €100.* ⊘ *Visitors: Mon. and Wed.–Fri. Practice area, caddies (reserve in advance), caddy carts, club rental, catering.*

Island Golf Club. Talk about exclusive—until 1960, the only way to reach this club was by boat. It was about as remote as you could get and still be only 24 km (15 mi) from Dublin. But things have changed. The Island has opened its doors to reveal a fine links course that rolls in and around sand hills, with small, challenging greens. ⊠ *Corballis, Donabate, Co. Dublin,* ☎ *01/843–6205. 18 holes. Yardage: 6,800. Par 71.* 🖃 *Fees: €100.* ⊘ *Visitors: Mon., Tues., and Fri. Practice area, caddies, caddy carts, catering.*

★ **Portmarnock Golf Club.** Across an estuary from the easternmost point of Ireland, Portmarnock is perhaps the most famous of Ireland's "Big Four" (Ballybunion, Royal County Down, and Royal Portrush are the others). Largely because of its proximity to Dublin, this links course has hosted numerous major championships. Known for its flat fairways and greens, it provides a fair test for any golfer who can keep it out of the heavy rough. ⊠ *Portmarnock, Co. Dublin,* ☎ *01/846–2968. 27 holes. Yardage: 7,300, 3,449. Par 72, 37.* 🖃 *Fees: weekdays, €130; weekends, €160.* ⊘ *Visitors: Mon., Tues., Thurs., and Fri. Practice area, driving range, caddies (reserve in advance), caddy carts, catering.*

Royal Dublin Golf Club. Links courses are usually in remote, even desolate areas, but this captivating one is only 6 km (4 mi) from the center of Dublin. On Bull Island, a bird sanctuary, Royal Dublin is the third-oldest club in Ireland and is routed in the old tradition of seaside links—the front 9 goes out in a line (wind helping), and the back 9 comes back in a line (wind against). Don't expect to make a comeback on the way home if you've struggled going out. ⊠ *Dollymount, Dublin 3,* ☎ *01/833–6346. 18 holes. Yardage: 6,963. Par 72.* 🖃 *Fees:*

weekdays €100; weekends €115. ☉ *Visitors: daily. Practice area, caddies, caddy carts, club rental, catering.*

St. Margaret's Golf and Country Club. Not all of the worthwhile golf in Ireland is played on century-old links courses. St. Margaret's, a parkland (inland) course, receives high praise from Ireland's golfing inner circle. If, after getting blown around on the seaside links, you long for a taste of Western golf, this is your haven. ⊠ *St. Margaret's, Co. Dublin,* ☎ *01/864–0400. 18 holes. Yardage: 6,929. Par 73.* ⌑ *Fees: weekdays €60; weekends €75.* ☉ *Visitors: daily. Practice area, driving range, caddy carts, club rental, shoe rental, catering.*

South of Dublin and the Southeast

Druids Glen Golf Club. Owner Hugo Flinn presented designers Pat Ruddy and Tom Craddock with the brief "Build me the finest parkland course in Ireland, whatever the cost." After an outlay of more than $16 million their handiwork was opened to the public. It has been chosen four times as the venue for the Murphy's Irish Open. Ruddy unashamedly admits to having copied some key elements of Augusta National—particularly the extensive use of water—in the layout. The course, situated about 40 km (25 mi) south of Dublin in County Wicklow, is remarkably beautiful, particularly around the glen from which its name derives. It is essentially an American-style target course incorporating some delightful changes in elevation, and its forbidding, par-3 17th has an island green, like the corresponding hole at TPC Sawgrass. ⊠ *Newtownmountkennedy, Co. Wicklow,* ☎ *01/287–3600. 18 holes. Yardage: 7,026. Par 71.* ⌑ *Fees: €125.* ☉ *Visitors: daily. Practice area, caddies, caddy carts, buggies, catering.*

★ **The K Club.** At just 27 km (17 mi) west of Dublin, this 18-hole, Arnold Palmer–designed parkland course offers a round of golf in lush, wooded surroundings bordered by the River Liffey. The generous fairways and immaculate greens are offset by formidable length, which makes it one of the most demanding courses in the Dublin vicinity. Additional stress is presented by negotiating the numerous doglegs, water obstacles, and sand bunkers. Facilities on the premises are of the highest standard, allowing a wide choice of sporting and nonsporting activities. ⊠ *Kildare Country Club, Straffan, Co. Kildare,* ☎ *01/627–3333. 18 holes. Yardage: 6,244. Par 72.* ⌑ *Fees: €175.* ☉ *Visitors: daily. Practice area, driving range, caddies, caddy carts, club rental, shoe rental, catering.*

★ **Mount Juliet Golf Course.** The Jack Nicklaus–designed championship parkland course, 19 km (11 mi) from Kilkenny Town, includes practice greens, a driving range, and, for those who feel a little rusty, a David Leadbetter golf academy. The heavily forested course has 8 holes that play over water, including the three signature par-3s. The back 9 presents a series of difficult bunker shots. A sporting day out comes to a welcome end in the Hunter's Yard or Rose Garden lodge, which cater to both the thirsty and the hungry. Greens fees are above average, and although visitors are always welcome, a weekday round is better than a weekend one, as tees can be crowded with members flocking to the course at week's end. ⊠ *Mount Juliet Estate, Thomastown, Co. Kilkenny,* ☎ *056/24455. 18 holes. Yardage: 7,112. Par 72.* ⌑ *Fees: weekdays, €135; weekends, €150.* ☉ *Visitors: daily. Practice area, driving range, caddies, caddy carts, club rental, lessons, catering.*

Tulfarris Golf Club. Less than a year after being officially opened, the $20 million development at Tulfarris was chosen as the venue for the Irish Senior Professional Open. Designed by Patrick Merrigan, it spans a 200-acre site beside Poulaphuca Lake, 50 km (31 mi) from Dublin, in an area of outstanding natural beauty. It's classic parkland, and has the potential to be among the country's leading venues. ⊠ *Blessington, Co. Wicklow,* ☎ *045/867–555. 18 holes. Yardage: 7,116. Par 72.* ⌐ *Fees: weekdays, €65; weekends, €80. Practice area, caddies, caddy carts, catering.*

Southwest

Adare Manor Golf Course. This charming parkland stretch is situated in the ancestral estate of the Earl of Dunraven. Its immediate success was virtually guaranteed by the international profile of its designer, Robert Trent Jones. The "grand old man" of golf-course architects seemed far more comfortable with the wooded terrain than he was when designing the second links at Ballybunion. As a result, he delivered a course with the potential to play host to events of the highest caliber. The front 9 is dominated by an artificial 14-acre lake with a $500,000 polyethylene base. It is in play at the 3rd, 5th, 6th, and 7th holes. The dominant hazards on the homeward journey are the River Mague and the majestic trees. Both combine to make the par-5 18th one of the most testing finishing holes imaginable. ⊠ *Adare, Co. Limerick,* ☎ *061/395–044. 18 holes. Yardage: 7,138. Par 72.* ⌐ *Fees: €110.* ☺ *Visitors: daily. Practice area, caddies, caddy carts, catering.*

★ **Ballybunion Golf Club.** This is one of the finest courses in the world. The Old Course was a virtual unknown until Herbert Warren Wind sang its praises in 1968, and today Ballybunion is universally regarded as one of golf's holiest grounds. On the shore of the Atlantic next to the southern entrance of the Shannon, it has the huge dunes of Lahinch without the blind shots. No pushover, but every hole is a pleasurable experience. Watch out for "Mrs. Simpson," a double fairway bunker on the 1st hole, named after the wife of Tom Simpson, the architect who remodeled the course in 1937. The New Course, which opened in 1985, was designed by Robert Trent Jones. ⊠ *Sandhill Rd., Ballybunion, Co. Kerry,* ☎ *068/27611. 36 holes. Yardage: 6,593 (Old), 6,216 (New). Par 71, 72.* ⌐ *Fees: €110 (Old), €75 (New), €135 (both on same day).* ☺ *Visitors: weekdays. Practice area, driving range, caddies, catering.*

Cork Golf Club. If you know golf-course architecture, you're familiar with the name Alister MacKenzie, who designed Cypress Point in California and Augusta National in Georgia. One of his few designs in Ireland is Cork, better known as Little Island. There's water on this parkland course, but it's not the temperamental ocean; instead, Little Island is in Cork Harbour, a gentle bay of the Irish Sea. The course is little known, but is one of the Emerald Isle's best. ⊠ *Little Island, Co. Cork,* ☎ *021/435–3451. 18 holes. Yardage: 6,119. Par 72.* ⌐ *Fees: weekdays, €70; weekends, €80.* ☺ *Visitors: Mon.–Wed. and Fri. Practice area, caddies, caddy carts, club rental, catering.*

Dooks Golf Club. On the second tier of courses in Ireland's Southwest, Dooks doesn't quite measure up to the world-class tracks. It is, nonetheless, a completely worthwhile day of golf if you're touring the area. Built in the old tradition of seaside links, it's shorter and a bit gentler, although the greens are small and tricky. It's an excellent way to take a breath. ⊠ *Dooks, Glenbeigh, Co. Kerry,* ☎ *066/976–8205. 18 holes. Yardage: 6,071. Par 70.* ⌐ *Fees: €40.* ☺ *Visitors: weekdays. Caddy carts, catering.*

Killarney Golf and Fishing Club. Freshwater fishing is the sport here, for this club is among a stunning mixture of mountains, lakes, and forests. There are three golf courses: the Killeen Course; Mahony's Point, set along the shores of Lough Leane; and the Lackabane, on the far side of the road from the main entrance. Killeen and Lackabane are longer; Mahony's places a premium on accuracy. Despite the abundance of seaside links, many well-traveled golfers name Killarney their favorite place to play in Ireland. ⊠ *Mahony's Point, Killarney, Co. Kerry,* ☎ *064/ 31034. 54 holes. Yardage: 6,474 (Killeen), 6,164 (Mahony's), 6,410 (Lackabane). All 3 courses: par 72.* ☞ *Fees: €70 on all 3 courses.* ☯ *Visitors: Mon.–Sat. Practice area, caddies, caddy carts, catering.*

Old Head Golf Links. On a celebrated 215-acre County Cork peninsula, which juts out into the wild Atlantic nearly 300 ft below, you'll find an awe-inspiring spectacle that defies comparison. The only golfing stretches that could be likened to it are the 16th and 17th holes at Cypress Point and small, Pacific sections of Pebble Beach, from the 7th to the 10th and the long 18th. Even if your golf is moderate, expect your pulse to race at the stunning views and wonderful wildlife. ⊠ *Kinsale, Co. Cork,* ☎ *021/477–8444. 18 holes. Yardage: 7,215. Par 72.* ☞ *Fees: €250.* ☯ *Visitors: daily. Practice area, caddies (reserve in advance), caddy carts, catering.*

Tralee Golf Club. Tralee is what all modern-golf-course architects *wish* they could do in the States: find unspoiled, seaside links and route a course on it that's designed for the modern game. This is an Arnold Palmer–Ed Seay design that opened in 1984, and the location is fantastic—cliffs, craters, dunes, and the gale-blowing ocean. Don't let the flat front 9 lull you to sleep—the back 9 can be a ferocious wake-up call. ⊠ *West Barrow, Ardfert, Co. Kerry,* ☎ *066/713–6379. 18 holes. Yardage: 6,738. Par 71.* ☞ *Fees: €110.* ☯ *Visitors: weekdays. Practice area, caddies, catering.*

Waterville Golf Links. Here's what you should know about Waterville before you play: the 1st hole of this course is aptly named "Last Easy." At 7,184 yards from the tips, Waterville is the longest course in Ireland or Britain, and it is generally regarded as their toughest test. Now the good news—the scenery is so majestic you may not care that your score is approaching the yardage. Six holes run along the cliffs by the sea, surrounding the other 12, which have a tranquil, if not soft, feel to them. ⊠ *Waterville, Co. Kerry,* ☎ *066/947–4545. 18 holes. Yardage: 7,225. Par 72.* ☞ *Fees: €125.* ☯ *Visitors: daily. Practice area, caddies, caddy carts, buggies, catering.*

West

Carne Golf Links. This is a newer, Eddie Hackett–designed links course that takes advantage of its location, far to the west on the shores of Blacksod Bay. From the elevated tees and greens you can see a string of Atlantic islands: Inishkea, Inishglora, and Achill. ⊠ *Carn, Belmullet, Co. Mayo,* ☎ *097/82292. 18 holes. Yardage: 6,608. Par 72.* ☞ *Fees: €40.* ☯ *Visitors: daily. Practice area, caddies, caddy carts, catering.*

Connemara Golf Club. The local club for the town of Clifden, Connemara is a links course where you can get carried away not only by the golf but by the scenery. Immediately to the west you'll see the Atlantic Ocean and Ballyconneely Bay, and to the east you'll see the Twelve Bens Mountains. The course starts flat, then rises into the hills for the final, challenging 6 holes. ⊠ *Ballyconneely, Clifden, Co. Galway,* ☎ *095/23502. 27 holes. Yardage: 7,229. Par 72.* ☞ *Fees: weekdays, €45; weekends, €50.* ☯ *Visitors: daily Practice area, caddies, caddy carts, catering.*

Lahinch Golf Club. The original course at Lahinch was designed by old Tom Morris, who, upon the unveiling in 1892, called it "as fine a natural course as it has ever been my good fortune to play over." That was when blind shots (those taken when you can't see your target) were in vogue; there are many here, as towering sand hills dominate every hole. Only a course with as much charm as this one could get away with that in today's modern game. The new Castle course is no less challenging, but conforms with today's standards. ✉ *Lahinch, Co. Clare,* ☎ *065/708–1003. 36 holes. Yardage: 6,220 (Old Course), 5,594 (Castle Course). Par 71, 70.* 📠 *Fees: €110 (Old Course), €50 (Castle).* ☉ *Visitors: daily. Practice area, caddies, caddy carts, catering.*

Westport Golf Club. Twice this inland course hosted the Irish Amateur Championship. It also lies in the shadows of religious history: rising 2,500 ft above Clew Bay, with its hundreds of islands, is Croagh Patrick, a mountain that legend connects with St. Patrick. The mountain is considered sacred, and it attracts multitudes of worshipers to its summit every year. All the prayers might pay off at the 15th, where your drive has to carry the ball over 200 yards of ocean. ✉ *Westport, Co. Mayo,* ☎ *098/28262. 18 holes. Yardage: 6,667. Par 73.* 📠 *Fees: weekdays, €38; weekends, €47.* ☉ *Visitors: weekdays. Practice area, caddies, caddy carts, catering.*

Northwest

County Sligo Golf Club. More than a century old, the course at Sligo is one of the grand old venues of Ireland, having hosted most of the country's major championships. At 6,565 yards, this links course isn't particularly long; however, it still manages to have seven par-4s of 400 yards or more. Typical of Ireland's hidden jewels, Rosses Point clings to cliffs above the Atlantic. The third tee offers views of the ocean, the hills, and the unusual mountain Ben Bulben. ✉ *Rosses Point, Co. Sligo,* ☎ *071/77186. 27 holes. Yardage: 6,043 (Old Course). Par 71.* 📠 *Fees: weekdays, €55; weekends, €70.* ☉ *Visitors: Mon., Tues., Thurs., and Fri. Practice area, caddies (summer only), caddy carts, club rental, catering.*

Donegal Golf Club. On the shores of Donegal Bay and approached through a forest, the windswept links are shadowed by the Blue Stack Mountains, with the Atlantic Ocean as a backdrop. The greens are large, but the rough is deep and penal, and there's a constant battle against erosion by the sea. Legendary golf writer Peter Dobereiner called it "hauntingly beautiful," perhaps recalling his experience on the par-3 5th, fittingly called "The Valley of Tears." ✉ *Murvagh, Laghey, Co. Donegal,* ☎ *073/34054. 18 holes. Yardage: 7,153. Par 73.* 📠 *Fees: weekdays, €40; weekends, €55.* ☉ *Visitors: daily. Practice area, caddies, caddy carts, catering.*

Enniscrone Golf Club. Enniscrone's setting is a natural for good golf— it's a combination of flatlands, foothills, and the Atlantic. It's not overly long on the scorecard, but the persistent winds can add yards to almost every hole (an extra 18 holes are being added). It's among the small number of clubs in Ireland with electric carts ("buggies"). ✉ *Enniscrone, Co. Sligo,* ☎ *096/36297. 27 holes. Yardage: 6,682. Par 73.* 📠 *Fees: weekdays, €45; weekends, €60.* ☉ *Visitors: weekdays, weekends by appointment. Practice area, caddies (weekends and holidays), caddy carts, buggies, club rental.*

Northern Ireland

Ballycastle Golf Club. Pleasure comes first here, with challenge as an afterthought. It's beautiful (5 holes wind around the remains of a 13th-century friary), short (less than 6,000 yards), and right next to Bushmills, the world's oldest distillery—at nearly 400 years. ✉ *2*

Cushendall Rd., Ballycastle BT54 6QP, Co. Antrim, ☎ *048/2076–2536.*
18 holes. Yardage: 5,927. Par 71. 🍴 *Fees: weekdays, U.K.£20; week-*
ends, U.K.£30. ☉ *Visitors: daily. Practice area, caddy cars, catering.*

Castlerock Golf Club. Where else in the world can you play a hole called
"Leg o' Mutton"? It's a 200-yard par-3 with railway tracks to the right
and a burn to the left—just one of several unusual holes at this course,
which claims, year-round, to have the best greens in Ireland. The finish is spectacular: from the elevated 17th tee, where you can see the
shores of Scotland, to the majestic 18th, which plays uphill to a plateau
green. ✉ *65 Circular Rd., Castlerock BT51 4TJ, Co. Derry,* ☎ *048/*
7084–8314. 27 holes. Yardage: 6,499, 2,678. Par 73, 35. 🍴 *Fees: week-*
days, U.K.£35, U.K.£12; weekends, U.K.£55, U.K.£15. ☉ *Visitors:*
Mon.–Thurs. Practice area, caddies (reserve in advance), caddy cars,
catering.

Malone Golf Club. Fishermen may find the 22-acre lake at the center
of this parkland layout distracting because it's filled with trout. The
golf, however, is just as well stocked—with large trees and well-man-
icured, undulating greens, this is one of the most challenging inland
tests in Ireland. Bring your power game—there are only three par-5s,
but they're all more than 520 yards. ✉ *240 Upper Malone Rd., Dun-*
murry, Belfast BT17 9LB, ☎ *048/9061–2695. 27 holes. Yardage:*
6,599, 3,138. Par 71, 36. 🍴 *Fees: weekdays, U.K.£40 (men), U.K.£30*
(women); Wed. and weekends, U.K.£45 (men), U.K.£35 (women). ☉
Visitors: Mon., Thurs., and Fri. Practice area, catering.

Portstewart Golf Club. Over a century old, Portstewart may scare you
with its opening hole, generally regarded as the toughest starter in Ireland. Picture a 425-yard par-4 that descends from an elevated tee to a
small green tucked between the dunes. The greens are known for uni-
formity and speed, and seven of the holes have been redesigned to
toughen the course. Also, if you want a break from the grand scale of
championship links, there's the Old Course 18 and the Riverside 9, 27
holes of downsize, executive-style golf. ✉ *117 Strand Rd., Portstew-*
art BT55 7PT, Co. Derry, ☎ *048/7083–2015. 45 holes. Yardage:*
6,779 (Championship), 4,730 (Old Course), 2,662 (Riverside). Par 72,
64, 32. 🍴 *Fees: weekdays, U.K.£60 (Championship), U.K.£10 (Old*
Course), U.K.£12 (Riverside); weekends, U.K.£80 (Championship),
U.K.£14 (Old Course), U.K.£17 (Riverside). ☉ *Visitors: Mon., Tues.,*
and Fri. Practice area, caddies, caddy cars, buggies, catering.

★ **Royal County Down.** Catch it on the right day at the right time and
you may think you're on the moon; Royal County Down is a links course
with a sea of craterlike bunkers and small dunes. It is, perhaps, the most
beautiful course in Ireland. And for better players, every day is the right
one. Harry Vardon labeled it the toughest course on the Emerald Isle,
and if you can't hit your driver long and straight, you might find it the
toughest course in the world. ✉ *Golf Links Rd., Newcastle BT33 0AN,*
Co. Down, ☎ *048/4372–2419. 36 holes. Yardage: 7,037 (Champi-*
onship), 4,708 (Annesley). Par 71, 65. 🍴 *Fees: weekdays, U.K.£90*
(Championship), U.K.£18 (Annesley); weekends, U.K.£100 (Cham-
pionship), U.K.£25 (Annesley). ☉ *Visitors: Mon., Tues., Thurs., and*
Fri. Practice area, caddies, caddy cars, catering.

★ **Royal Portrush.** The only club outside Scotland and England to have
hosted a British Open, Portrush is perhaps the most understated of Ireland's "Big Four." The championship Dunluce course is named for the
ruins of a nearby castle and is a sea of sand hills and curving fairways.
The Valley course is a less-exposed, tamer track. Both are conspicu-
ous for their lack of bunkers. The Dunluce, in a poll of Irish golf leg-

ends, was voted the best in Ireland. ✉ *Dunluce Rd., Portrush BT56 8JQ, Co. Antrim,* ☎ *048/7082–2311. 36 holes. Yardage: 6,845 (Dunluce), 6,304 (Valley). Par 72, 70.* 📧 *Fees: weekdays, U.K.£85 (Dunluce), U.K.£30 (Valley); weekends, U.K.£95 (Dunluce), U.K.£37.50. (Valley).* ⊙ *Visitors: weekdays. Practice area, caddies, caddy carts, buggies, catering.*

11 BACKGROUND AND ESSENTIALS

Portraits of Ireland

Books and Movies

Chronology

Irish Family Names

Map of Ireland

DIGGING UP THE PAST

DESPITE IRELAND'S ACCESSIBILITY, you may feel a sense of otherness, attributable not only to the evergreen climate and leisurely pace of life but also to the layering of history and legend dug deep under the country's rich, grassy surface. Standing stones and court graves, mottes and dolmens, raths and cairns, holy wells and mass stones, round towers and Celtic crosses, churches and country houses—the artifacts of Ireland's long, turbulent history are everywhere, from the barren limestone Burren in County Clare to the Neolithic tombs and defenses of Newgrange in County Meath. Even an island off the main island—Inishmore, one of the Aran Islands far out in Galway Bay—claims its antiquity: Dún Aengus, which is 5,000 years older than the pyramids of Giza. Given how tempestuous the fortunes of this small island have been, you may be surprised by just how many of these sights remain.

Iron Age Celts from Central Europe settled in Ireland in the 4th century BC and left a legacy of an agrarian society based on a democratic kingship, a justice system known as the Brehon laws, and an artisan caste proficient in working gold and precious metals. (The National Museum in Dublin displays heaps of this Bronze Age gold jewelry.) Christianity arrived in Ireland in 432 with St. Patrick (or, perhaps, as some scholars suggest, two and possibly more missionaries whose work became conflated into the Patrician story). By the 8th century, Ireland was in its golden age. In general, the country's proliferating religious orders received protection from God-fearing Irish kings. Monks labored for decades to produce the *Book of Kells* (now on display at Trinity College in Dublin). Having set up monasteries throughout Ireland, Irish monks set out for Europe, where they continued their expansion of monastic communities from England to northern Italy. According to the Thomas Cahill best-seller *How the Irish Saved Civilization*, the medieval Irish monks who copied and standardized the masterpieces of Virgil and Horace helped to prevent the loss of classical Latin, the written language of Rome, to the vernacular Romance tongues of Italy, Spain, and France.

About 800, Viking longboats scourged the island's coasts. The Norsemen established settlements in Wexford, Cork, and Dublin (and left the mark of bright-red hair behind on their Irish descendants). Brian Boru, last of the High Kings to sit at Tara, won the Battle of Clontarf, defeating a troop of Viking raiders off the coast near Dublin in 1014. But Boru's subsequent murder marked the end of an era. Without his leadership, the power of the Irish kings dissipated, and in 1155, English-born pope Adrian IV boldly granted dominion over Ireland to his fellow Englishman King Henry II. Fourteen years later Norman Strongbow arrived in Ireland, opening the door to more than 800 years of strife between the English and the Irish.

By 1609, the last of the Irish chieftains had lost their land to the British and sailed for exile, making way for the Plantation period. During this era 200,000 Scottish Lowlanders were "planted" on native Irish lands. Oliver Cromwell, "the Avenger," arrived with his troops in 1649, intent on making Ireland a Protestant country. He conducted a ruthless campaign of persecution against the already bitter Irish Catholics—a campaign that included beheading thousands of men, women, and children.

The Great Famine and Its Aftermath

Throughout the early 19th century, poverty was endemic and disease was a simple fact of life. Irish peasants worked for absentee British landlords and either paid exorbitant rents for land that had probably belonged to their parents or grandparents, or simply starved. The system was unjust, but somehow the bulk of Ireland survived the lean years prior to 1845. Within a year, however, potato blight ruined crops throughout the country. In a decade, the population was decimated, reduced from 8 to 6 million inhabitants. Starvation was largely to blame for the decline, but this period also marks the beginning of the large-scale emigration—to

America, Canada, and Australia—that continued, albeit at a slower pace, until the mid 1990s. More than 70 million of Ireland's descendants are scattered abroad in the Irish diaspora—including 44 million in the United States.

The mid-19th century also saw the rise of an Irish Nationalist movement. Various groups, including the Fenians and the Irish Republican Brotherhood, agitated for equal rights for Catholics, land reform, the revival of Ireland's Gaelic heritage, and the expulsion of the British from Ireland. The movement exploded—literally—on Easter Sunday 1916, when Nationalists proclaimed a republic. England's merciless vengeance on the patriots—it shot 15 of the uprising's leaders—galvanized the country to the bitter War of Independence, which ended in 1920 with the partitioning of Ireland into 26 counties in the South, constituting the Irish Free State, and 6 in the North, making up the British-ruled province of Northern Ireland. The defining event of modern Irish history, the severing of North from South eventually spawned more than 30 years of Troubles in the North (though the roots of the Troubles date back 800 years) and cast a dark shadow over the country.

The Irish Ascendant

There is a place in an ancient Irish myth called Tír na nóg ("the land of the ever young"). Ancient though it may be, it's a surprisingly relevant image for Ireland today. The fact that the country is, for the first time in more than 150 years, holding on to many of its young, speaks volumes—it is the era of the ascendant Irish. While past history is still treasured, there's a growing feeling among the young to look ahead, not back. "Get over it!" was the headline cover about Boston's young Irish population and their increasing focus on the years ahead, not on time-stained sto-

ries about the Great Famine. There's a growing body of evidence for this newfound Irish assuredness—both within Ireland's shores and among the Irish abroad.

Together both the North and South of Ireland welcome more visitors annually (5.2 million) than they have residents (5 million). Not surprisingly, Dublin, the booming capital of the Republic, is the best place to take the pulse of Ireland. One-third of the Republic's 3.6 million residents live in the capital. Dublin is the Celtic Tiger's beating heart, a far cry from Joyce's "our dear, dirty Dublin." Dozens of cranes hover over new office buildings and hotels, and Georgian terrace houses are being brought back to glorious life. Visitors—especially weekenders from the Continent—fill Dublin's buzzing cafés, pubs, restaurants, and hotels and pour out onto busy Grafton Street and the narrow cobblestone alleys of Temple Bar. Outside Dublin, the country's quickening pulse is also palpable. New golf courses, housing developments, and blue-signed divided highways indicate the changes afoot.

Less conspicuously, in villages throughout the country, heritage and genealogical centers have sprung up to accommodate the surge of interest among the Irish diaspora for information about their roots. This relationship between the past and the present, between those who left and those who stayed, is an elemental part of Ireland's identity. Today, throughout the Irish diaspora, there is a boundless yearning for all that Ireland embodies: indomitable strength against all odds, the romance of an ancient place, the longing for a lost world, the solace and transcendent possibility of art. It's likely that a trip to Ireland in 2003 will put you in touch with the sources— historical and concrete, ineffable and mysterious—of this longing.

PUB ETIQUETTE

Even if you're a veteran barfly who's been booted out of gin mills and clip joints from Bombay to Baton Rouge, there are still some aspects of Irish public house behavior that can perplex even the most seasoned drinker. Most of these complexities come down to language and the way the locals use it. The word "whore," for instance, has many interpretations—in much the same way that the Eskimoes have 84 different words for snow. For starters, it's gender-flexible but is usually applied by males to other males. Go figure. For instance, "He's a cute whore" signifies that the so-described person is a canny man to seal a business deal and is a phrase much heard in towns where cattle are being bought and sold. Likewise, all the other swear words that are little heard in other developed countries find liberal employ here. The Irish have always been experts at giving a sentence even greater poetry with the inclusion of one of these epithets—they have no intention of giving offense, it's simply another tool used to spin a good yarn.

Clear a path for the locals when the clock strikes half-past 11 and the owner flicks the lights to signify last call. Were Marilyn Monroe herself to offer all her charms to a sheep farmer from the Connemara highlands, at 11:30 he'd put her on hold to get up there for that last pint. Maybe Ireland's pubs close too early, or maybe that final pint sipped amidst the publican's plaintive cry, "Have ye no homes to go to?," is the sweetest of them all.

The round system is also, unfortunately, a mystery to many visitors. If you get into conversation with them, locals will automatically include you in the round—it's good manners as far as they're concerned, and the strongest means they have of saying, "Good to meet you." Having accepted, woe betide you if the compliment is not returned. The Irish won't care who you are or where you came from, but an absence of the required etiquette will not go down well.

Finally, a word to the ladies—know that most Irishmen under the age of 85 flirt outrageously with strangers. You'll hear poetry (Yeats continues to be the best aphrodisiac known on the island) and sonnets, and, as once witnessed at midnight on a rain-drenched street in Corofin, a man of 70 might just perform his version of a Fred Astaire tap dance for you. Don't be astonished. Consider it a form of theater, and take it as good fun. After all, that's what Irish women have been doing for generations.

BOOKS AND MOVIES

Autobiography

Angela's Ashes (1996), Frank McCourt's enormously affecting memoir of growing up desperately poor in Limerick, has garnered every major American literary accolade, from the Pulitzer Prize to the National Book Critics Circle Award. The memoir and its sequel, *'Tis* (1999), should definitely be on your must-read list. In *An Only Child* and *My Father's Son* (1969), Frank O'Connor, known primarily for his fiction and short stories, recounts his years as an Irish revolutionary and later as an intellectual in Dublin during the 1920s. Christy Brown's *My Left Foot* is the autobiographical account of a Dublin artist stricken with cerebral palsy. *On Another Man's Wound: A Personal History of Ireland's War of Independence* has been republished in 2002. Originally published more than 60 years ago, it's the classic account of the years 1916–1921. Author Ernie O'Malley was only 23 years old when he joined the IRA and reported directly to Michael Collins. His memoirs are fascinating. Irish journalist Nuala O'Faolain's unsentimental and wrenching memoir, *Are You Somebody? The Accidental Memoir of a Dublin Woman* (1999), is an account of her Dublin childhood and the plight of Irish women. When published in Ireland, it stayed on the bestseller list for 20 weeks.

Guidebooks and Travel Literature

Exploring Ireland (3rd ed.), published by Fodor's, is a full-color guide packed with photographs; it is an excellent companion guide to this edition.

Peter Somerville-Large's *Dublin* is filled with anecdotes relating to the famed Irish city. *Georgian Dublin,* by Desmond Guinness, the founder of the Irish Georgian Society, explores the city's architecture, with photographs and plans of Dublin's most admirable buildings. An excellent work on the Aran Islands is Tim Robinson's award-winning *The Stones of Aran: Pilgrimage.* Robinson has also written a long introduction to the Penguin edition of J. M. Synge's 1907 classic, *The Aran Islands.* Tomas Ó Crohán's *The Islandman* provides a good background on Dingle and the Blasket Islands.

In *Round Ireland in Low Gear* (1988), famed British travel writer Eric Newby breezily pens the story of his bicycle journey with his wife around the wet Emerald Isle. Fifty years older but no less fresh is H. V. Morton's *In Search of Ireland* (1938). Rebecca Solnit uses Ireland as a sounding board for her meditations on travel in *A Book of Migrations: Some Passages in Ireland* (1997).

History and Current Affairs

For two intriguing studies of Irish culture and history, consult Constantine Fitz-Gibbon's *The Irish in Ireland* and Sean O'Faolain's *The Irish: A Character Study,* which traces the history of Ireland from Celtic times. J. C. Beckett's *The Making of Modern Ireland,* a concise introduction to Irish history, covers the years between 1603 and 1923. *Modern Ireland,* by R. F. Foster, spans the years between 1600 and 1972. Thomas Cahill's *How the Irish Saved Civilization* is a lively look at how Irish scholars kept the written word and culture alive in the so-called Dark Ages. Cecil Woodham-Smith's *The Great Hunger* (1962) details the history of the Irish potato famine of the 1840s. For an acclaimed history of Irish nationalism, try Robert Kee's *The Green Flag.* Peter De Rosa's *Rebels: The Irish Rising of 1916* is a popular, novelistic take on the defining event of modern Irish history. John Ardagh's *Ireland and the Irish: Portrait of a Changing Society* (1997) is one of the best sociological and economic analyses of modern Ireland. *"We Wrecked the Place": Contemplating an End to the Northern Irish Troubles* (1996) by Belfast-based journalist Jonathan Stevenson gives an insightful take on the subject. John Conroy's *Belfast Diary: War as a Way of Life* (1995) was reissued with a new afterword on the cease-fire. *The Lost Lives* (1999) is a heart-wrenching collection of biographies about many who have died during the Troubles. Paddy Logue's *The Border: Personal Reflections from Ireland—North and South* (2000) presents impressions of activists, artists, athletes, and community workers on national ramifications and the significance of the border between North and South on their lives. Marie de Paor's book *Patrick: The Pilgrim Apostle of Ireland* (2002) is a very modern interpretation of St. Patrick and his role as the patron saint of Ireland. Senan Molony's book *The Irish Aboard the Titanic* (2002) explores class structure and ethnic racism amongst the Irish and against them from the building of the Titanic in Belfast to the moment the last Irish citizens boarded the lifeboats that fateful day. Every aspect of Irish involvement with the Titanic is investigated here.

Literature

Ulysses (1922) is the linguistically innovative masterpiece by James Joyce, one of the titans of 20th-century literature. Emulating the structure of *The Odyssey,* and using an unprecedented stream-of-consciousness technique, Joyce follows Leopold and Molly Bloom and Stephen Daedalus through the course of a single day—June 16, 1904—around Dublin. More accessible introductions to Joyce's writing include *A Portrait of the Artist as a Young Man* (1916) and *Dubliners* (1914), a collection of short stories. (Its most accomplished story, "The Dead," was made into a movie starring Angelica Huston in 1988.) Joyce aficionados may want to tackle his final, gigantic work, *Finnegan's Wake* (1939), which takes the linguistic experimentation of *Ulysses* to an almost incomprehensible level. Arguably the greatest literary challenge of the 20th century, its pages include word plays and phonetic metaphors in more than 100 languages. To prepare you for reading Joyce, you might seek out audio recordings in which he reads in his inimitable lilting tenor voice.

Samuel Beckett fills his story collection *More Pricks than Kicks* (1934) with Dublin characters; if you enjoy literary gamesmanship, you may also want to try Beckett's 1950s trilogy—*Molloy, Malone Dies,* and *The Unnameable.*

If you're drawn to tales of unrequited love, turn to Elizabeth Bowen's stories and her novel *The Last September* (1929), set in Ireland during the Irish Civil War. If you prefer reading more magical novels, take a look at James Stephens's *A Crock of Gold* (1912), a charming and wise fairy tale written for adults, and Flann

O'Brien's *At Swim-Two-Birds* (1939), a surrealistic tale full of Irish folklore.

One of Ireland's foremost fiction writers working today, Edna O'Brien began her career with the comic novel *The Country Girls* (1960) and continues today with *House of Splendid Isolation* (1994) and *Down by the River* (1997). She is a superb short-story writer; her collection *A Fanatic Heart* (1985) is one of her best.

Thomas Flanagan's *The Year of the French* (1979) is a historical novel about the people of County Mayo, who revolted in 1798 with the help of French revolutionaries. *A Nest of Simple Folk,* by Sean O'Faolain, follows three generations of an Irish family between 1854 and 1916. Leon Uris's *Trinity* covers the years 1840–1916, as seen through the eyes of British, Irish Catholic, and Ulster Protestant families. In *No Country for Young Men,* Julia O'Faolain writes of two Irish families struggling to overcome the effects of the Irish Civil War. In John McGahern's prizewinning novel *Amongst Women,* modern-day Ireland attempts to reconcile itself to the upheavals of the early years of this century. For a more contemporary look at life in urban Ireland, try the phenomenally successful Roddy Doyle. All three works from his "Barrytown Trilogy"—*The Snapper, The Commitments,* and *The Van*—have been made into films; *Paddy Clarke Ha Ha Ha* has followed suit as another success.

Movies

A plethora of movies have been made in or about Ireland, and the number of Irish characters on screen is legion (the most numerous being priests, drunks, New York cops, and Old Mother Riley). *Juno and the Paycock* (known in the United States as *The Shame of Mary Boyle*) and *The Plough and the Stars* (1936), about the months leading up to the Easter Uprising, are early screen adaptations of Sean O'Casey's theatrical masterpieces. John Ford's superb *The Informer* (1935) is a full-blooded and highly stylized tale of an IRA leader's betrayal during the struggle for independence by a simpleminded hanger-on who wants to emigrate to the United States. Ford's boisterous comedy *The Quiet Man* (1952) is an Irish-village version of *The Taming of the Shrew,* with John Wayne playing a boxer who returns to his ancestor's village in the west of Ireland to claim local beauty

Maureen O'Hara, and Barry Fitzgerald. David Lean's epic *Ryan's Daughter* (1970) is a four-hour pastoral melodrama of a village schoolmaster's wife falling for a British officer in the troubled Ireland of 1916; the film was a critical and commercial disaster for Lean, who didn't make another film for 14 years.

Daniel Day-Lewis and Brenda Fricker give Oscar-winning performances in Jim Sheridan's *My Left Foot* (1989), a biography of Christy Brown, the Irish writer and painter crippled from birth by cerebral palsy. *The Field* (1990), Ireland's first Oscar-nominated film, is a marker of just how far things have progressed in the Irish film business. Richard Harris and John Hurt played out the drama by John B. Keane around the village of Leenane in Connemara. Alan Parker's *The Commitments* (1991), from Roddy Doyle's best-seller, humorously recounts the efforts of a group of young, working-class northside Dubliners trying to make it as a soul band. *Into the West* has been embraced by movie-goers worldwide because of its fairytale-like plot. It follows two Irish traveler boys (gypsies) from Dublin projects to the West of Ireland in search of their beautiful horse Tír na nóg ("Land of Eternal Youth"), which was confiscated by an evil police officer. The film stars Gabriel Byrne. In *A Man of No Importance* (1994), Albert Finney plays a sexually repressed bus conductor whose passion for poetry leads him to stage Wilde's *Salomé*. John Sayles hooked up with acclaimed cinematographer Haskell Wexler to make *The Secret of Roan Inish* (1996), a magical realist fable about a Selkie—a creature from Celtic folklore who is a seal in the water and a woman on land—and the fisherman's family whose lives she changes. *Waking Ned Devine* (1998) is a sidesplitting comedy about a small Irish village thrown into turmoil by a dead man's lottery winnings. *The Butcher Boy* is a dark comedy about a young boy who goes insane as his family splits up. Interestingly, it stars musician Sinead O'Connor as the Virgin Mary. *This is the Sea,* a contemporary love story set in Northern Ireland after the 1994 ceasefire, was directed by Mary McGuickian. The film version of Frank McCourt's memoir *Angela's Ashes* (1999) has left an impact on some as strong as the book itself.

Some of the best movies made in Ireland deal with the Troubles that have afflicted Northern Ireland. *Four Days in July* (1984), directed by Mike Leigh in classic cinema verité style, is a poignant and compelling portrayal of the sectarian divide in working-class Belfast. Helen Mirren stars as the widow of an executed Protestant policeman in *Cal* (1984), based on Bernard MacLaverty's masterful novel about the Troubles. Daniel Day-Lewis was nominated for an Academy Award for his portrayal of Gerry Conlon, the wrongfully imprisoned Irish youth, in Jim Sheridan's *In the Name of the Father* (1993). Neil Jordan's *Michael Collins* (1996), with Liam Neeson and Julia Roberts, depicts the turbulent life of the heroic commander in chief of the Irish Republican Army from the Easter Uprising in 1916, when Collins was 25, until his assassination in West Cork six years later. Day-Lewis appears once again in *The Boxer* (1997), the story of an ex-boxer and former IRA man who tries to put his life back together in contemporary, sectarian Belfast.

Poetry

The poems of William Butler Yeats, Ireland's most celebrated poet, often describe the Irish landscape, including the Sligo and Coole countryside. Go for the formidably large but marvelous *Collected Poems: 1909 to 1962* (1996 2nd rev ed.), edited by Richard J. Finneran. A favorite poet among the Irish is Patrick Kavanagh, who wrote soberly—and exceptionally—about landscape, poverty, and rural farming life. His best-known and most controversial (long) poem, *The Great Hunger* (1942), caused some uproar when it was published, and won him a bit of notoriety. But now, finally, Kavanagh is seen as a tremendously important Irish poet. Born in Belfast in 1907 (his parents were from Connemara), Louis MacNeice is something of an anomaly. He is considered to be an Irish poet, though he spent much of his life in England. He worked as a writer and producer for BBC, for which he wrote some of his radio dramas. But MacNeice was mainly a poet, known for his long and marvelous poem *Autumn Journal,* which beautifully explores politics, history, and personal drama in alternating rhyming couplets. His poems are intimate, clever, and lyrical. MacNeice died in 1963.

For contemporary poetry, read Derek Mahon—the *Selected Poems* (1992) is a good start. Northern Ireland serves as the setting for many of Nobel Laureate Seamus Heaney's poems. *Opened Ground: Selected Poems 1966–1996* (1999) is a good overview of his lyrical, highly crafted style—like Yeats, Heaney is an intensely aural poet, a master of rhythm and sound. (He is also, thanks to his farmer father, obsessed with soil.) Diehard fans prefer his earlier, more rustic work. Take a look at his debut collection, *Death of a Naturalist* (1995 reprint), *The Haw Lantern* (1989), or *The Spirit Level* (1996) if you want options for smaller—and in some ways more worthwhile—collections. Paul Muldoon, from Belfast, is another major Irish poet. His *Selected Poems: 1968–1986* (1987) and *The Annals of Chile* (1994) are both good selections. Eavan Boland is widely regarded as among the top tier of Irish poets and the finest woman writing poetry in Ireland today. Two of her popular books are *Object Lessons: The Life of the Woman and the Poet in Our Time* (1995) and *An Origin Like Water: Collected Poems 1957–1987* (1996). One of Ireland's leading poets, Brendan Kennelly, selects and introduces his choices of the best Irish poetry in his book *Between Innocence and Peace: Favorite Poems of Ireland* (2002). He chooses from the works of Seamus Heaney, Eavan Boland, Michael Longley, Paul Durcan, and the grand masters—Yeats, Synge, and MacNeice.

Theater

Ireland's playwrights are as distinguished as its novelists and short-story writers. Samuel Beckett, who moved from Ireland to Paris and began writing in French, is the author of the comic modernist masterpiece *Waiting for Godot* (1952), among many other plays. Oscar Wilde's finest

plays, *The Importance of Being Earnest* and *An Ideal Husband* (both 1895), were playing to packed audiences in London when he was charged by his lover's father as a sodomite, setting in motion the trials that led to his downfall. Among the many plays of George Bernard Shaw, who grew up in Dublin, are *Arms and the Man* (1894), *Major Barbara* (1905), *Pygmalion* (1913), and *Saint Joan* (1923).

The history of Irish theater includes a number of controversial plays, such as J. M. Synge's *The Playboy of the Western World,* which was considered morally outrageous at the time of its opening in 1907 ("Playboy riots" took place in Dublin when the play was produced at the Abbey Theatre) but is appreciated today for its poetic language. Sean O'Casey wrote passionately about social injustice and working-class characters around the time of the Irish Civil War in such plays as *The Plough and the Stars* (1926) and *Juno and the Paycock* (1924). *The Quare Fellow* (1956), by Brendan Behan, challenged accepted mores in the 1950s and at the time could only be produced in London. Behan is also well known for his play *The Hostage* (1958) and for *Borstal Boy* (1958), his memoirs. Hugh Leonard (*Da* [1974] and *A Life* [1980]) and Brian Friel (*Philadelphia, Here I Come!* [1964], *The Faith Healer* [1979], and *Dancing at Lughnasa* [1990]), write works that often illuminate Irish small-town life. A group of young, brash Irish playwrights have taken London and Broadway by storm. Martin McDonagh's *The Beauty Queen of Linnane* (1996) and Conor McPherson's *The Weir* (1997) have won awards on both sides of the Atlantic.

IRELAND AT A GLANCE

ca. 3500 BC Neolithic (new Stone Age) settlers (origins uncertain) bring agriculture, pottery, and weaving. They also build massive megaliths—stone monuments with counterparts in England (Stonehenge), Brittany (Carnac), and elsewhere in Europe.

ca. 700 BC Celtic tribes begin to arrive via Britain and France; they divide Ireland into "fifths," or provinces, including Ulster, Leinster, Connaught, Meath, and Munster.

ca. AD 100 Ireland becomes the center of Celtic culture and trade without being settled by the Romans.

432 Traditional date for the arrival of St. Patrick and Christianity; in fact, Irish conversion to Christianity began at least a century earlier.

ca. 500–800 Golden age of Irish monasticism; as many as 3,000 study at Clonard (Meath). Irish missionaries carry the faith to barbarian Europe; art (exemplified by the *Book of Kells,* ca. 8th or 9th century) and Gaelic poetry flourish.

795 First Scandinavian Viking invasion; raids continue for the next 200 years. Viking towns founded include Dublin, Waterford, Wexford, Cork, and Limerick.

1014 Vikings decisively defeated at Clontarf by Irish troops under King Brian Boru of Munster. His murder cuts short hopes of a unified Ireland.

1172 Pope Alexander III confirms Henry II, king of England, as feudal lord of Ireland. Over the next two centuries, Anglo-Norman nobles establish estates, intermarry with the native population, and act in a manner similar to that of the neighboring Celtic chieftains. Actual control by the English crown is confined to a small area known as "the land of peace," or "the Pale," around Dublin.

1366 Statutes of Kilkenny attempt belatedly to enforce ethnic divisions by prohibiting the expression of Irish language and culture and intermarriage between the Irish and English, but Gaelic culture prevails and the Pale continues to contract. Constant warfare among the great landowners keeps Ireland poor, divided, and isolated from the rest of Europe.

1534–40 Henry VIII's break with the Catholic Church leads to insurrection in Ireland, led by Garret Mor's grandson Lord Offaly ("Silken Thomas"). He is executed with five of his brothers.

1558–1603 Reign of Queen Elizabeth I; her fear of Irish intrigue with Catholic enemies of England leads to expansion of English power.

1580–88 Edmund Spenser, an administrator for the Crown in Ireland, writes *The Faerie Queene.*

1591 Trinity College, Dublin, is founded.

1607 The Flight of the Earls and the beginning of the end of Gaelic Ireland. The earl of Tyrone and his ally Tyrconnell flee to Rome; their lands in Ulster are confiscated and opened to Protestant settlers, mostly Scots.

1641 Charles I's policies provoke insurrection in Ulster and, soon after, civil war in England.

1649   August: British leader Oliver Cromwell, having defeated Charles and witnessed his execution, invades Ireland, determined to crush Catholic opposition. Massacres at Drogheda and Wexford.

1652   Act of Settlement—lands of Cromwell's opponents are confiscated, and owners are forced across the Shannon to Connaught. Never fully carried out, this policy nonetheless establishes Protestant ascendancy.

1690   Battle of the Boyne—William of Orange lands in England and Catholic James II flees to Ireland to rally opposition. William pursues him with a large army and defeats him on the banks of the River Boyne in County Meath.

1775   American War of Independence begins, precipitating Irish unrest. Henry Grattan (1746–1820), a Protestant barrister, enters the Irish Parliament.

1782   Grattan's Parliament—Grattan asserts independence of Irish Parliament from Britain. Britain agrees, but independence is easier to declare than to sustain.

1823   Daniel O'Connell (1775–1847), "the Liberator," founds the Catholic Association to campaign for Catholic Emancipation.

1828   O'Connell's election to Parliament (illegal, because he was a Catholic) leads to passage of Catholic Emancipation Act in 1829; later, he works unsuccessfully for repeal of the Union.

1845–49   Failure of potato crop leads to famine; more than 1 million die, others migrate.

1856   Birth of George Bernard Shaw, playwright (d. 1950).

1858   Fenian Brotherhood founded in New York by Irish immigrants with the aim of overthrowing British rule. A revolt in 1867 fails, but it compels Gladstone, the British prime minister, to disestablish the Anglican Church (1869) and reform landholding (1870) in Ireland.

1865   Birth of William Butler Yeats, the great Irish poet (d. 1939).

1871   Isaac Butts founds parliamentary Home Rule Party, soon dominated by Charles Stewart Parnell (1846–91), descendant of English Protestants, who tries to force the issue by obstructing parliamentary business.

1890   Parnell is named corespondent in the divorce case of Kitty O'Shea; his career is ruined.

1893   Second Home Rule Bill passes Commons but is defeated by Lords. Subsequent policy is to "kill Home Rule with kindness" with land reform, but cultural nationalism revives with founding of Gaelic League to promote Irish language. Yeats, John Synge (1871–1909), and other writers find inspiration in Gaelic past.

1898   On the anniversary of Wolfe Tone's rebellion, Arthur Griffith (1872–1922) founds the Dublin newspaper the *United Irishman,* preaching *sinn féin* ("we ourselves")—secession from Britain; Sinn Féin party founded 1905. Socialist James Connolly (executed 1916) founds the *Workers' Republic.*

1904   William Butler Yeats and Lady Gregory found the Abbey Theatre in Dublin.

1914   Despite fierce opposition the Third Home Rule Bill passes the Commons and the Lords but is suspended due to the outbreak of World War I.

1916 Easter Uprising—Irish Republican Brotherhood (IRB) stages insurrection in Dublin and declares independence; the uprising fails, but the execution of 15 leaders by the British turns public opinion in favor of the insurgents. Yeats writes "a terrible beauty is born."

1919 January: Irish Parliamentarians meet as the Dáil Éireann (Irish Assembly) and declare independence. September: Dáil suppressed; Sinn Féin made illegal.

1920–21 War breaks out between Britain and Ireland: the "Black and Tans" versus the Irish Republican Army (IRA). Government of Ireland Act declares separate parliaments for North and South and continued ties to Britain. Elections follow, but the Sinn Féin majority in the South again declare themselves the Dáil Éireann under Eamon de Valera (1882–1975), rejecting British authority. December 1921: Anglo-Irish Treaty grants the South dominion status as the Irish Free State, allowing the North to remain under Britain.

1922 De Valera and his Republican followers reject the treaty; civil war results. The Irish Free State adopts a constitution; William T. Cosgrave becomes president. Michael Collins, chairman of the Irish Free State and commander in chief of the army, is shot dead in County Cork, not far from where he was born. In Paris, James Joyce's *Ulysses* is published.

1923 De Valera is arrested and the civil war ends, but Republican agitation and terrorism continue. William Butler Yeats is the first Irish writer to be awarded the Nobel Prize in Literature; he also takes a seat in the first Irish Parliament.

1938 New constitution creates Republic of Ireland with no ties to Britain.

1939–45 Despite strong pressure from Britain and the United States, Ireland remains neutral throughout World War II.

1959 Eamon de Valera resigns as Taoiseach (prime minister) and is later elected president.

1963 John F. Kennedy, the first Irish-American President of the United States, visits Ireland.

1972 Republic of Ireland admitted to European Economic Community. Troubles continue in the North. In Derry on January 30, British troops shoot 13 unarmed demonstrators on "Bloody Sunday." Stormont (the Northern Parliament) is suspended and direct rule from London is imposed. Acts of terrorism on both sides lead to draconian law enforcement by the British. "The Troubles," as the conflict is dubbed, will last 26 years and claim more than 3,000 lives.

1991 Mary Robinson becomes the first female President of the Republic of Ireland. Peace talks begin between the British and Irish governments and the main political parties of the North, excepting Sinn Féin.

1992 Ireland approves European Union. Sixty-two percent of the Irish vote yes in a referendum on whether to allow pregnant women to seek an abortion abroad.

1994 The IRA, in response to advances made by the Irish, British, and U.S. governments, announces a complete cessation of activities. Protestant paramilitary groups follow suit one month later. Gerry Adams, the leader of Sinn Féin, speaks on British TV and radio.

1996 Frustrated by the slow progress of the peace talks, the IRA explodes bombs on the British mainland, throwing the whole peace process into doubt. But violence has not returned to the province, and all parties say they are committed to peace.

1997 The Republic of Ireland legalizes divorce. Newly elected British prime minister Tony Blair apologizes for the British government's policies during Ireland's Great Famine, acknowledging that his predecessors' policies prolonged "a massive human tragedy." The IRA reestablishes its cease-fire.

1998 On Good Friday 1998, all sides in the conflict agree on an agreement for sharing power that guarantees the rights of the Catholic minority. Referenda in the North and the Republic show overwhelming support. A splinter IRA group opposed to the agreement explodes a bomb in Omagh, killing more than 20 people. Catholic leader John Hume and Protestant David Trimble share the Nobel Peace Prize.

1999 Despite sporadic violence by splinter loyalist groups, an executive branch of government, the Northern Ireland Assembly, is formed at Stormont in Belfast on November 27. Northern Ireland is no longer governed directly from Westminster.

2000 Proposals are made to reform the RUC (Royal Ulster Constabulary) by making it half Catholic and half Protestant and renaming it the "Northern Irish Police Force." Tensions remain high over the decommissioning of weapons.

2001 President Bill Clinton visits Dundalk and Belfast during the final weeks of his presidency to encourage continued implementation of the Good Friday Agreement. Due to a rise in pipe-bomb attacks, British troops are put back on patrol in certain neighborhoods in Belfast and Derry.

2002 The Republic of Ireland, which has some of the most restrictive abortion laws in the world, is faced with a voting referendum that could relax some restrictions in the primarily Catholic country. The IRA begins to decommission weapons in the wake of the September 11 attacks on the United States. The Euro is phased in as Northern Ireland and the Republic of Ireland's national currency.

Antrim
Lynch
McDonnell
McNeill
O'Hara
O'Neill
Quinn

Armagh
Hanlon
McCann

Carlow
Kinsella
Nolan
O'Neill

Cavan
Boylan
Lynch
McCabe
McGovern
McGowan
McNally
O'Reilly
Sheridan

Clare
Aherne
Boland
Clancy
Daly
Lynch
McGrath
McInerney
McMahon
McNamara
Molon(e)y
O'Brien
O'Dea
O'Grady
O'Halloran
O'Loughlin

Cork
Barry
Callaghan
Cullinane
Donovan
Driscoll
Flynn
Hennessey
Hogan
Lynch
McCarthy
McSweeney
Murphy
Nugent
O'Casey
O'Cullane
(Collins)

O'Keefe
O'Leary
O'Mahony
O'Riordan
Roche
Scanlon
Sheridan

Derry
Cahan
Hegarty
Kelly
McLaughlin

Donegal
Boyle
Clery
Doherty
Friel
Gallagher
Gormley
McGrath
McLoughlin
McSweeney
Mooney
O'Donnell

Down
Lynch
McGuinness
O'Neil
White

Dublin
Hennessey
O'Casey
Plunkett

Fermanagh
Cassidy
Connolly
Corrigan
Flanagan
Maguire
McManus

Galway
Blake
Burke
Clery
Fah(e)y
French
Jennings
Joyce
Kelly
Kenny
Kirwan
Lynch
Madden
Moran
O'Flaherty
O'Halloran

Kerry
Connor
Fitzgerald
Galvin
McCarthy
Moriarty
O'Connell
O'Donoghue
O'Shea
O'Sullivan

Kildare
Cullen
Fitzgerald
O'Byrne
White

Kilkenny
Butler
Fitzpatrick
O'Carroll
Tobin

Laois
Dempsey
Doran
Dunn(e)
Kelly
Moore

Leitrim
Clancy
O'Rourke

Limerick
Fitzgerald
Fitzgibbon
McKeough
O'Brien
O'Cullane
(Collins)
O'Grady
Woulfe

Longford
O'Farrell
Quinn

Louth
O'Carroll
Plunkett

Mayo
Burke
Costello
Dugan
Gormley
Horan
Jennings
Jordan
Kelly
Madden
O'Malley

Meath
Coffey
Connolly
Cusack
Dillon
Hayes
Hennessey
Plunkett
Quinlan

Monaghan
Boylan
Connolly
Hanratty
McKenna
McMahon
McNally

Offaly
Coghlan
Dempsey
Fallon
(Maher)
Malone
Meagher
Molloy
O'Carroll
Sheridan

Roscommon
Fallon
Flanagan
Flynn
Hanley
McDermot
McKeogh
McManus
Molloy
Murphy

Sligo
Boland
Higgins
McDonagh
O'Dowd
O'Hara
Rafferty

Tipperary
Butler
Fogarty
Kennedy
Lynch
Meagher
(Maher)
O'Carroll
O'Dwyer
O'Meara
Purcell
Ryan

Tyrone
Cahan
Donnelly
Gormley
Hagan
Murphy
O'Neill
Quinn

Waterford
Keane
McGrath
O'Brien
Phelan
Power

Westmeath
Coffey
Dalton
Daly
Dillon
Sheridan

Wexford
Doran
Doyle
Hartley
Kavanagh
Keating
Kinsella
McKeogh
Redmond
Walsh

Wicklow
Cullen
Kelly
McKeogh
O'Byrne
O'Toole

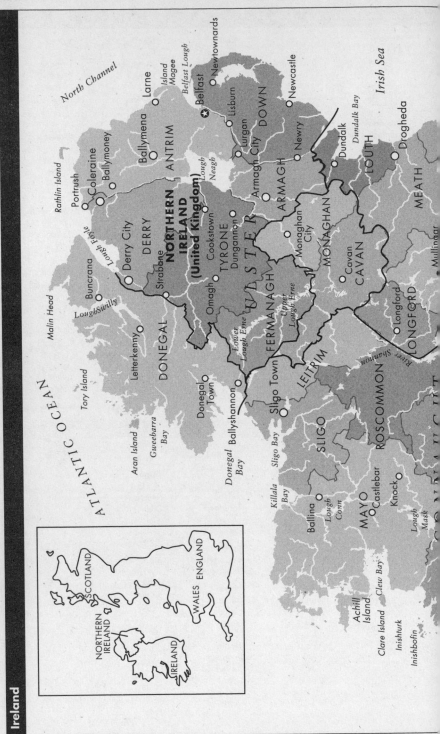

Ireland

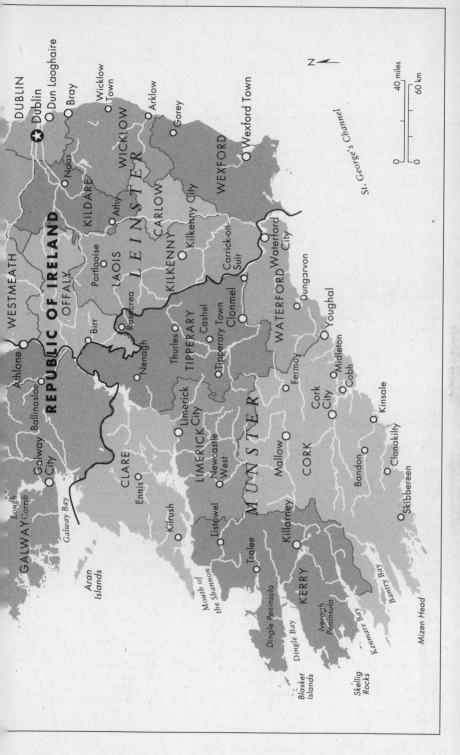

N

40 miles
60 km

St. George's Channel

DUBLIN
Dublin
Dun Laoghaire
Bray
Wicklow Town
Arklow
Gorey
Wexford Town
Naas
WICKLOW
KILDARE
Athy
CARLOW
WEXFORD
Kilkenny City
Carrick-on Suir
Waterford City
REPUBLIC OF IRELAND
WESTMEATH
LEINSTER
Portlaoise
LAOIS
OFFALY
KILKENNY
Dungarvon
Athlone
Birr
Roscrea
Thurles
Cashel
Tipperary Town
Clonmel
WATERFORD
Youghal
Galway
Ballinasloe
Nenagh
TIPPERARY
Midleton
Cobh
Galway City
Fermoy
Cork City
Kinsale
Lough Corrib
CLARE
Limerick City
Newcastle West
Mallow
CORK
Bandon
Clonakilty
Galway Bay
Ennis
LIMERICK
MUNSTER
Skibbereen
GALWAY
Kilrush
Listowel
Killarney
Aran Islands
Tralee
KERRY
Mouth of the Shannon
Dingle Peninsula
Iveragh Peninsula
Kenmare Bay
Bantry Bay
Dingle Bay
Mizen Head
Blasket Islands
Skellig Rocks

INDEX

Icons and Symbols

★ Our special recommendations

✕ Restaurant

🏨 Lodging establishment

✕🏨 Lodging establishment whose restaurant warrants a special trip

🐤 Good for kids (rubber duck)

☞ Sends you to another section of the guide for more information

✉ Address

☎ Telephone number

🕐 Opening and closing times

💷 Admission prices

Numbers in white and black circles ③ ❸ that appear on the maps, in the margins, and within the tours correspond to one another.

A

Abbey Presbyterian Church, 48, 49
Abbey Theatre, 17, 83
Abbeys. ☞ See Monasteries and abbeys
Achill Island, 329–330, 337
Adare, 272–274, 284
Addresses, *vii*
Aghadoe, 257–258
Ailt an Chorráin (Burtonport), 369
Ailwee Cave, 301
Albert Memorial Clock Tower, 390
Allihies, 249
An Clochan Liath, 369
Andrew Jackson Centre, 406
Andrew's Lane Theatre, 83
Anglican Parish Church (Monkstown), 104
Annaghmakerrig, 163
Annascaul, 264
Anne's Grove Gardens, 239
Annestown, 203
Antiques, shopping for, 8, 98, 232
Apartment and villa rentals, *xxvi–xxvii*
Apprentice Boys' Memorial Hall, 415
AquaDome, 269
Aquariums, 134, 427
Aran Heritage Centre, 317
Aranmore, 369
Arbour Hill Cemetery, 56
Ardara, 361–363

Ardboe, 420
Ardee, 130–131
Ardgillan Demesne (park), 132
Ardmore, 205–206, 213
Ards Forest Park, 367
Ark (children's theater), 37, 38
Arklow, 140
Armagh, 423–424, 434
Art galleries and museums
Dublin, 22, 27, 29, 34–35, 38, 40, 45, 48, 51–52, 81–82
Northern Ireland, 402, 418
Northwest, 346, 368, 371
Southwest, 224, 231, 253, 277
West, 314
Arthouse (exhibition space), 38
Astronomy Centre and Planetarium, 423
Athlone, 166–167, 173
Athlone Castle, 166
Athy, 146
ATMs (automatic teller machines), *xxx*
Augustine Abbey (Cong), 321
Avoca, 140
Avoca Handweavers, 140
Avondale Forest Park, 139–140
Avondale House, 140

B

Baily Lighthouse, 109
Ballina, 330, 331–332, 337
Ballinskelligs, 253
Ballsbridge, 67–68, 73–75, 89, 102
Ballybunion, 270
Ballycastle, 408–409, 434
Ballycotton, 237
Ballyferriter, 268
Ballyhack, 197
Ballyhack Castle, 197
Ballylane Farm, 190
Ballyliffin, 372
Ballymacarbery, 205
Ballymaloe Cookery School and Gardens, 237
Ballynahinch, 322
Ballyshannon, 356–357
Ballytore, 146–147
Ballyvaughan, 301–302
Balor's Fort, 368
Baltimore, 246–248
Baltray, 129
Banagher, 168
Bank of Ireland Arts Center, 23, 82
Bank of Ireland building, 22–23, 28
Banks, hours, *xii*
Dublin, 112
Bantry, 248–249, 284

Bantry Bay, 249
Bantry House, 248
Barnacle, Nora, 305, 308
Barry, John, statue of, 191
Beaghmore, 420
Beara Peninsula, 249–250
Bed-and-breakfasts, *xxvii*
Belfast Castle, 404
Belfast Zoo, 404
Bellamont Forest, 161
Bellamont House, 161
Belleek, 420
Belleek Pottery, 420
Belvedere House Gardens, 157
Bewley's Oriental Cafés, 18, 22, 23
Bicycling, *ix–x*, 6-7
Dublin, 91
Dublin environs, 120, 135
Midlands, 152, 167
Northern Ireland, 382, 429
Northwest, 341, 350, 362
Southeast, 177–178, 188, 194, 204
Southwest, 217, 232, 244, 246, 266, 270, 278
West, 295, 298, 314, 318, 324, 329, 330, 332
Bird sanctuary, 104, 193, 196
Bird-watching
Dublin, 104
Northern Ireland, 382, 431
Northwest, 367, 375
Southeast, 193, 196
Southwest, 254
Birr, 168–170, 173
Birr Castle Demesne, 169
Bishop Lucey Park, 223, 224
Bishop's Palace, 198
Bishop's Walk (Rock of Cashel), 208
Black Abbey, 185–186
Black Castle (Leighlinbridge), 184
Black Castle (Wicklow Town), 139
Blackfriars Abbey, 200
Blackrock, 104
Blarney, 233–234, 284
Blarney Castle, 233–234
Blarney Castle House, 234
Blasket Islands, 267
Blennerville, 268–269
Blessington, 144
Bloody Foreland Head, 369
Boardsailing. ☞ See Sailboarding
Boat and ferry travel, *x–xi*
Boating and sailing
Midlands, 152, 157, 167, 172
Northern Ireland, 421
Southwest, 235, 248, 252, 282
West, 289, 315, 325, 333–334

Bog tour, *168*
Bonamargy Friary, *408*
Book of Kells, *28–29, 126*
Books and movies, *448–451*
Bookshops, *98–99, 232, 249, 315*
Booterstown, *102, 104*
Bord na Mona Bog Rail Tour, *168*
Botanic Gardens (Belfast), *393*
Bowling, *91*
Boyle, *164–165, 173*
Boyle Abbey, *165*
Boyle Monument, *46*
Boyne Valley area, *122–133*
Brandon Hill, *189*
Bray, *134–135*
Breweries, *40, 44*
Brian Boru, High King, *423*
Bridge End, *373*
Brittas Bay, *140*
Browne's Hill Dolmen, *183*
Bruckless, *359–360*
Bullets (game), *382–383*
Buncrana, *372*
Bundoran, *355–356, 377*
Bunmahon, *203*
Bunratty Castle and Folk Park, *278*
Burren, *300–301*
Burren Centre, *300*
Bus travel, *xi–xii*
Dublin, *112–113*
Dublin environs, *147*
Midlands, *172*
Northern Ireland, *429–430*
Northwest, *374*
Southeast, *211*
Southwest, *281–282*
West, *334*
Bushmills, *409–410*
Business hours, *xii–xiii*
Dublin, *112*
Butler's Gate, *129*
Butterfly farm, *142*

C

Cahir, *207, 213*
Cahir Castle, *207*
Cahirciveen, *255, 284*
Calgach Centre (Derry), *415*
Cameras and photography, *xiii*
Camping, *xxvii*
Cape Clear Island, *247–248*
Car rentals, *xiii–xv*
Dublin, *113*
Midlands, *172*
Northern Ireland, *430*
Northwest, *374*
Southeast, *211*
Southwest, *281*
West, *334*
Car travel, *xv–xvi*
Dublin, *113*
Dublin environs, *148*
Midlands, *172–173*
Northern Ireland, *430*

Northwest, *374–375*
Southeast, *211–212*
Southwest, *281*
West, *335*
Caragh Lake, *255*
Carlingford, *133*
Carlow Castle, *183*
Carlow Town, *182–184, 213*
Carndonagh, *372*
Carnlough, *407–408*
Carraig Airt (Carrigart), *366*
Carrick-a-Rede, *408–409*
Carrickfergus, *405–406, 434*
Carrickfergus Castle, *406*
Carrick-on-Suir, *210–211, 213*
Carrigglas Manor, *159–160*
Carrowmore, *351*
Cashel (Southeast), *208–210, 213*
Cashel (West), *321–322*
Cashel of the Kings Heritage Center, *209*
Castle Archdale Country Park, *420–421*
Castle Coole, *422–423*
Castle Leslie, *162–163*
Castle Matrix, *272*
Castlebar, *330, 337*
Castledermot, *147*
Castlepollard, *158–159*
Castles
Dublin, *40, 42–43, 104, 109, 110*
Dublin environs, *124, 127, 128, 131, 133, 139, 142, 146*
Midlands, *156, 158–159, 162–163, 166, 169*
Northern Ireland, *404, 406, 410–411, 421*
Northwest, *352, 358, 367, 370*
Southeast, *182, 184, 186–187, 190, 195, 197, 206, 207, 210*
Southwest, *233–234, 237, 239, 240, 241, 245, 247, 258, 271, 272, 276, 278, 279*
West, *302, 303, 308, 318, 323*
Castletown House, *9, 141*
Castletownshend, *247*
Castlewellan Forest Park, *425*
Cathedral of Christ the King (Mullingar), *157*
Cathedral of Glendalough, *137*
Cathedral of Our Lady Assumed Into Heaven and St. Nicholas, *305, 306*
Cathedral of St. Declan, *205*
Cathedral of St. Fachan, *300–301*
Cathedral of the Assumption, *182*

Cathedral of the Immaculate Conception, *348*
Catholic Cathedral (Armagh), *423*
Cavalry Regimental Museum, *406*
Cavan, *160–161, 173*
Cavan Crystal, *160*
Cave Hill Heritage Center, *404*
Caverns
Dublin environs, *137*
West, *301*
Céide Fields (megalithic site), *332*
Cemeteries, *26, 56, 106, 348, 353–354*
Central Bank, *38*
Chapter House Museum, *417*
Charles Fort, *241*
Charleville Forest Castle, *156*
Chester Beatty Library, *40, 42, 43*
Children, travel tips for, *xvi–xvii*
Chimney (observation tower), *40, 42*
Chinaware, shopping for, *99–100, 342, 356, 357*
Christ Church Cathedral (Dublin), *40, 42*
Christ Church Cathedral (Waterford), *200*
Church of Kevin, *318*
Church of St. Teresa's (Dublin), *27*
Church of the Assumption (Wexford), *191*
Church of the Holy Trinity (Dublin), *43*
Church of the Immaculate Conception (Wexford), *191*
Churches
Dublin, *27, 31, 34, 36, 40, 42, 43, 45, 46, 47, 48, 49, 54, 104*
Dublin environs, *124, 126, 126, 129, 131, 132, 137, 139, 145, 146*
Midlands, *156, 157, 159, 167–168*
Northern Ireland, *388, 391, 395, 406, 415, 417, 423, 426*
Northwest, *348, 363, 373*
Southeast, *182, 185, 189, 190, 191, 200, 205, 208–209, 210*
Southwest, *225, 227, 235, 236, 255, 268, 274*
West, *300–301, 306, 318, 326*
City Hall (Belfast), *387–388*
City Hall (Dublin), *40, 42*
City Hall (Waterford), *198*
Clare Heritage Center, *302*
Clifden, *322–324, 337*
Clifden Castle, *323*

Cliffs of Moher, 297–298, 337
Climate, xl, xli
Clock House, 239
Clogher Strand, 267
Clogherhead, 129
Clonakilty, 245, 284
Clonea, 203
Clones, 163–164
Clones Lace Centre, 163
Clonmacnoise, 9, 167–168, 173
Clonmel, 210, 213
Cnoc an Linsigh (forest area), 124
Cobh, 235
Coleraine, 411, 434
Colleges and universities
Dublin, 18, 22, 28–30, 47
Dublin environs, 142
Northern Ireland, 393–394
Southwest, 227
West, 309
Collegiate Church of St. Nicholas, 305, 306
Collins, Michael, 245
Collins Barracks, 36, 57
Colmcille Heritage Centre, 371
Computers, travel with, xviii
Concerts. ☞ See Music, classical
Cong, 320–321
Connemara National Park, 325
Connemara region, 319
Connolly, James, 50–51, 56
Connor Pass, 268
Consumer protection, xviii
Cookstown, 420
Coolbanagher Church, 156
Coole Park, 302
Cooley Peninsula, 132–133
Cootehill, 161–162
Cork City Gaol, 223, 224
Cork Harbour, 234–235
Cork Opera House, 223, 224
Cork City Public Museum, 225
Cork Vision Centre, 223, 224
Cormac's Chapel, 208–209
Corofin, 302
Costs of the trip, xxix–xxx
Cottages, xxvii
County Antrim, 405–419
County Armagh, 419–428
County Derry, 405–419
County Down, 419–428
County Dublin, 101–110
dining, 105–106, 109–110
lodging, 79–80
pubs, 88
shopping, 97
County Fermanagh, 419–428
County Kildare, 141–147
County Louth. ☞ See Boyne Valley area
County Mayo, 319–332
County Museum (Carlow), 183

County Museum (Monaghan), 162
County Museum (Sligo), 347, 348
County Tyrone, 419–428
County Wexford Museum, 190
County Wicklow, 133–140
Court House (Cork), 223, 224
Courthouse (Dundalk), 132
Courthouse (Sligo Town), 347
Courtmacsherry, 245
Craggaunowen Castle, 279
Craggaunowen Project, 279
Crawford Municipal Art Gallery, 223, 224
Credit card abbreviations, xxx
Creeslough, 367
Creevelea Abbey, 352
Creevykeel, 355
Cricket, 382
Croagh Patrick (mountain), 327
Cromwell, Oliver, 191
Crookstown Heritage Centre, 146
Croppies Grave, 183
Crosses. ☞ See High crosses
Crown Liquor Saloon, 9, 387, 388
Cruises, xviii, 7, 167, 168, 200, 315, 421
Crystal, shopping for, 8, 99–100, 160, 200–201, 211
Curracloe Beach, 193
Curragh Main Barracks, 145
Curragh Racecourse, 144
Currency exchange, xxx, 431
Currency of Ireland, xxx
Cushendun, 408
Custom House (Belfast), 390
Custom House (Dublin), 43, 48, 49
Customs and duties, xviii–xx

D

Dalkey, 106
Dalkey Island, 106
Dalway's Bawn (farmhouse), 406
Damer House, 170–171
De Valera, Eamon, 108, 294
Department stores, 97–98, 233
Derrynane House, 253
Derrynane National Park, 253
Desmiond Castle and the International Museum of Wine, 241
Devenish Island, 421
Dingle, 264–266, 284

Dingle Peninsula, 263–270
Dining, xx–xxi, 5–6, 9–10.
price categories, xx, 59, 120, 151, 177, 216, 288, 340, 381
Disabilities and accessibility, xxi–xxii
Discount travel, xxii–xxiii
Distilleries, 40, 44–45, 157, 238, 409–410
Doctors. ☞ See Emergencies
Doe Castle, 367
Dolphin watching, 264
Dominican Friary (Sligo), 347–348
Donagh Cross, 372
Donegal Castle, 358
Donegal Irish Parian China factory, 356, 357
Donegal Town, 357–359, 377
Doolin, 298
Doolough Valley, 327
Dooney Rock, 353
Douglas Hyde Gallery of Modern Art, 29
Down Museum, 426
Downings, 366
Downpatrick, 426, 434
Drogheda, 128–129
Drumcliff, 348, 353–354
Dublin Castle, 40, 42–43
Dublin Civic Museum, 22, 23
Dublin Experience (audiovisual presentation), 30
Dublin Tourism, 22, 23, 26
Dublin Writers Museum, 17, 48, 49–50
Dublin Zoo, 57
Dublinia (audiovisual presentation), 40, 43
Dugoort, 330
Duiske Abbey, 189
Dún Aengus (prehistoric monument), 317
Dun Fionnachiad (Dunfanaghy), 367–368
Dun Laoghaire, 104–106
Dunbeg Fort, 266
Duncannon, 197
Duncannon Fort, 197
Dundalk, 131–132
Dundalk County Museum, 132
Dungarvan, 204–205, 213
Dunguaire Castle, 303
Dunlap, John, 419
Dunlewy Centre, 370
Dunluce Castle, 410
Dunluce Centre, 410
Dunmore East, 202
Dunquin, 267
Dursey Island, 249
Dysert O'Dea Castle Archaeology Center, 302

E

Electricity, xxiii
Embassies, xxiii, 114

Emergencies, *xxiii*
Dublin, 114
Dublin environs, 148
Midlands, 173
Northern Ireland, 431
Northwest, 375
Southeast, 212
Southwest, 281
West, 335
Emo Court and Gardens, 155–156
English Market (Cork), 223, 224–225
Ennis, 293–295, 337
Enniscorthy, 190, 213
Enniscorthy Castle, 190
Enniskerry, 135
Enniskillen, 421–422, 434
Enniskillen Castle, 421
Errigal Mountain, 369
Etiquette, *xxiii*
Europa Hotel (Belfast), 387, 388
Exploris (aquarium), 427

F

Fahan, 372
Fair Head, 408
Fal Carrach, 368
Fanad Peninsula, 366
Farm vacations, *xxvii*
Fastnet Rock Lighthouse, 247
Fermanagh County Museum, 421
Fermoy, 238–239
Ferries, *x–xi*
Dublin, 112
Northern Ireland, 429
Southeast, 211
Southwest, 271, 280
West, 296, 333–334
Festivals and seasonal events, *xli–xliv*
Film
Dublin, 82
Northern Ireland, 402
First Presbyterian Church (Belfast), 395
Fishing, *xxxi*, 7
Midlands, 152, 173
Northern Ireland, 382, 431–432
Northwest, 341, 356, 375–376
Southeast, 212
Southwest, 217, 232, 239, 244, 262, 278
West, 288, 314, 329, 332, 336
Fitzgerald's Park (Cork), 223, 225
Fleadh Nua (festival), 294
Flight of the Earls Heritage Centre, 365
Florence Court, 422
Flying Boat Museum, 271–272
Folk Village (Glencolumbkille), 361

Football, Gaelic
Dublin, 93–94
Northern Ireland, 382
Southeast, 178, 184, 188 195, 202, 204, 210; 212
Fore, 159
Fore Abbey, 159
Forts
Northern Ireland, 404, 424
Northwest, 368, 371–372
Southeast, 197
Southwest, 241, 252, 266
Forty Foot Bathing Pool, 105
Fota Island, 234–235
Four Courts building, 40, 43–44
Foxford Woollen Mills Visitor Center, 331
Franciscan Abbey (Donegal Town), 358
Franciscan Church (Wexford), 191
French Church, 200
Fry Model Railway Museum, 110

G

GAA Museum, 48, 50
G.P.A. Bolton Library, 209
Gaelic games, 7, 93, 178
Gaelic language, *xxv*
Gaiety Theatre, 83
Gallagher, Patrick, 369
Gallarus Oratory, 268
Gallery of Photography, 38
Galway City Museum, 305, 308
Gap of Dunloe, 258–259
Gap of Mamore, 372
Garden of Remembrance, 48, 50
Gardens
Dublin, 50, 57, 106, 108, 109, 110
Dublin environs, 135–136, 138, 146
Midlands, 155–156, 157, 158–159
Northern Ireland, 393
Northwest, 370
Southeast, 190, 195
Southwest, 237, 239, 245, 249
Garnish Island, 249
Garretstown Woods, 244
Gartan Lough, 370–371
Gate (theater), 48, 50, 54, 83
Gay and lesbian travelers, travel tips for, *xxiii–xxiv*
Genealogical Office, 30, 31
General Post Office (Cork), 223, 225
General Post Office (Dublin), 48, 50–51
George's Street Arcade, 22, 26
Giant's Causeway, 409, 434
Giant's Ring, 394
Glandore, 247

Glaslough, 163
Glasnevin, 106, 108
Glasnevin Cemetery, 106
Gleann Cholm Cille (Glencolumbkille), 361
Glebe House and Gallery, 371
Glen of Aherlow, 207
Glenariff Forest Park, 407–408
Glenbeigh, 255–256
Glencar Lough, 353
Glencolumbkille, 361
Glendalough, 136–138
Glengarriff, 249–250
Glens of Antrim, 406–407
Glenveagh Castle, 9, 370
Glenveagh National Park, 370
Glin, 271–272
Glin Castle, 271
Golf, *xxxi*, 7, 435–437
Dublin, 91–92, 437–439
Midlands, 152, 157, 158, 161, 162, 164, 167, 170, 171,172
Northern Ireland, 410–411, 426, 432, 441–443
Northwest, 342, 350, 362, 356, 359, 376, 441
Southeast, 178, 183, 188, 189, 196, 202, 203, 204, 209–210
Southwest, 217, 232, 234, 235, 237, 240, 249, 254, 256, 262–263, 270, 273, 278, 439–440
West, 293, 295, 296, 297, 314, 320, 324, 329, 332, 440–441
Gore-Booth family, 354
Gougane Barra National Park, 250
Gourmet Festival, 240–241
Government Buildings (Dublin), 30, 31
Graiguenamanagh, 189
Granard, 160
Grand Opera House (Belfast), 387, 388, 403
Gray's Print Shop, 419
Great Blasket, 267
Greenore, 133
Gregory, Lady Augusta, 302
Greyhound racing, 93, 188, 190, 382
Grianan Ailigh (fort), 371–372
Guest houses, *xxvii*
Guidebooks, *xxiv*
Guildhall (Derry), 413
Guinness Brewery and Storehouse, 40, 44
Gweedore Headland, 369
Gyles Quay, 132

H

Hatch's Castle, 131
Health clubs, 92

Health tips, *xxiv*
Heraldic Museum, *31*
Heritage Center (Bray), *134*
Heritage Center (Enniskillen), *421*
Heritage Center (Wicklow Town), *139*
Heritage Centre (Dalkey), *106*
Hermitage (Slane), *128*
High crosses
Dublin environs, *130, 137, 147*
Midlands, *163, 168*
Northern Ireland, *420*
Northwest, *354*
West, *301*
Hiking and walking, *xxxi, 7*
Dublin environs, *120, 135, 144, 148–149*
Midlands, *152*
Northern Ireland, *382, 432*
Northwest, *342, 376*
Southeast, *178*
Southwest, *217–218, 263*
West, *288–289, 336*
Hill, Derek, *371*
Hill of Tara, *125*
Holidays, *xxiv–xxv*
Holy Trinity Cathedral (Waterford), *200*
Holy Trinity Heritage Centre, *133*
Home exchanges, *xxvii–xxviii*
Homes, historic
Dublin, *26–27, 30, 31, 32, 33, 36, 110*
Dublin environs, *135–136, 140, 141, 143–144*
Midlands, *155–156, 159–160, 161, 164, 165, 170–171*
Northern Ireland, *422–423, 428*
Northwest, *354, 371*
Southeast, *186, 198*
Southwest, *234, 237, 248, 253, 258, 259*
West, *302, 308, 328*
Horn Head, *367*
Horse racing, *7*
Dublin, *93*
Dublin environs, *143, 144, 145*
Northern Ireland, *382*
Southeast, *188, 195, 203, 208, 210*
West, *289*
Horseback riding, *xxxii*
Dublin, *92*
Dublin environs, *148*
Midlands, *158*
Northern Ireland, *382, 423, 432*
Northwest, *350, 366, 373, 376*
Southeast, *178, 189, 194, 202, 205, 207*

Southwest, *232, 263, 270, 274, 278*
West, *295, 322, 324, 329*
Hospitals, historic, *45, 54*
Hostels, *xxviii*
Hot Press Irish Music Hall of Fame, *48, 51*
Hotels, *xxviii*
House of St. Columba, *361*
Howth, *109–110*
Howth Castle Gardens, *109*
Hugh Lane Municipal Gallery of Modern Art, *48, 51–52*
Huguenot Cemetery, *22, 26*
Hunt Museum, *274*
Hurling (Gaelic game)
Dublin, *93*
Northern Ireland, *382*
Southeast, *178, 184, 188, 195, 202, 204, 210, 212*

I

Icons and symbols, *vi, 460*
Ilnacullin, *249*
Imperial Hotel, *330*
Inagh Valley, *324*
Inchagoill Island, *319*
Inchydoney, *245*
Inisheer, *318–319*
Inishmaan, *318*
Inishmore, *317–318, 337*
Inishowen Head, *372*
Inishowen Peninsula, *372–373, 419*
Innisfallen Island, *258*
Innisfree, *352–353*
Inniskeen, *131*
Inniskeen Folk Museum, *131*
Insurance, *xiv, xxv*
International Museum of Wine, *241*
Ireland's Eye (island), *109*
Ireland's Historic Science Centre, *169*
Irish Famine Museum, *165*
Irish Film Centre, *37, 39, 82*
Irish Jewish Museum, *55*
Irish Linen Centre and Lisburn Museum, *404–405*
Irish Museum of Modern Art, *45*
Irish National Heritage Park, *193*
Irish Pewter Mill, *147*
Iveagh Gardens, *26–27*
Iveagh Market Hall (Dublin), *47*

J

Jackson, Andrew, *406*
Jails, *44, 224*
James Joyce Cultural Centre, *48, 52*
James Joyce Martello Tower, *105*
Jameson Heritage Centre, *238*
Japanese Gardens, *146*

Jeanie Johnston Visitor Shipyard, *268–269*
Jerpoint Abbey, *188*
Jewelry, shopping for, *99–100, 316*
Jogging, *92*
John F. Kennedy Arboretum, *190*
Johnstown Castle Gardens, *195*
Joyce, James, *35, 48, 52, 53, 105, 134, 308*

K

Kanturk, *240*
Kanturk Castle, *240*
Kate Kearney's Cottage (pub; Gap of Dunloe), *259*
Kavanagh, Patrick, *55–56, 131*
Kells, *126–127*
Kenmare, *250–252, 284*
Kennedy family, *190*
Kerry Bog Village Museum, *256*
Kerry the Kingdom, *269*
Kilbeggan Distillery, *157*
Kilcar, *361*
Kildare Town, *145–146*
Kilkee, *296, 337*
Kilkenny Castle, *186–187*
Killary Harbour, *326*
Killorglin, *256*
Killruddery House, *135*
Killybegs, *360–361*
Killyhoey Beach, *367*
Killykeen Forest Park, *160*
Kilmainham Gaol, *40, 44*
Kilmakedar Church, *268*
Kilmore Quay, *196–197*
Kilmore Quay Maritime Museum, *196*
Kilronan, *317*
Kilruddery House and Gardens, *135*
Kilrush, *295–296, 337*
Kilrush in Landlord Times (exhibition), *295*
King House (Boyle), *164*
King John's Castle (Carlingford), *133*
King John's Castle (Limerick), *276*
King William's Glen, *128*
Kinvara, *303–304*
Knappogue Castle, *279*
Knockbreda Parish Church, *395*
Knockmealdown Mountains, *206*
Knocknagriffin, *205*
Knocknarea, *351*
Knowth, *127*
Kylemore Abbey, *326*
Kylemore Valley, *325–326*
Kyteler's Inn, *186*

L

Lace making, 163
Ladies' View, 259
Lagan Lookout Visitor Centre (Belfast), 390, 391
Lahinch, 296–297
Lake Isle of Innisfree, 352–353
Lambert Puppet Theatre, 104
Language, xxv
Laracor, 124
Leenane, 326–327
Leighlinbridge, 184
Leinster House, 30, 31, 32, 33
Letterfrack, 325
Letterkenny, 363, 365, 377
Libraries
Dublin, 28–29, 30, 35–36, 40, 42, 44
Northern Ireland, 391
Southeast, 185, 209
Southwest, 272
Lighthouses
Howth, 109
North Bull Island, 108
South Wall, 102
Southwest, 247
West, 296
Limavady, 412, 434
Limerick Regional Archives, 274
Linen, shopping for, 9, 411, 411, 419
Linen Hall Arts Centre, 330
Linenhall Library, 390, 391
Lisdoonvarna, 299–300
Lisdoonvarna Spa and Bath House, 299
Lismore, 206–207, 225
Lismore Castle, 206
Lissadell House, 354
Listowel, 271
Locke's Distillery, 157
Lodging, xxv–xxviii, 10–11. price categories, xxvi, 70, 120, 152, 177, 216, 288, 341, 382
Londonderry. ☞ See Derry
Long-distance calls, xxxv–xxxvi
Longford, 159–160, 173
Loop Head Lighthouse, 296
Lord Brandon's Cottage, 259
Lough Beagh, 370
Lough Corrib, 319
Lough Dan, 136
Lough Derg, 170, 356
Lough Erne, 420–421
Lough Gill, 351–352
Lough Key Forest Park, 165
Lough Neagh, 420
Lough Swilly, 365
Lough Tay, 136
Louth, 131
Luggage, airline rules for, xxxii–xxxiii

Lynch Memorial Window, 305, 308
Lynch's Castle, 305, 308

M

Maam Cross, 320
Mail service, xxviii–xxix
Makemie, Francis, 365
Malahide, 110
Malahide Castle, 110
Malin Head, 372
Mallow, 239–240
Mallow Castle, 239
Manorhamilton, 353
Mansion House (Dublin), 31, 33
Mardyke, the (riverside walk; Cork), 223, 225
Marino Casino, 108
Maritime Museum (Arklow), 140
Markets, open-air, 98
Marlay Park, 102
Marsh's Library, 40, 44
Maynooth, 141–142
Maynooth Castle, 142
McArt's Fort (Belfast), 404
McCourt, Frank, 275
McSwyne's Gun (blowhole), 367
Meal plans, vi, xxvi
Meath Heritage and Genealogy Center, 124
Media, xxix
Medieval banquets, 262, 279
Meenlaragh, 368
Mellifont Abbey, 130
Mellon, Andrew, 419
Midleton, 238
Millmount Museum, 129
Milltown Malbray, 296
Mint Tower House, 133
Mizen Vision Visitor Centre, 246
Model Arts Centre and Niland Gallery, 346–347
Monaghan, 162, 173–174
Monasterboice, 130
Monasteries and abbeys
Dublin environs, 120, 130, 136–137
Midlands, 159, 165, 166, 167–168
Northwest, 347–348, 352, 358
Southeast, 185, 188 189, 191, 193, 200, 206
Southwest, 245, 247, 258
West, 321, 326
Money, xxix–xxx
Northern Ireland, 431
Monkstown, 104
Monkstown Castle, 104
Moone High Cross, 147
Motte of Granard, 160
Motte of Navan, 126
Mt. Brandon, 268
Mount Melleray Abbey, 206

Mount Stewart (estate), 428
Mount Street Bridge, 55
Mount Usher Gardens, 138
Mountains of Mourne, 424–426
Mountcharles, 359
Muckross Friary, 258
Muckross House, 258
Muireradach Cross, 130
Mullaghmore, 355
Mullingar, 157–158, 174
Murlough Bay, 408
Museums. ☞ Also Art galleries and museums
Dublin, 22, 23, 30, 31, 35–36, 45, 48, 49–50, 51, 55, 100, 102, 104–105, 109, 110
Dublin environs, 129, 130, 131, 132, 134,140, 142, 145, 146, 147
Midlands, 160, 162, 165
Northern Ireland, 393,394, 404–405, 406, 413, 415, 417, 420, 421, 426
Northwest, 347, 348, 361, 365, 371
Southeast, 183, 190, 195, 196, 208
Southwest, 225, 241, 248, 255, 268–269, 271–272, 274
West, 308, 317
Music, classical
Belfast, 403
Cork, 231
Dublin, 82
Music, contemporary
Dublin, 18, 82–83, 100
Music, shopping for, 100, 233, 316
Music, traditional, 6
Dublin, 89
Northern Ireland, 401–402, 403
Northwest, 350, 357, 359, 362
Southeast, 202
Southwest, 244, 252, 254, 266
West, 289, 297, 298, 300, 301, 304, 313, 318, 325, 329

N

Naas, 143
National Botanic Gardens, 106, 108
National College of Art and Design, 47
National Gallery of Ireland, 30, 34–35, 51
National Library, 30, 35
National Maritime Museum, 104–105
National Museum, 30, 35–36
National Museum Annexe, 36
National Museum of Agriculture and Rural Life, 195

National Sealife, *134*
National 1798 Center, *190*
National Stud Farm, *145*
National Stud Horse Museum, *145*
National Transport Museum, *109*
Natural History Museum, *30, 36*
Nature preserves
Dublin, 104
Saltee Islands, 196
Wexford, 193
Navan, *125–126*
Navan Fort, *424*
Nelson's Pillar, *52*
Nenagh, *171–172, 174*
Nenagh Castle Keep, *171*
Nenagh Heritage Centre, *171*
New Berkeley Library, *29*
New Project Arts Centre, *83*
New Ross, *189–190, 213*
Newbridge House, *110*
Newcastle, *425, 434*
Newgrange Farm, *9, 128*
Newgrange tombs, *127*
Newman House, *22, 26–27, 32*
Newmarket-on-Fergus, *293*
Newspapers and magazines, *xxix*
Newtown, *124*
Nire Valley, *205*
Nora Barnacle House, *305, 308*
North Bull Island, *108–109*
Number Twenty-Nine (historic home), *30, 36*

O
O'Brien's Castle, *318*
O'Brien's Tower, *297*
O'Carolan, Turlough, *46*
O'Conaire, Padraic, *306*
O'Connell, Daniel, *48, 52, 54, 106, 253, 255, 294*
O'Connell Memorial Church, *255*
Old Jameson Distillery, *40, 44–45*
Old Leighlin, *184*
Olympia Theatre, *18, 38, 39, 83*
Omagh, *420*
Omeath, *133*
One Martello Terrace, *134*
Opera
Dublin, 82
Northern Ireland, 388, 403, 418
Southeast, 194
Opera House (Cork), *223, 224*
Ormonde Castle, *210*
O'Rourke's Tower, *167*
Oughterard, *319–320, 337*
Oul' Lammas Fair, *408*

P
Packing, *xxxii–xxxiii*
Palace Stables Heritage Centre, *424*
Parke's Castle, *352*
Parks and forests
Dublin, 102, 108–109
Dublin environs, 124, 132, 139–140
Midlands, 160, 161, 162, 163, 165
Northern Ireland, 407–408, 420, 424–425
Northwest, 367, 370
Southeast, 193
Southwest, 224, 225, 250, 253
West, 325
Parnell, Charles Stewart, *44, 140*
Passports, *xxxiii*
Patrick, Saint, *160, 423, 426*
Patrick's Bridge, *223, 225*
Pearse Museum, *102*
People's Garden, *57*
Pewter, *147*
Phoenix Park (Dublin), *56–57*
Photography and equipment, travel tips for, *xiii*
Piper's Stones, *144*
Planetariums, *423*
Plane travel, *vii–ix*
airports, ix
Dublin, 111–112
luggage rules, xxxii–xxxiii
Midlands, 172
Northern Ireland, 428–429
Northwest, 373–374
Southeast, 211
Southwest, 279–280
West, 333
with children, xvii
Plassey, *276*
Plunkett, Saint Oliver, *129*
Poolbeg Lighthouse, *102*
Portaferry, *426–427*
Portarlington, *155–156*
Portora Royal School, *421*
Poulaphouca Reservoir, *144*
Powerscourt House, Gardens, and Waterfall, *135–136*
Powerscourt Townhouse Centre, *22, 27*
Prehistoric structures
Dublin environs, 120, 125, 127, 144
Northern Ireland, 420, 424
Northwest, 351, 355, 367, 368
Southeast, 183, 191
Southwest, 266
West, 317, 332
Price categories
dining, xx, 59, 120, 151, 177, 216, 288, 340, 381
lodging, xxvi, 70, 120, 152, 177, 216, 288, 341, 382

Pro-Cathedral (Dublin), *48, 54*
Protestant Cathedral (Armagh), *423*
Pubs, *7-8*
Puffin Island, *254*
Punchestown Racecourse, *143*

Q
Quaker Museum, *146*
Queen's University, *393–394*
Queenstown Story, *235*
Quiet Man Heritage Cottage, *321*

R
Radio and television, *xxix*
Rail passes, *xxxvii–xxxviii*
Ramelton, *365*
Rathcairn, *124–125*
Rathfarnham, *102*
Rathlin Island, *408*
Rathmullan, *365–366*
Recess, *320*
Reefert Church, *137*
Reginald's Tower, *198*
RHA Gallagher Gallery, *22, 27*
Ring (An Rinne), *204*
Ring of Beara, *249*
Ring of Hook, *197*
Ring of Kerry, *250–256*
Robertstown, *143*
Roches Point, *235*
Rock of Cashel, *9, 208*
Roscommon, *166, 174*
Roscommon Abbey, *166*
Roscommon Castle, *166*
Roscrea, *170–171*
Roscrea Heritage Centre, *171*
Rose of Tralee International Festival, *269*
Rosguill Peninsula, *366*
Ross Castle, *258*
Rossbeigh, *255*
Rosscarbery, *247*
Rosses (headland), *369*
Rosses Point, *353*
Rosslare, *195–196, 213*
Rossmore Forest Park, *162*
Rothe House, *186*
Rotunda Hospital, *48, 54*
Round Tower (Ardmore), *205–206*
Round Tower (Cashel), *208*
Round Tower (Castledermot), *147*
Round Tower (Clones), *163*
Round Tower (Clonmacnoise), *167*
Round Tower (Devenish Island), *421*
Round Tower (Drumcliff), *354*
Round Tower (Glendalough), *137*
Round Tower (Kells), *126*
Round Tower (Kildare), *145*

Round Tower (Killkenny City), *185*
Round Tower (Nenagh), *171*
Round Tower (Tory Island), *368*
Roundwood, *136*
Royal Hospital Kilmainham, *40*, *45*
Royal Inniskilling Fusiliers Regimental Museum, *421*
Royal Irish Academy, *31*, *36*
Rugby, *93–94*, *382*
Russborough House, *143–144*

S

Safety, *xxxiii*
Sailboarding, *244*, *248*, *282*, *315*, *336*
Sailing. ☞ *See* Boating and sailing
St. Aidan's Cathedral, *190*
St. Anne's Cathedral (Belfast), *390*, *391*
St. Anne's Church (Cork), *223*, *225*, *227*
St. Anne's Park, *108–109*
St. Ann's Church (Dublin), *31*, *36*
St. Begnet's Church, *106*
St. Brigid's Cathedral, *145*
St. Canice's Cathedral, *185*
St. Canice's Library, *185*
St. Colman's Cathedral, *235*
St. Colmcille's House, *126*
St. Columba's Church, *126*
St. Columb's Cathedral, *415*, *417*
St. Declan's Oratory, *205*
St. Enda's National Historic Park, *102*
St. Eunan's Cathedral, *363*
St. Fechin's Church, *159*
St. Finbarre's Cathedral, *223*, *227*
St. Francis Xavier (church), *48*, *54*
St. George's, *395*
St. John's Cathedral, *348*
St. Kevin's Bed (cave), *137*
St. Kevin's Church, *137*
St. Kevin's Cross, *137*
St. Laurence's Gate, *129*
St. Lavinius Church, *139*
St. Malachy's Church, *387*, *388*
St. Mary's Cathedral (Limerick), *274*
St. Mary's Church (Navan), *126*
St. Mary's Church of Ireland (Ardee), *131*
St. Mary's Church of Ireland (Clonmel), *210*
St. Mary's Collegiate Church, *236*
St. Mary's Pro-Cathedral (Cork), *227*
St. Michan's Church, *40*, *45*

St. Mochta's House, *131*
St. Mura cross slab, *372*
St. Nicholas of Myra's Church (Dublin), *46*, *47*
St. Nicholas's Church (Carrickfergus), *406*
St. Olaf's Church, *200*
St. Patrick Heritage Centre, *426*
St. Patrick's Cathedral (Cashel), *208*
St. Patrick's Cathedral (Dublin), *40*, *46*
St. Patrick's Cathedral (Dundalk), *132*
St. Patrick's Cathedral (Trim), *124*
St. Patrick's College, *142*
St. Patrick's Well, *46*
St. Peter's (Church of Ireland; Drogheda), *129*
St. Peter's Church (Drogheda), *129*
St. Stephen's Church (Dublin), *34*
Salmon Weir Bridge, *305*, *308*
Saltee Islands, *196*
Salthill, *305*, *308*, *337*
Samuel Beckett Centre, *84*
Sandycove, *104–106*
Sandymount Strand, *102*
Scruffy Murphy's (pub), *55*
Selskar Abbey, *191*, *193*
Senior citizens, travel tips for, *xxxiii–xxxiv*
Shanagarry, *237–238*
Shanagarry Castle, *237*
Shanagarry House, *237*
Shannon (river), *271*
Shannon Airport, *ix*, *284*
Shaw, George Bernard, *30*, *36*
Shelbourne Méridien Hotel, *22*, *27*, *28*
Sherkin Island, *247*
Shopping, *xii*, *xxxiv*, *8–9*
Silent Valley, *425*
Sinclair Seamen's Church, *395*
Skellig Experience, *254*
Skelligs (archaeological site), *254*
Skibbereen, *245–246*, *284*
Slane, *127–128*
Slane Castle, *127*, *128*
Slane Hill, *128*
Slea Head, *266–267*
Slieve Donard, *425*
Slieve League Mountains, *361*
Slieve Snaght, *372*
Sligo Abbey, *347*
Sligo Art Gallery. *346*
Sligo County Museum, *347*, *348*
Sneem, *252–253*
Soccer, *94*, *382*
South Wall, *102*

Spa Well, *239*
Spanish Arch, *305*, *308*
Spas, *299*
Sperrin Mountains, *419*
Sports and outdoor activities, *xxx–xxxii*, *6–7*
Staigue Fort, *252*
Steam Museum, *142*
Strabane, *419*
Stradbally, *203*
Straffan, *142–143*
Straffan Butterfly Farm, *142*
Strandhill, *351*
Stranmillis, *393*, *394*
Strokestown, *165*
Strokestown Park House, *165*
Student travel, *xxxiv*
Summerhill, *124*
Surfing, *297*, *342*, *351*, *376*, *411*
Swift, Jonathan, *46*, *124*
Swimming, *92–93*
Symbols and icons, *vi*, *460*
Synge, J. M., *316*

T

Taaffe's Castle, *133*
Tara, Hill of, *125*
Tara's Palace (dollhouse), *110*
Tarbert, *271*
Taxes, *xxxiv–xxxv*
Taxis, *115*
Teampaill na Skellig (Church of the Oratory), *137*
Telephones, *xxxv–xxxvi*
Temple Bar Music Centre, *18*
Tennis
  Dublin, *93*
  West, *315*
Terryglass, *170*
Theater
  Dublin, *48*, *50*, *83* *84*
  Northern Ireland, *403*, *418*
  Northwest, *350*
  Southwest, *231*, *270*
  West, *313–314*
Tholsel (Drogheda), *129*
Tholsel (Kilkenny City), *186*
Thomastown, *188–189*
Thoor Ballylee, *302–303*, *337*
Time, *xxxvi*
Timing the trip, *xl–xli*
Timoleague, *244–245*
Timoleague Castle Gardens, *245*
Tipperary Town, *207–208*, *213*
Tipping, *xxxvi*
Tivoli (theater), *84*
Tollymore Forest Park, *425*
Torc Waterfall, *258*
Torca Cottage, *106*
Tory Island, *368–369*
Tours and packages, *xxxvi–xxxvii*
Tower Museum, *413*, *415*
Townley Hall Estate, *128*

Train travel, *xxxvii–xxxviii*
Dublin, *116–117*
Dublin environs, *149*
Midlands, *168, 173*
Northern Ireland, *433–434*
Northwest, *376*
Southeast, *212*
Southwest, *269, 283–284*
West, *336–337*
Tralee, *269–270, 284*
Tramore, *203, 213*
Transportation, *xxxviii*
Travel agencies, *xxxviii–xxxix*
Traveler's checks, *xxx*
Trim, *124–125*
Trim Castle, *124*
Trinity College, *9, 18, 22, 28–30*
Triskel Arts Center, *223, 227*
Tullamore, *156–157, 174*
Tullynally Castle and Gardens, *158–159*
Tweeds, shopping for, *9, 100–101, 342, 361, 363, 366*

U

Ulster-American Folk Park, *419*
Ulster Folk and Transport Museum, *405*
Ulster Hall, *387, 388*
Ulster History Park, *419*
Ulster Museum, *393, 394*

Union Hall, *247*
Union Theological College (Belfast), *393, 394*
University College, Cork, *223, 227*
University College, Galway, *305, 309*
Upper Lake (Gap of Dunloe), *259*
Upperlands, *411–412*

V

Valentia Island, *254*
Value-added tax (VAT), *xxxiv–xxxv, 59*
Ventry, *266*
Victorian Clock Tower, *200*
Visas, *xxxiii*
Visitor information, *xxxix*

W

Walker Memorial, *415*
Water Gate, *421*
Waterfalls
Dublin environs, *135–136*
Northern Ireland, *407–408*
Northwest, *353*
Southwest, *258*
Waterford Glass Factory, *200–201*
Waterford Treasures, *200*
Waterville, *253*
Waterways Visitors Centre, *55, 56*

Weather information, *xi–xii, 434*
Web sites, *xxxix*
Wellbrook Beetling Mill, *420*
West Wicklow, *141–147*
Westgate Tower, *191*
Westport, *327–329, 337*
Westport House, *328*
Wexford Bull Ring, *191*
Wexford Wildfowl Reserve, *193*
W5: Whowhatwherewhywhen, *393*
White Island, *421*
White's Castle, *146*
Wicklow Town, *138–139*
Wicklow Way (trail), *102*
Wilson family home, *426*
Windmill, *268*
Wishing Stone, *368*
Woodfield, *245*
Workhouse Museum, *417*

Y

Yeats, W. B., *302–303, 346, 348, 352, 353–354*
Yeats Memorial Building, *346*
Yellow Steeple, *124*
Youghal, *236–237, 284*

Z

Zoos
Belfast, *404*
Dublin, *57*